13e

Cultural Anthropology
The Human Challenge

WILLIAM A. HAVILAND
University of Vermont

HARALD E. L. PRINS
Kansas State University

BUNNY McBRIDE
Kansas State University

DANA WALRATH
University of Vermont

WADSWORTH
CENGAGE Learning

Australia • Brazil • Japan • Korea • Mexico • Singapore • Spain • United Kingdom • United States

Cultural Anthropology: The Human Challenge,
Thirteenth Edition

William A. Haviland, Harald E. L. Prins, Bunny McBride, Dana Walrath

Anthropology Editor: Erin Mitchell

Developmental Editor: Lin Marshall Gaylord

Assistant Editor: Rachael Krapf

Editorial Assistant: Pamela Simon

Media Editor: Melanie Cregger

Marketing Manager: Andrew Keay

Marketing Coordinator: Dimitri Hagnéré

Marketing Communications Manager:
  Tami Strang

Content Project Manager: Samen Iqbal

Creative Director: Rob Hugel

Art Director: Caryl Gorska

Print Buyer: Karen Hunt

Rights Acquisitions Account Manager, Text:
  Roberta Broyer

Rights Acquisitions Account Manager, Image:
  Robyn Young

Production Service: Joan Keyes,
  Dovetail Publishing Services

Text Designer: Lisa Buckley

Photo Researchers: Billie Porter, Susan Kaprov

Copy Editor: Jennifer Gordon

Cover Designer: Lawrence R. Didona

Cover Images: Oriental Pearl TV Tower in
Shanghai: © Keren Su/Corbis; rice harvest near
Timbuktu, Mali: © Doco Dalfiano/Photolibrary;
whirling dervishes, Anatolia, Konya, Turkey:
© Bruno Morandi/Getty Images; woman with
laptop computer in Bhaktapur, Nepal: © Bill
Bachmann/The Image Works; herding llamas in
Huilco, Peru: © Frans Lemmens/Getty Images;
powwow circle: © Sean Schmidt

Compositor: Pre-PressPMG

For product information and technology assistance, contact us at
Cengage Learning Customer & Sales Support, 1-800-354-9706
For permission to use material from this text or product,
submit all requests online at **cengage.com/permissions**
Further permissions questions can be emailed to
permissionrequest@cengage.com

Library of Congress Control Number: 2009941338

Student Edition:

ISBN-13: 978-0-495-81082-7

ISBN-10: 0-495-81082-7

Loose-leaf Edition:

ISBN-13: 978-0-495-81178-7

ISBN-10: 0-495-81178-5

Wadsworth
20 Davis Drive
Belmont, CA 94002-3098
USA

Cengage Learning is a leading provider of customized learning solutions with office locations around the globe, including Singapore, the United Kingdom, Australia, Mexico, Brazil, and Japan. Locate your local office at **www.cengage.com/global.**

Cengage Learning products are represented in Canada by Nelson Education, Ltd.

To learn more about Wadsworth, visit **www.cengage.com/wadsworth**

Purchase any of our products at your local college store or at our preferred online store **www.CengageBrain.com.**

Printed in the United States of America
2 3 4 5 14 13 12 11

Dedicated to our parents who provided each of us with a nourishing environment, inspiring guidance, and an appreciation for cultural heritage. All of them fostered in all of us an eagerness to explore, experience, and enjoy other cultures, past and present.

Putting the World in Perspective

Although all humans that we know about are capable of producing accurate sketches of localities and regions with which they are familiar, **cartography** (the craft of map making as we know it today) had its beginnings in 16th-century Europe, and its subsequent development is related to the expansion of Europeans to all parts of the globe. From the beginning, there have been two problems with maps: the technical one of how to depict on a two-dimensional, flat surface a three-dimensional spherical object, and the cultural one of whose worldview they reflect. In fact, the two issues are inseparable, for the particular projection one uses inevitably makes a statement about how one views one's own people and their place in the world. Indeed, maps often shape our perception of reality as much as they reflect it.

In cartography, a **projection** refers to the system of intersecting lines (of longitude and latitude) by which part or all of the globe is represented on a flat surface. There are more than a hundred different projections in use today, ranging from polar perspectives to interrupted "butterflies" to rectangles to heart shapes. Each projection causes distortion in size, shape, or distance in some way or another. A map that correctly shows the shape of a landmass will of necessity misrepresent the size. A map that is accurate along the equator will be deceptive at the poles.

Perhaps no projection has had more influence on the way we see the world than that of Gerhardus Mercator, who devised his map in 1569 as a navigational aid for mariners. So well suited was Mercator's map for this purpose that it continues to be used for navigational charts today. At the same time, the Mercator projection became a standard for depicting landmasses, something for which it was never intended. Although an accurate navigational tool, the Mercator projection greatly exaggerates the size of landmasses in higher latitudes, giving about two thirds of the map's surface to the northern hemisphere. Thus the lands occupied by Europeans and European descendants appear far larger than those of other people. For example, North America (19 million square kilometers) appears almost twice the size of Africa (30 million square kilometers), while Europe

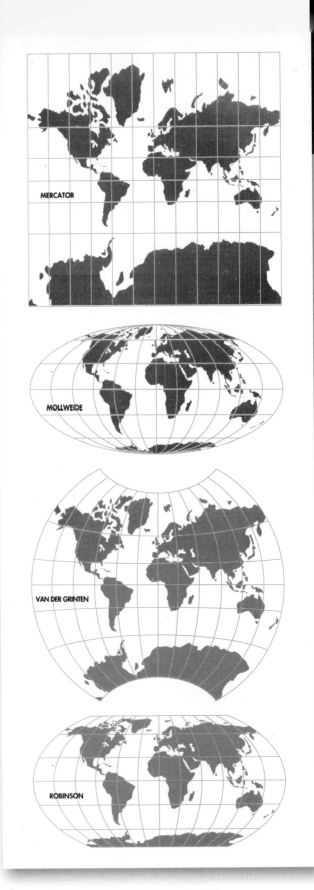

MERCATOR

MOLLWEIDE

VAN DER GRINTEN

ROBINSON

is shown as equal in size to South America, which actually has nearly twice the landmass of Europe.

A map developed in 1805 by Karl B. Mollweide was one of the earlier *equal-area projections* of the world. Equal-area projections portray landmasses in correct relative size, but, as a result, distort the shape of continents more than other projections. They most often compress and warp lands in the higher latitudes and vertically stretch landmasses close to the equator. Other equal-area projections include the Lambert Cylindrical Equal-Area Projection (1772), the Hammer Equal-Area Projection (1892), and the Eckert Equal-Area Projection (1906).

The Van der Grinten Projection (1904) was a compromise aimed at minimizing both the distortions of size in the Mercator and the distortion of shape in equal-area maps such as the Mollweide. Although an improvement, the lands of the northern hemisphere are still emphasized at the expense of the southern. For example, in the Van der Grinten, the Commonwealth of Independent States (the former Soviet Union) and Canada are shown at more than twice their relative size.

The Robinson Projection, which was adopted by the National Geographic Society in 1988 to replace the Van der Grinten, is one of the best compromises to date between the distortions of size and shape. Although an improvement over the Van der Grinten, the Robinson Projection still depicts lands in the northern latitudes as proportionally larger at the same time that it depicts lands in the lower latitudes (representing most Third World nations) as proportionally smaller. Like European maps before it, the Robinson Projection places Europe at the center of the map with the Atlantic Ocean and the Americas to the left, emphasizing the cultural connection between Europe and North America, while neglecting the geographic closeness of northwestern North America to northeastern Asia.

The following pages show four maps that each convey quite different cultural messages. Included among them is the Peters Projection, an equal-area map that has been adopted as the official map of UNESCO (the United Nations Educational, Scientific, and Cultural Organization), and a map made in Japan, showing us how the world looks from the other side.

The Robinson Projection

The map below is based on the Robinson Projection, which is used today by the National Geographic Society and Rand McNally. Although the Robinson Projection distorts the relative size of landmasses, it does so much less than most other projections. Still, it places Europe at the center of the map. This particular view of the world has been used to identify the location of many of the cultures discussed in this text.

The Peters Projection

The map below is based on the Peters Projection, which has been adopted as the official map of UNESCO. While it distorts the shape of continents (countries near the equator are vertically elongated by a ratio of 2 to 1), the Peters Projection does show all continents according to their correct relative size. Though Europe is still at the center, it is not shown as larger and more extensive than the Third World.

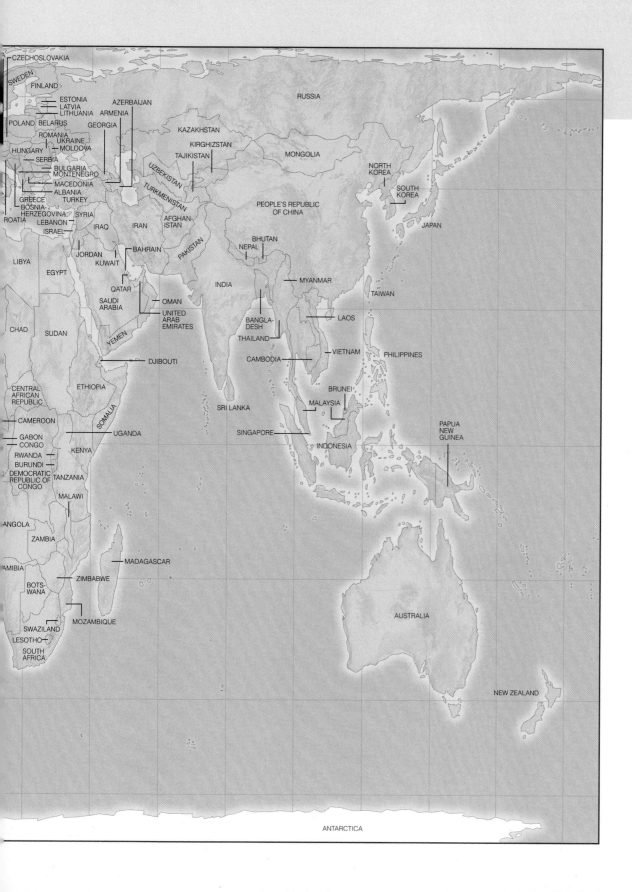

CZECHOSLOVAKIA
SWEDEN
FINLAND
ESTONIA
LATVIA
LITHUANIA
AZERBAIJAN
ARMENIA
POLAND BELARUS
GEORGIA
RUSSIA
KAZAKHSTAN
ROMANIA
UKRAINE
MOLDOVA
HUNGARY
SERBIA
BULGARIA
MONTENEGRO
MACEDONIA
ALBANIA
GREECE
BOSNIA-
HERZEGOVINA
ROATIA
LEBANON
ISRAEL
TURKEY
SYRIA
IRAQ
IRAN
UZBEKISTAN
TURKMENISTAN
KIRGHIZSTAN
TAJIKISTAN
MONGOLIA
NORTH
KOREA
SOUTH
KOREA
AFGHAN-
ISTAN
PEOPLE'S REPUBLIC
OF CHINA
JAPAN
LIBYA
EGYPT
JORDAN
KUWAIT
BAHRAIN
QATAR
SAUDI
ARABIA
OMAN
UNITED
ARAB
EMIRATES
PAKISTAN
INDIA
BHUTAN
NEPAL
BANGLA-
DESH
THAILAND
MYANMAR
LAOS
TAIWAN
CHAD
SUDAN
YEMEN
DJIBOUTI
CENTRAL
AFRICAN
REPUBLIC
ETHIOPIA
SOMALIA
SRI LANKA
CAMBODIA
VIETNAM
PHILIPPINES
BRUNEI
MALAYSIA
SINGAPORE
PAPUA
NEW
GUINEA
CAMEROON
GABON
CONGO
RWANDA
BURUNDI
UGANDA
KENYA
INDONESIA
DEMOCRATIC
REPUBLIC OF
CONGO
TANZANIA
MALAWI
ANGOLA
ZAMBIA
AMIBIA
MADAGASCAR
BOTS-
WANA
ZIMBABWE
SWAZILAND
LESOTHO
MOZAMBIQUE
SOUTH
AFRICA
AUSTRALIA
NEW ZEALAND
ANTARCTICA

Japanese Map

Not all maps place Europe at the center of the world, as this Japanese map illustrates. Besides reflecting the importance the Japanese attach to themselves in the world, this map has the virtue of showing the geographic proximity of North America to Asia, a fact easily overlooked when maps place Europe at their center.

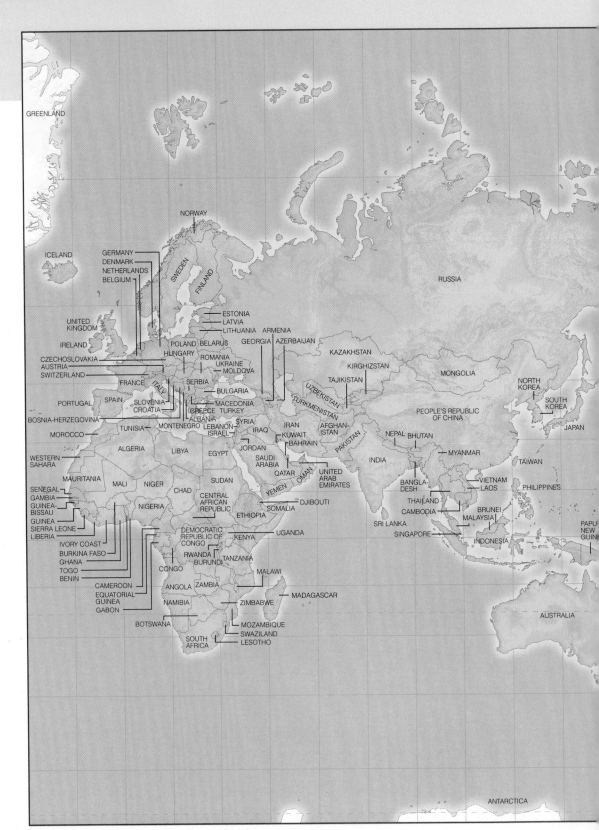

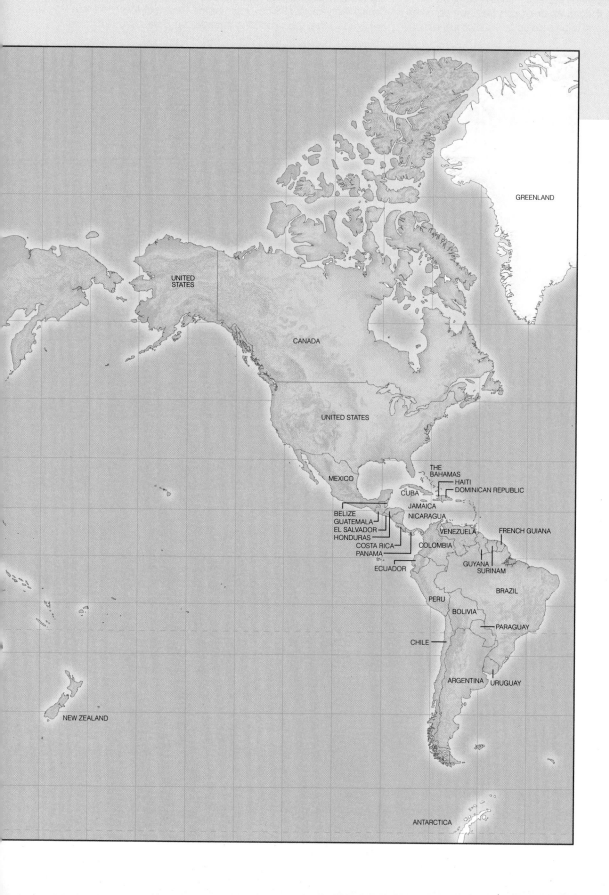

GREENLAND

UNITED
STATES

CANADA

UNITED STATES

MEXICO

THE
BAHAMAS
HAITI
DOMINICAN REPUBLIC
CUBA

JAMAICA

BELIZE
GUATEMALA
EL SALVADOR
HONDURAS
NICARAGUA

VENEZUELA

FRENCH GUIANA

COSTA RICA
PANAMA
COLOMBIA

GUYANA
SURINAM

ECUADOR

PERU

BRAZIL

BOLIVIA

PARAGUAY

CHILE

ARGENTINA
URUGUAY

NEW ZEALAND

ANTARCTICA

The Turnabout Map

The way maps may reflect (and influence) our thinking is exemplified by the Turnabout Map, which places the South Pole at the top and the North Pole at the bottom. Words and phrases such as "on top," "over," and "above" tend to be equated by some people with superiority. Turning things upside-down may cause us to rethink the way North Americans regard themselves in relation to the people of Central America. © 1982 by Jesse Levine Turnabout Map™—Dist. by Laguna Sales, Inc., 7040 Via Valverde, San Jose, CA 95135

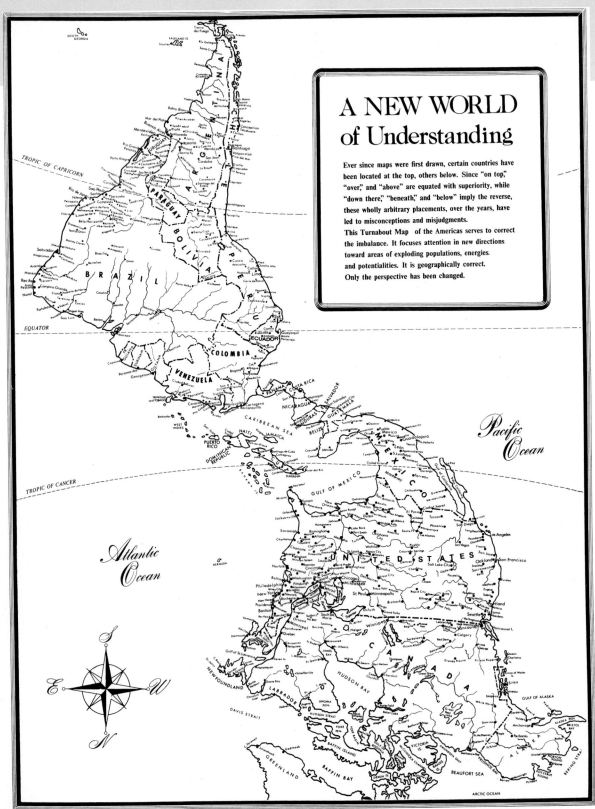

A NEW WORLD of Understanding

Ever since maps were first drawn, certain countries have been located at the top, others below. Since "on top," "over," and "above" are equated with superiority, while "down there," "beneath," and "below" imply the reverse, these wholly arbitrary placements, over the years, have led to misconceptions and misjudgments.

This Turnabout Map of the Americas serves to correct the imbalance. It focuses attention in new directions toward areas of exploding populations, energies, and potentialities. It is geographically correct. Only the perspective has been changed.

Brief Contents

Features Contents

Contents

© Julia Jean

Gai Ming-sheng/HK China Tourism Press

Chapter 10 Kinship and Descent   236

Chapter 11 Grouping by Gender, Age, Common Interest, and Social Class   260

Chapter 12 Politics, Power, and Violence   282

Chapter 13 Spirituality, Religion, and the Supernatural   310

Chapter 14 The Arts   340

Jochen Tack/Photo Library

Chapter 15 Processes of Change   362

Preface

Lucky 13. Working on this thirteenth edition of *Cultural Anthropology: The Human Challenge* has proved to us how fortunate we are to have the opportunity to revisit our textbook multiple times with the ambition of reaching well beyond mere updating to making the narrative and images ever more compelling, informative, and relevant to readers. Our efforts continue to be fueled by vital feedback from our students and from anthropology professors who have reviewed and used previous editions. Their input—combined with our own ongoing research and the surprisingly delightful task of rethinking familiar concepts that appear self-evident—has helped us bring fresh insight into classical themes.

With each new edition, we look anew at the archetypal examples of our discipline and weigh them against the latest innovative research methodologies, archaeological discoveries, genetic and other biological findings, linguistic insights, ethnographic descriptions, theoretical revelations, and significant examples of applied anthropology. These considerations, combined with attention to compelling issues in our global theater, go toward fashioning a thought-provoking textbook that presents both classical and fresh material in ways that stimulate students' interest, stir critical reflection, and prompt "ah-ha" moments.

Our Mission

Time and time again, we have observed that most students enter an introductory cultural anthropology class intrigued by the general subject but with little more than a vague sense of what it is all about. Thus the first and most obvious task of our text is to provide a thorough introduction to the discipline—its foundations as a domain of knowledge and its major insights into the rich diversity of humans as a culture-making species.

In doing this, we draw from the research and ideas of a number of traditions of anthropological thought, exposing students to a mix of theoretical perspectives and methodologies. Such inclusiveness reflects our conviction that different approaches offer distinctly important insights about human biology, behavior, and beliefs.

If most students start out with a vague sense of what anthropology is, they often have less clear and potentially more problematic views of the superiority of their own species and culture. A second task for this text, then, is to prod students to appreciate the richness and complexity of human diversity. Along with this is the aim of helping them understand why there are so many differences and similarities in the human condition, past and present.

Debates regarding globalization and notions of progress, the "naturalness" of the mother/father/child(ren) nuclear family, new genetic technologies, and how gender roles relate to biological variation all benefit greatly from the fresh and often fascinating insights gained through anthropology. This probing aspect of our discipline is perhaps the most valuable gift we can pass on to those who take our classes. If we, as teachers (and textbook authors), do our jobs well, students will gain a wider and more open-minded outlook on the world and a critical but constructive perspective on human origins and on their own biology and culture today. To borrow a favorite line from the famous poet T. S. Eliot, "the end of all our exploring will be to arrive where we started and know the place for the first time" (*Four Quartets*).

There has never been as great a need for students to acquire the anthropological tools to help them escape culture-bound ways of thinking and acting and to gain more tolerance for other ways of life. Thus we have written this text, in large part, to help students make sense of our increasingly complex world and to navigate through its interrelated biological and cultural networks with knowledge and skill, whatever professional path they take. We see the book as a guide for people entering the often bewildering maze of global crossroads in the 21st century.

Organization and Unifying Themes of the Book

In our own teaching, we have come to recognize the value of marking out unifying themes that help students see the big picture as they grapple with the vast array of material involved with the study of human beings. In *Cultural Anthropology* we employ three such themes:

1. We present anthropology as a study of humankind's responses through time to the fundamental **challenges of survival.** Each chapter is framed by this theme, opening with a Challenge Issue paragraph and photograph and ending with Questions for Reflection tied to that particular challenge.

2. We emphasize the integration of human culture and biology in the steps humans take to meet these challenges. The **Biocultural Connection** theme appears throughout the text—as a thread in the main narrative and in a boxed feature that highlights this connection with a topical example for each chapter.

3. We track the emergence of **globalization and its disparate impact on various peoples and cultures around the world.** While European colonization was a global force for centuries—leaving a significant, often devastating, footprint on the affected peoples in Asia, Africa, and the Americas—decolonization began about 200 years ago and became a worldwide wave in the mid-1900s. Since the 1960s, however, political and economic hegemony has taken a new and fast-paced form—namely, globalization (in many ways a concept that expands or builds on imperialism). Attention to both forms of global domination—colonialism and globalization—runs through *Cultural Anthropology,* culminating in the final chapter where we apply the concept of structural power to globalization, discussing it in terms of hard and soft power and linking it to structural violence.

Pedagogy

Cultural Anthropology features a range of learning aids, in addition to the three unifying themes described above. Each pedagogical piece plays an important role in the learning process—from clarifying and enlivening the material to revealing relevancy and aiding recall.

Accessible Language and a Cross-Cultural Voice

What could be more basic to pedagogy than clear communication? In addition to our standing as professional anthropologists, all four co-authors have made a specialty of speaking to audiences outside of our profession. Using that experience in the writing of this text, we consciously cut through a lot of unnecessary jargon to speak directly to students. Manuscript reviewers have recognized this, noting that even the most difficult concepts are presented in prose that is straightforward and understandable for today's first- and second-year college students. Where technical terms are necessary, they appear in bold-faced type, are carefully defined in the narrative, and are defined again in the running glossary in simple, clear language; these terms also appear in the glossary at the end of the book.

To make the narrative more accessible to students, we have broken it up into smaller bites, shortening the length of the paragraphs. We have also inserted additional subheads to provide visual cues to help students track what has been read and what is coming next.

Accessibility involves not only clear writing enhanced by visual cues but also a broadly engaging voice or style. The voice of *Cultural Anthropology* is distinct among introductory texts in the discipline, for it has been written from a cross-cultural perspective. We avoid the typical Western "we/they" voice in favor of a more inclusive one that will resonate with both Western and non-Western students and professors. Also, we highlight the theories and work of anthropologists from all over the world. Finally, we have drawn the text's cultural examples from industrial and postindustrial societies as well as nonindustrial ones. No doubt these efforts have played a role in the book's international appeal, evident in various translations and international editions.

Compelling Visuals

Haviland et al. texts repeatedly garner high praise from students and faculty for having a rich array of visuals, including maps, photographs, and figures. This is important since humans—like all primates—are visually oriented, and a well-chosen image may serve to "fix" key information in a student's mind. Unlike some competing texts, all of our visuals are in color, enhancing their appeal and impact. Notably, all maps and figures (many new to this edition) have been created with a color-blind sensitive palette.

PHOTOGRAPHS

Our pages feature a hard-sought collection of new and meaningful photographs. Large in size, many of them come with substantial captions that help students do a "deep read" of the image. Each chapter features at least fourteen pictures, including our popular Visual Counterpoints—side-by-side photos that effectively compare and contrast biological or cultural features.

MAPS

Map features include our "Putting the World in Perspective" map series, locator maps, and distribution maps that provide overviews of key issues such as pollution, endangered species, and energy consumption. Of special note are the Globalscape maps and stories, described in the boxed features section a bit further on.

Challenge Issues and Questions for Reflection

Each chapter opens with a Challenge Issue and accompanying photograph, which together carry forward the book's theme of humankind's responses through time to the fundamental challenges of survival within the context of the particular chapter. And each chapter closes with five Questions for Reflection, including one that relates back to the Challenge Issue presented in the chapter's opening. These questions are designed to stimulate and deepen thought, trigger class discussion, and link the material to the students' own lives.

Chapter Preview

Every chapter opening also presents three or four preview questions that mark out the key issues covered in the chapter. Beyond orienting students to the chapter contents, these questions provide study points useful when preparing for exams.

Barrel Model of Culture

Past and present, every culture is an integrated and dynamic system of adaptation that responds to a combination of internal and external factors. This is illustrated by a pedagogical device we refer to as the "barrel model" of culture. Depicted in a simple but telling drawing (Figure 2.2), the barrel model shows the interrelatedness of social, ideological, and economic factors within a cultural system along with outside influences of environment, climate, and other societies. Throughout the book examples are linked to this point and this image.

Integrated Gender Coverage

In contrast to many introductory texts, *Cultural Anthropology* integrates rather than separates gender coverage. Thus material on gender-related issues is included in *every* chapter. The result of this approach is a measure of gender-related material that far exceeds the single chapter that most books contain.

Why is the gender-related material integrated? Because concepts and issues surrounding gender are almost always too complicated to remove from their context. Moreover, spreading this material through all of the chapters has a pedagogical purpose, for it emphasizes how considerations of gender enter into virtually everything people do. Further, integration of gender into the book's "biological" chapters allows students to grasp the analytic distinction between sex and gender, illustrating the subtle influence of gender norms on biological theories about sex difference. Gender-related material ranges from discussions of gender roles in evolutionary discourse and studies of nonhuman primates, to intersexuality, homosexual identity, same-sex marriage, and female genital mutilation. Through a steady drumbeat of such coverage, this edition avoids ghettoizing gender to a single chapter that is preceded and followed by resounding silence.

Glossary as You Go

The running glossary is designed to catch the student's eye, reinforcing the meaning of each newly introduced term. It is also useful for chapter review, as the student may readily isolate the new terms from those introduced in earlier chapters. A complete glossary is also included at the back of the book. In the glossaries, each term is defined in clear, understandable language. As a result, less class time is required for going over terms, leaving instructors free to pursue other matters of interest.

Special Boxed Features

Our text includes five types of special boxed features. Every chapter contains a Biocultural Connection, along with two of the following three features: an Original Study, Anthropology Applied, and Anthropologist of Note. In addition, about half of the chapters include a Globalscape. All of these boxed features are carefully placed and introduced within the main narrative to alert students to their importance and relevance.

BIOCULTURAL CONNECTIONS

Now appearing in every chapter, this signature feature of the Haviland et al. textbooks illustrates how cultural and biological processes interact to shape human biology, beliefs, and behavior. It reflects the integrated biocultural approach central to the field of anthropology today. The sixteen Biocultural Connection titles hint at the intriguing array of topics covered by this feature:

- "The Anthropology of Organ Transplantation"
- "Adult Human Stature and the Effects of Culture: An Archaeological Example"
- "Pig Lovers and Pig Haters," by Marvin Harris
- "Paleolithic Prescriptions for the Diseases of Civilization"
- "The Biology of Human Speech"

- "A Cross-Cultural Perspective on Psychosomatic Symptoms and Mental Health"
- "Surviving in the Andes: Aymara Adaptation to High Altitude"
- "Cacao: The Love Bean in the Money Tree"
- "Marriage Prohibitions in the United States," by Martin Ottenheimer
- "Maori Origins: Ancestral Genes and Mythical Canoes"
- "African Burial Ground Project," by Michael Blakey
- "Sex, Gender, and Human Violence"
- "Change Your Karma and Change Your Sex?," by Hillary Crane
- Peyote Art: Divine Visions among the Huichol
- "Studying the Emergence of New Diseases"
- "Toxic Breast Milk Threatens Arctic Culture"

ORIGINAL STUDIES

Written expressly for this text, or selected from ethnographies and other original works by anthropologists, these studies present concrete examples that bring specific concepts to life and convey the passion of the authors. Each study sheds additional light on an important anthropological concept or subject area found in the chapter where it appears. Notably, these boxes are carefully integrated within the flow of the chapter narrative, signaling students that their content is not extraneous or supplemental. Appearing in twelve chapters, Original Studies cover a wide range of topics, evident from their titles:

- "Fighting HIV/AIDS in Africa: Traditional Healers on the Front Line," by Suzanne Leclerc-Madlala
- "The Importance of Trobriand Women," by Annette B. Weiner
- "Reconciliation and Its Cultural Modification in Primates," by Frans B. M. de Waal
- "Language and the Intellectual Abilities of Orangutans," by H. Lyn White Miles
- "The Blessed Curse," by R. K. Williamson
- "Gardens of the Mekranoti Kayapo," by Dennis Werner
- "Arranging Marriage in India," by Serena Nanda
- "Honor Killings in the Netherlands," by Clementine van Eck
- "The Jewish *Eruv*: Symbolic Place in Public Space," by Susan Lees
- "Sacred Law in Global Capitalism," by Bill Maurer
- "The Modern Tattoo Community," by Margo DeMello
- "Standardizing the Body: The Question of Choice," by Laura Nader

ANTHROPOLOGY APPLIED

These succinct and compelling profiles illustrate anthropology's wide-ranging relevance in today's world and give students a glimpse into a variety of the careers anthropologists enjoy. Featured in eleven chapters, they include

- "Forensic Anthropology: Voices for the Dead"
- "New Houses for Apache Indians," by George S. Esber
- "When Bambi Spoke Arapaho: Preserving Indigenous Languages," by S. Neyooxet Greymorning
- "Agricultural Development and the Anthropologist"
- "Global Ecotourism and Local Indigenous Culture in Bolivia," by Amanda Stronza
- "Resolving a Native American Tribal Membership Dispute," by Harald E. L. Prins
- "Anthropologists and Social Impact Assessment"
- "Dispute Resolution and the Anthropologist"
- "Reconciling Modern Medicine with Traditional Beliefs in Swaziland," by Edward C. Green
- "Bringing Back the Past," by Jennifer Sapiel Neptune
- "Development Anthropology and Dams"

ANTHROPOLOGISTS OF NOTE

Profiling pioneering and contemporary anthropologists from many corners of the world, this feature puts the work of noted anthropologists in historical perspective and draws attention to the international nature of the discipline in terms of both subject matter and practitioners. This edition highlights thirteen anthropologists from diverse areas of the discipline: Gregory Bateson, Ruth Fulton Benedict, Franz Boas, Paul Farmer, Jane Goodall, Kinji Imanishi, Claude Lévi-Strauss, Bronislaw Malinowski, Margaret Mead, Laura Nader, Matilda Coxe Stevenson, Eric R. Wolf, and Rosita Worl.

GLOBALSCAPES

Appearing in about half of the chapters, this unique feature charts the global flow of people, goods, and services, as well as pollutants and pathogens. With a map, a story, and a photo, the feature shows how the world is interconnected through human activity with topics geared toward student interests. Each one ends with a Global Twister— a question that prods students to think critically about globalization. Globalscapes in this edition are

- "A Global Body Shop?," investigating human organ trafficking around the world
- "How Much for a Red Delicious?," describing Jamaican migrant laborers working in Maine and Florida
- "Transnational Child Exchange?," chronicling international adoption
- "Football Diplomacy?," tracing the life of an Ivory Coast soccer star and the numerous countries in which he has trained and played
- "Pirate Pursuits in Puntland?," unveiling the complex economics behind piracy off the coast of Somalia

■ "Do Coffins Fly?," highlighting the work of a Ghanaian custom coffin maker gaining global recognition as art
■ "*Probo Koala*'s Dirty Secrets?," investigating the dumping of First World toxic waste in Third World countries

Changes and Highlights in the Thirteenth Edition

The pedagogical features described above strengthen each of the sixteen chapters in *Cultural Anthropology,* serving as threads that tie the text together and help students feel the holistic nature of the discipline. In addition, the engagingly presented concepts themselves provide students with a solid foundation in the principles and practices of anthropology today.

The text in hand has a significantly different feel to it than previous editions. All chapters have been revised extensively—the data, examples, and Suggested Readings updated, the chapter openers refreshed with new, up-to-date Challenge Issues and related photographs, and the writing further chiseled to make it all the more clear, lively, and engaging. Also, in addition to providing at least one new entry in the much-used Questions for Reflection at the end of the chapter, we have introduced a new question in each Biocultural Connection box.

Beyond these overall changes, each chapter has undergone specific modifications and additions. The inventory presented below provides brief previews of the chapter contents and changes in this edition.

CHAPTER 1: THE ESSENCE OF ANTHROPOLOGY
The book's opening chapter introduces students to the holistic discipline of anthropology, the unique focus of each of its fields, and the common philosophical perspective and methodological approaches they share. Touching briefly on fieldwork and the comparative method, along with ethical issues and examples of applied anthropology in all four fields, this chapter provides a foundation for understanding the methods shared by all four fields of anthropology. It also prepares students for the in-depth discussions of methods in primatology and the methods for studying the past shared by archaeology and paleoanthropology that follow in later chapters.

A new Challenge Issue dealing with global aspects of surrogate births that demonstrates the ways that an integrated holistic anthropological perspective contributes to the ability to negotiate the new technologies and practices of our ever-more interconnected world. The updated descriptions of the anthropological fields that follow take into account the excellent suggestions of our reviewers.

The section on linguistic anthropology has been expanded to include linguistic relativity, sociolinguistics, the work to save endangered languages, and the ways that languages continually change. The overview of physical anthropology was reorganized to improve the flow and includes an expanded discussion of developmental and physiological adaptation. Primate conservation issues are also highlighted. The archaeology section now includes historical archaeology and the work of James Deetz along with mention of other archaeological subspecializations. Technological innovations in archaeology such as GIS and GPR are included. Philippe Bourgois's work on the urban drug scene is included to illustrate range of the field sites open to ethnographers today.

The chapter also rejects the characterization of a liberal bias in anthropology, identifying instead the discipline's critical evaluation of the status quo. The ideological diversity among anthropologists is explored while emphasizing their shared methodology that avoids ethnocentrism. An expanded section on ethics includes the history of ethics, the changes of the AAA Code in response to classified or corporate fieldwork, and the effects of emergent technology. We emphasize the shared global environment in the section on globalization, with an updated Globalscape on organ trafficking.

CHAPTER 2: CHARACTERISTICS OF CULTURE
This foundational chapter addresses anthropology's core concept of culture, exploring the term and its significance for human individuals and societies. Elaborating on culture as the medium through which humans handle the problems of existence, we mark out its characteristics as something that is learned, shared, based on symbols, integrated, and dynamic. This chapter discusses ethnocentrism and cultural relativism, as well as culture and adaptation; the functions of culture; culture, society, and the individual; and culture and change. Ethnographic examples include a general look at the Amish of North America and a particular sketch of cremation rituals in Bali. We present a new figure showing China's ethnic groups, which accompanies a discussion about and photo of the Uyghur, a Turkish-speaking Muslim ethnic minority living in China's northwestern province of Xinjiang.

The section on culture and adaptation illustrates with several examples that what is adaptive in the short run may be maladaptive over time, including the fast-shrinking Ogallala aquifer in the U.S. Central Plains. The overhauled section on culture change features a wide-ranging discussion on topics from sustainability to fashion. A new Visual Counterpoint in the section on ethnocentrism compares the anti-immigration protests of Russian Nationalists with those of the American right-wing Minutemen Civil Defense Corps. Special features include a Biocultural Connection on adult stature and the effects of culture, an expanded Anthropologist of Note profile on Bronislaw

Malinowski, and George Esber's Anthropology Applied box on new housing for Apache Indians. This chapter also presents the "barrel model" illustration, conveying the key concepts of the integration of cultural infrastructure, social structure, and superstructure.

CHAPTER 3: ETHNOGRAPHIC RESEARCH: ITS HISTORY, METHODS, AND THEORIES

This chapter takes a unique approach to discussing ethnographic research. It begins with a historical overview on the subject—from the colonial era and salvage ethnography to acculturation studies, advocacy anthropology, and multi-sited ethnography in the era of globalization. The work of numerous anthropologists, past and present, is used to illustrate this historical journey. The chapter continues with an overview of research methods—marking out what is involved in choosing a research question and site and how one goes about doing preparatory research and participant observation. This section also covers ethnographic tools and aids, data-gathering methods, fieldwork challenges, and the creation of an ethnography in written, film, or digital formats.

The chapter also offers an overview of anthropology's theoretical perspectives, discusses the comparative method and the Human Relations Area Files, and explores the moral dilemmas and ethical responsibilities encountered in anthropological research. Special features include the Biocultural Connection "Pig Lovers and Pig Haters" by Marvin Harris, Annette Weiner's Original Study on Trobriand women, and an Anthropologists of Note box that profiles the pioneering visual anthropology work of Gregory Bateson and Margaret Mead. The chapter features new photographs of indigenous assistants trained by anthropologists collecting GPS data in the field and reviewing the downloaded data, alongside a map that is the result of their efforts. In addition, we have developed the section on advocacy anthropology and studying up, clarifying the link between the two, as well as the section on fieldwork challenges—especially the discussion of subjectivity and reflexivity. A new conclusion explores the ethical responsibilities of anthropological research in light of the idea that "knowledge is power."

CHAPTER 4: BECOMING HUMAN: THE ORIGIN AND DIVERSITY OF OUR SPECIES

This chapter gives an overview of race and racism, in the science of the past as well as current problems. With the politics of diversity changing globally, an understanding of the true nature of biological variation has become indispensable. The contributions of anthropology to debunking race as a biological category—starting with the work of Franz Boas and Ashley Montagu—are reviewed along with an emphasis on the interaction of cultural and biological influences on humans. We provide a brief overview

of the evolution of *Homo,* along with a discussion of some of the controversial issues of that development, including the Neandertal debate.

This chapter plays a key role in our effort to convey biology's role in culture. We establish the vital role of mammalian primate biology in being human. The chapter bypasses the terms *hominid* and *hominin* so that students will not get lost in disputes where scientists employ alternate taxonomies. Under the heading "Human Biological Variation and the Problem of Race," we discuss why the concept of race is not useful for studying human biological variation, presenting a historical overview on the creation of false racial categories. Subheads in this section explore race as a social construct and skin color as a biological adaptation.

Special features of the chapter include a Biocultural Connection titled "Paleolithic Prescriptions for the Diseases of Civilization" as well as an Original Study by Frans de Waal on primate reconciliation behavior. We also include Anthropologists of Note profiles on Jane Goodall and Kinji Imanishi.

CHAPTER 5: LANGUAGE AND COMMUNICATION

This chapter investigates the nature of language and the three branches of linguistic anthropology—descriptive linguistics, historical linguistics, and the study of language in its social and cultural settings (ethnolinguistics and sociolinguistics). The latter features new discussions of linguistic relativity and linguistic determinism. Also found here are sections on paralanguage and tonal languages and a fascinating new exploration of talking drums and whistled speech. We have retained and refined the sections on language and gender and body language (proxemics and kinesics) and provided updated material on the impact of electronic media on language and communication worldwide. A historical sketch about writing takes readers from traditional speech performatives and memory devices to Egyptian hieroglyphics to the conception and spread of the alphabet to the 2003 to 2012 Literacy Decade established by the United Nations. A revised and expanded discussion of language loss and revival features an intriguing look at new technology used by linguistic anthropologists collaborating on field research with speakers of endangered Khoisan "click" languages in southern Africa. That section also includes the latest data on the digital divide and its impact on ethnic minority languages—plus an updated chart showing Internet language populations.

This edition includes a revised Biocultural Connection on the biology of human speech, an updated Original Study on the language and intellectual abilities of orangutans, and a new and compelling Anthropology Applied piece, "When Bambi Spoke Arapaho: Preserving Indigenous Languages," by S. Neyooxet Greymorning.

A new conclusion recounts how the telecommunication revolution of the last two decades—mobile phones in particular—are transforming everything from social relations to economic dealings, even in the most remote corners of the world.

CHAPTER 6: SOCIAL IDENTITY, PERSONALITY, AND GENDER

Looking at individual identity within a sociocultural context, this chapter surveys the concept of self, enculturation and the behavioral environment, social identity through personal naming, the development of personality, the concepts of group and modal personality, and the idea of national character. Ethnographic examples include a Navajo naming and First Laugh Ceremony and a description of *sadhus* (ascetic Hindu monks). Our discussion on naming includes a new subsection describing name loss by Brule Sioux Luther Standing Bear and a brief recounting of how President Obama and his father both changed their given names and later reverted back to them. The revised discussion on normal and abnormal personality in a social context includes sobering statistics from a new global report on state-sponsored homophobia.

A substantial section of the chapter provides a thought-provoking historical overview of intersexuality, transsexuality, and transgendering, including current statistics on the incidence of intersexuality worldwide and a revised Original Study on intersexuality. In conjunction with the latter is a new photograph of the intersexed South African track star Caster Semenya, whose 2009 international championship was marred by accusations that she was not "fully female." Other special features include an Anthropologist of Note on Ruth Fulton Benedict and a Biocultural Connection about cross-cultural perspectives on psychosomatic symptoms and mental health. A new concluding section drives home the need for medical pluralism with a variety of healing modalities fit for humanity caught up in the worldwide dynamics of the 21st century.

CHAPTER 7: PATTERNS OF SUBSISTENCE

Here we investigate the various ways humans meet their basic needs and how societies adapt through culture to the environment. We begin with a discussion of adaptation, followed by profiles on modes of subsistence in which we look at food-foraging and food-producing societies—pastoralism, crop cultivation, and industrialization. In this edition, chapter headings, along with the narratives they introduce, have been significantly revised to provide greater clarity and a consistent focus on how—across time, space, and cultures—food is obtained, produced, and distributed. The section on adaptation and cultural evolution includes a new ethnohistorical example—the precontact Easter Island ecosystem collapse cause by deforestation. A new discussion of peasantry has been added, along with an extensive narrative about large-scale industrial food production, using chickens as an example.

The chapter's boxed features include a new Biocultural Connection on "Surviving in the Andes: Aymara Adaptation to High Altitude," along with an Original Study on swidden gardening in the Amazon basin in Brazil. We have included a newly illustrated Anthropology Applied piece about reviving ancient farming practices in Peru. Also in this chapter is a new Globalscape chronicling the international poultry industry.

A new conclusion summarizes the pros and cons of new subsistence strategies and technological innovations—how they impact different members of a society in the short and long run.

CHAPTER 8: ECONOMIC SYSTEMS

This chapter delves into such matters as the control of resources (natural, technological, labor) and types of labor division (gender, age, cooperative, task specialization). A section on distribution and exchange defines various forms of reciprocity (with a detailed and illustrated description of the Kula ring and a revised definition and new discussion of silent trade), along with redistribution and market exchange. The discussion on leveling mechanisms has been revised and expanded, with new narratives on cargos and the potlatch (including a rare and remarkable contemporary potlatch photograph). Our much revised concluding section, "Local Economies and Global Capitalism," includes a new discussion on guest laborers, the global tourism industry, the impact of mobile phones on small producers in remote areas, and genetically modified seeds developed and marketed worldwide—all indicating the economic opportunities and challenges of our era.

The chapter presents two new boxed features: Amanda Stronza's Anthropology Applied piece, "Global Ecotourism and Local Indigenous Culture in Bolivia," and an Anthropologist of Note profile on Rosita Worl, a Tlingit activist.

CHAPTER 9: SEX, MARRIAGE, AND FAMILY

Exploring the close interconnection among sexual reproductive practices, marriage, family, and household, we discuss the household as the basic building block in a culture's social structure, the center where childrearing, as well as shelter, economic production, consumption, and inheritance are commonly organized. Particulars addressed in this chapter include the incest taboo, endogamy and exogamy, dowry and bride-price, cousin marriage, same-sex marriage, divorce, residence patterns, and non-family households. Updated definitions of marriage, family, nuclear family, and extended family encompass current real-life situations around the world.

Among the various ethnographic examples, the presentation on the Nayar has been significantly revised to, among other things, clarify traditional practices from those of today. Updates include the most recent available figures concerning the makeup of U.S. households today and same-sex marriage around the world. The section on divorce has been expanded, with additional commentary on common cross-cultural reasons for ending marriages. Our revised concluding section," discusses how transnationalism, growing numbers of migrant laborers, international adoptions, and modern reproductive technologies are all impacting the ways humans think about and form families.

Boxed features include Serena Nanda's engaging Original Study on arranged marriage in India and a revised version of Martin Ottenheimer's Biocultural Connection on marriage prohibitions in the United States. The new Anthropologist of Note box commemorates the life and contributions of Claude Lévi-Strauss, who passed away at age 100 while this book was in production. Also, a new Globalscape investigates the blessings and issues of international adoption.

CHAPTER 10: KINSHIP AND DESCENT

This chapter marks out the various forms of descent groups and the roles descent plays as an integrated feature in a cultural system. Details and examples are presented concerning lineages, clans, phratries, and moieties (highlighting Hopi Indian matriclans and Scottish highland patriclans, among others), followed by illustrated examples of a representative range of kinship systems and their kinship terminologies.

The chapter includes a look at diasporic communities in today's globalized world and ethnographic examples from the Han Chinese, Maori of New Zealand, and Canela Indians of Brazil. A new section, "Making Relatives," features two subsections. The first is on fictive kin and ritual adoption, illustrating how, across cultures, people have developed ideas about how someone becomes "one of us," whether by birth, paternal recognition, or some other means. Examples include *compadrazgo* or "co-parenthood," established through a Roman Catholic baptismal ceremony and especially common in Latin America. The second part discusses kinship and new reproductive technologies, touching on the mind-boggling array of reproductive possibilities and how they are impacting humanity's conceptions of what it means to be biologically related.

This chapter includes an Anthropology Applied box on resolving Native American tribal membership disputes, a thought-provoking Original Study on honor killings among Turkish immigrants in the Netherlands, and a Biocultural Connection piece about ancient Maori mythical traditions that are now supported by genetic research.

CHAPTER 11: GROUPING BY GENDER, AGE, COMMON INTEREST, AND SOCIAL CLASS

This much-refined chapter includes discussions of grouping by gender, age, common interest, and social class. The section on age grouping features ethnographic material from the Mundurucu of Brazil and the Tiriki and Maasai of East Africa. Common-interest group examples range from the Shriners to the Crips to the Jewish diaspora. Also included is a new subsection describing the social networking platforms available to Internet and mobile phone users. In addition, we have expanded our discussion of women's organizations, profiling various groups such as SEWA, India's far-reaching Self-Employed Women's Association, which is having an enormous impact on the economic contributions of women. Our revised section on social class and caste includes three historical case studies: one on caste and its role in India's Hindu culture (accompanied by a new figure illustrating the traditional Hindu caste system) and two concerning racial segregation in South Africa and the United States.

Boxed features include Michael Blakey's Biocultural Connection on the African Burial Ground Project—the archaeological dig in New York City that revealed the physical stress of an entire community brought on by the social institution of slavery—and a shorter, punchier version of Susan Lees's Original Study on the Jewish *eruv*. Also included in this chapter is an updated version of our Globalscape about an Ivory Coast soccer star and the political impact of sports.

We conclude the chapter with a much-revised section on social mobility, noting that while great disparities in wealth, power, and prestige persist in many parts of the world, there are notable social changes in the opposite direction. Among them is a growing social justice movement among India's lowest castes and Untouchables, including a group of women known as the Pink Vigilantes.

CHAPTER 12: POLITICS, POWER, AND VIOLENCE

Looking at a range of uncentralized and centralized political systems—from kin-ordered bands and tribes to chiefdoms and states—this chapter explores the question of power, the intersection of politics and religion, and issues of political leadership and gender. Discussing the maintenance of order, we look at internalized and externalized controls (including a section on gossip's role in curbing socially unacceptable behavior), along with social control through witchcraft and through law. We mark the functions of law and the ways different societies deal with crime, including sentencing laws in Canada based on traditional Native American restorative justice techniques such as the Talking Circle.

Next, we shift our focus from maintaining order within a society to external affairs, including a discussion of violent conflict and warfare. In addition to a revised subsection that gives an overview of the 5,000-year history of armed conflicts among humans, we include material on current ideological and political conflicts and genocide, along with a map showing the frequency of armed conflicts in multinational states where one group suppresses other(s).

Special features include a Biocultural Connection exploring the relationship of sex, gender, and violence; an updated Anthropology Applied box on dispute resolution; and a new Globalscape profiling the surprising and complex economics behind piracy off the coast of Somalia. The revised final section of this chapter includes a new historical narrative on the concept of "crimes against humanity" and the International Criminal Court established in the Netherlands in 2002, which now has 110 member states.

CHAPTER 13: SPIRITUALITY, RELIGION, AND THE SUPERNATURAL

This chapter opens with a description of the anthropological approach to religion and the current distinctions between religion and spirituality, followed by an overview of the status of religion and spirituality today. The latter includes a chart showing the major religions of the world with their percentages of believers, along with a new world map depicting the global distribution of major religions that indicates where each is the majority. We then discuss beliefs concerning supernatural beings and spiritual forces (gods and goddesses, ancestral spirits, animism, and animatism), religious specialists (priests and priestesses, as well as shamans), and rituals and ceremonies (rites of passage and rites of intensification). The section on shamanism explores the origins of the term and presents our "shamanic complex" model of how shamanic healings take place. Ethnographic examples include the vision quests of Penobscot Indians of New England and the trance dancing and healing of Ju/'hoansi healers in southern Africa. We include a new subsection on taboos that discusses Mary Douglas's rituals of purity and impurity, along with a much-revised section on rites of passage, highlighting the original work of van Gennep.

A section on religion, magic, and witchcraft highlights Ibibio witchcraft, while another passage marks out religion's psychological and social functions, including efforts to heal physical, emotional, and social ills. Touching on religion and cultural change, this chapter looks at revitalization movements and new material on indigenous Christian churches in Africa.

Among other highlights in this chapter are discussions on sacred places and women's roles in religious leadership. Boxed features include Hillary Crane's arresting Biocultural Connection about Taiwanese Buddhist nuns, along with an Anthropology Applied piece on the mix of traditional beliefs and modern medicine in Swaziland. The chapter closes with a newly crafted section on the enduring nature of religion and spirituality that includes Bill Maurer's timely new Original Study on Shariah law and banking, "Sacred Law in Global Capitalism."

CHAPTER 14: THE ARTS

This chapter explores in detail three key categories of art—visual, verbal, and musical—illustrating what they reveal about and what functions they play in societies. It describes the distinctly holistic approach anthropologists bring to the study of art, noting the range of cultural insights art reveals—from kinship structures to social values, religious beliefs, and political ideas. Various approaches to analyzing art (such as, aesthetic and interpretive) are applied to rock art in southern Africa. Ethnographic examples in the section on verbal arts include the Abenaki creation myth of Tabaldak, one of many versions of the classic and culturally widespread father/son/donkey tale, as well as samples of modern urban legends in the United States.

The revised section on music now begins by stepping back in time to 40,000-year-old bone flutes and whistles unearthed by archaeologists and then marches forward to Abenaki shamans playing cedar flutes to summon game animals, traditional and New Age shamans playing drums to evoke trances, laborers on the edge of the Sahara working to the beat of a drum, and West African *griots* who recount their people's history through percussion and lyrics. Beyond such examples, this chapter discusses the elements of music, including tonality, rhythm, and melody. The chapter includes a Biocultural Connection about the role of peyote in Huichol art, along with a shorter, sharper version of Margo DeMello's Original Study, on the modern tattoo community.

The chapter's revised conclusion describes how endangered indigenous groups use aesthetic traditions as part of their cultural and economic survival strategy. It features a moving example of this in a new Applied Anthropology piece, "Bringing Back the Past," by Penobscot Indian anthropologist and master beader, Jennifer Sapiel Neptune.

CHAPTER 15: PROCESSES OF CHANGE

The themes and terminology of globalization are woven through this chapter, which includes definitions that distinguish *progress* from *modernization, rebellion* from *revolution,* and *acculturation* from *enculturation.* Here, we discuss mechanisms of change—innovation, diffusion, and cultural loss, as well as repressive change. Two new and very different examples have been added to the section on diffusion: We trace the spread of maize/corn and of the metric system. Our exploration of culture change and loss covers acculturation and ethnocide, citing a range of examples of repressive change from around the world—including a discussion of ethnocide in Tibet. This chapter also looks at reactions to such change, including revitalization movements, rebellions, and revolutions. A discussion on modernization touches on the issue of self-determination among indigenous peoples and highlights two contrasting cases: Skolt Lapp reindeer herders of Finland and Shuar Indians of Ecuador. Also featured are the historical profile of applied or practical anthropology and the emergence of action or advocacy anthropology in collaboration with indigenous societies, ethnic minorities, and other besieged or repressed groups. Among the many images in this chapter is a new United Nations Refugee Agency map showing the numbers and home countries of the 42 million forcibly displaced people in the world today.

Boxed features include a Biocultural Connection on the emergence of new diseases, an Anthropologist of Note profile on Eric R. Wolf, and an Anthropology Applied piece on development anthropology and dams, with a new and fascinating satellite image of China's Three Gorges Dam. The chapter concludes with a discussion of globalization as a worldwide process of accelerated modernization in which all parts of the earth are becoming interconnected in one vast, interrelated, and all-encompassing system.

CHAPTER 16: GLOBAL CHALLENGES, LOCAL RESPONSES, AND THE ROLE OF ANTHROPOLOGY

Our final chapter zeroes in on numerous global challenges confronting the human species today. We ask students to use the anthropological tools they have learned to think critically about these issues and take informed steps to help bring about a future in which humans live harmoniously with one another and with the natural world that sustains us. Sections on global culture and ethnic resurgence look at Westernization and its counterforce of growing nationalism and the breakup of multi-ethnic states. We present examples of resistance to globalization and discuss pluralism and multiculturalism.

We also recount the ever-widening gap between those who have wealth and power and those who do not. We define and illustrate the term *structural power* and its two branches—hard power (military and economic might) and soft power (media might that gains control through ideological influence). A substantial section about the rise of global corporations places this phenomenon in historical context and highlights the largest corporations (making particular note of media corporations and the emergence of the global "mediascape"). A new chart showing global distribution of military expenditure appears in this section, along with a graph comparing corporate profits to country GDPs.

We then address problems of structural violence—from pollution to epidemics of hunger and obesity. We also touch on the psychological problems that derive from powerful marketing messages shaping cultural standards concerning the ideal human body.

Special box features include an updated version of Laura Nader's Original Study "Standardizing the Body: The Question of Choice"; a Biocultural Connection about the threat to Arctic cultures from outside contamination; and an updated Globalscape on the practice of dumping toxic waste in the Third World.

We close with a summary of the meaning of this chapter's vast and sometimes troubling content—and discuss the role anthropology can play in helping to solve practical problems on local and global levels. Featured in this closing section is a heartening new Anthropologist of Note on Paul Farmer, world-renowned anthropologist, medical doctor, and human rights activist.

Supplements

Cultural Anthropology comes with a comprehensive supplements program to help instructors create an effective learning environment both inside and outside the classroom and to aid students in mastering the material.

Supplements for Instructors

ONLINE INSTRUCTOR'S MANUAL AND TEST BANK

The Instructor's Manual offers detailed chapter outlines, lecture suggestions, key terms, and student activities such as video exercises and Internet exercises. In addition, there are over seventy-five chapter test questions including multiple choice, true/false, fill-in-the-blank, short answer, and essay.

POWERLECTURE WITH JOININ™ AND EXAMVIEW®

On CD or DVD, this one-stop class preparation tool contains ready-to-use Microsoft PowerPoint slides, enabling you to assemble, edit, publish, and present custom lectures with ease. PowerLecture helps you bring together text-specific lecture outlines and art from Haviland's text along with videos and your own materials—culminating in powerful, personalized, media-enhanced presentations. The **JoinIn**™ content (for use with most "clicker" systems) available within PowerLecture delivers instant classroom assessment and active learning. Take polls and attendance, quiz, and invite students to actively participate while they learn. Featuring automatic grading, **ExamView**® is also available within PowerLecture, allowing you to create, deliver, and customize tests and study guides (both print and online) in minutes. See assessments onscreen exactly as they will print or display online. Build tests of up to 250 questions using up to twelve question types and enter an unlimited number of new questions or edit existing questions. PowerLecture also includes the text's Instructor's Resource Manual and Test Bank as Word documents.

WEBTUTOR ON BLACKBOARD AND WEBCT

Jumpstart your course with customizable, rich, text-specific content within your course management system. Simply load a content cartridge into your course management system to easily blend, add, edit, reorganize, or delete content, all of which is specific to Haviland et al.'s *Anthropology: The Human Challenge*, 13th edition, and includes media resources, quizzing, weblinks, discussion topics, and interactive games and exercises.

WADSWORTH ANTHROPOLOGY VIDEO LIBRARY

Qualified adopters may select full-length videos from an extensive library of offerings drawn from such excellent educational video sources as *Films for the Humanities and Sciences.*

ABC ANTHROPOLOGY VIDEO SERIES

This exclusive video series was created jointly by Wadsworth and ABC for the anthropology course. Each video contains approximately 60 minutes of footage originally broadcast on ABC within the past several years. The videos are broken into short 2- to 7-minute segments, perfect for classroom use as lecture launchers or to illustrate key anthropological concepts. An annotated table of contents accompanies each video, providing descriptions of the segments and suggestions for their possible use within the course.

AIDS IN AFRICA DVD

Southern Africa has been overcome by a pandemic of unparalleled proportions. This documentary series focuses on the new democracy of Namibia and the many actions there to control HIV/AIDS. Included in this series are four documentary films created by the Periclean Scholars at Elon University: (1) *Young Struggles, Eternal Faith,* which focuses on caregivers in the faith community; (2) *The Shining Lights of Opuwo,* which shows how young people share their messages of hope through song and dance; (3) *A Measure of Our Humanity,* which describes HIV/AIDS as an issue related to gender, poverty, stigma, education, and justice; and (4) *You Wake Me Up,* a story of two HIV-positive women and their acts of courage helping other women learn to survive. Cengage/Wadsworth is excited to offer these award-winning films to instructors for use in class. When presenting topics such as gender, faith, culture, poverty, and so on, the films will be enlightening for students and will expand their global perspective of HIV/AIDS.

Online Resources for Instructors and Students

ANTHROPOLOGY RESOURCE CENTER

This online center offers a wealth of information and useful tools for both instructors and students in all four fields of anthropology. It includes interactive maps, learning modules, video exercises, and breaking news in anthropology. For instructors, the Resource Center includes a gateway to time-saving teaching tools, such as image banks, sample syllabi, and more. Access to the website is available free when bundled with the text or for purchase at a nominal fee.

THE HAVILAND ET AL. COMPANION WEBSITE

The book's companion site includes chapter-specific resources for instructors and students. For instructors, the site offers a password-protected Instructor's Manual, Microsoft PowerPoint presentation slides, and more. For students, there are a multitude of text-specific study aids: tutorial practice quizzes that can be scored and e-mailed to the instructor, weblinks, flash cards, crossword puzzles, and much more.

INFOTRAC® COLLEGE EDITION

InfoTrac College Edition is an online library that offers full-length articles from thousands of scholarly and popular publications. Among the journals available are *American Anthropologist, Current Anthropology,* and *Canadian Review of Sociology and Anthropology.* Contact your local Cengage sales representative for details.

Supplements for Students

TELECOURSE STUDY GUIDE

The new distance learning course, **Anthropology: The Four Fields,** provides online and print companion study guide options that include study aids, interactive exercises, videos, and more.

Additional Student Resources

BASIC GENETICS FOR ANTHROPOLOGY CD-ROM: PRINCIPLES AND APPLICATIONS (STAND-ALONE VERSION), BY ROBERT JURMAIN AND LYNN KILGORE

This student CD-ROM expands on such biological concepts as biological inheritance (genes, DNA sequencing, and so on) and applications of that to modern human populations at the molecular level (human variation and adaptation—to disease, diet, growth, and development). Interactive animations and simulations bring these important concepts to life for students so they can fully understand the essential biological principles required for physical anthropology. Also available are quizzes and interactive flashcards for further study.

HOMINID FOSSILS CD-ROM: AN INTERACTIVE ATLAS, BY JAMES AHERN

The interactive atlas CD-ROM includes over seventy-five key fossils important for a clear understanding of human evolution. The QuickTime Virtual Reality (QTVR) "object" movie format for each fossil enables students to have a near-authentic experience of working with these important finds, by allowing them to rotate the fossil 360 degrees. Unlike some VR media, QTVR objects are made using actual photographs of the real objects and thus better preserve details of color and texture. The fossils used are high-quality research casts and real fossils. The organization of the atlas is nonlinear, with three levels and multiple paths, enabling students to see how the fossil fits into the map of human evolution in terms of geography, time, and evolution. The CD-ROM offers students an inviting, authentic learning environment, one that also contains a dynamic quizzing feature that will allow students to test their knowledge of fossil and species identification, as well as provide more detailed information about the fossil record.

VIRTUAL LABORATORIES FOR PHYSICAL ANTHROPOLOGY CD-ROM, FOURTH EDITION, BY JOHN KAPPELMAN

The new edition of this full-color, interactive CD-ROM provides students with a hands-on computer component for completing lab assignments at school or at home. Through the use of video clips, 3-D animations, sound, and digital images, students can actively participate in twelve labs as part of their physical anthropology and archaeology course. The labs and assignments teach students how to formulate and test hypotheses with exercises that include how to measure, plot, interpret, and evaluate a variety of data drawn from osteological, behavioral, and fossil materials.

Readings and Case Studies

CLASSIC AND CONTEMPORARY READINGS IN PHYSICAL ANTHROPOLOGY, EDITED BY M. K. SANDFORD WITH EILEEN M. JACKSON

This highly accessible reader emphasizes science—its principles and methods—as well as the historical development of physical anthropology and the applications of new technology to the discipline. The editors provide an introduction to the reader as well as a brief overview of the article so students know what to look for. Each article also includes discussion questions and Internet resources.

CLASSIC READINGS IN CULTURAL ANTHROPOLOGY, 2ND EDITION, EDITED BY GARY FERRARO

Now in its second edition, this reader includes historical and recent articles that have had a profound effect on the field of anthropology. Organized according to the major topic areas found in most cultural anthropology courses, this reader includes an introduction to the material as well

as a brief overview of each article, discussion questions, and InfoTrac College Edition key search terms.

GLOBALIZATION AND CHANGE IN FIFTEEN CULTURES: BORN IN ONE WORLD, LIVING IN ANOTHER, EDITED BY GEORGE SPINDLER AND JANICE E. STOCKARD

In this volume, fifteen case study authors write about culture change in today's diverse settings around the world. Each original article provides insight into the dynamics and meanings of change, as well as the effects of globalization at the local level.

CASE STUDIES IN CULTURAL ANTHROPOLOGY, EDITED BY GEORGE SPINDLER AND JANICE E. STOCKARD

Select from more than sixty classic and contemporary ethnographies representing geographic and topical diversity. Newer case studies focus on cultural change and cultural continuity, reflecting the globalization of the world.

CASE STUDIES IN CONTEMPORARY SOCIAL ISSUES, EDITED BY JOHN A. YOUNG

Framed around social issues, these new contemporary case studies are globally comparative and represent the cutting-edge work of anthropologists today.

CASE STUDIES IN ARCHAEOLOGY, EDITED BY JEFFREY QUILTER

These engaging accounts of new archaeological techniques, issues, and solutions—as well as studies discussing the collection of material remains—range from site-specific excavations to types of archaeology practiced.

EVOLUTION OF THE BRAIN MODULE: NEUROANATOMY, DEVELOPMENT, AND PALEONTOLOGY, BY DANIEL D. WHITE

The human species is the only species that has ever created a symphony, written a poem, developed a mathematical equation, or studied its own origins. The biological structure that has enabled humans to perform these feats of intelligence is the human brain. This module explores the basics of neuroanatomy, brain development, lateralization, and sexual dimorphism and provides the fossil evidence for hominid brain evolution. This module in chapter-like print format can be packaged for free with the text.

FORENSIC ANTHROPOLOGY MODULE: A BRIEF REVIEW, BY DIANE FRANCE

Diane France explores the myths and realities of forensic anthropology: the search for human remains in crime scenes, forensic anthropology in the courtroom, special challenges in mass fatality incident responses (such as plane crashes and terrorist acts), and what students should consider if they want to pursue a career in forensic anthropology.

MOLECULAR ANTHROPOLOGY MODULE,
BY LESLIE KNAPP

Leslie Knapp explores how molecular genetic methods are used to understand the organization and expression of genetic information in humans and nonhuman primates. Students will learn about the common laboratory methods used to study genetic variation and evolution in molecular anthropology. Examples are drawn from up-to-date research on human evolutionary origins and comparative primate genomics to demonstrate that scientific research is an ongoing process with theories frequently being questioned and reevaluated.

HUMAN ENVIRONMENT INTERACTIONS:
NEW DIRECTIONS IN HUMAN ECOLOGY,
BY CATHY GALVIN

Cathy Galvin provides students with an introduction to the basic concepts in human ecology, before discussing cultural ecology, human adaptation studies, human behavioral ecology, and political ecology. The module concludes with a discussion of resilience and global change as a result of human–environment interactions today.

Acknowledgments

In this day and age, no textbook comes to fruition without extensive collaboration. Beyond the shared endeavors of our author team, this book owes its completion to a wide range of individuals, from colleagues in the discipline to those involved in the production process. We are particularly grateful for the comments received through an electronic survey as well as the remarkable group of manuscript reviewers listed below. They provided unusually detailed and thoughtful feedback that helped us to hone and re-hone our narrative.

Stewart Brewer, Dana College

Kendall Campbell, Washington State University

Jennifer Coe, Jamestown Community College

Julie David, Orange Coast College and California Baptist University

Rene M. Descartes, State University of New York at Cobleskill

Sylvia Grider, Texas A&M University

Susan H. Krook, Normandale Community College

Barbara J. Michael, University of North Carolina, Wilmington

Renee B. Walker, SUNY College at Oneonta

Linda F. Whitmer, Hope International University

Holly E. Yatros, Oakland Community College and Macomb Community College

We carefully considered and made use of the wide range of comments provided by these individuals. Our decisions on how to utilize their suggestions were influenced by our own perspectives on anthropology and teaching, combined with the priorities and page limits of this text. Neither our reviewers nor any of the other anthropologists mentioned here should be held responsible for any shortcomings in this book. They should, however, be credited as contributors to many of the book's strengths.

Thanks, too, go to colleagues who provided material for some of the Original Study, Biocultural Connection, and Anthropology Applied boxes in this text: Michael Blakey, Hillary Crane, John Crock, Margo DeMello, Katherine Dettwyler, Frans B. M. de Waal, George S. Esber, Anabel Ford, Michele Goldsmith, Edward C. Green, S. Neyooxet Greymorning, Marvin Harris, Donna Hart, John Hawks, Michael M. Horowitz, Suzanne Leclerc-Madlala, Susan Lees, Roger Lewin, Anne Nacey Maggioncalda, Charles C. Mann, Jonathan Marks, Bill Maurer, Sir Robert May, H. Lyn White Miles, Laura Nader, Serena Nanda, Jennifer Sapiel Neptune, Martin Ottenheimer, Anna Roosevelt, Robert M. Sapolsky, Sherry Simpson, Meredith F. Small, Karen Springen, Amanda Stronza, William Ury, Clementine van Eck, Annette B. Weiner, Dennis Werner, R. K. Williamson, and Jane C. Waldbaum. Among these individuals we particularly want to acknowledge our admiration, affection, and appreciation for our mutual friend and colleague Jim Petersen, whose life came to an abrupt and tragic end while returning from fieldwork in the Brazilian Amazon. Jim's work is featured in one of the pieces by Charles C. Mann.

We have debts of gratitude to office workers in our departments for their cheerful help in clerical matters: Karen Rundquist, Emira Smailagic, Katie Weaver, and Sheri Youngberg. And to research librarian extraordinaire Nancy Bianchi and colleagues Yvette Pigeon, Paula Duncan, Lajiri Van Ness-Otunnu, and Michael Wesch for engaging in lively discussions of anthropological and pedagogical approaches. Also worthy of note here are the introductory anthropology teaching assistants who, through the years, have shed light for us on effective ways to reach new generations of students.

Our thanksgiving inventory would be incomplete without mentioning individuals at Wadsworth Publishing who helped conceive this text and bring it to fruition. Special gratitude goes to acquisitions editor Erin Mitchell and to senior development editor Lin Marshall Gaylord for her vision, vigor, and anthropological knowledge. Our thanks also go out to Wadsworth's skilled and enthusiastic editorial, marketing, design, and production team: Andrew Keay (marketing manager), Melanie Cregger (media editor), Pamela Simon (editorial assistant), Rachel Krapf (assistant editor), as well as Jerilyn Emori (content project manager) and Caryl Gorska (art director).

In addition to all of the above, we have had the invaluable aid of several most able freelancers, including our photo researchers Billie Porter and Susan Kaprov, who were always willing to go the extra mile to find the most telling and compelling photographs, and our skilled graphic designer Lisa Buckley. We are especially thankful to have had the opportunity to work once again with copy editor Jennifer Gordon and production coordinator Joan Keyes of Dovetail Publishing Services. Consummate professionals and generous souls, both of them keep track of countless details and bring calm efficiency and grace to the demands of meeting difficult deadlines. Their efforts and skills play a major role in making our work doable and pleasurable.

And finally, all of us are indebted to family members who have not only put up with our textbook preoccupation but cheered us on in the endeavor. Dana had the tireless support and keen eye of husband Peter Bingham—along with the varied contributions of their three sons Nishan, Tavid, and Aram Bingham. As co-author spouses under the same roof, Harald and Bunny have picked up slack for each other on every front to help this project move along smoothly. But the biggest debt of gratitude may be in Bill's corner for initiating this book more than three decades ago, building it into a leading introductory text used by hundreds of thousands of students around the world, and having the foresight to bring a trio of co-authors on board about a decade ago to maintain and build upon the established strengths of this long-term educational endeavor. Before putting together a team of co-authors several editions ago, he relied on the know-how of his spouse Anita de Laguna Haviland, whose varied skills played a vital role in this book's success.

About the Authors

Authors Bunny McBride, Dana Walrath, Harald Prins, and William Haviland

All four members of this author team share overlapping research interests and a similar vision of what anthropology is (and should be) about. For example, all are true believers in the four-field approach to anthropology and all have some involvement in applied work.

WILLIAM A. HAVILAND is Professor Emeritus at the University of Vermont, where he founded the Department of Anthropology and taught for thirty-two years. He holds a PhD in anthropology from the University of Pennsylvania.

He has carried out original research in archaeology in Guatemala and Vermont; ethnography in Maine and Vermont; and physical anthropology in Guatemala. This work has been the basis of numerous publications in various national and international books and journals, as well as in media intended for the general public. His books include *The Original Vermonters*, co-authored with Marjorie Power, and a technical monograph on ancient Maya settlement. He also served as consultant for the award-winning telecourse, *Faces of Culture,* and is co-editor of the series *Tikal Reports,* published by the University of Pennsylvania Museum of Archaeology and Anthropology.

Besides his teaching and writing, Dr. Haviland has lectured to numerous professional as well as non-professional audiences in Canada, Mexico, Lesotho, South Africa, and Spain, as well as in the United States. A staunch supporter of indigenous rights, he served as expert witness for the Missisquoi Abenakis of Vermont in an important court case over aboriginal fishing rights.

Awards received by Dr. Haviland include being named University Scholar by the Graduate School of the University of Vermont in 1990; a Certificate of Appreciation from the Sovereign Republic of the Abenaki Nation of Missisquoi, St. Francis/Sokoki Band in 1996; and a Lifetime Achievement Award from the Center for Research on Vermont in 2006. Now retired from teaching, he continues his research, writing, and lecturing from the coast of Maine. His most recent book is *At the Place of the Lobsters and Crabs* (2009).

HARALD E. L. PRINS is a University Distinguished Professor of Anthropology at Kansas State University. Born in the Netherlands, he studied at universities in Europe and the United States. He has done extensive fieldwork among indigenous peoples in South and North America, published many dozens of articles in seven languages, authored *The Mi'kmaq: Resistance, Accommodation, and Cultural Survival* (1996), co-authored *Indians in Eden* (2009), and co-edited *American Beginnings* (1994) and other books. Also trained in film, he has made award-winning documentaries and served as president of the Society for Visual Anthropology and visual anthropology editor of the *American Anthropologist.* Dr. Prins has won his university's most prestigious undergraduate teaching awards, held the Coffman Chair for University Distinguished Teaching Scholars (2004–2005), and was selected as Professor of the Year for the State of Kansas by the Carnegie Foundation for the Advancement of Teaching in 2008. Active in human rights, he served as expert witness in Native rights cases in the U.S. Senate and various Canadian courts, and was instrumental in the successful federal recognition and land claims of the Aroostook Band of Micmacs (1991). Dr. Prins was appointed Research Associate at the National Museum of Natural History, Smithsonian Institution (2008–2011), and served as guest professor at Lund University in Sweden (2010).

BUNNY MCBRIDE is an award-winning author specializing in cultural anthropology, indigenous peoples, international tourism, and nature conservation issues. Published in dozens of national and international print media, she has reported from Africa, Europe, China, and the Indian Ocean. Highly rated as a teacher, she served as visiting anthropology faculty at Principia College, the Salt Institute for Documentary Field

Studies, and since 1996 as adjunct lecturer of anthropology at Kansas State University. McBride's many publications include *Women of the Dawn* (1999), *Molly Spotted Elk: A Penobscot in Paris* (1995), and *Indians in Eden: Wabanakis and Rusticators on Maine's Mount Desert Island, 1850s–1920s* (co-authored, 2009). The Maine State legislature awarded her a special commendation for significant contributions to Native women's history (1999). A community activist and researcher for the Aroostook Band of Micmacs (1981–1991), McBride assisted this Maine Indian community in its successful efforts to reclaim lands, gain tribal status, and revitalize cultural traditions. She has curated various museum exhibits based on her research, most recently *Journeys West: The David & Peggy Rockefeller American Indian Art Collection* for the Abbe Museum in Bar Harbor, Maine. Currently she is working on a new book co-authored with Harald Prins (*From Indian Island to Omaha Beach: The Story of Charles Shay, Penobscot Indian War Hero,* 2010) and a series of museum exhibitions based on a two-volume study co-authored with Harald Prins for the National Park Service (*Asticou's Island Domain,* 2007). McBride also serves as oral history advisor for the Kansas Humanities Council and as board member and vice president of the Women's World Summit Foundation, based in Geneva, Switzerland.

DANA WALRATH is Assistant Professor of Family Medicine at the University of Vermont and a Women's Studies-affiliated faculty member. She earned her PhD in anthropology from the University of Pennsylvania and is a medical and biological anthropologist with principal interests in biocultural aspects of reproduction, the cultural context of biomedicine, genetics, and evolutionary medicine. She co-founded and directed an innovative educational program at the University of Vermont's College of Medicine that brings anthropological theory and practice to first-year medical students. Before joining the faculty at the University of Vermont in 2000, she taught at the University of Pennsylvania and Temple University. Her research has been supported by the National Science Foundation, Health Resources and Services Administration, the Centers for Disease Control, and the Templeton Foundation. Dr. Walrath's publications have appeared in *Current Anthropology, American Anthropologist,* and *American Journal of Physical Anthropology.* An active member of the Council on the Anthropology of Reproduction, she has also served on a national committee to develop women's health-care learning objectives for medical education and works locally to improve health care for refugees and immigrants.

Challenge Issue It is a challenge to make sense of who we are. Where did we come from? Why are we so radically different from some animals and so surprisingly similar to others? Why do our bodies look the way they do? How do we explain so many different beliefs, languages, and customs? Why do we act in certain ways? What makes us tick? While some people answer these questions with biological mechanisms and others with social or spiritual explanations, scholars in the discipline of anthropology address them through a holistic, integrated approach. Anthropology considers human culture and biology, in all times and places, as inextricably intertwined, each affecting the other in important ways. This photograph, taken in a specialized maternity clinic in Gujarat, India, provides a case in point. Since commercial surrogacy—the practice of paying a woman to carry another's fetus to term—was legalized in 2002, wealthy childless parents from all over the globe have traveled to India for this service. Chosen by foreigners because of their healthy drug-free lifestyle and lower fees, Indian women take on extra biological risk to make it possible for others to reproduce their genes. Global politics and local cultural practices interact with the seemingly purely biological process of birth. Understanding humanity in all its biological and cultural variety, past and present, is the fundamental contribution of anthropology. In the era of globalization, this contribution is all the more important. Indeed, the holistic and integrative anthropological perspective has become essential to human survival.

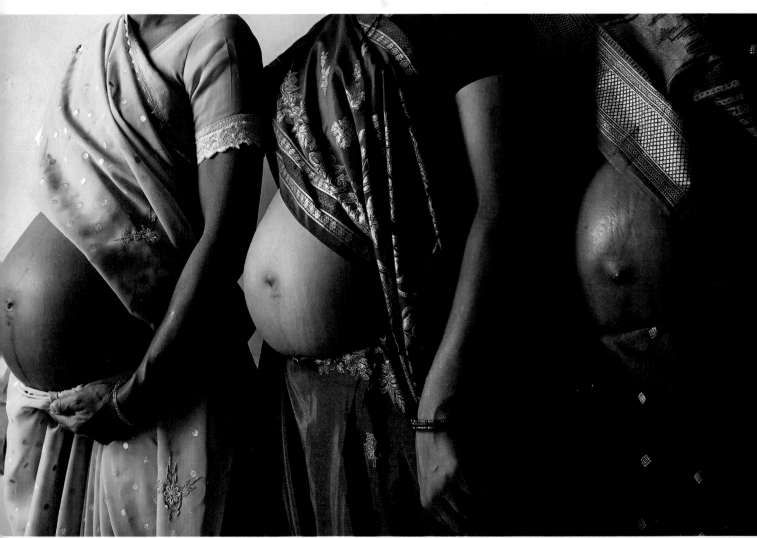

CHAPTER 1

The Essence of Anthropology

Chapter Preview

What Is Anthropology?

Anthropology, the study of humankind everywhere throughout time, produces knowledge about what makes people different from one another and what we all have in common. Anthropologists work within four fields of the discipline. While physical anthropologists focus on humans as biological organisms (tracing evolutionary development and looking at biological variations), cultural anthropologists investigate the contrasting ways groups of humans think, feel, and behave. Archaeologists try to recover information about human cultures—usually from the past—by studying material objects, skeletal remains, and settlements. Meanwhile, linguists study languages—communication systems by which cultures are maintained and passed on to succeeding generations. Practitioners in all four fields are informed by one another's findings and united by a common anthropological perspective on the human condition.

How Does Anthropology Compare to Other Disciplines?

In studying humankind, early anthropologists came to the conclusion that to fully understand the complexities of human thought, feelings, behavior, and biology, it was necessary to study and compare all humans, wherever and whenever. More than any other feature, this comparative, cross-cultural, long-term perspective distinguishes anthropology from other social sciences. Anthropologists are not the only scholars who study people, but they are uniquely holistic in their approach, focusing on the interconnections and interdependence of all aspects of the human experience, past and present. This holistic and integrative outlook equips anthropologists to grapple with an issue of overriding importance for all of us today: globalization.

How Do Anthropologists Do What They Do?

Anthropologists, like other scholars, are concerned with the description and explanation of reality. They formulate and test hypotheses—tentative explanations of observed phenomena—concerning humankind. Their aim is to develop reliable theories—interpretations or explanations supported by bodies of data—about our species. These data are usually collected through fieldwork—a particular kind of hands-on research that gives anthropologists enough familiarity with a situation that they can begin to recognize patterns, regularities, and exceptions. It is also through careful observation, combined with comparison, that anthropologists test their theories.

For as long as we have been on earth, people have sought to understand who we are, where we come from, and why we act as we do. Throughout most of human history, though, people relied on myth and folklore for answers, rather than on the systematic testing of data obtained through careful observation. Anthropology, over the last 150 years, has emerged as a tradition of scientific inquiry with its own approaches to answering these questions. Simply stated, **anthropology** is the study of humankind in all times and places. While focusing primarily on *Homo sapiens*—the human species—anthropologists also study our ancestors and close animal relatives for clues about what it means to be human.

The Development of Anthropology

Although works of anthropological significance have a considerable antiquity—about 2,500 years ago the Greek historian Herodotus chronicled the many different cultures he encountered during extensive journeys through territories surrounding the Mediterranean Sea and beyond, and nearly 700 years ago far-roving North African Arab scholar Ibn Khaldun wrote a "universal history"—anthropology as a distinct field of inquiry is a relatively recent product of Western civilization. The first anthropology program in the United States, for example, was established at the University of Pennsylvania in 1886, and the first doctorate in anthropology was granted by Clark University in 1892. If people have always been concerned about their origins and those of others, then why did it take such a long time for a systematic discipline of anthropology to appear?

   The answer to this is as complex as human history. In part, it relates to the limits of human technology. Throughout most of history, the geographic horizons of people have been restricted. Without ways to travel to distant parts of the world, observation of cultures and peoples far from one's own was a difficult—if not impossible—undertaking. Extensive travel was usually the privilege of an exclusive few; the study of foreign peoples and cultures could not flourish until improved modes of transportation and communication developed.

   This is not to say that people have been unaware of the existence of others in the world who look and act differently from themselves. The Old and New Testaments of the Bible, for example, are full of references to diverse ancient peoples, among them Babylonians, Egyptians, Greeks,

Anthropologists come from many corners of the world and carry out research in a huge variety of cultures all around the globe. Dr. Jayasinhji Jhala, pictured here, hails from the old city of Dhrangadhra in Gujarat, northwestern India. A member of the Jhala clan of Rajputs, an aristocratic caste of warriors, he grew up in the royal palace of his father, the maharaja. After earning a bachelor of arts degree in India, he came to the United States and earned a master's in visual studies from MIT, followed by a doctorate in anthropology from Harvard. Currently a professor and director of the programs of Visual Anthropology and the Visual Anthropology Media Laboratory at Temple University, he returns regularly to India with students to film cultural traditions in his own caste-stratified society.

Jews, and Syrians. However, the differences among these people are slight in comparison to those among peoples of arctic Siberia, the Amazon rainforest, and the Kalahari Desert of southern Africa.

   The invention of the magnetic compass allowed seafarers on better-equipped sailing ships to travel to truly faraway places and to meet people who differed radically from themselves. The massive encounter with previously unknown peoples—which began 500 years ago as Europeans sought to extend their trade and political

anthropology   The study of humankind in all times and places.

domination to all parts of the world—focused attention on human differences in all their amazing variety. With this attention, Europeans gradually came to recognize that despite all the differences, they might share a basic humanity with people everywhere. Initially, Europeans labeled these societies "savage" or "barbarian" because they did not share the same cultural values. Over time, however, Europeans acknowledged such highly diverse groups as fellow members of one species and therefore as relevant to an understanding of what it is to be human. This growing interest in human diversity coincided with increasing efforts to explain findings in scientific terms. It cast doubts on the traditional explanations based on religious texts such as the Torah, Bible, or Koran and helped set the stage for the birth of anthropology.

Although anthropology originated within the historical context of European cultures, it has long since gone global. Today, it is an exciting, transnational discipline whose practitioners come from diverse societies all around the world. Many professional anthropologists born and raised in Asian, African, Latin American, or American Indian cultures traditionally studied by European and North American anthropologists contribute substantially to the discipline. Their distinct non-Western perspectives shed new light not only on their own cultures but on those of others. It is noteworthy that in one regard diversity has long been a hallmark of the discipline: From its earliest days, women as well as men have entered the field. Throughout this text, we will be spotlighting individual anthropologists, illustrating the diversity of these practitioners and their work.

Anthropological Perspectives

Many academic disciplines are concerned in one way or another with our species. For example, biology focuses on the genetic, anatomical, and physiological aspects of organisms. Psychology is concerned primarily with cognitive, mental, and emotional issues, while economics examines the production, distribution, and management of material resources. And various disciplines in the humanities look into the historic, artistic, and philosophic achievements of human cultures. But anthropology is distinct because of its focus on the interconnections and interdependence of all aspects of the human experience in all places and times—both biological and cultural, past and present. It is this **holistic perspective** that best equips anthropologists to broadly address that elusive phenomenon we call human nature.

Anthropologists welcome the contributions of researchers from other disciplines and in return offer the benefit of their own findings. Anthropologists do not expect, for example, to know as much about the structure of the human eye as anatomists or as much about the perception of color as psychologists. As synthesizers, however, anthropologists are prepared to understand how these bodies of knowledge relate to color-naming practices in different human societies. Because they look for the broad basis of human ideas and practices without limiting themselves to any single social or biological aspect, anthropologists can acquire an especially expansive and inclusive overview of the complex biological and cultural organism that is the human being.

The holistic perspective also helps anthropologists stay keenly aware of ways that their own cultural ideas and values may impact their research. As the old saying goes, people often see what they believe, rather than what appears before their eyes. By maintaining a critical awareness of their own assumptions about human nature—checking and rechecking the ways their beliefs and actions might be shaping their research—anthropologists strive to gain objective knowledge about people. With this in mind, anthropologists aim to avoid the pitfalls of **ethnocentrism**, a belief that the ways of one's own culture are the only proper ones. Thus anthropologists have contributed uniquely to our understanding of diversity in human thought, biology, and behavior, as well as to our understanding of the many shared characteristics of humans.

To some, an inclusive, holistic perspective that emphasizes the inherent diversity within and among human cultures can be mistaken as shorthand for uniform liberal politics among anthropologists. This is not the case. Individual anthropologists are quite varied in their personal, political, and religious beliefs. At the same time, they apply a rigorous methodology for researching cultural practices from the perspective of the culture being studied—a methodology that requires them to check for the influences of their own biases. This is as true for an anthropologist analyzing the culture of the global banking industry as it is for one investigating trance dancing among contemporary hunter-gatherers. We might say that anthropology is a discipline concerned with unbiased evaluation of diverse human systems, including one's own. At times this requires challenging the status quo that is maintained and defended by the power elites of the system under study. This is true regardless of whether anthropologists focus on aspects of their own culture or on distant and different cultures.

holistic perspective A fundamental principle of anthropology: that the various parts of human culture and biology must be viewed in the broadest possible context in order to understand their interconnections and interdependence.

ethnocentrism The belief that the ways of one's own culture are the only proper ones.

Visual Counterpoint

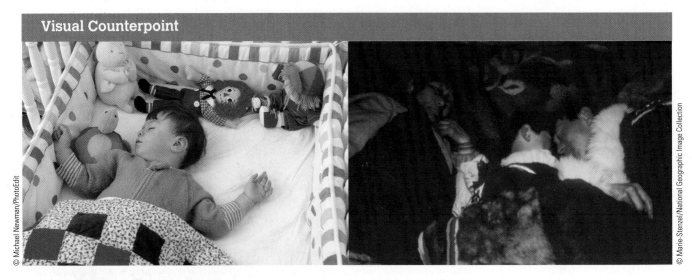

Although infants in the United States typically sleep apart from their parents, cross-cultural research shows that co-sleeping, of mother and baby in particular, is the rule. Without the breathing cues provided by someone sleeping nearby, an infant is more susceptible to sudden infant death syndrome (SIDS), a phenomenon in which a 4- to 6-month-old baby stops breathing and dies while asleep. The highest rates of SIDS are found among infants in the United States. The photo on the right shows a Nenet family sleeping together in their *chum* (reindeer-skin tent). Nenet people are arctic reindeer pastoralists living in Siberia.

While other social sciences have concentrated predominantly on contemporary peoples living in North American and European (Western) societies, historically anthropologists have focused primarily on non-Western peoples and cultures. Anthropologists work with the understanding that to fully access the complexities of human ideas, behavior, and biology, *all* humans, wherever and whenever, must be studied. Anthropologists work with a time depth that extends back millions of years to our pre-human ancestors. A cross-cultural, comparative, and long-term evolutionary perspective distinguishes anthropology from other social sciences. This all-encompassing approach also guards against **culture-bound** theories of human behavior: that is, theories based on assumptions about the world and reality that come from the researcher's own particular culture.

As a case in point, consider the fact that infants in the United States typically sleep apart from their parents. To people accustomed to multi-bedroom houses, cribs, and car seats, this may seem normal, but cross-cultural research shows that co-sleeping, of mother and baby in particular, is the norm. Further, the practice of sleeping apart favored in the United States dates back only about 200 years.

Recent studies have shown that separation of mother and infant has important biological and cultural consequences. For one thing, it increases the length of the infant's crying bouts. Some mothers incorrectly interpret the crying as indicating that the babies are receiving insufficient breast milk and consequently switch to feeding them bottled formula, proven to be less healthy. In extreme cases, a baby's cries may provoke physical abuse. But the benefits of co-sleeping go beyond significant reductions in crying: Infants who are breastfed receive more stimulation important for brain development, and they are apparently less susceptible to sudden infant death syndrome (SIDS or "crib death"). There are benefits to the mother as well: Frequent nursing prevents early ovulation after childbirth, it promotes loss of weight gained during pregnancy, and nursing mothers get at least as much sleep as mothers who sleep apart from their infants.[1]

Why do so many mothers continue to sleep separately from their infants? In the United States the cultural values of independence and consumerism come into play. To begin building individual identities, babies are provided with rooms (or at least space) of their own. This room also provides parents with a place for the toys, furniture, and other paraphernalia associated with "good" and "caring" childrearing in the United States.

Anthropology's historical emphasis on studying traditional, non-Western peoples has often led to findings that run

culture-bound Looking at the world and reality based on the assumptions and values of one's own culture.

---

[1] Barr, R. G. (1997, October). The crying game. *Natural History*, 47. Also, McKenna, J. J. (2002, September–October). Breastfeeding and bedsharing. *Mothering*, 28–37; and McKenna, J. J., & McDade, T. (2005, June). Why babies should never sleep alone: A review of the co-sleeping controversy in relation to SIDS, bedsharing, and breast feeding. *Pediatric Respiratory Reviews* 6 (2), 134–152.

counter to generally accepted opinions derived from Western studies. Thus anthropologists were the first to demonstrate

> that the world does not divide into the pious and the superstitious; that there are sculptures in jungles and paintings in deserts; that political order is possible without centralized power and principled justice without codified rules; that the norms of reason were not fixed in Greece, the evolution of morality not consummated in England.... We have, with no little success, sought to keep the world off balance; pulling out rugs, upsetting tea tables, setting off firecrackers. It has been the office of others to reassure; ours to unsettle.[2]

Although the findings of anthropologists have often challenged the conclusions of sociologists, psychologists, and economists, anthropology is absolutely indispensable to them, as it is the only consistent check against culture-bound assertions. In a sense, anthropology is to these disciplines what the laboratory is to physics and chemistry: an essential testing ground for their theories.

Anthropology and Its Fields

Individual anthropologists tend to specialize in one of four fields or subdisciplines: physical (biological) anthropology, archaeology, linguistic anthropology, or cultural anthropology (Figure 1.1). Some anthropologists consider archaeology and linguistics as part of the broader study of human cultures, but archaeology and linguistics also have close ties to biological anthropology. For example, while linguistic anthropology focuses on the cultural aspects of language, it has deep connections to the evolution of human language and to the biological basis of speech and language studied within physical anthropology.

Each of anthropology's fields may take a distinct approach to the study of humans, but all gather and analyze data that are essential to explaining similarities and differences among humans, across time and space. Moreover, all of them generate knowledge that has numerous practical applications. Many scholars within each of the four fields practice **applied anthropology,** which entails using anthropological knowledge and methods to solve practical problems. Applied anthropologists do not offer their perspectives from the sidelines. Instead, they actively collaborate with the communities in which they work—setting goals, solving problems, and conducting research together. In this book, numerous specific examples of how anthropology contributes to solving a wide range of challenges appear in Anthropology Applied features.

[2] Geertz, C. (1984). Distinguished lecture: Anti anti-relativism. *American Anthropologist 86*, 275.

Figure 1.1 The four fields of anthropology. Note that the divisions among them are not sharp, indicating that their boundaries overlap.

One of the earliest contexts in which anthropological knowledge was applied to a practical problem was the international public health movement that began in the 1920s. This marked the beginning of **medical anthropology**—a specialization that combines theoretical and applied approaches from the fields of cultural and biological anthropology with the study of human health and disease. The work of medical anthropologists sheds light on the connections between human health and political and economic forces, both locally and globally. Examples of this specialization appear in many of the Biocultural Connections featured in this text, including the one presented in this chapter, "The Anthropology of Organ Transplantation."

Physical Anthropology

Physical anthropology, also called *biological anthropology,* focuses on humans as biological organisms. Traditionally, biological anthropologists concentrated on human evolution, primatology, growth and development, human adaptation, and forensics. Today, **molecular anthropology,** or the anthropological study of genes and genetic relationships, contributes significantly to the contemporary study of human biological diversity. Comparisons among groups

applied anthropology The use of anthropological knowledge and methods to solve practical problems, often for a specific client.

medical anthropology A specialization in anthropology that combines theoretical and applied approaches from cultural and biological anthropology with the study of human health and disease.

physical anthropology The systematic study of humans as biological organisms; also known as biological anthropology.

molecular anthropology A branch of biological anthropology that uses genetic and biochemical techniques to test hypotheses about human evolution, adaptation, and variation.

The Anthropology of Organ Transplantation

In 1954, the first organ transplant occurred in Boston when surgeons removed a kidney from one identical twin to place it inside his sick brother. Though some transplants rely upon living donors, routine organ transplantation depends largely upon the availability of organs obtained from individuals who have died.

From an anthropological perspective, the meanings of death and the body vary cross-culturally. While death could be said to represent a particular biological state, social agreement about this state's significance is of paramount importance. Anthropologist Margaret Lock has explored differences between Japanese and North American acceptance of the biological state of "brain death" and how it affects the practice of organ transplants.

Brain death relies upon the absence of measurable electrical currents in the brain and the inability to breathe without technological assistance. The brain-dead individual, though attached to machines, still seems alive with a beating heart and pink cheeks. North Americans find brain death acceptable, in part, because personhood and individuality are culturally located in the brain. North American comfort with brain death has allowed for the "gift of life" through organ donation and subsequent transplantation.

By contrast, in Japan, the concept of brain death is hotly contested and organ transplants are rarely performed. The Japanese do not incorporate a mind–body split into their models of themselves and locate personhood throughout the body rather than in the brain. They resist accepting a warm pink body as a corpse from which organs can be harvested. Further, organs cannot be transformed into "gifts" because anonymous donation is not compatible with Japanese social patterns of reciprocal exchange.

Organ transplantation carries far greater social meaning than the purely biological movement of an organ from one individual to another. Cultural and biological processes are tightly woven into every aspect of this new social practice.

BIOCULTURAL QUESTION

What criteria do you use for death, and is it compatible with the idea of organ donation? Do you think that donated organs are fairly distributed in your society or throughout the globe?

(For more on this subject, see Lock, M. (2001). Twice dead: Organ transplants and the reinvention of death. Berkeley: University of California Press.)

---

separated by time, geography, or the frequency of a particular gene can reveal how humans have adapted and where they have migrated. As experts in the anatomy of human bones and tissues, physical anthropologists lend their knowledge about the body to applied areas such as gross anatomy laboratories, public health, and criminal investigations.

PALEOANTHROPOLOGY

Paleoanthropology is the study of the origins and predecessors of the present human species; in other words, it is the study of human evolution. Paleoanthropologists focus on biological changes through time to understand how, when, and why we became the kind of organisms we are today. In biological terms, we humans are primates, one of the many kinds of mammals. Because we share a common ancestry with other primates, most specifically apes, paleoanthropologists look back to the earliest primates (65 or so million years ago) or even the earliest mammals (225 million years ago) to reconstruct the complex path of human evolution. Paleoanthropology, unlike other evolutionary studies, takes a **biocultural** approach, focusing on the interaction of biology and culture.

The fossilized skeletons of our ancestors allow paleoanthropologists to reconstruct the course of human evolutionary history. To do this, paleoanthropologists compare the size and shape of these fossils to one another and to the bones of living species. Each new fossil discovery brings another piece to add to the puzzle of human evolutionary history. Biochemical and genetic studies add considerably to the fossil evidence. As we will see in later chapters, genetic evidence establishes the close relationship between humans and ape species—chimpanzees, bonobos, and gorillas. Genetic analyses indicate that the distinctive human line originated 5 to 8 million years ago. Physical anthropology therefore deals with much greater time spans than the other branches of anthropology.

PRIMATOLOGY

Studying the anatomy and behavior of the other primates helps us understand what we share with our closest living relatives and what makes humans unique. Therefore, **primatology,** or the study of living and fossil primates, is a vital part of physical anthropology. Primates include the Asian and African apes, as well as monkeys, lemurs, lorises, and tarsiers.

Biologically, humans are members of the ape family—large-bodied, broad-shouldered primates with no tail. Detailed studies of ape behavior in the wild indicate that the sharing of learned behavior is a significant part of their social life. Increasingly, primatologists designate the shared, learned behavior of nonhuman apes as *culture*. For example, tool use and communication systems indicate the elementary basis of language in some ape societies. Primate studies offer scientifically grounded perspectives on the behavior of our ancestors, as well as greater appreciation and respect for the abilities of our closest

paleoanthropology The study of the origins and predecessors of the present human species; the study of human evolution.
biocultural Focusing on the interaction of biology and culture.
primatology The study of living and fossil primates.

Though Jane Goodall originally began her studies of chimpanzees to shed light on the behavior of our distant ancestors, the knowledge she has amassed through over forty years in the field has reinforced how similar we are. In turn, she has devoted her career to championing the rights of our closest living relatives.

living relatives. As human activity encroaches on all parts of the world, the habitats of many primate species are endangered, thereby threatening the survival of the species themselves. Primatologists often advocate for the preservation of primate habitats so that these remarkable animals will be able to continue to inhabit the earth with us.

HUMAN GROWTH, ADAPTATION, AND VARIATION

Another specialty of physical anthropologists is the study of human growth and development. Anthropologists examine biological mechanisms of growth as well as the impact of the environment on the growth process. For example, Franz Boas, a pioneer of American anthropology of the early 20th century (see the Anthropologists of Note feature in this chapter) compared the heights of immigrants who spent their childhood in the "old country" (Europe) to the increased heights reached by their children who grew up in the United States. Today, physical anthropologists study the impact of disease, pollution, and poverty on growth. Comparisons between human and nonhuman primate growth patterns can provide clues to the evolutionary history of humans. Detailed anthropological studies of the hormonal, genetic, and physiological bases of healthy growth in living humans also contribute significantly to the health of children today.

Studies of human adaptation focus on the capacity of humans to adapt or adjust to their material environment—biologically and culturally. This branch of physical anthropology takes a comparative approach to humans living today in a variety of environments. Humans are remarkable among the primates in that they now inhabit the entire earth. Though cultural adaptations make it possible for humans to live in some environmental extremes, biological adaptations also contribute to survival in extreme cold, heat, and high altitude.

Some of these biological adaptations are built into the genetic makeup of populations. The long period of human growth and development provides ample opportunity for the environment to shape the human body. *Developmental adaptations* are responsible for some features of human variation, such as the enlargement of the right ventricle of the heart to help push blood to the lungs among the Quechua Indians of the Andean highlands known as the *altiplano.* In contrast, *physiological adaptations* are short-term changes in response to a particular environmental stimulus. For example, a woman who normally lives at sea level will undergo a series of physiological responses, such as increased production of oxygen-carrying red blood cells, if she suddenly moves to a high altitude. All of these kinds of biological adaptation contribute to present-day human variation.

Human differences include visible traits such as height, body build, and skin color, as well as biochemical factors such as blood type and susceptibility to certain diseases. Still, we remain members of a single species. Physical anthropology applies all the techniques of modern biology to achieve fuller understanding of human variation and its relationship to the different environments in which people have lived. Physical anthropologists' research on human variation has debunked false notions of biologically defined races, a belief based on widespread misinterpretation of human variation.

Forensic Anthropology: Voices for the Dead

Forensic anthropology is the analysis of skeletal remains for legal purposes. Law enforcement authorities call upon forensic anthropologists to use skeletal remains to identify murder victims, missing persons, or people who have died in disasters, such as plane crashes. Forensic anthropologists have also contributed substantially to the investigation of human rights abuses in all parts of the world by identifying victims and documenting the cause of their death.

Among the best-known forensic anthropologists is Clyde C. Snow. He has been practicing in this field for over forty years—first for the Federal Aviation Administration and more recently as a freelance consultant. In addition to the usual police work, Snow has studied the remains of General George Armstrong Custer and his men from the 1876 battle at Little Big Horn, and in 1985 he went to Brazil, where he identified the remains of the notorious Nazi war criminal Josef Mengele.

He was also instrumental in establishing the first forensic team devoted to documenting cases of human rights abuses around the world. This began in 1984 when he went to Argentina at the request of a newly elected civilian government to help with the identification of remains of the *desaparecidos,* or "disappeared ones," the 9,000 or more people who were eliminated by death squads during seven years of military rule. A year later, he returned to give expert testimony at the trial of nine junta members and to teach Argentineans how to recover, clean, repair, preserve, photograph, x-ray, and analyze bones. Besides providing factual accounts of the fate of victims to their surviving kin and refuting the assertions of revisionists that the massacres never happened, the work of Snow and his Argentinean associates was crucial in convicting several military officers of kidnapping, torture, and murder.

Since Snow's pioneering work, forensic anthropologists have become increasingly involved in the investigation of human rights abuses in all parts of the world, from Chile to Guatemala, Haiti, the Philippines, Rwanda, Iraq, Bosnia, and Kosovo. Meanwhile, they continue to do important work for more typical clients. In the United States these clients include the Federal Bureau of Investigation and city, state, and county medical examiners' offices.

Forensic anthropologists specializing in skeletal remains commonly work closely with forensic archaeologists. The relation between them is rather like that between a forensic pathologist, who examines a corpse to establish time and manner of death, and a crime scene

© AP Photo/Rodrigo Abd

The excavation of mass graves by the Guatemalan Foundation for Forensic Anthropology (Fernando Moscoso Moller, director) documents the human rights abuses committed during Guatemala's bloody civil war, a conflict that left 200,000 people dead and another 40,000 missing. In 2009, in a mass grave in the Quiche region, Diego Lux Tzunux uses his cell phone to photograph the skeletal remains believed to belong to his brother Manuel who disappeared in 1980. Genetic analyses allow forensic anthropologists to confirm the identity of individuals so that family members can know the fate of their loved ones. The analysis of skeletal remains provides evidence of the torture and massacre sustained by these individuals.

FORENSIC ANTHROPOLOGY

One of the many practical applications of physical anthropology is **forensic anthropology:** the identification of human skeletal remains for legal purposes. Although they are called upon by law enforcement authorities to identify murder victims, forensic anthropologists also investigate human rights abuses such as systematic genocide, terrorism, and war crimes. These specialists use details of skeletal anatomy to establish the age, sex, population affiliation, and stature of the deceased. Forensic anthropologists can also determine whether the person was right- or left-handed, exhibited any physical abnormalities, or had experienced trauma. While forensics relies upon differing frequencies of certain skeletal characteristics to establish population affiliation, it is nevertheless false to say that all people from a given population have a particular type of skeleton. (See the Anthropology Applied feature to read about the work of several forensic anthropologists and forensic archaeologists.)

forensic anthropology Applied subfield of physical anthropology that specializes in the identification of human skeletal remains for legal purposes.

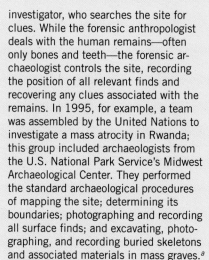

investigator, who searches the site for clues. While the forensic anthropologist deals with the human remains—often only bones and teeth—the forensic archaeologist controls the site, recording the position of all relevant finds and recovering any clues associated with the remains. In 1995, for example, a team was assembled by the United Nations to investigate a mass atrocity in Rwanda; this group included archaeologists from the U.S. National Park Service's Midwest Archaeological Center. They performed the standard archaeological procedures of mapping the site; determining its boundaries; photographing and recording all surface finds; and excavating, photographing, and recording buried skeletons and associated materials in mass graves.[a]

In another example, Karen Burns of the University of Georgia was part of a team sent to northern Iraq after the 1991 Gulf War to investigate alleged atrocities. On a military base where there had been many executions, she excavated the remains of a man's body found lying on its side facing Mecca, conforming to Islamic practice. Although no intact clothing existed, two polyester threads typically used in sewing were found along the sides of both legs. Although the threads survived, the clothing, because it was made of natural fiber, had decayed. "Those two threads at each side of the leg just shouted that his family didn't bury him," said Burns.[b] Proper though his position was, no Islamic family would bury their own in a garment sewn with polyester thread; proper ritual would require a simple shroud.

In recent years New York City has been the site of two major anthropological analyses of skeletal remains. To deal

with a present-day atrocity, Amy Zelson Mundorff, a forensic anthropologist for New York City's Office of the Chief Medical Examiner, supervised and coordinated the management, treatment, and cataloguing of people who lost their lives in the September 11 terrorist attack on the World Trade Center. Mundorff herself had been injured in the attack, but she was able to return to work two days after the towers fell.

And in 1991, just a short distance from the World Trade Center site, construction workers in lower Manhattan discovered an African burial ground from the 17th and 18th centuries. A bioarchaeological rather than strictly forensic approach allowed researchers to examine the complete cultural and historical context and lifeways of the entire population buried there. The African Burial Ground Project provided incontrovertible evidence of the horror of slavery in North America, in the busy northern port of New York City. The more than 400 individuals buried there, many of them children, were worked so far beyond their ability to endure that their spines were fractured. African American biological archaeologist Michael Blakey, who led the research team, noted the social impact of this work:

Descendants of the enslaved in different parts of the world have the right to know about the past and the right to memorialize history so that it might not happen again. With the project, we knew that we were peeling off layers of obscurity. We were also doing something that scholars within the African diaspora have been

doing for about 150 years and that is realizing that history has political implications of empowerment and disempowerment. That history is not just to be discovered but to be re-discovered, to be corrected, and that African-American history is distorted. Omissions are made in order to create a convenient view of national and white identity at the expense of our understanding our world and also at the expense of African-American identity. So that the project of history—in this case using archaeology and skeletal biology—is a project meant to help us understand something that has been systematically hidden from us.[c]

Thus several kinds of anthropologists analyze human remains for a variety of purposes, contributing to the documentation and correction of violence committed by humans of the past and present.

[a] Haglund, W. D., Conner, M., & Scott, D. D. (2001). The archaeology of contemporary mass graves. *Historical Archaeology 35* (1), 57–69.

[b] Cornwell, T. (1995, November 10). Skeleton staff. *Times Higher Education,* 20. http://www.timeshighereducation.co.uk/story.asp?storyCode=96035&sectioncode=26.

[c] "Return to the African Burial Ground: An interview with physical anthropologist Michael L. Blakey." (2003, November 20). *Archaeology.* http://www.archaeology.org/online/interviews/blakey/.

Cultural Anthropology

Cultural anthropology (also called *social* or *sociocultural anthropology*) is the study of patterns of human behavior, thought, and feelings. It focuses on humans as culture-producing and culture-reproducing creatures. Thus in order to understand the work of the cultural anthropologist, we must clarify what we mean by **culture**—a society's shared and socially transmitted ideas, values, and perceptions, which are used to make sense of experience and generate behavior and are reflected in that behavior. These standards are socially learned, rather than acquired through biological

inheritance. The manifestations of culture may vary considerably from place to place, but no person is "more cultured" in the anthropological sense than any other.

cultural anthropology Also known as social or sociocultural anthropology. The study of customary patterns in human behavior, thought, and feelings. It focuses on humans as culture-producing and culture-reproducing creatures.

culture A society's shared and socially transmitted ideas, values, and perceptions, which are used to make sense of experience and generate behavior and are reflected in that behavior.

Through his pioneering ethnographic studies of the culture of drug addicts and dealers, cultural anthropologist Philippe Bourgois opened up a new range of edgy field sites for cultural anthropologists. The insights from his detailed ethnographies about this world have been important not only for anthropological literature but for those concerned with the health of individuals and communities. Here Bourgois is pictured in one of his more recent field sites, a homeless encampment in North Philadelphia.

© Jeff Schonberg 2009

Cultural anthropology has two main components: ethnography and ethnology. An **ethnography** is a detailed description of a particular culture primarily based on **fieldwork,** which is the term all anthropologists use for on-location research. Because the hallmark of ethnographic fieldwork is a combination of social participation and personal observation within the community being studied, as well as interviews and discussions with individual members of a group, the ethnographic method is commonly referred to as **participant observation.** Ethnographies provide the information used to make systematic comparisons among cultures all across the world. Known as **ethnology,** such cross-cultural research allows anthropologists to develop anthropological theories that help explain why certain important differences or similarities occur among groups.

ETHNOGRAPHY

Through participant observation—eating a people's food, sleeping under their roof, learning how to speak and

ethnography A detailed description of a particular culture primarily based on fieldwork.

fieldwork The term anthropologists use for on-location research.

participant observation In ethnography, the technique of learning a people's culture through social participation and personal observation within the community being studied, as well as interviews and discussion with individual members of the group over an extended period of time.

ethnology The study and analysis of different cultures from a comparative or historical point of view, utilizing ethnographic accounts and developing anthropological theories that help explain why certain important differences or similarities occur among groups.

behave acceptably, and personally experiencing their habits and customs—the ethnographer seeks to gain the best possible understanding of a particular way of life. Being a participant observer does not mean that the anthropologist must join in battles to study a culture in which warfare is prominent; but by living among a warlike people, the ethnographer should be able to understand how warfare fits into the overall cultural framework. She or he must observe carefully to gain an overview without placing too much emphasis on one part at the expense of another. Only by discovering how *all* aspects of a culture—its social, political, economic, and religious practices and institutions—relate to one another can the ethnographer begin to understand the cultural system. This is the holistic perspective so basic to the discipline.

The popular image of ethnographic fieldwork is that it occurs among people who live in far-off, isolated places. To be sure, much ethnographic work has been done in the remote villages of Africa or South America, the islands of the Pacific Ocean, the Indian reservations of North America, the deserts of Australia, and so on. However, as the discipline has developed, Western industrialized societies have also become the focus of anthropological study. Some of this shift occurred as scholars from non-Western cultures became anthropologists. Ethnographic fieldwork has transformed from having expert Western anthropologists study people in "other" places to collaboration among anthropologists and the varied communities in which they work. Today, anthropologists from all around the globe employ the same research techniques that were used in the study of non-Western peoples to explore such diverse subjects as religious movements, street gangs, land rights, schools, marriage practices, conflict resolution, corporate bureaucracies, and health-care systems in Western cultures.

ETHNOLOGY

Largely descriptive in nature, ethnography provides the raw data needed for ethnology—the branch of cultural anthropology that involves cross-cultural comparisons and theories that explain differences or similarities among groups. Intriguing insights into one's own beliefs and practices may come from cross-cultural comparisons. Consider, for example, the amount of time spent on domestic chores by industrialized peoples and traditional food foragers (people who rely on wild plant and animal resources for subsistence). Anthropological research has shown that food foragers work far less time at domestic tasks and other subsistence pursuits compared to people in industrialized societies. Urban women in the United States who were not working for wages outside their homes put 55 hours a week into their housework—this despite all the "labor-saving" dishwashers, washing machines, clothes dryers, vacuum cleaners, food processors, and microwave ovens. In contrast, aboriginal women in Australia devoted 20 hours a week to their chores.[3] Nevertheless, consumer appliances have become important indicators of a high standard of living in the United States due to the widespread belief that household appliances reduce housework and increase leisure time.

By making systematic comparisons, ethnologists seek to arrive at scientific explanations concerning the function and operation of social practices and cultural features and patterns in all times and places. Today cultural anthropologists contribute to applied research in a variety of contexts—ranging from business to education to health care to government intervention to humanitarian aid.

Linguistic Anthropology

Perhaps the most distinctive feature of the human species is language. Although the sounds and gestures made by some other animals—especially apes—may serve functions comparable to those of human language, no other animal has developed a system of symbolic communication as complex as that of humans. Language allows people to preserve and transmit countless details of their culture from generation to generation.

The branch of anthropology that studies human languages is called **linguistic anthropology**. Although it shares data and methods with the more general discipline of linguistics, it differs in that it uses these to answer anthropological questions related to society and culture, such as language use within speech communities. When this field began, it emphasized the documentation of languages of cultures under ethnographic study—particularly those

whose future seemed precarious. Mastery of Native American languages—with grammatical structures so different from the Indo-European and Semitic languages to which Euramerican scholars were accustomed—prompted the notion of *linguistic relativity*. This refers to the idea that linguistic diversity reflects not just differences in sounds and grammar but differences in ways of looking at the world. For example, the observation that the language of the Hopi Indians of the American Southwest had no words for *past, present,* and *future* led the early proponents of linguistic relativity to suggest that the Hopi people had a different conception of time.[4] Similarly, the observation that English-speaking North Americans use a number of slang words—such as *dough, greenback, dust, loot, bucks, change, paper, cake, moolah, benjamins,* and *bread*—to refer to money could be a product of linguistic relativity. The profusion of names helps to identify a thing of special importance to a culture. For instance, the importance of money within North American culture is evident in the association between money and time, production, and capital in phrases such as "time is money" and "spend some time."

Complex ideas and practices integral to a culture's survival can also be reflected in language. For example, among the Nuer, a nomadic group that travels with grazing animals throughout southern Sudan, a baby born with a visible deformity is not considered a human baby. Instead it is called a baby hippopotamus. This name allows for the safe return of the hippopotamus to the river where it belongs. Such infants would not be able to survive in this society, and so linguistic practice is compatible with the compassionate choice the Nuer have had to make.

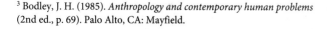

The notion of linguistic relativity has been challenged by theorists who propose that the human capacity for language is based on biological universals that underlie all human thought. Recently, Canadian cognitive scientist Stephen Pinker has even suggested that, at a fundamental

[3] Bodley, J. H. (1985). *Anthropology and contemporary human problems* (2nd ed., p. 69). Palo Alto, CA: Mayfield.

[4] Whorf, B. (1941). The relation of habitual thought and behavior to language. In L. Spier, A. I. Hallowell, & S. S. Newman (Eds.), *Language, culture, and personality: Essays in memory of Edward Sapir* (pp. 75–93). Menasha, WI: Sapir Memorial Publication Fund.

linguistic anthropology The study of human languages—looking at their structure, history, and relation to social and cultural contexts.

Linguistic anthropologist Gregory Anderson has devoted his career to saving indigenous languages. He founded and heads the Living Tongues Institute of Endangered Languages and works throughout the globe to preserve languages that are dying out at a shocking rate of about one every two weeks. Here he is working with Don Francisco Ninacondis and Ariel Ninacondis in Charazani, Bolivia, to preserve their language Kallawaya.

© Living Tongues Institute

level, thought is nonverbal.[5] A holistic anthropological approach considers language to have both a universal biological basis and specific cultural patterning.

Researching questions about human relations through language can involve focusing on specific speech events.[6] Such events form a **discourse** or an extended communication on a particular subject. These speech events reveal how social factors such as financial status, age, or gender affect the way an individual uses its culture's language. The linguistic anthropologist might examine whether the tendency for females in the United States to end statements with an upward inflection, as though the statement were a question, reflects a pattern of male dominance in this society. Because members of any culture may use a variety of different registers and inflections, the ones they choose to use at a specific instance convey particular meanings.

As with the anthropological perspective on culture, language is similarly regarded as alive, malleable, and changing. Online tools such as Urban Dictionary track the changes in North American slang, and traditional dictionaries include new words and usages each year. The implications of these language changes help increase our understanding of the human past. By working out relationships among languages and examining their spatial distributions, linguistic anthropologists may estimate how long the speakers of those languages have lived where they do. By identifying those words in related languages that have survived from an ancient ancestral tongue, these linguistic anthropologists can also suggest not only where, but how, the speakers of the ancestral language lived. Such work has shown, for example, linguistic ties between geographically distant groups such as the people of Finland and Turkey.

Linguistic anthropology is practiced in a number of applied settings. For example, linguistic anthropologists have collaborated with ethnic minorities in the revival of languages suppressed or lost during periods of oppression by another ethnic group. This work has included helping to create written forms of languages that previously existed only orally. This sort of applied linguistic anthropology represents the true collaboration that is characteristic of anthropological research today.

Archaeology

Archaeology is the branch of anthropology that studies human cultures through the recovery and analysis of material remains and environmental data. Such material products include tools, pottery, hearths, and enclosures that remain as traces of cultural practices in the past, as well as human, plant, and marine remains, some of which date back 2.5 million years. The arrangement of these traces when recovered reflects specific human ideas and behavior. For example, shallow, restricted concentrations of charcoal that include oxidized earth, bone fragments, and charred plant remains, located near pieces of fire-cracked rock, pottery, and tools suitable for food preparation, indicate cooking and food processing. Such remains can reveal much about

---

[5] Pinker, S. (1994). *The language instinct: How the mind creates language.* New York: Morrow.

[6] Hymes, D. (1974). *Foundations in sociolinguistics: An ethnographic approach.* Philadelphia: University of Pennsylvania Press.

discourse An extended communication on a particular subject.

archaeology The study of human cultures through the recovery and analysis of material remains and environmental data.

a people's diet and subsistence practices. Together with skeletal remains, these material remains help archaeologists reconstruct the biocultural context of past human lifeways. Archaeologists organize this material and use it to explain cultural variability and culture change through time.

Because archaeology is explicitly tied to unearthing material remains in particular environmental contexts, a variety of innovations in the geographic and geologic sciences have been readily incorporated into archaeological research. Innovations such as geographic information systems (GIS), remote sensing, and ground penetrating radar (GPR) complement traditional explorations of the past through archaeological digs.

Archaeologists can reach back for clues to human behavior far beyond the mere 5,000 years to which historians are confined by their reliance on written records. Calling this time period "prehistoric" does not mean that these societies were less interested in their history or that they did not have ways of recording and transmitting history. It simply means that written records do not exist. That said, archaeologists are not limited to the study of societies without written records; they may study those for which historic documents are available to supplement the material remains. In most literate societies, written records are associated with governing elites rather than with farmers, fishers, laborers, or slaves, and therefore they include the biases of the ruling classes. In fact, according to James Deetz, a pioneer in historical archaeology of the Americas, in many historical contexts, "material culture may be the most objective source of information we have."[7]

ARCHAEOLOGICAL SUBSPECIALTIES

While archaeologists tend to specialize in particular culture zones or time periods, connected with particular regions of the world, a number of topical subspecialties also exist. **Bioarchaeology,** for instance, is the archaeological study of human remains, emphasizing the preservation of cultural and social processes in the skeleton. For example, mummified skeletal remains from the Andean highlands in South America not only preserve this burial practice but also provide evidence of some of the earliest brain surgery ever documented. In addition, these bioarchaeological remains exhibit skull deformation techniques that distinguish nobility from other members of society. Other archaeologists specialize in *ethnobotany,* studying how people of a given culture made use of indigenous plants. Still others specialize in *zooarchaeology,* tracking the animal remains recovered in archaeological excavations.

Although most archaeologists concentrate on the past, some of them study material objects in contemporary settings. One example is the Garbage Project, founded

by William Rathje at the University of Arizona in 1973. This anthropological study of household waste of Tucson residents produced a wide range of thought-provoking information about contemporary social issues. For example, when surveyed by questionnaires, only 15 percent of households reported consuming beer, and no household reported consuming more than eight cans a week. Analysis of garbage from the same area showed that some beer was consumed in over 80 percent of the households, and 50 percent of households discarded more than eight cans per week.

In addition to providing actual data on beer consumption, the Garbage Project has tested the validity of research survey techniques, upon which sociologists, economists, other social scientists and policymakers rely heavily. The tests show a significant difference between what people *say* they do and what the garbage analysis shows they *actually* do. Therefore, ideas about human behavior based on simple survey techniques may be seriously in error.

In 1987, the Garbage Project began a program of excavating landfills in different parts of the United States and Canada. From this work came the first reliable data on what materials actually go into landfills and what happens to them there. And once again, common beliefs turned out to be at odds with the actual situation. For example, when buried in deep compost landfills, biodegradable materials such as newspapers take far longer to decay than anyone had expected. This kind of information is a vital step toward solving waste disposal problems.[8]

Ranging from technical to philosophical, the impact of the Garbage Project has been profound. Data from its landfill studies on hazardous waste and rates of decay of various materials play a major role in landfill regulation and management today. In terms of philosophy, the data gathered from the Garbage Project underscored the dire need for public recycling and composting that is now an accepted part of mainstream U.S. culture.

CULTURAL RESOURCE MANAGEMENT

While archaeology may conjure up images of ancient pyramids and the like, much archaeological fieldwork is carried out as **cultural resource management**. What

[7] Deetz, J. (1977). *In small things forgotten: The archaeology of early American life* (p. 160). Garden City, NY: Anchor/Doubleday.

[8] Details regarding the Garbage Project's history and legacy can be found at http://traumwerk.stanford.edu:3455/17/174.

bioarchaeology The archaeological study of human remains, emphasizing the preservation of cultural and social processes in the skeleton.

cultural resource management A branch of archaeology tied to government policies for the protection of cultural resources and involving surveying and/or excavating archaeological and historical remains threatened by construction or development.

distinguishes this work from traditional archaeological research is that it is specifically charged with preserving important aspects of a country's prehistoric and historic heritage. For example, in the United States, if the transportation department of a state government plans to replace an inadequate highway bridge, the state must first contract with archaeologists to identify and protect any significant prehistoric or historic resources that might be affected.

Since passage of the Historic Preservation Act of 1966, the National Environmental Policy Act of 1969, the Archaeological and Historical Preservation Act of 1974, and the Archaeological Resources Protection Act of 1979, cultural resource management is required for any construction project that is partially funded or licensed by the U.S. government. As a result, the field of cultural resource management has flourished. Many archaeologists are employed by such agencies as the Army Corps of Engineers, the National Park Service, the U.S. Forest Service, and the U.S. Natural Resource Conservation Service to assist in the preservation, restoration, and salvage of archaeological resources. Countries such as Canada and the United Kingdom have programs very similar to that of the United States, and from Chile to China, various governments use archaeological expertise to protect and manage their cultural heritage.

When cultural resource management work or other archaeological investigation unearths Native American cultural items or human remains, federal laws come into the picture again. The Native American Graves Protection and Repatriation Act (NAGPRA), passed in 1990, provides a process for the return of these remains to lineal descendants, culturally affiliated Indian tribes, and Native Hawaiian organizations. NAGPRA has become central to the work of anthropologists who study Paleo-Indian cultures in the United States. It has also been the source of controversy, such as that regarding Kennewick Man, a 9,300-year-old skeleton discovered near Kennewick, Washington, in 1996.

In addition to working in all the capacities mentioned, archaeologists also consult for engineering firms to help them prepare environmental impact statements. Some of these archaeologists operate out of universities and colleges, while others are on the staff of independent consulting firms. When state legislation sponsors any kind of archaeological work, it is referred to as *contract archaeology*.

empirical Based on observations of the world rather than on intuition or faith.
hypothesis A tentative explanation of the relationships between certain phenomena.

Anthropology, Science, and the Humanities

With its broad scope of subjects and methods, anthropology has sometimes been called the most humane of the sciences and the most scientific of the humanities—a designation that most anthropologists accept with pride. Given their intense involvement with people of all times and places, anthropologists have amassed considerable information about human failure and success, weakness and greatness—the real stuff of the humanities. While anthropologists steer clear of a cold, impersonal scientific approach that reduces people and the things they do and think to mere numbers, their quantitative studies have contributed substantially to the scientific study of the human condition. But even the most scientific anthropologists always keep in mind that human societies are made up of individuals with rich assortments of emotions and aspirations that demand respect.

Beyond this, anthropologists remain committed to the proposition that one cannot fully understand another culture by simply observing it; as the term *participant observation* implies, one must *experience* it as well. This same commitment to fieldwork and to the systematic collection of data, whether qualitative or quantitative, is also evidence of the scientific side of anthropology. Anthropology is an **empirical** social science based on observations or information about humans taken in through the senses and verified by others rather than on intuition or faith. But anthropology is distinguished from other sciences by the diverse ways in which scientific research is conducted within the discipline.

Science, a carefully honed way of producing knowledge, aims to reveal and explain the underlying logic, the structural processes that make the world tick. In their search for explanations, scientists do not assume that things are always as they appear on the surface. After all, what could be more obvious to the scientifically uninformed observer than the earth staying still while the sun travels around it every day? The creative scientific endeavor seeks testable explanations for observed phenomena, ideally in terms of the workings of hidden but unchanging principles or laws. Two basic ingredients are essential for this: imagination and skepticism. Imagination, though having the potential to lead us astray, helps us recognize unexpected ways phenomena might be ordered and to think of old things in new ways. Without it, there can be no science. Skepticism allows us to distinguish fact (an observation verified by others) from fancy, to test our speculations, and to prevent our imaginations from running wild.

Like other scientists, anthropologists often begin their research with a **hypothesis** (a tentative explanation or hunch) about the possible relationships between certain observed facts or events. By gathering various kinds of data that seem

Franz Boas (1858–1942) ■ *Matilda Coxe Stevenson (1849–1915)*

Franz Boas was not the first to teach anthropology in the United States, but it was Boas and his students, with their insistence on scientific rigor, who made anthropology courses common in college and university curricula. Born and raised in Germany where he studied physics, mathematics, and geography, Boas did his first ethnographic research among the Inuit (Eskimos) in arctic Canada in 1883 and 1884. After a brief academic career in Berlin, he came to the United States where he worked in museums interspersed with

ethnographic research among the Kwakiutl (Kwakwaka'wakw) Indians in the Canadian Pacific. In 1896, he became a professor at Columbia University in New York City. He authored an incredible number of publications, founded professional organizations and journals, and taught two generations of great anthropologists, including numerous women and ethnic minorities.

As a Jewish immigrant, Boas recognized the dangers of ethnocentrism and especially racism. Through ethnographic fieldwork and comparative analysis, he demonstrated that white supremacy theories and other schemes ranking non-European peoples and cultures as inferior were biased, ill-informed, and unscientific. Throughout his long and illustrious academic career, he promoted anthropology not only as a human science but also as an instrument to combat racism and prejudice in the world.

Among the founders of North American anthropology were a number of women who were highly influential among women's rights advocates in the late 1800s. One such pioneering anthropologist was **Matilda Coxe Stevenson,** who did fieldwork among the Zuni Indians of Arizona. In 1885, she founded the Women's Anthropological Society in Washington, DC, the first professional association for women scientists. Three years later, hired by the Smithsonian's Bureau of American Ethnology, she became one of the first women in the world

National Anthropological Archives Smithsonian 1895 Neg02871000

Mathilda Cox Stevenson in New Mexico about 1895.

to receive a full-time official position in science.

The tradition of women being active in anthropology continues. In fact, since World War II more than half the presidents of the now 12,000-member American Anthropological Association have been women.

Recording observations on film as well as in notebooks, Stevenson and Boas were also pioneers in visual anthropology. Stevenson used an early box camera to document Pueblo Indian religious ceremonies and material culture, while Boas photographed Inuit (Eskimos) in northern Canada in 1883 and Kwakiutl Indians from the early 1890s for cultural as well as physical anthropological documentation. Today, these old photographs are greatly valued not only by anthropologists and historians, but also by indigenous peoples themselves.

© Bildarchiv Preussischer Kulturbesitz/Art Resource, NY

Franz Boas on a sailing ship circa 1925.

to ground such suggested explanations on evidence, anthropologists come up with a **theory**—an explanation supported by a reliable body of data. In their effort to demonstrate links between *known* facts or events, anthropologists may discover *unexpected* facts, events, or relationships. An important function of theory is that it guides us in our explorations and may result in new knowledge. Equally important, the newly discovered facts may provide evidence that certain explanations, however popular or firmly believed, are unfounded. When the evidence is lacking or fails to support the suggested explanations, promising hypotheses or attractive hunches must be dropped. In other words, anthropology relies on empirical evidence. Moreover, no scientific theory—no matter how widely accepted by the international community of scholars—is beyond challenge.

It is important to distinguish between scientific theories—which are always open to future challenges born of new evidence or insights—and doctrine. A **doctrine**, or dogma, is an assertion of opinion or belief formally handed down by an authority as true and indisputable. For instance, those who accept a creationist doctrine on the origin of the human species as recounted in sacred texts or myths do so on the basis of religious authority;

theory In science, an explanation of natural phenomena, supported by a reliable body of data.

doctrine An assertion of opinion or belief formally handed down by an authority as true and indisputable.

they concede that their views may be contrary to explanations derived from genetics, geology, biology, or other sciences. Such doctrines cannot be tested or proved one way or another: They are accepted as matters of faith.

Straightforward though the scientific approach may seem, its application is not always easy. For instance, once a hypothesis has been proposed, the person who suggested it is strongly motivated to verify it, and this can cause one to unwittingly overlook negative evidence and unanticipated findings. This is a familiar problem in all science as noted by paleontologist Stephen Jay Gould: "The greatest impediment to scientific innovation is usually a conceptual lock, not a factual lock."[9] Because culture provides and shapes our very thoughts, it can be challenging to frame hypotheses or to develop interpretations that are not culture-bound. But by encompassing both humanism and science, the discipline of anthropology can draw on its internal diversity to overcome conceptual locks.

Fieldwork

All anthropologists think about whether their culture may have shaped the scientific questions they ask. In so doing, they rely heavily on a technique that has been successful in other disciplines: They immerse themselves in the data to the fullest extent possible. In the process, anthropologists become so thoroughly familiar with even the smallest details that they begin to recognize underlying patterns in the data, many of which might have been overlooked. Recognition of such patterns enables the anthropologist to frame meaningful hypotheses, which then may be subjected to further testing or validation in the field. Within anthropology, fieldwork provides additional rigor to the concept of total immersion in the data.

While fieldwork was introduced above in connection with cultural anthropology, it is characteristic of *all* the anthropological subdisciplines. Archaeologists and paleoanthropologists excavate in the field. A biological anthropologist interested in the effects of globalization on nutrition and growth will live in the field among a community of people to study this question. A primatologist might live among a group of chimpanzees or baboons just as a linguist would study the language of a culture by living in that community. Fieldwork, being fully immersed in another culture, challenges the anthropologist to be aware of the ways that cultural factors influence the research questions. Anthropological researchers monitor themselves by constantly checking their own biases and assumptions as they work; they present these self-reflections along with their observations, a practice known as *reflexivity*.

The validity or the reliability of a researcher's conclusions is established through the replication of observations and/or experiments by another researcher. Thus it becomes obvious if one's colleague has "gotten it right." But traditional validation by others is uniquely challenging in anthropology because observational access is often limited. Contact with a particular research site can be constrained by a number of factors. Difficulties of travel, obtaining permits, insufficient funding, or other conditions can interfere with access; also, what may be observed in a certain context at a certain time may not be observable at others. Thus one researcher cannot easily confirm the reliability or completeness of another's account. For this reason, anthropologists bear a special responsibility for accurate reporting. In the final research report, she or he must be clear about several basic issues: Why was a particular location selected as a research site? What were the research objectives? What were the local conditions during fieldwork? Which local individuals played a role in conducting the research? How were the data collected and recorded? How did the researcher check his or her own biases? Without such background information, it is difficult for others to judge the validity of the account and the soundness of the researcher's conclusions.

On a personal level, fieldwork requires the researcher to step out of his or her cultural comfort zone into a world that is unfamiliar and sometimes unsettling. Anthropologists in the field are likely to face a host of challenges—physical, social, mental, political, and ethical. They may have to deal with the physical challenge of adjusting to unaccustomed food, climate, and hygiene conditions. Typically, anthropologists in the field struggle with such mental challenges as being lonely, feeling like a perpetual outsider, being socially clumsy and clueless in their new cultural setting, and having to be alert around the clock because anything that is happening or being said may be significant to their research. Political challenges include the possibility of unwittingly letting oneself be used by factions within the community, or being viewed with suspicion by government authorities who may suspect the anthropologist is a spy. And there are ethical dilemmas as well: What does the anthropologist do if faced with a cultural practice he or she finds troubling, such as female circumcision? How does one deal with demands for food supplies and/or medicine? And is the fieldworker ever justified in using deception to gain vital information? Many such ethical questions arise in anthropological fieldwork.

At the same time, fieldwork often leads to tangible and meaningful personal, professional, and social rewards, ranging from lasting friendships to vital knowledge and insights concerning the human condition that make positive contributions to people's lives. Something of the meaning of anthropological fieldwork—its usefulness and its impact

---

[9] Gould, S. J. (1989). *Wonderful life* (p. 226). New York: Norton.

on researcher and subject—is conveyed in the following Original Study by Suzanne Leclerc-Madlala, an anthropologist who left her familiar New England surroundings about twenty-five years ago to do AIDS research among Zulu-speaking people in South Africa. Her research interest has changed the course of her own life, not to mention the lives of individuals who have AIDS/HIV and the type of treatment they receive.

Original Study

Fighting HIV/AIDS in Africa: Traditional Healers on the Front Line

by Suzanne Leclerc-Madlala

In the 1980s, as a North American anthropology graduate student at George Washington University, I met and married a Zulu-speaking student from South Africa. It was the height of apartheid, and upon moving to that country I was classified as "honorary black" and forced to live in a segregated township with my husband. The AIDS epidemic was in its infancy, but it was clear from the start that an anthropological understanding of how people perceive and engage with this disease would be crucial for developing interventions. I wanted to learn all that I could to make a difference, and this culminated in earning a PhD from the University of Natal on the cultural construction of AIDS among the Zulu. The HIV/AIDS pandemic in Africa became my professional passion.

Faced with overwhelming global health-care needs, the World Health Organization passed a series of resolutions in the 1970s promoting collaboration between traditional and modern medicine. Such moves held a special relevance for Africa where traditional healers typically outnumber practitioners of modern medicine by a ratio of 100 to 1 or more. Given Africa's disproportionate burden of disease, supporting partnership efforts with traditional healers makes sense. But what sounds sensible today was once considered absurd, even heretical. For centuries Westerners generally viewed traditional healing as a whole lot of primitive mumbo jumbo practiced by witchdoctors with demonic powers who perpetuated superstition. Yet, its practice survived. Today, as the African continent grapples with an HIV/AIDS epidemic of crisis proportion, millions of sick people who are either too poor or too distant to access modern health care are proving that traditional healers are an invaluable resource in the fight against AIDS.

Of the world's estimated 40 million people currently infected by HIV, 70 percent live in sub-Saharan Africa, and the vast majority of children left orphaned by AIDS are African. From the 1980s onward, as Africa became synonymous with the rapid spread of HIV/AIDS, a number of prevention programs involved traditional healers. My initial research in South Africa's KwaZulu-Natal province—where it is estimated that 36 percent of the population is HIV infected—revealed that traditional Zulu healers were regularly consulted for the treatment of sexually transmitted disease (STD). I found that such diseases, along with HIV/AIDS, were usually attributed to transgressions of taboos related to birth, pregnancy, marriage, and death. Moreover, these diseases were often understood within a framework of pollution and contagion, and like most serious illnesses, ultimately believed to have their causal roots in witchcraft.

In the course of my research, I investigated a pioneer program in STD and HIV education for traditional healers in the province. The program aimed to provide basic biomedical knowledge about the various modes of disease transmission, the means available for prevention, the diagnosing of symptoms, the keeping of records, and the making of patient referrals to local clinics and hospitals. Interviews with the healers showed that many maintained a deep suspicion of modern medicine. They perceived AIDS education as a one-way street intended to press them into formal health structures and convince them of the superiority of modern medicine. Yet, today, few of the 6,000-plus KwaZulu-Natal

Medical anthropologist Suzanne Leclerc-Madlala visits with "Doctor" Koloko in KwaZulu-Natal, South Africa. This Zulu traditional healer proudly displays her official AIDS training certificate.

CONTINUED

CONTINUED

healers who have been trained in AIDS education say they would opt for less collaboration; most want to have more.

Treatments by Zulu healers for HIV/AIDS often take the form of infusions of bitter herbs to "cleanse" the body, strengthen the blood, and remove misfortune and "pollution." Some treatments provide effective relief from common ailments associated with AIDS such as itchy skin rashes, oral thrush, persistent diarrhea, and general debility. Indigenous plants such as *unwele (Sutherlandia frutescens)* and African potato *(Hypoxis hemerocallidea)* are well-known traditional medicines that have proven immuno-boosting properties.

Both have recently become available in modern pharmacies packaged in tablet form. With modern anti-retroviral treatments still well beyond the reach of most South Africans, indigenous medicines that can delay or alleviate some of the suffering caused by AIDS are proving to be valuable and popular treatments.

Knowledge about potentially infectious bodily fluids has led healers to change some of their practices. Where porcupine quills were once used to give a type of indigenous injection, patients are now advised to bring their own sewing needles to consultations. Patients provide their own individual razor blades for making incisions on their skin, where previously healers reused the same razor on many clients. Some healers claim they have given up the practice of biting

clients' skin to remove foreign objects from the body. It is not uncommon today, especially in urban centers like Durban, to find healers proudly displaying AIDS training certificates in their inner-city "surgeries" where they don white jackets and wear protective latex gloves.

Politics and controversy have dogged South Africa's official response to HIV/AIDS. But back home in the waddle-and-daub, animal-skin-draped herbariums and divining huts of traditional healers, the politics of AIDS holds little relevance. Here the sick and dying are coming in droves to be treated by healers who have been part and parcel of community life (and death) since time immemorial. In many cases traditional healers have transformed their homes into hospices for AIDS patients. Because of the strong stigma that still plagues the disease, those with AIDS symptoms are often abandoned or sometimes chased away from their homes by family members. They seek refuge with healers who provide them with comfort in their final days. Healers' homes are also becoming orphanages as healers respond to what has been called the "third wave" of AIDS destruction: the growing legions of orphaned children.

The practice of traditional healing in Africa is adapting to the changing face of health and illness in the context of HIV/AIDS. But those who are suffering go to traditional healers not only in search of relief for physical symptoms. They go to learn about the ultimate cause of their disease—something other than the

immediate cause of a sexually transmitted "germ" or "virus." They go to find answers to the "why me and not him" questions, the "why now" and "why this." As with most traditional healing systems worldwide, healing among the Zulu and most all African ethnic groups cannot be separated from the spiritual concerns of the individual and the cosmological beliefs of the community at large. Traditional healers help to restore a sense of balance between the individual and the community, on one hand, and between the individual and the cosmos, or ancestors, on the other hand. They provide health care that is personalized, culturally appropriate, holistic, and tailored to meet the needs and expectations of the patient. In many ways it is a far more satisfactory form of healing than that offered by modern medicine.

Traditional healing in Africa is flourishing in the era of AIDS, and understanding why this is so requires a shift in the conceptual framework by which we understand, explain, and interpret health. Anthropological methods and its comparative and holistic perspective can facilitate, like no other discipline, the type of understanding that is urgently needed to address the AIDS crisis.

Adapted from: Leclerc-Madlala, S. (2002). Bodies and politics: Healing rituals in the democratic South Africa. In V. Faure (Ed.), Les cahiers de 'l'IFAS, no. 2. Johannesburg: The French Institute. (Leclerc-Madlala now works for USAID.)

Anthropology's Comparative Method

The end product of anthropological research, if properly carried out, is a coherent statement about a people that provides an explanatory framework for understanding the beliefs, behavior, or biology of those who have been studied. And this, in turn, is what permits the anthropologist to frame broader hypotheses about human beliefs, behavior, and biology. A single instance of any phenomenon is generally insufficient for supporting a plausible hypothesis. Without some basis for comparison, the hypothesis grounded in a single case may be no more than a particular historical coincidence. On the other hand, a single case may be enough to cast doubt on, if not refute, a theory that had previously been held to be valid. For example, the discovery in 1948 that Aborigines living in Australia's northern Arnhem Land put in an average workday of less than

6 hours, while living well above a bare-sufficiency level, was enough to call into question the widely accepted notion that food-foraging peoples are so preoccupied with finding scarce food that they lack time for any of life's more pleasurable activities. The observations made in the Arnhem Land study have since been confirmed many times over in various parts of the world.

To test hypothetical explanations of cultural and biological phenomena, researchers compare data gathered from several societies found in a region; these data are derived from a variety of approaches,

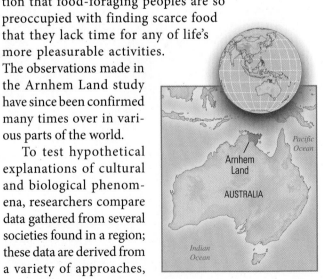

including archaeology, biology, linguistics, history, and ethnography. Carefully controlled comparison provides a broader basis for drawing general conclusions about humans than does the study of a single culture or population.

Ideally, theories in anthropology are generated from worldwide comparisons or comparisons across species or through time. The cross-cultural researcher examines a global sample of societies in order to discover whether hypotheses proposed to explain cultural phenomena or biological variation are universally applicable. The cross-cultural researcher depends upon data gathered by other scholars as well as his or her own. These data can be in the form of written accounts, artifacts and skeletal collections housed in museums, published descriptions of these collections, or recently constructed databases that allow for cross-species comparisons of the molecular structure of specific genes or proteins.

Questions of Ethics

The kinds of research carried out by anthropologists, and the settings within which they work, raise a number of important moral questions about the potential uses and abuses of our knowledge. In the early years of the discipline, many anthropologists documented traditional cultures they assumed would disappear due to disease, warfare, or acculturation imposed by colonialism, growing state power, or international market expansion. Some worked as government anthropologists, gathering data used to formulate policies concerning indigenous peoples or even to help predict the behavior of enemies during wartime. After the colonial era ended in the 1960s, anthropologists began to establish a code of ethics to ensure their research did not harm the groups they studied.

Today, this code grapples with serious questions: Who will utilize our findings and for what purposes? Who decides what research questions are asked? Who, if anyone, will profit from the research? For example, in the case of research on an ethnic or religious minority whose values may be at odds with the dominant mainstream society, will government or corporate interests use anthropological data to suppress that group? And what of traditional communities around the world? Who is to decide what changes should, or should not, be introduced for community "betterment"? And who defines what constitutes betterment—the community, a national government, or an international agency like the World Health Organization? What are the limits of cultural relativism when a traditional practice is considered a human rights abuse globally?

Today, many universities require that anthropologists, like other researchers, communicate in advance the nature, purpose, and potential impact of the planned study to individuals who provide information—and obtain their **informed consent,** or formal recorded agreement to participate in the research. Of course, this requirement is easier to fulfill in some societies or cultures than in others. When it is a challenge to obtain informed consent, or even impossible to precisely explain the meaning and purpose of this concept and its actual consequences, anthropologists may protect the identities of individuals, families, or even entire communities by altering their names and locations. For example, when Dutch anthropologist Anton Blok studied the Sicilian mafia, he did not obtain the informed consent of this violent secret group but opted not to disclose their real identities.[10]

Anthropologists deal with matters that are private and sensitive, including things that individuals would prefer not to have generally known about them. How does one write about such important but delicate issues and at the same time protect the privacy of the individuals who have shared their stories?

The dilemma facing anthropologists is also recognized in the preamble to the code of ethics of the American Anthropological Association (AAA), which was formalized in 1971 and revised in 1998 and again in 2009. This document outlines the various ethical responsibilities and moral obligations of anthropologists, including this central maxim: "Anthropological researchers must do everything in their power to ensure that their research does not harm the safety, dignity, or privacy of the people with whom they work, conduct research, or perform other professional activities." The recent healthy round of debates regarding this code has focused on the potential ethical breaches if anthropologists undertake classified contract work for the military, as some have in Afghanistan, or work for corporations. Some argue that in both cases the required transparency to the people studied cannot be maintained under these circumstances.

The AAA ethics statement is an educational document that lays out the rules and ideals applicable to anthropologists in all the subdisciplines. While the AAA has no legal authority, it does issue policy statements on research ethics questions as they come up. For example, recently the AAA recommended that field notes from medical settings should be protected and not subject to subpoena in malpractice lawsuits. This honors the ethical imperative to protect the privacy of individuals who have shared their stories with anthropologists.

[10] Blok, A. (1974). *The mafia of a Sicilian village 1860–1960: A study of violent peasant entrepreneurs.* New York: Harper & Row.

informed consent Formal recorded agreement to participate in research; federally mandated for all research in the United States and Europe.

The consumption habits of people in more temperate parts of the world are threatening the lifestyle of people from circumpolar regions. As global warming melts the polar ice caps, traditional ways of life, such as building an igloo, may become impossible. This Inuit man—in Iqaluit, the capital of the Canadian territory of Nunavut—may not be able to construct an igloo much longer. Therefore, the Inuit people consider global warming a human rights issue.

© The Canadian Press (Kevin Frayer)

Emerging technologies have ethical implications that impact anthropological inquiry. For example, the ability to sequence and patent particular genes has led to debates about who has the right to hold a patent—the individuals from whom the particular genes were obtained or the researcher who studies the genes? Given the radical changes taking place in the world today, a scientific understanding of the past has never been more important. Do ancient remains belong to the scientist, to the people living in the region under scientific investigation, or to whoever happens to have possession of them? Market forces convert these remains into very expensive collectibles and lead to systematic mining of archaeological and fossil sites. Collaboration between local people and scientists not only preserves the ancient remains from market forces but also honors the connections of indigenous people to the places and remains under study.

To sort out the answers to the all of the above questions, anthropologists recognize that they have special obligations to three sets of people: those whom they study, those who fund the research, and those in the profession who rely on published findings to increase our collective knowledge. Because fieldwork requires a relationship of trust between fieldworkers and the community in which they work, the anthropologist's first responsibility clearly is to the people who have shared their stories and the

globalization Worldwide interconnectedness, evidenced in global movements of natural resources, trade goods, human labor, finance capital, information, and infectious diseases.

greater community. Everything possible must be done to protect their physical, social, and psychological welfare and to honor their dignity and privacy.

This task is frequently complex. For example, telling the story of a people gives information both to relief agencies who might help them and to others who might take advantage of them. While anthropologists regard a people's right to maintain their own culture as a basic premise, any connections with outsiders can endanger the cultural identity of the community being studied. To surmount these obstacles, anthropologists frequently collaborate with and contribute to the communities in which they are working, allowing the people being studied to have some say about how their stories are told.

Anthropology and Globalization

A holistic perspective and a long-term commitment to understanding the human species in all its variety are the essence of anthropology. Thus anthropology is well equipped to grapple with an issue that has overriding importance for all of us at the beginning of the 21st century: **globalization.** This term refers to worldwide interconnectedness, evidenced in global movements of natural resources, trade goods, human labor, finance capital, information, and infectious diseases. Although worldwide travel, trade relations, and information flow have existed for several centuries, the pace and magnitude of these

Globalscape

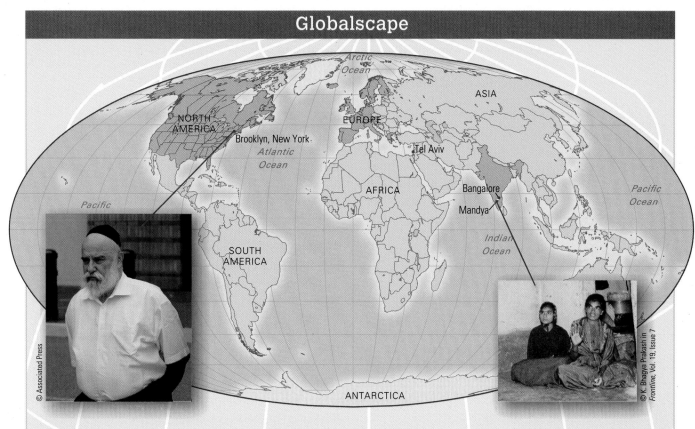

© Associated Press

© K. Bhagya Prakash in *Frontline*, Vol. 19, Issue 7

A Global Body Shop?

Lakshmamma, a mother in southern India's rural village of Holalu, near Mandya, has sold one of her kidneys for about 30,000 rupees ($650). This is far below the average going rate of $6,000 per kidney in the global organ transplant business. But the broker took his commission, and corrupt officials needed to be paid as well. Although India passed a law in 1994 prohibiting the buying and selling of human organs, the business is booming. In Europe and North America, kidney transplants can cost $200,000 or more, plus the waiting list for donor kidneys is long, and dialysis is expensive. Thus "transplant tourism," in India and several other countries, caters to affluent patients in search of "fresh" kidneys to be harvested from poor people like Lakshmamma, pictured here with her daughter.

The global trade network in organs has been documented by Israeli filmmaker Nick Rosen, who sold his own kidney for $15,000 through a broker in Tel Aviv to a Brooklyn, New York, dialysis patient. Rosen explained to the physicians at Mt. Sinai Hospital in New York City that he was donating his kidney altruistically. Medical anthropologist Nancy Scheper-Hughes has taken on the criminal and medical aspects of global organ trafficking for the past twenty years or so. She also co-founded Organs Watch in Berkeley, California, an organization working to stop the illegal traffic in organs.

The well-publicized arrest of Brooklyn-based organ broker Levy Izhak Rosenbaum in July 2009—part of an FBI sting operation that also led to the arrest of forty-three other individuals, including several public officials in New Jersey—represents progress made in combating illegal trafficking of body parts. According to Scheper-Hughes, "Rosenbaum wasn't the tip of an iceberg, but the end of something."[a] International crackdowns and changes in local laws are beginning to bring down these illegal global networks.

Global Twister Considering that $650 is a fortune in a poor village like Holalu, does medical globalization benefit or exploit people like Lakshmamma who are looked upon as human commodities? What factors account for the different values placed on the two donated kidneys?

[a] http://www.npr.org/templates/story/story.php?storyId=106997368.

long-distance exchanges have picked up enormously in recent decades; the Internet, in particular, has greatly expanded information exchange capacities.

The powerful forces driving globalization are technological innovations, cost differences among countries, faster knowledge transfers, and increased trade and financial integration among countries. Touching almost everybody's life on the planet, globalization is about economics as much as politics, and it changes human relations and ideas as well as our natural environments. Even geographically remote communities are quickly becoming interdependent through globalization.

Doing research in all corners of the world, anthropologists are confronted with the impact of globalization on human communities wherever they are located. As participant observers, they describe and try to explain how individuals and organizations respond to the massive changes confronting them. Anthropologists may also find out how local responses sometimes change the global flows directed at them. Dramatically increasing every year, globalization can be a two-edged sword. It may generate economic growth and prosperity, but it also undermines long-established institutions. Generally, globalization has brought significant gains to higher-educated groups in wealthier countries, while doing little to boost developing countries and actually contributing to the erosion of traditional cultures. Upheavals due to globalization are key causes for rising levels of ethnic and religious conflict throughout the world.

Since all of us now live in a global village, we can no longer afford the luxury of ignoring our neighbors, no matter how distant they may seem. In this age of globalization, anthropology may not only provide humanity with useful insights concerning diversity, but it may also assist us in avoiding or overcoming significant problems born of that diversity. In countless social arenas, from schools to businesses to hospitals to emergency centers, anthropologists have done cross-cultural research that makes it possible for educators, businesspeople, doctors, and humanitarians to do their work more effectively.

For example, in the United States today, discrimination based on notions of race continues to be a serious issue affecting economic, political, and social relations. Far from being the biological reality it is supposed to be, anthropologists have shown that the concept of race (and the classification of human groups into higher and lower racial types) emerged in the 18th century as an ideological vehicle for justifying European dominance over Africans and American Indians. In fact, differences of skin color are simply surface adaptations to different climactic zones and have nothing to do with physical or mental capabilities. Indeed, geneticists find far more biologic variation *within* any given human population than *among* them. In short, human "races" are divisive categories based on prejudice, false ideas of differences, and erroneous notions of the superiority of one's own group. Given the importance of this issue, race and other aspects of biologic variation will be discussed further in upcoming sections of the text.

A second example of the impact of globalization involves the issue of same-sex marriage. In 1989, Denmark became the first country to enact a comprehensive set of legal protections for same-sex couples, known as the Registered Partnership Act. At this writing, more than a half-dozen other countries and a growing number of individual U.S. states have passed similar laws, variously named, and numerous countries around the world are considering or have passed legislation providing people in homosexual unions the benefits and protections afforded by marriage.[11] In some societies—including Belgium, Canada, the Netherlands, Norway, South Africa, Spain, and Sweden—same-sex marriages are considered socially acceptable and allowed by law, even though opposite-sex marriages are far more common. The same is true for several U.S. states including Connecticut, Iowa, Massachusetts, New Hampshire, and Vermont.

As individuals, countries, and states struggle to define the boundaries of legal protections they will grant to same-sex couples, the anthropological perspective on marriage is useful. Anthropologists have documented same-sex marriages in human societies in various parts of the world, where they are regarded as acceptable under appropriate circumstances. Homosexual behavior occurs in the animal world just as it does among humans.[12] The key difference between people and other animals is that human societies possess beliefs regarding homosexual behavior, just as they do for heterosexual behavior. An understanding of global variation in marriage patterns and sexual behavior does not dictate that one pattern is more right than another. It simply illustrates that all human societies define the boundaries for social relationships.

A final example relates to the common confusion of *nation* with *state*. Anthropology makes an important distinction between these two: States are politically organized territories that are internationally recognized, whereas nations are socially organized bodies of people who share ethnicity—a common origin, language, and cultural heritage. For example, the Kurds constitute a nation, but their homeland is divided among several states: Iran, Iraq, Turkey, and Syria. The international boundaries among these states were drawn up after World War I, with little regard for the region's ethnic groups or nations. Similar processes have taken place throughout the world, especially in Asia and Africa, often making political conditions in these countries inherently unstable. As we will see in later chapters, states and nations rarely coincide—nations being split among different states, and states typically being controlled by members of one nation who commonly use their control to gain access to the land, resources, and labor of other nationalities within the state. Most of the armed conflicts in the world today, such as the many-layered conflicts in the Caucasus Mountains of Russia's

---

[11] Merin, Y. (2002). *Equality for same-sex couples: The legal recognition of gay partnerships in Europe and the United States.* Chicago: University of Chicago Press; "Court says same-sex marriage is a right." (2004, February 5). *San Francisco Chronicle;* current overviews and updates on the global status of same-sex marriage are posted on the Internet by the Partners Task Force for Gay & Lesbian Couples at www.buddybuddy.com.

[12] Kirkpatrick, R. C. (2000). The evolution of human homosexual behavior. *Current Anthropology 41,* 384.

southern borderlands, are of this sort and are not mere acts of "tribalism" or "terrorism," as commonly asserted.

As these examples show, ignorance about other cultures and their ways is a cause of serious problems throughout the world, especially now that our interactions and interdependence have been transformed by global information exchange and transportation advances. Anthropology offers a way of looking at and understanding the world's peoples—insights that are nothing less than basic skills for survival in this age of globalization.

Questions for Reflection

1. Anthropology uses a holistic approach to explain all aspects of human beliefs, behavior, and biology. How might anthropology challenge your personal perspective on the following questions: Where did we come from? Why do we act in certain ways? Does the example of legalized paid surrogacy, featured in the chapter opener, challenge your worldview?

2. From the holistic anthropological perspective, humans have one leg in culture and the other in nature. Are there examples from your life that illustrate the interconnectedness of human biology and culture?

3. Globalization can be described as a two-edged sword. How does it foster growth and destruction simultaneously?

4. The textbook definitions of *state* and *nation* are based on scientific distinctions between both organizational types. However, this distinction is commonly lost in everyday language. Consider, for instance, the names *United States of America* and *United Nations*. How does confusing the terms contribute to political conflict?

5. The Biocultural Connection in this chapter contrasts different cultural perspectives on brain death, while the Original Study features a discussion about traditional Zulu healers and their role in dealing with AIDS victims. What do these two accounts suggest about the role of applied anthropology in dealing with cross-cultural health issues around the world?

Suggested Readings

Bonvillain, N. (2007). *Language, culture, and communication: The meaning of messages* (5th ed.). Upper Saddle River, NJ: Prentice-Hall.

An up-to-date text on language and communication in a cultural context.

Fagan, B. M. (2005). *Archaeology: A brief introduction* (9th ed.). New York: Longman.

This primer offers an overview of archaeological theory and methodology, from field survey techniques to excavation to analysis of materials.

Kedia, S., & Van Willigen, J. (2005). *Applied anthropology: Domains of application*. New York: Praeger.

Compelling essays by prominent scholars on the potential, accomplishments, and methods of applied anthropology in domains including development, agriculture, environment, health and medicine, nutrition, population displacement and resettlement, business and industry, education, and aging. The contributors show how anthropology can be used to address today's social, economic, health, and technical challenges.

Marks, J. (2009). *Why I am not a scientist: Anthropology and modern knowledge*. Berkeley: University of California Press.

With his inimitable wit and deep philosophical insights, biological anthropologist Jonathan Marks shows the immense power of bringing an anthropological perspective to the culture of science.

Peacock, J. L. (2002). *The anthropological lens: Harsh light, soft focus* (2nd ed.). New York: Cambridge University Press.

This lively and innovative book gives the reader a good understanding of the diversity of activities undertaken by cultural anthropologists, while at the same time identifying the unifying themes that hold the discipline together. Additions to the second edition include such topics as globalization, gender, and postmodernism.

Challenge Issue   Born naked and speechless, we are naturally incapable of surviving alone. As humans, we rely on culture, a shared way of living, to meet the physical, social, economic, and ideological challenges of human survival. Each culture is distinct, expressing its unique qualities in numerous ways—by the clothes we wear, the way we speak, the food we eat, when and where we sleep, and the people who make up our household. Here we see Rabari camel nomads ranging the Kutch Desert in western India. The distinctive fabrics, forms, and colors of their objects and apparel mark the social identity of these herders who are easily recognized as Rabari, even from a distance. A key element in their successful adaptation to an arid environment is mobility. Thus nearly everything they own is movable and transportable. Ecological adaptation and symbolic expression of group identity are among the many interrelated functions of culture.

CHAPTER 2

Characteristics of Culture

Chapter Preview

What Is Culture?

Culture consists of the abstract ideas, values, and perceptions of the world that inform and are reflected in people's behavior. Culture is shared by members of a society and produces behavior that is intelligible to other members of that society. Culture is learned rather than inherited biologically, and all the different parts of a culture function as an integrated whole.

Why Do Cultures Exist?

Every culture provides a design for thought and action that helps people survive and deal with all the challenges of existence. To endure, a culture must satisfy the basic needs of those who live by its rules, and it must provide an orderly existence for the members of a society. In doing so, a culture must strike a balance between the self-interests of individuals and the needs of society as a whole. Moreover, it must have the capacity to change in order to adapt to new circumstances or to altered perceptions of existing circumstances.

Ethnocentrism: Are Some Cultures Better than Others?

Humans are born into families forming part of wider communities. Raised by relatives and other members of these groups, we learn to behave, speak, and think like others in our society. Because each of us is reared to regard the world from the vantage point of our own social group, the human perspective is typically ethnocentric—believing that the ways of one's own culture are the only proper ones. Crossing cultural boundaries, we discover that people everywhere have ethnocentric ideas and values. Anthropologists challenge ethnocentrism by striving to understand each culture in its own right.

Students of anthropology study a seemingly endless variety of human societies, each with its own distinctive environment and system of economics, politics, and religion. Yet for all this variety, these societies have one thing in common: Each is a group of people cooperating to ensure their collective survival and well-being. Group living and cooperation are impossible unless individuals know how others are likely to behave in any given situation. Thus some degree of predictable behavior is required of each person within the society. In humans, it is culture that sets the limits of behavior and guides it along predictable paths that are generally acceptable to those who fall within the culture.

The Concept of Culture

Anthropologists conceived the modern concept of culture toward the end of the 19th century. The first really clear and comprehensive definition came from the British anthropologist Sir Edward Tylor. Writing in 1871, he defined culture as "that complex whole which includes knowledge, belief, art, law, morals, custom, and any other capabilities and habits acquired by man as a member of society."[1]

Since Tylor's time, definitions of culture have proliferated, so that by the early 1950s, anthropologists A. L. Kroeber and Clyde Kluckhohn were able to collect over a hundred of them from the academic literature. Recent definitions tend to distinguish more clearly between actual behavior and the abstract ideas, values, and perceptions of the world that inform that behavior. To put it another way, **culture** goes deeper than observable behavior; it is a society's shared and socially transmitted ideas, values, and perceptions, which are used to make sense of experience and generate behavior and are reflected in that behavior.

Characteristics of Culture

Through the comparative study of many human cultures, past and present, anthropologists have gained an understanding of the basic characteristics evident in all of them: Every culture is socially learned, shared, based on symbols,

---

[1] Tylor, E. B. (1871). *Primitive culture: Researches into the development of mythology, philosophy, religion, language, art and customs* (p. 1). London: Murray.

culture A society's shared and socially transmitted ideas, values, and perceptions, which are used to make sense of experience and generate behavior and are reflected in that behavior.

enculturation The process by which a society's culture is passed on from one generation to the next and individuals become members of their society.

---

integrated, and dynamic. A careful study of these characteristics helps us to see the importance and the function of culture itself.

Culture Is Learned

All culture is learned rather than biologically inherited. One learns one's culture by growing up with it, and the process whereby culture is passed on from one generation to the next is called **enculturation.**

Most animals eat and drink whenever the urge arises. Humans, however, are enculturated to do most of their eating and drinking at certain culturally prescribed times and feel hungry as those times approach. These eating times vary from culture to culture, as does what is eaten, how it is prepared, how it is consumed, and where. To add complexity, food is used to do more than merely satisfy nutritional requirements. When used to celebrate rituals and religious activities, as it often is, food "establishes relationships of give and take, of cooperation, of sharing, of an emotional bond that is universal."[2]

Through enculturation every person learns socially appropriate ways of satisfying the basic biologically determined needs of all humans: food, sleep, shelter, companionship, self-defense, and sexual gratification. It is important to distinguish between the needs themselves, which are not learned, and the learned ways in which they are satisfied—for each culture determines in its own way how these needs will be met. For instance, a French Canadian fisherman's idea of a great dinner and a comfortable way to sleep may vary greatly from that of a Maasai nomadic herder in East Africa.

Learned behavior is exhibited in some degree by most, if not all, mammals. Several species may even be said to have elementary culture, in that local populations share patterns of behavior that, as among humans, each generation learns from the one before and that differ from one population to another. For example, research shows a distinctive pattern of behavior among lions of southern Africa's Kalahari Desert—behavior that fostered nonaggressive interaction with the region's indigenous hunters and gatherers and that each generation of lions passed on to the next.[3] Moreover, Kalahari lion culture changed over a thirty-year period in response to new circumstances. That said, it is important to note that not all learned behavior is cultural. For instance, a pigeon may learn tricks, but this behavior is reflexive, the result of conditioning by repeated training, not the product of enculturation.

---

[2] Caroulis, J. (1996). Food for thought. *Pennsylvania Gazette 95* (3), 16.

[3] Thomas, E. M. (1994). *The tribe of the tiger: Cats and their culture* (pp. 109–186). New York: Simon & Schuster.

Culture is passed on from one generation to the next. Here we see Meregeta Zewde Tadesi teaching his son the art of writing a prayer book in their village on the outskirts of Lalibela, one of Ethiopia's holiest cities. The village and town are located in northern Ethiopia's Amhara region, which is populated mostly by Ethiopian Orthodox Christians. Lalibela's population of about 14,500 includes more than 1,000 priests, deacons, and monks. Tadesi trained as a scribe in the medieval city of Gondar, a center of ecclesiastical learning about 200 km (125 mi) from their home.

© Sean Sprague/The Image Works

Beyond our species, examples of cultural behavior are particularly evident among other primates. A chimpanzee, for example, will take a twig, strip it of all leaves, and smooth it down to fashion a tool for extracting termites from their nest. Such tool making, which juveniles learn from their elders, is unquestionably a form of cultural behavior once thought to be exclusively human. In Japan, macaque monkeys have learned the advantages of washing sweet potatoes before eating them and passed the practice on to the next generation.

Within any given primate species, the culture of one population often differs from that of others, just as it does among humans. We have discovered both in captivity and in the wild that primates in general and apes in particular "possess a near-human intelligence, generally including the use of sounds in representational ways, a rich awareness of the aims and objectives of others, the ability to engage in tactical deception, and the faculty to use symbols in communication with humans and each other."[4]

Growing human awareness and understanding concerning such traits in our primate relatives have spawned numerous movements to extend human rights to apes. The movement reached a milestone in 2008 when Spain's parliament approved a resolution committing the country to the "Declaration on Great Apes," giving some human rights to gorillas, chimpanzees, bonobos, and orangutans.[5]

Culture Is Shared

As a shared set of ideas, values, perceptions, and standards of behavior, culture is the common denominator that makes the actions of individuals intelligible to other members of their society. It enables them to predict how others are most likely to behave in a given circumstance, and it tells them how to react accordingly. Society may be defined as an organized group or groups of interdependent people who generally share a common territory, language, and culture and who act together for collective survival and well-being. The ways in which these people depend upon one another can be seen in such features as their economic, communication, and defense systems. They are also bound together by a general sense of common identity.

Because culture and society are such closely related concepts, anthropologists study both. Obviously, there can be no culture without a society. Conversely, there are no known human societies that do not exhibit culture. This cannot be said for all other animal species. Ants and bees, for example, instinctively cooperate in a manner that clearly indicates a remarkable degree of social organization, yet this instinctual behavior is not a culture.

Although a culture is shared by members of a society, it is important to realize that all is not uniform. For one thing, no two people share the exact same version

[4] Reynolds, V. (1994). Primates in the field, primates in the lab. *Anthropology Today 10* (2), 4.

[5] O'Carroll, E. (2008, June 27). Spain to grant some human rights to apes. *Christian Science Monitor.*

society An organized group or groups of interdependent people who generally share a common territory, language, and culture and who act together for collective survival and well-being.

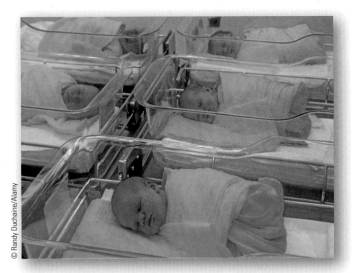

Newborn girls (under pink blankets) and boys (under blue blankets) in a U.S. hospital nursery. Euramerican culture requires that newborn infants be assigned a gender identity of either male or female. Yet, significant numbers of infants are born each year whose genitalia do not conform to cultural expectations. Because only two genders are recognized, the usual reaction is to make the young bodies conform to cultural requirements through gender assignment surgery that involves constructing male or female genitalia. This contrasts with many Native American cultures, which have traditionally recognized more than two genders.[6]

of their culture. And there are bound to be other variations. At the very least, there is some difference between the roles of men and women. This stems from the fact that women give birth but men do not and that there are obvious differences between male and female reproductive anatomy and physiology. Every society gives cultural meaning to biological sexual differences by explaining them in a particular way and specifying what their significance is in terms of social roles and expected patterns of behavior.

Because each culture does this in its own way, there can be tremendous variation from one society to another. Anthropologists use the term **gender** to refer to the cultural elaborations and meanings assigned to the biological differentiation between the sexes. So, although one's sex

is biologically determined, one's gender is socially constructed within the context of one's particular culture.

The distinction between sex, which is biological, and gender, which is cultural, is an important one. Presumably, gender differences are at least as old as human culture—about 2.5 million years—and arose from the biological differences between early human males and females. As with chimps and gorillas today, the species most closely related to humans, early human males were on average substantially larger than females (although size contrasts were not as great as among gorillas). Average male–female size difference in modern humans appears to be significantly less than among our remote ancestors. Moreover, technological advancements in the home and workplace over the last century or two have greatly diminished the cultural significance of many remaining male–female biological differences in societies all across the world.

Indeed, apart from sexual differences directly related to reproduction, any biological basis for contrasting gender roles has largely disappeared in modern industrial and postindustrial societies. (For example, hydraulic lifts used to move heavy automobile engines in an assembly line eliminate the need for muscular strength in that task.) Nevertheless, all cultures exhibit at least some gender role differentiation related to biological differences between the sexes—some far more so than others.

In addition to cultural variation associated with gender, there is also variation related to age. In any society, children are not expected to behave as adults, and the reverse is equally true. But then, who is a child and who is an adult? Again, although age differences are "natural," cultures give their own meaning and timetable to the human life cycle. In North America, for example, individuals are generally not regarded as adults until the age of 18; in many other cultures, adulthood begins earlier—often around age 12, an age closer to the biological changes of adolescence. That said, the status of adulthood often has less to do with age than with passage through certain prescribed rituals.

SUBCULTURES: GROUPS WITHIN A LARGER SOCIETY

Besides age and gender variation, there may be cultural variation between subgroups in societies that share an overarching culture. These may be occupational groups in societies where there is a complex division of labor, or social classes in a stratified society, or ethnic groups in some other societies. When such groups exist within a society, each functioning by its own distinctive standards of behavior while still sharing some common standards, we speak of **subcultures.** The word *subculture* carries no suggestion of lesser status relative to the word *culture.*

---

[6] For statistics on this, see Blackless, M., et al. (2000). How sexually dimorphic are we? Review and synthesis. *American Journal of Human Biology 12,* 151–166.

gender The cultural elaborations and meanings assigned to the biological differentiation between the sexes.

subculture A distinctive set of ideas, values, and behavior patterns by which a group within a larger society operates, while still sharing common standards with that larger society.

The Amish people have held onto their traditional agrarian way of life in the midst of industrialized North American society. Their strong community spirit—reinforced by close social ties between family and neighbors, common language, traditional customs, and shared religious beliefs that set them apart from non-Amish people—is also expressed in a traditional barn raising, a large collective construction project.

© Ian Adams Photography

Amish communities are one example of a subculture in North America. Specifically, they are an **ethnic group**—people who collectively and publicly identify themselves as a distinct group based on various cultural features such as shared ancestry and common origin, language, customs, and traditional beliefs. The Amish originated in western Europe during the Protestant revolutions that swept through Europe in the 16th century. Today members of this group number about 100,000 and live mainly in Pennsylvania, Ohio, Illinois, and Indiana in the United States, and in Ontario, Canada.

These rural pacifists base their lives on their traditional Anabaptist beliefs, which hold that only adult baptism is valid and that "true Christians" (as they define them) should not hold government office, bear arms, or use force. They prohibit marriage outside their faith, which calls for obedience to radical Christian teachings, including social separation from what they see as the wider "evil world" and rejection of material wealth as "vainglorious." Among themselves they usually speak a German dialect known as Pennsylvania Dutch (from *Deutsch,* meaning "German"). They use High German for religious purposes, and children learn English in school. Valuing simplicity, hard work, and a high degree of neighborly cooperation, they dress in a distinctive plain garb and even today rely on the horse for transportation as well as agricultural work.[7]

In sum, the Amish share the same **ethnicity.** This term, rooted in the Greek word *ethnikos* ("nation") and related to *ethnos* ("custom"), is the expression for the set of cultural ideas held by an ethnic group.

The goal of Amish education is to teach youngsters reading, writing, and arithmetic, as well as Amish values. Adults in the community reject what they regard as "worldly" knowledge and the idea of schools producing good citizens for the state. Resisting all attempts to force their children to attend regular public schools, they insist that education take place near home and that teachers be committed to Amish ideals.

Amish nonconformity to many standards of mainstream culture has frequently resulted in conflict with state authorities, as well as personal harassment from people outside their communities. Pressed to compromise, they have introduced "vocational training" beyond junior high to fulfill state requirements, but they have managed to retain control of their schools and to maintain their way of life.

Confronted with economic challenges that make it impossible for most Amish groups to subsist solely on farming,

ethnic group People who collectively and publicly identify themselves as a distinct group based on cultural features such as common origin, language, customs, and traditional beliefs.

ethnicity This term, rooted in the Greek word *ethnikos* ("nation") and related to *ethnos* ("custom"), is the expression for the set of cultural ideas held by an ethnic group.

---

[7] Hostetler, J., & Huntington, G. (1971). *Children in Amish society.* New York: Holt, Rinehart & Winston.

some work outside their communities. Many more have established cottage industries and actively market homemade goods to tourists and other outsiders. Yet, while their economic separation from mainstream society has declined somewhat, their cultural separation has not.[8] They remain a reclusive community, more distrustful than ever of the dominant North American culture surrounding them and mingling as little as possible with non-Amish people.

The Amish are but one example of the way a subculture may develop and be dealt with by the larger culture within which it functions. Different as they are, the Amish actually put into practice many values that other North Americans often respect only in the abstract: thrift, hard work, independence, a close family life. The degree of tolerance accorded to them, in contrast to some other ethnic groups, is also due in part to the fact that the Amish are "white" Europeans; they are defined as being of the same "race" as those who make up the dominant mainstream society. Although the concept of race has been shown to have no biological validity when applied to humans, it still persists as a powerful

social classification. This can be seen in the relative lack of tolerance shown toward American Indians, typically viewed as racially different by members of the dominant society.

Implicit in the discussion thus far is that subcultures may develop in different ways. On the one hand, Amish subculture in the United States developed gradually in response to how these European immigrants have communicated and interacted as members of a strict evangelical Protestant sect in pursuit of their common goals within the wider society. On the other hand, North American Indian subcultures are formerly independent cultural groups that underwent colonization by European settlers and were forcibly brought under the control of federal governments in the United States and Canada.

Although all American Indian groups have experienced enormous changes due to colonization, many have held onto traditions significantly different from those of the dominant Euramerican culture surrounding them, so that it is sometimes difficult to decide whether they remain as distinct cultures as opposed to subcultures. In this sense, *culture* and *subculture* represent opposite ends of a continuum, with no clear dividing line between them. The Anthropology Applied feature examines the intersection of culture and subculture with an example concerning Apache Indian housing.

[8] Kraybill, D. B. (2001). *The riddle of Amish culture* (pp. 1–6, 244, 268–269). Baltimore: Johns Hopkins University Press.

Anthropology Applied

New Houses for Apache Indians   *by George S. Esber*

The United States, in common with other industrialized countries of the world, contains a number of more or less separate subcultures. Those who live by the standards of one particular subculture have their closest relationships with one another, receiving constant reassurance that their perceptions of the world are the only correct ones and coming to take it for granted that the whole culture is as they see it. As a consequence, members of one subculture frequently have trouble understanding the needs and aspirations of other such groups. For this reason anthropologists, with their special understanding of cultural differences, are frequently employed as go-betweens in situations requiring interaction between peoples of differing cultural traditions.

As an example, while I was still a graduate student in anthropology, one of my professors asked me to work with architects and a community of Tonto Apache Indians to research housing needs for a new Apache community. Although the architects knew about cross-cultural differences in the use of space, they had no idea how to get relevant information from the Indian people. For

their part, the Apaches had no explicit awareness of their needs, for these were based on unconscious patterns of behavior. For that matter, few people are consciously aware of the space needs for their own social patterns of behavior.

My task was to persuade the architects to hold back on their planning long enough for me to gather, through participant observation and a review of written records, the data from which Apache housing needs could be abstracted. At the same time, I had to overcome Apache anxieties over an outsider coming into their midst to learn about matters as personal as their daily lives as they are acted out, in and around their homes. With these hurdles overcome, I was able to identify and successfully communicate to the architects those features of Apache life having importance for home and community design. At the same time, discussions of my findings with the Apaches enhanced their own awareness of their unique needs.

As a result of my work, the Apaches moved into houses that had been designed with *their* participation, for *their* specific needs. Among my findings was the realization that the Apaches

preferred to ease into social interactions rather than to shake hands and begin interacting immediately, as is more typical of the Anglo pattern. Apache etiquette requires that people be in full view of one another so each can assess the behavior of others from a distance prior to engaging in social interaction with them. This requires a large, open living space. At the same time, hosts feel compelled to offer food to guests as a prelude to further social interaction. Thus, cooking and dining areas cannot be separated from living space. Nor is standard middle-class Anglo kitchen equipment suitable, since the need for handling large quantities among extended families requires large pots and pans, which in turn calls for extra-large sinks and cupboards. Built with such ideas in mind, the new houses accommodated long-standing native traditions.

Adapted from Esber, G. S. (1987). Designing Apache houses with Apaches. In R. M. Wulff & S. J. Fiske (Eds.), Anthropological praxis: Translating knowledge into action. Boulder, CO: Westview. 2007 update by Esber.

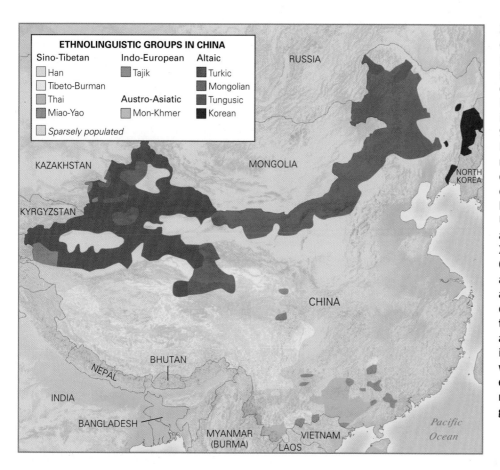

Figure 2.1 China is the largest country in the world, with a population of 1.3 billion people. A pluralistic country, it has fifty-five officially recognized nationalities. By far the largest ethnic group is the Han, comprising about 90 percent of the population. However, there are many ethnic minorities speaking radically different languages and having different cultural traditions. For example, the Uyghur (or Uighur), numbering 8.3 million, are a Turkic-speaking people in Xinjiang Province in northwestern China. Unlike most Han, who are Buddhists, most Uyghur are Sunni Muslims. Historically dominating the Chinese state, the Han typically see themselves as the "real" Chinese and ignore the ethnic minorities or view them with contempt. This ethnocentrism is also reflected in names historically used for these groups.

PLURALISM

Our discussion raises the issue of the multi-ethnic or **pluralistic society** in which two or more ethnic groups or nationalities are politically organized into one territorial state but maintain their cultural differences. Pluralistic societies could not have existed before the first politically centralized states arose a mere 5,000 years ago. With the rise of the state, it became possible to bring about the political unification of two or more formerly independent societies, each with its own culture, thereby creating a more complex order that transcends the theoretical one culture–one society linkage.

Pluralistic societies, which are common in the world today (see Figure 2.1 for an example), all face the same challenge: They are comprised of groups that, by virtue of their high degree of cultural variation, are all essentially operating by different sets of rules. Since social living requires predictable behavior, it may be difficult for the members of any one subgroup to accurately interpret and follow the different standards by which the others operate. This can lead to significant misunderstandings, such as the following case reported in the news:

Salt Lake City—Police called it a cross-cultural misunderstanding. When the man showed up to buy the Shetland pony advertised for sale, the owner asked what he intended to do with the animal. "For my son's birthday," he replied, and the deal was closed.

The buyer thereupon clubbed the pony to death with a two-by-four, dumped the carcass in his pickup truck and drove away. The horrified seller called the police, who tracked down the buyer. At his house they found a birthday party in progress. The pony was trussed and roasting in a *luau pit.* "We don't ride horses, we eat them," explained the buyer, a recent immigrant from Tonga [an island in the Pacific Ocean].[9]

Unfortunately, the difficulty members of one subgroup within a pluralistic society may have making sense of the standards by which members of other groups operate can go far beyond mere misunderstanding. It can intensify to the point of anger and violence. There are many examples of troubled pluralistic societies in the world today, including Bolivia, Iraq, and Kenya, where central governments face major challenges in maintaining peace and lawful order.

[9] *Wall Street Journal.* (1983, May 13).

pluralistic society A society in which two or more ethnic groups or nationalities are politically organized into one territorial state but maintain their cultural differences.

© TAO Images Limited/Alamy

The Uyghur, a Turkic-speaking Muslim ethnic minority in China, live in the country's northwestern province of Xinjiang. Politically dominated by China's Han ethnic majority, who comprise 90 percent of the population, Uyghurs are proud of their cultural identity and hold onto their distinctive traditional heritage—as evident in this photo of a Uyghur family group eating together on carpets woven with traditional Uyghur designs.

Culture Is Based on Symbols

Much of human behavior involves **symbols**—signs, sounds, emblems, and other things that are linked to something else and represent them in a meaningful way. Because often there is no inherent or necessary relationship between a thing and its representation, symbols are commonly arbitrary, acquiring specific meanings when people agree on usage in their communications.

In fact, symbols—ranging from national flags to wedding rings to money—enter into every aspect of culture, from social life and religion to politics and economics. We are all familiar with the fervor and devotion that a religious symbol can elicit from a believer. An Islamic crescent, Christian cross, or a Jewish Star of David—as well as the sun

among the Inca, a cow among the Hindu, a white buffalo calf among Plains Indians, or any other object of worship—may bring to mind years of struggle and persecution or may stand for a whole philosophy or religion.

The most important symbolic aspect of culture is language—using words to represent objects and ideas. Through language humans are able to transmit culture from one generation to another. In particular, language makes it possible to learn from cumulative, shared experience. Without it, one could not inform others about events, emotions, and other experiences to which they were not a party. Language is so important that an entire chapter in this book is devoted to the subject.

Culture Is Integrated

Culture, as we have seen, includes what people do for a living, the tools they use, the ways they work together, how they transform their environments and construct their dwellings, what they eat and drink, how they worship,

symbol A sign, sound, emblem, or other thing that is arbitrarily linked to something else and represents it in a meaningful way.

what they believe is right or wrong, what gifts they exchange and when, whom they marry, how they raise their children, how they deal with death, and so on. Because these and all other aspects of a culture must be reasonably well integrated in order to function properly, anthropologists seldom focus on one cultural feature in isolation. Instead, they view each in terms of its larger context and carefully examine its connections to related features.

For purposes of comparison and analysis, anthropologists customarily imagine a culture as a well-structured system made up of distinctive parts that function together as an organized whole. Although they may sharply distinguish each part as a clearly defined unit with its own characteristics and special place within the larger system, anthropologists recognize that social reality is complex and changeable and that divisions among cultural units are often blurry.

Broadly speaking, a society's cultural features fall within three categories: social structure, infrastructure, and superstructure, as depicted in our "barrel model" (Figure 2.2). **Social structure** concerns rule-governed relationships—with all their rights and obligations—that hold members of a society together. Households, families, associations, and power relations, including politics, are all part of social structure. It establishes group cohesion and enables people to consistently satisfy their basic needs, including food and shelter for themselves and their dependents, by means of

work. So, there is a direct relationship between a group's social structure and its economic foundation, which includes subsistence practices and the tools and other material equipment used to make a living.

Because subsistence practices involve tapping into available resources to satisfy a society's basic needs, this aspect of culture is known as **infrastructure.** Supported by this economic foundation, a society is also held together by a shared sense of identity and worldview. This collective body of ideas, beliefs, and values by which members of a society make sense of the world—its shape, challenges, and opportunities—and understand their place in it is known as ideology or **superstructure.** Including religion and national ideology, superstructure comprises their overarching ideas about themselves and everything else around them—and it gives meaning and direction to their lives. Influencing and reinforcing one another, and continually adapting to changing demographic and environmental factors, these three interdependent structures together constitute a cultural system.

KAPAUKU CULTURE AS INTEGRATED SYSTEM

The integration of economic, social, and ideological aspects of a culture can be illustrated by the Kapauku Papuans, a mountain people of Western New Guinea, studied in 1955 by anthropologist Leopold Pospisil.[10] The Kapauku economy relies on plant cultivation, along with pig breeding, hunting, and fishing. Although plant cultivation provides most of the people's food, it is through pig breeding that men achieve political power and positions of legal authority.

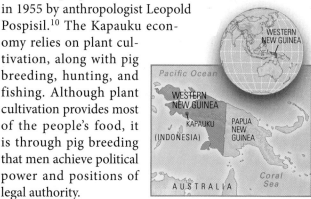

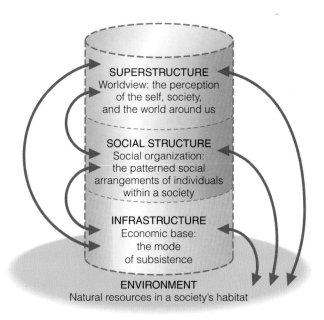

Figure 2.2 The barrel model of culture. Every culture is an integrated and dynamic system of adaptation that responds to a combination of internal factors (economic, social, ideological) and external factors (environmental, climatic). Within a cultural system, there are functional relationships among the economic base (infrastructure), the social organization (social structure), and the ideology (superstructure). A change in one leads to a change in the others.

[10] Pospisil, L. (1963). *The Kapauku Papuans of west New Guinea.* New York: Holt, Rinehart & Winston.

social structure The rule-governed relationships—with all their rights and obligations—that hold members of a society together. This includes households, families, associations, and power relations, including politics.

infrastructure The economic foundation of a society, including its subsistence practices and the tools and other material equipment used to make a living.

superstructure A society's shared sense of identity and worldview. The collective body of ideas, beliefs, and values by which members of a society make sense of the world—its shape, challenges, and opportunities—and understand their place in it. This includes religion and national ideology.

Among the Kapauku, pig breeding is a complex business. Raising a lot of pigs requires a lot of food to feed them. The primary fodder is sweet potatoes, grown in garden plots. According to Kapauku culture, certain garden activities and the tending of pigs are tasks that fall exclusively in the domain of women's work. To raise many pigs, a man needs numerous women in the household; so in Kapauku society multiple wives are not only permitted, they are highly desired. For each wife, however, a man must pay a bride-price, and this can be expensive. Furthermore, wives have to be compensated for their care of the pigs. Put simply, it takes pigs, by which wealth is measured, to get wives, without whom pigs cannot be raised in the first place. Needless to say, this requires considerable entrepreneurship. It is this ability that produces leaders in Kapauku society.

The interrelatedness of these elements with various other features of Kapauku culture is even more complicated. For example, one condition that encourages men to marry several women is a surplus of adult females, sometimes caused by loss of males through warfare. Among the Kapauku, recurring warfare has long been viewed as a necessary evil. By the rules of war, men may be killed but women may not. This system works to promote the imbalanced sex ratio that fosters the practice of having more than one wife. Having multiple wives tends to work best if all of them come to live in their husband's village, and so it is among the Kapauku. With this arrangement, the men of a village are typically "blood" relatives of one another, which enhances their ability to cooperate in warfare. Considering all of this, it makes sense that Kapauku typically trace descent (ancestry) through men.

Descent reckoning through men, coupled with near-constant warfare, tends to promote male dominance. So it is not surprising to find that positions of leadership in Kapauku society are held exclusively by men, who appropriate the products of women's labor in order to enhance their political stature. Such male dominance is by no means characteristic of all human societies. Rather, as with the Kapauku, it arises only under particular sets of circumstances that, if changed, will alter the way in which men and women relate to each other.

Culture Is Dynamic

Cultures are dynamic systems that respond to motions and actions within and around them. When one element within the system shifts or changes, the entire system strives to adjust, just as it does when an outside force applies pressure. To function adequately, a culture must be flexible enough to allow such adjustments in the face of unstable or changing circumstances.

All cultures are, of necessity, dynamic, but some are far less so than others. When a culture is too rigid or static and fails to provide its members with the means required for long-term survival under changing conditions, it is not likely to endure. On the other hand, some cultures are so fluid and open to change that they may lose their distinctive character. The Amish mentioned earlier in this chapter typically resist change as much as possible but are constantly making balanced decisions to adjust when absolutely necessary. North Americans in general, however, have created a culture in which change has become a positive ideal.

Functions of Culture

Polish-born British anthropologist Bronislaw Malinowski argued that people everywhere share certain biological and psychological needs and that the ultimate function of all cultural institutions is to fulfill these needs (see Anthropologist of Note). Others have marked out different criteria and categories, but the idea is basically the same: A culture cannot endure if it does not deal effectively with basic challenges. It must include strategies for the production and distribution of goods and services considered necessary for life. To ensure the biological continuity of its members, it must also provide a social structure for reproduction and mutual support. It must offer ways to pass on knowledge and enculturate new members so they can contribute to their community as well-functioning adults. It must facilitate social interaction and provide ways to avoid or resolve conflicts within their group as well as with outsiders.

Since a culture must support all aspects of life, as indicated in our barrel model, it must also meet the psychological and emotional needs of its members. This last function is met, in part, simply by the measure of predictability that each culture, as a shared design for thought and action, brings to everyday life. Of course it involves much more than that, including a worldview that helps individuals understand their place in the world and face major changes and challenges. For example, every culture provides its members with certain customary ideas and rituals that enable them to think creatively about the meaning of life and death. Many cultures even make it possible for people to imagine an afterlife. Invited to suspend disbelief and engage in such imaginings, people find the means to deal with the grief of losing a loved one.

In Bali, for instance, Hindu worshipers stage spectacular cremation rituals at special places where they burn the physical remains of their dead. After a colorful procession with musicians, the corpse is carried to a great cremation tower, or *wadah*, representing the three-layered cosmos. It is then transferred into a beautifully decorated sarcophagus, made of wood and cloth artfully shaped in the form

Bronislaw Malinowski (1884–1942)

Courtesy Phoebe Apperson Hearst Museum of Anthropology

Bronislaw Malinowski, born in Poland, earned his doctorate in anthropology at the London School of Economics and later, as a professor there, played a vital role in making it an important center of anthropology. Renowned as a pioneer in participant observation and particularly famous for his research among Trobriand

Islanders in the western Pacific, he stated that the ethnographer's goal is "to grasp the native's point of view . . . to realize *his* vision of *his* world."[a]

Writing about culture, Malinowski argued that people everywhere share certain biological and psychological needs and that the ultimate function of all cultural institutions is to fulfill those needs. Everyone, for example, needs to feel secure in relation to the physical universe. Therefore, when science and technology are inadequate to explain certain natural phenomena—such as eclipses or earthquakes—people develop religion and magic to account for those phenomena and to establish a feeling of security. The nature of the institution, according to Malinowski, is determined by its function.

Malinowski outlined three fundamental levels of needs that he claimed had to be resolved by all cultures:

1. A culture must provide for biological needs, such as the need for food and procreation.
2. A culture must provide for instrumental needs, such as the need for law and education.
3. A culture must provide for integrative needs, such as religion and art.

If anthropologists could analyze the ways in which a culture fills these needs for its members, Malinowski believed that they could also deduce the origin of cultural traits.

Although this belief was never justified, the quality of data called for by Malinowski's approach set new standards for anthropological fieldwork. He was the first to insist that it was necessary to settle into the community being studied for an extended period of time in order to really understand it. He demonstrated this approach with his work in the Trobriand Islands between 1915 and 1918. Never before had such fieldwork been done nor had such insights been gained into the workings of another culture. The quality of Malinowski's Trobriand research is said to have earned ethnography (the detailed description of a particular culture based primarily on fieldwork) recognition as a scientific enterprise.

[a]Malinowski, B. (1961). *Argonauts of the western Pacific* (p. 25). New York: Dutton.

---

of an animal—a bull when the deceased belonged to the highest caste of priests (*brahman*), a winged lion for the second highest caste of warriors and administrators (*satria*), and a half-fish/half-elephant for the next caste of merchants (*wesia*). After relatives and friends place their offerings atop or inside the sarcophagus, a Hindu priest sets the structure on fire. Soon, the body burns, and according to Balinese Hindu belief, the animal sarcophagus symbolically guides the soul of the deceased to Bali's "mother" mountain Gunung Angung. This is the sacred dwelling place of the island's gods and ancestors, the place to which many Balinese believe they return when they die. Freed from the flesh, the soul may later transmigrate and return in corporeal form. This belief in reincarnation of the soul allows the Balinese to cope with death as a celebration of life.

In sum, for a culture to function properly, its various parts must be consistent with one another. But consistency is not the same as harmony. In fact, there is friction and potential for conflict within every culture—among individuals, factions, and competing institutions. Even on the

most basic level of a society, individuals rarely experience the enculturation process in exactly the same way, nor do they perceive their reality in precisely identical fashion. Moreover, conditions may change, brought on by inside or outside forces.

Culture and Adaptation

In the course of their evolution, humans, like all animals, have continually faced the challenge of adapting to their environment. The term *adaptation* refers to a gradual process by which organisms adjust to the conditions of the locality in which they live. Organisms have generally adapted biologically as the frequency of advantageous anatomical and physiological features increases in a population through a process known as *natural selection*. For example, body hair protects mammals from extremes of temperature; specialized teeth help them to procure the kinds of food they need; and so on. Short-term physiological responses to

Adult Human Stature and the Effects of Culture: An Archaeological Example

Among human beings, each of us is genetically programmed at conception to achieve a certain stature as an adult. Whether or not we actually wind up as tall as our genes would allow, however, is influenced by experiences during our period of growth and development.

For example, if an individual becomes severely ill, this may arrest growth temporarily, a setback that will not be made up when growth resumes. Critically important as well is the quality of diet. Without adequate nutrition, a person will not grow to be as tall as would otherwise be possible. Thus

in stratified societies, higher-ranked people have tended to be the tallest individuals, as they generally have access to the best diets and are shielded from many of life's harsher realities. Conversely, lower-ranked individuals have tended to be shorter, owing to poor diets and generally harsher lives.

At the ancient Maya city of Tikal, in the Central American country of Guatemala, analysis of human skeletons from burials reveals stature differences characteristic of stratified societies. On average, males interred in rich tombs were taller than those in simple graves associated with relatively small houses.

Those buried near intermediate-sized houses were generally taller than those from simple graves but not as tall as those from tombs.

Thus the analysis provides strong support for a reconstruction of Tikal society into three strata: lower class commoners, higher class commoners, and (at the top) the ruling elite.

BIOCULTURAL QUESTION

If you look around in your own society today, do you notice any differences in physical height between the wealthy elite and the working poor?

the environment—along with responses that become incorporated into an organism through interaction with the environment during growth and development—are other kinds of biological adaptations.

Humans, however, have increasingly come to depend on **cultural adaptation**, a complex of ideas, technologies, and activities that allows them to survive and even thrive in their environment. Biology has not provided them with built-in fur coats to protect them in cold climates, but it has given them the ability to make their own coats, build fires, and construct shelters to shield themselves against the cold. They may not be able to run as fast as a cheetah, but they are able to invent and build vehicles that can carry them faster and farther than any other creature. Through culture and its many constructions, the human species has secured not just its survival but its expansion as well—at great cost to other species and, increasingly, to the planet at large. By manipulating environments through cultural means, people have been able to move into a vast range of environments, from the icy Arctic to the searing Sahara Desert.

This is not to say that everything that humans do they do *because* it is adaptive to a particular environment. For one thing, people do not just react to an environment as given; rather, they react to it as they perceive it, and different groups of people may perceive the same environment

in radically different ways. They also react to things other than the environment: their own biological natures, their beliefs and attitudes, and the short- and long-term consequences of their behavior for themselves and other people and life forms that share their habitats. (See the Biocultural Connection.) Although people maintain cultures to deal with problems, some cultural practices have proved to be maladaptive and have actually created new problems—such as toxic water and air caused by certain industrial practices, or North America's obesity epidemic brought on by the culture of cars, fast food, television, and computers.

A further complication is the relativity of any given adaptation: What is adaptive in one context may be seriously maladaptive in another. For example, the sanitation practices of food-foraging peoples—their toilet habits and methods of garbage disposal—are appropriate for populations with low density and some degree of residential mobility. But these same practices become serious health hazards for large, fully sedentary populations.

Similarly, behavior that is adaptive in the short run may be maladaptive over a longer period of time. For instance, the development of irrigation in ancient Mesopotamia (southern Iraq) made it possible for people to increase their food production, but it also caused a gradual accumulation of salt in the soil, which contributed to the downfall of that civilization over 4,000 years ago.

Today the development of prime farmland in the eastern United States, for purposes other than food production, increases our dependency on food raised elsewhere, in less than optimal environments. Marginal farmlands can produce high yield with costly technology; however,

cultural adaptation A complex of ideas, activities, and technologies that enables people to survive and even thrive in their environment.

What is adaptive at one time may not be at another. In the Central Plains of the United States, a principal region for grain cultivation, irrigation systems and chemical fertilizers have resulted in large but unsustainable crop yields. Here we see crop fields in western Kansas, watered by a center-pivot irrigation system fed by the Ogallala aquifer, which underlies eight states, from southern South Dakota to northwestern Texas, and yields about 30 percent of the nation's groundwater used for irrigation, plus drinking water to 82 percent of the people who live within the aquifer boundary. Heavy use of the aquifer has resulted in large but unsustainable crop yields all across the largely semi-arid region. Over the past five decades, the aquifer's water table has dropped dramatically, and some experts estimate it will dry up in as little as twenty-five years. Moreover, semi-arid regions are vulnerable to salinization as steady winds hasten evaporation of surface water and leave salts in the soil. Chemical fertilizers also contribute to the pollution problem.

over time, these yields will not be sustainable due to loss of topsoil, increasing salinity of soil, and silting of irrigation works, not to mention the high cost of water and fossil fuel. For a culture to be successful, it must produce collective human behavior that is generally adaptive to the natural environment.

Culture and Change

Cultures have always changed over time, although rarely as rapidly or as massively as many are doing today. Change takes place in response to such events as population growth, technological innovation, environmental crisis, the intrusion of outsiders, or modification of behavior and values within the culture.

While cultures must have some flexibility to remain adaptive, cultural change can also bring unexpected and sometimes disastrous results. For example, consider the relationship between culture and the droughts that periodically afflict so many people living in African countries just south of the Sahara Desert. The lives of some 14 million pastoral nomadic people native to this region are centered on cattle and other livestock, herded from place to place as needed to provide them with pasture and water. For thousands of years these nomads have efficiently utilized vast areas of arid lands in ways that allowed them to survive severe droughts many times in the past. Unfortunately, the nomadic way of life is frowned upon by the central governments of modern states in the region because it involves moving back and forth across relatively new international boundaries, making the nomads difficult to track for purposes of taxation and other government controls.

Seeing nomads as a challenge to their authority, these governments have tried to stop the migratory herders from ranging through their traditional grazing territories and to convert them into sedentary villagers. Simultaneously, governments have aimed to press pastoralists into a market

Climate and politics have conspired to create serious cultural change among pastoralists. Moving across vast territories to provide pasture and water for their livestock, these nomadic peoples have long depended upon mobility for survival. For generations, they commonly crossed unmarked international borders to meet the needs of their animals. Difficult to control by central governments trying to impose taxes on them, they now face major obstacles in pursuing their customary way of life. Increasingly restricted from moving across their traditional grazing territories, these African herders are hit all the harder when droughts occur. So it is in this photo taken in Kenya, where the combination of limited grazing lands and severe drought resulted in the death of many animals and turned others into "bones on hoofs." Such catastrophes have forced many pastoralists to give up their old lifeways entirely.

© Tony Karumba/AFP/Getty Images

economy by giving them incentives to raise many more animals than required for their own needs so that the surplus could be sold to add to the tax base. Combined, these policies have led to overgrazing, erosion, and a lack of reserve pasture during recurring droughts. Thus droughts today are far more disastrous than in the past because when they occur, they jeopardize the nomads' very existence.

The market economy that led nomads to increase their herds beyond sustainability is a factor in a huge range of cultural changes, including shifts in fashion. In many countries where swift change is driven by capitalism and its demand for market growth, clothing styles transform with stunning rapidity. Fashion trends also illustrate the interplay of the infrastructure, social structure, and superstructure tiers in our barrel model of culture. For example, the emergence of unisex clothing reflects diminishing gender differences in the Western labor market and in the division of labor in many societies around the world.

Culture, Society, and the Individual

Ultimately, a society is no more than a union of individuals, all of whom have their own special needs and interests. To survive, it must succeed in balancing the immediate self-interest of its individual members with the needs and demands of the collective well-being of society as a whole. To accomplish this, a society offers rewards for adherence to its culturally prescribed standards. In most cases, these rewards assume the form of social approval. For example, in contemporary North American society a person who holds a good job, takes care of family, pays taxes, and does volunteer work in the neighborhood may be spoken of as a "model citizen" in the community. To ensure the survival of the group, each person must learn to postpone certain immediate personal satisfactions. Yet the needs of the individual cannot be overlooked entirely or emotional stress and growing resentment may erupt in the form of protest, disruption, and even violence.

Consider, for example, the matter of sexual expression, which, like anything that people do, is shaped by culture. Sexuality is important in every society for it helps to strengthen cooperative bonds among members, ensuring the perpetuation of the social group itself. Yet sex can be disruptive to social living. If the issue of who has sexual access to whom is not clearly spelled out, competition for sexual privileges can destroy the cooperative bonds on which human survival depends. Uncontrolled sexual activity, too, can result in reproductive rates that cause a society's population to outstrip its resources. Hence, as it shapes sexual behavior, every culture must balance the needs of society against the individual's sexual needs and desires so that frustration does not build up to the point of being disruptive in itself.

Cultures vary widely in the way they go about this. On one end of the spectrum, societies such as the Amish in North America or the Muslim Brotherhood in Egypt have taken an extremely restrictive approach, specifying no sex outside of marriage. On the other end are societies such as

© Wire Image/Getty Images

In the world of fashion, driven by capitalism's relentless demand for market growth, styles change so swiftly that few trends remain "in" or "hot" for more than a year. Here we see Paris Hilton at the 2009 launch of the new JC Penney fashion sportswear clothing line I "Heart" Ronson, targeted at 21- to 35-year-old women. Her underwear-as-outerwear look, echoing a growing permissiveness about body exposure, may well be "out" by the time students read this caption!

the Norwegians who generally accept premarital sex and often choose to have children outside marriage, or even more extreme, the Canela Indians in Brazil, whose social codes guarantee that, sooner or later, everyone in a given village has had sex with just about everyone of the opposite sex. Yet, even as permissive as the latter situation may sound, there are nonetheless strict rules as to how the system operates.[11]

Not just in sexual matters, but in all life issues, cultures must strike a balance between the needs and desires of individuals and those of society as a whole. When those of

society take precedence, people may experience excessive stress. Symptomatic of this are increased levels of mental illness and behavior regarded as antisocial: violence, crime, abuse of alcohol and other drugs, depression, suicide, or simply alienation. If not corrected, the situation can result in cultural breakdown. But just as problems develop if the needs of society take precedence over those of the individual, so too do they develop if the balance is upset in the other direction.

Ethnocentrism and the Evaluation of Cultures

There are numerous highly diverse cultural solutions to the challenges of human existence. Anthropologists have been intrigued to find that people in most cultures tend to see their own way of life as the best of all possible worlds. This is reflected in the fact that in many cultures the traditional name for one's own society translates roughly into "true human beings." In contrast, their names for outsiders commonly translate into various unflattering or even insulting versions of contempt, including "barbarians," "monkeys," "dogs," "weird-looking people," "funny talkers," and so forth. As noted in Chapter 1, any adequately functioning culture regards its own ways in positive terms, and often as the only proper ones: this view is known as *ethnocentrism*.

Anthropologists have been actively engaged in the fight against ethnocentrism ever since they started to study and actually live among traditional peoples with radically different cultures—thus learning by personal experience that these "others" were no less human than anyone else. Resisting the common urge to rank cultures, anthropologists have instead aimed to understand individual cultures and the general concept of culture. To do so, they have examined each culture on its own terms, aiming to discern whether the culture satisfied the needs and expectations of the people themselves. If a people practiced human sacrifice or capital punishment, for example, anthropologists asked about the circumstances that made the taking of human life acceptable according to that particular group's values.

This brings us to the concept of **cultural relativism**— the idea that one must suspend judgment on other peoples' practices in order to understand those practices in their own cultural terms. Only through such an approach

[11] Crocker, W. A., & Crocker, J. (1994). *The Canela, bonding through kinship, ritual and sex* (pp. 143–171). Fort Worth: Harcourt Brace.

cultural relativism The idea that one must suspend judgment of other people's practices in order to understand them in their own cultural terms.

Visual Counterpoint

Many people in the world consider their own nation superior to others, framing their nationalist pride by proclaiming to be a "master race," "divine nation," or "chosen people," and viewing their homeland as sacred. Such nationalist ideology is associated with militant ethnocentrism and dislike, fear, or even hatred of foreigners, immigrants, and ethnic minorities. For instance, most Russians now agree with the nationalist slogan "Russia for the Russians," and almost half believe their nation has a natural right to dominate as an empire. The photo on the right shows Russian Nationalists, ten thousand of whom recently marched to St. Petersburg to protest the immigration of Azeri Tajiks, Turks, and other foreigners into Russia. In their extremism, they are matched by the Minutemen Civil Defense Corps in the United States. Active nationwide, Minutemen view whites as the only "true" Americans and are also strongly against immigrants. The left-hand picture shows Minutemen in Palominas, Arizona, erecting a U.S.–Mexico border fence on private ranchland.

can one gain a meaningful view of the values and beliefs that underlie the behaviors and institutions of other peoples and societies, as well as insights into the underlying beliefs and practices of one's own society.

Take, for example, the 16th-century Aztec practice of sacrificing humans for religious purposes. Few (if any) North Americans today would condone such practices, but by suspending judgment one can get beneath the surface and discern how it functioned to reassure the populace that the Aztec state was healthy and that the sun would remain in the heavens.

Moreover, an impartial and open-minded exploration of Aztec sacrifice rituals may offer a valuable comparative perspective on the death penalty that exists today in a handful of countries, including the United States. Numerous studies by social scientists have clearly shown that the death penalty does not deter violent crime, any more than Aztec sacrifice really provided sustenance for the sun. In fact, cross-cultural studies show that homicide rates mostly decline after its abolition.[12] Similar to Aztec human sacrifice, capital punishment may be seen as an institutionalized magical response to perceived disorder—an act that "reassures many that society is not out of control after all, that the majesty of the law reigns, and that God is indeed in his heaven."[13]

Cultural relativism is essential as a research tool. However, employing it for research does not mean suspending judgment forever, nor does it require that anthropologists defend a people's right to engage in any cultural practice, no matter how destructive. All that is necessary is that we avoid *premature* judgments until we have a full understanding of the culture in which we are interested. Then, and only then, may anthropologists adopt a critical stance and in an informed way consider the advantages and disadvantages particular beliefs and behaviors have for a society and its members. As British anthropologist David Maybury-Lewis emphasized, "One does not avoid making judgments, but rather postpones them in order to make informed judgments later."[14]

[12] Ember, C. R., & Ember, M. (1996). What have we learned from cross-cultural research? *General Anthropology 2* (2), 5.

[13] Paredes, J. A., & Purdum, E. D. (1990). "Bye, bye Ted . . . " *Anthropology Today 6* (2), 9.

[14] Maybury-Lewis, D.H.P. (1993). A special sort of pleading. In W. A. Haviland & R. J. Gordon (Eds.), *Talking about people* (2nd ed., p. 17). Mountain View, CA: Mayfield.

A valid question to ask is how well does a given culture satisfy the biological, social, and psychological needs of those whose behavior it guides.[15] Specific indicators of this are found in the nutritional status and general physical and mental health of its population; the incidence of violence, crime, and delinquency; the demographic structure, stability, and tranquility of domestic life; and the group's relationship to its resource base. The culture of a people who experience high rates of malnutrition (including obesity), violence, crime, delinquency, suicide, emotional disorders and despair, and environmental degradation may be said to be operating less well than that of another people who exhibit few such problems. In a well-working culture, people "can be proud, jealous, and pugnacious, and live a very satisfactory life without feeling 'angst,' 'alienation,' 'anomie,' 'depression,' or any of the other pervasive ills of our own inhuman and civilized way of living."[16] When traditional ways of coping no longer seem to work, and people feel helpless to shape their own lives in their own societies, symptoms of cultural breakdown become prominent.

In short, a culture is essentially a maintenance system to ensure the continued well-being of a group of people. Therefore, it may be deemed successful as long as it secures the survival of a society in a way that its members find to be reasonably fulfilling. What complicates matters is that any society is made up of groups with different interests, raising the possibility that some people's interests may be better served than those of others. Notably, the cultural system in stratified societies generally favors the ruling elite, while the groups scraping by on the bottom benefit the least. The difference may be measured in terms of material wealth as well as physical health.

For this reason, anthropologists must always ask *whose* needs and *whose* survival are best served by the culture in question. Only by looking at the overall situation can a reasonably objective judgment be made as to how well a culture is working. But anthropologists today recognize that few peoples still exist in isolation; globalization affects the dynamics of cultural change in almost every corner of our global village. Accordingly, as will be detailed in many of the following chapters, we must widen our scope and develop a truly worldwide perspective that enables us to appreciate cultures as increasingly open and interactive systems.

A high rate of crime and delinquency is one sign that a culture is not adequately satisfying a people's needs and expectations. This San Quentin Prison cell block can be seen as such evidence. It is sobering to note that 25 percent of all imprisoned people in the world are incarcerated in the United States. In the past decade the country's jail and prison population jumped by more than 700,000—from 1.6 to 2.3 million. Ironically, people in the United States think of their country as "the land of the free," yet it has the highest incarceration rate in the world (751 per 100,000 inhabitants). The median among all nations is about 125, roughly a sixth of the American rate.

---

[15] Bodley, J. H. (1990). *Victims of progress* (3rd ed., p. 138). Mountain View, CA: Mayfield.

[16] Fox, R. (1968). *Encounter with anthropology* (p. 290). New York: Dell.

Questions for Reflection

1. Like everyone else in the world, you are meeting daily challenges of survival through your culture. Do you live in an environment that is still primarily natural, or is it modified by human technology and construction? And how does your culture provide you with the necessary means to effectively adapt to that environment?

2. Many large modern societies are pluralistic. Are you familiar with any subcultures in your own society? Could you make friends with or even marry someone from another subculture? What kind of problems would you be likely to encounter?

3. Although all cultures across the world display some degree of ethnocentrism, some are more ethnocentric than others. In what ways is your own society ethnocentric?

Considering today's globalization (as described in Chapter 1), do you think ethnocentrism poses more of a problem than in the past?

4. The barrel model offers you a simple framework to imagine what a culture looks like from an analytical point of view. How would you apply that model to your own community?

5. An often overlooked first step for developing an understanding of another culture is having knowledge and respect for one's own cultural traditions. Do you know the origins of the worldview commonly held by most people in your community? How do you think it developed over time, and what makes it so accepted or popular in your group today?

Suggested Readings

Bergendorff, S. (2009). *Simple lives, cultural complexity: Rethinking culture in terms of complexity theory.* Lanham, MD: Rowman & Littlefield.

The author, a globalization expert from Denmark, explores how people manage to live relatively simple lives while remaining seemingly unaware of the cultural complexity they produce while doing so. He argues that people do not need to know their entire "cultural order" and its formal logics to cope with everyday life. His book offers an innovative perspective on the concept of culture and the many ways that it is deployed and understood by its bearers.

Brown, D. E. (1991). *Human universals.* New York: McGraw-Hill.

Fascination with cultural diversity should not eclipse the study of human universals; this book examines the relevance of universals for our understanding of the nature of all humanity and raises issues transcending boundaries of biological and social science, as well as the humanities.

Hatch, E. (1983). *Culture and morality: The relativity of values in anthropology.* New York: Columbia University Press.

The author traces anthropological grapplings with the concept of cultural relativity—looking at it in relation to relativity of knowledge, historical relativism, and ethical relativism.

Lewellen, T. C. (2002). *The anthropology of globalization: Cultural anthropology enters the 21st century.* Westport, CT: Greenwood.

This is a useful and digestible undergraduate textbook on the anthropology of globalization—looking at theory, migration, and local–global relationships.

Urban, G. (2001). *Metaculture: How cultures move through the modern world.* Westport, CT: Greenwood.

Urban examines the dynamics and implications of the rapid circulation of contemporary capitalist culture with its constant striving for "newness."

Challenge Issue Anthropologists take on the challenge of studying and describing cultures around the world and finding scientific explanations for their differences and similarities. Why do people think, feel, and act in certain ways—and find it wrong or impossible to do otherwise? Answers must come from fact-based knowledge about cultural diversity—knowledge that is not culture-bound and is widely recognized as significant. Over the years, anthropology has generated such knowledge through various theories and research methods. In particular, anthropologists obtain information through long-term, full-immersion fieldwork based on participant observation. Here we see anthropologist Lucas Bessire demonstrating his new handheld GPS receiver to Ayoreo Indian friends during a break in a hunting expedition in the dry forest of the Gran Chaco in Paraguay, South America—one involved moment among many in the all-engaging challenge of anthropological fieldwork.

CHAPTER 3

Ethnographic Research: Its History, Methods, and Theories

Chapter Preview

How and Why Did Ethnographic Research Evolve?

In the early years of the discipline, many anthropologists documented traditional cultures they assumed would disappear due to disease, warfare, or acculturation imposed by colonialism, growing state power, or international market expansion. Some worked as government anthropologists, gathering data used to formulate policies concerning indigenous peoples or to help predict the behavior of enemies during wartime. After the colonial era ended in the 1960s, anthropologists established a code of ethics to ensure their research did not harm the groups they study. Today it is common for anthropologists to collaborate with minority groups and communities under siege and to assist in cultural revitalization efforts. Anthropological methods and knowledge are also applied to a range of globalization challenges, including economic development, conflict resolution, business, and politics. Finally, anthropologists do research to better understand what makes us tick and to explain cross-cultural differences and similarities.

How Is Research Related to Theory?

Data resulting from research, whether collected through fieldwork or another method, provide anthropologists with material needed to produce a comprehensive written (or filmed) ethnography, or description, of a culture. Moreover, they supply details that are fundamental to ethnology—cross-cultural comparisons and theories that explain different cultural beliefs and behaviors. Beyond offering explanations, theories help us frame new questions that deepen our understanding of cultural phenomena. Anthropologists have come up with a wide variety of theories, some of which have been replaced or improved by new information or better explanations. Gradually, much of what was puzzling or unknown about our complex species and its fascinating social and cultural diversity is exposed, revealed, or clarified through theoretically informed research.

What Are Ethnographic Research Methods?

Although anthropology relies on various research methods, its hallmark is extended fieldwork in a particular community or cultural group. This fieldwork features participant observation in which the researcher not only observes and documents the daily life of the community being studied but also participates in that life. Typically, an anthropologist's initial fieldwork is carried out solo and lasts a full year. However, some anthropologists work in teams, and some field stays may be briefer or longer. It is not uncommon for anthropologists to return to their field sites periodically over the course of several decades.

As briefly discussed in Chapter 1, cultural anthropology has two main scholarly components: *ethnography* and *ethnology*. Ethnography is a detailed description of a particular culture primarily based on fieldwork. Ethnology is the study and analysis of different cultures from a comparative or historical point of view, utilizing ethnographic accounts and developing anthropological theories that help explain why certain important differences or similarities occur among groups.

Historically, anthropology focused on non-Western traditional peoples whose languages were not written down—people whose communication was often direct and face to face, and whose knowledge about the past was based primarily on oral tradition. Even in societies where writing exists, not much of what is of interest to anthropologists is recorded in writing. Thus anthropologists have made a point of going to these places in person to observe and experience peoples and their cultures firsthand. This is called *fieldwork*.

Today, anthropological fieldwork takes place not only in small-scale communities in distant corners of the world, but also in modern urban neighborhoods in industrial or postindustrial societies. Anthropologists can be found doing fieldwork in a wide range of places and within a host of diverse groups and institutions, including global corporations, nongovernmental organizations (NGOs), migrant labor communities, and peoples scattered and dispersed because of natural or human-made catastrophes.

In our unsettled and globalizing world, where long-standing boundaries between cultures are being erased, new social networks and cultural constructs are emerging, made possible by long-distance mass transportation and communication technologies. Anthropologists today are adjusting their research methods to better describe, explain, and understand these complex but fascinating dynamics in the rapidly changing human condition of the 21st century.

History of Ethnographic Research and Its Uses

Anthropology emerged as a formal discipline during the heyday of colonialism (1870s–1950s) when many European anthropologists focused on the study of traditional peoples and their cultures in the colonies overseas. For instance, French anthropologists did most of their research in North and West Africa and Southeast Asia; British anthropologists in southern and East Africa; Dutch anthropologists in what has become Indonesia, Western New Guinea, and Suriname; and Belgian anthropologists in Congo of Africa.

Meanwhile, anthropologists in North America focused primarily on their own countries' Native Indian and Eskimo communities—usually residing on tracts of land known as reservations, or in remote Arctic villages. Because these indigenous groups are surrounded by a dominant society that has settled on what used to be exclusively Native lands, and they are no longer completely independent from that larger society's national government, their reservations are sometimes described as *internal colonies.*

At one time it was common practice to compare peoples still pursuing traditional lifeways—based on hunting, fishing, gathering, and/or small-scale farming or herding—with the ancient prehistoric ancestors of Europeans and to categorize the cultures of these traditional peoples as "primitive." Although anthropologists have long abandoned such ethnocentric terminology, many others still think and speak of these traditional cultures as underdeveloped or even undeveloped. This misconception helped state societies, commercial enterprises, and other powerful outside groups justify expanding their activities and invading the lands belonging to these peoples, often exerting overwhelming pressure on them to change their ancestral ways.

Salvage Ethnography or Urgent Anthropology

In this disturbing and often violent historical context, the survival of thousands of traditional communities worldwide has been at stake. In fact, many of these threatened peoples have become physically extinct. Others survived but were forced to surrender their territories or their way of life. Although anthropologists have seldom been able to prevent such tragic events, they have tried to make a record of these cultural groups. This important early anthropological practice of documenting endangered cultures was initially called *salvage ethnography* and later became known as **urgent anthropology.**

By the late 1800s, many European and North American museums were sponsoring anthropological expeditions to collect cultural artifacts and other material remains (including skulls, bones, utensils, weapons, clothing, and ceremonial objects), as well as vocabularies, myths, and other relevant cultural data. Early anthropologists also began taking ethnographic photographs, and by the 1890s some began shooting documentary films or recording the speech, songs, and music of these so-called vanishing peoples.

urgent anthropology Ethnographic research that documents endangered cultures; also known as salvage ethnography.

Until recently, Ayoreo Indian bands lived largely isolated in the Gran Chaco, a vast wilderness in South America's heartland. One by one, these migratory foragers have been forced to "come out" due to outside encroachment on their habitat. Today, most dispossessed Ayoreo Indians find themselves in different stages of acculturation. This photo shows Ayoreo women of Zapocó in Bolivia's forest. Dressed in Western hand-me-downs and surrounded by plastic from the modern society that is pressing in on them, they weave natural plant fibers into traditionally patterned bags to sell for cash, while men make money by cutting trees for logging companies.

Although the first generation of anthropologists often began their careers working for museums, those coming later were academically trained in the emerging discipline and became active in newly founded anthropology departments. In North America, most of the latter did their fieldwork on tribal reservations where indigenous communities were falling apart in the face of disease, poverty, and despair brought on by pressures of forced cultural change. These anthropologists interviewed American Indian elders still able to recall the ancestral way of life prior to the disruptions forced upon them. The researchers also collected oral histories, traditions, myths, legends, and other information, as well as old artifacts for research, preservation, and public display.

Beyond documenting social practices, beliefs, artifacts, and other disappearing cultural features, anthropologists also sought to reconstruct abandoned traditional lifeways remembered only by surviving elders. Although anthropological theories have come and gone during the past hundred years, the plight of indigenous peoples struggling for cultural survival endures. Anthropologists can and still do contribute to that effort, assisting in cultural preservation efforts. In that work, utilizing a variety of new methods, they can tap into and continue to build on

a professional legacy of salvage ethnography and urgent anthropology.

Acculturation Studies

Since the 1930s, anthropologists have been studying asymmetrical (sharply uneven) cultural contact or *acculturation*. This is the often disruptive process of cultural change occurring in traditional societies as they come in contact with more powerful state societies—in particular, industrialized or capitalist societies.

Typically, as the dominant (often foreign) power establishes its superiority, local indigenous cultures are made to appear inferior, ridiculous, or otherwise not worth preserving; and they are often forced to adopt the ways of the dominant society pressing in on them. Government-sponsored programs designed to compel indigenous groups to abandon their ancestral languages and cultural traditions for those of dominant society have ripped apart the unique cultural fabric of one group after another. These programs left many indigenous families impoverished, demoralized, and desperate.

One of the first anthropologists to study acculturation was Margaret Mead in her 1932 fieldwork among the Omaha Indians of Nebraska. In that research (one of many projects she undertook), she focused on community breakdown and cultural disintegration of this traditional American Indian tribe. In the course of the 20th century, numerous other anthropologists carried out acculturation studies in Asia, Africa, Australia, Oceania, the Americas, and even in parts of Europe, thereby greatly contributing to our knowledge of complex and often disturbing processes of cultural change.

Applied Anthropology

In identifying the disintegrating effects of asymmetrical cultural contact, acculturation studies gave birth to *applied anthropology*—the use of anthropological knowledge and methods to solve practical problems in communities confronting new challenges. For traditional groups in colonized territories or on reservations, government officials began looking at how anthropological research might help these communities struggling with imposed economic, social, and political changes. Voicing the need for an applied anthropology to address the negative effects of colonial policies, Polish-born British anthropologist Bronislaw Malinowski commented, "The anthropologist who is unable to register the tragic errors committed at times with the best intentions remains an antiquarian covered with academic dust and in fool's paradise."[1]

In 1937 the British government set up an anthropological research institute in what is now Zambia to study the impact of international markets on Central Africa's traditional societies. In the next decade, anthropologists worked on a number of problem-oriented studies throughout Africa, including the disruptive effects of the mining industry and labor migration on domestic economies and cultures.

Facing similar issues in North America, the U.S. Bureau of Indian Affairs (BIA), which oversees federally recognized tribes on Indian reservations, established an applied anthropology branch in the mid-1930s. Beyond studying the problems of acculturation, the handful of applied anthropologists hired by the BIA were to identify culturally appropriate ways for the U.S. government to introduce social and economic development programs to reduce poverty, promote literacy, and solve a host of other problems on the reservations.

In 1941, the international Society for Applied Anthropology was founded to promote scientific investigation of the principles controlling human relations and the encouragement of their practical application. Today, many academically trained anthropologists specialize in applied research, working for a variety of local, regional, national, and international institutions, in particular nongovernmental organizations (NGOs), and are active on numerous fronts in every corner of the world.

Studying Cultures at a Distance

During World War II (1939–1945) and the early years of the Cold War (over forty years of political hostility and sharp conflict in diplomacy, economics, and ideology between blocks of capitalist countries led by the United States and rival blocks of communist countries led by Russia), some anthropologists shifted their attention from small-scale traditional communities to modern state societies. Aiming to discover basic personality traits, or psychological profiles, shared by the majority of the people in modern state societies, several U.S. and British anthropologists became involved in a wartime government program of "national character" studies. Such studies were considered useful in efforts to better understand and deal with the newly declared enemy states of Japan and Germany (in World War II) and later Russia and others.

During wartime, on-location ethnographic fieldwork was impossible in enemy societies and challenging at best in most other foreign countries. So, Mead and her close friend Ruth Benedict (one of her former professors at Columbia University), along with several other anthropologists, developed innovative techniques for studying "culture at a distance." Their methods included the analysis of newspapers, literature, photographs, and popular films. They also collected information through structured interviews with immigrants and refugees from the enemy nations, as well as foreigners from other countries.[2]

For instance, the efforts of these anthropologists to portray the "national character" of peoples inhabiting distant countries included investigating topics such as childrearing beliefs, attitudes, and practices, in conjunction with examining print or film materials for recurrent cultural themes and values. This cultural knowledge was also used for propaganda and psychological warfare. After the war, some of the information and insights based on such long-distance anthropological studies were found useful in temporarily governing the occupied territories and dealing with newly liberated populations in other parts of the world.

---

[1] In Mair, L. (1957). *An introduction to social anthropology* (p. 4). London: Oxford University Press. See also Malinowski, B. (1945). *The dynamics of culture change: An inquiry into race relations in Africa* (pp. 1–13). New Haven and London: Yale University Press.

[2] Mead, M., & Métraux, R. (Eds.). (1953). *The study of culture at a distance.* Chicago: University of Chicago Press.

Studying Contemporary State Societies

Although there were theoretical flaws in the national character studies and methodological problems in studying cultures at a distance, anthropological research on contemporary state societies was more than just a war-related endeavor. Even when anthropologists devoted themselves primarily to researching non-Western small-scale communities, they recognized that a generalized understanding of human relations, ideas, and behavior depends upon knowledge of *all* cultures and peoples, including those in complex, large-scale industrial societies organized in political states, such as modern France or the United States. Already during the years of the Great Depression (1930s) several anthropologists worked in their own countries in settings ranging from factories to farming communities and suburban neighborhoods.

One interesting example of an early anthropologist doing research on the home front is Hortense Powdermaker. Born in Philadelphia, Powdermaker went to London to study anthropology under Malinowski and did her first major ethnographic fieldwork among Melanesians in the southern Pacific. When she returned to the United States, she researched a racially segregated town in Mississippi in the 1930s.[3] During the next decade, she focused on combating U.S. dominant society's racism against African Americans and other ethnic minorities.

While in the South, Powdermaker became keenly aware of the importance of the mass media in shaping people's worldviews.[4] To further explore this ideological force in modern culture, she cast her critical eye on the domestic film industry and did a year of fieldwork in Hollywood (1946–1947).

As Powdermaker was wrapping up her Hollywood research, several other anthropologists were launching other kinds of studies in large-scale societies. Convinced that governments and colonial administrations, as well as new global institutions such as the United Nations (founded in 1945), could and should benefit from anthropological insights, Ruth Benedict and Margaret Mead initiated a team project in comparative research on contemporary cultures based at Columbia University in New York (1947–1952).

In 1950, Swiss anthropologist Alfred Métraux put together an international team of U.S., French, and Brazilian researchers to study contemporary race relations in Brazil. The project, sponsored by UNESCO (the United Nations Education, Science, and Culture Organization), was part of the UN's global campaign against racial prejudice and discrimination. Headquartered in Paris, Métraux selected this South American country as a research site primarily for comparative purposes. Like the United States, it was a former European colony with a large multi-ethnic population and a long history of black slavery. Brazil had abolished slavery twenty-five years later than the United States but had made much more progress in terms of its race relations. In contrast to the racially segregated United States, Brazil was believed to be an ideal example of harmonious, tolerant, and overall positive cross-racial relations. The research findings yielded unexpected results, showing that dark-skinned Brazilians of African descent did face systemic social and economic discrimination—albeit not in the political and legal form of racial segregation that pervaded the United States at the time.[5]

In 1956 and 1957, anthropologist Julian Steward left the United States to supervise an anthropological research team in developing countries such as Kenya, Nigeria, Peru, Mexico, Japan, Myanmar (Burma), Malaya, and Indonesia. His goal was to study the comparative impact of industrialization and urbanization upon these different populations. Other anthropologists launched similar projects in other parts of the world.

Peasant Studies

In the 1950s, as anthropologists widened their scope to consider the impact of complex state societies on the traditional indigenous groups central to early anthropological study, some zeroed in on peasant communities. Peasants represent an important social category, standing midway between modern industrial society and traditional subsistence foragers, herders, farmers, and fishers. Part of larger, more complex societies, peasant communities exist worldwide, and peasants number in the many hundreds of millions.

Peasantry represents the largest social category of our species so far. Because peasant unrest over economic and social problems fuels political instability in many developing countries, anthropological studies of these rural populations in Latin America, Africa, Asia, and elsewhere are considered significant and practical.[6] In addition to improving policies aimed at social and economic development in rural communities, anthropological peasant studies may offer insights into how to deal with peasants resisting challenges to their traditional way of life. Such anthropological research may be useful in promoting

---

[3] Powdermaker, H. (1939). *After freedom: A cultural study in the Deep South.* New York: Viking.

[4] Wolf, E. R., & Trager, G. L. (1971). Hortense Powdermaker 1900–1970. *American Anthropologist* 73 (3), 784.

[5] Prins, H.E.L., & Krebs, E. (2006). Toward a land without evil: Alfred Métraux as UNESCO anthropologist 1948–1962. In *60 years of UNESCO history. Proceedings of the international symposium in Paris, 16–18 November 2005.* Paris: UNESCO.

[6] Redfield, R. (1953). *The primitive world and its transformations* (pp. 40–41). Ithaca, NY: Cornell University Press; Wolf, E. R. (1966). *Peasants* (p. 1). Englewood Cliffs, NJ: Prentice-Hall.

© Harald E. L. Prins

Peasant studies came to the fore during the 1950s as anthropologists began investigating rural peoples in state societies and the impact of capitalism on traditional small-scale communities. Here a Guarani-speaking peasant leader addresses a crowd in front of the presidential palace in Paraguay's capital city of Asunción at a massive protest rally against land dispossession.

social justice by helping to solve, manage, or avoid social conflicts and political violence, including rebellions and guerrilla warfare or insurgencies.[7]

Advocacy Anthropology and Studying Up

By the 1960s, European colonial powers had relinquished almost all of their overseas domains. Many anthropologists turned their attention to the newly independent countries in Africa and Asia, while others focused on South and Central America. However, as anti-Western sentiment and political upheaval seriously complicated fieldwork in many parts of the world, significant numbers of anthropologists investigated important issues of cultural change and conflict inside Europe and North America. Many of these issues, which remain focal points to this day, involve immigrants and refugees coming from places where anthropologists have conducted research.

Some anthropologists have gone beyond studying such groups to playing a role in helping them adjust to their new circumstances—an example of applied anthropology. Others have become advocates for peasant communities, ethnic or religious minorities, or indigenous groups struggling to hold onto their ancestral lands, natural resources, and customary ways of life. Both focus on identifying, preventing, or solving problems and challenges in groups that form part of complex societies and whose circumstances and affairs are conditioned or even determined by powerful outside institutions or corporations over which they generally have little or no control.

Although anthropologists have privately long championed the rights of indigenous peoples and other cultural groups under siege, one of the first anthropological research projects explicitly and publicly addressing the quest for social justice and cultural survival took place among the Meskwaki, or Fox Indians, on their reservation in the state of Iowa (1948–1959). Based on long-term fieldwork with this North American Indian community, anthropologist Sol Tax challenged government-sponsored applied anthropological research projects and proposed instead that researchers work directly with "disadvantaged, exploited, and oppressed communities [to help *them*] identify and solve their [*own*] problems."[8]

Over the past few decades, anthropologists committed to social justice and human rights have become actively and increasingly involved in efforts to assist indigenous groups, peasant communities, and ethnic minorities. Today, most anthropologists committed to community-based and politically involved research refer to their work as **advocacy anthropology.**

Anthropologist Robert Hitchcock has practiced advocacy anthropology for over three decades. Specializing in development issues, he has focused primarily on land rights, as well as the social, economic, and cultural rights, of indigenous peoples in southern Africa—especially Bushmen (San, Basarwa) groups in Botswana. Hitchcock's

---

[7] Firth, R. (1946). *Malay fishermen: Their peasant economy* (pp. ix–x). London: Kegan Paul; see also Wolf, E. R. (1969). *Peasant wars of the twentieth century* (pp. ix–xiii, 276–302). New York: Harper & Row.

advocacy anthropology   Research that is community based and politically involved.

---

[8] Field, L. W. (2004). Beyond "applied" anthropology. In T. Biolsi (Ed.), *A companion to the anthropology of American Indians* (pp. 472–489). Oxford: Blackwell; see also Lurie, N. O. (1973). Action anthropology and the American Indian. In *Anthropology and the American Indian: A symposium* (p. 6). San Francisco: Indian Historical Press.

Dr. Rodolfo Stavenhagen, UN Special Rapporteur on the Situation of Human Rights and Fundamental Freedom of the Indigenous People. Here he appears with Victoria Tauli-Corpuz, chairperson of the UN Permanent Forum on Indigenous Issues, at a press conference near Manilla in the Phillipines in 2007.

work has involved helping Bushmen to ensure their rights to land—for foraging, pasturing, farming, and income-generation purposes—in the face of development projects aimed at setting aside land for the ranching, mining, or conservation interests of others. He helped draw up legislation on subsistence hunting in Botswana, making it the only country in Africa that allows broad-based hunting rights for indigenous peoples who forage for part of their livelihood.[9]

Today's most wide-ranging advocacy anthropologist is Rodolfo Stavenhagen, the UN's specialist on indigenous rights. A research professor at the Colegio de Mexico since 1965, he is founder and first president of the Mexican Academy of Human Rights. Stavenhagen leads investigations on the human rights and fundamental freedoms of indigenous peoples throughout the world.

Because of anthropology's mission to gain a more comprehensive understanding of the human condition in its full cross-cultural range and complexity, not just in distant places or at the margins of our own societies, some scholars have urged ethnographic research in the centers of political and economic power in the world's dominant societies. This widening of the anthropological scope is especially important for applied and advocacy anthropologists doing research on groups or communities embedded in larger and more complex processes of state-level politics

and economics or even transnational levels of global institutions and multinational corporations. Of particular note in this effort is anthropologist Laura Nader. Coining the term *study up*, she has called upon anthropologists to focus on Western elites, government bureaucracies, global corporations, philanthropic foundations, media empires, business clubs, and so on.

Studying up is easier said than done, because it is a formidable challenge to do participant observation in such well-guarded circles. And when these elites are confronted with research projects or findings not of their liking, they have the capacity and political power to stop or seriously obstruct the research or the dissemination of its results.

Globalization and Multi-Sited Ethnography

As noted in Chapter 1, the impact of globalization is everywhere. Distant localities are becoming linked in such a way that local events and situations are shaped by forces and activities occurring thousands of miles away, and vice versa. Connected by modern transportation, world trade, finance capital, transnational labor pools, and information superhighways, even the most geographically remote communities become increasingly interdependent. Indeed, all of humanity now exists in what we refer to in this text as a *globalscape*—a worldwide interconnected landscape with multiple intertwining and overlapping peoples and cultures on the move.

One consequence of globalization is the formation of *diasporic* populations (*diaspora* is a Greek word,

[9] Hitchcock, R. K., & Enghoff, M. (2004). *Capacity-building of first people of the Kalahari, Botswana: An evaluation.* Copenhagen: International Work Group for Indigenous Affairs.

originally meaning "scattering"), living and working far from their original homeland. Some diasporic groups feel uprooted and fragmented, but others are able to transcend vast distances and stay in touch with family and friends through communication technologies. With Internet access to blogs and other sources of news, combined with e-mail, text messaging, and a variety of social media platforms, geographically dispersed individuals spend more and more of their time in cyberspace.[10] This electronically mediated environment enables people who are far from home to remain informed, to maintain their social networks, and even to hold onto a historical sense of ethnic identity that culturally distinguishes them from those with whom they share their daily routines in actual geographic space..

Globalization has given rise to a new trend in anthropological research and analysis known as **multi-sited ethnography**—the investigation and documentation of peoples and cultures embedded in the larger structures of a globalizing world, utilizing a range of methods in various locations of time and space. Engaged in such mobile ethnography, researchers seek to capture the emerging dimension of the global by following individual actors, organizations, objects, images, stories, conflicts, and even pathogens as they move about in various interrelated transnational situations and locations.[11]

An example of multi-sited ethnographic research on a diasporic ethnic group is a recent study on transnational Han Chinese identities by Chinese American anthropologist Andrea Louie. Louie's fieldwork carried her to an array of locations in San Francisco, Hong Kong, and southern China—including her ancestral home in the Cantonese village Tiegang in Guangdong Province. Her paternal great-grandfather left the village in the 1840s, crossing the Pacific Ocean to work on railroad construction during the California Gold Rush. But other family members remained in their ancestral homeland. Here, Louie describes her research investigating Chinese identities from different and changing perspectives:

My fieldwork on Chinese identities employed a type of mobile [ethnography] aimed at examining

A young girl born in China shares her China adoption workbook with anthropologist Andrea Louie at the child's home in St. Louis, Missouri. The interactive workbook encouraged the girl to draw a picture of what she imagined her birth mother looked like, to write down questions about her birth family, and to document the process of becoming a family through adoption. She received the book from her mother on her seventh "Gotcha Day," which marks the day that they first "got" each other in Wuhan, China. Andrea Louie helped film that important moment when she traveled to China with several adoptive parents on a fieldwork trip that was part of her larger multi-sited project on Chinese adoptee identities.

various parts of a "relationship" being forged anew across national boundaries that draws on metaphors of shared heritage and place. In my investigation of "Chineseness" I conducted participant observation and interviews in San Francisco with Chinese American participants of the In Search of Roots program,[12] as well as later in China when they visited their ancestral villages and participated in government-sponsored Youth Festivals. . . . I interviewed people in their homes, and apartments; in cafes, culture centers, and McDonald's restaurants; and in rural Chinese villages and on jet planes, focusing on various moments and contexts of interaction within which multiple and often discrepant discourses of Chineseness are brought together.[13]

Also emerging in multi-sited ethnography are greater interdisciplinary approaches to fieldwork, bringing in theoretical ideas and research methods from cultural studies, media studies, and mass communication. One example is

---

[10] Appadurai, A. (1996). *Modernity at large: Cultural dimensions of globalization*. Minneapolis: University of Minnesota Press.

[11] Marcus, G. (1995). Ethnography in/of the world system: The emergence of multi-sited ethnography. *Annual review of anthropology 24*, 95–117; Robben, A.C.G.M., & Sluka, J. A. (Eds.). (2007). *Ethnographic fieldwork: An anthropological reader*. Malden, MA: Blackwell.

multi-sited ethnography The investigation and documentation of peoples and cultures embedded in the larger structures of a globalizing world, utilizing a range of methods in various locations of time and space.

---

[12] This program, run by organizations in Guangzhou and San Francisco, provides an opportunity for young adults (ages 17 to 25) of Cantonese descent to visit their ancestral villages in China.

[13] Louie, A. (2004). *Chineseness across borders: Renegotiating Chinese identities in China and the United States* (pp. 8–9). Durham and London: Duke University Press.

the emergence of ethnographic studies of online "imagined communities" or *cyberethnography.*

Even in the fast-changing, globalizing world of the 21st century, core ethnographic research methods developed about a century ago continue to be relevant and revealing. New technologies have been added to the anthropologist's tool kit, but the hallmarks of our discipline—holistic research through fieldwork with participant observation—is still a valued and productive tradition. Having presented a sweeping historical overview of shifting anthropological research challenges and strategies, we turn now to the topic of research methods.

Doing Ethnography

Every culture comprises underlying rules or standards that are rarely obvious. A major challenge to the anthropologist is to identify and analyze those rules. Fundamental to the effort is **ethnographic fieldwork**—extended on-location research to gather detailed and in-depth information on a society's customary ideas, values, and practices through participation in its collective social life.

While it is true that the scope of cultural anthropology has expanded to include urban life in complex industrial and postindustrial societies, ethnographic methods developed for fieldwork in traditional small-scale societies continue to be central to anthropological research in all types of communities. The methodology still includes personal observation of and participation in the everyday activities of the community, along with interviews, mapping, collection of genealogical data, and recording of sounds and visual images. It all begins with selecting a research site and a research problem or question.

Site Selection and Research Question

Anthropologists usually work outside their own culture, society, or ethnic group, most often in a foreign country. Although it has much to offer, anthropological study within one's own society may present special problems, as described by noted British anthropologist Sir Edmund Leach:

> Surprising though it may seem, fieldwork in a cultural context of which you already have intimate firsthand experience seems to be much more difficult than fieldwork which is approached from the naïve viewpoint of a total stranger. When anthropologists study facets of their own society their vision seems to become distorted by prejudices

which derive from private rather than public experience.[14]

For this reason, most successful anthropological studies of societies to which the researchers themselves belong are done by individuals who first worked in some other culture. The more one learns of other cultures, the more one gains a fresh and more revealing perspective on one's own.

But wherever the site, research requires advance planning that usually includes obtaining funding and securing permission from the community to be studied (and, where mandated, permission from government officials as well). If possible, researchers make a preliminary trip to the site to make these and other arrangements before moving there for more extended research. After exploring the local conditions and circumstances, they have the opportunity to better define their specific research question or problem. For instance, what is the psychological impact of a new highway on members of a traditionally isolated farming community? Or how does the introduction of new electronic media such as cell phones influence long-established gender relations in cultures with religious restrictions on social contact between men and women?

Preparatory Research

Before heading into the field, anthropologists do preparatory research. This includes delving into any existing written, visual, or sound information available about the people and place one has chosen to study. It may involve contacting and interviewing others who have some knowledge about or experience with the community, region, or country.

Because anthropologists must be able to communicate with the people they have chosen to study, they will also have to learn the language used in the community selected for fieldwork. Many of the more than 6,000 languages currently spoken in the world have now been recorded and written down, especially during the past century, so it is possible to learn some foreign languages prior to fieldwork. However, as in the early days of the discipline, some of today's anthropologists do research among peoples whose native languages have not

---

[14] Leach, E. (1982). *Social anthropology* (p. 124). Glasgow: Fontana.

ethnographic fieldwork Extended on-location research to gather detailed and in-depth information on a society's customary ideas, values, and practices through participation in its collective social life.

yet been written down. In this case, the researcher may be able to find someone who is minimally bilingual to help the anthropologist gain some proficiency with the language. Another possibility is to first learn an already recorded and closely related language, which provides some elementary communication skills during the early phase of the actual fieldwork.

Finally, anthropologists prepare for fieldwork by studying theoretical, historical, ethnographic, and other literature relevant to the research. For instance, anthropologists interested in understanding violence, both between and within groups, will read studies describing and theoretically explaining conflicts such as wars, insurgencies, raids, feuds, vengeance killings, and so on. Having delved into the existing literature, they may then formulate a theoretical framework and research question to guide them in their fieldwork. Such was the case when anthropologist Napoleon Chagnon applied sociobiological theory to his study of violence within Yanomami Indian communities in South America's tropical rainforest, suggesting that males with an aggressive reputation

as killers are reproductively more successful than those without such a status.[15]

Christopher Boehm took a different theoretical approach in his research on blood revenge among Slavic mountain people in Montenegro. He framed his research question in terms of the ecological function of this violent tradition, as it regulated relations between groups competing for survival in a harsh environment with scarce natural resources.[16]

Participant Observation: Ethnographic Tools and Aids

Once in the field, anthropologists rely on *participant observation*—a research method in which one learns about a group's behaviors and beliefs through social

---

[15] Chagnon, N. A. (1988). Life histories, blood revenge, and warfare in a tribal population. *Science 239*, 935–992.

[16] Boehm, C. (1984). *Blood revenge.* Lawrence: University of Kansas Press.

The hallmark research methodology for anthropologists is participant observation—illustrated by this photo of anthropologist Julia Jean (center), who is both observing *and* participating in a Hindu ritual at a temple for the Goddess Kamakhya in northeastern India.

involvement and personal observation within the community, as well as interviews and discussion with individual members of the group over an extended stay in the community. This work requires an ability to socially and psychologically adapt to a strange community with a different way of life. Keen personal observation skills are also essential, employing *all* the senses—sight, touch, smell, taste, and hearing—in order to perceive collective life in the other culture.

When participating in an unfamiliar culture, anthropologists are often helped by one or more generous individuals in the village or neighborhood. They may also be taken in by a family, and through participation in the daily routine of a household, they will gradually become familiar with the community's basic shared cultural features.

Anthropologists may also formally enlist the assistance of **key consultants**—members of the society being studied who provide information to help researchers understand the meaning of what they observe. (Early anthropologists referred to such individuals as *informants.*) Just as parents guide a child toward proper behavior, so do these insiders help researchers unravel the mysteries of what at first is a strange, puzzling, and unpredictable world. To compensate local individuals for their help in making anthropologists feel welcome in the community and gain access to the treasure troves of inside information, fieldworkers may thank them for their time and expertise with goods, services, or cash.

Beyond the skills and resources noted above, an anthropologist's most essential ethnographic tools in the field are notebooks, pen/pencil, camera, and sound and video recorders. Increasingly, researchers also use laptop computers equipped with data processing programs.

Although researchers may focus on a particular cultural aspect or issue, they will consider the culture as a whole for the sake of context. This holistic and integrative approach—a hallmark of anthropology—requires being tuned in to nearly countless details of daily life—both the ordinary and the extraordinary. By taking part in community life, anthropologists learn why and how events are organized and carried out. Through alert and sustained participation—carefully watching, questioning, listening, and analyzing over a period of time—they can usually identify, explain, and often predict a group's behavior.

Data Gathering: The Ethnographer's Approach

Information collected by ethnographers falls into two main categories: quantitative and qualitative data. **Quantitative data** consist of statistical or measurable information, such as population density, demographic composition of people and animals, and the number and size of houses; the hours worked per day; the types and quantities of crops grown; the amount of carbohydrates or animal protein consumed per individual; the quantity of wood, dung, or other kinds of fuel used to cook food or heat dwellings; the number of children born out of wedlock; the ratio of spouses born and raised within or outside the community; and so on.

Qualitative data concern nonstatistical information about such features as settlement patterns, natural resources, social networks of kinship relations, customary beliefs and practices, personal life histories, and so on. Often, these nonquantifiable data are the most important part of ethnographic research because they capture the essence of a culture; this information provides us with deeper insights into the unique lives of different peoples, helping us truly understand what, why, and how they feel, think, and act in their own distinctive ways.

Beyond the generalities of participant observation, how exactly do ethnographers gather data? Field methods include formal and informal interviewing, mapping, collection of genealogical data, and recording sounds and images. Cultural anthropologists may also use surveys, but not in the way you might think. Below we touch on several key methods for collecting information.

TAKING SURVEYS

Unlike many other social scientists, anthropologists do not usually go into the field equipped with predetermined surveys or questionnaires; rather, they recognize that there are many things that can be discovered only by keeping an open mind while thoughtfully watching, listening, participating, and asking questions. As fieldwork proceeds, anthropologists sort their complex impressions and observations into a meaningful whole, sometimes by formulating and testing limited or low-level hypotheses, but just as often by making use of imagination or intuition and following up on hunches. What is important is that the results are constantly checked for accuracy and consistency, for if the parts fail to fit together in a way that is internally

key consultant A member of the society being studied who provides information that helps researchers understand the meaning of what they observe; early anthropologists referred to such individuals as informants.

quantitative data Statistical or measurable information, such as demographic composition, the types and quantities of crops grown, or the ratio of spouses born and raised within or outside the community.

qualitative data Nonstatistical information such as personal life stories and customary beliefs and practices.

During fieldwork, anthropologists use computers not only for recording and processing data, but as a means of communicating with the peoples being studied. Here we see ecologist James Kremer (pointing at the computer) and anthropologist Stephen Lansing (behind Kremer) who have researched the traditional rituals and network of water temples linked to the irrigation management of rice fields on the island of Bali in Indonesia. They are explaining a computer simulation of this system to the high priest of the Supreme Water Temple, as other temple priests look on. Located on the crater rim above the caldera and lake of Mount Batur, this temple is associated with the Goddess of the Crater Lake. Every year people from hundreds of villages bring offerings here, expressing gratitude to this deity for the gift of water.

coherent, it may be that a mistake has been made and further inquiry is necessary.

This is not to say that anthropologists do not conduct surveys. Some do. But these are just one part of a much larger research strategy that includes a considerable amount of qualitative data as well as quantitative. Also, in ethnographic fieldwork, surveys are usually carried out after one has spent enough time on location to have gained the community's confidence and to know how to compose a questionnaire with categories that are culturally relevant.

Two studies of a village in Peru illustrate the problem of gathering data through surveys alone. One was carried out by a sociologist who, after conducting the survey by questionnaire, concluded that people in the village invariably worked together on one another's privately owned plots of land. By contrast, a cultural anthropologist who lived in the village for over a year (including the brief period when the sociologist did his study) witnessed that particular practice only once. The anthropologist's long-term participant observation revealed that although the idea of labor exchange relations was important to the

people's sense of themselves, it was not a common economic practice.[17]

The point here is that questionnaires all too easily embody the concepts and categories of the researcher, who is an outsider, rather than those of the people being studied. Even where this is not a problem, questionnaires tend to concentrate on what is measurable, answerable, and acceptable as a question, rather than probing the less obvious and more complex qualitative aspects of society or culture.

Moreover, for a host of reasons—fear, ignorance, hostility, hope of reward—people may give false, incomplete, or biased information.[18] Keeping culture-bound ideas, which are often embedded in standardized questionnaires, out of research methods is an important point in all ethnographic research.

_____

[17] Chambers, R. (1983). *Rural development: Putting the last first* (p. 51). New York: Longman.

[18] Sanjek, R. (1990). On ethnographic validity. In R. Sanjek (Ed.), *Field notes* (p. 395). Ithaca, NY: Cornell University Press.

INTERVIEWING

Asking questions is fundamental to ethnographic field-work and takes place in **informal interviews** (unstructured, open-ended conversations in everyday life) and **formal interviews** (structured question/answer sessions carefully noted as they occur and based on prepared questions). Informal interviews may be carried out at any time and in any place—on horseback, in a canoe, by a cooking fire, during ritual events, while walking through the community with a local inhabitant, and the list goes on. Such casual exchanges are essential, for it is often in these conversations that people share most freely. Moreover, questions put forth in formal interviews typically grow out of cultural knowledge and insights gained during informal ones.

Getting people to open up is an art born of a genuine interest in both the information and the person who is sharing it. It requires dropping all assumptions and cultivating the ability to *really* listen. It may even require a willingness to be the village idiot by asking simple questions to which the answers may seem obvious. Also, effective interviewers learn early on that numerous followup questions are vital since first answers may mask truth rather than reveal it. Questions generally fall into one of two categories: broad, *open-ended questions* (Can you tell me about your childhood?) and *closed questions* seeking specific pieces of information (Where and when were you born?).

In ethnographic fieldwork, interviews are used to collect a vast range of cultural information: from life histories, genealogies, and myths to craft techniques and midwife practices to beliefs concerning everything from illness to food taboos. Genealogical data can be especially useful, as they provide information about a range of social customs (such as cousin marriage), worldviews (such as ancestor worship), political relations (such as alliances), and economic arrangements (such as hunting or harvesting on clan-owned lands).

Researchers employ numerous **eliciting devices**—activities and objects used to draw out individuals and encourage them to recall and share information. There are countless examples of this: taking a walk with a local and asking about songs, legends, and place names linked to geographic features; sharing details about one's own family and neighborhood and inviting a telling in return; joining in a community activity and asking a local to explain the practice and why they are doing it; taking and sharing photographs of cultural objects or activities and asking locals to explain what they see in the pictures.

MAPPING

Many anthropologists have done fieldwork in remote places where there is little geographic documentation. Even if cartographers have mapped the region, standard maps seldom show geographic and spatial features that are culturally significant to the people living there. People inhabiting areas that form part of their ancestral homeland have a particular understanding of the area and their own names for local places. These native names may convey essential geographic information, describing the distinctive features of a locality such as its physical appearance, its specific dangers, or its precious resources.

Place names may derive from certain political realities such as headquarters, territorial boundaries, and so on. Others may make sense only in the cultural context of a local people's worldview as recounted in their myths, legends, songs, or other narrative traditions. Thus to truly understand the lay of the land, some anthropologists make their own detailed geographic maps documenting culturally relevant geographic features in the landscape inhabited by the people they study.

Especially since the early 1970s, anthropologists have become involved in indigenous land use and occupancy studies for various reasons, including the documentation of traditional land claims. Researchers constructing individual map biographies may gather information from a variety of sources: local oral histories; early written descriptions of explorers, traders, missionaries, and other visitors; and data obtained from archaeological excavations.

One such ethnogeographic research project took place in northwestern Canada, during the planning stage of the building of the Alaska Highway natural gas pipeline. Since the line would cut directly though Native lands, local indigenous community leaders and federal officials insisted that a study be done to determine how the new construction would affect indigenous inhabitants. Canadian anthropologist Hugh Brody, one of the researchers in this ethnogeographic study, explained: "These maps are the key to the studies and their greatest contribution. Hunters, trappers, fishermen, and berry-pickers mapped out all the land they had ever used in their lifetimes, encircling hunting areas species by species, marking gathering location and camping sites—everything their life on the land had entailed that could be marked on a map."[19]

In addition to mapping the local place names and geographic features, anthropologists may also map out

---

[19] Brody, H. (1981). *Maps and dreams* (p.147). New York: Pantheon.

informal interview An unstructured, open-ended conversation in everyday life.

formal interview A structured question/answer session carefully notated as it occurs and based on prepared questions.

eliciting device An activity or object used to draw out individuals and encourage them to recall and share information.

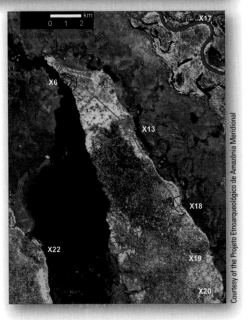

For anthropologist Michael Heckenberger, doing fieldwork among the Kuikuro people of the Upper Xingu River in the southern margins of the Amazon rainforest has become a collaborative undertaking. Together with other specialists on his research team, he has trained local tribespeople to help with the research project about their ancestral culture, which includes searching for the remains of ancient earthworks and mapping them. Here we see Laquai Kuikuro, one of the trained assistants, collecting GPS data (in this case, collecting points of a modern manioc field—manioc being a primary dietary staple of indigenous Amazonian communities in Brazil) and then reviewing the downloaded data. On the right is a map showing GPS-charted indigenous earthworks in the Upper Xingu superimposed over a Landsat satellite image.

information relevant to the local subsistence, such as animal migration routes, favorite fishing areas, places where medicinal plants can be harvested or firewood cut, and so on.

Today, by means of the technology known as global positioning system (GPS), researchers can measure precise distances by triangulating the travel time of radio signals from various orbiting satellites. They can create maps that pinpoint human settlement locations and the layout of dwellings, gardens, public spaces, watering holes, pastures, surrounding mountains, rivers, lakes, seashores, islands, swamps, forests, deserts, and any other relevant feature in the regional environment.

To store, edit, analyze, integrate, and display this geographically referenced spatial information, some anthropologists use cartographic digital technology, known as geographic information systems (GIS). GIS makes it possible to map the geographic features and natural resources in a certain environment—and to link these data to ethnographic information about population density and distribution, social networks of kinship relations, seasonal patterns of land use, private or collective claims of ownership, travel routes, sources of water, and so on. With GIS researchers can also integrate information about beliefs, myths, legends, songs, and other culturally relevant data associated with distinct locations. Moreover, they can create interactive inquiries for analysis

of research data as well as natural and cultural resource management.[20]

PHOTOGRAPHING AND FILMING

Most anthropologists use cameras for fieldwork, as well as notepads, computers, or sound recording devices to document their observations. Photography has been instrumental in anthropological research for more than a century. For instance, Franz Boas took photographs during his first fieldwork among the Inuit in the Canadian Arctic in the early 1880s. And just a few years after the invention of the moving picture camera in 1894, anthropologists began filming traditional dances by indigenous Australians and other ethnographic subjects of interest.

---

[20] Schoepfle, M. (2001). Ethnographic resource inventory and the National Park Service. *Cultural Resource Management 5*, 1–7.

Margaret Mead (1901–1978) ▪ *Gregory Bateson (1904–1980)*

From 1936 to 1938 **Margaret Mead** and **Gregory Bateson** did collaborative ethnographic fieldwork in Bali. Bateson, Mead's husband at the time, was a British anthropologist trained by Alfred C. Haddon, who led the 1898 Torres Strait expedition and is credited with making the first ethnographic film in the field. During their stay in Bali, Bateson took about 25,000 photographs and shot 22,000 feet of motion picture film. Afterward, the couple co-authored the photographic ethnography *Balinese Character: A Photographic Analysis* (1942).

That same year, Bateson worked as an anthropological film analyst studying German motion pictures. Soon Mead and a few other anthropologists became involved in thematic analysis of foreign fictional films. She later compiled a number of such visual anthropology studies in a co-edited volume titled *The Study of Culture at a Distance* (1953).

Mead became a tireless promoter of the scholarly use of ethnographic

Library of Congress

In 1938, after two years of fieldwork in Bali, Margaret Mead and Gregory Bateson began research in Papua New Guinea, where they staged this photograph of themselves to highlight the importance of cameras as part of the ethnographic tool kit. (Note camera on tripod behind Mead and other cameras atop the desk.)

photography and film. In 1960, the year the portable sync-sound film camera was invented, Mead was serving as president of the American Anthropology Association. In her presidential address at the association's annual gathering, she pointed out what she saw as shortcomings in the discipline and urged anthropologists to use cameras more effectively.[a] Chiding her colleagues for not fully utilizing new technological developments, she complained that anthropology had come "to depend on words, and words, and words."

Mead's legacy is commemorated in numerous venues, including the Margaret Mead Film Festival hosted annually since 1977 by the American Museum of Natural History in New York City. Thus it was fitting that during the Margaret Mead Centennial celebrations in 2001 the American Anthropological Association endorsed a landmark visual media policy statement urging academic committees to consider ethnographic visuals—and not just ethnographic writing—when evaluating scholarly output of academics up for hiring, promotion, and tenure.

---

[a]Mead, M. (1960). Anthropology among the sciences. *American Anthropologist 63,* 475–482.

Especially following the invention of the portable synchronous-sound camera in 1960, ethnographic film-making took off. New technological developments made it increasingly obvious that visual media could serve a wide range of cross-cultural research purposes. Some anthropologists employed still photography in community surveys and elicitation techniques. Others turned to film to document and research traditional patterns of non-verbal communication such as body language and social space use. Cameras have also been (and continue to be) instrumental in documenting the disappearing world of traditional foragers, herders, and farmers surviving in remote places.

Since the digital revolution that began in the 1980s, we are witnessing an explosive growth in visual media all across the world. It is not unusual for anthropologists to arrive in remote villages where at least a few native inhabitants take their own pictures or record their own stories and music. For researchers in the field, native-made audio-visual documents may represent a wealth of precious cultural information. The Anthropologists of Note feature details the long history of such equipment in anthropology.

Challenges of Ethnographic Fieldwork

While ethnographic fieldwork offers a range of opportunities to gain better and deeper insight into the community being studied, it comes with a Pandora's box of challenges. At the least, it usually requires researchers to step out of their cultural comfort zone into an unknown world that is sometimes unsettling. As touched upon in Chapter 1, anthropologists in the field are likely to face a wide array of challenges—physical, social, mental, political, and ethical.

While they are handling these challenges, they must be fully engaged in work and social activities with the community. In addition, they are doing a host of other things, such as interviewing, taking copious notes, and analyzing data. In the following paragraphs we offer details on some of the most common personal struggles anthropologists face in the field.

Social Acceptance

Having decided where to do ethnographic research and what to focus on, anthropologists embark on the journey to their field site. Because few choose to do research in their own home communities, most experience culture shock and loneliness at least during the initial stages of their work—work that requires them to establish social contacts with strangers who have little or no idea who they are, why they have come, or what they want from them. In short, a visiting anthropologist is as much a mystery to those she or he intends to study as the group is to the researcher.

Although there is no sure way of predicting how one will be received, it is certain that success in ethnographic fieldwork depends on mutual goodwill and the ability to develop friendships and other meaningful social relations. As New Zealand anthropologist Jeffrey Sluka notes, "The classic image of successful rapport and good fieldwork relations in cultural anthropology is that of the ethnographer who has been 'adopted' or named by the tribe or people he or she studies."[21]

Among the numerous ethnographic examples of anthropologists being adopted by a family, lineage, or clan is the case of Canadian anthropologist Richard Lee, adopted by a group of Ju/'hoansi (Bushmen) foragers in the Kalahari Desert. He describes the informal way in which this took place:

> One day in March 1964, I was visiting a !Xabe village, when Hwan//a, a woman about my age who was married to one of the Tswana Headman Isak's three sons, playfully began to call me, "Uncle, uncle, /Tontah, come see me."
>
> Puzzled, I drew closer; until that time the Ju had referred to me simply as the White Man (/Ton) or the bearded one.... Hwan//a smiled and said, "You are all alone here and I have no children, so I will name you /Tontah after my tsu /Tontah who is dead, and, as I have named you, you shall call me mother."
>
> .... The name stuck. Soon people all over the Dobe area were calling me /Tontah.[22]

Anthropologists adopted into networks of kinship relations not only gain social access and certain rights but also assume social obligations associated with their new kinship status. These relationships can be deep and enduring—as illustrated by Smithsonian anthropologist William Crocker's description of his 1991 return to the Canela tribal community after a twelve-year absence. He had lived among these Amazonian Indians in Brazil off and on for a total of sixty-six months from the 1950s through the 1970s. When he stepped out of the single-motor missionary plane that had brought him back in 1991, he was quickly surrounded by Canela:

> Once on the ground, I groped for names and terms of address while shaking many hands. Soon my Canela mother Tutkhwey (dove-woman), pulled me over to the shade of a plane's wing and pushed me down to a mat on the ground. She put both hands on my shoulders and, kneeling beside me, her head by mine, cried out words of mourning in a loud yodeling manner. Tears and phlegm dripped onto my shoulder and knees. According to a custom now abandoned by the younger women, she was crying for the loss of a grown daughter, Tsepkhwey (bat-woman), as well as for my return.[23]

Since that 1991 reunion, Crocker has visited the Canela community every other year—always receiving a warm welcome and staying with locals. Although many anthropologists are successful in gaining social acceptance and even adoption status in communities where they do participant observation, they rarely go completely native and abandon their own homeland—for even after long stays in a community, after learning to behave appropriately and communicate well, few become complete insiders.

Political Tension

Challenges during fieldwork include the possibility of being caught in political rivalries and used unwittingly by factions within the community; also, the anthropologist may be viewed with suspicion by government authorities who suspect the anthropologist of spying.

Anthropologist June Nash, for instance, has faced serious political and personal challenges doing fieldwork in various Latin American communities experiencing violent changes. As an outsider, Nash tried to avoid becoming embroiled in local conflicts but could not maintain her position as an impartial observer while researching a tin mining community in the Bolivian highlands. When the conflict between local

[21] Sluka, J. A. (2007). Fieldwork relations and rapport: Introduction. In A.C.G.M. Robben & J. A. Sluka (Eds.), *Ethnographic fieldwork: An anthropological reader* (p. 122). Malden, MA: Blackwell.

[22] Lee, R. B. (1993). *The Dobe Ju/'hoansi* (p. 61). Ft. Worth: Harcourt Brace.

[23] Crocker, W. H., & Crocker, J. G. (2004). *The Canela: Kinship, ritual, and sex in an Amazonian tribe* (p. 1). Belmont, CA: Wadsworth.

© Smithsonian Institution/Photographer unknown

Anthropologist William Crocker did fieldwork among Canela Indians in Brazil over several decades. He still visits the community regularly. In this 1964 photograph, a Canela woman (M~i~i- kw'ej, or Alligator Woman) gives him a traditional haircut while other members of the community look on. She is the wife of his adoptive Canela "brother" and therefore a "wife" to Crocker in Canela kinship terms. Among the Canela, it is improper for a mother, sister, or daughter to cut a man's hair.

miners and bosses controlling the armed forces became violent, Nash found herself in a revolutionary setting in which miners viewed her tape recorder as an instrument of espionage and suspected her of being a CIA agent.[24]

All anthropologists face the overriding challenge of winning the trust that allows people to be themselves and share an unmasked version of their culture with a newcomer. Some do not succeed in meeting this challenge. So it was with anthropologist Lincoln Keiser in his difficult fieldwork in the remote town of Thull, situated in the Hindu Kush Mountains of northwestern Pakistan. Keiser ventured there to explore customary blood feuding among a Kohistani tribal community of 6,000 Muslims making their living by a mix of farming and herding in the rugged region. However, the people he had traveled so far to study did not appreciate his presence. As Keiser recounted, many of the fiercely independent tribesmen in this area, "where the AK-47 [sub-machine gun] symbolizes the violent quality of male social relations," treated him with great disdain and suspicion, as a foreign "infidel":

> Throughout my stay in Thull, many people remained convinced I was a creature sent by the devil to harm the community. . . . [Doing fieldwork there] was a test I failed, for a *jirga* [political council] of my most vocal opponents ultimately forced me to leave Thull three months before

I had planned. . . . Obviously, I have difficulty claiming the people of Thull as "my people" because so many of them never ceased to despise me. . . . Still, I learned from being hated.[25]

Gender, Age, Ideology, Ethnicity, and Skin Color

Keiser's fieldwork challenges stemmed in part from his non-Muslim religious identity, marking him as an outsider in the local community of the faithful. Gender, age, ethnicity, and skin color can also impact a researcher's access to a community. For instance, male ethnographers may face prohibitions or severe restrictions in interviewing women or observing certain women's activities. Similarly, a female researcher may not find ready reception among males in communities with gender-segregation traditions. With respect to skin color, African American anthropologist Norris Brock-Johnson encountered social obstacles while doing fieldwork in the American Midwest, but his dark skin helped him gain "admission to the world of black Caribbean shipwrights" on the island of Bequia where he studied traditional boatmaking.[26]

[24] Nash, J. (1976). Ethnology in a revolutionary setting. In M. A. Rynkiewich & J. P. Spradley (Eds.), *Ethics and anthropology: Dilemmas in fieldwork* (pp. 148–166). New York: Wiley.

[25] Keiser, L. (1991). *Friend by day, enemy by night: Organized vengeance in a Kohistani community* (p. 103). Fort Worth: Holt, Rinehart & Winston.

[26] Robben, A.C.G.M. (2007). Fieldwork identity: Introduction. In A.C.G.M. Robben & J. A. Sluka (Eds.), *Ethnographic fieldwork: An anthropological reader* (p. 61). Malden, MA: Blackwell; Johnson, N. B. (1984). Sex, color, and rites of passage in ethnographic research. *Human Organization* 43 (2), 108–120.

Subjectivity and Reflexivity

Whether working near home or abroad, when endeavoring to identify the rules that underlie each culture, ethnographers must grapple with the very real challenge of bias or subjectivity—his or her own and that of members in the community being studied. Because perceptions of reality may vary, an anthropologist must be extremely careful in describing a culture. To do so accurately, the researcher needs to seek out and consider three kinds of data:

1. The people's own understanding of their culture and the general rules they share—that is, their ideal sense of the way their own society ought to be.
2. The extent to which people believe they are observing those rules—that is, how they think they really behave.
3. The behavior that can be directly observed—that is, what the anthropologist actually sees happening.

Clearly, the way people think they *should* behave, the way in which they think they *do* behave, and the way in which they *actually* behave may be distinctly different. By carefully examining and comparing these elements, anthropologists can draw up a set of rules that may explain the acceptable range of behavior within a culture.

Beyond the possibility of drawing false conclusions based on a group's ideal sense of itself, anthropologists run the risk of misinterpretation due to personal feelings and biases shaped by their own culture, as well as gender and age. It is important to recognize this challenge and make every effort to overcome it, for otherwise one may seriously misconstrue what one sees.

A case in point is the story of how male bias in the Polish culture in which Malinowski was raised caused him to ignore or miss significant factors in his pioneering study of the Trobrianders. Unlike today, when anthropologists receive special training before going into the field, Malinowski set out to do fieldwork early in the 20th century with little formal preparation. The following Original Study, written by anthropologist Annette Weiner who ventured to the same islands sixty years after Malinowski, illustrates how gender can impact one's research findings—both in terms of the bias that may affect a researcher's outlook and in terms of what key consultants may feel comfortable sharing with a particular researcher.

In anthropology, researchers are expected to self-monitor through constantly checking their own personal or cultural biases and assumptions as they work. They must present these self-reflections along with their observations. This practice of critical self-examination is known as *reflexivity*.

Original Study

The Importance of Trobriand Women   *by Annette B. Weiner*

Walking into a village at the beginning of fieldwork is entering a world without cultural guideposts. The task of learning values that others live by is never easy. The rigors of fieldwork involve listening and watching, learning a new language of speech and actions, and most of all, letting go of one's own cultural assumptions in order to understand the meanings others give to work, power,

death, family, and friends. During my fieldwork in the Trobriand Islands of Papua New Guinea, I wrestled doggedly with each of these problems—and with the added challenge that I was working in the footsteps of a celebrated anthropological ancestor, Bronislaw Kasper Malinowski. . . .

In 1971, before my first trip to the Trobriands, I thought I understood many things about Trobriand customs and beliefs from having read Malinowski's exhaustive writings. Once there, however, I found that I had much more to discover about what I thought I already knew. For many months I worked with these discordant realities, always conscious of Malinowski's shadow, his words, his explanations. Although I found significant differences in areas of importance, I gradually came to understand how he reached certain conclusions. The answers we both received from informants were not so dissimilar, and I could actually trace how Malinowski had analyzed what his informants told him in a way

that made sense and was scientifically significant—given what anthropologists generally then recognized about such societies. Sixty years separate our fieldwork, and any comparison of our studies illustrates not so much Malinowski's mistaken interpretations but the developments in anthropological knowledge and inquiry from his time to mine. . . .

My most significant point of departure from Malinowski's analyses was the attention I gave to women's productive work. In my original research plans, women were not the central focus of study, but on the first day I took up residence in a village I was taken by them to watch a distribution of their own wealth—bundles of banana leaves and banana fiber skirts—which they exchanged with other women in commemoration of someone who had recently died. Watching that event forced me to take women's economic roles more seriously than I would have from reading Malinowski's studies. Although Malinowski noted the high status of

Trobriand women, he attributed their importance to the fact that Trobrianders reckon descent through women, thereby giving them genealogical significance in a matrilineal society. Yet he never considered that this significance was underwritten by women's own wealth because he did not systematically investigate the women's productive activities. Although in his field notes he mentions Trobriand women making these seemingly useless banana bundles to be exchanged at a death, his published work only deals with men's wealth.

My taking seriously the importance of women's wealth not only brought women as the neglected half of society clearly into the ethnographic picture but also forced me to revise many of Malinowski's assumptions about Trobriand men. For example, Trobriand kinship as described

by Malinowski has always been a subject of debate among anthropologists. For Malinowski, the basic relationships within a Trobriand family were guided by the matrilineal principle of "mother-right" and "father-love." A father was called "stranger" and had little authority over his own children. A woman's brother was the commanding figure and exercised control over his sister's sons because they were members of his matrilineage rather than their father's matrilineage. . . .

In my study of Trobriand women and men, a different configuration of matrilineal descent emerged. A Trobriand father is not a "stranger" in Malinowski's definition, nor is he a powerless figure as the third party to the relationship between a woman and her brother. The father is one of the most important

persons in his child's life, and remains so even after his child grows up and marries. Even his procreative importance is incorporated into his child's growth and development. He gives his child many opportunities to gain things from his matrilineage, thereby adding to the available resources that he or she can draw upon.

At the same time, this giving creates obligations on the part of a man's children toward him that last even beyond his death. Thus, the roles that men and their children play in each other's lives are worked out through extensive cycles of exchanges, which define the strength of their relationships to each other and eventually benefit the other members of both their matrilineages. Central to these exchanges are women and their wealth.

That Malinowski never gave equal time to the women's side of things, given the deep significance of their role in societal and political life, is not surprising. Only recently have anthropologists begun to understand the importance of taking women's work seriously. . . . In the past, both women and men ethnographers generally analyzed the societies they studied from a male perspective. The "women's point of view" was largely ignored in the study of gender roles, since anthropologists generally perceived women as living in the shadows of men—occupying the private rather than the public sectors of society, rearing children rather than engaging in economic or political pursuits.

In the Trobriand Islands, women's wealth consists of banana leaves and banana-fiber skirts, large quantities of which must be given away on the death of a relative.

From Weiner, A. B. (1988). The Trobrianders of Papua New Guinea *(pp. 4–7). New York: Holt, Rinehart & Winston.*

Validation

As the Original Study makes clear, determining the accuracy of anthropological descriptions and conclusions can be difficult. In the natural sciences, one can replicate observations and experiments to try to establish the reliability of a researcher's conclusions. Thus one can see for oneself if one's colleague has "gotten it right." But validating ethnographic research is uniquely challenging because access to sites may be limited or barred altogether, due to a number of factors: insufficient funding, logistical difficulties in reaching the site, problems in obtaining permits, and changing cultural and environmental conditions. These factors mean that what could be observed in

a certain context at a certain time cannot be observed at others. Thus one researcher cannot easily confirm the reliability or completeness of another's account.

For this reason, anthropologists bear a heavy responsibility for factual reporting, including disclosing key issues related to their research: Why was a particular location selected as a research site and for which research objectives? What were the local conditions during fieldwork? Who provided the key information and major insights? How were data collected and recorded? Without such background information, it is difficult to judge the validity of the account and the soundness of the researcher's conclusions.

Putting It All Together: Completing an Ethnography

After collecting ethnographic information, the next challenge is to piece together all that has been gathered into a coherent whole that accurately describes the culture. Traditionally, ethnographies are detailed written descriptions comprised of chapters on topics such as the circumstances and place of fieldwork itself; historical background; the community or group today; its natural environment; settlement patterns; subsistence practices; networks of kinship relations and other forms of social organization; marriage and sexuality; economic exchanges; political institutions; myths, sacred beliefs, and ceremonies; and current developments. These may be illustrated with photographs and accompanied by maps, kinship diagrams, and figures showing social and political organizational structures, settlement layout, floor plans of dwellings, seasonal cycles, and so on.

Visual Anthropology and Digital Media

Sometimes ethnographic research is documented not only in writing but also with sound recordings and on film. Visual records may be used for documentation and illustration as well as for analysis or as a means of gathering additional information in interviews. Moreover, footage shot for the sake of documentation and research may be edited into a documentary film. Not unlike a written ethnography, such a film is a structured whole composed of numerous selected sequences, visual montage, juxtaposition of sound and visual image, and narrative sequencing, all coherently edited into an accurate visual representation of the ethnographic subject.[27]

In recent years anthropologists have experimented with digital media.[28] With the emergence of **digital ethnography**—the use of digital technologies (audio and visual) for the collection, analysis, and representation of ethnographic data—the potential for anthropological research, interpretation, and presentation is greater than ever before. Digital recording devices provide ethnographers with a wealth of material to analyze and utilize toward building hypotheses. They also open the door to sharing findings in new, varied, and interactive ways in the far-reaching digitalized realm of the Internet.[29] Digital ethnographers, having amassed a wealth of digital material while researching, are able to share their findings through DVDs, CD-ROMs, photo essays, podcasts, blogs, or vlogs (video blogging).

Ethnohistory

Ethnohistory is a kind of historical ethnography that studies cultures of the recent past through oral histories; the accounts of explorers, missionaries, and traders; and analysis of such records as land titles, birth and death records, and other archival materials. The ethnohistorical analysis of cultures is a valuable approach to understanding change and plays an important role in theory building.

---

[27] See Collier, J., & Collier, M. (1986). *Visual anthropology: Photography as a research method.* Albuquerque: University of New Mexico Press; El Guindi, F. (2004). *Visual anthropology: Essential method and theory.* Walnut Creek, CA: Altamira.

[28] See also Ginsburg, F. D., Abu-Lughod, L., & Larkin, B. (Eds.). (2009). *Media worlds: Anthropology on new terrain.* Berkeley: University California Press.

---

[29] Michael Wesch, personal communication.

Courtesy of Hu Tai-Li

Anthropologist-filmmaker Hu Tai-Li filming the Maleveq ceremony in the Paiwan village Kulalao, southern Taiwan. An award-winning pioneer of ethnographic films in Taiwan, Tai-Li is a research fellow at the Institute of Ethnology, Academia Sinica, a professor at National Chin-Hua University, and the president of the Taiwan International Ethnographic Film Festival. Since earning an undergraduate degree in history from the National Taiwan University and a PhD in anthropology from City University of New York, she has directed and produced a half-dozen documentaries on a range of topics—including traditional rituals and music, development issues, and national and ethnic identity.

digital ethnography The use of digital technologies (audio and visual) for the collection, analysis, and representation of ethnographic data.

ethnohistory A study of cultures of the recent past through oral histories; accounts of explorers, missionaries, and traders; and analysis of records such as land titles, birth and death records, and other archival materials.

Ethnology: From Description to Interpretation and Theory

Largely descriptive in nature, ethnography provides the basic data needed for *ethnology*—the branch of cultural anthropology that makes cross-cultural comparisons and develops theories that explain why certain important differences or similarities occur between groups. As noted in Chapter 1, the end product of anthropological research, if properly carried out, is a coherent statement about culture or human nature that provides an explanatory framework for understanding the ideas and actions of the people being studied. In short, such an explanation or interpretation supported by a reliable body of data is a **theory.** As discussed in Chapter 1, theory is distinct from *doctrine* or *dogma*—an assertion of opinion or belief formally handed down by an authority as indisputably true and accepted as a matter of faith.

Anthropologists do not claim that any one theory about culture is the absolute truth. Rather they judge or measure a theory's validity and soundness by varying degrees of probability; what is considered to be "true" is what is most probable. But while anthropologists are reluctant about making absolute statements about complex issues such as exactly how cultures function or change, they can and do provide fact-based evidence about whether assumptions have support or are unfounded and thus not true. Thus a theory, contrary to widespread misuse of the term, is much more than mere speculation; it is a critically examined explanation of observed reality.

Always open to future challenges born of new evidence or insights, scientific theory depends on demonstrable, fact-based evidence and repeated testing. So it is that, as our cross-cultural knowledge expands, the odds favor some anthropological theories over others. Old explanations or interpretations must sometimes be discarded as new theories based on better or more complete evidence are shown to be more effective or probable.

Ethnology and the Comparative Method

A single instance of any phenomenon is generally insufficient for supporting a plausible hypothesis. Without some basis for comparison, the hypothesis grounded in a single case may be no more than a hunch born of a unique happenstance or particular historical coincidence. Theories in anthropology may be generated from worldwide cross-cultural or historical comparisons or even comparisons with other species. For instance, anthropologists may examine a global sample of societies in order to discover whether a hypothesis proposed to explain certain phenomena is supported by fact-based evidence. Of necessity, the cross-cultural researcher depends upon evidence gathered by other scholars as well as his or her own.

A key resource that makes this possible is the **Human Relations Area Files (HRAF),** which is a vast collection of cross-indexed ethnographic and archaeological data catalogued by cultural characteristics and geographic location. This ever-growing data bank classifies more than 700 cultural characteristics and includes nearly 400 societies, past and present, from all around the world. Archived in about 300 libraries (on microfiche or online) and approaching a million pages of information, the HRAF facilitates comparative research on almost any cultural feature imaginable—warfare, subsistence practices, settlement patterns, marriage, rituals, and so on.

Among other things, anthropologists interested in finding explanations for certain social or cultural beliefs and practices can use HRAF to test their hypotheses. For example, Peggy Reeves Sanday examined a sample of 156 societies drawn from HRAF in an attempt to answer her comparative research questions concerning dominance and gender in different societies. Her study, published in 1981 (*Female Power and Male Dominance*), disproves the common misperception that women are universally subordinate to men, sheds light on the way men and women relate to each other, and ranks as a major landmark in the study of gender.

Cultural comparisons are not restricted to contemporary ethnographic data. Indeed, anthropologists frequently turn to archaeological or historical data to test hypotheses about cultural change. Cultural characteristics thought to be caused by certain specified conditions can be tested archaeologically by investigating similar situations where such conditions actually occurred. Also useful are data provided in ethnohistories.

Anthropology's Theoretical Perspectives: A Brief Overview

Entire books have been written about each of anthropology's numerous theoretical perspectives. Here we offer a general overview to convey the scope of anthropological theories and their role in explaining and interpreting cultures.

In the previous chapter, we presented the barrel model of culture as a dynamic system of adaptation in which social structure, infrastructure, and superstructure intricately

theory In science an explanation of natural phenomena, supported by a reliable body of data.

Human Relations Area Files (HRAF) A vast collection of cross-indexed ethnographic and archaeological data catalogued by cultural characteristics and geographic locations; archived in about 300 libraries (on microfiche or online).

interact. Helping us to imagine culture as an integrated whole, this model allows us to think about something very complex by reducing it to a highly simplified scheme or basic design.

Although most anthropologists generally conceptualize culture as holistic and integrative, they may have very different takes on the relative significance of different elements that make up the whole and exactly how they relate to one another. We touch on these contrasting perspectives below—in broad strokes.

Idealist

When analyzing a culture, some argue that humans act primarily on the basis of their ideas, concepts, or symbolic representations. In their research and analysis, these anthropologists usually emphasize that to understand or explain why humans behave as they do, one must first get into other people's heads and try to understand how they imagine, think, feel, and speak about the world in which they live. Because of the primacy of the superstructure (ideas, values), this is known as an **idealist perspective** (not to be confused with idealism in the sense of fantasy or hopeful imagination).

Examples of idealist perspectives include psychological and cognitive anthropology (culture and personality), ethnoscience, structuralism, and postmodernism, as well as symbolic and interpretive anthropology. The latter approach is most famously associated with anthropologist Clifford Geertz, who viewed humans primarily as "symbolizing, conceptualizing, and meaning-seeking" creatures. Drawing on words from German historical sociologist Max Weber, Geertz wrote: "Man is an animal suspended in webs of significance he himself has spun. I take culture to be those webs, and the analysis of it to be therefore not an experimental science in search of law but an interpretive one in search of meaning."[30] Geertz developed an artful ethnographic research strategy in which a culturally significant event or social drama (for instance, a Balinese cockfight) is chosen for observation and analysis as a form of "deep play" that may provide essential cultural insights. Peeling back layer upon layer of socially constructed meanings, the anthropologist offers what Geertz called a "thick description" of the event in a detailed ethnographic narrative.

---

[30] Geertz, C. (1973). *The interpretation of culture.* London: Hutchinson.

idealist perspective A theoretical approach stressing the primacy of superstructure in cultural research and analysis.
materialist perspective A theoretical approach stressing the primacy of infrastructure (material conditions) in cultural research and analysis.

Materialist

Many other anthropologists hold a theoretical perspective in which they stress explaining culture by first analyzing the material conditions that they see as determining people's lives. They may begin their research with an inventory of available natural resources for food and shelter, the number of mouths to feed and bodies to keep warm, the tools used in making a living, and so on. Anthropologists who highlight such environmental or economic factors as primary in shaping cultures basically share a **materialist perspective.**

Examples of materialist theoretical approaches include Marxism, neo-evolutionism, cultural ecology, sociobiology, and cultural materialism. In cultural ecology, anthropologists focus primarily on the subsistence mechanisms in a culture that enable a group to successfully adapt to its natural environment. Building on cultural ecology, some anthropologists include considerations of political economy such as industrial production, capitalist markets, wage labor, and finance capital. A political economy perspective is closely associated with Marxist theory, which essentially explains major change in society as the result of growing conflicts between opposing social classes, namely those who possess property and those who do not.

One result of widening the scope—combining cultural ecology and political economy to take into account the emerging world systems of international production and trade relations—is known as *political ecology*. Closely related is *cultural materialism*, a theoretical research strategy identified with Marvin Harris.[31] Placing primary emphasis on the role of environment, demography, technology, and economy in determining a culture's mental and social conditions, he argues that anthropologists can best explain ideas, values, and beliefs as adaptations to economic and environmental conditions (see the Biocultural Connection).

Structural-Functionalist

Not all anthropologists can be easily grouped in idealist or materialist camps. Giving primacy to social structure, many analyze a cultural group by first and foremost focusing on this middle layer in our barrel model. Although it is difficult to neatly pigeonhole various perspectives in this group, theoretical explanations worked out by pioneering French social thinkers like Emile Durkheim and his student Marcel Mauss influenced the development of *structural-functionalism*. Primarily associated with British anthropologists in the mid-1900s, this approach focuses on the underlying patterns or structures of social relationships, attributing functions to cultural institutions in terms of the contributions they make toward maintaining a group's social order.

---

[31] Harris, M. (1979). *Cultural materialism: The struggle for a science of culture.* New York: Random House.

Pig Lovers and Pig Haters *by Marvin Harris*

In the Old Testament of the Bible, the Israelite's God (Yahweh) denounced the pig as an unclean beast that pollutes if tasted or touched. Later, Allah conveyed the same basic message to his prophet Muhammad. Among millions of Jews and Muslims today, the pig remains an abomination, even though it can convert grains and tubers into high-grade fats and protein more efficiently than any other animal.

What prompted condemnation of an animal whose meat is relished by the greater part of humanity? For centuries, the most popular explanation was that the pig wallows in its own urine and eats excrement. But linking this to religious abhorrence leads to inconsistencies. Cows kept in a confined space also splash about in their own urine and feces.

These inconsistencies were recognized in the 12th century by Maimonides, a widely respected Jewish philosopher and physician in Egypt, who said God condemned swine as a public health measure because pork had "a bad and damaging effect upon the body." The mid-1800s discovery that eating undercooked pork caused trichinosis appeared to verify Maimonides's reasoning. Reform-minded Jews then renounced the taboo, convinced that if well-cooked pork did not endanger public health, eating it would not offend God. But others held to it.

Scholars have suggested this taboo stems from the idea that the animal was once considered divine—but this explanation falls short since sheep, goats, and cows were also once worshiped in the Middle East, and their meat is enjoyed by all religious groups in the region.

I think the real explanation lies in the fact that pig farming threatened the integrity of the basic cultural and natural ecosystems of the Middle East. Until their conquest of the Jordan Valley in Palestine over 3,000 years ago, the Israelites were nomadic herders, living almost entirely from sheep, goats, and cattle. Like all pastoralists, they maintained close relationships with sedentary farmers who held the oases and the great rivers. With this mixed farming and pastoral complex, the pork prohibition constituted a sound ecological strategy. The pastoralists could not raise pigs in their arid habitats, and among the semi-sedentary farming populations pigs were more of a threat than an asset.

The basic reason for this is that the world zones of pastoral nomadism correspond to unforested plains and hills that are too arid for rainfall agriculture and that cannot easily be irrigated. The domestic animals best adapted to these zones are ruminants (including cattle, sheep, and goats), which can digest grass, leaves, and other cellulose foods more effectively than other mammals.

The pig, however, is primarily a creature of forests and shaded riverbanks. Although it is omnivorous, its best weight gain is from foods low in cellulose (nuts, fruits, tubers, and especially grains), making it a direct competitor of man. It cannot subsist on grass alone and is ill-adapted to the hot, dry climate of the grasslands, mountains, and deserts in the Middle East. . . .

Among the ancient mixed farming and pastoralist communities of the Middle East, domestic animals were valued primarily as sources of milk, cheese, hides, dung, fiber, and traction for plowing. Goats, sheep, and cattle provided all of this, plus an occasional supplement of lean meat. From the beginning, therefore, pork must have been a luxury food, esteemed for its succulent, tender, and fatty qualities.

Between 4,000 and 9,000 years ago, the human population in the Middle East increased sixty-fold. Extensive deforestation accompanied this rise, largely due to damage caused by sheep and goat herds. Shade and water, the natural conditions appropriate for raising pigs, became ever more scarce, and pork became even more of a tempting luxury. . . . People find it difficult to resist such temptations on their own. Hence Yahweh and Allah were heard to say that swine were unclean—unfit to eat or touch.

In short, in the Middle East it was ecologically maladaptive . . . to raise pigs in substantial numbers, and small-scale production would only increase the temptation. Better then, to prohibit the consumption of pork entirely.

BIOCULTURAL CONNECTION

Consider a taboo you follow and come up with an explanation for it other than the conventional one that most people accept.

Adapted from Harris, M. (1989). Cows, pigs, wars, and witches: The riddles of culture *(pp. 35–60). New York: Vintage/ Random House.*

Beyond these three general groups, there are various other anthropological approaches. Some stress the importance of identifying general patterns or even discovering laws. Early anthropologists believed that they could discover such laws by means of the theory of *unilinear cultural evolution* of universal human progress, beginning with what was then called "savagery," followed by "barbarism," and gradually making progress toward a condition of human perfection known as "high civilization."[32]

Although anthropologists have long abandoned such sweeping generalizations as unscientific and ethnocentric, some continued to search for universal laws in the general development of human cultures by focusing on technological development as measured in the growing capacity for energy capture per capita of the population. This theoretical perspective is sometimes called *neo-evolutionism*. Others seek to explain recurring patterns in human social behavior in terms of laws of natural selection by focusing on possible relationships with human genetics, a theoretical perspective identified with sociobiology. Yet others stress that broad generalizations are impossible because each culture is distinct and can only be understood as resulting from unique historical processes and circumstances. Some even go a step further and focus on in-depth description and analysis of personal life histories of individual members in a group in order to reveal the work of a culture.

---

[32] Carneiro, R. L. (2003). *Evolutionism in cultural anthropology: A critical history.* Boulder, CO: Westview.

Beyond these cultural historical approaches, there are other theoretical perspectives that do not aim for laws or generalizations to explain culture. Theoretical perspectives that reject measuring and evaluating different cultures by means of some sort of universal standard, and stress that they can only be explained or interpreted in their own unique terms, are associated with the important anthropological principle known as *cultural relativism,* discussed in the previous chapter.

Ethical Responsibilities in Anthropological Research

As explained in this chapter, anthropologists obtain information about different peoples and their cultures through long-term, full-immersion fieldwork based on personal observation of and participation in the everyday activities of the community. Once they are admitted and allowed to stay, anthropologists are usually befriended and sometimes even adopted, gradually becoming familiar with the local social structures and cultural features and even with highly personal or politically sensitive details known only to trusted insiders.

Because the community is usually part of a larger and more powerful complex society, anthropological knowledge about how the locals live, what they own, what motivates them, and how they are organized has the potential to make the community vulnerable to exploitation and manipulation. In this context, it is good to be reminded of the ancient Latin maxim *scientia potentia est* ("knowledge is power"). In other words, anthropological knowledge may have far-reaching—and possibly negative—consequences for the peoples being studied.

This problematic relationship between knowledge and power is an uncomfortable one. Are there any rules that may guide anthropologists in their ethical decision making and help them judge right from wrong? This important issue is addressed in the American Anthropological Association's Code of Ethics (discussed in Chapter 1). First formalized in 1971 and modified in its current form in 1998, this document outlines the various ethical responsibilities and moral obligations of anthropologists, including this central maxim: "Anthropological researchers must do everything in their power to ensure that their research does not harm the safety, dignity, or privacy of the people with whom they work, conduct research, or perform other professional activities."

The first step in this endeavor is to communicate in advance the nature, purpose, and potential impact of the planned study to individuals who provide

Former social science teacher Major Robert Holbert takes notes while drinking tea with local school administrators in a small Afghan town in 2007. Embedded with a U.S. Army brigade combat unit, the officer conducted sociocultural assessments as part of the "Human Terrain System" (HTS). Designed to improve the military's ability to understand the complexities of the "human terrain" (civilian population) as it applies to operations in war-torn Afghanistan, HTS has been part of a counterinsurgency strategy against Taliban guerillas since 2006. American social scientists, including anthropologists, participated in its development and implementation. Anthropological involvement in "the struggle for hearts and minds" has been controversial since the mid-1960s, sparking intense debates over ethical concerns that militarizing anthropology may harm communities.

information—and to obtain their informed consent or formal recorded agreement to participate in the research. But protecting the community one studies requires more than that; it demands constant vigilance and alertness. There are some situations where this is particularly challenging—such as working for a global business corporation, international bank, or government agency, such as the foreign service, police, or military.[33] Moreover, it may not be possible to fully anticipate all the cross-cultural and long-term consequences of publishing one's research findings. Navigating this ethical gray area is challenging, but it is the anthropologist's responsibility to be aware of moral responsibilities and to take every possible caution to ensure that one's research does not jeopardize the well-being of the people being studied.

[33]American Anthropological Association. (2007). Executive board statement on the Human Terrain System Project. http://www.aaanet.org/pdf/ EB_Resolution_110807.pdf; González, R. J. (2009). *American counterinsurgency: Human science and the human terrain.* Chicago: University of Chicago Press; McFate, M. (2007). *Role and effectiveness of socio-cultural knowledge for counterinsurgency.* Alexandria, VA: Institute for Defense Analysis.

Questions for Reflection

1.   In describing and interpreting human cultures, anthropologists have long relied on ethnographic fieldwork, including participant observation. What makes this research method uniquely challenging and effective? Of what use might the findings be for meeting the unique challenges of our globalizing world?

2.   Early anthropologists engaged in salvage ethnography (urgent anthropology) to create a reliable record of indigenous cultures once widely expected to vanish. Although many indigenous communities did lose customary practices due to acculturation, descendants of those cultures can now turn to anthropological records to revitalize their ancestral ways of life. Do you think this is a good thing? Why or why not?

3.   In our globalizing world, a growing number of anthropologists carry out multi-sited ethnography rather than conduct research in a single community. If you would do such a multi-sited research project, what would you focus on, and where would you conduct your actual participant observations and interviews?

4.   If you were invited to "study up," on which cultural group would you focus? How would you go about getting access to that group for participant observation, and what serious obstacles might you encounter?

5.   In light of professional ethics, what moral dilemmas might anthropologists face in choosing to advise a government in exploring or implementing a nonviolent solution to a military conflict? How is military anthropology different from other forms of applied anthropology, such as working for the Foreign Service, the World Bank, the Roman Catholic Church, or an international business corporation such as IBM and Intel?

Suggested Readings

Bernard, H. R. (2002). *Research methods in anthropology: Qualitative and quantitative approaches* (3rd ed.). Walnut Creek, CA: Altamira.

Written in a conversational style and rich with examples, this extremely useful and accessible book has twenty chapters divided into three sections: preparing for fieldwork, data collection, and data analysis. It touches on all the basics, from literature search and research design to interviewing, field note management, multivariate analysis, ethics, and more.

Boškovic, A. (Ed.). (2009). *Other people's anthropologies: Ethnographic practice on the margins.* Oxford, England: Berghahn.

This volume with contributions from prominent and promising anthropologists from many different countries is based on a workshop of the European Association of Social Anthropologists held in Vienna in 2004. The collection offers fresh and alternative perspectives on a discipline historically dominated by scholars in the core of the world system, representing the so-called great traditions (Anglo-American, French, and German).

Dicks, B., et al (2005). *Qualitative research and hypermedia: Ethnography for the digital age (New technologies for social research).* Thousand Oaks, CA: Sage.

Introducing emerging ethnographic research methods that utilize new technologies, the authors explain how to conduct data collection, analysis, and representation using new technologies and hypermedia; they also discuss how digital technologies may transform ethnographic research.

Erickson, P. A., & Murphy, L. D. (2003). *A history of anthropological theory* (2nd ed.). Peterborough, Ontario: Broadview.

A clear and concise survey from antiquity to the modern era, effectively drawing the lines between the old and new. This edition features several new and expanded sections on topics including feminist anthropology, globalization, and medical anthropology.

Gordon, R., Lyons, H., and Lyons, A. (Eds.). (2010). *Fifty key anthropologists.* New York: Routledge.

 A collection of engaging essays on some of the most significant figures who have shaped and defined the discipline of anthropology. The fifty anthropologists featured were selected based on their contributions to the discipline through theory, fieldwork, or institutional development.

Pink, S. (2001). *Doing visual ethnography: Images, media and representation in research.* Thousand Oaks, CA: Sage.

Exploring the use and potential of photography, video, and hypermedia in ethnographic and social research, this text offers a reflexive approach to the practical, theoretical, methodological, and ethical issues of using these media. Following each step of research, from planning to fieldwork to analysis and representation, the author suggests how visual images and technologies can be combined to form an integrated product..

Robben, A.C.G.M., & Sluka, J. A. (Eds.). (2007). *Ethnographic fieldwork: An anthropology reader.* Malden, MA: Blackwell.

This up-to-date text provides a comprehensive selection of classic and contemporary reflections, examining the tensions between self and other, the relationships between anthropologists and key consultants, conflicts and ethical challenges, various types of ethnographic research (including multi-sited fieldwork), and different styles of writing about fieldwork.

John Reader/Photo Researchers, Inc.

Challenge Issue   A 23-meter (75-foot) trail of ancient footprints is all that is left of a small group of early human ancestors walking upright across a field of volcanic ash about 3.6 million years ago. Discovered at Laetoli in East Africa in 1976, about a day's walk from Olduvai Gorge, this trail was found in the same layer of hardened ash as fossil bones and footprints of ancient antelopes, baboons, hyenas, and other mammals (including a gigantic prehistoric relative of modern-day elephants). How did these two-legged primates meet the challenge of physical survival in this natural environment? What did they look like? Did they swing sticks, throw stones, or make tools with their free hands? Could they talk? Where do they fit in the natural order between humans and apes, and why did they become extinct as a species? And what do such fossil finds tell us about the emergence of our own species as modern humans with complex cultures? Anthropologists play a key role in unlocking the answers to such fascinating questions.

CHAPTER 4

Becoming Human: The Origin and Diversity of Our Species

Chapter Preview

To What Group of Animals Do Humans Belong?

Biologists classify humans as *Homo sapiens,* members of the primates—a subgroup of mammals. Biological species are defined by reproductive isolation and designated by a two-part name including genus (*Homo*) and species (*sapiens*). Other primates include lemurs, lorises, tarsiers, monkeys, and apes. Because human culture is rooted in our mammalian primate biology, studying the anatomy and behavior of other primates, particularly our closest living ape relatives, helps us understand how and why early humans developed as they did.

When and How Did Humans Evolve?

Present evidence suggests that humans evolved from small African apes between 5 and 8 million years ago (mya). Bipedalism, or walking on two feet, was the first change to distinguish the human evolutionary line. The behavior of these early "bipeds" was comparable to that of modern-day chimpanzees. Several million years after the evolution of bipedalism, brain size began to expand, along with the development of cultural activities such as making stone tools. The earliest stone tools date to between 2.5 and 2.6 mya, coinciding with the appearance of the first members of the genus *Homo* in the fossil record. From then on, shared, learned behavior—culture—has played an increasingly important role in human survival.

Is the Biological Concept of Race Useful for Studying Physical Variation in Humans?

No. Biologically defined, "race" refers to subspecies, and no subspecies exist within modern *Homo sapiens*. The vast majority of biological variation within our species occurs *within* populations rather than among them. Furthermore, the differences that do exist among populations occur in gradations from one neighboring population to another, without sharp breaks. For these and other reasons, anthropologists have actively worked to expose the fallacy of race as a biological concept while recognizing its significance as a social category.

Anthropologists gather information from a variety of sources to piece together an understanding of evolutionary history and humankind's place in the animal kingdom. Studies of living primates (our closest mammal relatives), ancient fossils, and even molecular biology contribute to the story of how humans evolved.

On one level, human evolutionary studies are wholly scientific, formulating and testing hypotheses about biological and behavioral processes in the past. At the same time, like all scientists, anthropologists are influenced by changing cultural values. *Paleoanthropologists,* who study human evolutionary history, and *primatologists,* who study living primates, as well as the physical or biological anthropologists who study contemporary biological diversity, must be critically aware of their personal beliefs and cultural assumptions as they construct their theories.

Evolution Through Adaptation

In a general sense, **evolution** (from the Latin word *evolutio,* literally "rolling forth" or unfolding) refers to change through time. Biologically, it refers to changes in the genetic makeup of a population over generations. Passed from parents to offspring, **genes** are the basic physical units of heredity that specify the biological traits and characteristics of each organism. While some evolution takes place through a process known as **adaptation**— a series of beneficial adjustments of organisms to their environment—random forces also contribute substantially to evolutionary change.

Adaptation is the cornerstone of the theory of evolution by **natural selection,** originally formulated by English naturalist Charles Darwin. Simply put, this theory holds that individuals having biological characteristics best suited to a particular environment survive and reproduce with greater frequency than do individuals without those characteristics.

In this chapter, we will discuss the evolutionary history of our species. Looking at the biology and behavior of our closest living relatives, the other primates, will complement the examination of our past. We will also explore some aspects of human biological variation and the cultural meanings given to this variation.

Distinct among humans is the biological capacity to produce a uniquely rich array of *cultural adaptations,* a complex of ideas, technologies, and activities that enable people to survive and even thrive in their environment. Early humans, like all other creatures, greatly depended on physical attributes for survival. But in the course of time, humans came to rely increasingly on culture as an effective way of adapting to the environment. They figured out how to manufacture and utilize tools; they organized into social units that made food foraging more successful; and they learned to preserve and share their traditions and knowledge through the use of symbols that ultimately included spoken language.

The ability to solve a vast array of challenges through culture has made our species unusual among creatures on this planet. Humans do not merely adapt to the environment through biological change; we shape the environment to suit human needs and desires. Today, computer technology enables us to organize and manipulate an ever-increasing amount of information to keep pace with the environmental changes we have wrought. Space technology may enable us to propagate our species in extraterrestrial environments. If we manage to avoid self-destruction through misuse of our sophisticated tools, biomedical technology may eventually enable us to control genetic inheritance and thus the future course of our biological evolution.

The fundamental elements of human culture came into existence about 2.5 mya. Using scientific know-how to reach far back in time, we can trace the roots of our species and reconstruct the origins of human culture. Before stepping back that far, it is useful to have a glimpse at the work of two 19th-century scholars whose pioneering research and theoretical contributions are important foundation stones in this line of inquiry: Charles Darwin (1809–1882) and Gregor Mendel (1822–1884).

evolution Changes in the genetic makeup of a population over generations.

genes The basic physical units of heredity that specify the biological traits and characteristics of each organism.

adaptation A series of beneficial adjustments of organisms to their environment.

natural selection The principle or mechanism by which individuals having biological characteristics best suited to a particular environment survive and reproduce with greater frequency than individuals without those characteristics.

A Brief History of Research on Evolution and Genetics

Charles Darwin came to the idea of natural selection through personal discoveries and observations experienced during a five-year (1831–1836) scientific journey around the world aboard the two-masted British sloop *H.M.S. Beagle.* His findings forced him to radically rethink long-established ideas about the natural order.

Aware that his new theory, which proposed the evolutionary idea of natural selection, would provoke controversy in conservative religious circles, Darwin waited over two decades to publish his research. As expected, his book, *On the Origin of Species by Means of Natural Selection, or the Preservation of Favoured Races in the Struggle for Life,* created a storm upon its release in 1859. Within its pages, Darwin presented this famous passage:

> It may be said that natural selection is daily and hourly scrutinising, throughout the world, every variation, even the slightest; rejecting that which is bad, preserving and adding up all that is good; silently and insensibly working, whenever and wherever opportunity offers, at the improvement of each organic being in relation to its organic and inorganic conditions of life. We see nothing of these slow changes in progress, until the hand of time has marked the long lapses of ages, and then so imperfect is our view into long past geological ages, that we only see that the forms of life are now different from what they formerly were.[1]

A few years after the publishing of Darwin's landmark book, a Roman Catholic monk named Gregor Mendel presented results from the biological experiments he carried out in the vegetable garden of his monastery in Brno, a city in today's Czech Republic. Raised on a small farm and having studied physics after entering the priesthood, Mendel had a keen and scientific interest in plant variations—so much so that over a seven-year period he cultivated and tested 29,000 pea plants at the monastery. Based on this research, he determined that the inheritance of each biological trait is determined by "units" or "factors" (later called genes) that are passed on to descendents unchanged. Moreover, he found that an individual inherits one such unit from each parent for each trait. And, finally, he demonstrated that a trait may not show up in an individual but can still be passed on to the next generation.

Mendel introduced his findings in an 1865 conference paper "Experiments in Plant Hybridisation." Published the following year, this article was the first to formulate the basic laws of biological inheritance. Although almost completely ignored for nearly four decades, Mendel's findings came to be recognized as a major theoretical contribution, and today, long after his death, the monk is honored as the father of genetics.

Mendel based his laws on statistical frequencies of observed characteristics—the color and surface texture in generations of peas. Later, with the benefit of increasingly precise research instruments (especially more powerful microscopes), his inferences about the mechanisms of inheritance were confirmed through the discovery of the cellular and molecular basis of inheritance.

When chromosomes, the cellular structures containing the genetic information, were discovered at the start of the 20th century, they provided a visible vehicle for transmission of traits proposed in Mendel's laws. In the 1930s and 1940s, combining Mendelian genetics and Darwin's theory of natural selection, a small international group of pioneering zoologists, botanists, and biochemists developed the new field of population genetics, formulating a comprehensive theoretical model.

Known as the *modern evolutionary synthesis,* this neo-Darwinist theory explains that evolution is gradual, based on environmental adaptation and small genetic changes within geographically separated populations after many generations of natural selection. A key building block in this theory is the discovery of DNA (deoxyribonucleic acid) within cells. Microscopic, DNA was first isolated in 1869, but scientists did not discover that these molecules carry genetic information until many decades later. Based on breakthroughs by molecular biologists since the early 1950s, we now understand that the main function of DNA is long-term storage of genetic information used in the development and functioning of all living organisms, including our own species.

Today, scientists understand that random genetic *mutation*—an abrupt change in a DNA gene, altering the genetic message carried by that cell—is the source of variation that gives organisms their reproductive edge.

Humans and Other Primates

Humans are one of 10 million species on earth, 4,000 of which are fellow mammals. **Species** are populations or groups of populations having common attributes and the ability to interbreed and produce live, fertile offspring. Different species are reproductively isolated from one another. Biologists organize or classify species into larger groups of biologically related organisms. The human species is one kind of **primate,** a subgroup of mammals that also includes lemurs, lorises, tarsiers, monkeys, and apes. Among fellow primates, humans are most closely related

---

[1] Darwin, C. (2007). *On the origin of species by means of natural selection, or the preservation of favoured races in the struggle for life* (p. 53). New York: Cosimo. (orig. 1859)

species A population or group of populations having common attributes and the ability to interbreed and produce live, fertile offspring. Different species are reproductively isolated from one another.

primate The subgroup of mammals that includes lemurs, lorises, tarsiers, monkeys, apes, and humans.

Chimpanzi 21 Months Old brought from Angola in 1738. 2 f. 4 In. high: the Dam was more than 5 foot from the Life.

© Hulton-Deutsch Collection/Corbis

Early scientific struggles to classify great apes, and to identify and weigh the significance of the similarities and differences between them and humans, are reflected in early European renderings of apes, including this 18th-century image of a chimpanzee portrayed as a biped equipped with a walking stick.

to apes—chimpanzees, bonobos, gorillas, orangutans, and gibbons—all of particular interest to primatologists.

European scientists have argued long and hard over issues of species classification, especially since the start of the age of exploration about 500 years ago that brought them to distant lands inhabited by life forms they had never seen. Most vexing was the question concerning the difference between apes and humans. In 1698, after dissecting a young male chimpanzee captured in West Africa and brought to Europe, an English physician concluded the creature was almost human and classified it as *Homo sylvestris* ("man of the forest").

A few decades later, Swedish naturalist Carolus Linnaeus (1707–1778) published the first edition of his famous *System of Nature* (1735). In it he classified humans with sloths and monkeys in the same order: Anthropomorpha ("human-shaped"). By the time Linnaeus published the tenth edition of his famous book in 1758, he had replaced the name

"Anthropomorpha" with "Primate" and included lemurs, monkeys, and humans in that category. Moreover, he now recognized not just one human species but two: *Homo sapiens* or *Homo diurnus* ("active during daylight") and an apelike human he called *Homo nocturnus* ("active during night"). He also referred to the latter as *Homo troglodytes* ("cave-dweller"). Linnaeus's shifting categories typify the struggle of early scientists to classify humans precisely within the natural system.

Perhaps the best illustration of the perplexity involved is a comment made by an 18th-century French bishop upon seeing an orangutan in a menagerie. Uncertain whether the creature before him was human or beast, he proclaimed: "Speak and I shall baptize thee!"[2]

In the course of the 18th century, European scientists continued to debate the proper classification of the great apes (as well as human "savages" encountered overseas) and placed chimpanzees and orangutans (gorillas were not recognized as a separate species until 1847) squarely between humans and the other animals. Perhaps going further than any other reputable scholar in Europe at the time, the famous Scottish judge Lord Mondobbo argued in several widely read scholarly publications in the 1770s and 1780s that orangutans should be considered part of the human species. He pointed out that they could walk erect and construct shelters and that they used sticks to defend themselves. He even suggested that at least in principle these "savages" were capable of speech.[3]

Still, most Europeans clung to the notion of a marked divide between humans on the one hand and animals on the other. Debates about the exact relationship between humans and other animals continue to this day. These debates include biological data on ancient fossils and genetics, as well as philosophical stances on the "humane" treatment of our closest ape relatives.

One could question the value of including nonhuman primates in this textbook when the distinctive cultural capacities of humans are our major concern. However, humans have a long evolutionary history as mammals and primates that set the stage for the cultural beings we are today. By studying our evolutionary history as well as the biology and behavior of our closest living relatives, we gain a better understanding of how and why humans developed as they did.

Evidence from ancient skeletons indicates the first mammals appeared over 200 mya as small nocturnal (night-active) creatures. The earliest primatelike creatures came into being about 65 mya when a new, mild climate favored the spread of dense tropical and subtropical forests over much of

[2] Corbey, R. (1995). Introduction: Missing links, or the ape's place in nature (p. 1). In R. Corbey & B. Theunissen (Eds.), *Ape, man, apeman: Changing views since 1600*. Leiden: Department of Prehistory, Leiden University.

[3] Barnard, A. (1995). Mondobbo's *Orang outang* and the definition of man (pp. 71–85). In R. Corbey & B. Theunissen (Eds.), *Ape, man, apeman: Changing views since 1600*. Leiden: Department of Prehistory, Leiden University.

the earth. The change in climate and habitat, combined with the sudden extinction of dinosaurs, favored mammal diversification, including the evolutionary development of arboreal (tree-living) mammals from which primates evolved.

The ancestral primates possessed biological characteristics that allowed them to adapt to life in the forests. Their relatively small size enabled them to use tree branches not accessible to larger competitors and predators. Arboreal life opened up an abundant new food supply. The primates were able to gather leaves, flowers, fruits, insects, bird eggs, and even nesting birds, rather than having to wait for them to fall to the ground. Natural selection favored those who judged depth correctly and gripped the branches tightly. Those individuals who survived life in the trees passed on their genes to the succeeding generations.

Although the earliest primates were nocturnal, today most primate species are diurnal (active in the day). The transition to diurnal life in the trees required important biological adjustments that helped shape the biology and behavior of humans today.

Anatomical Adaptation

Ancient and modern primate groups possess a number of anatomical characteristics described below. However, compared to other mammals, primates have only a few anatomical specializations while their behavior patterns are very diverse and flexible.

PRIMATE DENTITION

The varied diet available to arboreal primates—shoots, leaves, insects, and fruits—required relatively unspecialized teeth, compared to those found in other mammals. Comparative anatomy and the fossil record reveal that mammals ancestral to primates possessed three incisors, one canine, four premolars, and three molars on each side of the jaw, top and bottom, for a total of forty-four teeth. The incisors (in the front of the mouth) were used for gripping and cutting, canines (behind the incisors) for tearing and shredding, and molars and premolars (the "cheek teeth") for grinding and chewing food.

The evolutionary trend for primate dentition has been toward a reduction in the number and size of the teeth (Figure 4.1).

PRIMATE SENSORY ORGANS

The primates' adaptation to arboreal life involved changes in the form and function of their sensory organs. The sense of smell was vital for the earliest ground-dwelling, night-active mammals. It enabled them to operate in the dark, to sniff out their food, and to detect hidden predators. However, for active tree life during daylight, good vision is a better guide than smell in judging the location of the next branch or tasty morsel. Accordingly, the sense of smell declined in primates, while vision became highly developed.

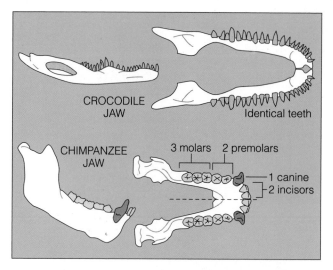

Figure 4.1 As seen in all reptiles, the crocodile jaw pictured above contains a series of identically shaped teeth. If a tooth breaks or falls out, a new tooth will emerge in its place. By contrast, primates, like all mammals, have only two sets of teeth: "baby" and adult teeth. Apes and humans possess precise numbers of specialized teeth, each with a particular shape, as indicated on this chimpanzee jaw: Incisors in front are shown in blue, canines behind in red, followed by two premolars and three molars in yellow (the last being the wisdom teeth in humans).

Traveling through trees demands judgments concerning depth, direction, distance, and the relationships of objects hanging in space, such as vines or branches. Monkeys and apes achieved this through binocular stereoscopic color vision (Figure 4.2), the ability to see the world in the three dimensions of height, width, and depth.

Tree-living primates also possess an acute sense of touch. An effective feeling and grasping mechanism helps keep them from falling and tumbling while speeding through the trees. The early mammals from which primates evolved possessed tiny touch-sensitive hairs at the tips of their hands and feet. In primates, sensitive pads backed up by nails on the tips of the animals' fingers and toes replaced these hairs. In some monkeys from Central and South America, this feeling and grasping ability extends to the tail.

THE PRIMATE BRAIN

An increase in brain size, particularly in the cerebral hemispheres—the areas supporting conscious thought—occurred in the course of primate evolution. In monkeys, apes, and humans the cerebral hemispheres completely cover the cerebellum, the part of the brain that coordinates the muscles and maintains body balance. One of the most significant outcomes of this is the flexibility seen in primate behavior. Rather than relying on reflexes controlled by the cerebellum, primates constantly react to a variety of features in the environment and, of course, to one another.

Figure 4.2 Anthropoid primates possess binocular stereoscopic vision. Binocular vision refers to overlapping visual fields due to forward-facing eyes. Three-dimensional or stereoscopic vision comes from binocular vision and the transmission of information from each eye to both sides of the brain.

Primary receiving area for visual information

THE PRIMATE SKELETON

The skeleton gives vertebrates—animals with internal backbones—their basic shape or silhouette, supports the soft tissues, and helps protect vital internal organs. Some evolutionary trends are evident in the primate skeleton. For example, as primates relied increasingly on vision rather than smell, the eyes rotated forward to become enclosed in a protective layer of bone. Simultaneously, the snout reduced in size. The opening at the base of the skull for the spinal cord to pass assumed a more forward position, reflecting some degree of upright posture rather than a constant four-footed stance.

The limbs of the primate skeleton follow the same basic ancestral plan seen in the earliest vertebrates. The upper portion of each arm or leg has a single long bone, the lower portion has two bones, and then hands or feet with five radiating digits. Other animals possess limbs specialized to optimize a particular behavior, such as speed. In nearly all of the primates, the big toe and thumb are *opposable,* making it possible to grasp and manipulate objects such as sticks and stones with their feet as well as their hands. Humans and their direct ancestors are the only exceptions, having lost the opposable big toe. The generalized limb pattern allows for flexible movements by primates.

In the apes, a sturdy collarbone (clavicle) orients the arms at the side rather than at the front of the body, allowing for heightened flexibility. With their broad flexible shoulder joints, apes can hang suspended from tree branches and swing from tree to tree.

The retention of the flexible vertebrate limb pattern in primates was a valuable asset to evolving humans. It was, in part, having hands capable of grasping that enabled our own ancestors to manufacture and use tools and thus alter the course of their evolution.

Behavioral Adaptation

Primates adapt to their environments not only anatomically but also through a wide variety of behaviors. Young apes spend more time reaching adulthood than do most other mammals. During their lengthy growth and development, they learn the behaviors of their social group. While biological factors play a role in the duration of primate dependency, many of the specific behaviors learned during childhood derive solely from the traditions of the group. The behavior of primates, particularly apes, provides anthropologists with clues about the earliest development of human cultural behavior.

Many studies of the behavior of apes in their natural habitat also provide models for paleoanthropologists interested in reconstructing the behavior of our earliest human ancestors. While no living primate lives exactly as evolving humans did, these studies have revealed remarkable variation and sophistication in ape behavior. Primatologists increasingly interpret these variations as cultural because they are learned rather than genetically programmed or instinctive. We shall look at the behavior of two closely related African species of chimpanzee: common chimpanzees and bonobos.

CHIMPANZEE AND BONOBO BEHAVIOR

Like nearly all primates, chimpanzees and bonobos are highly social animals. Among chimps, the largest social organizational unit is a group usually composed of fifty or more individuals who collectively inhabit a large geographic area. Rarely, however, are all of these animals together at one time. Instead, they are usually found ranging singly or in small subgroups consisting of adult males, or females with their young, or males and females together with young. In the course of their travels, subgroups may join forces and forage together, but sooner or later these will break up again into smaller units. Typically, when some individuals split off, others join, so the composition of subunits shifts frequently.

Relationships among individuals within the ape communities are relatively harmonious. In the past, primatologists believed that male dominance hierarchies, in

Jane Goodall (b. 1934) ▪ Kinji Imanishi (1902–1992)

In July 1960, **Jane Goodall** arrived with her mother at the Gombe Chimpanzee Reserve on the shores of Lake Tanganyika in Tanzania. Goodall was the first of three women Kenyan anthropologist Louis Leakey sent out to study great apes in the wild (the others were Dian Fossey and Biruté Galdikas, who were to study gorillas and orangutans, respectively); her task was to begin a long-term study of chimpanzees. Little did she realize that, more than forty years later, she would still be at it.

Born in London, Goodall grew up and was schooled in Bournemouth, England. As a child, she dreamed of going to live in Africa, so when an invitation arrived to visit a friend in Kenya, she jumped at the opportunity. While in Kenya, she met Leakey, who gave her a job as an assistant secretary. Before long, she was on her way to Gombe. Within a year, the outside world began to hear the most extraordinary things about this pioneering woman: tales of tool-making apes, cooperative hunts by chimpanzees, and what seemed like exotic chimpanzee rain dances. By the mid-1960s, her work had earned her a doctorate from Cambridge University, and Gombe was on its way to becoming one of the most dynamic field stations for the study of animal behavior anywhere in the world.

Although Goodall is still very much involved with her chimpanzees, she spends a good deal of time these days lecturing, writing, and overseeing the work of others. She is heavily committed to primate conservation. Goodall is also passionately dedicated to halting illegal trafficking in chimps as well as fighting for the humane treatment of captive chimpanzees.

Kinji Imanishi—a naturalist, explorer, and mountain climber—profoundly influenced primatology in Japan and throughout the world. Like all Japanese scholars, he was fully aware of Western methods and theories but developed a radically different approach to the scientific study of the natural world.

He dates his transformation to a youthful encounter with a grasshopper: "I was walking along a path in a valley, and there was a grasshopper on a leaf in a shrubbery. Until that moment I had happily caught insects, killed them with chloroform, impaled them on pins, and looked up their names, but I realized I knew nothing at all about how this grasshopper lived in the wild."[a] In his most important work, *The World of Living Things,* first published in 1941, Imanishi developed a comprehensive theory about the natural world rooted in Japanese cultural beliefs and practices.

Imanishi's work challenged Western evolutionary theory in several ways. First, Imanishi's theory, like Japanese culture, does not emphasize differences between humans and other animals. Second, rather than focusing on the biology of individual organisms, Imanishi suggested that naturalists examine "specia" (a species society) to which individuals belong as the unit of analysis. Rather than focusing on time, Imanishi emphasized space

in his approach to the natural world. He highlighted the harmony of all living things rather than conflict and competition among individual organisms.

Imanishi's research techniques, now standard worldwide, developed directly from his theories: long-term field study of primates in their natural societies using methods from ethnography.

With his students, Imanishi conducted pioneering field studies of African apes and Japanese and Tibetan macaques, long before Louis Leakey sent the first Western primatologists into the field. Japanese primatologists were the first to document the importance of kinship, the complexity of primate societies, patterns of social learning, and the unique character of each primate social group. Because of the work by Imanishi and his students, we now think about the distinct cultures of primate societies.

[a] Heita, K. (1999). Imanishi's world view. *Journal of Japanese Trade and Industry 18* (2), 15.

which some animals outrank and can dominate others, formed the basis of primate social structures. They noted that physical strength and size play a role in determining an animal's rank. By this measure males generally outrank females. However, with the benefit of detailed field studies over the last fifty years, including cutting-edge research by primatologists such as Jane Goodall (see Anthropologists of Note), the nuances of primate social behavior and the importance of female primates have been documented.

High-ranking female chimpanzees may dominate low-ranking males. And among bonobos, female rank determines the social order of the group far more than male rank. While greater strength and size do contribute to an animal's higher rank, several other factors also come into play in determining its social position. These include the rank of its mother, which is largely determined through her cooperative social behavior and how effective each individual animal is at creating alliances with others.

On the whole, bonobo females form stronger bonds with one another than do chimpanzee females. Moreover, the strength of the bond between mother and son interferes with bonds among males. Not only do bonobo males defer to females in feeding, but *alpha* (high-ranking) females have been observed chasing alpha males; such males may even yield to low-ranking females, particularly when groups of females form alliances.[4]

Widening his gaze beyond social ranking and attack behavior among great apes, Japanese primatologist Kinji Imanishi (see Anthropologists of Note) initiated field studies of bonobos, investigating and demonstrating the importance of social cooperation rather than competition. Likewise, Dutch primatologist Frans de Waal's research, highlighted in the following Original Study, shows that reconciliation after an attack may be even more important from an evolutionary perspective than the actual attack.

---

[4] de Waal, F., Kano, T., & Parish, A. R. (1998). Comments. *Current Anthropology 39*, 408, 410, 413.

Original Study

Reconciliation and Its Cultural Modification in Primates

by Frans B. M. de Waal

Despite the continuing popularity of the struggle-for-life metaphor, it is now recognized that there are drawbacks to open competition, hence that there are sound evolutionary reasons for curbing it. The dependency of social animals on group life and cooperation makes aggression a socially costly strategy. The basic dilemma facing many animals, including humans, is that they sometimes cannot win a fight without losing a friend.

This photo shows what may happen after a conflict—in this case between two female bonobos. About 10 minutes after their fight, the two females approach each other, with one clinging to the other and both rubbing their clitorises and genital swellings together in a pattern known as genito-genital rubbing, or GG-rubbing. This sexual contact, typical of bonobos, constitutes a so-called reconciliation. Chimpanzees, which are closely related to bonobos (and to us: bonobos and chimpanzees are our closest animal relatives), usually reconcile in a less sexual fashion, with an embrace and mouth-to-mouth kiss.

We now possess evidence for reconciliation in more than twenty-five different primate species, not just in apes but also in many monkeys—and in studies conducted on human children in the schoolyard. Researchers have even found reconciliation in dolphins, spotted hyenas, and some other nonprimates. Reconciliation seems widespread: a common mechanism found whenever relationships need to be maintained despite occasional conflict.[a,b]

The definition of reconciliation used in animal research is a friendly reunion between former opponents not long after a conflict. This is somewhat different from definitions in the dictionary, primarily because we look for an empirical definition that is useful in observational studies—in our case, the stipulation that the reunion happen not long after the conflict.

Let me describe two interesting elaborations on the mechanism of reconciliation. One is *mediation*. Chimpanzees are the only animals known to use mediators in conflict resolution. To be able to mediate conflict, one needs to understand relationships outside of oneself, which may be the reason why other animals fail to show this aspect of conflict resolution. For example, if two male chimpanzees have been involved in a fight, even on a very large island as where I did my studies, they can easily avoid each other, but instead they will sit opposite from each other, not too far apart, and avoid eye contact. They can sit like this for a long time. In this situation, a third party, such as an older female, may move in and try to solve the issue. The female will approach one of the males and groom him for a brief while. She then gets up and walks slowly to the other male, and the first male walks right behind her.

Two adult female bonobos engage in so-called GG-rubbing, a sexual form of reconciliation typical of the species.

© Amy Parish/Anthro-Photo

We have seen situations in which, if the first male failed to follow, the female turned around to grab his arm and make him follow. So the process of getting the two males in proximity seems intentional on the part of the female. She then begins grooming the other male, and the first male grooms her. Before long, the female disappears from the scene, and the males continue grooming: She has in effect brought the two parties together.

There exists a limited anthropological literature on the role of conflict resolution, a process absolutely crucial for the maintenance of the human social fabric in the same way that it is crucial for our primate relatives. In human societies, mediation is often done by high-ranking or senior members of the community, sometimes culminating in feasts in which the restoration of harmony is celebrated.[c]

The second elaboration on the reconciliation concept is that it is not purely instinctive, but a learned social skill subject to what primatologists now increasingly call "culture" (meaning that the animal behavior is subject to learning from others as opposed to genetic transmission).[d] To test the learnability of reconciliation, I conducted an experiment with young rhesus and stumptail monkeys. Not nearly as conciliatory as stumptail monkeys, rhesus monkeys have the reputation of being rather aggressive and despotic. Stumptails are considered more laid-back and tolerant. We housed members of the two species together for 5 months. By the end of this period, they were a fully integrated group: They slept, played, and groomed together.

After 5 months, we separated them again, and measured the effect of their time together on conciliatory behavior. The research controls—rhesus monkeys who had lived with one another, without any stumptails—showed absolutely no change in the tendency to reconcile. Stumptails showed a high rate of reconciliation, which was also expected, because they also do so if living together. The most interesting group was the experimental rhesus monkeys, those who had lived with stumptails. These monkeys started out at the same low level of reconciliation as the rhesus controls, but after they had lived with the stumptails, and after we had segregated them again so that they were now housed only with other rhesus monkeys who had gone through the same experience, these rhesus monkeys reconciled as much as stumptails do. This means that we created a "new and improved" rhesus monkey, one that made up with its opponents far more easily than a regular rhesus monkey.[e]

This was in effect an experiment on monkey culture: We changed the culture of a group of rhesus monkeys and made it more similar to that of stumptail monkeys by exposing them to the practices of this other species. This experiment also shows that there exists a great deal of flexibility in primate behavior. We humans come from a long lineage of primates with great social sophistication and a well-developed potential for behavioral modification and learning from others.

---

[a] de Waal, F. B. M. (2000). *Primates—A natural heritage of conflict resolution. Science 28,* 586–590.

[b] Aureli, F., & de Waal, F. B. M. (2000). *Natural conflict resolution.* Berkeley: University of California Press.

[c] Reviewed by Frye, D. P. (2000). Conflict management in cross-cultural perspective. In F. Aureli & F. B. M. de Waal, *Natural conflict resolution* (pp. 334–351). Berkeley: University of California Press.

[d] For a discussion of the animal culture concept, see de Waal, F. B. M. (2001). *The ape and the sushi master.* New York: Basic.

[e] de Waal, F. B. M., & Johanowicz, D. L. (1993). Modification of reconciliation behavior through social experience: An experiment with two macaque species. *Child Development 64,* 897–908.

Prior to the 1980s primates other than humans were thought to be vegetarians. However, groundbreaking research by Jane Goodall, among others, showed otherwise. This British researcher's fieldwork among chimpanzees in their forest habitat at Gombe, a wildlife reserve on the eastern shores of Lake Tanganyika in Tanzania, revealed that these apes supplement their primary diet of fruits and other plant foods with insects and also meat. Even more surprising, she found that in addition to killing small invertebrate animals for food, they also hunted and ate monkeys, usually flailing them to death.

Chimpanzee females sometimes hunt, but males do so far more frequently and may spend hours watching, following, and chasing intended prey. Moreover, in contrast to the usual primate practice of each animal finding its own food, hunting frequently involves teamwork, particularly when the prey is a baboon. Once a potential victim has been isolated from its troop, three or more adult chimps will carefully position themselves so as to block off escape routes while another pursues the prey. Following the kill, most who are present get a share of the meat, either by grabbing a piece as chance affords or by begging for it.

Whatever the nutritional value of meat, hunting is not done purely for dietary purposes but for social and sexual reasons as well. Anthropologist Craig Stanford, who has done fieldwork among the chimpanzees of Gombe in Tanzania since the early 1990s, found that these sizable apes (100-pound males are common) frequently kill animals weighing up to 25 pounds and eat much more meat than previously believed. Although somewhat different chimpanzee hunting practices have been observed elsewhere in Africa, hunts at Gombe usually take place during the dry season when plant foods are less readily available and female chimps display genital swelling, which signals that they are ready to mate. Notably, fertile females are more successful than others at begging for meat, and males often share the meat after copulation.[5] For chimps

---

[5] Stanford, C. B. (2001). *Chimpanzee and red colobus: The ecology of predator and prey.* Cambridge, MA: Harvard University Press.

ready for motherhood, a supply of protein-rich food helps support the increased nutritional requirements of pregnancy and lactation.

Beyond sharing meat to attract sexual partners, males use their catch to reward friends and allies, gaining status in the process. In other words, although Stanford links male hunting and food-sharing behavior with female reproductive biology, these behaviors are part of a complex social system that may be rooted more in the cultural traditions and history of Gombe than in chimpanzee biology.

Among bonobos, hunting is primarily a female activity. Also, female hunters regularly share carcasses with other females but less often with males. Even when the most dominant male throws a tantrum nearby, he may still be denied a share of meat.[6] Such discriminatory sharing among female bonobos is also evident when it comes to other foods such as fruits.

The sexual practices of chimpanzees and bonobos differ as much as their hunting strategies. For chimps, sexual activity—initiated by either the male or the female—occurs only during the periods when females signal their fertility through genital swelling. By most human standards, chimp sexual behavior is promiscuous. A dozen or so males have been observed to have as many as fifty copulations in one day with a single female. Dominant males try to monopolize sexually receptive females, although cooperation from the female is usually required for this to succeed. An individual female and a lower-ranking male sometimes form a temporary bond, leaving the group together for a few private days during the female's fertile period. Thus dominant males do not necessarily father all (or even most) of the offspring in a social group. Social success, achieving alpha male status, does not translate neatly into the evolutionary currency of reproductive success.

Among bonobos (as among humans) sexuality goes far beyond male–female mating for purposes of biological reproduction. Primatologists have observed virtually every possible combination of ages and sexes engaging in a remarkable array of sexual activities, including oral sex, tongue-kissing, and massaging each other's genitals. Male bonobos may mount each other, or one may rub his scrotum against that of the other. Among females, genital rubbing is particularly common. As described in this chapter's Original Study, the primary function of most of this sex, both hetero- and homosexual, is to reduce tensions and resolve social conflicts. Notably, although forced copulation among chimpanzees is known to occur, such rape has never been observed among bonobos.[7]

CHIMPANZEE AND BONOBO CHILDHOOD DEVELOPMENT

Chimpanzee and bonobo dependence on learned social behavior is related to their extended period of childhood development. Born without built-in responses dictating specific behavior in complex situations, the young chimp or bonobo, like the young human, learns by observation, imitation, and practice how to strategically interact with others and even manipulate them for his or her own benefit. Making mistakes along the way, young primates modify their behavior based on the reactions of other members of the group. They learn to match their interactive behaviors according to each individual's social position and temperament. Anatomical features such as a free upper lip (unlike lemurs or cats, for example) allow monkeys and apes varied facial expression, contributing to greater communication among individuals.

Young chimpanzees and bonobos also learn other functional behaviors from adults, such as how to make and use tools. Beyond deliberately modifying objects to make them suitable for particular purposes, chimps and bonobos can to some extent modify them to regular patterns and may even prepare objects at one location in anticipation of future use at another place. For example, chimps commonly select a long, slender branch, strip off its leaves, and carry it on a "fishing" expedition to a termite nest. Reaching their destination, they insert the stick into the nest, wait a few minutes, and then pull it out to eat the insects clinging to it.

There are numerous examples of chimpanzees using tools: They use leaves as wipes or sponges to get drinking water out of a hollow. Large sticks may serve as clubs or as missiles (as may stones) in aggressive or defensive displays. Recently a chimp group in Senegal has even been observed fashioning sticks into spears and using them to hunt.[8] Stones are used as hammers and anvils to crack open certain kinds of nuts. Twigs are used as toothpicks to clean teeth as well as to extract loose baby teeth.[9]

Bonobos in the wild have not been observed making and using tools to the extent that chimpanzees do. But tool-making capabilities have been shown by a captive bonobo who independently made stone tools remarkably similar to the earliest tools made by our own ancestors.

Primates have a great range of calls that are often used together with movements of the face or body to convey a message. Observers have not yet established the meaning of all the sounds, but a good number have been distinguished, such as warning calls, threat calls, defense calls, and gathering calls. Experiments with captive apes

[6] Ingmanson, E. J. (1998). Comment. *Current Anthropology 39,* 409.

[7] de Waal, F. (1998). Comment. *Current Anthropology 39,* 407.

[8] Hopkin, M. (2007, February 22). Chimps make spears to catch dinner. *Nature,* doi:10.1038/news070219-11.

[9] McGrew, W. C. (2000). Dental care in chimps. *Science 288,* 1747.

have revealed even greater communication abilities using American Sign Language and keyboards.

Primatologists are uncovering increasing evidence of the remarkable behavioral sophistication and intelligence of chimpanzees and other apes—including a capacity for conceptual thought previously unsuspected by most scientists. The widespread practice of caging our primate cousins and exploiting them for entertainment or medical experimentation has become increasingly controversial.

Human Ancestors

Figuring out biological links between ancient human fossils and related but long-extinct species within the animal kingdom is as controversial and challenging today as it was in the 18th century when Linnaeus was working on his *System of Nature.* Today, paleoanthropologists developing taxonomic schemes for humans and their ancestors reach beyond Linnaeus's focus on shared physical characteristics to consider genetic makeup. Humans are classified as **hominoids,** the broad-shouldered tailless group of primates that includes all living and extinct apes and humans. Humans and their ancestors are distinct among the hominoids for **bipedalism** ("two-footed")—walking upright on both hind legs.

Over the past few decades, genetic and biochemical studies have confirmed that the African apes—chimpanzees, bonobos, and gorillas—are our closest living relatives (Figure 4.3). By comparing genes and proteins among all the apes, scientists have estimated that gibbons, followed by orangutans, were the first to diverge from a very ancient common ancestral line. At some time between 5 and 8 mya, humans, chimpanzees, and gorillas began to follow separate evolutionary courses. Chimpanzees later diverged into two separate species: the common chimpanzee and the bonobo. Early human evolutionary development followed a path that produced, eventually, only one surviving bipedal species: *Homo sapiens.*

Larger brains and bipedal movement constitute the most striking differences between humans and our closest primate relatives. Although we might like to think that it is our larger brains that make us special among fellow primates, it is now clear that bipedalism appeared at the beginning of the ancestral line leading to humans and played a pivotal role in setting us apart from the apes. Brain expansion came later.

The First Bipeds

Between 5 and 15 mya, various kinds of hominoids lived throughout Africa, Asia, and Europe. One of these apes living in Africa between 5 and 8 mya was a direct ancestor

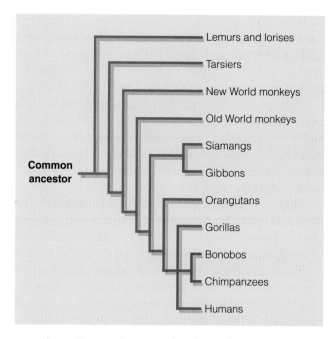

Figure 4.3 The relationship among monkeys, apes, and humans can be established by molecular similarities and differences. Molecular evidence indicates that the split between the human and African ape lines took place between 5 and 8 million years ago. Several important fossil finds dating from 5 to 7 million years ago have been discovered in the last few years.

to the human line. Each new fossil from this critical time period (such as the 6-million-year-old *Orrorin* fossils discovered in Kenya in 2001[10] or the 6- to 7-million-year-old skull discovered in Chad, Central Africa[11]) is proposed as the latest "missing link" in the evolutionary chain leading to humans.

For a hominoid fossil to be definitively classified as part of the human evolutionary line, evidence of bipedalism is required. However, all early bipeds are not necessarily direct ancestors to the humans. Nevertheless, new discoveries of ancient humanlike fossils, especially in East Africa, repeatedly stir the scientific and popular imagination that a "missing link" has been identified in "the great chain" between the earliest bipeds and the human species today.

---

[10] Senut, B., et al. (2001). First hominid from the Miocene (Lukeino formation, Kenya). *Comptes Rendus de l Academie de Sciences 332,* 137–144.

[11] Brunet, M., et al. (2002). A new hominid from the Upper Miocene of Chad, Central Africa. *Nature 418,* 145–151.

hominoid The broad-shouldered tailless group of primates that includes all living and extinct apes and humans.

bipedalism "Two-footed"—walking upright on both hind legs—a characteristic of humans and their ancestors.

Between 4 and 5 mya, the environment of eastern and southern Africa was mostly a mosaic of open country with pockets of woodland. Some early bipeds seem to have lived in such closed wooded areas. One forested pocket existed in what is now the Afar desert of northeastern Ethiopia, where a large number of fossil bone fragments of a very early biped were recently found. Dated to 4.4 mya, they were identified as belonging to a hominoid species called *Ardipithecus ramidus* (in the region's Afar language, *ardi* means "ground" or "floor"; *pithekos* is Greek for "ape"; *ramid* is Afar for "root").

This fossil find included the remains of about thirty-six individuals who hunted small animals and gathered plants and nuts in what was then a humid tropical woodland, especially dense with palm and fig trees. Already very different from chimps, with whom they shared a common ancestor about 2 million years earlier, these ancient hominoids could walk upright. As bipeds, they could carry food in their very long arms as they explored the woodland floor on two short legs. They were also quadrupeds—when climbing and moving about in the trees where they lived.

The most complete skeleton is that of a small-brained 1.22-meter (4-foot) tall adult female who weighed about 50 kilograms (120 pounds). Skeletal analysis revealed her bipedalism. First unearthed in 1994, she was named Ardi by the team that found her in the arid floodplain along the middle stretch of the Awash River. Although it is possible that Ardi and the other ardipithecines found in this area represent a species that did not further evolve, many scholars accept them as belonging to the human branch of the primate family tree and, as such, possibly direct ancestors in the evolutionary process that ultimately led to the development of our own species.[12]

Later human ancestors inhabited more open country known as savannah—grasslands with scattered trees and groves—and are assigned to one or another species of the genus ***Australopithecus*** (from Latin *australis,* meaning "southern," and Greek *pithekos,* meaning "ape"). Opinions vary on just how many species there were in Africa between about 1 and 4 mya. For our purposes and the sake of simplicity, it suffices to refer to them collectively as "australopithecines." The earliest definite australopithecine fossils date back 4.2 million years,[13] whereas the most recent ones

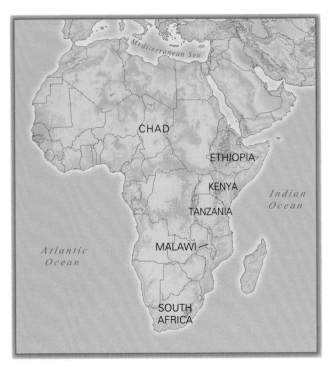

Figure 4.4 Australopithecine fossils have been found in South Africa, Malawi, Tanzania, Kenya, Ethiopia, and Chad. Among recent important finds is the 3.3-million-year-old skull and partial skeleton of a 3-year-old *Australopithecus afarensis* unearthed by Ethiopian paleoanthropologist Zeresenay Alemseged in his home country. Some experts refer to the young ape as "Lucy's baby" after the famous adult female australopithecine skeleton discovered in 1974 and known as Lucy even though the toddler's fossil is tens of thousands of years older. This fossil provides rare evidence of what young australopithecines were like. Also, unlike Lucy, the child's fossil includes fingers, a foot, a complete torso, and a face.

are only about 1 million years old. They have been found up and down the length of eastern Africa from Ethiopia to South Africa and westward into Chad (Figure 4.4).[14]

None of the australopithecines were as large as most modern humans. Whereas all were much more muscular for their size, males were quite a bit larger than females. Australopithecines possessed small brains comparable to those of modern African apes, but the size and structure of their teeth were more like those of contemporary humans (except for the robust australopithecines, who had massive teeth and jaws).

Although first evolving among ardipithecines inhabiting Africa's tropical woodlands, bipedalism is a particularly important adaptive feature in the more open savannah environment.[15] A biped could not run as fast as a quadruped

---

[12] White, T. D., et al. (2009, October). *Ardipithecus ramidus* and the paleobiology of early hominids. *Science 326* (5949), 64, 75–86.

[13] Alemseged, Z., et al. (2006, September 21). *Nature 443,* 296–301.

Australopithecus   The genus including several species of early bipeds from southern, eastern, and Central Africa (Chad) living between about 1.1 and 4.4 million years ago, one of whom was directly ancestral to humans.

---

[14] Wolpoff, M. (1996). *Australopithecus:* A new look at an old ancestor. *General Anthropology 3* (1), 2.

[15] Lewin, R. (1987). Four legs bad, two legs good. *Science 235,* 969.

but could travel long distances in search of food and water without tiring. With free hands, a biped could take food to places where it could be eaten in relative safety and could carry infants rather than relying on the babies hanging on for themselves. As bipeds, australopithecines could use their hands to wield sticks or other objects effectively in threat displays and to protect themselves against predators. Also, erect posture exposes a smaller area of the body to the direct heat of the sun than a quadrupedal position, helping to prevent overheating on the open savannah. Furthermore, a biped with its head held high could see farther, spotting food as well as predators from a distance (Figure 4.5).

Although adapted fully to bipedalism, curved toe bones and relatively long arms indicate australopithecines had not given up tree climbing altogether. However, to survive in their savannah environment, early bipeds may have been forced to try out supplementary sources of food on the ground, as they likely did around the time when the first members of the genus *Homo* appeared about 2.5 mya. In addition to whatever plant foods were available,

the major new source was animal protein. This was not protein from monkey meat obtained as a result of coordinated hunting parties like those of the chimpanzees and bonobos of today, but rather the fatty marrow and whatever other edible leftover flesh remained in and on the bones of dead animals.

Early *Homo*

Increased meat consumption by our early ancestors was important for human evolution. On the savannah, it is hard for a primate with a humanlike digestive system to satisfy its protein requirements from available plant resources. Moreover, failure to do so has serious consequences: stunted growth, malnutrition, starvation, and death. Leaves and legumes (nitrogen-fixing plants, familiar modern examples being beans and peas) provide the most readily accessible plant sources of protein. However, these are hard for primates like us to digest unless they are cooked.

Chimpanzees have a similar problem today when out on the savannah. In such a setting, they spend more than a third of their time going after insects like ants and termites on a year-round basis, while at the same time increasing their search for edible eggs and hunting for small vertebrate animals. Not only are such animal foods easily digestible, but they provide high-quality proteins that contain all the essential amino acids, the building blocks of protein, in just the right proportions.

Our remote ancestors probably solved their dietary problems in much the same way that chimps on the savannah do today (and in some ways, as discussed in this chapter's Biocultural Connection on the next page, their dietary habits and the physical effort it took to secure food made these early human ancestors healthier than many millions of present-day people). However, without the daggerlike teeth for ripping and cutting flesh, they were at a disadvantage. Even chimpanzees, whose canine teeth are far larger and sharper than ours, frequently have trouble tearing through the skin of other animals. It appears then that for more efficient utilization of animal protein, our ancestors needed sharp tools for butchering carcasses.

The earliest *identifiable* stone tools have been found in Africa (in Ethiopia, in northern Kenya near Lake Turkana, and in Tanzania at Olduvai Gorge), often in the same geological strata–distinctive layers of soil, clay, or rock—as the earliest *Homo* fossils. They include flakes and choppers. Flakes were obtained from a "core" stone by striking it with another stone or against a large rock. The flakes that broke off from the core had two sharp edges, effective for cutting meat and scraping hides. Leftover cores were transformed into choppers, used to break open bones.

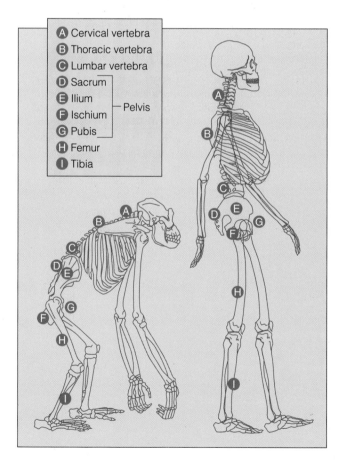

A Cervical vertebra
B Thoracic vertebra
C Lumbar vertebra
D Sacrum
E Ilium
F Ischium — Pelvis
G Pubis
H Femur
I Tibia

Figure 4.5 Changes in anatomy associated with bipedalism are evident in this comparison of chimp and human skeletons.

Paleolithic Prescriptions for the Diseases of Civilization

Though increased life expectancy is often hailed as one of modern civilization's greatest accomplishments, in some ways we in the developed world lead far less healthy lifestyles than our ancestors. Throughout most of our evolutionary history, humans led more physically active lives and ate a more varied low-fat diet than we do now. They did not drink or smoke. They spent their days scavenging or hunting for animal protein while gathering vegetable foods with some insects thrown in for good measure. They stayed fit through traveling great distances each day over the savannah and beyond.

Today we may survive longer, but in old age we are beset by chronic disease. Heart disease, diabetes, high blood pressure, and cancer shape the experience of old age in wealthy industrialized nations. The prevalence of these "diseases of civilization" has increased rapidly over the past sixty years, fueled by many modern factors including processed foods and physical inactivity. Anthropologists Melvin Konner and Marjorie Shostak and physician Boyd Eaton have suggested that our Paleolithic ancestors have provided a prescription for a cure. They propose that as "stone-agers in a fast lane," people's health will improve by returning to the lifestyle to which their bodies are adapted.[a] Such Paleolithic prescriptions are an example of evolutionary medicine—a branch of medical anthropology that uses evolutionary principles to contribute to human health.

Evolutionary medicine bases its prescriptions on the idea that rates of cultural change exceed the rates of biological change. Our food-forager physiology was shaped over millions of years, while the cultural changes leading to contemporary lifestyles have occurred rapidly.

Anthropologists George Armelagos and Mark Nathan Cohen suggest that the downward trajectory for human health began with the earliest human village settlements some 10,000 years ago.[b] When humans began farming rather than gathering, they often switched to single-crop diets. In addition, settlement into villages led directly to the increase in infectious disease. While the cultural invention of antibiotics has cured many infectious diseases, it also led to the increase in chronic diseases.

Our evolutionary history offers clues about the diet and lifestyle to which our bodies evolved. By returning to our ancient lifeways, we can make the diseases of civilization a thing of the past.

BIOCULTURAL QUESTION

What sort of Paleolithic prescriptions would our evolutionary history contribute toward behaviors such as childrearing practices, sleeping, and work patterns? Are there any ways that your culture or personal lifestyle are well aligned with past lifeways?

Gusto/Photo Researchers, Inc.

[a] Eaton, S. B., Konner, M., & Shostak, M. (1988). Stone-agers in the fast lane: Chronic degenerative diseases in evolutionary perspective. *American Journal of Medicine 84* (4), 739–749.

[b] Cohen, M. N., & Armelagos, G. J. (Eds.). (1984). *Paleopathology at the origins of agriculture.* Orlando: Academic.

The appearance of stone flakes and choppers marks the beginning of the **Lower Paleolithic,** the first part of the Old Stone Age, spanning from about 200,000 or 250,000 to 2.6 million years ago. At Olduvai and Lake Turkana, these tools are nearly 2 million years old; those found at the Ethiopian sites are older, at 2.5 to 2.6 million years. All of these early Lower Paleolithic tools are part of the **Oldowan tool tradition,** a name first given to the tools found at Olduvai Gorge in the 1960s.

Prior to the Lower Paleolithic, australopithecines probably used tools such as heavy sticks to dig up roots or ward off animals, unmodified stones to hurl as weapons or to crack open nuts and bones, and simple carrying devices made of hollow gourds or knotted plant fibers. These tools, however, are not traceable in the long-term archaeological record.

Since the late 1960s, a number of sites in southern and eastern Africa have been discovered with fossil remains of a lightly built biped with a body all but indistinguishable from that of the earlier australopithecines, except that the teeth are smaller and the brain is significantly larger relative to body size.[16] Furthermore, the inside of the skull

Lower Paleolithic The first part of the Old Stone Age spanning from about 200,000 or 250,000 to 2.6 million years ago.

Oldowan tool tradition The first stone tool industry, beginning between 2.5 and 2.6 million years ago at the start of the Lower Paleolithic.

[16] Conroy, G. C. (1997). *Reconstructing human origins: A modern synthesis* (pp. 264–265, 269–270). New York: Norton.

 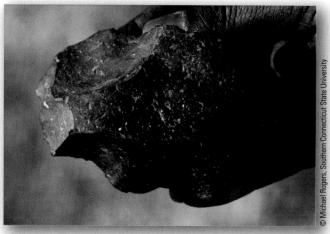

The earliest stone tools dated to the beginning of the lower Paleolithic or Old Stone Age between 2.5 and 2.6 million years ago were discovered by Ethiopian paleoanthropologist Sileshi Semaw (pictured here) at Gona, located in the west-central Afar region of Ethiopia. The 2.6-million-year-old Gona core on the right is a well-struck cutting/chopping tool with sharp edges.

shows a pattern in the left cerebral hemisphere that, in contemporary people, is associated with language. While this does not prove that these bipeds could speak, it suggests a marked advance in information-processing capacity over that of australopithecines.

Since major brain-size increase and tooth-size reduction are important trends in the evolution of the genus *Homo,* paleoanthropologists designated these fossils as a new species: ***Homo habilis*** ("handy man").[17] Significantly, the earliest fossils to exhibit these trends appeared around 2.5 to 2.6 mya, about the same time as the earliest evidence of stone tool making.

Tools, Food, and Brain Expansion

Evolutionary transformations often occur suddenly as large random mutations produce novel organisms that, by chance, are well adapted to a particular environment. Sometimes natural selection produces change more gradually. This appears to have taken place following the arrival of *Homo habilis,* the first species in the genus *Homo;* with the demonstrated use of tools, our human ancestors began a course of gradual brain expansion that continued until some 200,000 years ago. By then, brain size had approximately tripled and reached the levels of today's humans.

Many scenarios proposed for the adaptation of early *Homo*—such as the relationship among tools, food, and brain expansion—rely upon a feedback loop between brain size and behavior. The behaviors made possible by

larger brains confer advantages to large-brained individuals, contributing to their increased reproductive success. Over time, their genetic variance becomes more common in successive generations, and the population gradually evolves into a larger-brained form.

In the case of tool making, the archaeological record provides us with tangible data concerning our ancestors' cultural abilities fitting with the simultaneous biological expansion of the brain. Tool making itself puts a premium on manual dexterity as opposed to hand use emphasizing power. In addition, the patterns of stone tools and fossilized animal bones at Oldowan sites in Africa suggest improved organization of the nervous system.

The sources for stone used to make cutting and chopping tools were often far from the sites where tools were used to process parts of animal carcasses. Also, the high density of fossil bones at some Oldowan sites and patterns of seasonal weathering indicate such sites were used repeatedly over a period of years. It appears that the Oldowan sites were places where tools and the raw materials for making them were stockpiled for later use in butchering. This implies advanced preparation for meat processing and thereby attests to the growing importance of foresight and the ability to plan ahead. Beginning with *Homo habilis* in Africa about 2.5 to 2.6 mya, human evolution began a sure course of increasing brain size relative to body size and increasing cultural development, each acting upon and thereby promoting the other.

---

[17] Some have argued that *Homo habilis* was not the only species of early *Homo.*

Homo habilis "Handy man." The first fossil members of the genus *Homo* appearing 2.5 to 2.6 million years ago, with larger brains and smaller faces than australopithecines.

Homo erectus and Spread of the Genus *Homo*

Shortly after 2 mya, at a time when *Homo habilis* and Oldowan tools had become widespread in Africa, a new species, **Homo erectus** ("upright man"), appeared on that continent. Unlike *H. habilis,* however, *H. erectus* did not remain confined to Africa. In fact, evidence of *H. erectus* fossils almost as old as those discovered in Africa have been found in the Caucasus Mountains of Georgia (between Turkey and Russia), South Asia, China, the island of Java (Indonesia), and western Europe.

Because the fossil evidence also suggests some differences within and among populations of *H. erectus* inhabiting discrete regions of Africa, Asia, and Europe, some paleoanthropologists prefer to split *H. erectus* into several distinct groups. Nonetheless, regardless of species designation, it is clear that beginning 1.8 mya, these larger-brained members of the genus *Homo* lived not only in Africa but also had spread to Eurasia (Figure 4.6).

The emergence of *H. erectus* as a new species in the long course of human evolution coincided with the beginning of the Pleistocene epoch or Ice Age, which spanned from about 2 million to 10,000 years ago. During this period of global cooling, Arctic cold conditions and abundant snowfall in the earth's northern hemisphere created vast ice sheets that temporarily covered much of Eurasia and North America. These fluctuating but major glacial periods often lasted tens of thousands of years, separated by intervening warm periods. During interglacial periods the world warmed up to the point that the ice sheets melted and sea levels rose, but during much of this time sea levels were much lower than today, exposing large surfaces of low-lying lands now under water.[18]

Of all the epochs in the earth's 4.6-*billion*-year history, the Pleistocene is particularly significant for our species, for this era of dramatic climate shifts is the period in which humans—from *H. erectus* to *H. sapiens*—evolved and spread all across the globe. Confronted by environmental changes due to climatic fluctuations or movements into different geographic areas, our early human ancestors were constantly challenged to make biological and, especially, cultural adaptations in order to survive and successfully reproduce.

In the course of this long evolutionary process, random mutations introduced new characteristics into evolving populations in different regions of the world. The principle

Homo erectus "Upright man." A species within the genus *Homo* first appearing just after 2 million years ago in Africa and ultimately spreading throughout the Old World.

[18] Fagan, B. M. (2000). *Ancient lives: An introduction to archaeology* (pp. 125–133). Englewood Cliffs, NJ: Prentice-Hall.

Figure 4.6
Paleoanthropological sites, with dates, at which *Homo erectus* remains have been found. The arrows indicate the proposed routes by which *Homo* spread from Africa to Eurasia.

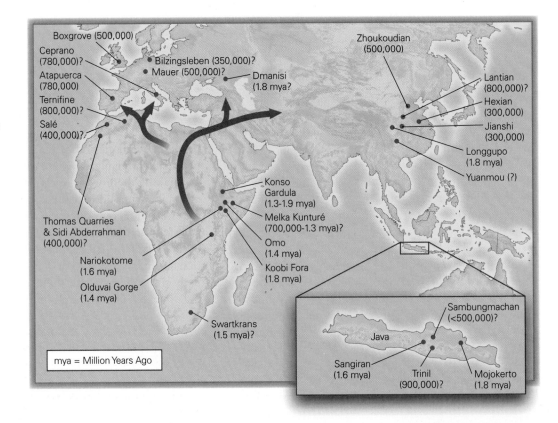

Boxgrove (500,000)?
Ceprano (780,000)?
Atapuerca (780,000)?
Ternifine (800,000)?
Salé (400,000)?
Bilzingsleben (350,000)?
Mauer (500,000)?
Dmanisi (1.8 mya?)
Zhoukoudian (500,000)
Lantian (800,000)?
Hexian (300,000)
Jianshi (300,000)
Longgupo (1.8 mya)
Yuanmou (?)
Thomas Quarries & Sidi Abderrahman (400,000)?
Konso Gardula (1.3-1.9 mya)
Melka Kunturé (700,000-1.3 mya)?
Omo (1.4 mya)
Koobi Fora (1.8 mya)
Nariokotome (1.6 mya)
Olduvai Gorge (1.4 mya)
Swartkrans (1.5 mya)?
Java
Sambungmachan (<500,000)?
Sangiran (1.6 mya)
Trinil (900,000)?
Mojokerto (1.8 mya)

mya = Million Years Ago

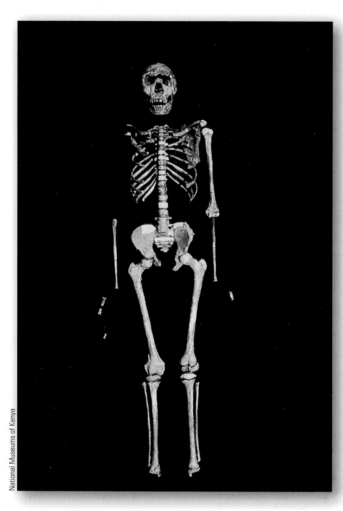

One of the oldest—at 1.6 million years—and most complete fossils of *Homo erectus* is the "strapping youth" from Lake Turkana, Kenya: a tall and muscular boy who was already 5 feet 3 inches tall when he died at about the age of 13.

of natural selection was at work on humans as it was on all forms of life, favoring the perpetuation of certain characteristics within particular environmental conditions. At the same time, other characteristics that conferred no particular advantage or disadvantage also appeared by random mutation in geographically removed populations. The end result was a gradually growing physical variation in the human species. In this context, it is not surprising that *H. erectus* fossils found in Africa, Asia, and Europe reveal levels of physical variation not unlike those seen in modern human populations living across the globe today.

Available fossil evidence indicates that *H. erectus* had a body size and proportions similar to modern humans, though with heavier musculature. Differences in body size between the sexes diminished considerably compared to earlier bipeds, perhaps to facilitate successful childbirth. Based on fossil skull evidence, *H. erectus'* average brain size fell within the higher range of *H. habilis* and within the lower range of modern human brain size.

The dentition was fully human, though relatively large by modern standards.

As one might expect, given its larger brain, *H. erectus* outstripped its predecessors in cultural development. In Africa and Eurasia, the Oldowan chopper was replaced by the more sophisticated hand axe. At first, the hand axes—shaped by regular blows giving them a larger and finer cutting edge than chopper tools—were probably all-purpose implements for food procurement and processing, and defense. But *H. erectus* also developed cleavers (like hand axes but without points) and various scrapers to process animal hides for bedding and clothing. In addition, this human ancestor relied on flake tools used "as is" to cut meat and process vegetables, or refined by "retouching" into points and borers for drilling or punching holes in materials.

Improved technological efficiency is also evident in *H. erectus'* use of raw materials. Instead of making a few large tools out of big pieces of stone, these ancestors placed a new emphasis on smaller tools, thus economizing their raw materials.

Fire Making in Early Human Development

Remains found in southern Africa suggest that *H. erectus* may have learned to use fire by 1 mya. Although there exists considerable variation in physiological conditioning among different human groups and even among individuals within each group, studies of modern humans indicate that most people can remain reasonably comfortable down to 10 degrees Celsius (50 degrees Fahrenheit) with minimal clothing as long as they keep active. Without controlled use of fire, it is unlikely that early humans could have moved successfully into regions where winter temperatures regularly dropped much below that point—as they must have in northern China and most of Europe, where *H. erectus* spread some 800,000 years ago.

Fire gave our human ancestors more control over their environment. It permitted them to continue activities after dark and provided a means to frighten away predators. It supplied them with the warmth and light needed for cave dwelling, and it enabled them to cook food.

The ability to modify food culturally through cooking may have contributed to the eventual reduction in the tooth size and jaws of later fossil groups since cooked food requires less chewing. However, cooking does more than tenderize food. It detoxifies a number of otherwise poisonous plants. In addition, it alters substances in plants, allowing important vitamins, minerals, and proteins to be absorbed by the gut rather than passing unused through the intestines. And, finally, it makes high-energy complex carbohydrates, such as starch, digestible. In short, when our human ancestors learned to employ fire to warm and protect themselves and to cook their food, they dramatically increased their geographic range and nutritional options.

With *H. erectus* we also have evidence of organized hunting as the means for procuring meat, animal hides, horn, bone, and sinew. Early evidence demonstrating the hunting technology of these ancestors includes 400,000-year-old wooden spears discovered in a peat bog (what was originally marsh or swamp land) in northern Germany, although it is likely that evolving humans had begun to hunt before then. Increased organizational ability is also indicated in prehistoric sites such as Ambrona and Torralba in Spain where group hunting techniques were used to drive a variety of large animals (including elephants) into a swamp for killing.[19]

With *H. erectus,* then, we find a clearer manifestation than ever before of the complex interplay among biological, cultural, and ecological factors. Social organization and technology developed along with an increase in brain size and complexity and a reduction in tooth and jaw size. The appearance of cultural adaptations such as controlled use of fire, cooking, and more complex tool kits may have facilitated language development. (See Chapter 5 for more on language origins and the linguistic capacity of our ape cousins.)

Improvements in communication and social organization brought about by language undoubtedly contributed to better methods for food gathering and hunting, to a population increase, and to territorial expansion. Continuous biological and cultural change through natural selection in the course of hundreds of thousands of years gradually transformed *H. erectus* into the next emerging species: *Homo sapiens.*

Beginnings of *Homo sapiens*

At various Paleolithic sites in Africa, Asia, and Europe, a large number of human fossils have been found that date between roughly 200,000 and 1 million years ago. Among the most notable are those discovered in the mountains of Atapuerca in northern Spain, where paleontologist Juan Luis Arsuaga and his team have excavated various caves over the past few decades. In a huge cave called Gran Dolina, they found fossil remains dating to 800,000 years ago. Arguing that these fossils represent the last common ancestor of modern humans and Neandertals (discussed below), Arsuaga ascribed them to a new species: *Homo antecessor* ("antecessor" is Latin for "forerunner").

Whether one chooses to call these or any other humanlike fossils from that period *H. erectus, H. heidelbergensis,* or *H. antecessor* is more than a name game. Fossil names indicate researchers' perspectives about evolutionary relationships among groups. When specimens are given separate species names, it signifies that they form part of a reproductively isolated group.

The most famous site in the Atapuerca Mountains is Sima de los Huesos ("Pit of Bones") at the bottom of a deep chimney in one of the large cave systems. There, researchers discovered more than 5,000 human bones, including the fossil remains of thirty individuals of both sexes and all ages, up to about 40 years. Dated to about 400,000 years ago, these are thought to be early ancestors of the Neandertals, which evolved in Europe in conditions of geographic and genetic isolation in the late Pleistocene.[20]

The Neandertal Debate

As we proceed along the human evolutionary trajectory, the fossil record provides us with many more human specimens compared to earlier periods. The record is particularly rich when it comes to the Neandertals, a distinct and certainly controversial ancient member of the genus *Homo.* Typically, they are represented as the classic cavemen, stereotyped in Western popular media and even in natural history museum displays as wild and hairy club-wielding brutes.

Based on abundant fossil evidence, we know that **Neandertals** were a distinct and extremely muscular group within the genus *Homo* inhabiting Europe and Southwest Asia from about 30,000 to 125,000 years ago. Although they had brains on average somewhat larger than modern humans, their faces and skulls were quite different from those of later fossilized remains referred to as "anatomically modern humans." Their large noses and teeth projected forward more than is the case with modern people. They generally had a sloping forehead and prominent brow ridges over their eyes, and on the back of the skull, a bony mass provided for attachment of powerful neck muscles. These features, while not exactly in line with modern ideals of European beauty, are common in Norwegian and Danish skulls dating to about 1,000 years ago—the time of the Vikings.[21] Nevertheless, these characteristics do little

---

[19] Freeman, L. G. (1992). *Ambrona and Torralba: New evidence and interpretation.* Paper presented at the 91st Annual Meeting, American Anthropological Association.

Neandertals A distinct group within the genus *Homo* inhabiting Europe and Southwest Asia from approximately 30,000 to 125,000 years ago.

[20] Arsuaga, J. L., et al. (2000). The Atapuerca human fossils. *Human Evolution 15,* 1–2.

[21] Ferrie, H. (1997). An interview with C. Loring Brace. *Current Anthropology 38,* 861.

In a cave beneath the hillside in Atapuerca, Spain, lies one of the most remarkable sites in all of paleoanthropology: the Sima de los Huesos ("Pit of Bones"). The bottom of the pit is crammed with animal bones, including cave bears, lions, foxes, and wolves. Even more remarkable, thousands of early human fossils dating back 400,000 years have been found here. The well-preserved remains come from about thirty individuals and comprise the greatest single cache of ancient *Homo* fossils in the world.

to negate the popular image of Neandertals as cave-dwelling brutes.

The rude reputation of Neandertals may also derive from the time of their discovery, as the first widely publicized Neandertal skull was found in 1856, well before scientific theories to account for human origins had gained acceptance. This odd-looking old skull, happened upon near Düsseldorf in Germany's Neander Valley ("valley" is *Tal* in German), took German scientists by surprise. Initially, they explained its extraordinary features as evidence of some disfiguring disease in an invading "barbarian" from the east who had crawled into a deep cave to die. Although it became evident that the skull belonged to an ancient human fossil, Neandertals are still a perplexing group surrounded by controversy.

We now understand that many aspects of the Neandertal's unique skull shape and body form represent its biological adaptation to an extremely cold climate. We also know that its intellectual capacity for cultural adaptation was noticeably superior to that of earlier members of the genus *Homo*.

One of the most hotly debated arguments in paleoanthropology has been the genetic relationship of Neandertals to anatomically modern humans. Were they a separate species that became extinct less than 30,000 years ago? Or were they an archaic subspecies of *Homo sapiens?* And if they were not a dead end and inferior side branch in human evolution, did they actually contribute to our modern human gene pool? In that case, so the argument goes, their direct descendants walk the earth today.[22]

Meanwhile, other parts of the world were inhabited by variants of archaic *H. sapiens,* lacking the mid-facial

---

[22] See Orlando, L., et al. (2006, June 6). Correspondence: Revisiting Neandertal diversity with a 100,000 year old mtDNA sequence. *Current Biology* *16*, 400–402; Hawks, J. (2006, July 21). Neandertal Genome Project. http://johnhawks.net/weblog.

As this face-off between paleoanthropologist Milford Wolpoff and his reconstruction of a Neandertal shows, the latter did not differ all that much from modern humans of European descent.

© Paul Jaronski/UM Photo Service

projection and massive muscle attachments on the back of the skull common among the Neandertals. Human fossil skulls found near the Solo River in Java are a prime example. Dates for these specimens range between about 27,000 and 200,000 years ago. The fossils, with their modern-sized brains, display certain features of *H. erectus* combined with those of archaic as well as more modern *H. sapiens.* Human fossils from various parts of Africa, the most famous being a skull from Kabwe in Zambia, also show a combination of ancient and modern traits. Finally, similar remains have been found at several places in China.

Adaptations to a wide range of different natural environments by archaic *Homo sapiens* were, of course, both biological and cultural, but their capacity for cultural adaptation was predictably superior to what it had been in earlier members of the genus *Homo.* Neandertals' extensive use of fire, for example, was essential to survival in a cold climate like that of Europe during the various glacial periods. They lived in small bands or single-family units, both in the open and in caves, probably communicating through language (see Chapter 5). Evidence of deliberate burials of the deceased among Neandertals reflects a measure of ritual behavior in their communities. Moreover, the fossil remains of an amputee discovered in Iraq and an arthritic man excavated in France imply that Neandertals

took care of the disabled, something not seen previously in the human fossil record.

The tool-making tradition of all but the latest Neandertals is called the **Mousterian tool tradition** after a site (Le Moustier) in the Dordogne region of southern France. We see this tradition among Neandertals in Europe and Southwest Asia and among their human contemporaries in northern Africa during the Middle Paleolithic, generally dating from about 40,000 to 125,000 years ago.

Although considerable variability exists, Mousterian tools are generally lighter and smaller than those of earlier traditions. Whereas previously only two or three flakes could be obtained from the entire stone core, Mousterian toolmakers obtained many smaller flakes, which they skillfully retouched and sharpened. Their tool kits also contained a greater variety of types than the earlier ones: hand axes, flakes, scrapers, borers, notched flakes for shaving wood, and many types of points that could be attached to wooden shafts to make spears. This variety of tools facilitated more effective use of food resources and enhanced the quality of clothing and shelter. These types of stone tools were used by *all* people, Neandertals and their contemporaries elsewhere, including North Africa and Southwest Asia, during this time period.

For archaic *H. sapiens,* improved cultural adaptive abilities relate to the fact that the brain had achieved modern size. Such a brain made possible not only sophisticated technology but also conceptual thought of considerable intellectual complexity. Decorative pendants and objects with carved and engraved markings also appear in the archaeological record from this period. Objects were also commonly colored with pigments such as manganese

Mousterian tool tradition   The tool industry found among Neandertals in Europe and Southwest Asia, and their human contemporaries in northern Africa, during the Middle Paleolithic, generally dating from about 40,000 to 125,000 years ago.

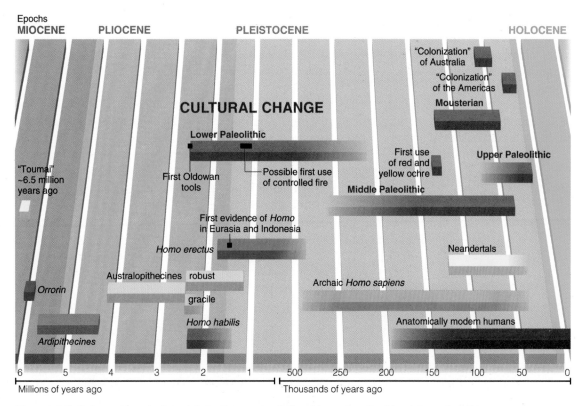

Epochs
MIOCENE   **PLIOCENE**   **PLEISTOCENE**   **HOLOCENE**

CULTURAL CHANGE

"Colonization"
of Australia

"Colonization"
of the Americas

Mousterian

Lower Paleolithic

First use
of red and
yellow ochre   **Upper Paleolithic**

First Oldowan
tools   Possible first use
of controlled fire

Middle Paleolithic

"Toumaï"
~6.5 million
years ago

First evidence of *Homo*
in Eurasia and Indonesia

Homo erectus

Australopithecines   robust   **Neandertals**

Orrorin   gracile   Archaic *Homo sapiens*

Homo habilis   Anatomically modern humans

Ardipithecines

6   5   4   3   2   1   500   250   200   150   100   50   0

Millions of years ago   Thousands of years ago

Figure 4.7 Paleoanthropologists debate the exact relationship among the bipedal species along with the number of species that existed over the past 5 to 8 million years. The time spans for the Lower, Middle, and Upper Paleolithic vary tremendously by region. Note also that the time scale is expanded for the most recent 250,000 years.

dioxide and red or yellow ochre. The ceremonial burial of the dead and creation of nonutilitarian, decorative objects provide additional evidence supporting theoretical arguments in favor of symbolic thinking and language use in these ancient populations.

Establishing the relationship between anatomical change and cultural change over the course of human evolutionary history is complex (Figure 4.7). In the course of the Middle Paleolithic (beginning around 200,000 years ago), individuals with a somewhat more anatomically modern human appearance began to appear in Africa and Southwest Asia. While the earliest of these fossils are associated with the Mousterian tool industries used by Neandertals, over time new tool industries and other forms of cultural expression appeared. Whether these changes in skull shape are linked with superior cultural abilities is at the heart of the modern human origins debate. In Europe, the transition to the tools of the Upper Paleolithic occurred between 35,000 and 40,000 years ago. By this time, Neandertal technology was also comparable to the industries used by these anatomically modern *H. sapiens*.[23]

Anatomically Modern Peoples and the Upper Paleolithic

A veritable explosion of tool types and other forms of cultural expression beginning about 40,000 years ago constitutes what is known as the **Upper Paleolithic** transition. Upper Paleolithic tool kits include increased prominence of "blade" tools: long, thin, precisely shaped pieces of stone demonstrating the considerable skill of their creators. The Upper Paleolithic, lasting until about 10,000 years ago, is best known from archaeological evidence found in Europe where numerous distinctive tool industries from successive time periods have been documented. In addition, the European archaeological record is rich with cave wall paintings, engravings, and bas-relief sculptures as well as many portable nonutilitarian artifacts from this period.

In Upper Paleolithic times, humans began to manufacture tools for more effective hunting and fishing, as well as gathering. Cultural adaptation also became more

[23] Mellars, P. (1989). Major issues in the emergence of modern humans. *Current Anthropology 30*, 356–357.

Upper Paleolithic The last part (10,000–40,000 years ago) of the Old Stone Age, featuring tool industries characterized by long slim blades and an explosion of creative symbolic forms.

highly specific and regional, thus enhancing people's ability to survive under a wide variety of environmental conditions. Instead of manufacturing all-purpose tools, Upper Paleolithic populations inhabiting a wide range of environments—mountains, marshlands, tundra, forests, lake regions, river valleys, and seashores—all developed specialized devices suited to the resources of their particular habitat and to the different seasons. This versatility

also permitted humans to spread out by crossing open water and Arctic regions to places never previously inhabited by humans, most notably Australia (between 40,000 and 60,000 years ago) and the Americas (about 15,000 to 20,000 years ago).

This degree of specialization required improved manufacturing techniques. The blade method of manufacture (Figure 4.8), invented by archaic *H. sapiens* and later used widely in Europe and western Asia, required less raw material than before and resulted in smaller and lighter tools with a better ratio between weight of flint and length of cutting edge (Figure 4.9).

Invented by Mousterian toolmakers, the *burin* (a stone tool with chisel-like edges) came into common use in the Upper Paleolithic. The burin provided an excellent means of working bone and antler used for tools

Figure 4.8 During the Upper Paleolithic, this new, more refined technique of manufacturing stone tools became common. The stone was broken to create a striking platform. Then, with another hard object, long, almost parallel-sided flakes were struck from the sides, resulting in sharp-edged blades to be used for a variety of cutting purposes.

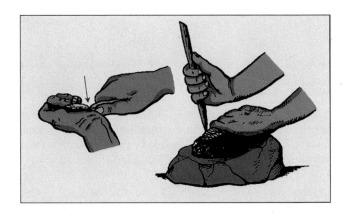

Figure 4.9 Pressure flaking—in which a bone, antler, or wooden tool is used to press rather than strike off small flakes—is another technique of tool manufacture that became widespread during the Upper Paleolithic. Here we see two pressure flaking methods.

The techniques of the Upper Paleolithic allowed for the manufacture of a variety of tool types. The finely wrought Solutrean bifaces of Europe, made using a pressure flaking method as illustrated in Figure 4.9, are shaped like plant leaves.

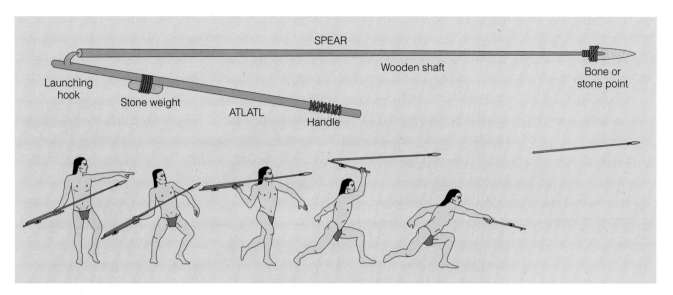

Figure 4.10 Invented by early humans in the late Ice Age about 15,000 years ago, the atlatl or spear-thrower continued to be used by hunting peoples in many parts of the world until quite recently. Devised many thousands of years before the bow and arrow, this remarkable tool enhanced a hunter's success, making it possible to throw light spears much farther and with great force and accuracy. The entire atlatl would have been a foot or two long, with a handle on one end and a hook on the other that fitted into the blunt end of the spear. The hook was sometimes made of beautifully carved antler, bone, or stone.

such as fishhooks and harpoons. The spear-thrower, or *atlatl* (a Nahuatl word used by Aztec Indians in Mexico, referring to a wooden device, 1 to 2 feet long, with a hook on the end for throwing a spear), also appeared at this time. By effectively elongating the arm, the atlatl gave hunters increased force behind the spear throw (Figure 4.10).

Art was an important aspect of Upper Paleolithic cultures. As far as we know, humans had not produced representational artwork before. In some regions, tools and weapons were engraved with beautiful animal figures; pendants were made of bone and ivory, as were female figurines; and small sculptures were carved out of stone or modeled out of clay. Spectacular paintings and engravings depicting humans and animals of this period have been found on the walls of caves and rock shelters in Spain, France, Australia, and Africa. Because the southern African rock art tradition spans 27,000 years and lasted into historic times, documented accounts tell us that much of it depicts visions artists have when in altered states of consciousness related to spiritual practices. Along with the animals, the art also includes a variety of geometric motifs based on mental images spontaneously generated by the human nervous system when in trance.

Australian cave art, some of it older than European cave art and also associated with trancing, includes similar motifs. The occurrence of the same geometric designs in the cave art of Europe suggests trancing was a part of these prehistoric foraging cultures as well. The geometric motifs in Paleolithic art have also been interpreted as stylized human figures and patterns of descent. Given the great importance of kinship in all historically known communities of hunters, fishers, and gatherers, this should not be surprising. Whether or not a new kind of human—anatomically modern with correspondingly superior intellectual abilities—is responsible for this cultural explosion is hotly debated within paleoanthropology.

Hypotheses on the Origins of Modern Humans

On a biological level the great debate can be distilled to a question of whether one, some, or all populations of the archaic groups played a role in the evolution of modern *H. sapiens*. Those supporting the **multiregional hypothesis** argue that the fossil evidence suggests a simultaneous local transition from *H. erectus* to modern *H. sapiens* throughout the parts of the world inhabited by early members of the genus *Homo*. By contrast, those

multiregional hypothesis The hypothesis that modern humans originated through a process of simultaneous local transition from *Homo erectus* to *Homo sapiens* throughout the inhabited world.

These 31,000-year-old images, painted on a wall in the multichambered Chauvet Cave in the Ardèche region of southern France, provide spectacular evidence of early artistic creativity among our ancestors. In addition to the Ice Age animals depicted here—horses, wild ox, rhino, and bison—the chambers of Chauvet feature renderings of ten other species: bear, lion, mammoth, mountain goat, giant deer, owl, panther, red deer, and reindeer, as well as human hand prints.

Courtesy of the Minister of Culture and Communications, France

supporting the **recent African origins hypothesis** (also known as the *Eve* or *out of Africa* hypothesis) use genetic and other evidence to argue that all anatomically modern humans living today descend directly from one single population of archaic *H. sapiens* in Africa. Improved cultural capabilities then allowed members of this group to replace other archaic human forms as they began to spread out of Africa some time after 100,000 years ago. So while both models place human origins firmly in Africa, the first argues that our human ancestors began moving into Asia and Europe as early as 1.8 mya, whereas the second maintains that anatomically modern *H. sapiens* evolved only in Africa, completely replacing other members of the genus *Homo* as they spread throughout the world.

Though the recent African origins hypothesis is accepted by many paleoanthropologists, not every scholar supports it. Among those with opposing views, Chinese paleoanthropologists generally favor the multiregional hypothesis in part because it fits better with the fossil discoveries from Australia and Asia. The claim of ancient human

roots in eastern Asia also resonates well with the region's traditional ethnocentric ideas about China as the place of human origins and the world's most ancient civilization. Traditionally, it is imagined as "the Middle Kingdom"— the center of humanity on earth.

By contrast, the recent African origins hypothesis depends more upon the interpretation of genetic evidence, fossils, and cultural remains from Europe, Africa, and Southwest Asia. However, this model can be critiqued on several grounds. For example, the molecular evidence upon which it is based has been strongly criticized, as more recent genetic studies indicate that Africa was not the sole source of DNA in modern humans.[24] Recent African origins proponents argue that anatomically modern people coexisted for a time with other archaic populations until the superior cultural capacities of the moderns resulted in extinction of the archaic peoples.

That said, by 30,000 years ago, many of the distinctive anatomical features seen in archaic groups like Neandertals seem to disappear from the fossil record in Europe. Instead, individuals with generally higher foreheads, smoother brow ridges, and more distinct chins seemed to have Europe to themselves. However, a comparative

recent African origins hypothesis The hypothesis that all modern people are derived from one single population of archaic *Homo sapiens* from Africa who migrated out of Africa after 100,000 years ago, replacing all other archaic forms due to their superior cultural capabilities; also called the Eve or out of Africa hypothesis.

[24] Gibbons, A. (1997). Ideas on human origins evolve at anthropology gathering. *Science 276,* 535–536; Pennisi, E. (1999). Genetic study shakes up out of Africa theory. *Science 283,* 1828.

Some living people, such as this indigenous Australian, do not all meet the problematic definition of anatomical modernity according to skull shape proposed in the recent African origins model. Therefore, some paleoanthropologists suggest that this narrow definition of anatomical modernity is flawed, perhaps even ethnocentric, because all living people are clearly full-fledged members of the species *Homo sapiens.*

examination of skulls representing the full range of individual human variation found in every part of the world today reveals now living people with skulls not meeting the anatomical definition of modernity proposed in the recent African origins model.[25]

Human Biological Variation and the Problem of Race

The Neandertal debate raises fundamental questions about the complex relationship between biological and cultural human variation. As we reviewed the human fossil record throughout this chapter, inferences were made about the cultural capabilities of our ancestors partially based on biological features. Such questions are deeply embedded within a discipline that has a long history of studying cultural and biological variation within the human species and how it relates to the concept of **race** as a subspecies or discrete biological division within a species.

Today, anthropologists agree that no subspecies exist within currently surviving *Homo sapiens.* Consequently,

as far as contemporary humanity is concerned, race is not a valid biological category. In fact, anthropologists work actively to expose the concept of race as scientifically inapplicable to humans. At the same time, they recognize the powerful symbolic significance of race as a social and political category in many countries, including the United States, Germany, Brazil, and South Africa.

Race as a Social Construct

To deal with the politically divisive aspects of racial symbolism, we must begin by understanding how the notion of distinct human races came to be. Earlier in this chapter, we discussed how European scholars struggled to make sense of the massive amounts of new information generated since the age of exploration, beginning about 500 years ago. Coming to them from the most remote corners of the world, this information forced them to critically rethink deeply rooted ideas about humanity and its relationship to other forms of life. In the quest for understanding, they reasoned not only on the basis of scientific facts but also from the perspective of their particular religious beliefs and cultural traditions. Looking back on their writings, we are now painfully aware of how ethnocentrism and other prejudices clouded their findings.

Among the most telling examples of this is the racial categorizing done by German anatomist Johann Blumenbach (1752–1840). Initially, Blumenbach adopted the classification system devised by the Swedish naturalist Linnaeus in 1758, which divided the human species into four major groups according to geographic area and classified all Europeans as "white," Africans as "black," American Indians as "red," and Asians as "yellow."

Later, in the 1795 edition of his book *On the Natural Variety of Mankind,* Blumenbach introduced some significant changes to this four-race scheme. Based on a comparative examination of his human skull collection, he judged as most beautiful the skull of a woman from the Caucasus Mountains between Russia and Turkey. It was more symmetrical than the others, and he thought it reflected nature's ideal form: the circle. Surely, Blumenbach reasoned, this perfect specimen resembled God's original creation. Moreover, he thought that the living inhabitants of the Caucasus region were the most beautiful in the world. Based on these criteria, he concluded that this high mountain range not far from the lands mentioned in the Bible was near the place of human origins.

---

[25] Wolpoff, M., & Caspari, R. (1997). *Race and human evolution* (pp. 344–345, 393). New York: Simon & Schuster.

race In biology, a subgroup within a species, not scientifically applicable to humans because there exist no subspecies within modern *Homo sapiens.*

Building on his idea that the southeastern Europeans inhabiting the Caucasus looked most like the first humans, Blumenbach decided that all light-skinned peoples in Europe and adjacent parts of western Asia and northern Africa belonged to the same race. On this basis, he dropped the European race label and replaced it with "Caucasian." Although he continued to distinguish American Indians as a separate race, he regrouped dark-skinned Africans as "Ethiopian" and split those Asians not considered Caucasian into two separate races: "Mongolian" (referring to most inhabitants of Asia, including China and Japan) and "Malay" (indigenous Australians, Pacific Islanders, and others).

But, Blumenbach did more than change labels: He also introduced a formal hierarchical ordering of the races he delineated. Convinced that Caucasians were closest to the original ideal humans created in God's image, he ranked them as superior. The other races, he argued, were the result of "degeneration." Moving away from their place of origin and adapting to different environments and climates, they had degenerated physically and morally into what many Europeans came to think of as inferior races.[26]

Critically reviewing this and other early historical efforts to classify humanity in higher and lower forms, we now clearly recognize their factual errors and ethnocentric biases with respect to the concept of race. Especially disastrous is the notion of superior and inferior races, as this has been used as justification for brutalities ranging from repression to slavery to mass murder and genocide. It has also been employed to justify stunning levels of mockery, as painfully illustrated in the following tragic story of Ota Benga, an Mbuti Pygmy man from Africa who in the early 1900s was caged in a New York zoo with an orangutan.

RACISM ON PUBLIC DISPLAY: A PYGMY IN THE BRONX ZOO

Captured in a raid in Congo, Ota Benga somehow came into the possession of Samuel Verner, a North American missionary-explorer looking for exotic "savages" for exhibition in the United States. In 1904, Ota and a group of fellow Pygmies were shipped across the Atlantic and exhibited at a World's Fair in Saint Louis, Missouri. About 23 years old at the time, Ota was 4 feet 11 inches in height and weighed 103 pounds. Throngs of visitors came to see displays of dozens of indigenous peoples from around the globe, shown in their traditional dress and living in replica villages doing their customary things. The fair was a success for the organizers, and all the Pygmies survived to be shipped back to their homeland.

The enterprising Verner also returned to Congo and with Ota's help collected artifacts to be sold to the American

About 25 years old, Ota Benga is shown here holding a young chimpanzee in the Bronx Zoo in 1906. This Mbuti Pygmy had been captured in a raid in Congo and exhibited at the World's Fair in Saint Louis, Missouri.

Museum of Natural History in New York City. In the summer of 1906 Verner returned to the United States, along with Ota. Soon thereafter, Verner went bankrupt and lost his entire collection to the bank. Left stranded in the big city, Ota was placed in the care of the museum and then taken to the Bronx Zoo where he was put on exhibit in the monkey house, with an orangutan as company. Ota's sharpened teeth (a cultural practice among his own people) were seen as evidence of his supposedly cannibal nature.

After intensive protest, zoo officials released the unfortunate Pygmy from his cage and during the day let him roam free in the park, where he was often harassed by teasing visitors. Ota (usually referred to as a "boy") was then turned over to an orphanage for African American children. In 1916, upon hearing that he would never return to his homeland, he took a revolver and shot himself through the heart.[27]

---

[26] Gould, S. J. (1994). The geometer of race. *Discover 15* (11), 65–69.

[27] Bradford, P. V., & Blume, H. (1992). *Ota Benga: The Pygmy in the zoo.* New York: St. Martin's.

CHALLENGING RACISM

The racist display at the Bronx Zoo a century ago was by no means unique. Just a tip of the ethnocentric iceberg, it was the manifestation of a powerful ideology in which one small part of humanity sought to demonstrate and justify its claims of biological and cultural superiority. This had particular resonance in North America, where people of European descent were thrown together in a society with Native Americans, African slaves, and later Asians imported as a source of cheap labor. Indeed, such claims, based on false notions of race, have resulted in the oppression and genocide of millions of humans because of the color of their skin or the shape of their skulls.

Fortunately, by the early 20th century, some scholars began to challenge the concept of racial superiority. Among the strongest critics was Franz Boas (1858–1942), a Jewish scientist who immigrated to the United States because of rising anti-Semitism in his German homeland and who became the founder of North America's academic anthropology. As president of the American Association for the Advancement of Science, Boas criticized hierarchical notions of race in an important speech titled "Race and Progress," published in the prestigious journal *Science* in 1909.

Ashley Montagu (1905–1999), a British student of Boas's and one of the best-known anthropologists of his time, devoted much of his career to combating scientific racism. Like Boas, he was born into a Jewish family and personally felt the sting of anti-Semitism. Originally named Israel Ehrenberg, he changed his name in the 1920s and emigrated from England to the United States, where he fought racism in his writings and in academic and public lectures. Of all his works, none is more important than his book *Man's Most Dangerous Myth: The Fallacy of Race*. Published in 1942, it took the lead in exposing, on purely scientific grounds, the fallacy of human races as clearly bounded biological categories.

The dogma of "the inequality between humans and the races"[28] provided ideological fodder to Nazi German politicians who capitalized on these ideas to dehumanize, enslave, and kill millions of Jews and Gypsies in Europe during the Second World War.

Although several leading anthropologists, including Ruth Benedict, publicly challenged racial segregation policies and a host of other discriminatory laws and practices in the United States and elsewhere, theories claiming an intellectual and genetic basis for "racial inferiority"

of black Africans and their descendents in the Americas remained popular in the postwar period of the mid-20th century. In many parts of the United States, official racial segregation policies discriminating against African Americans were publicly defended and promoted by powerful political agents and news media.

Taught by well-established scholars at universities and medical schools on both sides of the Atlantic Ocean, theories justifying racial discrimination were also used in support of a regime based on white supremacy in South Africa. There, an apartheid system was officially established in 1948 by an ethnic minority of European descent.

Proclaiming racist discrimination a violation of universal human rights, the United Nations and its various agencies were instrumental in challenging race theories as obstructive to peaceful international coexistence. In its campaign to combat racial prejudice and discrimination, the UN secured the cooperation of an international group of anthropologists, biologists, geneticists, and other scholars demonstrating "the absurdity of the so-called 'scientific' bases of racial prejudice."[29]

Race as a Biological Construct

Social constructions of race are often tied up in the false but tenacious idea that there really is a biological foundation to the concept of human races. As already mentioned, in biology a race is defined as a subspecies: a population within a species that differs in terms of genetic variance from other populations of the same species. Simple and straightforward though such a definition may seem, there are three very important things to note about it.

First, it is arbitrary; there is no agreement on how many differences it takes to make a race. For some who are interested in the topic, different frequencies in the variants of one gene are sufficient; for others, different frequencies involving several genes are necessary. Ultimately, it has been impossible to reach agreement not just on the number of genes, but also on precisely which ones are the most important for defining races.

After arbitrariness, the second important thing to note about the biological definition of race is that it does not mean that any one so-called race has exclusive possession of any particular variant of any gene or genes. In human terms, the frequency of a trait like type O blood, for example, may be high in one racial population and low in another, but it is present in both. In other words, populations

[28] Métraux, A. (1953). Applied anthropology in government: United Nations. In A. A. Kroeber (Ed.), *Anthropology today: An encyclopedic inventory* (pp. 880–894). Chicago: University of Chicago Press.

[29] Alfred Métraux, cited in Prins, H. E. L., & Krebs, E. (2007). Toward a land without evil: Alfred Métraux a UNESCO anthropologist 1948–1962. In *60 years of UNESCO history. Proceedings of the international symposium in Paris, 16–18 November 2005* (pp. 115–125). Paris: UNESCO.

© Associated Press

Many people have become accustomed to viewing so-called racial groups as natural and separate divisions within our species based on visible physical differences. However, these groups differ from one another in only 6 percent of their genes. For many thousands of years, individuals belonging to different human social groups have been in sexual contact. Exchanging their genes, they maintained the human species in all its colorful variety and prevented the development of distinctive subspecies (biologically defined races). This continued genetic mixing is effectively illustrated by the above photo of distant relatives, all of whom are descendents of Sally Hemings, an African American slave, and Thomas Jefferson, the Euramerican gentleman-farmer who had 150 slaves working for him at his Virginia plantation and served as third U.S. president (1801–1809).

are genetically "open," meaning that genes flow between them. Because human populations are genetically open, no fixed racial groups have developed within our modern species.

The third important thing to note about the scientifically inappropriate use of the term *race* with respect to humans is that the differences among individuals within a particular population are generally greater than the differences among populations.

In sum, the biological concept of race does not apply to *Homo sapiens*. That said, to dismiss race as a biologically invalid category is not to deny the reality of human biological diversity. The task for anthropologists is to explain that diversity and the social meanings given to it rather than to try to falsely split our species into discrete categories called races.

SKIN COLOR: A CASE STUDY IN ADAPTATION

The popular idea of race is commonly linked to skin color, a complex biological trait. Skin color is subject to great variation and is attributed to several key factors: the transparency or thickness of the skin; a copper-colored pigment called carotene; reflected color from the blood vessels (responsible for the rosy color of lightly pigmented people); and, most significantly, the amount of melanin

(from *melas,* a Greek word meaning "black")—a dark pigment in the skin's outer layer. People with dark skin have more melanin-producing cells than those with light skin, but everyone (except those with albinism) has a measure of melanin.

Exposure to sunlight increases melanin production, causing skin color to deepen. Melanin is known to protect skin against damaging ultraviolet solar radiation;[30] consequently, dark-skinned peoples are less susceptible to skin cancers and sunburn than are those with less melanin. Because the highest concentrations of dark-skinned people tend to be found in the tropical regions of the world, it appears that natural selection has favored heavily pigmented skin as a protection against exposure where ultraviolet radiation is most constant.[31]

In northern latitudes, light skin has an adaptive advantage as the manufacturer of vitamin D through a

---

[30] Neer, R. M. (1975). The evolutionary significance of vitamin D, skin pigment, and ultraviolet light. *American Journal of Physical Anthropology 43,* 409–416.

[31] Branda, R. F., & Eatoil, J. W. (1978). Skin color and photolysis: An evolutionary hypothesis. *Science 201,* 625–626.

chemical reaction dependent upon sunlight. Vitamin D is vital for maintaining the balance of calcium in the body. In northern climates with little sunshine, light skin allows enough sunlight to penetrate the skin and stimulate the formation of vitamin D, essential for healthy bones. Dark pigmentation interferes with this process. The severe consequences of vitamin D deficiency can be avoided through culture. Until recently, children in northern Europe and North America were regularly fed a spoonful of cod liver oil during the dark winter months. Today, pasteurized milk is often fortified with vitamin D.

Given what we know about the adaptive significance of human skin color, and the fact that, until 800,000 years ago, members of the genus *Homo* were exclusively creatures of the tropics, it is likely that lightly pigmented skins are a recent development in human history. Conversely, and consistent with humanity's African origins, darkly pigmented skins likely are quite ancient. The enzyme tyrosinase, which converts the amino acid tyrosine into the compound that forms melanin, is present in lightly pigmented peoples in sufficient quantity to make them very "black." The reason it does not is that they have genes that inactivate or inhibit it.[32]

Human skin, more liberally endowed with sweat glands and lacking heavy body hair compared to other primates, effectively eliminates excess body heat in a hot climate. This would have been especially advantageous to our ancestors on the savannah, who could have avoided confrontations with large carnivorous animals by carrying

[32] Wills, C. (1994). The skin we're in. *Discover 15* (11), 79.

out most of their activities in the heat of the day. For the most part, tropical predators rest during this period, hunting primarily from dusk until early morning. Without much hair to cover their bodies, selection would have favored dark skin in our human ancestors. In short, based on available scientific evidence, all humans appear to have a "black" ancestry, no matter how "white" some of them may appear to be today.

Obviously, one should not conclude that, because it may be a more recent development, lightly pigmented skin is better, or more highly evolved, than heavily pigmented skin. The latter is clearly better evolved to the conditions of life in the tropics or at high altitudes where exposure to ultraviolet light increases, although with cultural adaptations like protective clothing, hats, and more recently invented sunscreen lotions, lightly pigmented peoples can survive there. Conversely, the availability of supplementary sources of vitamin D allows more heavily pigmented peoples to do quite well far away from the tropics. In both cases, culture has rendered skin color differences largely irrelevant from a purely biological perspective. With time and with the efforts we see being made in many cultures today, skin color may lose its social significance as well.

Over the course of several million years, humans have gradually developed into a highly diverse and yet still unified single species inhabiting the entire earth. Biological adaptation to a wide geographic range of natural environments is responsible for some aspects of human variation. However, while evolution continues into the present, different cultures shape both the expression and the interpretation of human biological variation at every step. We humans do indeed stand with one foot in nature and another in culture.

Questions for Reflection

1. Over the course of their evolutionary history, humans increasingly used the medium of culture to face the challenges of existence. How does studying the biological basis of human culture through living primates and human evolution help address the challenge of knowing ourselves?

2. In the mid-1600s, a Dutch inventor built the first practical microscope that enabled him to see and describe bacteria, sperm, and the circulation of protoplasmic particles in small blood vessels. What do you think was the impact of this invention on educated Europeans and their perspective on long-term human development and biological variations?

3. How might you relate the Neandertal debates to stereotyping or racism in contemporary society?

4. Some aspects of human variation derive clearly from biological adaptations to the environment. As humans came to rely more upon cultural adaptations, what were the effects on our biology? How has culture shaped our interpretations of our biology?

5. Considering the historical context of slavery and racist behavior, do you think "Caucasian" as an ethnocentric label of superiority played a role in how Europeans and their descendents in America and elsewhere justified white supremacy as normal? Why are racial categories such as "Caucasian" still used?

Suggested Readings

de Waal, F. B. M. (2001). *The ape and the sushi master.* New York: Basic.

In an accessible style, one of the world's foremost experts on bonobos demonstrates ape culture and challenges theories that exclude animals from the "culture club." His discussion takes the concept of ape culture beyond anthropocentrism and ties it to communication and social organization.

Goodall, J. (2000). *Reason for hope: A spiritual journey.* New York: Warner.

A personal memoir linking this famous primatologist's lifework with chimpanzees in Tanzania's Gombe wildlife preserve to her spiritual convictions. Exploring difficult topics such as environmental destruction, animal abuse, and genocide, Goodall expands the concept of humanity and advocates basic human rights for chimpanzees.

Jones, S., Martin, R., & Pilbeam, D. (Eds.). (1994). *Cambridge encyclopedia of human evolution.* New York: Cambridge University Press.

Over seventy scholars contributed to this comprehensive introduction to the human species, covering the gamut—from genetics, primatology, and the fossil evidence to contemporary human ecology, demography, and disease.

Klein, R. G., & Edgar, B. (2002). *The dawn of human culture.* New York: Wiley.

Reexamining the archaeological evidence and bringing in new discoveries in the study of the human brain, the authors detail the changes that enabled humans to think and behave in far more sophisticated ways than before, resulting in the incredibly rapid evolution of new skills.

Marks, J. (2002). *What it means to be 98 percent chimpanzee: Apes, people, and their genes.* Berkeley: University of California Press.

This provocative book places the ongoing study of the relationship between genes and behavior in historical and cultural contexts. Marks uses the close genetic relationship of chimps and humans to demonstrate the limits of genetics for explaining differences in complex traits such as behavior or appearance. His discussion of the absence of a genetic basis for race is particularly good.

Wolpoff, M., & Caspari, R. (1997). *Race and human evolution: A fatal attraction.* New York: Simon & Schuster.

A historical account of efforts to develop a scientific theory of race in Western societies is joined with an analysis of the fossil evidence for modern human origins in this fascinating book. Its authors, champions of the multiregional hypothesis, document the social processes leading to the division of contemporary humans into racial groups suggesting that the division of fossil groups into separate species represents a similar application of the false concept of biological race.

Challenge Issue   As social creatures dependent upon one another for survival, humans face the challenge of communicating clearly in a multiplicity of situations about countless things connected to our well-being. We do this with a variety of distinctive gestures, sounds, touches, and body postures. Our most sophisticated means of sharing large amounts of complex information is through language—a foundation stone of every human culture. Today, as shown in this photo of a Tuareg nomad talking on his satellite phone while astride a camel in the Sahara Desert, modern technology enables people to communicate instantly from even the most remote corners of the earth. But to make sense of messages, they must share a language, no matter how sophisticated their electronic gadgets.

CHAPTER 5

Language and Communication

Chapter Preview

What Is Language?

A language is a system of symbolic communication using sounds and/or gestures that are put together according to rules, resulting in meanings that are based on agreement by a society and intelligible to all who share that language. Although humans rely heavily on spoken language, or speech, to communicate with one another, it is not their sole means of communication. Human language is embedded in an age-old gesture-call system in which body motions and facial expressions, along with vocal features such as tone and volume, play vital roles in conveying messages. The anthropological study of language can be divided into three key branches: descriptive linguistics, historical linguistics, and the investigation of language in relation to social and cultural settings.

How Is Language Related to Culture?

A culture consists of ideas and perceptions of the world that inform and are reflected in people's behavior. This complex of ideas and perceptions is encoded in a coherent system of symbols that serves as communication between members of a society. As such, language is fundamental to the functioning of human cultures. Social variables—such as age, gender, and economic status—may influence how people use language. Moreover, people communicate what is meaningful to them, and that is largely defined by their particular culture. Our use of language has an effect on, and is influenced by, our culture.

How Do Languages Change?

All languages are constantly transforming—new words are adopted or coined, others are dropped, and some shift in meaning. Languages change for various reasons, ranging from selective borrowing from another language to the need for new vocabulary to deal with technological innovations or altered social realities. On one hand, domination of one society by another may result in erosion or loss of a particular language. On the other, cultural revitalization may result in the resurgence or revival of a threatened or even extinct language. Today's global telecommunication revolution is transforming both written and spoken language all around the world.

The human ability to communicate through language rests squarely on our biological makeup. We are programmed for language, be it through sounds or gestures. (Sign languages, such as the American Sign Language—ASL—used by the hearing impaired, are fully developed languages in their own right.) Beyond the cries of babies, which are not learned but which do communicate, humans must learn their language. So it is that any normal child from anywhere in the world readily learns the language of his or her culture.

Language is a system of communication using sounds and/or gestures that are put together according to certain rules, resulting in meanings that are intelligible to all who share that language. These sounds and gestures are **symbols**—marks, sounds, gestures, motions, or other signs that are arbitrarily linked to something else and represent it *in a meaningful way*. For example, the word *crying* is a symbol, a combination of sounds to which we assign the meaning of a particular action and which we can use to communicate that meaning, whether or not anyone around us is actually crying.

Signals, unlike culturally learned symbols, or meaningful signs, are instinctive sounds and gestures that have a natural or self-evident meaning. Screams, sighs, and coughs, for example, are signals that convey some kind of emotional or physical state.

Today's language experts are not certain how much credit to give to animals, such as dolphins or chimpanzees, for the ability to use symbols as well as signals. But it has become evident that these animals and many others communicate in remarkable ways.[1] Apes have demonstrated an ability to understand language quite well, even using rudimentary grammar. Several chimpanzees, gorillas, and orangutans have been taught American Sign Language. Researchers have discovered that even vervet monkeys utilize distinct calls for communication. These calls go

beyond merely signaling levels of fear or arousal. Among other things, these small African monkeys have specific calls to signify the type of predator threatening the group. According to primatologist Allison Jolly,

> [The calls] include which direction to look in or where to run. There is an audience effect: calls are given when there is someone appropriate to listen . . . monkey calls are far more than involuntary expressions of emotion.[2]

What are the implications for our understanding of the nature and evolution of language? Before we can answer this, we need a better understanding of the various systems of animal communication. Meanwhile, even as debate continues over how human and animal communication relate to each other, we cannot dismiss communication among nonhuman species as a set of simple instinctive reflexes or fixed action patterns.[3]

A remarkable example of the many scientific efforts under way on this subject is the story of an orangutan named Chantek, featured in the following Original Study on the opposite page. Among other things, it illustrates the creative process of language development and the capacity of a nonhuman primate to recognize symbols.

While language studies such as the one involving Chantek are fascinating and reveal much about primate cognition, the fact remains that human culture is ultimately dependent on an elaborate system of communication far more complex than that of any other species—including our fellow primates. The reason for this is the sheer amount of knowledge that must be learned by each person from other individuals in order to fully participate in society. Of course, a significant amount of learning can and does take place in the absence of language by way of observation and imitation, guided by a limited number of meaningful signs or symbols. However, all known human cultures are so rich in content that they require communication systems that not only can give precise labels to various classes of phenomena but also permit people to think and talk about their own and others' experiences and expectations—past, present, and future.

The central and most highly developed human system of communication is language. Knowledge of the workings of language, then, is essential to a full understanding of what culture is about and how it operates.

---

[1] Among many references on this, see Bekoff, M., et al. (Eds.). (2002). *The cognitive animal: Empirical and theoretical perspectives on animal cognition.* Cambridge, MA: MIT Press; Patterson, F. G. P., & Gordon, W. (2002). Twenty-seven years of Project Koko and Michael. In B. Galdikas et al. (Eds.), *All apes great and small* (vol. 1): *Chimpanzees, bonobos, and gorillas* (pp. 165–176). New York: Kluwer Academic.

language A system of communication using sounds or gestures that are put together in meaningful ways according to a set of rules.

symbol A mark, sound, gesture, motion, or other sign that is arbitrarily linked to something else and represents it in a meaningful way.

signal An instinctive sound or gesture that has a natural or self-evident meaning.

---

[2] Jolly, A. (1991). Thinking like a vervet. *Science 251,* 574; see also Seyfarth, R. M., et al. (1980). Monkey responses to three different alarm calls: Evidence for predator classification and semantic communication. *Science 210,* 801–803.

[3] Armstrong, D. F., Stokoe, W. C., & Wilcox, S. E. (1993). Signs of the origin of syntax. *Current Anthropology 34,* 349–368; Burling, R. (1993). Primate calls, human language, and nonverbal communication. *Current Anthropology 34,* 25–53.

Language and the Intellectual Abilities of Orangutans *by H. Lyn White Miles*

In 1978, after researchers began to use American Sign Language for the deaf to communicate with chimpanzees and gorillas, I began the first long-term study of the language ability of an orangutan named Chantek. There was criticism that symbol-using apes might just be imitating their human caregivers, but there is now growing agreement that orangutans, gorillas, and both chimpanzee species can develop language skills at the level of a 2- to 3-year-old human child.

Chantek beginning the sign for "tomato."

The goal of Project Chantek was to investigate the mind of an orangutan through a developmental study of his cognitive and linguistic skills. It was a great ethical and emotional responsibility to engage an orangutan in what anthropologists call "enculturation," since I would not only be teaching a form of communication, I would be teaching aspects of the culture upon which that language was based. . . .

A small group of caregivers at the University of Tennessee, Chattanooga, began raising Chantek when he was 9 months old. They communicated with him by using gestural signs based on the American Sign Language for the deaf. After a month, Chantek produced his own first sign and eventually learned to use approximately 150 different signs, forming a vocabulary similar to that of a very young child. Chantek learned names for people (LYN, JOHN), places (YARD, BROCK-HALL), things to eat (YOGURT, CHOCOLATE), actions (WORK, HUG), objects (SCREWDRIVER, MONEY), animals (DOG, APE), colors (RED, BLACK), pronouns (YOU, ME), location (UP, POINT), attributes (GOOD, HURT), and emphasis (MORE, TIME-TO-DO).

We found that Chantek's signing was spontaneous and nonrepetitious. He did not merely imitate his caregivers, but rather he actively used signs to initiate communications and meet his needs. Almost immediately, he began using signs in combinations with slight changes in how he articulated and arranged his signs. He commented "COKE DRINK" after drinking his coke, "PULL BEARD" while pulling a caregiver's hair through a fence, and "TIME HUG" while locked in his cage as his caregiver looked at her watch. But, beyond using signs in this way, could he use them as symbols, that is, more abstractly to represent a person, thing, action, or idea, even apart from its context or when it was not present?

One indication of the capacity of both deaf and hearing children to use symbolic language is the ability to point, which some researchers argued that apes could not do spontaneously. Chantek began to point to objects when he was 2 years old, somewhat later than human children. First, he showed and gave us objects, and then he began pointing where he wanted to be tickled and to where he wanted to be carried. Finally, he could answer questions like WHERE HAT? WHICH DIFFERENT? and WHAT WANT? by pointing to the correct object.

As Chantek's vocabulary increased, the ideas that he was expressing became more complex, such as when he signed BAD BIRD at noisy birds giving alarm calls, and WHITE CHEESE FOOD-EAT for cottage cheese. He understood that things had characteristics or attributes that could be described. He also created combinations of signs that we had never used before.

In the way that a child learns language, Chantek began to over- or under-extend the meaning of his signs, which gave us insight into his emotions and how he was beginning to classify his world. For example, he used the sign DOG for actual dogs, as well as for a picture of a dog in his Viewmaster, orangutans on television, barking noises on the radio, birds, horses, a tiger at the circus, a herd of cows, a picture of a cheetah, and a noisy helicopter that presumably sounded like it was barking. For Chantek, the sign BUG included crickets, cockroaches, a picture of a cockroach, beetles, slugs, small moths, spiders, worms, flies, a picture of a graph shaped like a butterfly, tiny brown pieces of cat food, and small bits of feces. He signed BREAK before he broke and shared pieces of crackers, and after he broke his toilet. He signed BAD to himself before he grabbed a cat, when he bit into a radish, and for a dead bird.

We also discovered that Chantek could comprehend our spoken English (after the first couple of years we used speech as well as signing). When he was 2 years old, Chantek began to sign for things that were not present. He frequently asked to go to places in his yard to look for animals, such as his pet squirrel and cat, who served as playmates. He also made requests for ICE CREAM, signing CAR RIDE and pulling us toward the parking lot for a trip to a local ice cream shop.

We learned that an orangutan can tell lies. Deception is an important indicator of language abilities since it requires a deliberate and intentional misrepresentation of reality. In order to deceive, you must be able to see events from the other person's perspective and negate his or her perception. Chantek began to deceive from a relatively early age, and we caught him in lies about three times a week. He learned that he could sign DIRTY to get into the bathroom to play with the washing machine, dryer, soap, and so on, instead of using the toilet. He also used his signs deceptively to gain social advantage in games, to divert attention in social interactions, and to avoid testing situations and to delay coming home after walks on campus.

CONTINUED

© H. Lyn Miles, PhD, Chantek Foundation

CONTINUED

On one occasion, Chantek stole a pencil eraser, pretended to swallow it, and "supported" his case by opening his mouth and signing FOOD-EAT, as if to say that he had swallowed it. However, he really held the eraser in his cheek, and later it was found in his bedroom where he commonly hid objects.

We carried out tests of Chantek's mental ability using measures developed for human children. Chantek reached a mental age equivalent to that of a 2- to 3-year-old child, with some skills of even older children. On some tasks done readily by children, such as using one object to represent another and pretend play, Chantek performed as well as children, but less frequently. He engaged in chase games in which he would look over his shoulder as he darted about, although no one was chasing him. He also signed to his toys and offered them food and drink.

By 4½ years of age, Chantek showed evidence of planning, creative simulation, and the use of objects in novel relations to one another to invent new meanings. For example, he simulated the context for food preparation by giving his caregiver two objects needed to prepare his milk formula

and staring at the location of the remaining ingredient.

Chantek was extremely curious and inventive. When he wanted to know the name of something, he offered his hands to be molded into the shape of the proper sign. But language is a creative process, so we were pleased to see that Chantek began to invent his own signs. He invented: NO-TEETH (to show us that he would not use his teeth during rough play); EYE-DRINK (for contact lens solution used by his caregivers); and DAVE-MISSING-FINGER (a name for a favorite university employee who had a hand injury). Like our ancestors, Chantek had become a creator of language.

(Adapted from Miles, H.L.W. (1993). Language and the orangutan: The old "person" of the forest. In P. Cavalieri & P. Singer (Eds.), The Great Ape Project (pp. 45–50). New York: St. Martin's Press.)

Update

My relationship and research with Chantek continue through the Chantek Foundation and Animal Nation, Inc. of Kennesaw, Georgia. Chantek now uses several hundred signs and has invented some new ones of his own—such as

KATSUP (by combining TOMATO and TOOTHPASTE). He uses a computer and makes stone tools, paintings, and other arts and crafts, including small percussion instruments used in my Native American rock band Animal Nation. Chantek also makes unique jewelry and found art assemblages of semi-precious stones for the foundation, which helps to fund the research.

As someone of Abenaki Indian heritage, I believe that animals are "persons of the nonhuman kind." There is a growing movement across the globe for recognition of the intelligence, personhood, and even legal protection of all great apes, based on their culture in natural settings and on what we have learned from Chantek's abilities. Plans are in the making for Chantek and other enculturated apes to live in culture-based preserves where they have more range of choices and learning opportunities than zoos or research centers are willing to provide. An exciting new project under the auspices of Animal Nation, Inc., will give great apes an opportunity to communicate with one another via the Internet. As rock musician Peter Gabriel says in his song "Animal Nation" about communicating with ages, "Who knows where this will end?" (For more information, see www.chantek.org.)

Linguistic Research and the Nature of Language

Any human language—Chinese, English, Swahili, or whatever—is obviously a means of transmitting information and sharing with others both collective and individual experiences. It is a system that enables us to translate our concerns, beliefs, and perceptions into symbols that can be understood and interpreted by others.

In spoken language, this is done by taking sounds—no language uses more than about fifty—and developing rules for putting them together in meaningful ways. Sign languages, such as American Sign Language, do the same with gestures rather than sounds. The vast array of languages in the world—some 7,000 or so different ones—may well astound and mystify us by their great variety and complexity, yet language experts have found that all languages, as far back as we can trace them, are organized in the same basic way.

The roots of **linguistics**—the systematic study of all aspects of language—go back a long way, to the works of

ancient language specialists in India more than 2,000 years ago. The European age of exploration, from the 16th through the 18th centuries, set the stage for a great leap forward in the scientific study of language. Explorers, invaders, and missionaries accumulated information about a huge diversity of languages from all around the world. More than 10,000 languages still existed when they began their inquiries.

Linguists in the 19th century, including anthropologists, made a significant contribution in comparative research—discovering patterns, relationships, and systems in the sounds and structures of different languages and tentatively formulating laws and principles concerning language. In the 20th century, while still collecting data, these researchers made considerable progress in unraveling the reasoning process behind language construction, testing and working from new and improved theories.

Insofar as theories and facts of language are verifiable by independent researchers looking at the same materials, it can now be said that we have a science of linguistics. This science has three main branches: descriptive linguistics, historical linguistics, and a third branch that focuses on language in relation to social and cultural settings.

linguistics The modern scientific study of all aspects of language.

For linguists studying language in the field, laptops and recording devices are indispensable tools. Here Tiffany Kershner of Kansas State University works with native Sukwa speakers in northern Malawi, Africa.

Descriptive Linguistics

How can an anthropologist, a trader, a missionary, a diplomat, or any other outsider research a foreign language that has not yet been described and analyzed, or for which there are no readily available written materials? There are hundreds of such undocumented languages in the world. Fortunately, effective methods have been developed to help with the task. Descriptive linguistics involves unraveling a language by recording, describing, and analyzing all of its features. It is a painstaking process, but it is ultimately rewarding in that it provides deeper understanding of a language—its structure, its unique linguistic repertoire (figures of speech, word plays, and so on), and its relationship to other languages.

The process of unlocking the underlying rules of a spoken language requires a trained ear and a thorough understanding of how multiple different speech sounds are produced. Without such know-how, it is extremely difficult to write out or make intelligent use of any data concerning a particular language. To satisfy this preliminary requirement, most people need special training in phonetics, discussed below.

Phonology

Rooted in the Greek word *phone* (meaning "sound"), **phonetics** is defined as the systematic identification and description of the distinctive sounds in a language. Phonetics is basic to **phonology,** the study of language sounds.

In order to analyze and describe any language, one needs first an inventory of all its distinctive sounds.

While some of the sounds used in other languages may seem very much like those of the researcher's own speech pattern, others may be unfamiliar. For example, the *th* sound common in English does not exist in the Dutch language and is difficult for most Dutch speakers to pronounce, just as the *r* sound used in numerous languages is tough for Japanese speakers. And the unique "click" sounds used in Bushman languages in southern Africa are difficult for speakers of just about every other language.

While collecting speech sounds or utterances, the linguist works to isolate the **phonemes**—the smallest units of sound that make a difference in meaning. This isolation and analysis may be done by a process called the *minimal-pair test.* The researcher tries to find two short words that appear to be exactly alike except for one sound, such as *bit* and *pit* in English. If the substitution of *b* for *p* in this minimal pair makes a difference in meaning, as it does in English, then those two sounds have been identified as distinct phonemes of the language and will require two different symbols to record. If, however, the linguist

phonetics The systematic identification and description of distinctive speech sounds in a language.

phonology The study of language sounds.

phonemes The smallest units of sound that make a difference in meaning in a language.

finds two different pronunciations (as when "butter" is pronounced "budder") and then finds that there is no difference in their meaning for a native speaker, the sounds represented will be considered variants of the same phoneme. In such cases, for economy of representation only one of the two symbols will be used to record that sound wherever it is found.

Morphology, Syntax, and Grammar

While making and studying an inventory of distinctive sounds, linguists also look into **morphology,** the study of the patterns or rules of word formation in a language (including such things as rules concerning verb tense, pluralization, and compound words). They do this by marking out specific sounds and sound combinations that seem to have meaning. These are called **morphemes**—the smallest units of sound that carry a meaning in a language.

Morphemes are distinct from phonemes, which can alter meaning but have no meaning by themselves. For example, a linguist studying English in a North American farming community would soon learn that *cow* is a morpheme—a meaningful combination of the phonemes *c, o,* and *w.* Pointing to two of these animals, the linguist would elicit the word *cows* from local speakers. This would reveal yet another morpheme—the *s*—which can be added to the original morpheme to indicate plural.

The next step in unraveling a language is to identify its **syntax**—the patterns or rules by which morphemes are arranged into phrases and sentences. The **grammar** of the language will ultimately consist of all observations about its morphemes and syntax.

One of the strengths of modern descriptive linguistics is the objectivity of its methods. For example, English-speaking anthropologists who specialize in this will not approach a language with the idea that it must have nouns, verbs, prepositions, or any other of the form classes identifiable in English. Instead they see what turns up in the language and attempt to describe it in terms of its own inner workings. This allows for unanticipated discoveries. For instance, unlike many other languages, English does not distinguish between feminine and masculine nouns. So it

is that English speakers use the definite article *the* in front of any noun, while French requires two types of such definite articles: *la* for feminine nouns and *le* for masculine—as in *la lune* (the moon) and *le soleil* (the sun).

German speakers go one step farther, utilizing three types of articles: *der* in front of masculine nouns, *die* for feminine, and *das* for neutral. It is also interesting to note that in contrast to their French neighbors, Germans consider the moon as masculine, so they say *der Mond,* and the sun as feminine, which makes it *die Sonne.* In another part of the world, the highlands of Peru and Bolivia in South America, indigenous peoples who speak Quechua are not concerned about whether nouns are gendered or neutral, for their language has no definite articles.

Historical Linguistics

While descriptive linguistics focuses on all features of a particular language at any one moment in time, historical linguistics deals with the fact that languages change. In addition to deciphering "dead" languages that are no longer spoken, specialists in this field investigate relationships between earlier and later forms of the same language, study older languages to track the processes of change into modern ones, and examine interrelationships among older languages. For example, they attempt to sort out the development of Latin (spoken almost 1,500 years ago in southern Europe) into the Romance languages of Italian, Spanish, Portuguese, French, and Romanian by identifying natural shifts in the original language and tracking modifications brought on by centuries of direct contact with Germanic-speaking invaders from northern Europe.

Historical linguists are not limited to the faraway past, for even modern languages are constantly transforming—adding new words, dropping others, or changing meaning. Technological breakthroughs resulting in new equipment and products prompt linguistic shifts. For instance, the electronic revolution that brought us radio, television, and computers has created entirely new vocabularies. Over the last decade or so, Internet use has widened the meaning of a host of already existing English words—from *hacking* and *surfing* to *spam.* Entirely new words, such as *blogging* and *vlogging* (video blogging), have been coined, leading to the creation of Internet dictionaries such as netlingo.com.

Increasing professional specialization is another driving force in language transformation. We see one of many examples in the field of biomedicine where today's students must learn the specialized vocabulary and idioms of the profession—over 6,000 new words in the first year of medical school.

Especially when focusing on long-term processes of change, historical linguists depend on written records of

morphology The study of the patterns or rules of word formation in a language (including such things as rules concerning verb tense, pluralization, and compound words).

morphemes The smallest units of sound that carry a meaning in language. They are distinct from phonemes, which can alter meaning but have no meaning by themselves.

syntax The patterns or rules by which words are arranged into phrases and sentences.

grammar The entire formal structure of a language, including morphology and syntax.

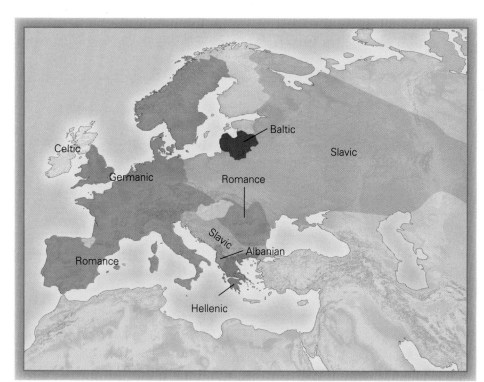

Figure 5.1 Indo-European language subgroups in Europe. Not all languages spoken in Europe are part of the Indo-European family. Basque, for example, is an ancient language still spoken in the French-Spanish borderland. Moreover, languages spoken by Hungarians, Estonians, Finns, Komi (in northeast Russia), and Saami (in northern Scandinavia) belong to the Uralic language family.

travel comm (tv)

languages. They have achieved considerable success in working out the relationships among different languages, and these are reflected in schemes of classification. For example, English is one of approximately 140 languages classified in the larger Indo-European language family (Figure 5.1). A **language family** is a group of languages descended from a single ancestral language. This family is subdivided into some eleven subgroups (Germanic, Romance, and so on), indicating that there has been a long period (6,000 years or so) of **linguistic divergence** from an ancient unified language (reconstructed as Proto-Indo-European) into separate "daughter" languages. English is one of several languages in the Germanic subgroup (Figure 5.2), all of which are more closely related to one another than they are to the languages of any other subgroup of the Indo-European family. *span, port, It-span*

So, despite the differences between them, the languages of one subgroup share certain features when compared to those of another. As an illustration, the word for "father" in the Germanic languages always starts with an *f* or closely related *v* sound (Dutch *vader,* German *Vater,* Gothic *Fadar*). Among the Romance languages, by contrast, the comparable word always starts with a *p*: French *père,* Spanish and Italian *padre*—all derived from the Latin *pater.* The original Indo-European word for "father" was *p'tēr,* so in this case, the Romance languages have retained the earlier pronunciation, whereas the Germanic languages have diverged. Thus many words that begin with *p* in the Romance languages, like Latin *piscis* and *pes,* become words like English *fish* and *foot* in the Germanic languages.

In addition to describing the changes that have taken place as languages have diverged from ancient parent languages, historical linguists have also developed methods to estimate when such divergences occurred. One such technique is known as **glottochronology,** a term derived from the Greek word *glottis,* which means "tongue" or "language." This method compares the **core vocabularies** of languages—pronouns, lower numerals, and names for body parts and natural objects. It is based on the assumption that these basic vocabularies change more slowly than other words and at a more or less constant rate of 14 to 19 percent per 1,000 years. That means that after about 1,000 years, two "sister languages" still share nearly 75 percent of the core vocabulary. (Linguists determined this rate by calculating changes documented in thirteen historic written languages.) By applying a mathematical formula to two related core vocabularies, one can roughly determine the approximate number of years since the languages separated.

language family A group of languages descended from a single ancestral language.

linguistic divergence The development of different languages from a single ancestral language.

glottochronology In linguistics, a method for identifying the approximate time that languages branched off from a common ancestor; based on analyzing core vocabularies.

core vocabulary The most basic and long-lasting words in any language—pronouns, lower numerals, and names for body parts and natural objects.

Latin-french, Spanish, Romanian, Italian, Por

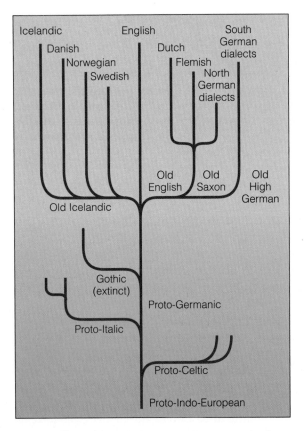

Figure 5.2 **English is one of a group of languages in the Germanic subgroup of the Indo-European family. This diagram shows its relationship to other languages in the same subgroup. The root was Proto-Indo-European, an ancestral language originally spoken by early farmers and herders who spread north and west over Europe, bringing with them both their customs and their language.**

Although not as precise we might like, glottochronology, in conjunction with other chronological dating methods such as those based on archaeological and genetic data, can help determine the time of linguistic divergence.

Processes of Linguistic Divergence

Studying modern languages in their specific cultural contexts can help us understand the processes of change that may have led to linguistic divergence. Clearly, one force for change is selective borrowing by one language from another. This is evident in the many French words present in the English language—and in the growing number of English words cropping up in languages all around the world due to globalization.

There is also a tendency for any group within a larger society to create its own unique vocabulary, whether it is a street gang, sorority, religious group, prison inmates, or platoon of soldiers. By changing the meaning of existing words or inventing new ones, members of the "in-group" can communicate with fellow members while effectively excluding outsiders who may be within hearing range.

Finally, there seems to be a human tendency to admire the person who comes up with a new and clever idiom, a useful word, or a particularly stylish pronunciation, as long as these do not seriously interfere with communication. All of this means that no language stands still.

Phonological differences among groups may be regarded in the same light as vocabulary differences. In a class-structured society, for example, members of the upper class may try to keep their pronunciation distinct from that of lower classes, or vice versa, as a means of reinforcing social boundaries.

Language Loss and Revival

Perhaps the most powerful force for linguistic change is the domination of one society over another, as demonstrated during 500 years of European colonialism. Such dominations persist today in many parts of the world, such as Taiwan's indigenous peoples being governed by Mandarin-speaking Chinese, Tarascan Indians by Spanish-speaking Mexicans, or Bushmen by English-speaking Namibians.

In many cases, foreign political control has resulted in linguistic erosion or even complete disappearance, sometimes leaving only a faint trace in old, indigenous names for geographic features such as hills and rivers. Over the last 500 years about 3,000 of the world's 10,000 or so languages have become extinct as a direct result of warfare, epidemics, and forced assimilation brought on by colonial powers and other aggressive outsiders. Most of the remaining 7,000 languages are spoken by very few people, and many of them are losing speakers rapidly due to globalization. Half have fewer than 10,000 speakers each, and a quarter have fewer than 1,000. Put another way, half of the world's languages are spoken by just 2 percent of the world's population.[4]

In North America, only 150 of the original 300 indigenous languages still exist, and many of these surviving tongues are moving toward extinction at an alarming rate. Thousands of indigenous languages elsewhere in the world are also threatened, such as Defaku, spoken by just 200 people in Nigeria. Fewer than ten people still speak N/u, a "click" language traditionally spoken in South Africa's Kalahari Desert. It is the only surviving member of the !Ui branch of the Tuu language family (previously called Southern Khoisan).

Anthropologists predict that the number of languages still spoken in the world today will be cut in half by the year 2100, in large part because children born into ethnic minority groups no longer use the ancestral language when they go to school, migrate to cities, join the larger workforce, and are exposed to printed and electronic media.

[4] Harrison, K. D. *Pop!Tech 2008: Scarcity and abundance: Global and local trends in language extinction.* www.poptech.org/popcasts/k_david_harrison__poptech_2008

© Bonny Sands

© Bonny Sands

Collaborative efforts between community members and researchers to preserve fast-disappearing languages sometimes require creative solutions. Several linguistic anthropologists are collaborating on field research with speakers of endangered Khoisan "click" languages such as Nluu and !Xun in southern Africa. Using a portable ultrasound imaging machine, they capture the tongue movements of the click consonants. On the left, Johanna Brugman holds an ultrasound probe under the chin of one of the ten last remaining Nluu speakers, Ouma Katrina Esau, who is helping to document how click sounds are made. On the right, !Xun speaker Jenggu Rooi Fransisko wears a stabilization headset that anchors the probe under his chin. The blue tubes are Palatron sticks used to measure head and jaw movement in order to determine exactly how much movement is caused by the tongue alone. An image of the tongue appears on the ultrasound monitor. Clicks are produced by creating suction within a cavity formed between the front and back parts of the tongue—except in the case of bilabial clicks in which the cavity is made between the lips and the back of the tongue. Nluu is one of only three languages remaining in the world that use bilabial clicks as consonants.

Various media—the print press, radio, satellite television, Internet, and text messaging on cell phones—are driving the need for a shared language, and increasingly that is English. In the past 500 years, this language—originally spoken by about 2.5 million people living only in part of the British Isles in northwestern Europe—has spread around the world. Today some 375 million people (nearly 6 percent of the global population) claim English as their native tongue. Close to a billion others (about 15 percent of humanity) speak it as a second or foreign language.

While a common language allows people from different ethnic backgrounds to communicate, there is the risk that a global spread of one language may contribute to the disappearance of others. And with the extinction of each language, we lose "hundreds of generations of traditional knowledge encoded in these ancestral tongues"—a vast repository of knowledge about the natural world, plants, animals, ecosystems, and cultural traditions.[5] Among many examples is the inventory of 1,000 medicinal plants held in the threatened language of Kallawaya, an ancient "secret" language used by Indian herbal healers in the Bolivian highlands.

The United Nations Educational, Scientific, and Cultural Organization (UNESCO) recently marked out key factors used to assess the endangerment status of a language.[6] Beyond obvious points—such as declining numbers of

speakers, discriminatory governmental policies, illiteracy, and insufficient means for language education—a key issue is the impact electronic media such as the Internet have on language groups.

Today, Internet content exists in only a handful of languages, and 84 percent of Internet users are native speakers of just ten of the world's 7,000 languages. On one hand, there is the serious risk that the overwhelming presence of a few already dominant languages on the Internet further threatens endangered languages. On the other hand, the Internet offers a powerful tool for maintaining and revitalizing disappearing languages and the cultures to which they are tied—as indicated in the ever-growing number of indigenous groups developing computer programs to help teach their native tongues.

Ensuring digital access to local content is a new and important component in language preservation efforts. In 2001, UNESCO established Initiative B@bel, which uses information and communication technologies to support linguistic and cultural diversity. Promoting multilingualism on the Internet, this initiative aims to bridge the digital divide—to make access to Internet content and services more equitable for users worldwide (Figure 5.3).

Sometimes, in reaction to a real or perceived threat of cultural dominance by powerful foreign societies, ethnic groups and even entire countries may seek to maintain or reclaim their unique identity by purging their vocabularies of "foreign" terms. Emerging as a significant force

---

[5] www.livingtongues.org/background.html.

[6] www.unesco.org/webworld/babel.

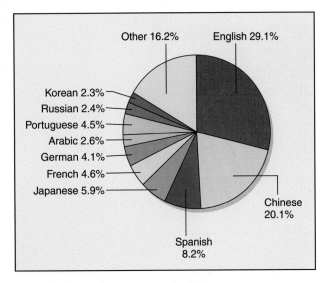

Figure 5.3 Although the world's digital divide is diminishing, it is still dramatic. As illustrated here, nearly 84 percent of today's 1.6 billion Internet users are native speakers of just ten of the world's 7,000 languages. Among the fastest-growing Internet language groups since 2005 are Arabic, Chinese, and Russian. (Source: www.internetworldstats.com, 2009)

for linguistic change, such **linguistic nationalism** is particularly characteristic of the former colonial countries of Africa and Asia today. It is by no means limited to those countries, however, as one can see by periodic French attempts to purge their language of such Americanisms as *le hamburger*. Another example of this is France's decision to substitute the word *e-mail* with the government-approved term *couriel*.

For many ethnic minorities, efforts to counter the threat of linguistic extinction or to resurrect already extinct languages form part of their struggle to maintain a sense of cultural identity and dignity. A prime means by which powerful groups try to assert their dominance over minorities living within their borders is to actively suppress their languages. Examples of this include 20th-century government-sanctioned efforts to repress Native American cultures in Canada and the United States and fully absorb them into mainstream society. Government policies included taking Indian children away from their parents and putting them in boarding schools where only English was allowed, and students were often punished for speaking their traditional

---

linguistic nationalism The attempt by ethnic minorities and even countries to proclaim independence by purging their language of foreign terms.

sociolinguistics The study of the relationship between language and society through examining how social categories (such as age, gender, ethnicity, religion, occupation, and class) influence the use and significance of distinctive styles of speech.

gendered speech Distinct male and female speech patterns, which vary across social and cultural settings.

---

languages. Upon returning to their homes, many could no longer communicate with their own close relatives and neighbors.

While now abolished, these institutions and the historical policies that shaped them did lasting damage to American Indian groups striving to maintain their cultural heritage. Especially over the past three decades many of these besieged indigenous communities have been actively involved in language revitalization efforts. Among numerous examples of this is the work of S. Neyooxet Greymorning, a Southern Arapaho, who has devoted three decades to developing and implementing ways to revive indigenous languages, including his own. Greymorning, a professor of anthropology and Native American studies at the University of Montana, tells his story in the Anthropology Applied feature.

Language in Its Social and Cultural Settings

As discussed in the section on descriptive linguistics, language is not simply a matter of combining sounds according to certain rules to come up with meaningful utterances. It is important to remember that languages are spoken by people who are members of distinct societies. In addition to the fact that most societies have their own unique cultures, individuals within each society tend to vary in the ways they use language based on social factors such as gender, age, class, and ethnicity.

We choose words and sentences to communicate meaning, and what is meaningful in one community or culture may not be in another. Our use of language reflects, and is reflected by, the rest of our culture. For that reason, linguistic anthropologists also research language in relation to its various distinctive social and cultural contexts. This third branch of linguistic study falls into two categories: sociolinguistics and ethnolinguistics.

Sociolinguistics

Sociolinguistics, the study of the relationship between language and society, examines how social categories (such as age, gender, ethnicity, religion, occupation, and class) influence the use and significance of distinctive styles of speech.

LANGUAGE AND GENDER

As a major factor in personal and social identity, gender is often reflected in language use, so it is not surprising that numerous thought-provoking sociolinguistic topics fall under the category of language and gender. These include research on **gendered speech**—distinct male and

When Bambi Spoke Arapaho: Preserving Indigenous Languages

by S. Neyooxet Greymorning

In life, there are experiences later recognized as defining moments. For me, a moment like that happened in my second year of college when some mysterious individual stood over me and asked, "What are you doing to help your people?" I remember getting up, going to the library, and walking along the stacks. Trailing my fingers over books, I randomly stopped and pulled one out. It was about the overall status of American Indian languages in the United States. Curious, I opened it, looked up Arapaho, and read that it was among the healthiest Native languages. Comforted by this, it didn't occur to me that a rapidly dwindling number of young Arapaho speakers was signaling the demise of my ancestral tongue. Years later when I told tribal Elder Francis Brown about this, he said, "The Elders called your name."

Perhaps they continued to call. When I went on to graduate school and studied anthropology, I felt driven to take almost every linguistic class available. By 1981, I understood that to lose a language is to lose aspects of how a people make sense of themselves and the world they live in, and the values that culturally and psychologically bind a people together shaping their identity. Feeling the need to do something, I decided to spend the summer on the Wind River Reservation in central Wyoming putting together an Arapaho dictionary. Then I learned that University of Massachusetts professor Dr. Zdeněk Salzmann, a Czech anthropologist who did linguistic work with the Arapaho, had the same idea. I called him, and he suggested we work together.

As a graduate student I dedicated myself to gaining the knowledge, skills, and experience that could contribute to revitalizing languages. Upon completing my doctorate, 1992, I was invited to direct a language and culture program on the Wind River Reservation where Arapaho language instruction had been introduced within the public school system in the late 1970s. By 1993, although Arapaho was taught from kindergarten–high school, my assessment revealed students were only able to say a few basic phrases and vocabulary words having to do with

Courtesy of S. Neyooxet Greymorning

food, animals, colors, and numbers—nothing near fluency and the goal of keeping Arapaho alive.

Recognizing the need for a different approach, I began laying the groundwork to establish one of the first full-day language immersion preschools on a reservation: Hinono'eitiino'oowu'—the Arapaho Language Lodge. The aim was for language "providers" to only speak Arapaho and use a multifaceted approach that included not only word and phrase acquisition, but also response exercises, visual association, and interaction with videos and audio cassettes of songs.

Around this time I contacted Disney Studios and convinced them to allow us to translate *Bambi* into Arapaho as a learning aid.[a] *Bambi* seemed like a good choice because it echoed traditional stories in which animals speak, it was a story that most children on the reservation knew, and as the story unfolds Bambi uses simple childlike language as he learns to talk.

However, even a multifaceted approach that included Bambi speaking Arapaho was not turning the tide of language demise, so I began to think through the challenges with increased focus. From 1996–2002 I gradually developed a new approach, Accelerated Second Language Acquisition (ASLA©™). During 2003, using

my children as language learners, I tested and honed ASLA into a workable methodology that helps re-tune the brain so people learn to visualize the language rather than continually translate back and forth in their minds between the language they know and the one they're learning.

In an effort to encourage language teachers on the reservation to adopt this approach, I have modeled teaching Arapaho through ASLA at the University of Montana with remarkable results. Beyond efforts to help preserve Arapaho, I'm regularly asked to give ASLA workshops for others who are committed to Indigenous language revitalization. To date, I have had contact with over 1,200 individual language instructors from more than 60 different communities in the US, Canada, and Australia, representing over 40 different languages.[b]

The challenge of preserving languages (and the countless keys to life that each one holds) is daunting in our age of globalization. But something my uncle told me during a boyhood visit with him encourages me to be counted among those who keep trying. He woke me at dawn and took me to a pond. There was no wind, and the water was like glass. After instructing me to pick up a small stone, he said, "Now drop it in the pond and tell me what you see." Releasing the stone, I watched it make ever-widening circles on the water. "I want you to always remember," said my uncle, "that nothing is so small that it can't put something larger than itself into motion."

---

[a]See Greymorning, S. N. (2001). Reflections on the Arapaho Language Project or, when Bambi spoke Arapaho and other tales of Arapaho language revitalization efforts. In K. Hale & L. Hinton, *The green book of language revitalization in practice* (pp. 287–297). New York: Academic.

[b]For video examples of students of ASLA speaking Arapaho, plus written comments from language instructors and students about ASLA, go to www.nsilc.org.

Makers of the feature film *Dances with Wolves* aimed for cultural authenticity by casting Native American actors and hiring a female language coach to teach Lakota to those who did not know how to speak it. However, the lessons did not include the "gendered speech" aspect of Lakota—the fact that females and males follow different rules of syntax. Consequently, when Native speakers of the language saw the film, they were amused to hear the actors who portrayed the Lakota warriors speaking like women.

© Orion Pictures Corporation/Everett Collection

female speech patterns, which vary across social and cultural settings.

One of the first in-depth studies in this vein, done in the early 1970s, asserted that neither language nor gender could be studied independently of the socially constructed communities in which we live. Exploring the relationship of gender and power, it addressed specific issues including social factors said to contribute to North American women exhibiting less decisive speech styles than men. This study and a subsequent wave of related scholarly works have produced new insights about language as a social speech "performance" in both private and public settings.[7]

Gendered speech research also includes the study of distinct male and female syntax exhibited in various languages around the world, such as the Lakota language, still spoken at the Pine Ridge and Rosebud Indian reservations in South Dakota. When a Lakota woman asks someone, "How are you?" she says, "Tonikt*hkahe*?" But when her brother poses the same question, he says, "Tonikt*ukahwo*?" As explained by Michael Two Horses, "Our language is gender-specific in the area of commands, queries, and a couple of other things."[8]

---

[7] See Lakoff, R. T. (2004). *Language and woman's place.* M. Bucholtz (Ed.). New York: Oxford University Press.

[8] Personal communication, April 2003.

dialects Varying forms of a language that reflect particular regions, occupations, or social classes and that are similar enough to be mutually intelligible.

SOCIAL DIALECTS

Sociolinguists are also interested in **dialects**—varying forms of a language that reflect particular regions, occupations, or social classes and that are similar enough to be mutually intelligible.

Distinguishing dialects from languages and revealing the relationship between power and language, the noted linguist-political activist Noam Chomsky often quoted the saying that a dialect is a language without an army.[9] Technically, all dialects are languages—there is nothing partial or sublinguistic about them—and the point at which two different dialects become distinctly different languages is roughly the point at which speakers of one are almost totally unable to communicate with speakers of the other.

Boundaries may be psychological, geographic, social, or economic, and they are not always very sharp. In the case of regional dialects, there is frequently a transitional territory, or perhaps a buffer zone, where features of both are found and understood, as between central and southern China. The fact is that if you learn the Chinese of Beijing, you will find that a Chinese person from Canton or Hong Kong will understand almost nothing of what you say, although both languages—or dialects—are usually lumped together as Chinese.

A classic example of the kind of dialect that may set one group apart from others within a single society is one

---

[9] See biographical entry for Chomsky in Shook, J. R., et al. (Eds.). (2004). *Dictionary of modern American philosophers, 1860–1960.* Bristol, England: Thoemmes Press. The saying is attributed to Yiddish linguist Max Weinreich.

TV Biggest culprit

spoken by many inner-city African Americans. Technically known as African American Vernacular English (AAVE), it has often been referred to as "black English" and "Ebonics." Unfortunately, there is a widespread misperception among non-AAVE speakers that this dialect is somehow substandard or defective. A basic principle of linguistics is that the selection of a so-called prestige dialect—in this case, what we may call Standard English as opposed to AAVE—is determined by social and historical forces such as wealth and power and is not dependent on virtues or shortcomings of the dialects themselves. In fact, AAVE is a highly structured mode of speech with patterned rules of sounds and sequences like any other language or dialect. Many of its distinctive features stem from the retention of sound patterns, grammatical rules concerning verbs, and even words of the West African languages spoken by the ancestors of present-day African Americans.[10]

In many societies where different dialects are spoken, individuals often become skilled at switching back and forth between them, depending on the situation in which they are speaking. Without being conscious of it, we all do the same sort of thing when we switch from formality to informality in our speech, depending upon where we are and to whom we are talking. The process of changing from one language mode to another as the situation demands, whether from one language to another or from one dialect of a language to another, is known as **code switching,** and it has been the subject of a number of sociolinguistic studies.

Ethnolinguistics

The study of the relationships between language and culture, and how they mutually influence and inform each other, is the domain of **ethnolinguistics.**

LINGUISTIC RELATIVITY

In this type of research, anthropologists may investigate how a language reflects the culturally significant aspects of a people's traditional natural environment. Among the Inuit in the Canadian Arctic, for instance, we find numerous words for different types of snow, whereas Americans in a city like Detroit most likely possess a rich vocabulary allowing them to precisely distinguish between many different types of cars, categorized by model, year, and manufacturer. This is an example of **linguistic relativity**—the idea that distinctions encoded in one language are unique to that language.

Another example concerns cultural categories of color. Languages have different ways of dividing and naming elements of the color spectrum, which is actually a continuum of multiple hues with no clear-cut boundaries between them. In English we speak of red, orange, yellow, green, blue, indigo, and violet, but other languages mark out different groupings. For instance, Indians in Mexico's northwestern mountains speaking Tarahumara have just one word for both "green" and "blue"—*siyoname.*

LINGUISTIC DETERMINISM

Related to linguistic relativity is the principle of **linguistic determinism**—the idea that language to some extent shapes the way in which people view and think about the world around them. An extreme version of this principle holds that language actually determines thought and thereby shapes behavior and culture itself. A more widely accepted view holds that thought is merely influenced by language.

Linguistic determinism is associated with the pioneering ethnolinguistic research of anthropologist Edward Sapir and his student Benjamin Lee Whorf during the 1930s and 1940s. Their research resulted in what is now known as the *Sapir-Whorf hypothesis:* Each language provides particular grooves of linguistic expression that predispose speakers of that language to perceive the world in a certain way. In Whorf's own words, "The structure of the language one habitually uses influences the manner in which one understands his environment. The picture of the universe shifts from tongue to tongue."[11]

Whorf gained many of these insights while translating English into Hopi, a North American Indian language still spoken in Arizona. Doing this work, he discovered that Hopi differs from English not only in vocabulary but also in terms of its grammatical categories such as nouns and

[10] Monaghan, L., Hinton, L., & Kephart, R. (1997). Can't teach a dog to be a cat? The dialogue on ebonics. *Anthropology Newsletter 38* (3), 1, 8, 9.

[11] Quoted in Hoebel, E. A. (1958). *Man in the primitive world: An introduction to anthropology* (p. 571). New York: McGraw-Hill.

code switching Changing from one mode of speech to another as the situation demands, whether from one language to another or from one dialect of a language to another.

ethnolinguistics A branch of linguistics that studies the relationships between language and culture and how they mutually influence and inform each other.

linguistic relativity The idea that distinctions encoded in one language are unique to that language.

linguistic determinism The idea that language to some extent shapes the way in which we view and think about the world around us.

verbs. For instance, Hopi use numbers for counting and measuring things that have physical existence, but they do not apply numbers in the same way to abstractions like time. They would have no problem translating an English sentence such as, "I see fifteen sheep grazing on three acres of grassland," but an equally simple sentence such as, "Three weeks ago, I enjoyed my fifteen minutes of fame" would require a much more complex translation into Hopi.

It is also of note that Hopi verbs express tenses differently than English verbs. Rather than marking past, present, and future, with -*ed*, -*ing*, or *will*, Hopi requires additional words to indicate if an event is completed, is still ongoing, or is expected to take place. So instead of saying, "Three strangers stayed for fifteen days in our village," a Hopi would say something like, "We remember three strangers stay in our village until the sixteenth day." In addition, Hopi verbs do not express tense by their forms. Unlike English verbs that change form to indicate past, present, and future, Hopi verbs distinguish among a statement of fact (if the speaker actually witnesses a certain event), a statement of expectation, and a statement that expresses regularity. For instance, when you ask an English-speaking athlete "Do you run?" he may answer "Yes," when in fact he may at that moment be sitting in an armchair watching TV. A Hopi athlete asked the same question in his own language might respond "No," because in Hopi the statement of fact "he runs" translates as *wari* ("running occurs"), whereas the statement that expresses regularity—"he runs" (such as, on the track team)—translates as *warikngwe* ("running occurs characteristically").

This shows that the Hopi language structures thinking and behavior with a focus on the present—on getting ready and carrying out what needs to be done right now. Whorf summed it up like this: "A characteristic of Hopi behavior is the emphasis on preparation. This includes announcing and getting ready for events well beforehand, elaborate precautions to insure persistence of desired conditions, and stress on good will as the preparer of good results."[12]

In the 1990s linguistic anthropologists devised new research strategies to actually test Sapir and Whorf's original hypothesis.[13] One study found that speakers of Swedish and Finnish (neighboring peoples who speak radically different languages) working at similar jobs in similar regions under similar laws and regulations show significantly different rates of on-the-job accidents. The rates are substantially lower among the Swedish speakers.

What emerges from comparison of the two languages is that Swedish (one of the Indo-European languages) emphasizes information about movement in three-dimensional space. Finnish (a Ural-Altaic language unrelated to Indo-European languages) emphasizes more static relations among coherent temporal entities. As a consequence, it seems that Finns organize the workplace in a way that favors the individual person over the temporal organization in the overall production process. This in turn leads to frequent production disruptions, haste, and (ultimately) accidents.

A more obvious ethnolinguistic observation is that language mirrors or reflects, rather than determines, cultural reality. Aymara Indians living in the Bolivian highlands, for example, depend on the potato (or *luki*) as their major source of food. Their language has over 200 words for potatoes, reflecting the many varieties they traditionally grow and the many different ways that they preserve and prepare this food. Similarly, anthropologists have noted that the language of the Nuer, a nomadic African people of southern Sudan, is rich in words and expressions having to do with cattle; not only are more than 400 words used to describe cattle, but Nuer boys actually take their names from them. By studying the language, we can determine the significance of cattle in Nuer culture and the whole etiquette of human and cattle relationships.

If language does mirror cultural reality, it would follow that changes in a culture will sooner or later be reflected in changes in the language. We see this happening all around the world today, including in the English language.

Linguists have found that although language is generally flexible and adaptable, established terminologies do tend to perpetuate themselves, reflecting and revealing the social structure and worldview of groups and people. For example, American English has a wide array of words having to do with conflict and warfare. It also features an abundance of militaristic metaphors, such as "conquering" space, "fighting" the "battle" of the bulge, carrying out a "war" against drugs, making a "killing" on the stock market, "shooting down" an argument, "torpedoing" a plan, "spearheading" a movement, "decapitating" a foreign government, or "bombing" on an exam, to mention just a few. An observer from a different and perhaps less aggressive culture, such as the Hopi in Arizona or the Jain in India, could gain considerable insight into the importance of open competition, winning, and military might in the United States simply by paying attention to such commonly used phrases.

[12] Carroll, J. B. (Ed.). (1956). *Language, thought and reality: Selected writings of Benjamin Lee Whorf* (p. 148). Cambridge, MA: MIT Press.

[13] Lucy, J. A. (1997). Linguistic relativity. *Annual Review of Anthropology 26*, 291–312.

Aymara Indians living in the highlands of Bolivia and Peru in South America depend on the potato as their major source of food. Their language has over 200 words for this vegetable, reflecting the many varieties they traditionally grow and the many different ways they preserve and prepare it.

Language Versatility

In many societies throughout the world, it is not unusual for individuals to be fluent in two, three, or more languages. They succeed in this in large part because they experience training in multiple languages as children—not as high school or college students, which is the educational norm in the United States.

In some regions where groups speaking different languages coexist and interact, people often understand one another but may choose not to speak the other's language. Such is the case in the borderlands of northern Bolivia and southern Peru where Quechua-speaking and Aymara-speaking Indians are neighbors. When an Aymara farmer speaks to a Quechua herder in Aymara, the Quechua will reply in Quechua, and vice versa, each knowing that the other understands both languages even if speaking just one. The ability to comprehend two languages but express oneself in only one is known as *receptive* or *passive bilingualism*.

In the United States, perhaps reflecting the country's enormous size and power, many citizens are not interested in learning a second or foreign language. This is especially significant—and troubling—since the United States is not only one of the world's most ethnically diverse countries, but also the world's largest economy and heavily dependent on international trade relations. In our globalized world, being bilingual or multilingual may open doors of communication not only for trade but for work, diplomacy, art, and friendship. Ironically, reluctance to learn another language prevails in the United States despite the fact that the majority language in the Americas is not English but Spanish; Spanish is not only the majority language of the hemisphere but also the fastest-growing language in the United States.

Beyond Words: The Gesture-Call System

As efficient as they are at naming and talking about ideas, actions, and things, all languages are to some degree inadequate at communicating certain kinds of information that people need to know in order to fully understand what is being said. For this reason, human speech is always embedded within a *gesture-call system* of a type that we share with nonhuman primates.

The various sounds and gestures of this system serve to "key" speech, providing listeners with the appropriate frame for interpreting what a speaker is saying. Messages about human emotions and intentions are effectively communicated by this gesture-call system: Is the speaker happy, sad, mad, enthusiastic, tired, or in some other emotional state? Is he or she requesting information, denying something, reporting factually, or lying? Very little of this information is conveyed by spoken language alone. In English, for example, at least 90 percent of emotional information is transmitted not by the words spoken but by body language and tone of voice.

Body Language

The **gesture** component of the gesture-call system consists of facial expressions and body postures and motions that convey intended as well as subconscious messages. The method for notating and analyzing this body language is known as **kinesics**.

Humanity's repertoire of body language is enormous. This is evident if you consider just one aspect of it: the fact that a human being has about fifty facial muscles and is thereby capable of making more than 7,000 facial expressions! Thus it should not be surprising to hear that at least 60 percent of our total communication takes place nonverbally. Often, gestural messages complement spoken messages—for instance, nodding the head while affirming something verbally, raising eyebrows when asking a question, or using hands and fingers to illustrate or emphasize what is being talked about. However, nonverbal signals are sometimes at odds with verbal ones, and they have the power to override or undercut them. For example, a person may say the words "I love you" a thousand times to someone, but if the person does not mean it, the nonverbal signals will likely communicate that falseness.

Little scientific notice was taken of body language prior to the 1950s, but since then a great deal of research has been devoted to this intriguing subject. Cross-cultural studies in this field have shown that there are many similarities around the world in such basic facial expressions as smiling, laughing, crying, and displaying shock or anger. The smirks, frowns, and gasps that we have inherited from our primate ancestry require little learning and are harder to fake than conventional or socially obtained gestures that are shared by members of a group, albeit not always consciously so.

Routine greetings are also similar around the world. Europeans, Balinese, Papuans, Samoans, Bushmen, and at least some South American Indians all smile and nod, and if the individuals are especially friendly, they will raise their eyebrows with a rapid movement, keeping them raised for a fraction of a second. By doing so, they signal a readiness for contact. The Japanese, however, suppress the eyebrow flash, regarding it as indecent. This example illustrates that there are important differences, as well as similarities, cross-culturally.

Another example can be found in gestural expressions for yes and no. In North America, one nods the head down then up for yes or shakes it left and right for no. The people of Sri Lanka also nod to answer yes to a factual question, but if asked to do something, a slow sideways movement of the head means yes. In Greece, the nodded head means yes, but no is indicated by jerking the head back so as to lift the face, usually with the eyes closed and the eyebrows raised.

Another aspect of body language has to do with social space: how people position themselves physically in relation to others. **Proxemics,** the cross-cultural study of social space, came to the fore through the work of anthropologist Edward Hall (1914–2009), who coined the term. Growing up in the culturally diverse southwestern United States, Hall glimpsed the complexities of intercultural relations early on in life. As a young man in the 1930s, he worked with construction crews of Hopi and Navajo Indians, building roads and dams. In 1942 he earned his doctorate in anthropology under the famous Franz Boas, who stressed that communication is the core of culture.

During World War II, Hall commanded an African American regiment in Europe and the Philippines, and in the early 1950s, he worked with the U.S. State Department to develop the new field of intercultural communication at the Foreign Service Institute. While training some 2,000 Foreign Service workers, his ideas about nonverbal communication began to crystallize. He articulated them in his 1959 book *The Silent Language,* now recognized as the founding document for the field of intercultural communication.

Hall's research showed that people from different cultures have different frameworks for defining and organizing social space—the personal space they establish around their bodies, as well as the macrolevel sensibilities that shape cultural expectations about how streets, neighborhoods, and cities should be arranged. Among other things, his investigation of personal space revealed that every culture has distinctive norms for closeness. (You can see this for yourself if you are watching a foreign film, visiting a foreign country,

---

gestures Facial expressions and body postures and motions that convey intended as well as subconscious messages.

kinesics A system of notating and analyzing postures, facial expressions, and body motions that convey messages.

proxemics The cross-cultural study of people's perception and use of space.

Visual Counterpoint

Cultures around the world have noticeably different attitudes concerning proxemics or personal space—how far apart people should be positioned in nonintimate social encounters. How does the gap between the U.S. businessmen pictured here compare with that of the robed men of Saudi Arabia?

or taking part in a multicultural group. How close to one another do people stand when talking in the street or riding in a subway or elevator? Does the pattern match the one you are accustomed to in your own cultural corner?)

Hall identified the range of cultural variation in four categories of proxemically relevant social spaces: intimate (0–18 inches), personal-casual (1½–4 feet), social-consultive (4–12 feet), and public distance (12 feet and beyond). Hall warned that different cultural definitions of socially accepted use of space within these categories can lead to serious miscommunication and misunderstanding in cross-cultural settings. His research has been fundamental for the present-day training of international businesspeople, diplomats, and others involved in intercultural work.

Paralanguage

The second component of the gesture-call system is **paralanguage**—specific voice effects that accompany speech and contribute to communication. These include vocalizations such as giggling, groaning, or sighing, as well as voice qualities such as volume, intensity, pitch, and tempo.

The importance of paralanguage is suggested by the comment, "It's not so much *what* was said as *how* it was said." Obviously, whispering or shouting can make a big difference in meaning, even though the uttered words would be the same when written down. Minor differences in pitch, tempo, and phrasing may seem less obvious, but they still impact how words are perceived. Studies show, for example, that even *subliminal* messages, which are communicated

below the threshold of conscious perception, can be far more important in courtroom proceedings than even the most perceptive trial lawyer may have realized. Among other things, *how* a witness gives testimony alters the reception it gets from jurors and influences the witness's credibility.[14]

Communication has changed radically over the past two decades with the rise of e-mail, text messaging, and instant messaging. These technologies resemble the spontaneity and speed of face-to-face communication but lack the body signals and voice qualifiers that nuance what is being said (and hint at how it is being received). According to a recent study, the intended tone of e-mail messages is perceived correctly only 56 percent of the time.[15] Misunderstood messages can quickly create problems and even hostility. Because the risk of miscommunication with these technologies abounds, certain sensitive exchanges are better made in person.

---

[14] O'Barr, W. M., & Conley, J. M. (1993). When a juror watches a lawyer. In W. A. Haviland & R. J. Gordon (Eds.), *Talking about people* (2nd ed., pp. 42–45). Mountain View, CA: Mayfield.

[15] Kruger, J., et al. (2005, December). Egocentrism over e-mail: Can people communicate as well as they think? *Journal of Personality and Social Psychology 89* (6), 925–936.

paralanguage Voice effects that accompany language and convey meaning. These include vocalizations such as giggling, groaning, or sighing, as well as voice qualities such as pitch and tempo.

Tonal Languages

Beyond communicating emotions, voice tones—rises and falls in pitch—may encode a much wider range of meanings. This brings us to so-called **tonal languages** in which the various distinctive sound pitches of spoken words not only are an essential part of their pronunciation but are also central to their meaning. In addition to hundreds of vowels and consonants, sounds can be divided into tones that play a fundamental role in distinguishing one word from another. Worldwide, at least one-third of humanity speaks a tonal language. About 70 percent of the world's languages are tonal, including many in Africa, Central America, and East Asia.

For example, Mandarin Chinese, the most common language in China, has four contrasting tones: flat, rising, falling, and falling then rising. These tones are used to distinguish among normally stressed syllables that are otherwise identical. So, depending on intonation, *ba* can mean "to uproot," "to hold," "eight," or "a harrow" (farm tool).[16] Cantonese, the primary language in southern China and Hong Kong, uses six contrasting tones, and some Chinese dialects have as many as nine.

In nontonal languages such as English, tone can be used to convey an attitude or to change a statement into a question. But tone alone does not change the meaning of individual words as it does in Mandarin, where careless use of tones with the syllable *ma* could cause one to call someone's mother a horse!

Telecommunication: Talking Drums and Whistled Speech

When told that friends live within shouting distance, one might assume that their home is within easy reach. After all, even a very loud human voice has its natural limits beyond which our ears cannot pick up the sound. Of course, sounds carry farther in some environments than in others. When shouting to each other in a canyon or rocky valley, for example, people can communicate across much greater distances than in a thick forest where sounds are quickly

---

[16] Catford, J. C. (1988). *A practical introduction to phonetics* (p. 183). Oxford, England: Clarendon.

tonal language A language in which the sound pitch of a spoken word is an essential part of its pronunciation and meaning.

whistled speech An exchange of whistled words using a phonetic emulation of the sounds produced in spoken voice; also known as whistled language.

Whistled speech, occurring in about thirty languages around the world, allows community members to exchange essential information in an abridged form of everyday spoken language. Here we see two people engaged in whistled speech: Elaine Kingeekuk, a Siberian Yupik speaker from St. Lawrence Island, Alaska, and Juan Casimiro Nava, a Mazatec speaker from Oaxaca, Mexico. Both are retired schoolteachers, assisting French linguist Julien Meyer in documenting their whistled languages.

swallowed up. But until the telecommunication inventions of the 19th century, acoustic space was limited by natural factors.

Yet, long before the invention of these modern devices, people found ways to expand their acoustic range, sounding information far beyond their loudest vocal reach. One fascinating example is the *talking drum* (also known as the *signaling drum* or *tambour-téléphone*). Widespread among tonal-speaking peoples in West Africa, these large, wooden slit drums can transmit coded information that can be heard from as far away as 12 kilometers (7½ miles)—well beyond human shouting range. On the periphery or at the outer range limit, messages can be picked up and relayed by drum again until all the villages in the district have received it.

Another traditional telecommunication system used to expand acoustic space is **whistled speech,** or whistled language—an exchange of whistled words using a phonetic emulation of the sounds produced in spoken voice.[17] Whistling does not involve vocal cords. Instead, sounds are generated by blowing, producing air vibrations at the mouth's aperture; the faster the air stream, the higher the noise. Whistled speech can be more effective across greater

---

[17] Meyer, J., Meunier, F., & Dentel, L. (2007). Identification of natural whistled vowels by non-whistlers. *Proceedings of Interspeech 2007* (pp. 1593–1596). Antwerpen, Belgium.

distances than shouted talk because it occurs at a higher pitch or frequency range and takes place primarily in the narrow bandwidth (2,500–3,000 Hz) where the human ear has a peak response. Also, because whistling overcomes other noises in the environment more effectively than the human voice, it retains a higher level of intelligibility as the distance of communication increases. In short, whistling has a greater range of audibility than talking.

Whistling techniques vary. Some involve both lips (bilabial). Others involve lips and teeth (labiodental), or the mouth roof and tongue tip, or a retroflexed tongue with various finger combinations. In particular, two-finger whistling can produce very loud sounds, and in a ravine can be picked up by the human ear from as far away as 8 kilometers (5 miles).

Whistling lends itself to playing with melodies, and whistled speech may have developed from the whistling of purely musical phrases. While its precise origins are not known, whistled speech still occurs in more than thirty languages around the world.

Typically dealing with the recurring concerns and activities of people who share a culture, whistled speech allows members of a community to exchange essential information in an abridged form of everyday spoken language. Encoding that information in what might be described as a whistled shorthand, the vocabulary can be considerable. In Silbo, for instance, traditionally used by Spanish-speaking inhabitants of La Gomera off the northwest African coast, islanders can whistle some 2,000 words.

For obvious reasons, whistled speech occurs more often in tonal languages. Bilabial and labiodental techniques in particular lend themselves to short and medium-distance discussions. Such is the case with Yupik Eskimos of St. Lawrence Island, who may have felt the need to develop whistled speech to aid them when kayaking through dense fog or hunting in snow fields. A similar environmental factor may have inspired the Piraha, a small Amazonian Indian community: When hunting in the thick rainforest where visibility is limited, they communicate by whistling their melodious language, in a rhythmic succession of tones varying in pitch and duration.

Like the talking drum, whistled speech is an endangered tradition—disappearing in part because the communities where the practice once thrived are no longer isolated or because the ancestral lifeways are vanishing or already gone. Moreover, the ever-expanding reach of mobile phones and other electronic telecommunication technologies has contributed to the demise of whistled language.[18]

The Origins of Language

Cultures all around the world have sacred stories or myths addressing the age-old question of the origins of human language. Anthropologists collecting these stories have often found that cultural groups tend to locate the place of origin in their own ancestral homelands and believe that

---

[18] Meyer J., & Gautheron, B. (2006). Whistled speech and whistled languages. In K. Brown (Ed.), *Encyclopedia of language & linguistics* (2nd ed., vol. 13, pp. 573–576). Oxford, England: Elsevier; Meyer, J. (2008). Typology and acoustic strategies of whistled languages: Phonetic comparison and perceptual cues of whistled vowels. *Journal of the International Phonetic Association 38*, 69–94.

The unfinished Tower of Babel, described in the first book of the Bible, symbolizes an ancient West Asian myth about the origins of language diversity. According to this story, a united people speaking one language, set out to build a tower to signify their power and link earth to heaven. Angered by their pride, their god, Yaweh, stopped the effort by confusing their languages and scattering them across the globe.

the first humans also spoke their language. For example, the Incas of Peru told the story of Pacha Camac ("Earth Maker"), the divine creator, who came to the valley of Tiwanaku in the Andean highlands in ancient times and drew people up from the earth—creating from clay a person of each nation, painting each with particular clothing, and giving each a language to speak and songs to sing.

On the other side of the globe, ancient Israelites believed that it was Yahweh, the divine creator, who had given them Hebrew, the original tongue spoken in paradise. Later, when humans began building the high Tower of Babel to signify their own power and to link earth and heaven, Yahweh intervened. He created a confusion of tongues so that people could no longer understand one another, and he scattered them all across the face of the earth, leaving the massive tower unfinished.

Early scientific efforts to explain the origin of language suffered from a lack of solid data. Today, there is more scientific evidence, including genetic information, to work with—better knowledge of primate brains, new studies of primate communication, more information on the development of linguistic competence in children, more human fossils that can be used to tentatively reconstruct what ancient brains and vocal tracts were like, and a better understanding of the lifeways of early human ancestors. We still cannot conclusively prove how, when, and where human language first developed, but we can now theorize reasonably on the basis of more and better information.

The archaeological record shows that the archaic humans known as Neandertals (living from 30,000 to 125,000 years ago in Europe and southwestern Asia) had the neurological and anatomical features necessary for speech. Fossilized brain casts from earlier members of the genus *Homo* provide evidence of specializations in the left hemisphere of the brain and associated with the development of language. In addition, the observation that the earliest stone tools were made predominantly by right-handed individuals also supports the idea that lateral specialization had occurred by this time.

Because human language is embedded within a gesture-call system of a type that we share with nonhuman primates (especially great apes), anthropologists have gained considerable insight into human language by observing the communication systems of fellow primates, as we saw in the Original Study about Chantek at the beginning of the chapter. Like humans, apes are capable of referring to events removed in time and space, a phenomenon known as **displacement** and one of the distinctive features of human language.[19]

Since there is continuity between gestural and spoken language, the latter could have emerged from the former through increasing emphasis on finely controlled movements of the mouth and throat. This scenario is consistent

---

[19] For a discussion covering thirty years of chimpanzee sign language studies and some neurological and behavioral data accounting for the similarity between human and nonhuman communication systems, see Fouts, R. S., & Waters, G. (2001). Chimpanzee sign language and Darwinian continuity: Evidence for a neurology continuity of language. *Neurological Research 23,* 787–794.

displacement Referring to things and events removed in time and space.

Several species of apes have been taught to use American Sign Language. Some chimpanzees have acquired signing vocabularies surpassing 400 words, and a lowland gorilla named Koko has a working vocabulary of more than 1,000 words.

© Susan Kuklin/Photo Researchers, Inc.

with the appearance of neurological structures underlying language in the earliest representatives of the genus *Homo* and steady enlargement of the human brain 200,000 to 2.5 million years ago. The soft tissues of the vocal tract related to speech are not preserved in the fossil record. But as outlined in the Biocultural Connection, a comparison of the vocal anatomy of chimps and humans allows paleoanthropologists to identify the anatomical differences responsible for human speech that appeared over the course of human evolution.[20]

[20] Leading evolutionary theorist Philip Lieberman argues that human language ability is the confluence of a succession of separate evolutionary developments rigged together by natural selection for an evolutionarily unique ability. See Lieberman, P. (2006). *Toward an evolutionary biology of language.* Cambridge, MA: Belknap.

Biocultural Connection

The Biology of Human Speech

While other primates have shown some capacity for language (a socially agreed upon code of communication), actual speech is unique to humans; this ability is linked to humans' distinct anatomical development of the vocal organs.

Of particular importance are the positions of the human larynx (voice box) and the epiglottis. The larynx, situated in the respiratory tract between the pharynx (throat) and trachea (wind pipe), contains the vocal chords. The epiglottis is the structure that separates the esophagus or food pipe from the wind pipe as food passes from the mouth to the stomach. (See the figure for comparative diagrams of the anatomy of this region in chimps and humans.)

As humans mature and develop the neurological and muscular coordination for speech, the larynx and epiglottis shift to a downward position. The human tongue bends at the back of the throat and is attached to the pharynx, the region of the throat where the food and airways share a common path. Sound occurs as air exhaled from the lungs passes over the vocal cords and causes them to vibrate.

Through continuous interactive movements of the tongue, pharynx, lips, and teeth, as well as nasal passages, the sounds are alternately modified to produce speech—the uniquely patterned sounds of a particular language. Based on longstanding socially learned patterns of speech, different languages stress certain distinctive types of sounds as significant and ignore others. For instance, languages belonging to the Iroquoian family, such as Mohawk, Seneca, and Cherokee, are among the few in the world that have no bilabial stops (*b* and *p* sounds). They also lack the labiodental spirants (*f* and *v* sounds), leaving the bilabial nasal *m* sound as the only consonant requiring lip articulation.

It takes many years of practice for people to master the muscular movements needed to produce the precise sounds of any particular language. But no human could produce the finely controlled speech sounds without a lowered position of the larynx and epiglottis.

BIOCULTURAL QUESTION
Sharing a capacity for speech, humans say and understand many thousands of words. Since macaws and other parrots also learn many words, do they have speech? And if so, do they actually think?

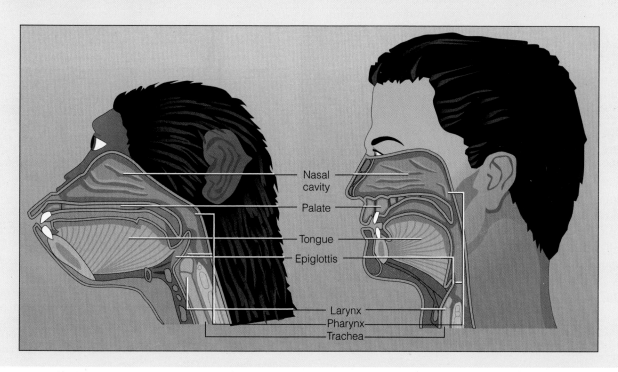

Nasal cavity
Palate
Tongue
Epiglottis
Larynx
Pharynx
Trachea

There are obvious advantages to spoken over gestural language for a species increasingly dependent on tool use for survival. To talk with one's hands, the person must stop whatever else he or she is doing with them; speech does not interfere with that. Other benefits include being able to talk in the dark, past opaque objects, or among speakers whose attention is diverted. Precisely when the changeover to spoken language took place is not known, although all would agree that spoken languages are at least as old as the species *Homo sapiens*.

Early anthropologists searched for a truly "primitive" language spoken by a living people that might show the processes of language just beginning or developing. That search has now been abandoned, for anthropologists have come to realize that there is no such thing as a "primitive" language in the world today, or even in the recent past. So far, all human languages that have been described and studied, even among people with something approximating a Stone Age technology, are highly developed, complex, and capable of expressing infinite meanings. Every language or dialect now known has a long history and has developed its own particular subtleties and complexities that reflect its speakers' way of life and what they want or need to communicate with others. Thus anthropologists recognize that all languages are more or less equally effective as systems of communication within their own particular cultural contexts.

From Speech to Writing

When anthropology developed as an academic discipline over a century ago, it concentrated its attention on small traditional communities that relied primarily on personal interaction and oral communication for survival. Cultures that depend on talking and listening often have rich traditions of storytelling and speechmaking, which play a central role in education, conflict resolution, political decision making, spiritual or supernatural practices, and many other aspects of life.

Traditional orators (from the Latin *orare*, "to speak") are usually trained from the time they are young. Their memorization skills are often enhanced by rhyme, rhythm, and melody. Orators may also employ special objects to help them remember—notched sticks, knotted strings, bands embroidered with shells, and so forth. Traditional Iroquois Indian orators often performed their formal speeches with wampum belts made of hemp string with white and bluish-purple shell beads woven into distinctive

writing system A set of visible or tactile signs used to represent units of language in a systematic way.

patterns symbolizing important messages or agreements, including treaties with other nations.

Thousands of languages, past and present, have existed only in spoken form, but many others have been documented in visual graphic symbols of some sort. Over time, simplified pictures of things (pictographs) and ideas (ideographs) evolved into more stylized symbolic forms.

Although different peoples invented a variety of graphic styles, anthropologists distinguish an actual **writing system** as a set of visible or tactile signs used to represent units of language in a systematic way. Recently discovered symbols carved into 8,600-year-old tortoise shells found in western China may represent the world's earliest evidence of elementary writing.[21]

---

[21] Li, X., et al. (2003). The earliest writing? Sign use in the seventh millennium BC at Jiahu, Henan Province, China. *Antiquity 77*, 31–44.

Hendrick Tejonihokarawa ("Open the Door"), a Mohawk chief of the Iroquois Confederacy, holding a wampum belt made of hemp string and shell beads (quahog and whelk shells). Wampum designs were used to symbolize a variety of important messages or agreements, including treaties with other nations. (Painting is by the Dutch artist Johannes Verelst in 1710.)

A fully developed early writing system is Egyptian hieroglyphics, developed some 5,000 years ago and in use for about 3,500 years. Another very old system is *cuneiform,* an arrangement of wedge-shaped imprints developed primarily in Mesopotamia (southern Iraq), which lasted nearly as long. About two millennia after these systems were established, others began to appear, developing independently in distant locations around the world.[22]

Inscriptions discovered in Egypt's western desert suggest that our **alphabet** (a series of symbols representing the *sounds* of a language) was invented almost 4,000 years ago by Semitic-speaking peoples in that region. Inscriptions carved into a natural limestone wall alongside hundreds of Egyptian hieroglyphs show that these Semites adopted a limited number of hieroglyphs as symbols for sounds in their own language. For instance, they took the glyph for "ox" and determined that it would stand for the sound at the start of the Semitic word for "ox," which is *aleph.* (This symbol looks like the horned head of an ox—and like the letter *A* upside-down.) Likewise, they chose the Egyptian glyph for "house" to stand for the opening sound of the Semitic word for "house," which is *beth.* (This symbol looks like a two-room house—and like the letter *B* tipped back.) The result was a writing system with characters based on a selection of Egyptian glyphs but representing sounds in early Semitic. Over the next thousand years, Semitic-speaking peoples inhabiting the eastern Mediterranean, including Phoenicians, adopted this system and developed the script into a more linear form.[23]

Most of the alphabets used today descended from the Phoenician one. The Greeks adopted it about 2,800 years ago, modifying the characters to suit sounds in their own language. The word *alphabet* comes from the first two letters in the Greek writing system, *alpha* and *beta* (otherwise meaningless words in Greek). From Greece, the writing system spread to Rome. When Latin-speaking Romans expanded their empire throughout much of Europe, northern Africa, and western Asia, they used a modified Greek alphabet. From the 15th century onward, as European nations grew their trade networks and built colonial empires, the Latin alphabet spread far and wide, making it possible to mechanically reproduce writings in any human language.

Although other writing systems, such as Chinese (which routinely uses 4,000 characters, about 10 percent of the total), are used by hundreds of millions of

people, modern inventions such as the Internet continue to expand the use of the Latin alphabet as a global writing system.

Literacy and Modern Telecommunication in Our Globalizing World

Thousands of years have passed since literacy first emerged, yet today more than 800 million adults worldwide cannot read and write. Illiteracy condemns already disadvantaged people to ongoing poverty—migrant rural workers, refugees, ethnic minorities, and those living in rural backlands and urban slums throughout the world. For example, a third of India's 1 billion inhabitants cannot read and write, and 75 million children around the world are not enrolled in school.[24]

Rural women are especially disadvantaged. Once again taking India as an example, less than half of the rural women there can read and write, and in some of the northeastern districts only one in five is literate. Yet, all across the globe, including India, literacy is rising more swiftly than ever. Declaring literacy a human right, the United Nations established September 8 as International Literacy Day and proclaimed the period 2003 to 2012 as the Literacy Decade with the objective of extending literacy to all humanity.[25]

Taking a historical look at the development of literacy in European nations, we find that in the 17th century, most English, French, and German adults were illiterate. And before that time, so few had mastered the skill of writing that, for long-distance communication, illiterate people relied on someone in town who for a fee would write a dictated note or letter, or read one that had been received. And even today, there are many adults in Europe and North America who have varying competencies in reading but little or none in writing—a more difficult skill.

While many people in the world still rely on others to write and read for them, the global telecommunication revolution has reached the most remote villagers on earth. The demand for cell phones is high, even among the

---

[22] del Carmen Rodriguez Martinez, M., et al. (2006). Oldest writing in the New World. *Science 313* (5793), 1610–1614.

[23] Himmelfarb, E. J. (2000, January/February). First alphabet found in Egypt. Newsbrief. *Archaeology 53* (1).

[24] UNESCO Institute for Statistics. (2007). http://stats.uis.unesco.org.

[25] www.unesco.org/education/litdecade.

alphabet A series of symbols representing the sounds of a language arranged in a traditional order.

poor in rural backlands and urban slums—and they make long-distance communication possible without literacy. Bypassing regular landline phone networks, which have not yet reached many locations, modern telecommunication systems are now transforming the cultural fabric everywhere—thanks to satellite phones and cell phone towers powered by fossil fuel, solar, or wind. Perhaps nowhere is this truer than in India, which has the fastest growing mobile phone market in the world.

Over the last two decades, the telecommunications revolution has expanded our acoustic space to global dimensions. Hundreds of millions of people now rely on mobile phones for communication beyond natural speaking range. Many, including those who are illiterate, use these phones only for voice calls. But others also use them to download e-mails, exchange text messages, and explore the Internet.

Beyond maintaining social networks, mobile phones are also used in everyday subsistence strategies. For example, they enable tens of millions of poor rural dwellers in developing countries to locate the best prices for their produce—making it possible for growers to deal directly with district markets rather than going through intermediaries.[26]

In today's fast-changing globalizing world, the mobile phone is more than a means of communication. It has become a survival tool—perhaps nowhere more so than in Japan, which now ranks as the world's top "cellular nation." On the move and surrounded by strangers, people use their mobiles to get and give information, to express their individuality, and to stay in touch—twittering instead of whistling to avoid feeling lost in the global jungle.

<hr />

[26] See also Horst, H. A., & Miller, D. (Eds.). (2006). *The cell phone: An anthropology of communication.* New York: Berg.

© Charles Sturge/Alamy

The telecommunication revolution is reaching even the most remote places on earth thanks to satellite phones and cell phone towers powered by fossil fuel, the sun, or the wind. Those without phones of their own can often find mobile phone stands such as this one in Kampala, Uganda, in East Africa.

Questions for Reflection

1. In what ways do you feel prepared or unprepared to meet the challenge of communicating effectively in our increasingly globalized world?

2. Over 3,000 languages have disappeared over the last 500 years, most of them vanishing without a trace. Fewer than 7,000 remain. It is now estimated that about 30 languages per year will become extinct during the current century. Do you see this demise as positive or negative?

3. Applying the principle of linguistic determinism to your own language, consider how your perceptions of objective reality might have been shaped by your language. How might your sense of reality be different if you grew up speaking Hopi?

4. What distinguishes us from apes like Chantek the orangutan? What words might Chantek choose to tell us about his confined existence as a subject of scientific research?

5. Since much of our communication is nonverbal, how effective do you think text message codes like OJ (only joking), XD (excited), VSF (very sad face), or G (grin) are in digital communication when e-mailing or texting? Have your digital messages ever been misunderstood? If so, what do you think was at the root of the miscommunication, and how was it resolved?

Suggested Readings

Duranti, A. (2001). Linguistic anthropology: History, ideas, and issues. In A. Duranti (Ed.), *Linguistic anthropology: A reader* (pp. 1–38). Oxford, England: Blackwell.

A good summary of the development of the field of linguistic anthropology.

Gladdol, D. (2006). *English next.* London: British Council.

A fascinating overview of the rise of English as a global language—and the socioeconomic problems this spread presents to monolingual English-speaking people. (free PDF available online)

Harrison, K. D. (2008). *When languages die: The extinction of the world's languages and the erosion of human knowledge.* New York: Oxford University Press.

This compelling and thought-provoking catalogue of disappearing languages all around the world reveals, case by case, the great loss of human knowledge that accompanies their demise—knowledge about the natural world, cultural heritage, plus our understanding of the capacities of the human mind.

Lieberman, P. (2006). *Toward an evolutionary biology of language.* Cambridge, MA: Belknap.

A leading evolutionary theorist of language draws on evidence from evolutionary biology, genetics, physical anthropology, anatomy, and neuroscience.

Morse, D., et al. (1979). *Gestures: Their origins and distribution.* New York: Stein & Day.

This well-illustrated text explores the derivations and distributions of dozens of gestures, as well as the varied meanings they have in different parts of the world.

Yip, M. (2002). *Tone.* New York: Cambridge University Press.

A comprehensive and clearly organized introduction to tone and tonal phonology, covering the main types of tonal systems found in Africa, the Americas, and Asia.

Challenge Issue Every society faces the challenge of humanizing its children, teaching them the values, social codes, and skills that will enable them to be functioning and contributing members in the community. This is vital, for it helps ensure that the society will perpetuate itself culturally as well as biologically. Most traditional communities raise children in ways that condition them for their future social status as adult men and women—making sure they have the appropriate appearance, apparel, attitude, and other culturally significant features that indicate gender differences. (A good number also provide cultural models for an alternative gender role.) This photo shows a Kazakh father and son setting out on a hunting expedition with a golden eagle in the Altai Mountains of western Mongolia. Kazakhs are semi-nomadic herders living in northern Central Asia (especially Kazakhstan, but also in western Mongolia and parts of Uzbekistan, China, and Russia). For centuries, they have trained golden eagles to partner them in hunting rabbit, marmot, fox, and even wolf—primarily for fur. They refer to this mighty bird of prey as a *berkut* and to the man who hunts with them as a *berkutchi*. Eagle hunting is a male tradition. Boys learn from their fathers and uncles how to capture, raise, train, and confidently handle an eagle from fledgling to maturity; how to ride high and proud on their horse stirrups with this huge raptor on their arm; when and how to release the bird to pursue the prey; and how to gallop across the steppes as fast as the wind to claim it.

CHAPTER 6

Social Identity, Personality, and Gender

Chapter Preview

What Is Enculturation?

Enculturation is the process by which culture is passed from one generation to the next and through which individuals become members of their society. This process begins soon after birth with the development of self-awareness—the ability to perceive oneself as a unique being in time and space and to judge one's own actions. The way a person perceives and gets oriented to surrounding creatures and objects is specified by the culture in which he or she grows up. Along with object orientation, an individual's behavioral environment includes spatial, temporal, and normative orientations. In the past few decades, many cultures have rapidly transformed in response to technological advances, and individuals in these settings now experience a cyberspace reality as well as their material reality.

How Does Enculturation Influence Personality?

Studies suggest a relationship between enculturation and personality development. While each individual begins life with certain broad potentials and limitations that are genetically inherited, the distinct childrearing practices of each culture socialize children toward the particular norms and standards of their society and thereby impact personality. For example, childrearing practices in some cultures seem to promote the development of compliant personalities, while others seem to foster more independent, self-reliant personalities.

Are Different Personalities Characteristic of Different Cultures?

Each culture emphasizes certain personality traits as good and others as bad, and each has distinct ways of encouraging or discouraging those traits accordingly. Nonetheless, it is difficult to characterize cultures in terms of particular personalities. Of the several attempts made, the concept of modal personality is the most satisfactory. This recognizes that any human society has a range of individual personalities, but some will be more typical than others. Those that approximate the modal personality of a particular culture are thought of as normal. Since modal personalities may differ from one culture to another and since the acceptable range of variation from the standard may also differ per culture, it is clear that normal and abnormal are culturally relative concepts. This observation also applies to the range of socially acceptable gender expressions in different cultures.

In 1690 English philosopher John Locke presented the *tabula rasa* theory in his book *An Essay Concerning Human Understanding*. This notion holds that a newborn human is like a blank slate, and what the individual becomes in life is written on the slate by his or her life experiences. The implication is that at birth all individuals are basically the same in their potential for character development and that their adult personalities are exclusively the products of their postnatal experiences, which differ from culture to culture.

Locke's idea offered high hopes for the all-embracing impact of intellectual and moral instruction on a child's character formation, but it missed the mark, as we now know, for it did not take into consideration genetic contributions to human behavior. Based on recent breakthroughs in human genetic research, anthropologists have come to recognize that an identifiable portion of our behavior is genetically influenced.[1] This means each person is born with a particular set of inherited tendencies that help mark out his or her adult personality. While this genetic inheritance sets certain broad potentials and limitations, an individual's cultural environment, gender, social status, and unique life experiences, particularly in the early childhood years, also play a significant role in personality formation.

Since different cultures handle the raising and education of children in different ways, these practices and their effects on adult personalities are important subjects of anthropological inquiry. Such cross-cultural studies gave rise to the specialization of psychological anthropology and are the subjects of this chapter.

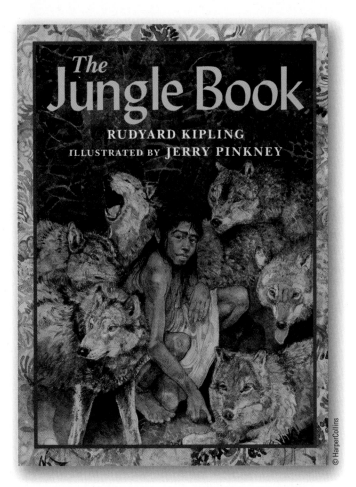

In 1916 the international Boy Scout movement expanded to include younger boys in a "cub scout" program inspired by Rudyard Kipling's *The Jungle Book* (1894). Born in former British India (1865), Kipling wrote this story about a young boy in India named Mowgli being raised by a wolf as one of her own cubs. Translated into some forty languages, including Hindi, Swahili, and Chinese, the book has been the subject of many cartoons and movies. Despite happy wild-child legends, human infants are biologically ill-equipped to survive successfully without culture.

Enculturation: The Human Self and Social Identity

From the moment of birth, a person faces multiple survival challenges. Obviously, newborns cannot take care of their own biological needs. Only in myths and romantic fantasies do we encounter stories about children successfully coming of age alone in the wilderness or accomplishing this feat having been raised by animals in the wild. For example, Italians in Rome still celebrate the mythological founders of their city, the twin brothers Romulus and Remus, who according to legend were suckled as infants by a she-wolf. And millions of children around the world have been fascinated by stories about Tarzan and the apes or the jungle boy Mowgli and the wolves. Moreover, young and old alike have been captivated by newspaper hoaxes about "wild" children, such as a 10-year-old boy reported to have been found running among gazelles in the Syrian desert in 1946.

Fanciful imaginations aside, human children are biologically ill-equipped to survive without culture. This point has been driven home by several documented cases about feral children (*feral* comes from *fera*, which is Latin for "wild animal") who grew up deprived of human contact. None of them had a happy ending. For instance, there was nothing romantic about the girl Kamala, supposedly rescued from a wolf den in India in 1920: She moved about on all fours and could not feed herself. And everyone in Paris considered the naked "wild boy" captured in the woods outside Aveyron village in 1800 an incurable idiot. Clearly, the biological capacity for what we think of as human, which entails culture, must be nurtured to be realized.

---

[1] Harpending, H., & Cochran, G. (2002). In our genes. *Proceedings of the National Academy of Sciences USA 99* (1), 10–12.

Visual Counterpoint

© James Balog

© Laura Dwight/Corbis

Self-awareness is not restricted to humans. This chimpanzee knows that the individual in the mirror is himself and not some other chimp, just as the girl recognizes herself.

Because culture is socially constructed and learned rather than biologically inherited, all societies must somehow ensure that culture is adequately transmitted from one generation to the next—a process we have already defined as *enculturation*. Since each group lives by a particular set of cultural rules, a child will have to learn the rules of his or her society in order to survive. Most of that learning takes place in the first few years when a child learns how to feel, think, speak, and, ultimately, act like an adult who embodies being Japanese, Kikuyu, Lakota, Norwegian, or whatever ethnic or national group into which it is born.

The first agents of enculturation in all societies are the members of the infant's household, especially the child's mother. (In fact, cultural factors are at work even before birth through what a pregnant mother eats, drinks, and inhales, as well as the sounds, rhythms, and activity patterns of her daily life.) Who the other members are depends on how households are structured in each particular society.

As the young person matures, individuals outside the household are brought into the enculturation process. These usually include other relatives and certainly the individual's peers. In some societies, professionals are brought into the process to provide formal instruction. In many societies, however, children are allowed to learn through observation and participation, at their own speed.

Self-Awareness

Enculturation begins with the development of **self-awareness**—the ability to identify oneself as an individual creature, to reflect on oneself, and to evaluate oneself. Humans do not have this cognitive ability at birth, even though it is essential for their successful social functioning. It is self-awareness that permits one to take social responsibility for one's conduct, to learn how to react to others, and to assume a variety of roles in society. An important aspect of self-awareness is the attachment of positive value to one's self. Without this, individuals cannot be motivated to act to their advantage.

self-awareness The ability to identify oneself as an individual, to reflect on oneself, and to evaluate oneself.

Self-awareness does not come all at once. In modern industrial and postindustrial societies, for example, self and non-self are not clearly distinguished until a child is about 2 years of age, lagging somewhat behind other cultures. Self-awareness develops in concert with neuromotor development, which is known to proceed at a slower rate in infants from industrial societies than in infants in many, perhaps even most, small-scale farming or foraging communities. The reasons for this slower rate are not yet clear, although the amount of human contact and stimulation that infants receive seems to play an important role.

As discussed in Chapter 1, infants in the United States, for example, generally do not sleep with their parents, most often being put in rooms of their own. This is seen as an important step in making them into individuals, "owners" of themselves and their capacities. As a consequence, they do not experience the steady stream of personal stimuli, including smell, movement, and warmth, that they would if co-sleeping. Private sleeping also takes away the opportunity for frequent nursing through the night.

In the majority of the world's societies, infants routinely sleep with their parents, or at least their mothers. Also, they are carried or held most other times, usually in an upright position. The mother typically responds to a cry or "fuss" within seconds, usually offering the infant her breast. So it is among traditional Ju/'hoansi (pronounced "zhutwasi") people of southern Africa's Kalahari Desert, whose infants breastfeed on demand in short frequent bouts—commonly nursing about four times an hour, for 1 or 2 minutes at a time. Overall, a 15-week-old Ju/'hoansi infant is in close contact with its mother about 70 percent of the time (compared to 20 percent for home-reared infants in the United States). Moreover, Ju/'hoansi babies usually have considerable contact with numerous other adults and children of all ages.

This steady stream of varied stimuli is significant, for recent studies show that stimulation plays a key role in the hardwiring of the brain; it is necessary for development of the neural circuitry. Looking at breastfeeding in particular, the longer a child is breastfed, the better his or her overall health, the higher he or she will score on cognitive tests, and the lower the risk of obesity, allergies, and attention deficit hyperactivity disorder.[2] Because our biological heritage as primates has programmed us to develop in response to social stimuli, it is not surprising that self-awareness and a variety of other beneficial qualities develop more rapidly in response to close contact with other humans.

Social Identity Through Personal Naming

Personal names are important devices for self-definition in all cultures. It is through naming that a social group acknowledges a child's birthright and establishes its social identity. Among the many cultural rules that exist in each society, those having to do with naming are unique because they individualize a person and at the same time identify one as a group member. In fact, names often express and represent multiple aspects of one's group identity—ethnic, gender, religious, political, or even rank, class, or caste. Without a name, an individual has no identity, no self. For this reason, many cultures consider name selection to be an important issue and mark the naming of a child with a special event or ritual known as a **naming ceremony**.

NAMING PRACTICES ACROSS CULTURES

Worldwide, there are countless contrasting approaches to naming. For instance, Aymara Indians in the Bolivian highland village of Laymi do not consider an infant truly human until they have given it a name. And naming does not happen until the child begins to speak the Aymara language, typically around the age of 2. Once the child shows the ability to speak like a human, he or she is considered fit to be recognized as such with a proper name. The naming ceremony marks the toddler's social transition from a state of "nature" to "culture" and consequently to full acceptance into the Laymi community.

Unlike the Aymara, Icelanders name babies at birth. Following ancient custom, Icelandic infants receive their father's personal given name as their last name. The suffix *sen* is added to a boy's name and *dottir* to a girl's name. Thus a brother and sister whose father is named Sven Olafsen would have the last names Svensen and Svendottir.

Among the Netsilik Inuit in Arctic Canada, a mother experiencing a difficult delivery would call out the names of deceased people of admirable character. The name being called at the moment of birth is thought to enter the infant's body and help the delivery, and the child would bear that name thereafter. Inuit parents may also name their children for deceased relatives in the belief that the spiritual identification will help shape their character.[3]

---

[2] Dettwyler, K. A. (1997, October). When to wean. *Natural History*, 49; World Health Organization. (2003). *Global strategy on infant and young child feeding*. Geneva: Author.

naming ceremony A special event or ritual to mark the naming of a child.

---

[3] Balikci, A. (1970). *The Netsilik Eskimo*. Garden City, NY: Natural History.

Navajo babies begin to learn the importance of community at a special First Laugh Ceremony (*Chi Dlo Dil*). At this event, the person who prompted an infant's first laugh teaches the child (and reminds the community) about the joy of generosity by helping the baby to give symbolic gifts of sweets and rock salt to each guest. Pictured here is the baby daughter of a pediatrician working at a remote clinic on the reservation. She celebrates her first laugh wearing a Navajo dress and jewelry given to her by her mother's Navajo patients.

In many cultures, a person receives a name soon after birth but may acquire new names during subsequent life phases. We see this in examples from two neighboring American Indian groups in the southwestern United States.

In the Hopi culture, on the twentieth day of a child's life, the father's sister gives the baby its name in a sunrise ceremony. At age 6, the child receives another name in a religious ceremony. Reaching adulthood, the person gets yet another name and keeps that one until the end of her or his life. Yet one more name is bestowed upon a Hopi at death, a name that is not to be mentioned after it is given.

In contrast, a Navajo child receives a name at birth. If born into a family that follows traditions, the baby is likely to be given an ancestral clan name soon after he or she laughs for the first time. Among the Navajo, laughter is seen as the earliest expression of human language, a signal that life as a social being has started. Thus it is an occasion for celebration. The person who prompted that very first laugh invites family and close friends to a First Laugh Ceremony. At the gathering, the party sponsor places rock salt in the baby's hand and helps slide the salt all over the little one's body. Representing tears—of both laughter and crying—the salt is said to provide strength and protection, leading to a long, happy life. Then the ancestral name is given. Next, because a central purpose of the occasion is to ensure that the child will become a generous person, the sponsor helps the baby give sweets and a piece of salt to each guest as they step forward to welcome the child into the embrace of the community. By accepting these symbolic gifts, guests also receive strength and protection. The ceremony reminds young and old alike of the importance of generosity and sharing.[4]

_____

[4] Authors' participant observation at traditional Navajo First Laugh ceremony of Wesley Bitsie-Baldwin; personal communication, LaVerne Bitsie-Baldwin and Anjanette Bisie.

Name-giving customs play an important role in a person's life journey as a socially accepted member of a culture. But what about naming in multi-ethnic or pluralistic societies?

NAMING AND IDENTITY POLITICS

Because names symbolically express and represent an individual's cultural self, they may gain particular significance in personal and collective identity politics. For instance, when an ethnic group or nation falls under the control of a more powerful and expanding neighboring group, its members may be forced to assimilate and give up their cultural identity. One early indicator may be that families belonging to the subjugated or overwhelmed group decide to abandon their own ancestral naming traditions. Such was the case when Russia expanded its empire into Siberia and colonized the Turkic-speaking Xakas. Within a few generations, most Xakas had Russian names.[5]

The identity politics of personal naming practices can also be seen in North America, where cultural origins are rooted primarily in a British colonial past. The continent was long dominated by Anglo-Saxon Protestants who controlled the government, fashioned the collective cultural fabric, and pressed a political agenda of national assimilation in "melting pot" terms. For example, American Indian families, whether they lived on or off their tribal reservations, came under pressure to forgo their cultural traditions, including their customary personal and family names. As part of the assimilation process, many agreed or were compelled to have their indigenous names translated into English. In particular, those who became Christian converts adopted European names, at least for public identification and self-presentation.

Among countless examples of this is the personal story of Luther Standing Bear, a Sicangu (Brule Sioux) tribesman from the Rosebud Indian Reservation in South Dakota. In 1879, he and numerous other Lakota-speaking children were taken from the familiar grasslands of the Great Plains to a U.S. government-run boarding school in Pennsylvania "to learn the ways of white men." Years later he recalled the traumatic day when government agents took him from his family's tipi encampment at the recently established reservation:

> They wrote my name in a big book. At that time I was entered as "Oka Kte, or Plenty Kill, son of Standing Bear." After my name was in the book, all the white people shook hands with me and said something in the white man's language which I did not understand. . . .

> [After a long journey, we arrived at the Carlisle Indian school] where there was a lot of writing on one of the blackboards. We did not know what it meant, but our interpreter came into the room and said, "Do you see all these marks on the blackboard? Well, each word is a white man's name. They are going to give each one of you one of these names by which you will hereafter be known." None of the names were read or explained to us, so of course we did not know the sound or meaning of any of them.

> [Forbidden to speak our own languages, each of the Indian boys was handed a long stick and told to point to] any name he wanted. . . . I had selected the name "Luther"—not "Lutheran" as many people called me. . . . The teacher took a piece of white tape and wrote the name on it. Then she cut off a length of the tape and sewed it on the back of the boy's shirt. . . . Soon we all had the names of white men sewed on our backs."[6]

Name change stories are also common among immigrants hoping to avoid racial discrimination or ethnic stigmatization. For instance, it was not uncommon for Jewish immigrants and their U.S.-born children trying to "make it" in the entertainment industry to Americanize their names: Issur Danielovitch became Kirk Douglas, Jonathan Stuart Leibowitz switched to Jon Stewart, and Joyce Frankenberg turned into Jane Seymour.

A similar, more recent name shift example comes from U.S. President Barack Hussein Obama, born of (and named after) a Luo father from western Kenya and a Euramerican mother from Kansas. While studying in the United States, his East African father had "Americanized" his name into Barry, and the younger Obama did the same during his growing up years in Hawaii. Later, as a 19-year-old studying in New York, Barry found himself in an identity quest and reverted to Barack.[7]

In identity politics, naming can also be a resistance strategy by a minority group asserting its cultural pride or even rights of self-determination against a dominant society. For instance, a minority group in Bulgaria known as the Pomak defied the Bulgarian state and refused to convert to Eastern Orthodox Christianity. Moreover, in an act of cultural resistance, they held on to their own Turkish-Arabic naming traditions as an expression of their ethnic identity, no matter the political reality.[8]

[5] Butanayev, V. (n.d.). *Xooray attari* [Xakas names]. Cited by Harrison, K. D. (2002). Naming practices and ethnic identity in Tuva. *Proceedings of the Chicago Linguistics Society 35* (2).

[6] Standing Bear, L. (1975). *My People the Sioux* (pp. 125, 137–138). Lincoln: University of Nebraska Press.

[7] Wolffe, R., Ramirez, J., & Bartholet, J. (2008, March 31). When Barry became Barack. *Newsweek.*

[8] See Harrison, K. D. (2002). Naming practices and ethnic identity in Tuva. *Proceedings of the Chicago Linguistics Society 35* (2).

Barack Hussein Obama, Senior and Junior, 1971. Both Americanized their first name to Barry for a time. The father reverted to Barack
when he returned to his home country of Kenya after studying in the
United States. President Obama did the same at age 19 as an undergraduate in search of his identity.

In the United States, African Americans with inherited
Christian names that were imposed upon their enslaved
ancestors have, in growing numbers, rejected those names.
Many have also abandoned the faith tradition represented
by those names to become members of the Nation of Islam
("Black Muslims"). An enduringly famous example of this
is champion boxer Cassius Clay, who converted to Islam
in the mid-1960s. Like others, he rejected his "slave name"
and adopted the name Muhammad Ali.

Among American Indians as well, name reversion
has become quite common since the 1960s. For example,
Lakota activist Russell Means of Pine Ridge Reservation
recently announced that he wanted to be known as Oyate
Wacinyapin ("Works for the People").

The Self and the Behavioral Environment

The development of self-awareness requires basic orientations that structure the psychological fields in which the
self acts. These include object orientation, spatial orientation, temporal orientation, and normative orientation—
discussed below.

Each individual must learn about a world of objects
other than the self. Through this *object orientation,* each
culture singles out for attention certain environmental
features, while ignoring others or lumping them together
into broad categories. A culture also explains the perceived

environment. This is important, for a cultural explanation
of one's surroundings imposes a measure of order and provides the individual with a sense of direction needed to act
meaningfully and effectively.

Behind this lies a powerful psychological drive to reduce uncertainty—part of the common human need for a
balanced and integrated perspective on the relevant universe. When confronted with ambiguity and uncertainty,
people invariably strive to clarify and give structure to the
situation; they do this in ways that their particular culture
deems appropriate. Thus our observations and explanations of the universe are largely culturally constructed and
mediated symbolically through language. In fact, everything in the physical environment varies in the way it is
perceived and experienced by humans. In short, we perceive the world around us through a cultural lens.

The behavioral environment in which the self acts also
involves *spatial orientation,* or the ability to get from one
object or place to another. Notably, when we speak of trying to *orient* ourselves, we are using an ancient word for
"rising" that refers to the east where the sun comes up.
Traditionally, place names commonly contain references
to significant geographic features in the landscape. For
instance, the name Mississippi in North America means
literally "big river"; the English coastal city of Plymouth is
located at the mouth of the river Plym; and the riverside
city of Bamako, Mali, in West Africa translates as "crocodile river."

Finding your way to class, remembering where you
left your car keys, directing someone to the nearest bus
stop, and traveling through deep underground networks
in subway tunnels are examples of highly complex cognitive tasks based on spatial orientation and memory. So is
a desert nomad's ability to travel long distances from one
remote oasis to another—determining the route by means
of a mental map of the vast open landscape and gauging
his location by the position of the sun in daytime, the stars
at night, and even by the winds and smell of the air.

Technological revolutions in the 20th century have led
to the invention of a newly created media environment,
where we learn to orient ourselves in cyberspace. Without
our spatial orientations, whether in natural or virtual reality, navigating through daily life would be impossible.

Temporal orientation, which gives people a sense of
their place in time, is also part of the behavioral environment. Connecting past actions with those of the present and future provides a sense of self-continuity. This is
the function of a calendar. Derived from the Latin word
kalendae, which originally referred to a public announce-
ment at the first day of a new month, or moon, such a chart
gives people a framework for organizing their days, weeks,
months, and even years. Just as the perceived environment
of objects is organized in cultural terms, so too are time
and space.

Dark and foreboding to outsiders, the Ituri forest in the tropical heart of Africa is viewed with affection by the Mbuti foragers who live there. In their eyes, it is like a benevolent parent, providing them with all they ask for: sustenance, protection, and security.

A final aspect of the behavioral environment is the *normative orientation*. Moral values, ideals, and principles, which are purely cultural in origin, are as much a part of the individual's behavioral environment as are trees, rivers, and mountains. Without them people would have nothing by which to gauge their own actions or those of others. Normative orientation includes standards that indicate what ranges of behavior are acceptable for males, females, and whichever additional gender roles exist in a particular society.

Personality

In the process of enculturation, each individual is introduced to a society's natural and human-made environment along with a collective body of ideas about the self and others. The result is the creation of a kind of internalized

personality The distinctive way a person thinks, feels, and behaves.

cultural blueprint of the world in which the individual will feel, think, and act as a social being. It is his or her particular map of how to run the maze of life. When we speak of someone's personality, we are generalizing about that person's internalized map over time. Hence, personalities are products of enculturation, as experienced by individuals, each with his or her distinctive genetic makeup.

Personality does not lend itself to a formal definition, but we take it as the distinctive way a person thinks, feels, and behaves. Derived from the Latin word *persona,* meaning "mask," the term relates to the idea of learning to play one's role on the stage of daily life. Gradually, the "mask," as it is "placed" on the face of a child, begins to shape that person until there is little sense of the mask as a superimposed alien force. Instead it feels natural, as if one were born with it. The individual has successfully internalized the culture.

Personality Development

Although *what* one learns is important to personality development, most anthropologists assume that *how* one learns is no less important. Along with psychological theorists, anthropologists view childhood experiences as strongly influencing adult personality. Indeed, many pioneering psychological anthropologists have been attracted to Freudian psychoanalytic theory, while maintaining a critical eye.

Psychological literature tends to be long on speculative concepts, clinical data, and studies that are culture-bound. Anthropologists, for their part, are more interested in studies that seek to prove, modify, or at least shed light on the roles of different cultural influences in shaping personality. For example, traditionally the cultural ideal for the white middle class in Western societies has been for men to be tough, aggressive, assertive, dominant, and self-reliant, whereas women have been expected to be gentle, passive, obedient, and caring. To many, these personality contrasts between male and female seem so natural that they are thought to be biologically grounded and therefore fixed and universal. But are they? Have anthropologists identified any psychological or personality characteristics that universally differentiate the sexes?

ADOLESCENCE AND GENDER IDENTITY
Margaret Mead, a pioneer in anthropological study of gender identity and personality development, was a 24-year-old doctoral candidate when she set out for the Pacific Ocean island of Samoa. Mead wanted to test the theory (then widely accepted) that the biological changes of adolescence were always fraught with social, psychological, and emotional stress. Based on her fieldwork there, she later wrote the book *Coming of Age in Samoa: A Psychological Study of Primitive Youth for Western Civilization.*

In it she explained that adolescence does not have to be a time of stress and strain, but cultural conditions may make it so. Published in 1928, this book is generally credited with marking the beginning of psychological anthropology (culture and personality).

Pioneering works, however, are rarely without their faults, and *Coming of Age* is no exception. For one, Mead's time in the field (nine months) was not enough to understand fully the nuances of native speech and body language necessary to comprehend the innermost feelings of her informants. Furthermore, her sample of Samoan adolescents was a mere fifty, half of whom had not yet passed puberty.

Despite its faults, Mead's book stands as a landmark for several reasons: Not only was it a deliberate test of a Euramerican psychological hypothesis, but it also showed psychologists the value of modifying intelligence tests to make them appropriate for the population under study. Furthermore, by emphasizing the lesson to be drawn for Mead's own society, it laid the groundwork for the popularization of anthropology and advanced the cause of applied anthropology.

Other work by Mead has been equally foundational to the study of personality and gender. In the early 1930s she studied three ethnic groups in Papua New Guinea—the Arapesh, the Mundugamor, and the Tchambuli. This comparative research suggested that whatever biological differences exist between men and women, they are extremely malleable. In short, she concluded, biology is not destiny. Mead found that among the Arapesh, relations between men and women were expected to be equal, with both genders exhibiting what most North Americans traditionally consider feminine traits (cooperative, nurturing, and gentle).[9] She also discovered gender equality among the Mundugamor (now generally called Biwat); however, in that community both genders displayed supposedly masculine traits (individualistic, assertive, volatile, aggressive). Among the Tchambuli (now called Chambri), however, Mead found that women dominated men.

More recent anthropological research suggests that some of Mead's interpretations of gender roles were incorrect—for instance, neither do Chambri women dominate Chambri men nor vice versa. Yet, as with Mead's pioneering research in Samoa, her cross-cultural findings in Papua New Guinea remain valuable, despite their flaws, for they generated new insights into the human condition, showing that male dominance is not genetically fixed in our human "nature." Instead, it is socially constructed in the context of particular cultural adaptations and, consequently, alternative gender arrangements can be created. (See the Anthropologist of Note feature on Mead's teacher, colleague, and close friend Ruth Benedict for her pathbreaking work on personality as a cultural construct.) Although biological factors in male–female behavior do play a role (in fact, debate continues about the genetic and hormonal factors involved), it has nonetheless become clear that each culture provides different opportunities and has different expectations for ideal or acceptable behavior.[10]

CHILDREARING AND GENDER AMONG THE JU/'HOANSI

To understand the importance of childrearing practices for the development of gender-related personality characteristics, we may take another brief look at the already mentioned Ju/'hoansi, people native to the Kalahari Desert of Namibia and Botswana in southern Africa. The Ju/'hoansi are one of a number of groups traditionally referred to as Bushmen, who were once widespread through much of southern Africa.

Reo Fortune/Library of Congress

Anthropologist Margaret Mead in Pere, a small village on the island of Manus, now part of Papua New Guinea. Researching the thought processes of children through their drawings, she determined that what is considered childlike in thought varies according to the emphases of the culture. She published her findings in *Growing Up in New Guinea* (1930), a book written for a general audience.

[9] Mead, M. (1950). *Sex and temperament in three primitive societies.* New York: New American Library. (orig. 1935)

[10] Errington, F. K., & Gewertz, D. B. (2001). *Cultural alternatives and a feminist anthropology: An analysis of culturally constructed gender interests in Papua New Guinea.* Cambridge, England, and New York: Cambridge University Press.

Ruth Fulton Benedict (1887–1947)

Ruth Fulton Benedict came late to anthropology. After her graduation from Vassar College, she taught high school English, published poetry, and tried her hand at social work. At age 31, she began studying anthropology, first at the New School for Social Research in New York City, and then at Columbia University. Having earned her doctorate under Franz Boas, she joined his department. One of her first students was Margaret Mead.

As Benedict herself once said, the main purpose of anthropology is "to make the world safe for human differences." In anthropology, she developed the idea that culture was a collective projection of the personality of those who created it. In her most famous book *Patterns of Culture* (1934), she compared the cultures of three peoples—the Kwakiutl Indians of the Pacific Northwest coast in Canada, the Zuni Indians of the Arizona desert in the United States, and the Melanesians of Dobu Island off the southern shore of Papua New Guinea. She held that each was comparable to a great work of art, with an internal coherence and consistency of its own.

Seeing the Kwakiutl as egocentric, individualistic, and ecstatic in their rituals, she labeled their cultural

© The Granger Collection, New York

configuration "Dionysian" (named after the Greek god of wine and noisy feasting). The Zuni, whom she saw as living by the golden mean, wanting no part of excess or disruptive psychological states and distrusting of individualism, she characterized as "Apollonian" (named after the Greek god of poetry who exemplified beauty). The Dobuans, whose culture seemed to her magic-ridden, with everyone fearing and hating everyone else, she characterized as "paranoid."

Another theme of *Patterns of Culture* is that deviance should be understood as a conflict between an individual's personality and the norms of the culture to which the person belongs. Still in print today, *Patterns* has sold close to 2 million copies in a dozen languages. It had great influence on Mead during her cross-cultural gender studies among the Papuans in New Guinea.

Although *Patterns of Culture* still enjoys popularity in some nonanthropological circles, anthropologists have long since abandoned its approach as impressionistic. To compound the problem, Benedict's characterizations of cultures are misleading (the supposedly Apollonian Zunis, for example, indulge in such seemingly Dionysian practices as sword swallowing and walking over hot coals), and the use of such value-laden terms as "paranoid" prejudices others against the culture so labeled. Nonetheless, the book did have an enormous and valuable influence by focusing attention on the problem of the interrelation between culture and personality and by popularizing the reality of cultural variation.

Traditionally subsisting as nomadic hunter-gatherers (foragers), in the past three decades many Ju/'hoansi have been forced to settle down—tending small herds of goats, planting gardens for their livelihood, and engaging in occasional wage labor.[11]

Among those Ju/'hoansi who traditionally forage for a living, equality is stressed, and dominance and aggressiveness

are not tolerated in either gender. Men are as mild-mannered as the women, and women are as energetic and self-reliant as the men. By contrast, among the Ju/'hoansi who have recently settled in permanent villages, men and women exhibit personality characteristics resembling those traditionally thought of as typically masculine and feminine in North America and other industrial societies.

Among these food foragers, each newborn child receives extensive personal care from its mother during the first few years of life, for the space between births is typically four to five years. This is not to say that mothers are constantly with their children. For instance, when women go to collect wild plant foods in the bush, they do not always take their offspring along. At such times, the children are supervised by their fathers or other community adults, nearly half of whom are found in camp on any given day. Because these include men as well as women, children are as much habituated to the male as to the female presence.

Traditional Ju/'hoansi fathers spend much time with their offspring, interacting with them in nonauthoritarian

---

[11] Draper, P. (1975). !Kung women: Contrasts in sexual egalitarianism in foraging and sedentary contexts. In R. Reiter (Ed.), *Toward an anthropology of women* (pp. 77–109). New York: Monthly Review.

In traditional Ju/'hoansi society, fathers as well as mothers show great indulgence to children, who do not fear or respect men more than they do women.

ways. Although they may correct their children's behavior, so may women who neither defer to male authority nor use the threat of paternal punishment. Thus, among Ju/'hoansi foragers, no one grows up to respect or fear male authority any more than female authority. In fact, instead of being punished, a child who misbehaves will simply be carried away and introduced to some other more agreeable activity.

Children of both sexes do equally little work. Instead, they spend much of their time in playgroups that include boys and girls of widely different ages. And when it comes to older children keeping an eye out for the younger ones, this is done spontaneously rather than as an assigned task, and the burden does not fall more heavily on girls than boys. In short, Ju/'hoansi children in traditional foraging groups have few experiences that set one gender apart from the other.

The situation is different among Ju/'hoansi who have been forced to abandon their traditional life as foragers and now reside in permanent settlements: Women spend much of their time in and around the home preparing food, doing other domestic chores, and tending the children. Men, meanwhile, spend many hours outside the household growing crops, raising animals, or doing wage labor. As a result, children are less habituated to their presence. This remoteness of the men, combined with their greater knowledge of the outside world and their access to cash, tends to strengthen male influence in the household.

Within village households, gender typecasting begins early. As soon as girls are old enough, they are expected to attend to many of the needs of their younger siblings, thereby allowing their mothers time to deal with other domestic tasks. This not only shapes but also limits the behavior of girls, who cannot range as widely or explore as freely and independently as they could without little brothers and sisters in tow. Boys, by contrast, have little to do with babies and toddlers, and when they are assigned work, it generally takes them away from the household. Thus the space that village girls occupy becomes restricted, and they are trained in behaviors that promote passivity and nurturance, whereas village boys begin to learn the distant, controlling roles they will later play as adult men.

When comparing childrearing traditions in different cultures, we find that a group's economic organization and the social relations in its subsistence practices impact the way a child is brought up, and this, in turn, affects the adult personality. Cross-cultural comparisons also show that alternatives exist to the way that children are raised—which means that changing the societal conditions in which one's children grow up can alter significantly the way men and women act and interact.

With this in mind, we turn to a discussion about traditions of dependence and independence training. As you read, bear in mind that many cultures employ a mixture of these types of customary childrearing techniques.

DEPENDENCE TRAINING

Some years after Margaret Mead's pioneering comparative research on gender, psychological anthropologists carried out a significant and more wide-ranging series of cross-cultural studies on the effects of childrearing on personality. Among other things, their work showed that it is possible to distinguish between two general patterns of childrearing. These patterns stem from a number of practices that, regardless of the reason for their existence, have the effect of emphasizing dependence on the one hand and independence on the other. For convenience, we will call these "dependence training" and "independence training."[12]

Dependence training socializes people to think of themselves in terms of the larger whole. Its effect is to create community members whose idea of selfhood transcends individualism, promoting compliance in the

---

[12] Whiting, J. W. M., & Child, I. L. (1953). *Child training and personality: A cross-cultural study.* New Haven, CT: Yale University Press.

> **dependence training** Childrearing practices that foster compliance in the performance of assigned tasks and dependence on the domestic group, rather than reliance on oneself.

performance of assigned tasks and keeping individuals within the group. This pattern is typically associated with extended families, which consist of several husband-wife-children units within the same household. It is most likely to be found in societies with an economy based on subsistence farming but also in foraging groups where several family groups may live together for at least part of the year. Big extended families are important, for they provide the labor force necessary to till the soil, tend whatever flocks are kept, and carry out other part-time economic pursuits considered necessary for existence.

These large families, however, have built into them certain potentially disruptive tensions. For example, important family decisions must be collectively accepted and followed. In addition, the in-marrying spouses—husbands and/or wives who come from other groups—must conform themselves to the group's will, something that may not be easy for them.

Dependence training helps to keep these potential problems under control and involves both supportive and corrective aspects. On the supportive side, parents are easygoing, and mothers yield to the desires of their young, particularly when it comes to breastfeeding, which is provided on demand and continues for several years. This may be interpreted as rewarding the child for seeking support within the family, the main agent in meeting the child's needs. Also on the supportive side, children at a relatively early age are assigned a number of child-care and domestic tasks, all of which make significant and obvious contributions to the family's welfare. Thus family members all actively work to help and support one another.

On the corrective side, behavior the adults interpret as aggressive or selfish is likely to be actively discouraged. Moreover, the adults tend to be insistent on overall obedience, which commonly inclines the individual toward being subordinate to the group. This combination of encouragement and discouragement in the socialization process teaches individuals to put the group's needs above their own—to be obedient, supportive, noncompetitive, and generally responsible, to stay within the fold and not do anything potentially disruptive. Indeed, a person's very definition of self comes from the individual being a part of a larger social whole rather than from his or her mere individual existence.

INDEPENDENCE TRAINING

Independence training fosters individual self-reliance and personal achievement. It is typically associated with societies in which a basic social unit consisting of

parent(s) and offspring fends for itself. Independence training is particularly characteristic of mercantile (trading), industrial, and postindustrial societies where self-sufficiency and personal achievement are important traits for success, if not survival—especially for men, and increasingly for women.

This pattern of training involves both encouragement and discouragement. On the negative side, infant feeding is prompted more by schedule than demand. In North America, as noted above, babies are rarely nursed for more than a year, if that. Many parents resort to an artificial nipple or teething ring (pacifier) to satisfy the baby's sucking instincts—typically doing so to calm the child rather than out of an awareness that infants need sucking to strengthen and train coordination in the muscles used for feeding and speech.

North American parents are comparatively quick to start feeding infants baby food and even try to get them to feed themselves. Many are delighted if they can prop their infants up in the crib or playpen so that they can hold their own bottles. Moreover, as soon after birth as possible, children are commonly given their own private space, away from their parents.

Displays of individual will, assertiveness, and even aggression are encouraged or at least tolerated to a greater degree than where dependence training is the rule. In schools, and even in the family, competition and winning are emphasized. Schools in the United States, for example, devote considerable resources to competitive sports. Competition is fostered within the classroom as well—overtly through practices such as spelling bees and awards and covertly through customs such as grading on a curve. In addition, there are various popularity contests, such as crowning a prom queen and king or holding an election to choose the classmate who is "best looking" or "most likely to succeed." Thus by the time individuals have grown up in U.S. society, they have received a clear message: Life is about winning or losing, and losing is equal to failure.[13]

In sum, independence training generally encourages individuals to seek help and attention rather than to give it and to try to exert individual dominance. Such qualities are useful in societies with hierarchical social structures that emphasize personal achievement and where individuals are expected to look out for their own interests. Its socialization patterns match cultural values and expectations increasingly prevalent in the spread of global capitalism.

One kind of training—independence, dependence, or a combination of both—is not inherently better or worse

---

independence training Childrearing practices that foster independence, self-reliance, and personal achievement.

[13] Turnbull, C. M. (1983). *The human cycle* (p. 74). New York: Simon & Schuster.

than any other. If compliant adults who are accepting of authority are required, then independence training will not work well in that society. Nor will dependence training serve very well a society whose adults are expected to be self-reliant, questioning of authority, and ready to explore and embrace new ways of doing things. Building on this basic cross-cultural dichotomy in childrearing practices, comparative research by psychological anthropologists has greatly added to our increasingly sophisticated understanding of the complex relationship between culture and personality.

Group Personality

From the holistic perspective that anthropologists bring to the comparative study of childrearing, it is clear that these customary practices, personality development, and other aspects of culture are systemically interrelated. This insight has prompted research to explore whether whole societies might be analyzed in terms of particular personality types. Certainly, common sense suggests that personalities fitting for one culture may be less suitable for others. For example, an egocentric, aggressive personality would be out of place where self-effacement, cooperation, and sharing are the keys to success.

Unfortunately, common sense, like conventional wisdom in general, is not always true. Anthropologists asked themselves whether it would be possible to describe a group personality without falling into the trap of stereotyping. The answer is a qualified yes, especially with respect to traditional communities. The larger and more complex a society becomes, the greater its variegation in personalities. In an abstract way, we may speak of a generalized "cultural personality" for a society, as long as we do not expect to find a uniformity of personalities within that society.

Put another way, a person develops certain personality characteristics that, from common experience, resemble those of other people. Yet, each human being also acquires distinct personality traits because every individual is exposed to unique sets of experiences and may react to shared experiences in novel ways. Moreover, each person brings to these experiences a one-of-a-kind genetic potential (except in the case of identical twins) that plays a role in determining personality development.

Consider for example the Yanomami Indians, who subsist on foraging and horticulture in the tropical forests of northern Brazil and southern Venezuela. Commonly, Yanomami men strive to achieve a reputation for fierceness and aggressiveness, and they defend that reputation at the risk of serious personal injury and death. Yet, among the Yanomami there are men who have quiet and somewhat retiring personalities. It is all too easy for an

outsider to overlook these individuals when other, more "typical" Yanomami are in the front row, pushing and demanding attention.

Modal Personality

Obviously, any productive approach to the problem of group personality must recognize that each individual is unique to a degree in both genetic inheritance and life experiences, and it must leave room for a range of different personality types in any society. In addition, personality traits that may be regarded as appropriate in men may not be so regarded in women, and vice versa. Given all this, we may focus our attention on the **modal personality**, defined as those character traits that occur with the highest frequency in a social group and are therefore the most representative of its culture.

Modal personality is a statistical concept rather than the personality of an average person in a particular society. As such, it opens up for investigation the questions of how more complex societies organize diversity and how diversity relates to cultural change. Such questions are easily missed if one associates a certain type of personality with one particular culture, as did some earlier anthropologists (see Ruth Benedict in Anthropologist of Note). At the same time, modal personalities of different groups can be compared.

Data on modal personality are best gathered by means of psychological tests (such as the Rorschach or "ink blot" test) administered to a sample of the population. In addition, observing and recording the frequency of certain behaviors, collecting and analyzing life histories and dreams, and analyzing popular tales, jokes, legends, and traditional myths can yield useful data on modal personality.

While having much to recommend it, the concept of modal personality as a means of dealing with group personality nevertheless presents certain difficulties. One is the complexity of the measurement techniques, which may be hard to do in the field. For instance, an adequate representative sample of subjects is necessary. The problem here is twofold: making sure the sample is really representative and having the time and personnel necessary to administer the tests, conduct interviews, and so on, all of which can be lengthy proceedings.

Also, the tests themselves constitute a problem, for those devised in one cultural setting may not be appropriate in another. Moreover, language differences or conflicting cultural values between the researcher and

modal personality Those character traits that occur with the highest frequency in a social group and are therefore the most representative of its culture.

the individuals being studied may inhibit communication and/or lead to misinterpretation. For example, just what is aggression? Does everyone define it the same way? Is it an elemental analytical concept, or does it involve other variables? In addition to the problem of test questions being culture-bound, it is worth noting that the concept of testing itself is culturally embedded, especially in hierarchically structured mass societies that value ranking systems based on people's potential capacity in production.

National Character

Several years ago, Italy's tourism minister publicly commented on "typical characteristics" of Germans, referring to them as "hyper-nationalistic blondes" and "beer-drinking slobs" holding "noisy burping contests" on Italy's beaches.[14] Outraged (and proud of his country's excellent beer), Germany's chancellor canceled his planned vacation to Italy and demanded an official apology. Of course, many Germans think of Italians as dark-eyed, hot-blooded spaghetti eaters. To say so in public, however, might cause an uproar.

Unflattering stereotypes about foreigners are deeply rooted in cultural traditions everywhere. Many Japanese believe Koreans are stingy, crude, and aggressive, while many Koreans see the Japanese as cold and arrogant. Similarly, we all have in mind some image, perhaps not well defined, of the typical citizen of Russia or Mexico or England. And Americans traveling abroad may be insulted that others in the world hold the negative image of loud, brash, and arrogant Yankees. Although these are simply stereotypes, we might ask if these stereotypes have any basis in fact. In reality, does such a thing as *national character* exist?

Some anthropologists once thought that the answer might be yes. So, they embarked on national character studies in the 1930s and 1940s, aiming to discover basic personality traits shared by the majority of the people of modern state societies. In what came to be known as the *culture and personality* movement, their research emphasized childrearing practices and education as the factors theoretically responsible for such characteristics.

Early on it was recognized that the national character studies were flawed, mainly because they made generalizations based on limited data, relatively small samples of informants, and questionable assumptions about developmental psychology. These flaws notwithstanding,

The collectively shared core values of Chinese culture promote the integration of the individual into a larger group, as we see in this large gathering of Taipei residents doing Tai Chi together.

national character studies were important in that they helped change the anthropological focus from traditional small-scale communities of foragers, herders, and farmers in exotic places to large-scale contemporary state societies. Moreover, they prompted new theoretical and methodological approaches to serious interdisciplinary group research.[15]

Core Values

An alternative approach to national character—one that allows for the fact that not all personalities will conform to cultural ideals—is that of Chinese American

---

[14] "Italy-Germany verbal war hots up." (2003, July 9). *Deccan Herald* (Bangalore, India).

[15] See Beeman, W. O. (2000). Introduction: Margaret Mead, cultural studies, and international understanding. In M. Mead & R. Métraux (Eds.), *The study of culture at a distance* (pp. xiv–xxxi). New York and Oxford: Berghahn.

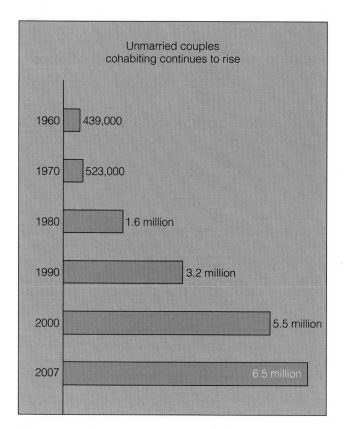

Figure 6.1 **The number of opposite-sex couples cohabiting in the United States, by year. Cohabiting couples now make up almost 10 percent of all opposite-sex U.S. couples, married and unmarried.**
Source: U.S. Census Bureau, 2007.

anthropologist Francis Hsu. His approach is to study **core values** (values especially promoted by a particular culture) and related personality traits. The Chinese, he suggests, value kin ties and cooperation above all else. To them, mutual dependence is the very essence of personal relationships and has been for thousands of years. Compliance and subordination of one's will to that of family and kin transcend all else, while self-reliance is neither promoted nor a source of pride.

Perhaps the core value held in highest esteem by North Americans of European descent is rugged individualism. Each individual is supposed to be able to achieve anything he or she likes, given a willingness to work hard enough. From their earliest years, individuals are subjected to relentless pressures to excel, and as we have already noted, competition and winning are crucial to this. Undoubtedly, this contributes to the restlessness and drive seen as characteristic for much of North American society today—and increasingly common wherever people compete for survival, wealth, and power in the global market.

Also, to the degree that it motivates individuals to work hard and to go where the jobs are, this individualism fits well with the demands of a global market economy. Thus, while individuals in Chinese traditional society are firmly bound into a larger group to which they have lifelong obligations, most urban North Americans and western Europeans live isolated from relatives other than their young children and spouse—and even the commitment to marriage has lessened (Figure 6.1). Many people in western Europe, North America, and other industrial or postindustrial societies choose to remain single or postpone marriage. This growing individualism is also indicated by the declining rates of formal marriage and rising rates of divorce—with close to 50 percent of marriages now failing.[16]

Alternative Gender Models from a Cross-Cultural Perspective

As touched on earlier, the gender roles assigned to each sex vary from culture to culture and have an impact on personality formation. But what if the sex of an individual is not self-evident, as revealed in the following Original Study? Written when its author was an undergraduate student of philosophy at Bryn Mawr College in Pennsylvania, this narrative offers a compelling personal account of the emotional difficulties associated with intersexuality and gender ambiguity, while making the important point that attitudes toward gender vary cross-culturally. However, some of the cultural information is overly generalized and therefore not quite accurate, including the idea that all or most Native American spiritual-religious worldviews were and are nonhierarchical.[17]

---

[16] Observations on North American culture in this section are drawn primarily from Natadecha-Sponsal, P. (1993). The young, the rich and the famous: Individualism as an American cultural value. In P. R. DeVita & J. D. Armstrong (Eds.), *Distant mirrors: America as a foreign culture* (pp. 46–53). Belmont, CA: Wadsworth. See also Whitehead, B. D., & Popenoe, D. (2004). *The state of our unions: The social health of marriage in America 2004.* Rutgers, NJ: Rutgers University National Marriage Project; Noack, T. (2001). Cohabitation in Norway: An accepted and gradually more regulated way of living. *International Journal of Law, Policy, and the Family 15* (1), 102–117.

[17] For scholarly accounts of the issues presented here, readers may turn to several excellent books, including the one mentioned in the Original Study: Roscoe, W. (1991). *The Zuni man-woman.* Albuquerque: University of New Mexico Press.

core values   Those values especially promoted by a particular culture.

The Blessed Curse   *by R. K. Williamson*

One morning not so long ago, a child was born. This birth, however, was no occasion for the customary celebration. Something was wrong: something very grave, very serious, very sinister. This child was born between sexes, an "intersexed" child. From the day of its birth, this child would be caught in a series of struggles involving virtually every aspect of its life. Things that required little thought under "ordinary" circumstances were, in this instance, extraordinarily difficult. Simple questions now had an air of complexity: "What is it, a girl or a boy?" "What do we name it?" "How shall we raise it?" "Who (or what) is to blame for this?"

A Foot in Both Worlds

The child referred to in the introductory paragraph is myself. As the great-granddaughter of a Cherokee woman, I was exposed to the Native American view of people who were born intersexed, and those who exhibited transgendered characteristics. This view, unlike the Euramerican one, sees such individuals in a very positive and affirming light. Yet my immediate family (mother, father, and brothers) were firmly fixed in a negative Christian Euramerican point of view. As a result, from a very early age I was presented with two different and conflicting views of myself. This resulted in a lot of confusion within me about what I was, how I came to be born the way I was, and what my intersexuality meant in terms of my spirituality as well as my place in society.

I remember, even as a small child, getting mixed messages about my worth as a human being. My grandmother, in keeping with Native American ways, would tell me stories about my birth. She would tell me how she knew when I was born that I had a special place in life, given to me by God, the Great Spirit, and that I had been given "a great strength that girls never have, yet a gentle tenderness that boys never know" and that I was "too pretty and beautiful to be a boy only and too strong to be a girl only." She rejoiced at this "special gift" and taught me that it meant that the Great Spirit had "something important for me to do in this life." I remember how good I felt inside when she told me these things and how I soberly contemplated, even at the young age of 5, that I must be diligent and try to learn and carry out the purpose designed just for me by the Great Spirit.

My parents, however, were so repulsed by my intersexuality that they would never speak of it directly. They would just refer to it as "the work of Satan." To them, I was not at all blessed with a "special gift" from some "Great Spirit," but was "cursed and given over to the Devil" by God. My father treated me with contempt, and my mother wavered between contempt and distant indifference. I was taken from one charismatic church to another in order to have the "demon of mixed sex" cast out of me. At some of these "deliverance" services I was even given a napkin to cough out the demon into!

In the end, no demon ever popped out of me. Still I grew up believing that there was something inherent within me that caused God to hate me, that my intersexuality was a punishment for this something, a mark of condemnation.

Whenever I stayed at my grandmother's house, my fears would be allayed, for she would once again remind me that I was fortunate to have been given this special gift. She was distraught that my parents were treating me cruelly and pleaded with them to let me live with her, but they would not let me stay at her home permanently. Nevertheless, they did let me spend a significant portion of my childhood with her. Had it not been for that, I might not have been able to survive the tremendous trials that awaited me in my walk through life.

Blessed Gift: The Native American View

It is now known that most, if not all, Native American societies had certain individuals that fell between the categories of "man" and "woman." The various nations had different names for such people, but a term broadly used and recognized is *berdache*, a word of French origin that designated a male, passive homosexual. [The preferred term today is *two-spirit*.] Some of these individuals were born physically intersexed. Others appeared to be anatomically normal males, but exhibited the character and the manners of women—or vice versa. The way native people treated such individuals reveals some interesting insights into Native American belief systems.

The Spirit

The extent to which Native Americans see spirituality is reflected in their belief that all things have a spirit: "Every object—plants, rocks, water, air, the moon, animals, humans, the earth itself—has a spirit. The spirit of one thing (including a human) is not superior to the spirit of any other. . . . The function of religion is not to try to condemn or to change what exists, but to accept the realities of the world and to appreciate their contributions to life. Everything that exists has a purpose."

This paradigm is the core of Native American thought and action. Because everything has a spirit, and no spirit is superior to that of another, there is no "above" or "below," no "superior" or "inferior," no "dominant" and "subordinate." These are only illusions that arise from unclear thinking. Thus, an intersexed child is not derided or viewed as a "freak of nature" in many traditional Native American cultures. Intersexuality (as well as masculinity in a female or effeminacy in a male) is seen as the manifestation of the spirit of the child, so an intersexed child is respected as much as a girl child or a boy child. It is the spirit of the child that determines what the gender of the child will ultimately be. According to a Lakota, Lame Deer, "the Great Spirit made them *winktes* [two-spirit], and we accepted them as such." In this sense, the child has no control over what her or his gender will be. It follows that where there is no choice, there can be no accountability on the part of the child. Indeed, the child who is given the spirit of a *winkte* is unable to resist becoming one.

> When an Omaha boy sees the Moon Being [a feminine Spirit] on his vision quest, the spirit holds in one hand a man's bow and arrow and in the other a woman's pack strap. . . . "When the youth tried to grasp the bow and arrows, the Moon Being crossed hands very quickly, and if the youth was not very careful he seized the pack strap instead of the bow and arrows, thereby fixing his lot in later life. In such a case he could not help acting [like a] woman, speaking, dressing, and working just as . . . women . . . do."

The Curse: The Euramerican View

In contrast to the view of respect and admiration of physical intersexuality and transgendered behavior traditionally held by Native Americans, the Europeans who came to "Turtle Island" (the Cherokee name for North America) brought with them their worldview, shaped by their Judeo-Christian beliefs. According to this religious perspective, there had to be, by mandate of God, a complete dichotomy of the sexes. . . .

Will Roscoe, in his book *The Zuni Man-Woman*, reports (pp. 172–173):

Spanish oppression of "homosexual" practices in the New World took brutal forms. In 1513, the explorer Balboa had some forty berdaches thrown to his dogs [to be eaten alive]—"a fine action by an honorable and Catholic Spaniard," as one Spanish historian commented. In Peru, the Spaniards burned "sodomites, . . . and in this way they frightened them in such a manner that they left this great sin."

It is abundantly clear that Christian Euramericans exerted every effort to destroy Native American culture:

In 1883, the U.S. Office of Indian Affairs issued a set of regulations that came to be known as the Code of Religious Offenses, or Religious Crimes Code. . . . Indians who refused to adopt the habits of industry, or to engage in "civilized pursuits or employments" were subject to arrest and punishment. . . . By interfering with native sexuality [and culture], the agents of assimilation effectively undermined the social fabric of entire tribes. (Roscoe, p. 176)

A Personal Resolution

For me, the resolution to the dual message I was receiving was slow in coming, largely due to the fear and self-hatred instilled in me by Christianity. Eventually, though, the spirit wins out. I came to adopt my grandmother's teaching about my intersexuality. Through therapy, and a new, loving home environment, I was able to shed the constant fear of eternal punishment I felt for something I had no control over. After all, I did not create myself.

Because of my own experience, and drawing on the teaching of my grandmother, I am now able to see myself as a wondrous creation of the Great Spirit—but not only me. All creation is wondrous. There is a purpose for everyone in the gender spectrum. Each person's spirit is unique in her or his or her-his own way. It is only by living true to the nature that was bestowed upon us by the Great Spirit, in my view, that we are able to be at peace with ourselves and be in harmony with our neighbor. This, to me, is the Great Meaning and the Great Purpose. . . .

Adapted from Williamson, R. K. (1995). The blessed curse: Spirituality and sexual difference as viewed by Euramerican and Native American cultures. The College News 18 (4). Reprinted with permission of the author.

The biological facts of human nature are not always as clear-cut as most people assume. At the level of chromosomes, biological sex is determined according to whether a person's 23rd chromosomal set is XX (female) or XY (male). Some of the genes on these chromosomes control sexual development. This standard biological package does not apply to all humans, and a considerable number are **intersexuals**—people who are born with reproductive organs, genitalia, and/or sex chromosomes that are not exclusively male or female. These individuals do not fit neatly into a binary gender standard.[18]

For example, some people are born with a genetic disorder that results in them having only one X chromosome instead of the usual two. A person with this chromosomal complex, known as Turner syndrome, develops female external genitalia but has nonfunctional ovaries and is therefore infertile. Other individuals are born with the XY sex chromosomes of a male but have an abnormality on the X chromosome that affects the body's sensitivity to androgens (male hormones). This is known as androgen insensitivity syndrome (AIS). An adult XY person with complete AIS appears fully female with a normal clitoris, labia, and breasts. Internally, these individuals possess testes (up in the abdomen, rather than in their usual descended position in the scrotal sac), but they are otherwise born without a complete set of either male or female internal genital organs. They generally possess a short, blind-ended vagina.

"Hermaphrodites" make up a distinct category of intersexuality—although the terms "male pseudohermaphrodite" and "female pseudohermaphrodite" are often used to refer to a range of intersex conditions. The name, now objected to by many activists, comes from a figure in Greek mythology: Hermaphroditus (son of Hermes, messenger of the gods, and Aphrodite, goddess of beauty and love) who became half-male and half-female when he fell in love with a nymph and his body fused with hers.[19]

More obviously intersexed individuals ("true hermaphrodites") have both testicular and ovarian tissue. They may have a separate ovary and testis, but more commonly they have an ovotestis—a gonad containing both sorts of tissue. About 60 percent of hermaphrodites possess XX (female) sex chromosomes, and the remainder may have XY or a mosaic (a mixture). Their external genitalia may be ambiguous or female, and they may have a uterus or (more commonly) a hemi-uterus (half uterus).[20]

---

[18] This section is based on several sources: Chase, C. (1998). Hermaphrodites with attitude. *Gay and Lesbian Quarterly 4* (2), 189–211; Dumurat-Dreger, A. (1998, May/June). "Ambiguous sex" or ambivalent medicine? *The Hastings Center Report 28* (3), 2,435 (posted on the Intersex Society of North America website: www.isna.org); Fausto-Sterling, A. (1993). The five sexes: Why male and female are not enough. *The Sciences 33* (2), 20–24; the Mayo Clinic website: http://www.mayoclinic.com/.

[19] The Intersex Society of North America suggests using DSD (disorders of sexual development) rather than "hermaphrodites" as part of an effort to urge clinicians to shift from focusing on gender and genitals to the exclusion of the real medical problems people with DSD face.

[20] Fausto-Sterling, A. (2000, July). The five sexes revisited. *The Sciences*, 20–24.

intersexual A person born with reproductive organs, genitalia, and/or sex chromosomes that are not exclusively male or female.

Caster Semenya, an 18-year-old runner from the South African village of Limpopo. After winning the women's 800-meter race at the 2009 world championships in Berlin, Caster faced a barrage of media reports with headlines such as "Gold Awarded Amid Dispute Over Runner's Sex." Gender tests, subsequently ordered by the International Sports Federation, revealed that the runner has internal male sexual organs. Horrified by the way the issue has been handled, South African Sports Minister Makhenkesi Stofile told *Sports Illustrated*, "We think her human rights have been violated and her privacy invaded."

© AP Photo Anja Niedringhaus

Biologist Anne Fausto-Sterling, a specialist in this area, notes that the concept of intersexuality is rooted in "an idealized biological world in which our species is perfectly divided into two kinds:

> That idealized story papers over [that] some women have facial hair, some men have none; some women speak with deep voices, some men veritably squeak. Less well known is the fact that on close inspection, absolute dimorphism disintegrates even at the level of basic biology. Chromosomes, hormones, the internal sex structures, the gonads and external genitalia all vary more than most people realize. Those born outside of the . . . dimorphic mold are called intersexuals.[21]

Intersexuality may be unusual but is not uncommon. In fact, about 1 percent of all humans are intersexed in some (not necessarily visible) way—in other words, nearly 70 million people worldwide.[22] Until recently, it was rarely discussed publicly in many societies. Since the mid-20th century, individuals with financial means in technologically advanced parts of the world have had the option of reconstructive surgery and hormonal treatments to alter such conditions, and many parents faced with raising a visibly intersexed child in a culture intolerant of such minorities have chosen this option for their baby. However, there is a growing movement to put off such irreversible procedures indefinitely or until the child becomes old enough to be the one to make the choice. Obviously, a society's attitude toward these individuals can impact their personality—their fundamental sense of self and how they express it.

In addition to people who are biologically intersexed, throughout history some individuals have been subjected to a surgical removal of some of their sexual organs. In many cultures, male prisoners or war captives have undergone forced castration, a crushing or cutting of the testicles. While castration of adult males does not eliminate the sex drive or the possibility of having an erection, it does put an end to the production of sperm necessary for reproduction.

Archaeological evidence from ancient Egypt, Iraq, Iran, and China suggests that the cultural practice of castrating war captives may have begun several thousand years ago. Young boys captured during war or slave-raiding expeditions were often castrated before being sold and shipped off to serve in foreign households, including royal courts. In the Ottoman empire of the Turks, where these individuals could occupy a variety of important functions in the sultan's household from the

---

[21] Ibid.

[22] Fausto-Sterling, A. (2003, August 2). Personal e-mail communication from this recognized expert on the subject. For published statistics, see her article co-authored with Blackless, M., et al. (2000). How sexually dimorphic are we? Review and synthesis. *American Journal of Human Biology 12,* 151–166.

mid-15th century onward, they were known as *eunuchs*. As suggested by the original meaning of the word, which is Greek for "guardian of the bed," castrated men were often put in charge of a ruler's harem, the women's quarters in a household. Eunuchs could also rise to high status as priests and administrators and were even appointed to serve as military commanders, as happened in the great Persian, Byzantine, and Chinese empires. Some powerful lords, kings, and emperors kept hundreds of eunuchs in their castles and palaces.[23]

Other than forced castration, there were also men who engaged in self-castration or underwent voluntary castration. For example, early Christian monks in Egypt and neighboring regions voluntarily abstained from sexual relationships and sometimes castrated themselves for the sake of the kingdom of heaven. Such genital mutilation was also practiced among Coptic monks in Egypt and Ethiopia until the early 20th century.[24]

In the late 15th century, Europe saw the emergence of a category of musical eunuchs known as *castrati*. These eunuchs sang female parts in church choirs after Roman Catholic authorities banned women singers on the basis of Saint Paul's instruction, "Let your women keep silence in the churches." Simultaneously, castrati began performing female roles in operas. Castrated before they reached puberty so as to retain their high voices, these selected boys were often orphaned or came from poor families. Without functioning testes to produce male sex hormones, physical development into manhood is aborted, so deeper voices—as well as body hair, semen production, and other usual male attributes—were not part of a castrati's biology.

The phenomenon of castrati continued until about 1900, when Roman Catholic authorities in the Vatican banned their role in church music. By then, the eunuch systems in the Chinese and Ottoman empires were also about to be abolished.[25]

Mapping the sexual landscape, anthropologists have come to realize that gender bending exists in many cultures all around the world, playing a significant role in shaping behaviors and personalities. For example, indigenous communities in the U.S. Great Plains and Southwest created social space for **transgenders,** people who cross over or occupy an alternative position in the binary male–female gender construction. The Lakota of the northern Plains had a third gender category of culturally accepted transgendered males who dressed as women

Admiral Sheng Ho (or Zhèng Hé, 1371–1433) of the Chinese imperial fleet was a famous military commander. He was also a eunuch, as were other military officers in the great ancient empires of China, Persia, and Byzantium. Born and raised in a Muslim family, he was captured as an 11-year-old boy in Yunnan, southwestern China. Soon afterward, he was castrated and sent to the household of the Prince of Yen, one of the Chinese emperor's twenty-six sons. Growing to a height above 2 meters (6.5 feet), Sheng Ho entered the army and rose as a military officer. When the Prince of Yen became emperor in 1402, Sheng Ho became the Grand Imperial Eunuch. Three years later, he was appointed admiral over a fleet of sixty-two sailing ships and 28,000 men. In the next three decades, this powerful eunuch headed five major exploratory and trading expeditions throughout the Indian Ocean, reaching as far as East Africa. In 1431, with a fleet of 100 ships, Sheng Ho set out for his final voyage. He died on the east coast of India en route back to China and was buried at sea.

and were thought to possess both male and female spirits. They called (and still call) these third-gender individuals *winkte,* applying the term to a male "who wants to be a woman." Thought to have special curing powers,

---

[23] Herdt, G. (Ed.). (1996). *Third sex, third gender: Beyond sexual dimorphism in culture and history.* New York: Zone.

[24] Abbot, E. (2001). *A history of celibacy.* Cambridge, MA: Da Capo Press.

[25] Taylor, G. (2000). *Castration: Abbreviated history of western manhood* (pp. 38–44, 252–259). New York: Routledge.

transgender A person who crosses over or occupies an alternative position in the binary male–female gender construction.

winktes traditionally enjoyed considerable prestige in their communities. Among the neighboring Cheyenne, such a person was called *hemanah,* literally meaning "half-man, half-woman."[26] The preferred term among most North American Indians today is "two-spirits."[27]

Such third-gender individuals are well known in Samoa, where males who take on the identity of females are referred to as *fa'afafines* ("the female way"). Becoming a *fa'afafine* is an accepted option for boys who prefer to dance, cook, clean house, and care for children and the elderly. In large families, it is not unusual to find two or three boys being raised as girls to take on domestic roles in their households. As anthropologist Lowell Holmes reported,

> In fact, they tend to be highly valued because they can do the heavy kinds of labor that most women find difficult. A Samoan nun once told me how fortunate it is to have a fa'afafine in the family to help with the household chores. [There] is also the claim made that fa'afafines never have sexual relations with each other but, rather, consider themselves to be "sisters." [They] are religious and go to church regularly dressed as women and . . . some are even Sunday school teachers. Fa'afafines often belong to women's athletic teams, and some even serve as coaches.[28]

These transgendered cultural types cannot be simply lumped together as homosexuals. For example, the Tagalog-speaking people in the Philippines use the word *bakla* to refer to a man who views himself "as a male with a female heart." These individuals cross-dress on a daily basis, often becoming more "feminine" than Philippine women in their use of heavy makeup, in the clothing they wear, and in the way they walk. Like the Samoan *fa'afafines,* they are generally not sexually attracted to other *bakla* but are drawn to heterosexual men instead.

In addition, some people are gender variants—permanent or incidental transvestites (cross-dressers) without being homosexuals—making it obvious that the cross-cultural sex and gender scheme is complex. Indeed, the late 19th-century "homosexuality" label is quite inadequate to cover the full range of sex and gender diversity.

In sum, human cultures in the course of thousands of years have creatively dealt with a wide range of inherited and artificially imposed sexual features. Studying

Transgendering occurs in many cultures, but it is not always publicly tolerated. Among Polynesians inhabiting Pacific Ocean islands such as Tonga and Samoa, however, such male transvestites are culturally accepted. Samoans refer to these third-gender individuals as *fa'afafines* ("the female way").

complex categories involving intersexuality and transgendering allows us to recognize the existing range of gender alternatives and to debunk false stereotypes. It is one more piece of the human puzzle—an important one that prods us to rethink social codes and the range of forces that shape personality as well as each society's definition of normal.

Normal and Abnormal Personality in a Social Context

The cultural standards that define normal behavior for any society are determined by that society itself. While the societies just noted have accepted transgender behaviors, many others regard them as culturally abnormal and show intolerance toward those who deviate from commonly accepted social standards of sexual behavior. For instance,

[26] Medicine, B. (1994). Gender. In M. B. Davis (Ed.), *Native America in the twentieth century.* New York: Garland.

[27] Jacobs, S. E. (1994). Native American two-spirits. *Anthropology Newsletter 35* (8), 7.

[28] Holmes, L. D. (2000). *Paradise bent* (film review). *American Anthropologist 102* (3), 604–605.

according to a recent global report on state-sponsored homophobia:

> With Panama decriminalising homosexuality in 2008 and Burundi for the first time in its history criminalizing homosexuality in 2009, the world now counts 80 countries with State-sponsored homophobic laws: 72 countries and 3 entities (Turkish Cyprus, Gaza and Cook Islands) punish consenting adults with imprisonment, while 5 countries (Iran, Mauritania, Saudi Arabia, Sudan, Yemen and parts of Nigeria and Somalia) punish them with the death penalty.[29]

If a male in one of these sexually restrictive societies dresses as a woman, he is widely viewed as emotionally troubled, or even mentally ill, and his abnormal behavior may lead to punitive measures or psychiatric intervention.

There are countless such examples of the fact that what is considered normal and acceptable (if not always popular) in one society is abnormal and unacceptable (ridiculous, shameful, and sometimes criminal) in another. As well, the standards that define normal behavior may shift over time. In England, for instance, homosexuality was decriminalized in 1967. And six years later, the American Psychiatric Association removed same-sex orientation from its authoritative list of clinical mental disorders.[30]

Of course, there is a substantial difference between no longer regarding a sexual minority as criminal or as mentally ill and ending all discrimination against them for being "abnormal." And it almost goes without saying that such discrimination is problematic not only for people whose sexual orientation is different from that of the mainstream but for anyone who deviates significantly in appearance or behavior from general social standards or norms.

However, in many cultures, individuals may stand out as "different" without being considered "abnormal" in the strictest sense of the word—and without suffering social rejection, ridicule, censure, condemnation, imprisonment, or some other penalty. Moreover, some cultures not only tolerate or accept a much wider range of diversity than others, but they may actually accord special status to the deviant or eccentric as unique, extraordinary, even sacred, as illustrated by the following example.

---

[29] International Lesbian, Gay, Bisexual, Trans and Intersex Association (ILGA). (2009). *The 2009 report on state-sponsored homophobia.* See also the Pew Research Center. (2007). *Global attitudes survey.*

[30] Bayer, R. (1987). *Homosexuality and American psychiatry: The politics of diagnosis.* Princeton, NJ: Princeton University Press.

Sadhus: Holy Men in Hindu Culture

Sadhus, religious mystics in India and Nepal, present a fascinating ethnographic example of abnormal individuals living in cultures where they are socially accepted and even honored. Their lives also illustrate the degree to which one's social identity and sense of personal self are cultural constructs.

When a young Hindu man in India or Nepal decides to become an ascetic monk, or *sadhu,* he must transform his personal identity, change his sense of self, and leave his place in the social order. Detaching himself from the pursuit of earthly pleasures (*kama*) and power and wealth (*artha*), he makes a radical break with his family and friends and abandons the moral principles and rules of conduct prescribed for his caste (*dharma*). Symbolically expressing his "death" as a typical Hindu, he participates in his own funeral ceremony, followed by a ritual rebirth. As a born-again, he acquires a new identity as a *sadhu* and is initiated into a particular ascetic order or sect.

Having surrendered all social, material, and even sexual attachments to normal human pleasures and delights, the *sadhu* dedicates himself to achieving spiritual union with the divine or universal soul. This is done through intense meditation (chanting sacred hymns or mystical prayer texts—mantras) and yoga (an ascetic and mystic discipline involving prescribed postures and controlled breathing). The goal is to become a fully enlightened soul, liberated from the physical limits of the individual mortal self, including the cycle of life and death.

The *sadhu* path to this divine state of pure consciousness and total inner freedom (*mokshe*) is acutely challenging. It demands extraordinary concentration and near superhuman effort, as can be seen in the most extreme yoga postures. This chosen life of suffering may even include self-torture as a form of extreme penance. For instance, some *sadhus* pierce their tongue or cheek with a long iron rod, stab a long knife through their arm or leg, or stick their head into a small hole in the ground for hours on end. Among the more extreme examples, one *sadhu* is known to have kept his right arm continuously stretched up into the air for twenty-five years (transforming his hand into a useless stump).

Most Hindus revere and sometimes even fear *sadhus.* When they encounter one—by a temple or cemetery, or

Shaivite *sadhu* of the Aghori sub-sect drinks from a human skull bowl (symbolizing human mortality). He is a
strict follower of the Hindu god Shiva, whose image can be seen behind him.

perhaps near a forest, riverbank, or mountain cave—they
typically offer him food or other alms. Sightings are not
uncommon since an estimated 5 million *sadhus* live in
India and Nepal. They belong to different sub-sects of ascetic orders, each with its own characteristics and ritual
practices. Some *sadhus* are believed to have succeeded in
achieving divine status as *jivan mukta* ("a soul liberated
while still alive") and are devoutly honored as great saints
or as gods on earth.

Perhaps the most remarkable *sadhus* belong to a very
small sub-sect of the Shaivite Order, devoted to worshiping Shiva, the Hindu god of destruction and reproduction.
Known as *aghoris* (meaning "not terrible," one of Shiva's
names), these extremely ascetic monks challenge the cosmic order itself and turn normal rules of Hindu conduct
upside-down. Naked or near naked ("sky-clad"), they
spend most of their time around cremation grounds. On a
regular basis they apply ashes to their body, face, and long
matted hair. As a daily reminder of human mortality, they
drink and eat from human skull bowls, occasionally challenging themselves in their devotion to Shiva by eating

their own excrement or decomposed human flesh torn
from a body awaiting cremation.[31]

If one of these bearded, long-haired Hindu monks,
especially an *aghori,* practiced his sacred devotions as a
Shiva worshiper in western Europe or North America—
walking around naked and drinking from a human skull
bowl—surely he would be viewed not as a holy man but as
severely mentally disturbed.

Mental Disorders Across Time and Culture

Many anthropologists believe that the only meaningful
criterion for personality evaluation is the correlation between personality and social conformity. From their point

[31] See Kelly, T. L. (2006). *Sadhus, the great renouncers.* Photography exhibit,
Indigo Gallery, Naxal, Kathmandu, Nepal. www.asianart.com/exhibitions/
sadhus/index.html. See also Heitzman, J., & Wordem, R. L. (Eds.). (2006).
India: A country study (sect. 2, 5th ed.). Washington, DC: Federal Research
Division, Library of Congress.

A Cross-Cultural Perspective on Psychosomatic Symptoms and Mental Health

Biomedicine, the dominant medical system of Euramerican cultures, sometimes identifies physical ailments experienced by individuals as "psychosomatic"—a term derived from *psyche* ("mind") and *soma* ("body"). These ailments can be serious and painful, but because a precise physiological cause cannot be identified through scientific methods, the illness is viewed as something rooted in mental or emotional causes—and thus on some level not quite real.

Each culture possesses its own historically developed ideas about health, illness, and associated healing practices. While biomedicine is based in modern Western traditions of science, it is also steeped in the cultural beliefs and practices of the societies within which it operates. Fundamentally informed by a dualistic mind–body model, biomedicine represents the human body as a complex machine with parts that can be manipulated by experts. This approach has resulted in spectacular treatments, such as antibiotics that have eradicated certain infectious diseases.

Today, the remarkable breakthroughs of biomedicine are spreading rapidly throughout the world, and people from cultures with different healing systems are moving into countries where biomedicine dominates. This makes treating illnesses defined by biomedicine as

psychosomatic disorders all the more difficult.

Indicative of our biocultural complexity, psychological factors such as emotional stress, worry, and anxiety may stem from cultural contexts and result in increased physiological agitation like irregular heart pounding or palpitations, heightened blood pressure, headaches, stomach and intestinal problems, muscle pains and tensions, rashes, appetite loss, insomnia, fatigue, and a range of other troubles. Indeed, when individuals are unable to deal successfully with stressful situations in daily life and do not get the opportunity for adequate mental rest and relaxation, even their natural immune systems may weaken, increasing their chances of getting a cold or some other infection. For people forced to adapt to a quickly changing way of life in their own country or immigrants adjusting to a foreign culture, these pressures may result in a range of disorders that are difficult to explain from the perspective of biomedicine.

Medical and psychological approaches developed in European and North American societies are often unsuccessful in dealing with these problems, for a number of reasons. For one, the various immigrant ethnic groups have different concepts of mind and body than do medical practitioners trained in Western (Euramerican)

medicine. Among many Caribbean peoples, for example, a widely held belief is that spiritual forces are active in the world and that they influence human identity and behavior. For someone with a psychosomatic problem, it is normal to seek help from a local *curandero* or *curandera* ("folk healer"), a *santiguadora* ("herbalist"), or even a *santéro* (a Santéria priest) rather than a medical doctor or psychiatrist. Not only does the client not understand the symbols of Western psychiatry, but a psychiatric visit is often too expensive and may imply that the person is *loco*.

During the past few decades, however, anthropologists have become increasingly involved in cross-cultural medical mediation, challenging negative biases and correcting misinformation about non-Western indigenous perceptions of mind–body connections. The inclusion of culturally appropriate healing approaches has gained growing acceptance among the Western medical and psychological establishment in Europe, North America, and many other parts of the world.

BIOCULTURAL QUESTION

Given the cross-cultural differences in concepts of mind and body, should authorities in a pluralistic society apply the same standards to faith healers as to medical doctors?

---

of view, insanity is a culturally constructed mental illness, and people are considered insane when they fail to conform to a culturally defined range of normal behavior.

No matter how eccentric or bizarre certain behaviors might seem in a particular place and time, those behaviors are not necessarily abnormal in all cultures, and it is possible for the "abnormal" to become socially accepted in cultures that are changing. Such is the case with manic depression (now more properly called *bipolar disorder*) and attention deficit hyperactivity disorder (ADHD), both previously regarded as dreaded liabilities.

In western Europe and North America, the manic and hyperactivity aspects of these conditions have gradually become viewed as assets in the quest for success.[32] Just as

social attitudes concerning a wide range of both psychological and physical differences change over time within a society, they also vary across cultures—as is evident in this chapter's Biocultural Connection.

CULTURAL RELATIVITY OF ABNORMALITY

Is "normal" is a meaningless concept when applied to personality? Within the context of a particular culture, the concept of normal personality is quite meaningful. Irving Hallowell, a major figure in the development of psychological anthropology, ironically observed that it is normal to share the delusions traditionally accepted by one's society. Abnormality involves the development of a delusional system of which the culture does not approve. The individual who is disturbed because he or she cannot adequately measure up to the norms of society and be happy may be termed "neurotic." When a person's delusional system is

---

[32] Martin, E. (1999). Flexible survivors. *Anthropology News 40* (6), 5–7.

so different that it in no way reflects his or her society's norms, the individual may be termed "psychotic."

If severe enough, culturally induced conflicts can produce psychosis and also determine its particular form. In a culture that encourages aggressiveness and suspicion, the insane person may be one who is passive and trusting. In a culture that encourages passivity and trust, the insane person may be the one who is aggressive and suspicious. Just as each society establishes its own norms, each individual is unique in his or her perceptions.

Although it is true that each particular culture defines what is and is not normal behavior, the situation is complicated by findings suggesting that major categories of mental disorders may be universal types of human affliction. Take, for example, schizophrenia—probably the most common of all psychoses and one that may be found in any culture, no matter how it may manifest itself. Individuals afflicted by schizophrenia experience distortions of reality that impair their ability to function adequately, so they often withdraw from the social world into their own psychological shell.

Although environmental factors play a role, evidence suggests that schizophrenia is caused by a biochemical disorder for which there is an inheritable tendency. One of its more severe forms is paranoid schizophrenia. Those suffering from it fear and mistrust nearly everyone. They hear voices that whisper dreadful things to them, and they are convinced that someone is "out to get them." Acting on this conviction, they engage in bizarre sorts of behaviors, which lead to their removal from society.

CULTURE-BOUND SYNDROME

A **culture-bound syndrome,** or ethnic psychosis, is a mental disorder specific to a particular cultural group (Table 6.1).[33] A historical example is Windigo psychosis, limited to northern Algonquian groups such as the Cree and Ojibwa. In their traditional belief systems, these Indians recognized the existence of cannibalistic monsters called Windigos. Individuals afflicted by the psychosis developed the delusion that, falling under the control of these monsters, they were themselves transformed into Windigos, with a craving for human flesh. As this happened, the psychotic individuals perceived people around them turning into edible animals—fat beavers, for instance. Although there are no known instances where sufferers of

Windigo psychosis actually devoured humans, they were acutely afraid of doing so, and people around them feared that they might.

Windigo psychosis may seem different from clinical cases of paranoid schizophrenia found in Euramerican cultures, but a closer look suggests otherwise. The disorder was merely being expressed in ways compatible with traditional northern Algonquian cultures. Ideas of persecution, instead of being directed toward other humans, were directed toward supernatural beings (the Windigo monsters); cannibalistic panic replaced panic expressed in other forms.

Windigo behavior has seemed exotic and dramatic to Euramericans, but psychotic individuals draw upon whatever imagery and symbolism their culture has to offer. For instance, the delusions of Irish schizophrenics draw upon the images and symbols of Irish Catholicism and feature Virgin and Savior motifs. In short, the underlying biomedical structure of the mental disorder may be the same in all cases, but its expression is culturally specific.

A Western example of a culture-bound syndrome is "hysteria," expressed by fainting spells, choking fits, and even seizures and blindness. Identified in industrializing societies of 19th-century Europe and North America, this disorder was particularly associated with young urban women in well-to-do social circles. In fact, the term invented for this "nervous disease" is derived from the Greek word for uterus. Not only has the diagnosis of this disorder declined in the course of the 20th century, but the term itself was banished from the medical nomenclature.[34]

In more recent decades, we have seen the rise of two related culture-bound syndromes: *bulimia nervosa* and *anorexia nervosa.* Bulimia is characterized by frequent binge eating followed by vomiting or other frantic efforts to avoid gaining weight. Anorexia is an obsession to remain thin, evidenced in self-starvation that may result in death. This neurotic "fear of fatness" manifests itself in Western consumer societies where a growing percentage of the population is overweight or obese. Bulimia and anorexia are primarily diagnosed in female adolescents who reside in a culture that exalts thinness, even as fast food and leisure snacking are more prevalent. With the globalization of consumer society's fat–thin contradiction, its associated psychological eating disorders are also crossing borders.[35] Today, Japan is just behind the United States in deaths related to psychological eating disorders.[36]

---

[33] Simons, R. C., & Hughes, C. C. (Eds.). (1985). *The culture-bound syndromes: Folk illnesses of psychiatric and anthropological interest.* Dordrecht, Netherlands: Reidel.

culture-bound syndrome A mental disorder specific to a particular cultural group.

---

[34] Gordon, R. (2000). *Eating disorders: Anatomy of a social epidemic* (2nd ed.). New York: Wiley-Blackwell.

[35] Littlewood, R. (2004). Commentary: Globalization, culture, body image, and eating disorders. *Culture, Medicine, and Psychiatry 28* (4), 597–602.

[36] World Health Organization. (2004). Statistical information system. See also http://www.nationmaster.com/graph/mor_eat_dis-mortality-eating-disorders.

Table 6.1 Culture-Bound Syndromes

Name of Disorder	Culture	Description
Amok	Malaysia (also observed in Java, Philippines, Africa, and Tierra del Fuego)	A disorder characterized by sudden, wild outbursts of homicidal aggression in which the afflicted person may kill or injure others. The rage disorder is usually found in males who are rather withdrawn, quiet, and inoffensive prior to the onset of the disorder. Stress, sleep deprivation, extreme heat, and alcohol are among the conditions thought to precipitate the disorder. Several stages have been observed: Typically in the first stage the person becomes more withdrawn; then a period of brooding follows in which a loss of reality contact is evident. Ideas of persecution and anger predominate. Finally, a phase of automatism, or *amok*, occurs, in which the person jumps up, yells, grabs a knife, and stabs people or objects within reach. Exhaustion and depression usually follow, with amnesia for the rage.
Anorexia nervosa	Western countries (becoming global)	A disorder occurring most frequently among young women in which a preoccupation with thinness produces a refusal to eat. This condition can result in death.
Latah	Malaysia	A fear reaction often occurring in middle-aged women who are subservient and self-effacing. The disorder is precipitated by the word *snake* or by tickling. It is characterized by echolalia (repetition of the words and sentences of others). The disturbed individual may also react with negativism and the compulsive use of obscene language.
Koro	Southeast Asia (particularly Malaysia)	A fear reaction or anxiety in males in which the person fears that his penis will withdraw into his abdomen and he will die. This reaction may appear after sexual overindulgence or excessive masturbation. The anxiety is typically very intense and of sudden onset. The condition is "treated" by having the penis held firmly by the patient or by family members or friends. Often the penis is clamped to a wooden box.
Windigo	Algonquian Indians of Canada and northern United States	A fear reaction in which a hunter becomes anxious and agitated, convinced that he is bewitched. Fears center on his being turned into a cannibal by the power of a monster with an insatiable craving for human flesh.
Kitsunetsuki	Japan	A disorder in which victims believe that they are possessed by foxes and are said to change their facial expressions to resemble foxes. Entire families are often possessed and banned by the community.
Pibloktoq and other Arctic hysterias	Circumpolar peoples from Lapland eastward across Siberia, northern Alaska, and Canada to Greenland	A disorder brought on by fright, which is followed by a short period of bizarre behavior; victim may tear clothes off, jump in water or fire, roll in snow, try to walk on the ceiling, throw things, thrash about, and "speak in tongues." Outburst is followed by a return to normal behavior.

Source: Based on Carson, R. C., Butcher, J. N., & Coleman, J. C. (1990). *Abnormal psychology and modern life* (8th ed., p. 85). Glenview, IL: Scott Foresman.

Personal Identity and Mental Health in Globalizing Society

Anthropologists view childrearing, gender issues, social identity, and emotional and mental health issues in their cultural context; this perspective recognizes that each individual's unique personality, feelings of happiness, and overall sense of health are shaped or influenced by the particular culture within which the person is born and raised to function as a valued member of the community. These communities, however, are seldom stable.

As illustrated by the spread of consumer culture and its associated psychological disorders, people all across the world face sometimes bewildering challenges hurled at them by the forces of globalization. These forces impact how people raise their children, how their personalities are influenced, and how they maintain their individual and collective social, psychological, and mental health.

In the past few decades, medical and psychological anthropologists have made valuable contributions to improving health care, not only in so-called developing countries far away, but also in their own societies. However, mental health practices prevailing in Europe and North America remain ethnocentric when theorizing and treating psychological disorders—a problem reinforced by a reductionist biomedical mindset that largely ignores the role of cultural factors in the etiology, expression, course, and outcome of mental disorders. Furthermore, commercial pressures on the health-care establishment favor bioscience and pharmacotherapy, with drug companies providing a quick and cheap fix for the problem.[37]

_____

[37] Luhrmann, T. M. (2001). *Of two minds: An anthropologist looks at American psychiatry.* New York: Vintage; Marsella, A. J., & White, G. (1982). *Cultural conceptions of mental health and therapy.* New York: Springer.

Informed by cultural relativist views on normality and deviance, anthropological perspectives on identity, mental health, and psychiatric disorders are especially useful in pluralistic societies where people from different ethnic groups, each with a distinctive culture, coexist and interact. Intensified by globalization, this multi-ethnic convergence drives home the need for a medical pluralism providing multiple healing modalities suited for the cultural dynamics of the 21st century.

Questions for Reflection

1. Every society faces the challenge of humanizing its children, teaching them the values and social codes that will enable them to be functioning, contributing members in the community. What childrearing practices did you experience that embody the values and social codes of your society?

2. Considering the cultural significance of naming ceremonies in so many societies, what do you think motivated your parents when they named you? Does that have any influence on your sense of self?

3. Margaret Mead's cross-cultural research on gender relations suggests that male dominance is a cultural construct and, consequently, that alternative gender arrangements can be created. Looking at your grandparents, parents, and siblings, do you see any changes in your own family? What about your own community? Do you think such changes are positive?

4. Given that nearly 70 million people in today's world are intersexed and in light of the fact that a very small fraction of these people have access to reconstructive surgery, what do you think of societies that have created cultural space for a third-gender option?

5. Do you know someone in your family, neighborhood, or school who is "abnormal"? What is the basis for that judgment, and do you think everyone shares that opinion? Can you imagine that personal habits you consider normal would be viewed as deviant in the past or in another country?

Suggested Readings

Barnouw, V. (1985). *Culture and personality* (4th ed.). Homewood, IL: Dorsey.

This is a revision of a well-respected text designed to introduce students to psychological anthropology.

Brettell, C. B., & Sargent, C. F. (Eds.). (2000). *Gender in cross-cultural perspective* (3rd ed.). Upper Saddle River, NJ: Prentice-Hall.

Classic and contemporary gender readings on a range of topics, including the cultural construction of femininity and masculinity and the impact of globalization on gender issues.

LaFont, S. (Ed.). (2003). *Constructing sexualities: Readings in sexuality, gender, and culture.* Upper Saddle River, NJ: Prentice-Hall.

A broad yet detailed look at sexuality and gender behavior. Statistics, ethnographic examples, and theoretical insights on numerous themes—from the biological basics and sex categories to sexual orientation and transsexuality.

Levine, R. A. (2007). Ethnographic studies of childhood: A historical overview. *American Anthropologist 109* (2), 247–260.

This article offers a succinct survey and discussion of the ethnographic literature on childhood studies in the 20th century, from psychoanalytically informed studies by Malinowski, Mead, and others in the 1920s and 1930s to comparative psychocultural studies launched by Whiting et al. in the 1950s, followed by diverse anthropological trends in infant studies from the 1960s onward.

Quinn, N. (2005). Universals of child rearing. *Anthropological Theory 5*, 475–514.

Based on cross-cultural comparisons of childrearing strategies, the author identifies four universal features of childrearing that together explain how every society so effectively enculturates children into valued adults.

Suárez-Orozoco, M. M., Spindler, G., & Spindler, L. (1994). *The making of psychological anthropology*, II. Fort Worth: Harcourt Brace.

This collection of articles consists of firsthand accounts of the objectives, accomplishments, and failures of well-known specialists in psychological anthropology.

Challenge Issue Facing the challenge of getting food, fuel, shelter, and other necessities, humans must gather, produce, or buy the means to satisfy such needs. During the span of human existence, this has been accomplished in a range of highly contrasting natural environments by different biological and cultural adaptations. Inventing and applying various technologies, humans have developed distinctive subsistence arrangements to harness energy and process required resources. Thus we may find hunters in Namibia's desert, fishers in Norway, manioc planters in Brazil's rainforest, goat herders in Iran's mountains, steel-mill laborers in South Korea, computer techs in India's cities, and poultry farmers in rural Alabama. While all human activities impact their environments, some are more invasive than others—as we see in this photo showing peasant farmers of Dazhai village practicing wet-rice cultivation on the mountainous slopes of Guangxi Province in southern China. They have created terraces to capture rainwater, prevent soil erosion, and increase food production.

CHAPTER 7

Patterns of Subsistence

Chapter Preview

What Is Adaptation?

Adaptation refers to beneficial adjustments of organisms to their environment, a process that not only leads to changes in the organisms but also impacts their environment. Such dynamic interaction is necessary for the survival of all life forms, including human beings. The human species adapts not only biologically but culturally. In fact, in the course of evolution humans came to rely increasingly on cultural rather than biological change as a means of effectively adapting to different and changing environments.

How Do Humans Adapt Culturally?

Through cultural adaptation, humans develop ways of doing things that are compatible with the resources they have available to them and within the limitations of the various habitats in which they live. In a particular region, people living in similar environments tend to borrow from one another customs that work well in those settings. Once achieved, adaptations may be remarkably stable for long periods of time, even thousands of years. Humankind's unique creative capacity to adapt by means of culture has enabled our species to inhabit an extraordinary variety of environments.

What Cultural Adaptations Have Humans Achieved?

Food foraging is the oldest and most universal human adaptation and typically involves geographic mobility. Other adaptations, based on the domestication of plants and animals, began to develop in some parts of the world about 10,000 years ago. Horticulture (cultivating plants with hand tools) led to more permanent settlements (villages and towns) while pastoralism (herding grazing animals) required mobility to seek out pasture and water. Cities began to develop as early as 5,000 years ago in some world regions, as intensive agriculture and long-distance trading produced sufficient resources to support larger populations and various full-time specialists. And only about two centuries ago, a worldwide transition from an economy based on manual labor and draft animals toward one based on machines was set into motion by the industrial revolution, which radically transformed manufacturing, agriculture, mining, and transportation. These changes led to increasingly complex and large-scale social organizations—but did not necessarily improve the overall conditions of human existence. Two of the unanticipated negative consequences of a machine technology energized by fossil-fuel burning are environmental pollution and global warming, contributing to regional climate changes.

All living beings must satisfy certain basic needs to stay alive—including food, water, and shelter. Moreover, because these needs must be met on an ongoing basis, no creature could long survive if its relations with its environment were random and chaotic. All require regular access to a supply of food along with reliable means of obtaining and using it. A lion would die if all its prey disappeared, if its teeth and claws grew soft, or if its digestive system failed.

Although people face similar sorts of problems, they have an overwhelming advantage over other creatures: People have culture. If the rains do not come and the hot sun turns grassland into desert, we may pump water from deep wells, quenching our thirst, irrigating the pastures, and feeding our grazing animals. Conversely, if the rains do not end and our pastures turn into marshlands, we may choose to build earth mounds for our villages or dig canals to drain flooded fields. And to keep our food supplies from rotting, we can preserve them by drying or roasting and keep them in safe storage places for protection and future use. When our tools fail or are inadequate, we may choose to replace them or invent better ones. And if our stomachs are incapable of digesting a particular food, we can prepare it by cooking.

We are, nonetheless, subject to similar basic needs and pressures as are all other living creatures, and it is important to understand human survival from this point of view. The crucial concept that underlies such a perspective is adaptation: how humans adjust to and act upon the burdens and opportunities presented in daily life.

Adaptation

As discussed earlier in this book, *adaptation* is the process organisms undergo to achieve a beneficial adjustment to a particular environment. What makes human adaptation unique among all other species is our capacity to produce and reproduce culture, enabling us to creatively adapt to an extraordinary range of radically different environments. The biological underpinnings of this capacity include large brains and a long period of growth and development.

How humans adjust to the burdens and opportunities presented in daily life is the basic concern of all cultures. As defined earlier in the book, a people's *cultural adaptation* consists of a complex of ideas,

activities, and technologies that enable them to survive and even thrive; that adaptation, in turn, impacts their environment.

The process of adaptation establishes an ever-shifting balance between the needs of a population and the potential of its environment. This process can be illustrated by the Tsembaga people of Papua New Guinea, one of about twenty local groups of Maring speakers who support themselves chiefly through cultivating crops using simple hand tools such as digging sticks or hoes.[1] Although the Tsembaga also raise pigs, they eat them only under conditions of illness, injury, warfare, or celebration. At such times the pigs are sacrificed to ancestral spirits, and their flesh is ritually consumed. (This guarantees a supply of high-quality protein when it is most needed.)

Traditionally, the Tsembaga and their neighbors are bound together in a unique cycle of pig sacrifices that serves to mark the end of hostilities between groups. Hostilities are periodically fueled by ecological pressures in which pigs play a significant role. Because they fulfill important functions in the community, pigs are rarely slaughtered. Omnivorous eaters, they keep the village free of garbage and even human feces; moreover, they serve as status symbols for their owners who reserve them for important ritual feasts. But there are drawbacks to keeping the pigs alive and allowing them to multiply, since their numbers grow quickly. Invading the village gardens, the hungry pigs eat the sweet potatoes and other crops, leaving almost nothing for their human owners. In short, they become a problem.

The need to expand food cultivation in order to feed the prestigious but pesky pigs puts a strain on the land best suited for farming. Sooner or later, fighting breaks out between the Tsembaga and their neighbors. Hostilities usually end after several weeks, followed by a pig feast ritual. For this event, the Tsembaga butcher and roast almost all of their pigs and feast heartily on them with invited allies. By means of this feast, the Tsembaga not only pay their debts to their allies and gain prestige, but also eliminate a major source of irritation and complaint between neighbors. Moreover, the feast leaves everyone well fed and physically strengthened as a result of the animal protein intake. Even without hostilities over scarce land, such large pig feasts have been held whenever the pig population has become unmanageable—every five to ten years, depending on the groups' success in growing crops and raising animals. Thus the cycle of

---

[1] Rappaport, R. A. (1969). Ritual regulation of environmental relations among a New Guinea people. In A. P. Vayda (Ed.), *Environment and cultural behavior* (pp. 181–201). Garden City, NY: Natural History.

Surviving in the Andes: Aymara Adaptation to High Altitude

However adaptable we are as a species through our diverse cultures, some natural environments pose such extreme climatic challenges that the human body must make physical adaptations to successfully survive. The central Andean highlands of Bolivia offer an interesting example of complex biocultural interaction, where a biologically adapted human body type has emerged due to natural selection.

Known as the *altiplano,* this high plateau has an average elevation of 4,000 meters (13,000 feet). Many thousands of years ago, small groups of human foragers in the warm lowlands climbed up the mountain slopes in search of game and other food. The higher they moved, the harder it became to breathe due to decreasing molecular concentration, or partial pressure, of oxygen in the inspired air. However, upon reaching the cold and treeless highlands, they found herds of llamas and hardy food plants, including potatoes—reasons to stay. Eventually (about 4,000 years ago) their descendants domesticated both the llamas and the potatoes and developed a new way of life as high-altitude agropastoralists.

The llamas provided meat and hides, as well as milk and wool. And the potatoes, a rich source of carbohydrates, became their staple food. In the course of many centuries, the Aymara selectively cultivated more than 200 varieties of these tubers on small family-owned tracts of land. They boiled them fresh for immediate consumption and also freeze-dried and preserved them as *chuño,* which is the Aymara's major source of nutrition to this day.

© Victor Englebert

Still surviving as highland subsistence farmers and herders, these Aymara Indians have adapted culturally and biologically to the cold and harsh conditions of Bolivia's altiplano. They live and go about their work at extremely high altitudes (up to 4,800 meters/15,600 feet), where partial pressure of oxygen in the air is far lower than that to which most humans are biologically accustomed.

Experiencing a marked hypoxemia (insufficient oxygenation of the blood), a person's normal physiological response to being active at such heights is quick and heavy breathing. Most outsiders visiting the altiplano typically need several days to acclimatize to these conditions. Going too high too quickly can cause *soroche* (mountain sickness), with physiological problems such as pulmonary hypertension, increased heart rates, shortness of breath, headaches, fever, lethargy, and nausea. These symptoms usually disappear when one becomes fully acclimated, but most people will still be quickly exhausted by otherwise normal physical exercise.

For the Aymara Indians whose ancestors have inhabited the altiplano for many thousands of years, the situation is different. Through generations of natural selection, their bodies have become biologically adapted to the low oxygen levels. Short-legged and barrel-chested, their small bodies have an unusually large thoracic volume compared to their tropical lowland neighbors and most other humans. Remarkably, their expanded heart and lungs possess about 30 percent greater pulmonary diffusing capacity to oxygenate blood. In short, the distinctly broad chests of the Aymara Indians are biological evidence of their adaptation to the low-oxygen atmosphere of a natural habitat in which they survive as high-altitude agropastoralists.

BIOCULTURAL QUESTION

If a group of Aymara Indians abandons their high-altitude homeland in the Bolivian altiplano and settles for a new life in the coastal lowlands, will their descendents still living in this low-altitude environment a dozen generations later have smaller chests?

For more information see Baker, P. (Ed.). (1978). The biology of high altitude peoples. London: Cambridge University Press; Rupert, J. L., & Hochachka, P. W. (2001). The evidence for hereditary factors contributing to high altitude adaptation in Andean natives: A review. High Altitude Medicine & Biology 2 *(2), 235–256.*

fighting and feasting keeps the ecological balance among humans, land, and animals.

Through their distinctive cultures, different human groups have managed to adapt to a very diverse range of natural environments—from Arctic snowfields to Polynesian coral islands, from the Sahara Desert to the Amazon rainforest. Adaptation occurs not only when humans make changes in their natural environment but also when they are biologically changed by their natural environment, as illustrated in this chapter's Biocultural Connection.

The Unit of Adaptation

The unit of adaptation includes both organisms and their environment. Organisms, including human beings, exist as members of a population; populations, in turn, must have the flexibility to cope with variability and change within the natural environment that sustains them. In biological terms, this flexibility means that different organisms within the population have somewhat differing genetic endowments. In cultural terms, it means that variation occurs among individual skills, knowledge, and personalities. Indeed, organisms and environments form dynamic interacting systems. And although environments do not determine culture, they do present certain possibilities and limitations: People might just as easily farm as fish, but we do not expect to find farmers in Siberia's frozen tundra or fishermen in the middle of North Africa's Sahara Desert.

Some anthropologists have adopted the ecologists' concept of **ecosystem,** defined as a system composed of both the natural environment and all the organisms living within it. The system is bound by the activities of the organisms, as well as by such physical processes as erosion and evaporation.

Adaptation in Cultural Evolution

Human groups adapt to their environments by means of their cultures. However, cultures may change over the course of time; they evolve. This is called **cultural evolution.** The process is sometimes confused with the idea of **progress**—the notion that humans are moving forward to a better, more advanced stage in their development toward perfection. Yet not all changes turn out to be positive in the long run, nor do they improve conditions for every member of a society even in the short run. Complex, urban societies are not more highly evolved than those of food foragers. Rather, both are highly evolved, but in quite different ways.

Cultural adaptation must also be understood from a historical point of view. To fit into an ecosystem, humans (like all organisms) must have the potential to adjust to or become a part of it. A good example of this is the Comanche, whose known history begins in the highlands of southern Idaho.[2] Living in that harsh,

---

[2] Wallace, E., & Hoebel, E. A. (1952). *The Comanches.* Norman: University of Oklahoma Press.

---

ecosystem A system, or a functioning whole, composed of both the natural environment and all the organisms living within it.

cultural evolution Cultural change over time; not to be confused with progress.

progress The notion that humans are moving forward to a better, more advanced stage in their cultural development toward perfection.

convergent evolution In cultural evolution, the development of similar cultural adaptations to similar environmental conditions by different peoples with different ancestral cultures.

arid region, these North American Indians traditionally subsisted on wild plants, small animals, and occasionally larger game. Their material equipment was simple and limited to what they (and their dogs) could carry or pull. The size of their groups was restricted, and what little social power could develop was in the hands of the shaman, who was a combination of healer and spiritual guide.

At some point in their nomadic history, the Comanche moved east onto the Great Plains, attracted by enormous bison herds. As much larger groups could be supported by the new and plentiful food supply, the Comanche needed a more complex political organization. Eventually they acquired horses and guns from European and neighboring Indian traders. This enhanced their hunting capabilities significantly and led to the emergence of powerful hunting chiefs.

The Comanche became raiders in order to get horses (which they did not breed for themselves), and their hunting chiefs evolved into war chiefs. The once materially unburdened and peaceful hunter-gatherers of the dry highlands became wealthy, and raiding became a way of life. In the late 18th and early 19th centuries, they dominated the southern Plains (now primarily Texas and Oklahoma). In moving from one regional environment to another and in adopting a new technology, the Comanche were able to take advantage of existing cultural capabilities to thrive in their new situation.

Sometimes societies that developed independently of one another find similar solutions to similar problems. For example, the Cheyenne Indians moved from the woodlands of the Great Lakes region to the Great Plains and took up a form of Plains Indian culture resembling that of the Comanche, even though the cultural historical backgrounds of the two groups differed significantly. (Before they transformed into horse-riding bison hunters, the Cheyenne had cultivated crops and gathered wild rice, which fostered a distinct set of social, political, and religious practices.) This is an example of **convergent evolution**—the development of similar cultural adaptations to similar environmental conditions by different peoples with different ancestral cultures. (See Figure 7.1 for a map of Native American culture areas.)

Especially interesting is that the Cheyenne gave up crop cultivation completely and focused exclusively on hunting and gathering after their move into the vast grasslands of the northern High Plains. Contrary to the popular notion of evolution as a progressive movement toward increased manipulation of the environment, this ethnographic example shows that cultural historical changes in subsistence practices do not always go from dependence on wild food to farming; they may go the other way as well.

A Comanche bison hunt as painted by artist George Catlin (1796–1872). Plains Indians such as the Comanche and Lakota developed similar cultures as they had to adapt to similar environmental conditions.

© Smithsonian American Art Museum, Washington, DC/Art Resource, NY

Related to the phenomenon of convergent evolution is **parallel evolution,** in which similar cultural adaptations to similar environmental conditions are achieved by peoples whose ancestral cultures were already somewhat alike. For example, the development of farming in Southwest Asia and Mesoamerica took place independently, as people in both regions, whose lifeways were already comparable, became dependent on a narrow range of plant foods that required human intervention for their protection and reproductive success. Both developed intensive forms of agriculture, built large cities, and created complex social and political organizations.

It is important to recognize that stability as well as change is involved in cultural adaptation and evolution; episodes of major adaptive change may be followed by long periods of relative stability in a cultural system. Moreover, not everybody benefits from changes, especially if change is forced upon them. As history painfully demonstrates, all too often humans have made changes that have had disastrous results, leading to the deaths of countless people—not to mention other creatures—and to the destruction of the natural environment.

Among the many examples of environmental destruction with catastrophic results is Easter Island in the southern Pacific. First settled by Polynesian seafarers about a thousand years ago, it became the homeland of the Rapanui people. Like other Polynesians, they subsisted on growing crops and raising chickens, as well as fishing, hunting, and gathering. Prospering, they produced surplus and formed chiefdoms. Success, however, did not last.

Within several generations, the energetic Rapanui had deforested their beautiful island, and their ecosystem began to collapse. Crop failure led to famines and social tensions, triggering violent conflicts leading to cycles of destruction. Warfare and disease decimated the population by about 75 percent. Their numbers had dropped to about 3,000 by the time Europeans first landed on their shores in the 18th century—bringing new diseases and other miseries that nearly wiped the Rapanui from the face of the earth.[3]

Environmental destruction on a much more massive scale has occurred in many other parts of the world, especially in the course of the 20th century, ruining the lives of millions. Considering such catastrophes, we must avoid falling into the ethnocentric trap of equating change with progress or with seeing everything as adaptive.

CULTURE AREAS

From early on, anthropologists recognized that ethnic groups living within the same broad habitat often share certain cultural traits. This reflects the fact that there

[3] Diamond, J. (2005). *Collapse: How societies choose to fail or succeed* (Ch. 2, pp. 79–119). New York: Penguin; Van Tilburg, J. A. (1994). *Easter Island archaeology, ecology and culture.* London: British Museum Press.

parallel evolution In cultural evolution, the development of similar cultural adaptations to similar environmental conditions by peoples whose ancestral cultures were already somewhat alike.

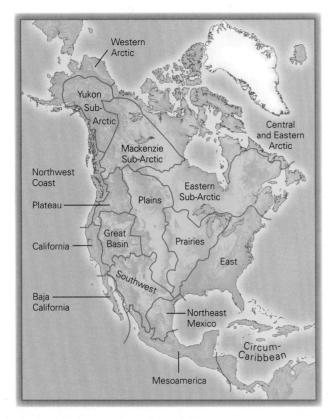

Figure 7.1 This map shows the major culture areas that have been identified for North and Central America. Within each, there is an overall similarity of Native cultures, as opposed to the differences that distinguish the cultures of one area from those of all others.

exists a basic relationship among their similar natural environment, available resources, and subsistence practices and that neighboring peoples are in contact and engage in exchange with one another.

Classifying groups according to their cultural traits, anthropologists have mapped geographic regions in which a number of societies have similar ways of life. Known as **culture areas,** such regions often correspond to ecological regions (Figure 7.1). In sub-Arctic North America, for example, migratory caribou herds graze across the vast tundra. For dozens of different groups that have made this area their home, these animals provide a major source of food as well as material for shelter and clothing. Adapting to more or less the same ecological resources in this sub-Arctic landscape, these groups have developed similar subsistence technologies and practices in the course of generations. They may speak very different languages, but they may all be said to form part of the same culture area.

culture area A geographic region in which a number of societies follow similar patterns of life.

Because of changes in the natural environment such as habitat destruction and the extinction of plant and animal species, culture areas are not always stable. Moreover, new species may be introduced and technologies may be invented or adopted from more distant cultures. Such was the case with the indigenous culture area of the Great Plains in North America (see Figure 7.1). For thousands of years, many indigenous groups with similar ways of life existed in this vast ecological area between the Mississippi River and the Rocky Mountains. Until the mid-1800s, when European immigrants invaded the region and almost completely annihilated the millions of free-ranging bison, these large grazing herds provided an obvious and practical source of food and materials for clothing and shelter.

The efficiency of indigenous groups in the southern grasslands increased greatly in the 1600s when they gained access to Spanish horses on the northern Mexican frontier and became mounted bison hunters. During the next century, the new horse complex spread northward to almost every indigenous group ranging in the Great Plains culture area. A total of thirty-one politically independent peoples, including the Cheyenne and Comanche just mentioned, reached a similar adaptation to this particular environment.

So it was that by the time of the Euramerican invasion of their vast hunting territories in the 19th century, the Indians of the Great Plains were all bison hunters, dependent on this animal for food, clothing, shelter, and bone tools. Each nation was organized into a number of warrior societies, and prestige came from hunting and fighting skills. Their villages were typically arranged in a distinctive circular pattern, and they shared many religious rituals, such as the Sun Dance.

During the 1870s and 1880s, railroads were built across the Great Plains, and mass slaughter of bison followed. More than 1 million of these animals were killed every year, mostly by non-Indians interested only in their hides and tongues (tongues were a luxury meat commodity, easily removed and compact to ship). With their herds almost exterminated, Indians of the Plains faced starvation, which made it impossible to effectively defend their homeland. This resulted in the near collapse of their traditional cultures from the 1890s onward.

CULTURE CORE

Environment and technology are not the only factors that determine a society's pattern of subsistence; social structure and political organization also influence how a society solves its food problem. For instance, if we wish to understand the rise of irrigation agriculture in the great centers of ancient civilization (such as in what are now Egypt, China, Peru, and Iraq), we need to know not only the technological and environmental factors that made the building of large-scale irrigation works possible but also the social structure and political organization that made it

In Bali, gatherings for rituals at water temples allowed farmers to arrange schedules for flooding their rice paddies.

© Joe Carini/The Image Works

feasible to mobilize the many workers necessary to build and maintain the systems and to grow and harvest the crops. For this understanding, we must examine the political elites and administrators that coordinated the work, decided where the water would be used, and determined how the agricultural products of this collective venture would be distributed.

The cultural features that are fundamental to the society's way of making its living are called its **culture core.** This includes the society's food-producing techniques, knowledge of available resources in its environment, and the work arrangements involved in applying those techniques to the local environment.

The culture core comprises other aspects of culture that bear on the production and distribution of food. Among these is worldview or ideology, evidenced in the ways religious beliefs sometimes prohibit the use of certain readily available and highly nutritious foods. For example, most Muslims and Jews abstain from eating pork because doing so is prohibited by their religion, and most Hindus do not eat beef because they revere cows as sacred animals. There are countless other food taboos, all varying across cultures: horse meat (regularly part of French fare but generally abhorred in England), dogs (not eaten by Europeans but a typical ingredient in Korean meals), monkeys (appreciated by Amazonian Indians but excluded from North American menus), insects (an important source of nutrition in many tropical cultures but considered creepy in most other parts of the world), and humans (not eaten by most humans).[4]

A number of anthropologists focus on identifying the principles behind native idea systems and how they inform a people about their environment. For example, on the Indonesian island of Bali, ritual meetings were held regularly at water temples, located at the forks of rivers. Part of the ritual included negotiating seasonal schedules for flooding the farmers' rice fields. Without the water temple rituals, irrigation coordination risks falling apart, resulting in water shortages, pest infestation, and lower productivity. In short, cultural beliefs, no matter how irrelevant they seem to uninformed outsiders, may offer the key to understanding another society's subsistence or any other long-established collective practice.

Modes of Subsistence

Human societies everywhere have developed a cultural infrastructure that is compatible with the natural resources they have available to them and within the limitations of their various habitats. Each mode of subsistence involves not only resources but also the technology required to effectively capture and utilize them, as well as the kinds of work arrangements that are developed to best suit a society's needs. In the next few pages,

---

[4] Pelto, G. H., Goodman, A. H., & Dufour, D. L. (Eds.). (2000). *Nutritional anthropology: Biocultural perspectives on food and nutrition.* Mountain View, CA: Mayfield.

culture core Cultural features that are fundamental in the society's way of making its living—including food-producing techniques, knowledge of available resources, and the work arrangements involved in applying those techniques to the local environment.

we will discuss the major types of cultural infrastructure, beginning with the oldest and most universal mode of subsistence: food foraging.

Food-Foraging Societies

Before the domestication of food plants and animals, all people supported themselves through **food foraging,** a mode of subsistence involving some combination of hunting, fishing, and gathering wild plant foods. When food foragers had the earth to themselves, they had their pick of the best environments. But gradually areas with rich soils and ample supplies of water were appropriated by farming societies and, more recently, by industrial and postindustrial societies. As a result, small foraging communities were edged out of their traditional habitats by these expanding groups.

Today at most a quarter of a million people (less then 0.005 percent of the world population of over 6.8 billion) still support themselves mainly as foragers. They are found only in the world's most marginal areas—frozen Arctic tundra, deserts, and inaccessible forests—and typically lead a migratory existence that makes it impractical to accumulate many material possessions. Because foraging

food foraging   Hunting, fishing, and gathering wild plant foods.

cultures have nearly disappeared in areas having a natural abundance of food and fuel resources, anthropologists are necessarily cautious when it comes to making generalizations about the ancient human past based on in-depth studies of still-existing foraging groups that have adapted to more marginal habitats.

Typically, foragers have ample and balanced diets and are less likely to experience severe famine than farmers. Their material possessions are limited, but so is their desire to amass things. Notably, they have plenty of leisure time for concentrating on family ties, social life, and spiritual development—apparently far more than people living in farming and industrial societies. Such findings clearly challenge the once widely held view that food foragers live a miserable existence.

It is important to note that present-day people who subsist by hunting, fishing, and wild plant collection are not following an ancient way of life because they do not know any better. Rather, they have been forced by circumstances into situations where foraging is the best means of survival or they simply prefer to live this way. In fact, foraging constitutes a rational response to particular ecological, economic, and sociopolitical realities. Moreover, for at least 2,000 years, hunters, fishers, and gatherers have met the demands for commodities such as furs, hides, feathers, ivory, pearls, fish, nuts, and honey within larger trading networks. Like everyone else, most food foragers are now part of a larger system with social, economic, and political relations extending far beyond regional, national, or even continental boundaries.

Human groups (including food foragers) do not exist in isolation except occasionally, and even then not for long. The bicycle this Bushman of southern Africa is riding is indicative of his links with the wider world. For 2,000 years, Bushmen have been interacting regularly with neighboring farmers and pastoralists. As well, food foragers have supplied much of the commodities desired by the rest of the world, such as the elephant ivory used for keyboards on pianos so widely sought in 19th-century North America.

© Anthony Bannister, Gallo Images/CORBIS

Characteristics of Foraging Communities

The hallmarks of food-foraging societies (particularly those few that still or until recently survive in marginal areas that are not as naturally rich in food and fuel) include mobility, small group size, flexible division of labor by gender, food sharing, egalitarianism, communal property, and rarity of warfare.

Although much has been written on the theoretical importance of hunting for shaping the supposedly competitive and aggressive nature of the human species, most anthropologists are unconvinced by these arguments. To be sure, warlike behavior on the part of food-foraging peoples is known, but such behavior is a relatively recent phenomenon in response to pressure from expansionist states. In the absence of such pressures, food-foraging peoples are remarkably nonaggressive and place more emphasis on peacefulness and cooperation than they do on violent competition. We touch on each of the other characteristics below.

MOBILITY

Food foragers move as needed within a circumscribed region that is their home range to tap into naturally available food sources. Some groups, such as the Ju/'hoansi in the Kalahari Desert of southern Africa who depend on the reliable and highly drought-resistant mongongo nut, may keep to fairly fixed annual routes and cover only a restricted territory. Others, such as the traditional Shoshone in the western highlands of North America, had to cover a wider territory, their course determined by the local availability of the erratically productive pine nut.

A crucial factor in this mobility is availability of water. The distance between the food supply and water must not be so great that more energy is required to fetch water than can be obtained from the food.

SMALL GROUP SIZE

Another characteristic of the food-foraging adaptation is the small size of local groups, typically fewer than a hundred people. No completely satisfactory explanation for this has been offered, but both ecological and social factors are involved. Among the ecological factors is the **carrying capacity** of the land—the number of people that the available resources can support at a given level of food-getting techniques. This requires adjusting to seasonal and long-term changes in resource availability. Carrying capacity involves not only the immediate presence of food and water but also the tools and work necessary to secure them, as well as short- and long-term fluctuations in their availability.

In addition to seasonal or local adjustments, food foragers must make long-term adjustments to resources. Food-foraging populations usually stabilize at numbers well below the carrying capacity of their land. In fact, the home ranges of most food foragers can support from three to five times as many people as they typically do. In the long run, it may be more adaptive for a group to keep its numbers low rather than to expand indefinitely and risk destruction by a sudden and unexpected natural reduction in food resources. The population density of foraging groups surviving in marginal environments today rarely exceeds one person per square mile—a very low density.

How food-foraging peoples regulate population size relates to two things: how much body fat they accumulate and how they care for their children. Ovulation requires a certain minimum of body fat, and in traditional foraging societies, this is not achieved until early adulthood. Hence, female reproductive maturity typically occurs between the early and mid-20s, and teenage pregnancies—at least, successful ones—are virtually unknown.[5] Once a child is born, its mother nurses it several times each hour, even at night, and this continues over a period of four or five years. The constant stimulation of the mother's nipple suppresses the level of hormones that promote ovulation, making conception less likely, especially if work keeps the mother physically active and she does not have a large store of body fat to draw on for energy.[6] Continuing to nurse for several years, women give birth only at widely spaced intervals. Thus the total number of offspring remains low but sufficient to maintain stable population size.

FLEXIBLE DIVISION OF LABOR BY GENDER

Division of labor exists in all human societies and is probably as old as human culture. Among food foragers, the hunting and butchering of large game as well as the processing of hard or tough raw materials are almost universally masculine occupations. By contrast, women's

---

[5] Hrdy, S. B. (1999). Body fat and birth control. *Natural History 108* (8), 88; see also Frisch, R. (2002). *Female fertility and the body fat connection.* Chicago: University of Chicago Press.

[6] Small, M. F. (1997). Making connections. *American Scientist 85,* 503; see also Konner, M., & Worthman, C. (1980). Nursing frequency, gonadal function, and birth spacing among !Kung hunter-gatherers. *Science 207,* 788–791.

carrying capacity The number of people that the available resources can support at a given level of food-getting techniques.

Frequent nursing of children over four or five years acts to suppress ovulation among food foragers such as Ju/'hoansi. As a consequence, women give birth to relatively few offspring at widely spaced intervals.

work in foraging societies usually focuses on collecting and processing a variety of plant foods, as well as other domestic chores that can be fit to the demands of breast-feeding and that are more compatible with pregnancy and childbirth.

Among food foragers today, the work of women is no less arduous than that of men. Ju/'hoansi women, for example, may walk 12 miles a day, two or three times a week, to gather food, carrying not only their children but also, on the return home, between 15 and 33 pounds of food. Still, they do not have to travel quite as far as do men on the hunt, and their work is usually less dangerous. Also, their tasks require less rapid mobility, do not need complete and undivided attention, and are readily resumed after interruption.

All of this is compatible with those biological differences that remain between the sexes. Certainly women who are pregnant or have infants to nurse cannot travel long distances in pursuit of game as easily as men can. By

the same token, of course, women may have preferred and been better at the less risky task of gathering.

But, saying that differing gender roles among food foragers is compatible with the biological differences between men and women is *not* saying that these roles are biologically determined. Among the Great Plains Indians of North America, for example, there are quite a few reports of women who gained fame as hunters and warriors—both historically regarded as men's activities. In fact, the division of labor by gender is often far less rigid among food foragers than it is in most other types of society. Thus, Ju/'hoansi males, willingly and without embarrassment, as the occasion demands, will gather wild plant foods, build huts, and collect water, even though all are regarded as women's work.

Notably, the food-gathering activities of women play a major role in the survival of their group: Research shows that contemporary food foragers may obtain up to 60 or 70 percent of their diets from plant foods, with perhaps some fish and shellfish also provided primarily by women (the exceptions tend to be food foragers living in Arctic regions, where plant foods are not available for much of the year).

Although women in foraging societies commonly spend some time each day gathering plant foods, men rarely hunt on a daily basis. The amount of energy expended in hunting, especially in hot climates, is often greater than the energy return from the kill. Too much time spent searching out game might actually be counterproductive. Energy itself is derived primarily from plant carbohydrates, and it is usually the female gatherers who bring in the bulk of the calories. A certain amount of meat in the diet, though, guarantees high-quality protein that is less easily obtained from plant sources, for meat contains exactly the right balance of all of the amino acids (the building blocks of protein) the human body requires. No one plant food does this, and in order to get by without meat, people must hit on exactly the right combination of plants to provide the essential amino acids in the correct proportions.

FOOD SHARING

Another key feature of human social organization associated with food foraging is the sharing of food. Among the Ju/'hoansi, women have control over the food they collect and can share it with whomever they choose. Men, by contrast, are constrained by rules that specify how much meat is to be distributed and to whom. For the individual hunter, meat sharing is really a way of storing it for the future: His generosity, obligatory though it might be, gives him a claim on the future kills of other hunters. As a cultural trait, food sharing has the obvious survival value of distributing resources needed for subsistence.

Visual Counterpoint

Typically, food foragers such as the Ju/'hoansi have a division of labor in which women gather and prepare "bush" food (here an ostrich egg omelet) and men usually do the hunting.

EGALITARIAN SOCIAL RELATIONS

An important characteristic of the food-foraging society is its egalitarianism. Because foragers are usually highly mobile and lack animal or mechanical transportation, they must be able to travel without many encumbrances, especially on food-getting expeditions. By necessity, the material goods they carry with them are limited to the barest essentials, which include implements for hunting, gathering, fishing, building, and cooking. (For example, the average weight of an individual's personal belongings among the Ju/'hoansi is just under 25 pounds.) In this context, it makes little sense for them to accumulate luxuries or surplus goods, and the fact that no one owns significantly more than another helps to limit status differences. Age and sex are usually the only sources of important status differences.

It is important to realize that status differences by themselves do not constitute inequality, a point that is easily misunderstood, especially where relations between men and women are concerned. In most traditional food-foraging societies, women did not and do not defer to men. To be sure, women may be excluded from some rituals in which males participate, but the reverse is also true. Moreover, the fruits of women's labor are controlled by them, not by men. Nor do women sacrifice their autonomy even in societies in which male hunting, rather than female gathering, brings in the bulk of the food.

Such was the case, for example, among the Innu (Montagnais) Indians of Labrador. Theirs was a society in which the hunt was of overwhelming importance. For their part, women manufactured clothing and other necessities, but provided much less of the food than is common among food foragers in most other natural environments. Until recently, women as well as men could be shamans. Nevertheless, women were excluded from ritual feasts having to do with hunting—but then, so were men excluded from ritual feasts held by women. Basically, each gender carried out its own activities, with neither meddling in those of the other. Early missionaries to the Innu hunting bands lamented that men had no inclination to make their wives obey them and worked long and hard to convince the Indians that civilization required men to impose their authority on women. But after 300 years of

pressing this point, missionaries achieved only limited success.

Food foragers make no attempt to accumulate surplus foodstuffs, often an important source of status in agrarian societies. This does not mean that they live constantly on the verge of starvation, for their environment is their natural storehouse. Except in the coldest climates (where a surplus must be set aside to see people through the long, lean winter season) or in times of acute ecological disaster, some food can almost always be found in a group's territory. Because food resources are typically shared and distributed equally throughout the group (share and share alike is the order of the day), no one achieves the wealth or status that hoarding might bring. In such a society, having more than others is a sign of deviance rather than a desirable characteristic.

The food forager's concept of territory contributes as much to social equality as it does to the equal distribution of resources. Most groups have home ranges within which access to resources is open to all members. What is available to one is available to all. If an Mbuti Pygmy hunter living in the forests of Central Africa discovers a honey tree, he has first rights; but when he has taken his share, others have a turn. In the unlikely possibility that he does not take advantage of his discovery, others will. No individual within the community privately owns the tree; the system is first come, first served. Therefore, knowledge of the existence of food resources circulates quickly throughout the entire group.

How Technology Impacts Cultural Adaptations among Foragers

Like habitat, technology plays an important role in shaping the characteristics of the foraging life discussed above. The mobility of food-foraging groups may depend on the availability of water, as among the Ju/'hoansi, or of game animals and other seasonal resources, as among the Mbuti in the Democratic Republic of Congo in Central Africa. Different hunting technologies and techniques may also play a part in determining movement, as well as population size and division of labor by gender.

Consider, for example, the Mbuti Pygmies in the Ituri tropical forest. All Mbuti bands hunt elephants with spears. However, for other game, some of the bands use bows and others use large nets. Those equipped with nets have a cooperative division of labor in which

men, women, and children collaborate in driving antelope and other game into the net for the kill. Usually, this involves very long hours and movement over great distances as participants surround the animals and beat the woods noisily to chase the game in one direction toward the great nets. Since this sort of "beat-hunt" requires the cooperation of seven to thirty families, those using this method have relatively large camps. Among Mbuti bow hunters, on the other hand, only men go after the game. These archers tend to stay closer to the village for shorter periods of time and live in smaller groups, typically of no more than six families. While there is no significant difference in overall population density between net and bow hunting areas, archers generally harvest a greater diversity of animal species, including monkeys.[7]

Food-Producing Societies

Obviously, habitat and technology do not tell the whole story of how we humans feed ourselves. After the emergence of tool making, which enabled humans to consume significant amounts of meat as well as plant foods, the next truly momentous event in human history was the domestication of plants and animals. Over time, this achievement transformed cultural systems, with humans developing new economic arrangements, social structures, and ideological patterns based on plant cultivation, breeding and raising animals, or a mixture of both.

The transition from food foraging to food production first took place about 10,000 years ago in Southwest Asia (the Fertile Crescent, including the Jordan River Valley and neighboring regions in the Middle East). This was the beginning of the **Neolithic** or New Stone Age (from the Greek *neo* meaning "new" and *lith* meaning "stone"), in which people possessed stone-based technologies and depended on domesticated plants and/or animals. Within the next few thousand years, similar early transitions to agricultural economies took place independently in other parts of the world where human groups began to raise and (later) alter wild cereal plants such as wheat, maize (corn), and rice; legumes such as beans; gourds such as squash; and tubers such as potatoes. Doing the same with a number of wild animal species ranging in their hunting territories, they began to domesticate goats, sheep, pigs, cattle, and llamas (Figure 7.2).

Neolithic The New Stone Age; prehistoric period beginning about 10,000 years ago in which peoples possessed stone-based technologies and depended on domesticated plants and/or animals.

---

[7] Bailey, R. C., & Aunger, R. (1989). Net hunters vs. archers: Variation in women's subsistence strategies in the Ituri forest. *Human Ecology 17*, 273–297; Terashima, H. (1983). Mota and other hunting activities of the Mbuti archers: A socio-ecological study of subsistence technology. *African Studies Monograph* (Kyoto), 71–85.

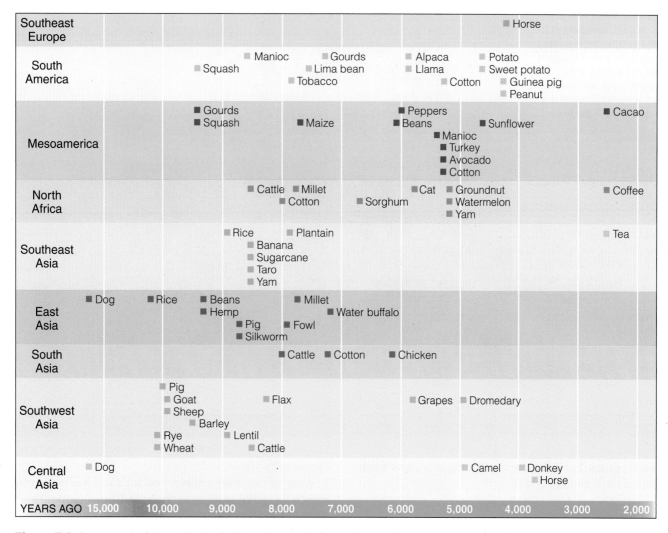

Figure 7.2 Appearance of domesticates in the archaeological record.

Because these activities brought about a radical transformation in almost every aspect of their cultural systems, Australian-born archaeologist Gordon Childe introduced the term **Neolithic revolution** to refer to the profound cultural change associated with the early domestication of plants and animals. As humans became increasingly dependent on domesticated crops, they mostly gave up their mobile way of life and settled down to till the soil, sow, weed, protect, harvest, and safely store their crops. No longer on the move, they could build more permanent dwellings and began to make pottery for storage of water, food, and so on.

Just why this change came about is one of the important questions in anthropology. Because food production requires more work than food foraging, is more monotonous, and is often a less secure means of subsistence, it is unlikely that people became food producers voluntarily.

Initially, it appears that food production arose as a largely unintended byproduct of existing food management practices. Among many examples, we may consider the Paiute Indians, whose desert habitat in the western highlands of North America includes some oasis-like marshlands. These foragers discovered how to irrigate wild crops in their otherwise very dry homeland, thus increasing the quantity of wild seeds and bulbs to be harvested. Although their ecological intervention was very limited, it allowed them to settle down for longer periods in greater numbers than otherwise would have been possible.

Unlike the Paiute, who stopped just short of a Neolithic revolution, other groups elsewhere in the world continued to transform their landscapes in ways that favored the appearance of new varieties of particular plants

Neolithic revolution The profound cultural change beginning about 10,000 years ago and associated with the early domestication of plants and animals and settlement in permanent villages.

In preparation for new planting, this old, overgrown plot in the Amazon forest in Venezuela is burned. Although it looks destructive, if done properly, slash-and-burn cultivation is an ecologically sound way of growing crops in the tropics.

© Jacques Jangoux/Alamy

and animals, which came to take on increasing importance for people's subsistence. Although probably at first accidental, it became a matter of necessity as growth outstripped people's ability to sustain themselves through food foraging. For them, food production became a subsistence option of last resort.

Producing Food in Gardens: Horticulture

With the advent of plant domestication, some societies took up **horticulture** (from the Latin *hortus,* meaning "garden") in which small communities of gardeners cultivate crops with simple hand tools, using neither irrigation nor the plow. Typically, horticulturists cultivate several varieties of food plants together in small, hand-cleared gardens. Because they do not usually fertilize the soil, they use a given garden plot for only a few years before abandoning it in favor of a new one. Often, horticulturists grow enough food for their subsistence, and occasionally they produce a modest surplus that can be used for

other purposes such as inter-village feasts and exchange. Although their major food supplies may come from their gardens, many horticulturists will also hunt game, fish, and collect wild plants foods in the forest when need and opportunity arise.

One of the most widespread forms of horticulture, especially in the tropics, is **slash-and-burn cultivation,** or *swidden farming,* in which the natural vegetation is cut, the slash is subsequently burned, and crops are then planted among the ashes. This is an ecologically sophisticated and sustainable way of raising food, especially in the tropics, when carried out under the right conditions: low population densities and adequate amounts of land. It mimics the diversity of the natural ecosystem, growing several different crops in the same field. Mixed together, the crops are less vulnerable to pests and plant diseases than a single crop.

Not only is the system ecologically sound, but it is far more energy efficient than modern farming methods used in developed countries such as the United States, where natural resources such as land and fuel are still relatively cheap and abundant, and many farms operate with financial support in the form of government subsidies or tax breaks. While high-tech farming requires more energy input than it yields, slash-and-burn farming produces between 10 and 20 units of energy for every unit expended. A good example of how such a system works is provided by the Mekranoti Kayapo Indians of Brazil's Amazon forest, profiled in the following Original Study.

horticulture Cultivation of crops carried out with simple hand tools such as digging sticks or hoes.

slash-and-burn cultivation An extensive form of horticulture in which the natural vegetation is cut, the slash is subsequently burned, and crops are then planted among the ashes; also known as swidden farming.

Gardens of the Mekranoti Kayapo   *by Dennis Werner*

The planting of a Mekranoti garden always follows the same sequence. First, men clear the forest and then burn the debris. Then, in the ashes, both men and women plant sweet potatoes, manioc, bananas, corn, pumpkins, papaya, sugar cane, pineapple, cotton, tobacco, and annatto, whose seeds yield achiote, the red dye used for painting ornaments and people's bodies. Since the Mekranoti don't bother with weeding, the forest gradually invades the garden. After the second year, only manioc, sweet potatoes, and bananas remain. And after three years or so there is usually nothing left but bananas. Except for a few tree species that require hundreds of years to grow, the area will look like the original forest twenty-five to thirty years later.

This gardening technique, known as slash-and-burn, is one of the most common in the world. At one time critics condemned the technique as wasteful and ecologically destructive, but today we know that, especially in the humid tropics, slash-and-burn may be one of the best gardening techniques possible.

Continuous high temperatures encourage the growth of the microorganisms that cause rot, so organic matter quickly breaks down into simple minerals. The heavy rains dissolve these valuable nutrients and carry them deep into the soils, out of the reach of plants. The tropical forest maintains its richness because the heavy foliage shades

the earth, cooling it and inhibiting the growth of the decomposers. A good deal of the rain is captured by leaves before ever reaching the ground.

When a tree falls in the forest and begins to rot, other plants quickly absorb the nutrients that are released. In contrast, with open-field agriculture, the sun heats the earth, the decomposers multiply, and the rains quickly leach the soils of their nutrients. In a few years a lush forest, if cleared for open one-crop agriculture, can be transformed into a barren wasteland.

A few months after the Mekranoti plant banana and papaya, these trees shade the soil, just as the larger forest trees do. The mixing of different kinds of plants in the same area means that minerals can be absorbed as soon as they are released; corn picks up nutrients very fast, while manioc is slow. Also, the small and temporary clearings mean that the forest can quickly reinvade its lost territory.

Because decomposers need moisture as well as warmth, the long Mekranoti dry season could alter this whole picture of soil ecology. But soil samples from recently burned Mekranoti fields and the adjacent forest floor showed that, as in most of the humid tropics, the high fertility of the Indians' garden plots comes from the trees that are burned there, not from the soil, as in temperate climates.

Getting a good burn is a tricky operation. Perhaps for this reason the more experienced and knowledgeable members of the community oversaw its timing. If done too early, the rains will leach out the minerals in the ash before planting time. If too late, the debris will be too wet to burn properly. Then, insects and weeds that could plague the plants will not die and few minerals will be released into the soil. If the winds are too weak, the burn will not cover the entire plot. If they are too strong, the fire can get out of hand.

Shortly after burning the plots and clearing away of some of the charred debris, people began the long job of planting, which took up all of September and lasted into October. In the center of the circular garden plot the women dug holes and threw in a few pieces of sweet potatoes. After covering the tubers with dirt, they usually asked a male to stomp on the mound and

make a ritual noise resembling a Bronx cheer—magic to ensure a large crop. Forming a large ring around the sweet potatoes, the Indians rapidly thrust pieces of manioc stems into the ground, one after the other.

When grown, manioc stems form a dense barrier to the sweet potato patch, and some of the plants must be cut down to gain entrance. Outside of the ring of manioc, the women planted yams, cotton, sugar cane, and annatto. Banana stalks and papaya trees, planted by simply throwing the seeds on the ground, form the outermost circle. The Indians also planted corn, pumpkins, watermelons, and pineapple throughout the garden. Rapid growers, they were harvested long before the manioc matured. The garden appeared to change magically from corn and pumpkins to sweet potatoes and manioc without replanting.

Mekranoti gardens grew well. A few Indians complained now and then about a peccary that had reduced their corn harvest or eaten a watermelon they had looked forward to enjoying, but in general the animals seemed to leave the crops alone. Even the leaf-cutting ants that are problems in other areas did not bother the Mekranoti. Occasionally a neighbor who had not planted a new garden would make off with a prized first-year crop, such as pumpkin, watermelon, or pineapple. But even these thefts were rare. In general, the Mekranoti could depend on harvesting whatever they planted.

Eventually, I wanted to calculate the productivity of Mekranoti gardens. Western agronomists knew very little about slash-and-burn crop cultivation. They were accustomed to experiments in which a field was given over to a single crop and the harvest happened all at once. Here, the plants were all mixed together, and people harvested piecemeal whenever they needed something. The manioc could stay in the ground, growing for several years before it was dug up.

I began measuring off areas of gardens to count how many manioc plants, ears of corn, or pumpkins were found there. The women thought it strange to see me struggling through the tangle of plants to measure off

CONTINUED

CONTINUED

areas, 10 meters by 10 meters, placing string along the borders, and then counting what was inside. Sometimes I asked a woman to dig up all of the sweet potatoes within the marked-off area. My requests were bizarre, but the women cooperated just the same, holding on to the ends of the measuring tapes, or sending their children to help. For some plants, like bananas, I simply counted the number of clumps of stalks in the garden, and the number of banana bunches I could see growing in various clumps. By watching how long it took the bananas to grow, from the time I could see them until they were harvested, I could

calculate a garden's total banana yield per year.

After returning from the field, I was able to combine the time allocation data with the garden productivities to get an idea of how hard the Mekranoti need to work to survive. The data showed that for every hour of gardening one Mekranoti adult produces almost 18,000 kilocalories of food. (As a basis for comparison, people in the United States consume approximately 3,000 kilocalories of food per day.) As insurance against bad years, and in case they receive visitors from other villages, they grow far more produce than they need. But even so, they don't need to work very hard to survive. A look at the average amount of time adults spend on different tasks every

week shows just how easygoing life in horticultural societies can be:

8.5 hours	Gardening
6.0 hours	Hunting
1.5 hours	Fishing
1.0 hour	Gathering wild foods
33.5 hours	All other jobs

Altogether, the Mekranoti need to work less than 51 hours a week, and this includes getting to and from work, cooking, repairing broken tools, and all of the other things we normally don't count as part of our work week.

From Werner, D. (1990). Amazon journey *(pp. 105–112). Englewood Cliffs, NJ: Prentice-Hall.*

Producing Food on Farms: Agriculture

In contrast to horticulture, **agriculture** (from the Latin *agri,* meaning "field") is growing food plants like grains, tubers, fruits, and vegetables in soil prepared and maintained for crop production. This form of more intensive food production involves using technologies other than hand tools, such as irrigation, fertilizers, and plows pulled by harnessed draft animals. In the so-called developed countries of the world, agriculture relies on fuel-powered tractors to produce food on large plots of land. But the ingenuity of some early agriculturalists is illustrated in this chapter's Anthropology Applied feature, highlighting an ecologically sound mountain terracing and irrigation system established 1,000 years ago.

Among agriculturists, surplus crop cultivation is generally substantial—providing food not only for their own needs but also for those of various full-time specialists and nonproducing consumers. This surplus may be traded or sold for cash, or it may be coerced out of the farmers through taxes, rent, or tribute (forced gifts acknowledging submission or protection) paid to landowners or other dominant groups. These landowners and specialists—such as traders, carpenters, blacksmiths, sculptors, basketmakers, and stonecutters—typically reside in substantial towns or cities, where political power is centralized in the hands

of a socially elite class. Dominated by more powerful groups and markets, much of what the farmers do is governed by political and economic forces over which they have little control.

It is not always easy to make the distinction between horticulture and agriculture. For example, the Hopi Indians of the North American Southwest, in addition to flood plain farming, also irrigate plots near springs, while using simple hand tools. Moreover, they produce for their own immediate needs and live in small towns without centralized political government.

Early food producers have developed several major crop complexes: two adapted to dry uplands and two to tropical wetlands. In the dry uplands of Southwest Asia, for example, farmers time their agricultural activities with the rhythm of the changing seasons, cultivating wheat, barley, oat, flax, rye, and millet. In the tropical wetlands of Southeast Asia, rice and tubers such as yams and taro are cultivated. In the Americas, people have adapted to natural environments similar to those of Africa and Eurasia, but have cultivated their own indigenous plants. Typically, maize, beans, squash, and the potato are grown in drier areas, whereas manioc is extensively grown in the tropical wetlands.

CHARACTERISTICS OF CROP-PRODUCING SOCIETIES

One of the most significant correlates of crop cultivation was the development of fixed settlements, in which farming families reside together near their cultivated fields. The task of food production lent itself to a different kind of social organization. Because the hard work of some members of the group could provide food for all, others became free to devote their time to inventing

agriculture The cultivation of food plants in soil prepared and maintained for crop production. Involves using technologies other than hand tools, such as irrigation, fertilizers, and the wooden or metal plow pulled by harnessed draft animals.

Agricultural Development and the Anthropologist

Gaining insight into the traditional practices of indigenous peoples, anthropologists have often been impressed by the ingenuity of their knowledge. This awareness has spread beyond the profession to the Western public at large, giving birth to the popular notion that indigenous groups invariably live in some sort of blissful oneness with the environment. But this was never the message of anthropologists, who know that traditional people are only human, and like all human beings, are capable of making mistakes. Just as we have much to learn from their successes, so can we learn from their failures.

Archaeologist Ann Kendall is doing just this in the Patacancha Valley in the Andes Mountains of southern Peru. Kendall is director and founder of the Cusichaca Trust, near Oxford, England, a rural development organization that revives ancient farming practices. In the late 1980s, after working for ten years on archaeological excavations and rural development projects, she invited botanist Alex Chepstow-Lusty of Cambridge University to investigate climatic change and paleoecological data. His findings, along with Kendall's, provided evidence of intensive farming in the Patacancha Valley, beginning about 4,000 years ago. The research showed that over time widespread clearing to establish and maintain farm plots, coupled with minimal terracing of the hillsides, had resulted in tremendous soil loss through erosion. By 1,900 years ago, soil degradation and a cooling climate had led to a dramatic reduction in farming. Then, about 1,000 years ago, farming was revived, this time with soil-sparing techniques.

Kendall's investigations have documented intensive irrigated terrace construction over two periods of occupation, including Inca development of the area. It was a sophisticated system, devised to counteract erosion and achieve maximum agricultural production. The effort required workers to haul load after load of soil up from the valley floor. In addition, they planted alder trees to stabilize the soil and to provide both firewood and building materials.

So successful was this farming system by Inca times that the number of people living in the valley quadrupled to some 4,000, about the same as it is now. However, yet another reversal of fortune occurred when the Spanish took over Peru and the terraces and trees here and elsewhere were allowed to deteriorate.

Armed with these research findings and information and insights gathered through interviews and meetings with locals, the Cusichaca Trust supported the restoration of the terraces and 5.8 kilometers of canal. The effort relied on local labor working with traditional methods and materials—clay (with a cactus mix to keep it moist), stone, and soil. Local families have replanted 160 hectares of the renovated pre-conquest terraces with maize, potatoes, and wheat, and the plots are up to ten times more productive than they were. Among other related accomplishments, twenty-one water systems have been installed, which reach more than 800 large families, and a traditional concept of home-based gardens has been adapted to introduce European-style vegetable gardens to improve diet and health and to facilitate market gardening. Since 1997, these projects have been under an independent local rural development organization known as ADESA.

The Cusichaca Trust has continued its pioneering work in areas of extreme poverty in Peru further to the north, such as Apurimac and Ayacucho, using tried and tested traditional technology in the restoration of ancient canal and terrace systems.

Adapted from Krajick, K. (1998). Greenfarming by the Incas? Science 281, 323. *The 2003 update and elaboration by textbook authors are based on personal communication with Kendall and Cusichaca Trust reports. For more information, see www.cusichaca.org.*

and manufacturing the equipment needed for a new sedentary way of life. Tools for digging and harvesting, pottery for storage and cooking, clothing made of woven textiles, and housing made of stone, wood, or sun-dried bricks all came out of the new sedentary living conditions and the altered division of labor.

The Neolithic revolution also brought important changes in social structure. At first, social relations were egalitarian and hardly different from those that prevailed among food foragers. As settlements grew, however, and large numbers of people had to share important resources such as land and water, society became more elaborately organized.

Transhumance festival, Saint-Rémy-de-Provence, France. Before winter sets in, Saint-Rémy farmers lead their livestock from the high-altitude summer grazing grounds of the Alpilles Mountains to fields situated in the valley near the village. There the animals feed on the stubble of harvest crops, as well as hay (long and nutritious sun-dried grass harvested in the summer for winter feeding). In early summer, the animals are taken back to the cooler mountain pastures. Their seasonal comings and goings are often celebrated with festivals in which the herds are paraded through town.

Mixed Farming: Crop Growing and Animal Breeding

As noted above, indigenous food-producing cultures in the western hemisphere depended primarily on growing domesticated indigenous crops such as manioc, corn, and beans. With some exceptions, including the Aymara and Quechua, who traditionally also keep llamas and alpacas in their high-altitude homeland in the Andes Mountains of South America (see the Biocultural Connection feature), American Indians obtained sufficient meat, fat, leather, and wool from wild game.

On the other side of both oceans, however, Eurasian and African food-producing peoples often do not have an opportunity to obtain enough vitally important animal proteins from wild game, fish, or fowl (although they would not pass up a rare chance to catch some). Instead, many of these farming cultures have developed a mixed subsistence strategy and combine crop cultivation with animal husbandry. In addition to growing crops like cereals, tubers, or vegetables, they may also breed and raise animals for food and other purposes, including selling or trading. The variety of wild animals domesticated by humans in Africa and Eurasia includes chickens, ducks, geese, rabbits, pigs, goats, sheep, cattle, camels, dromedaries, donkeys, and horses.

Depending on cultural traditions, ecological circumstances, and animal habits, some species are kept in barns or fenced-off fields, while others may range quite freely in and around the settlement or designated pastures, albeit under supervision, branded or otherwise marked by their owners

as private property. For instance, in some English farming communities (not unlike Papua villages in New Guinea) historically it was not unusual to find ear-marked pigs freely roaming in the surrounding woodlands in search of acorns and any other food appealing to their omnivorous appetite.

Likewise, many ancient agricultural communities adapted to mountainous environments from the Alps to the Himalayas have traditionally herded livestock (cows, sheep, horses, and so on) in high summer pastures, leaving their narrow lowland valleys for alternative use—farming grains, keeping orchards, and growing vegetables and hay for animal winter food. After the crop harvest, before the weather turns cold and snow covers the higher pastures, those who left the village to tend the herds bring the animals back to the valley and settle in for the winter season. This "vertical" seasonal movement of herders and their livestock between high-altitude summer pastures and lowland valleys is an example of *transhumance* (*trans* means "across"; *humus* means "earth").

In contrast to transhumance, in which a number of men from the village annually move with their herds to seasonal pastures while other community members remain home in the settlement, there are also cultures in which the entire community migrates with the herds to their alternate grazing grounds—as described in the next section.[8]

---

[8] Cole, J. W., & Wolf, E. R. (1999). *The hidden frontier: Ecology and ethnicity in an alpine valley* (with a new introduction). Berkeley: University of California Press; see also Jones, S. (2005). Transhumance re-examined. *Journal of the Royal Anthropological Institute 11* (4), 841–842.

Herding Grazing Animals: Pastoralism

One of the more striking examples of human adaptation to the environment is **pastoralism**—breeding and managing large herds of domesticated herbivores (grazing and browsing animals), such as goats, sheep, cattle, horses, llamas, or camels. Unlike the forms of animal husbandry discussed above, pastoralism is a specialized way of life centered on breeding and herding animals.

Dependent on livestock for daily survival, families in pastoral cultures own herds of grazing animals whose need for food and drink determines the pastoralists' everyday routines. When a dozen or more herding families join together, their collective herds may number in the thousands and sometimes even a few hundred thousand. Unlike crop cultivators who need to remain close to their fields, pastoral peoples do not usually establish permanent settlements since they must follow or drive their large herds to new pastures on a regular basis. Like their herds, most pastoralists must be mobile and have adjusted their way of life accordingly.

CASE STUDY: BAKHTIARI HERDERS IN THE ZAGROS MOUNTAINS

Nomadic pastoralism is an effective way of living—far more so than sheep or cattle ranching—in environments that are too dry, cold, steep, or rocky for farming, such as the vast, arid grasslands that stretch eastward from North Africa through the Arabian Desert, across the plateau of Iran and into Turkistan and Mongolia. Today, in Africa and Asia alone, more than 21 million people are pastoralists, still migrating with their herds. These nomadic groups regard movement as a natural part of life.

Counted among the world's pastoral groups are the Bakhtiari, a fiercely independent people who live in the unforgiving Zagros Mountains of western Iran.[9] The Bakhtiari way of life, uniquely adapted to the seasonal fluctuations in their rugged mountainous environment, involves moving with their grazing animals from winter pastures in low steppe lands to summer pastures on high plateaus. For many thousands of years the Bakhtiari have tended herds of goats and fat-tailed sheep this way. Their lives revolve around these major seasonal migrations needed to provide good grazing lands for their flocks—hazardous journeys as long as 200 miles, over mountains as high as 12,000 feet, and through deep chasms and churning watercourses.

Each fall, before the harsh winter comes to the mountains, these nomads load their tents and other belongings on donkeys and drive their flocks down to the warm plains that border Iraq in the west. Here the grazing land is excellent and well watered during the winter months. In the spring, when the low-lying pastures dry up, the Bakhtiari return to the mountain valleys, where a new crop of grass is sprouting. For this trek, they split into five groups, each containing about 5,000 individuals and 50,000 animals.

The return trip north is especially dangerous because the mountain snows are melting and the gorges are full of turbulent, ice-cold water rushing down from the mountain peaks. This long trek is further burdened by the newborn spring lambs and goat kids. Where the watercourses are not very deep, the nomads ford them. Deeper channels, including one river that is a half-mile wide, are crossed with the help of inflatable goatskin rafts, on which they place infants and elderly or infirm family members, as well as lambs and kids. Men swim alongside the rafts, pushing them through the icy water. If they work from dawn to dusk, the nomads can get all of the people and animals across the river in five days. Not surprisingly, dozens of animals drown each day.

In the mountain passes, where a biting wind numbs the skin and brings tears to the eyes, the Bakhtiari trek a rugged slippery trail. Climbing the steep escarpments is dangerous, and often the stronger men must carry their children and the baby goats on their shoulders as they make their way over the ice and snow to the lush mountain valley that is their destination. During each migration the nomads may cover as many as 200 miles. The journey is familiar but not predictable. It can take weeks, for the flocks travel slowly and require constant attention. Men and older boys walk the route, driving the sheep and goats as they go. Women and children usually ride atop donkeys, along with tents and other equipment.

Reaching their destination, the Bakhtiari set up tents—traditionally black goat-hair shelters woven by the women. The tents are a fine example of adaptation to a changing environment. The goat-hair cloth retains heat and repels

---

[9] Material on the Bakhtiari is drawn mainly from Barth, F. (1960). Nomadism in the mountain and plateau areas of Southwest Asia. *The problems of the arid zone* (pp. 341–355). Paris: UNESCO; Coon, C. S. (1958). *Caravan: The story of the Middle East* (2nd ed., ch. 13). New York: Holt, Rinehart & Winston; Salzman, P. C. (1967). Political organization among nomadic peoples. *Proceedings of the American Philosophical Society 111*, 115–131.

pastoralism Breeding and managing large herds of domesticated grazing and browsing animals, such as goats, sheep, cattle, horses, llamas, or camels.

In the Zagros Mountains region of Iran, pastoral nomads follow seasonal pastures, migrating with their flocks over rugged terrain that includes perilously steep snowy passes and fast ice-cold rivers.

water during the winter and keeps out heat during the summer. These portable homes are easy to erect, take down, and transport. Inside, the furnishings are sparse and functional, but also artful. Heavy felt pads or elaborate wool rugs, also woven by the women, cover the ground, and pressed against the inside walls of the tent are stacks of blankets, goatskin containers, copper utensils, clay jugs, and bags of grain.

Central to Bakhtiari subsistence, sheep and goats provide milk, cheese, butter, meat, hides, and wool. Women and girls spend considerable time spinning wool into yarn—sometimes doing so while riding atop donkeys on the less rugged parts of their migration. They use the yarn to make not only rugs and tents, but also clothing, storage bags, and other essentials. With men owning and controlling the animals, which are of primary importance in Bakhtiari life, women generally have less economic and political power than their fathers, brothers, or husbands—but are by no means without influence.

The Bakhtiari live in the political state of Iran but have their own traditional system of justice, including laws and a penal code. They are governed by tribal leaders, or *khans,* men who are elected or inherit their office. Most Bakhtiari *khans* grew wealthy when oil was discovered in their homeland around the start of the 20th century, and many of them are well educated, having attended Iranian or foreign universities.

Despite this, and although some of them own houses in cities, the *khans* spend much of their lives among their people in the mountains. Such prominence of men in both economic and political affairs is common among pastoral nomads; theirs is very much a man's world. That said, elderly Bakhtiari women eventually may gain a good deal of power. And some women of all ages today are gaining a measure of economic control by selling their beautiful handmade rugs to traders, which brings in cash to their households.

While pastoral nomads like the Bakhtiari depend largely on their herds to meet their basic daily needs, they also trade surplus animals, leather, and wool (and various crafts such as woven rugs) with farmers or merchants in exchange for crops and valued commodities such as flour, dried fruit, spices, tea, metal knives, pots and kettles, cotton or linen textiles, guns, and (more recently) lightweight plastic containers, sheets, and so on. In other words, there are many ties that connect them to surrounding agricultural and industrial societies.

Intensive Agriculture: Urbanization and Peasantry

With the intensification of agriculture, some farming villages grew into towns and even cities (Figure 7.3). In these larger population centers, individuals who had previously

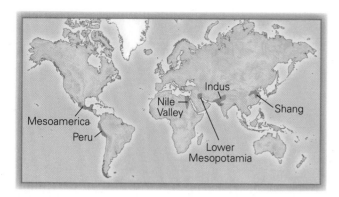

Figure 7.3 Locations of major early civilizations. Those of Central and South America developed wholly independently of those in Africa and Eurasia. Chinese civilization may have developed independently of those that developed earlier in Mesopotamia, the Egyptian Valley, and the Indus Valley.

been engaged in farming were freed to specialize in other activities. Thus craft specialists such as carpenters, blacksmiths, sculptors, basket makers, and stonecutters contribute to the vibrant, diversified life of the city.

Unlike horticulturists and pastoralists, city dwellers are only indirectly concerned with adapting to their natural environment. Far more important is the need to adapt to living and getting along with their fellow urbanites. Urbanization brings with it a new social order: Marked inequality develops as society becomes more complex, and people are ranked according to how much control they hold over resources, the kind of work they do, their gender, or the family they are born into. As social institutions cease to operate in simple, face-to-face groups of relatives, friends, and acquaintances, they become more formal and bureaucratic, with specialized political institutions.

With urbanization came a sharp increase in the tempo of human cultural change. Writing was created, trade intensified and expanded, the wheel and the sail were invented, and metallurgy and other crafts were developed. In many early cities, monumental buildings, such as royal palaces and temples, were built by thousands of men, often slaves taken in war. These feats of engineering still amaze modern architects and engineers. The inhabitants of these buildings—the ruling class composed of nobles and priests—formed a central government that dictated the social and religious rules to be followed and carried out by the merchants, craft specialists, warriors, servants, and other city dwellers.

Notably, these urbanized populations mostly depended for much of their daily food (such as bread, tortillas, vegetables, meat, fish, fruit, milk, butter, and cheese) and fuel (especially firewood for cooking and heating their dwellings) on what was produced or foraged in surrounding areas. For this reason, the urban ruling class sought to widen its territorial power and political control over rural populations. This is how farmers who raised their own crops and livestock as they saw fit, and who determined themselves if and how much surplus they would produce, lost that traditional self-determination.

Once a powerful group managed to dominate a community of farmers, it also imposed its rules on them, forcing them to work harder and obliging them to make payments in farm produce or labor services as fees for protection, as acknowledgment of submission, or other forms of exploitation. Thus burdened by taxes to feed those repressing them, these farmers were left with little to feed their own families and lost their independence. In short, subjected to an ever more dominant group, these farmers turned into **peasants.** One of the first anthropologists to study peasant communities was Eric Wolf, who defined them as "rural cultivators whose surpluses are transferred to a dominant group of rulers that uses the surpluses both to underwrite its own standard of living and to distribute the remainder to groups in society that do not farm but must be fed for their specific goods and services in turn."[10]

With their growing numbers trying to survive on less and less fertile land, and forced to pay tribute or taxes, the exploited peasant masses could expect little more than poverty. And so it continues in many parts of the world today. No matter how hard they work, most peasants possess too little land of their own to go beyond meeting the most basic needs of their families. Unable to produce enough of a surplus to sell for cash, they rarely have capital to buy the labor-saving equipment that could increase their production. Thus most peasants remain stuck in poverty, struggling to make ends meet. Meanwhile, big landowners and wealthy merchants have had the means to expand their holdings and invest in new machinery that leads to increased productivity and profitability.

Industrial Food Production

Until about 200 years ago, human societies all across the world had developed cultural infrastructures based on foraging, horticulture, agriculture, or pastoralism. This changed with the invention of the steam engine in England, which brought about an industrial revolution

---

[10] Wolf, E. R. (1966). *Peasants* (pp. 4–5). Englewood Cliffs, NJ: Prentice-Hall.

peasant A rural cultivator whose surpluses are transferred to a dominant group of rulers that uses the surpluses both to underwrite its own standard of living and to distribute the remainder to groups in society that do not farm but must be fed for their specific goods and services in turn.

Chickens ready for butchering are usually grabbed by their feet, stuffed in crates, and trucked off to the slaughterhouse. But some farmers use mechanical harvesters. Moving through a chicken barn, a harvester can pick up about 200 birds in 30 seconds. Once full, it places the birds in holding containers. From there, the chickens are mechanically transferred to a "packing unit," which automatically counts them and places them into drawers that are stacked, loaded onto a truck, and transported to a processing plant. There the chickens are mass-killed, cut up, and packaged.

that quickly spread to other parts of the globe. Replacing animal and human labor, as well as hand tools, new machines were invented, first powered by steam, then by biofuels (coal, gas, oil), sharply increasing factory production and boosting mass transportation.

Throughout the 1800s and 1900s, this resulted in large-scale industrialization of many societies. Technological inventions utilizing electricity and (since the 1940s) nuclear energy brought about more dramatic changes in social and economic organization on a worldwide scale.

Modern industrial technologies not only affect manufacturing but also impact food production. In contrast to traditional farms and plantations, which historically depended on human labor (often forced) and on animal power in many places, modern agriculture depends on newly invented labor-saving devices such as tractors, combines, milk machines, and so on. With large machines plowing, seeding, weeding, mowing, and harvesting crops, the need for farm hands and other rural workers is sharply diminished. This has also happened with livestock—in particular, hogs, cattle, and poultry.

Since the 1960s, food production in industrialized countries has become large-scale, enormously efficient,

and often very profitable, especially for corporate owners and shareholders. Industrial food production has had far-reaching economic, social, and political consequences, not all of which are readily recognized as related and intertwined. Today, large food-producing corporations own enormous tracts of land on which they mass-produce tons of mechanically harvested crops and/or raise huge numbers of meat animals. Crops and animals alike are harvested, processed, packed, and shipped with ever-greater efficiency to supermarkets to feed largely urban masses.

Although meat, poultry, and other agricultural products are relatively cheap and thus affordable, even for millions of poorer people around the world, industrial food production by **agribusiness** has often been a disaster for millions of peasants and small farmers. Even medium-sized farms growing corn, wheat, or potatoes, or raising cows, hogs, and chickens can rarely compete without government subsidies. For that reason, the number of family-owned farms in western Europe and North America has dramatically declined in the past few decades. This process has led to huge drops in many rural populations, decimating many farming communities.

For the family farms that have managed to survive, there is seldom enough income to cover the costs of a large household, including education, health care, farm and household insurance, and taxes. This situation forces individuals to seek money-earning opportunities elsewhere, often far away. Ironically, some hire on as cheap wage laborers in poultry- or meat-packing plants where working conditions are distasteful and often dangerous.

agribusiness Large-scale businesses involved in food production, including farming, contract farming, seed supply, agrichemicals, farm machinery, distribution, processing, and marketing. Also known as corporate farming, it stands in contrast to smaller family-owned farms.

Globalscape

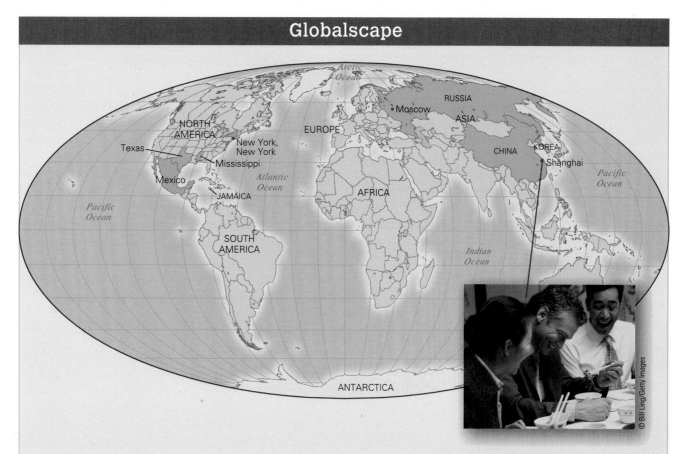

© Bill Ling/Getty Images

Chicken Out: Bush's Legs or Phoenix Talons?

Every evening in Moscow, Russians can be found enjoying a traditional dinner that may begin with *borscht* (beet soup) and *smetana* (sour cream), followed by a main course of *kotleta po-kievski* (boneless fried chicken breast)—or, if the budget is a bit tight, *nozhki busha* (chicken legs), baked, fried, or roasted—served with cabbage and potatoes.

Foreign visitors may recognize the breast entrée as chicken Kiev, but may be baffled to learn that the specialty *nozhki busha* translates as "Bush's legs." That is because these big meaty legs are imported from the United States and first appeared on Russian menus when the Soviet Union collapsed in 1991, during George H. W. Bush's

presidency (1989–1993). At the time, the Russian economy was dismal, and few people could afford beef or pork. Even chicken legs were too expensive for ordinary Russians. To help the transition to a capitalist democracy, the U.S. government promoted the advantages of free markets and global trade. What better propaganda than cheap chicken—especially since the American preference for white meat resulted in a surplus of dark meat legs. And so it was that the U.S. poultry industry entered the Russian market. Today, Russia imports more U.S. chicken than it produces on its own farms, especially legs—over a billion!

What happens with a typical 6-pound "broiler" chicken butchered by a Mexican immigrant working for minimum wage in a Mississippi poultry

plant? As we have seen, its legs are served up in Moscow, while its breasts end up on U.S. dining tables or on the menus of international airlines. And the rest of the bird? One of its frozen wings goes into a giant container shipped to Korea; the other to West Africa. The offal (neck, heart, liver, and guts) is transported to Jamaica where it is boiled and dished up in soup. The excess fat gets converted into biodiesel fuel at an experimental refinery in Texas. And what about its cute yellow feet? Both are exported to Shanghai, deep-fried, stewed, and served up as a delicacy called *fèngzhuâ*, or Phoenix talons, last seen being nibbled on by a visiting New York banker.

Global Twister What happens to the feathers?

Maximizing profits, agribusinesses are constantly streamlining food production and seeking ways to reduce labor costs by trimming the number of workers, minimizing employee benefits, and driving down wages. Pushing for market expansion beyond regional or even national boundaries, the largest among them have gone global. In the United States, for example, the poultry industry, which

requires vast quantities of corn and soy to feed the fast-growing roosters known as "broilers," now has a worldwide market in addition to growing domestic demand.

During the past half century, per capita consumption of chicken in the United States has increased tenfold to about 85 pounds per year. Considerably cheaper than pork or beef, it now represents nearly half of all meat eaten. Even so, U.S. consumption does not begin to match U.S. production, for the United States is the world's largest producer of chicken meat—some 36 billion pounds per year.

Most large-scale poultry farmers raise these broilers in enclosed "chicken houses." Each building is big enough to hold about 23,000 birds until they reach the butchering size (about 5 or 6 pounds), which takes just seven weeks. Chicken farms are located primarily in the southeastern states where there is ready access to corn and soy feed. The country's biggest broiler processing plant, located in Carthage, Mississippi, and owned by Tyson Food, is capable of slaughtering almost 2.5 million chickens per week. The $55-billion U.S. poultry business exports billions of tons of chicken annually to dozens of countries around the world. Nearly a quarter of its frozen chicken meat goes to Russia (over 900,000 tons comprised of more than a billion chicken legs). Another 400,000 tons go to China (primarily chicken feet, more than 1.2 billion of them). (See this chapter's Globalscape for more about chicken farming.)

Today's industrial food production and global marketing complex, involving a network of interlinked distribution centers, is made possible by an electronic-digital revolution that began in the late 20th century. That revolution is currently under way primarily in parts of North America, western Europe, Japan, and a few other wealthy countries where economies are increasingly based on the research and development of new knowledge and technologies, as well as providing information, services, and finance capital on a global scale.[11]

---

[11] Ritzer, G. (2007). *The coming of post-industrial society* (2nd ed.). New York: McGraw-Hill.

Concluding Remarks

New subsistence strategies over the past few centuries that use technological inventions to more effectively harness energy are commonly valued as progress. Yet, as discussed in this chapter, not all innovations turn out to be positive in the long run, nor do they improve the quality of life for every member of a society even in the short run.

Thousands of generations ago, our human ancestors emerged in Africa. They multiplied and dispersed, ultimately occupying every continent on earth. Adjusting as they went, each of these migrating groups developed its own cultural repertoire of ideas and practices to secure food, fuel, and safety for themselves and their offspring. Measured in terms of population growth, geographic expansion, and technological know-how, our species has been enormously successful in adapting itself to a wide range of different natural environments and developing the means required to satisfy its needs.

As long as the collective needs of a population remain within its means, the group can be said to enjoy a degree of relative abundance, or affluence. However, when its needs grow beyond the means available, it faces shortages, or scarcity.

Because abundance and shortage are based on the relationship between means and needs, affluence and scarcity are relative concepts. And for that reason, anthropologists tend to be cautious about the uncritical use of the term "progress" as applied to "economic development." Although there is no question that millions of people do enjoy a life of health and abundance, perhaps more so than their own ancestors, many must work harder and longer hours to put food on the table, and millions more live in poverty, are malnourished, and die too young. For them, the idea of human progress is unreal and difficult to swallow as truth.

Questions for Reflection

1. Since the beginning of human history, our species has met the challenge of survival by adapting to different environments. In capturing essential natural resources, we have also modified these environments. Do you know any examples of landscapes radically transformed for economic reasons? Who benefits from such environmental changes in the long run?

2. When buying a chicken breast sandwich in a deli, try to imagine where the food that fed your particular bird was cultivated; where the chicken was cooped up; how, where, and by whom it was slaughtered and packaged. And finally, while enjoying that breast stuck between slices of bread, ask yourself who might be chewing on the bird's feet somewhere on the other side of the world.

3. What was so radical about the domestication of plants and animals that led to it being referred to as the Neolithic *revolution*? Can you think of any equally radical changes in subsistence practices going on in the world today?

4. Consider the ideas of change and progress in light of the agricultural development project described in the Anthropology Applied feature. Come up with your own definition of progress that goes beyond the standard idea of technological and material advancement.

5. Technological development in industrial societies often results in highly productive machines effectively replacing animal and human workers. Think of a useful mechanical device and consider its benefits and costs, not only to you but also to others.

Suggested Readings

Bates, D. G. (2001). *Human adaptive strategies: Ecology, culture, and politics* (2nd ed.). Boston: Allyn & Bacon.

This book explores different adaptive practices and their correlative political structures. Theoretical issues are made accessible through the use of readable ethnographic case studies.

Bogucki, P. (1999). *The origins of human society*. Oxford, England: Blackwell.

The author provides a comprehensive global history of the human species, tracing the process of cultural evolution from our prehistoric beginnings as foragers to the creation of agricultural economies leading to complex societies and empires. As a record of human achievements, this book successfully incorporates the explosion in archaeological data accumulated since 1950.

Chatty, D. (1996). *Mobile pastoralists: Development planning and social change in Oman*. New York: Columbia University Press.

This study looks at the forces of modernization in a nomadic community and the resulting shift from herding to wage labor, as well as the changing role of women.

Lee, R. B., & Daly, R. H. (1999). *The Cambridge encyclopedia of hunters and gatherers*. New York: Cambridge University Press.

This is an essential reference text on foragers.

Pollan, M. (2008). *In defense of food: An eater's manifesto*. New York: Penguin.

This keen analysis of the American diet follows up on Pollan's *The Omnivore's Dilemma,* which firmly linked the industrialization of our food supply to the degradation of the environment. It chronicles how basic understanding of a balanced diet has been confused, complicated, and distorted by food industry marketers and nutritional scientists, who profit from the confusion. "Edible foodlike substances," writes Pollan, are often packaged with labels bearing health claims that are typically false or misleading, while "real food" is disappearing from the marketplace and is replaced by "nutrients," thereby ruining our health.

Challenge Issue   All humans face the challenge of securing resources needed for immediate and long-term survival. Whatever we lack, we may seek to get through exchange or trade. In today's capitalist societies people can exchange almost anything of value without ever actually meeting in person. But the market in traditional societies is a real location where people personally meet to exchange goods at designated times. So it is at this market in the Guatemalan highlands where Maya peasants meet. Growing more food than they need to feed their families, they barter the surplus for merchandise they do not grow or make themselves—from sugar and plastic containers to blue jeans, rubber boots, steel axes, knives, shovels, and machetes. They also sell their produce for money to pay for goods and services, such as medicine and the bus or truck that carries them to their villages. The distinctly embroidered blouse (*huipile*) worn by each of the Maya women reveals where she lives and whether she is single or married. All around the world, at marketplaces like this one, people from different places forge and affirm social networks of friends, neighbors, and allies needed for their safety and well-being.

CHAPTER 8

Economic Systems

Chapter Preview

How Do Anthropologists Study Economic Systems?

Anthropologists study the means by which goods are produced, distributed, and consumed in the context of the total culture of particular societies. Although they have adopted theories and concepts from economists, most anthropologists recognize that theoretical principles derived from the study of capitalist market economies have limited applicability to economic systems in societies that are not industrialized and where people do not produce and exchange goods for private profit. This is because, in these non-state societies, the economic sphere of behavior is not separate from the social, religious, and political spheres.

How Do Different Societies Organize Their Economic Resources and Labor?

In small-scale nonindustrial societies, land and other valuable resources are usually controlled by groups of relatives, and individual ownership is rare. Division of labor is by age and gender with some craft specialization. Production takes place in the quantity and at the time required, and most goods are consumed by the group that produces them. This is notably different from the economic arrangements in large-scale industrial and postindustrial societies where there is a much more complex division of labor, individuals or business corporations own property, producers and consumers rarely know each other, and transactions take place by means of money.

How and Why Are Goods Exchanged or Redistributed?

People exchange goods through reciprocity, redistribution, and/or market exchange. Reciprocity involves the exchange of goods and services of roughly equivalent value and is often undertaken for ritual or prestige purposes. Redistribution requires a government and/or religious elite to collect and reallocate resources, in the form of either goods or services. Leveling mechanisms ensure that no one accumulates significantly more goods than anyone else. Market exchange in nonindustrial societies takes place in designated locations where people trade goods, meet friends and strangers, and find entertainment. In modern societies, market exchange may be indirect, impersonal, and mediated by money or capital in the form of shares or stock. With the advent of digital technology, trading is also conducted on the Internet where individuals or corporations buy and sell "financial instruments" measured in minuscule percentages of large numbers with minute fluctuations on a global scale with lightning speed. The worldwide growth of mobile phone use also enables people in geographically remote or difficult to reach locations to be better informed economically and to engage directly in business transactions in larger markets.

An **economic system** is an organized arrangement for producing, distributing, and consuming goods. Since people, in pursuing a particular means of subsistence, necessarily produce, distribute, and consume things, our discussion of subsistence patterns in the previous chapter obviously involved economic matters. Yet economic systems encompass much more than we have covered so far. Now comes the rest of the story.

Economic Anthropology

Studying the economies of traditional small-scale societies, researchers from industrial and postindustrial capitalist societies run the risk of interpreting anthropological data in terms of their own technologies, their own values of work and property, and their own determination of what is rational. Take, for example, the following statement from a classic textbook in economics: "In all societies, the prevailing reality of life has been the inadequacy of output to fill the wants and needs of the people."[1]

This assertion fails to consider that in many societies people's wants and needs are maintained at levels that can be fully and continuously satisfied, and that without repressing or exploiting fellow human beings. In such societies, people gather or produce goods in the quantity and at the time required, and to do more than this makes no sense at all. No matter how hard they may work when hard work is called for, at other times they will have available hours, days, or even weeks on end to devote to "unproductive" (in the economic sense) activities.

To many observers enculturated in industrial or postindustrial societies, such people may seem lazy—and if they happen to be hunters and gatherers, even the skillful or strenuous work they do is likely to be misinterpreted. To those whose livelihoods depend on farming, trading, or factory or office work, hunting is typically defined as a sport. Hence, the male hunters in foraging societies are often perceived as spending virtually all of their time in recreational pursuits, while the female food gatherers are seen as working themselves to the bone.

To understand how the schedule of wants or demands of a given society is balanced against the supply of goods and services available, it is necessary to introduce a noneconomic variable: the anthropological variable of culture. In any given economic system, economic processes cannot be interpreted without culturally defining the demands and understanding the conventions that dictate how and when they are satisfied. The fact is, the economic sphere of behavior is *not* separate from the social, religious, and political spheres and thus is not completely free to follow its own purely economic logic. To be sure, economic behavior and institutions can be analyzed in strictly economic terms, but to do so is to ignore crucial noneconomic cultural considerations, which do, after all, have an impact on the way things are in real life. As a case in point, we may look briefly at yam production among the Trobriand Islanders, who inhabit a group of coral islands that lie in the southern Pacific Ocean off the eastern tip of New Guinea.[2]

Case Study: The Yam Complex in Trobriand Culture

Trobriand men spend a great deal of their time and energy raising yams—not for themselves or their own households, but to give to others, normally their sisters and married daughters. The purpose of cultivating these starchy edible roots is not to provision the households that receive them, because most of what people eat they grow for themselves in gardens where they plant taro, sweet potatoes, tapioca, greens, beans, and squash, as well as breadfruit and banana trees. The reason a man gives yams to a woman is to show his support for her husband and to enhance his own influence.

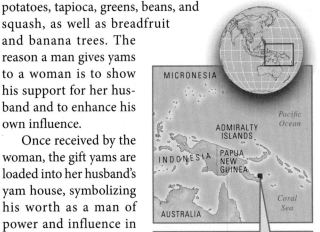

Once received by the woman, the gift yams are loaded into her husband's yam house, symbolizing his worth as a man of power and influence in his community. He may use some of these yams to purchase a variety of things, including arm shells, shell necklaces and earrings, betel nuts, pigs, chickens, and locally

---

[1] Heilbroner, R. L., & Thurow, L. C. (1981). *The economic problem* (6th ed., p. 327). Englewood Cliffs, NJ: Prentice-Hall.

economic system An organized arrangement for producing, distributing, and consuming goods.

[2] Weiner, A. B. (1988). *The Trobrianders of Papua New Guinea.* New York: Holt, Rinehart & Winston.

Trobriand Island men devote a great deal of time and energy to raising yams, not for themselves but to give to others. These yams, which have been raised by men related through marriage to a chief, are about to be loaded into the chief's yam house.

produced goods such as wooden bowls, combs, floor mats, lime pots, and even magic spells. Some he must use to fulfill social obligations. For instance, a man is expected to present yams to the relatives of his daughter's husband when she marries and again when death befalls a member of the husband's family. Finally, any man who aspires to high status and power is expected to show his worth by organizing a yam competition, during which he gives away huge quantities of yams to invited guests. As anthropologist Annette Weiner explains: "A yam house, then, is like a bank account; when full, a man is wealthy and powerful. Until yams are cooked or they rot, they may circulate as limited currency. That is why, once harvested, the usage of yams for daily food is avoided as much as possible."[3]

By giving yams to his sister or daughter, a man not only expresses his confidence in the woman's husband, but also makes the latter indebted to him. Although the recipient rewards the gardener and his helpers by throwing a feast, at which they are fed cooked yams, taro, and—what everyone especially looks forward to—ample pieces of pork, this in no way pays off the debt. The debt can only be repaid in women's wealth, which consists of bundles of banana leaves and skirts made of the same material dyed red.

Although the banana leaf bundles are of no utilitarian value, extensive labor is invested in their production, and large quantities of them, along with skirts, are regarded as essential for paying off all the members of other family groups who were close to a recently deceased relative in life and who assisted with the funeral. Also, the wealth and vitality of the dead person's family group are measured by the quality and quantity of the bundles and skirts so distributed. Because a man has received yams from his wife's brother, he is obligated to provide his wife with yams for purchasing the necessary bundles and skirts, beyond those she has produced, to help with payments following the death of a member of her family. Because deaths are unpredictable and can occur at any time, a man must have yams available for his wife when she needs them. This, and the fact she may require all of his yams, acts as an effective check on a man's wealth.

Like people the world over, the Trobriand Islanders assign meanings to objects that make those objects worth far more than their cost in labor or materials. Yams, for example, establish long-term relationships that lead to other advantages, such as access to land, protection, assistance, and other kinds of wealth. Thus yam exchanges are as much social and political transactions as they are economic ones. Banana leaf bundles and skirts, for their part, are symbolic of the political status of families and of their immortality. In their distribution, which is related to rituals associated with death, we see how men in Trobriand society are ultimately dependent on women and their valuables.

So important are these matters to Trobrianders that even with the infiltration of Western culture—money, education, religion, and law—they remain committed to yam cultivation and to the production of women's wealth. Looked at in terms of modern capitalist economics, these activities appear meaningless, but viewed in terms of Trobriand values and concerns, they make a great deal of sense.

Production and Its Resources

In every society, particular customs and rules govern the kinds of work done, who does the work, attitudes toward the work, how it is accomplished, and who controls the resources necessary to produce desired goods, knowledge,

---

[3] Ibid., p. 86.

and services. The primary resources in any culture are raw materials, technology, and labor. The rules directing the use of these are embedded in a people's culture and determine the way the economy operates within any given natural environment.

Land and Water Resources

All societies regulate allocation of valuable natural resources—especially land and water. Food foragers must determine who will hunt game and gather plants in their home range and where these activities take place. Groups that rely on fishing or growing crops need to make similar decisions concerning who carries out which task on which stretch of water or land. Farmers must have some means of determining title to land and access to water supplies for irrigation. Pastoralists require a system that determines rights to watering places and grazing land, as well as the right of access to land where they move their herds.

In Western capitalist societies, a system of private ownership of land and rights to natural resources generally prevails. Although elaborate laws have been enacted to regulate the buying, owning, and selling of land and water resources, if individuals wish to reallocate valuable farmland to some other purpose, for instance, they generally can.

In traditional nonindustrial societies, land is often controlled by kinship groups such as the family or band rather than by individuals. For example, among the Ju/'hoansi of the Kalahari Desert, each band of ten to thirty people lives on roughly 250 square miles of land, which they consider to be their territory— their own country. These territories are not defined by boundaries but in terms of water holes that are located within them. The land is said to be "owned" by those who have lived the longest in the band, usually a group of brothers and sisters or cousins. Their concept of landholding, however, is not something easily translated into modern Western terms

A Ju/'hoansi water hole. The practice of defining territories on the basis of core features such as water holes is typical of food foragers, such as these people of the Kalahari Desert in southern Africa.

of private ownership. Within their traditional worldview, no part of their homeland can be sold for money or traded away for goods. Outsiders must ask permission to enter the territory—but denying the request would be unthinkable.

The practice of defining territories on the basis of core features—be they water holes (as among the Ju/'hoansi), watercourses (as among Indians of the northeastern United States), unique sites in the landscape where ancestral spirits are thought to dwell (as among the Aborigines in Australia), or whatever—is typical of food foragers. Territorial boundaries tend to be rather vaguely defined, and to avoid friction, foragers may designate part of their territory as a buffer zone between them and their neighbors. The adaptive value of this is obvious: The size of band territories, as well as the size of the bands, can adjust to keep in balance with availability of resources in any given place. Such adjustment would be more difficult under a system of individual ownership of clearly bounded land.

Among some West African farming groups, a tributary system of land ownership prevails. All land is said to belong to the head chief, who allocates it to various subchiefs, who in turn distribute it to family groups. Then the family group leaders assign individual plots to each farmer. Just as in traditional Europe, these African people owe allegiance to the subchiefs (or nobles) and the head chief (or king). The people who work the land must pay tribute in the form of products or special services such as fighting for the king when necessary.

These people do not really own the land; rather, it is a kind of lease. Yet as long as the land is kept in use, rights to such use will pass to their heirs. No user, however, can give away, sell, or otherwise dispose of a plot of land without approval from the elder of the family group. When an individual no longer uses the allocated land, it reverts to the head of the large family group, who reallocates it to some other group member. The important operative principle here is that the system extends the individual's right to use land for an indefinite period, but the land is not "owned" outright. This serves to maintain the integrity of valuable farmland as such, preventing its loss through subdivision and conversion to other uses.

Technology Resources

All societies have some means of creating and allocating tools that are used to produce goods, as well as traditions for passing them on to succeeding generations. A society's **technology**—the number and types of tools employed, combined with knowledge about how to make and use them—is directly related to the lifestyles of its members. Food foragers and pastoral nomads who are frequently on the move are apt to have fewer and simpler tools than more settled peoples such as sedentary farmers. A great

number of complex tools would hinder mobility. Thus, as noted in the previous chapter, the average weight of an individual's personal belongings among the Ju/'hoansi is just under 25 pounds, limited to the barest essentials such as implements for hunting, gathering, fishing, building, and cooking. Pastoral nomads, aided by pack animals, typically have more material possessions than foragers, but still less than people who live in permanent settlements.

Food foragers make and use a variety of tools, many of which are ingenious in their effectiveness. Some of these they make for their individual use, but codes of generosity are such that a person may not refuse to give or loan what is requested. Tools may be given or loaned to others in exchange for the products resulting from their use. For example, a Ju/'hoansi who gives his arrow to another hunter has a right to a share in any animals the hunter kills. Game is considered to "belong" to the man whose arrow killed it, even when he is not present on the hunt. In this context, it makes little sense for them to accumulate luxuries or surplus goods, and the fact that no one owns significantly more than another helps to limit status differences.

Among horticulturists, the axe, digging stick, and hoe are the primary tools. Since these are relatively easy to produce, almost everyone can make them. Whoever makes a tool has first rights to it, but when he or she is not using it, any family member may ask to use it, and the request is rarely denied. Refusal would cause people to treat the tool owner with scorn for this singular lack of concern for others. If a relative helps raise the crop traded for a particular tool, that relative becomes part owner of the implement, and it may not be traded or given away without his or her permission.

In permanently settled agricultural communities, tools and other productive goods are more complex, heavier, and costlier to make. In such settings, individual ownership tends to be more absolute, as are the conditions under which people may borrow and use such equipment. It is easy to replace a knife lost by a relative during palm cultivation but much more difficult to replace an iron plow or a diesel-fueled harvesting machine. Rights to the ownership of complex tools are more rigidly applied; generally the person who has funded the purchase of a complex piece of machinery is considered the sole owner and may decide how and by whom it will be used.

Labor Resources and Patterns

In addition to raw materials and technology, labor is a key resource in any economic system. A look around the world reveals many different labor patterns, but two features are

---

technology Tools and other material equipment, together with the knowledge of how to make and use them.

Often, work that is considered inappropriate for women (or men) in one society is performed by them in another. Here we see female stone construction laborers in Bangalore, India, who carry concrete atop their heads.

© David Wells/The Image Works

almost always present in human cultures: a basic division of labor by gender and by age.

DIVISION OF LABOR BY GENDER

Anthropologists have studied extensively the social division of labor by gender in cultures of all sorts. Whether men or women do a particular job varies from group to group, but typically work has been and often continues to be divided into the tasks of either one or the other. For example, the practices most commonly regarded as "women's work" have tended to be those that can be carried out near home and that are easily resumed after interruption. The tasks historically often regarded as "men's work" have tended to be those requiring physical strength, rapid mobilization of high bursts of energy, frequent travel at some distance from home, and assumption of high levels of risk and danger.

Many exceptions occur, however, as in societies where women regularly carry burdensome loads or put in long hours of hard work cultivating crops in the fields. In some societies, women perform almost three quarters of all work, and in several societies they have served as warriors. For example, in the 19th-century West African kingdom of Dahomey (in what is now called Benin), thousands of women served in the armed forces of the Dahomean king, and some considered the women to be better fighters than their male counterparts. Also, there are references to female warriors in ancient Ireland, and archaeological evidence indicates their presence among Vikings.

During World War II in the early 1940s, some 58,000 Soviet women engaged in frontline combat defending their homeland against German invaders, and North Vietnamese women fought in mixed-gender army units during the Vietnam War in the 1960s and early 1970s. Today, women serve in the military of most countries, but only Canada, Denmark, France, Germany, and a few others permit them to join combat units.

Instead of looking for key biological factors to explain the social division of labor, a more useful strategy is to examine the kinds of work that men and women do in the context of specific societies to see how it relates to other cultural and historical factors. Researchers find a continuum of patterns, ranging from flexible integration of men and women to rigid segregation by gender.[4]

The *flexible/integrated pattern* is exemplified by the Ju/'hoansi discussed above and is seen most often among food foragers (as well as communities where crops are traditionally cultivated primarily for family consumption). In such societies, men and women perform up to 35 percent of activities with approximately equal participation, and tasks deemed especially appropriate for one gender may be performed by the other, without loss of face, as the situation warrants. Where these practices prevail, boys and

---

[4] Sanday, P. R. (1981). *Female power and male dominance: On the origins of sexual inequality* (pp. 79–80). Cambridge, England: Cambridge University Press.

girls grow up in much the same way, learn to value cooperation over competition, and become equally habituated to adult men and women, who interact with one another on a relatively equal basis.

Societies following a *segregated pattern* define almost all work as either masculine or feminine, so men and women rarely engage in joint efforts of any kind. In such societies, it is inconceivable that someone would even think of doing something considered the work of the opposite sex. This pattern is frequently seen in pastoral nomadic, intensive agricultural, and industrial societies, where men's work keeps them outside the home for much of the time. Typically, men in such societies are expected to be tough, aggressive, and competitive—and this often involves assertions of male superiority, and hence authority, over women. Historically, societies segregated by gender often have imposed their control on societies featuring integration, upsetting the egalitarian nature of the latter.

In the third pattern of labor division by gender, sometimes called the *dual sex configuration,* men and women carry out their work separately, as in societies segregated by gender, but the relationship between them is one of balanced complementarity rather than inequality. Although competition is a prevailing ethic, each gender manages its own affairs, and the interests of both men and women are represented at all levels. Thus, as in integrated societies, neither gender exerts dominance over the other. The dual sex orientation may be seen among certain American Indian peoples whose economies were based upon subsistence farming, as well as among several West African kingdoms, including that of the aforementioned Dahomeans.

In postindustrial societies, the division of labor by gender becomes blurred and even irrelevant, resembling the flexible/integrated pattern of traditional foragers briefly discussed above. Although gender preferences and discrimination in the workplace exist in societies making the economic transition, cultural ideas more fitting agricultural or industrial societies predictably change in due time, adjusting to postindustrial challenges and opportunities.

DIVISION OF LABOR BY AGE
Division of labor according to age is also typical of human societies. Among the Ju/'hoansi, for example, children are not expected to contribute significantly to subsistence until they reach their late teens. Indeed, until they possess adult levels of strength and endurance, many "bush" foods are tough for them to gather. Until that point, youngsters contribute primarily by taking care of their littlest siblings while grownups deal with subsistence needs.

The Ju/'hoansi equivalent of retirement comes somewhere around the age of 60. Elderly people, while they

will usually do some foraging for themselves, are not expected to contribute much food. However, older men and women alike play an essential role in spiritual matters. Freed from food taboos and other restrictions that apply to younger adults, they may handle ritual substances considered dangerous to those still involved with hunting or having children. By virtue of their old age, they have memories of customary practices and events that happened far in the past. Thus they are repositories of accumulated wisdom—the libraries of a nonliterate people—and are able to suggest solutions to problems younger adults have never before had to face. Considered useful for their knowledge, they are far from being unproductive members of society.

In some food-foraging societies, women do continue to make a significant contribution to provisioning in their later years. Among the Hadza of East Africa, the input of older women is critical to their daughters, whose foraging abilities are significantly hindered when they have new infants to nurse. The energy costs of lactation, along with the tasks of holding, carrying, and nursing an infant, all encumber the mother's foraging efficiency. Those most immediately affected by this are a woman's weaned children not yet old enough to forage effectively for themselves. The problem is solved by the foraging efforts of grandmothers.[5]

In many traditional farming societies, children as well as older people may make a greater contribution to the economy in terms of work and responsibility than is common in industrial or postindustrial societies. For instance, in Maya peasant communities in southern Mexico and Guatemala, children not only look after their younger brothers and sisters but also help with housework. Girls begin to make a substantial contribution to the work of the household by age 7 or 8. By age 11 they are constantly busy with an array of chores—grinding corn, making tortillas, fetching wood and water, sweeping, and so forth. Young boys have less to do but are given small tasks, such as bringing in the chickens or playing with a baby. However, by age 12 they are carrying toasted tortillas to the men out working in the fields and returning with loads of corn.[6]

Children also work in industrial societies, where poor families depend on every possible contribution to the household. There, however, economic desperation may easily lead to the cold exploitation of children in factory settings. The use of child labor has become a

[5] Hawkes, K., O'Connell, J. F., & Blurton Jones, N. G. (1997). Hadza women's time allocation, offspring, provisioning, and the evolution of long postmenopausal life spans. *Current Anthropology 38,* 551–577.
[6] Vogt, E. Z. (1990). *The Zinacantecos of Mexico, a modern Maya way of life* (2nd ed., pp. 83–87). Fort Worth: Holt, Rinehart & Winston.

This Hmong girl in a Thailand factory exemplifies the use of child labor in many parts of the world, often by large corporations. Even in Western countries, child labor plays a major economic role.

matter of increasing concern as large capitalist corporations rely more and more on the low-cost manufacture of goods in the world's poorer countries. Reliable figures are hard to come by, but it is estimated that there are some 200 million child laborers under age 14, almost all living in Third World countries where their families depend on the extra income they bring home. Many enter the labor force when they are only 6 or 7 years old, working full-time, from dawn to dusk, for extremely low wages, which helps keep the labor costs down.

Although the United States long ago passed laws prohibiting institutionalized child labor, the country imports at least $100 million worth of products manufactured by poorly paid children, ranging from rugs and carpets to clothing and soccer balls.[7]

COOPERATIVE LABOR

Cooperative work groups can be found everywhere—in foraging as well as food-producing and in nonindustrial as well as industrial societies. Often, if the effort involves the whole community, a festive spirit permeates the work. Jomo Kenyatta, a Kikuyu leader who was trained as an anthropologist before becoming Kenya's first president, described a happy moment in a communal workday of an East African farming village such as his own:

> If a stranger happens to pass by, he will have no idea that these people who are singing and dancing have completed their day's work. This is why most Europeans have erred by not realizing that the African in his own environment does not count hours or work by the movement of the clock, but works with good spirit and enthusiasm to complete the tasks before him.[8]

In some parts of East Africa, work parties begin with the display of a pot of millet beer to be consumed after the tasks have been finished. Home-brewed from millet, their major cereal crop, the beer is not really payment for the work; indeed, the labor involved is worth far more than the beer consumed. Rather, drinking the low-alcohol but highly nutritious beverage together is more of a symbolic activity to celebrate the spirit of friendship and mutual support, whereas recompense comes as individuals sooner or later participate in work parties for others. In rural areas all around the world, farmers commonly help one another during harvest and haying seasons, often sharing major pieces of equipment.

In most human societies, the basic unit within which cooperation takes place is the household. It is both a unit of production and consumption; only in industrial societies have these two things been separated.

TASK SPECIALIZATION

In contemporary industrial and postindustrial societies, there is a great diversity of specialized tasks to be performed, and no individual can even begin to know all of those customarily seen as fitting for his or her age and gender. However, although specialization has increased in these societies, modern technologies are making labor divisions based on gender less relevant. By contrast, in small-scale foraging and traditional crop-cultivating societies, where division of labor typically occurs along lines of age and gender, each person has knowledge and competence in all aspects of work appropriate to his or her age and gender. Yet, even in these nonindustrial societies there is a measure of specialization.

An example of task specialization can be found among the Afar people of the Danakil Depression in the borderlands of Eritrea and Ethiopia, one of the lowest and hottest places on earth.[9] The Danakil's desolate

[7] "It's the law: Child labor protection." (1997, November/December). *Peace and Justice News*, 11.

[8] Herskovits, M. (1952). *Economic anthropology: A study in comparative economics* (2nd ed., p. 103). New York: Knopf.

Scorching hot and dry, the Danakil Desert in northeastern Africa lies some 113 meters (370 feet) below sea level—remains of what was once part of the Red Sea—with enormous salt flats. Afar nomads and their pack camels periodically travel to this desert, cutting blocks of rock salt that they trade with peoples in the interior highlands. Here we see them preparing and packing their quarry for the long journey.

landscape features sulfur fields, smoking fissures, volcanic tremors, and vast salt plains. Since ancient times, groups of Afar men periodically mine the salt, hacking blocks from the plain's crust. The work is backbreaking, all the more so with temperatures soaring to 140 degrees Fahrenheit.

Along with the physical strength required for such work under the most trying conditions, successful mining demands specialized planning and organization skills for getting to and from the work site. Pack camels have to be fed in advance, since importing sufficient fodder for them interferes with their ability to carry out salt. Food and water, packed by Afar women at the desert's edge, must be carried in for the miners, typically numbering thirty to forty per group. Travel is arranged for nighttime to avoid the scorching sun.[10]

In the past few decades, we have seen the emergence of new forms of task specialization in an international division of labor and in response to global markets of supply and demand. Many of these specializations are linked to tourism, now one of the largest industries in the world. Estimates vary, but in 2007 the industry employed some 230 million people and generated about $5 trillion—nearly 10 percent of the total value of goods and services produced worldwide. The recent global economic crisis beginning in 2008 slowed tourism's rapid rise, but the industry continues to grow, albeit at a slower space.[11] Some communities that still hold on to a natural habitat with a wealth of plant and animal life are able to tap into a specialized niche known as ecotourism, as detailed in this chapter's Anthropology Applied feature.

[9] Nesbitt, L. M. (1935). *Hell-hole of creation.* New York: Knopf.

[10] Mesghinua, H. M. (1966). Salt mining in Enderta. *Journal of Ethiopian Studies 4* (2); O'Mahoney, K. (1970). The salt trade. *Journal of Ethiopian Studies 8* (2).

[11] World Travel & Tourism Council: www.wttc.org. See also the UN's World Tourism Organization's annual report: www.unwto.org.

Global Ecotourism and Local Indigenous Culture in Bolivia

by Amanda Stronza

We traveled in a small fleet of motorized canoes. As the sun dipped behind the trees one steamy afternoon in April 2002, we turned the last few bends of the Tuichi River and arrived to our destination, the Chalalán Ecolodge of northern Bolivia. Our group included eighteen indigenous leaders from various parts of the Amazon rainforest, a handful of regional tour operators, conservationists, environmental journalists, and me—an applied anthropologist studying the effects of ecotourism on local livelihoods, cultural traditions, and resource use. We had been navigating for nine hours through lowland rainforest to visit one of the first indigenous, community-run ecotourism lodges in the world.

As we wended our way, combing the riverbanks for caimans, capybaras, tapirs, and jaguars, our conversations meandered too. Mostly, the indigenous leaders shared stories of how ecotourism had affected their own forests and communities. They spoke of tourists who brought both opportunities and conflicts, and of their own efforts to balance conservation and development. They compared notes on wildlife in their regions, the kinds of visitors they had attracted, the profits they'd earned, the new skills they had gained, and the challenges they were facing as they sought to protect their lands and cultural traditions while also engaging with the global tourism industry.

Having studied ecotourism in the Amazon since 1993, I felt honored to be on board participating in these discussions. With support from the Critical Ecosystem Partnership Fund, I had the opportunity that year—the International Year of Ecotourism—to assemble leaders from three indigenous ecotourism projects in South America. All three were partnerships between local communities and private tour companies or nongovernmental organizations. For example, the lodge we were visiting, Chalalán, came about through a partnership between the Quechua-Tacana community of San José de Uchupiamonas, Bolivia, and two global organizations, Conservation International and the Inter-American Development Bank. Much of the $1,450,000 invested in Chalalán went toward preparing community members to assume full ownership and management of the lodge within five years. After a successful transfer in 2001, the lodge now belonged to San José's 600-member Quechua-Tacana community.

The indigenous leaders who gathered for this trip had keen, first-hand knowledge about the costs and benefits ecotourism can bring. They were former hunters, now leading tourists as birding and wildlife guides; small farmers and artisans making traditional handicrafts to sell to visitors; river-savvy fishermen supplementing their incomes by driving tour boats; and local leaders whose intimate knowledge of their communities helped them manage their own tour companies. Among them was Chalalán's general manager Guido Mamani, who recounted the benefits Chalalán had brought to the Tacana of San José. "Ten years ago," he recalled, "people were leaving San José because there were few ways to make a living. Today they are returning because of pride in the success of Chalalán. Now, they see opportunity here." As a result of their renewed pride in their mix of Quechua and Tacana histories, the community has begun hosting tourists for cultural tours in San José. "We want to give tourists presentations about the community and our customs," Mamani explained, "including our legends, dances, traditional music, the coca leaves, the traditional meals. We want to show our culture through special walks focusing on medicinal and other useful plants."

Mamani and the other indigenous ecotourism leaders characterized the success of their lodges in three ways: economic, social, and environmental. Chalalán, for example, counted its economic success in terms of employment and new income. It directly employs eighteen to twenty-four people at a time, and additional families supply farm produce and native fruits to the lodge. With artisans selling handicrafts to tourists, the community has gained regional fame for its wooden carved masks. The social benefits of Chalalán include new resources for education, health care, and communication. With their profits from tourism, the community built a school, a clinic, and a potable water system. They also purchased an antenna, solar panels, and a satellite dish to connect with the world from their remote forests along the Tuichi River.

Beyond these sorts of material improvements, ecotourism has catalyzed symbolic changes for the people of San José. "We have new solidarity in our cultural traditions," one woman noted, "and now we want to show who we are to the outside world." These experiences of Chalalan and similar projects suggest that ecotourism may be more than just a conservation and development idea—it may also be a source of pride, empowerment, and strengthened cultural identity among indigenous peoples.

Distribution and Exchange

In societies without a money economy, the rewards for labor are usually direct. The workers in a family group consume what they harvest, eat what the hunter or gatherer brings home, and use the tools they themselves make. But even where no formal medium of exchange such as money exists, some distribution of goods takes place.

Anthropologists often classify the cultural systems of distributing material goods into three modes: reciprocity, redistribution, and market exchange.[12]

---

[12] Polanyi, K. (1968). The economy as instituted process. In E. E. LeClair, Jr., & H. K. Schneider (Eds.), *Economic anthropology: Readings in theory and analysis* (pp. 127–138). New York: Holt, Rinehart & Winston.

These Ju/'hoansi men are cutting up meat that will be shared by others in the camp. Food distribution practices of such food foragers are an example of generalized reciprocity.

© Stan Washburn/Anthro-Photo

Reciprocity

Reciprocity refers to the exchange of goods and services, of roughly equal value, between two parties. This may involve gift giving. Notably, individuals or groups in most cultures like to think that the main point of the transaction is the gift itself, yet what actually matters are the social ties that are created or reinforced between givers and receivers. Because reciprocity is about a relationship between the self and others, gift giving is seldom really selfless. The overriding (if unconscious) motive is to fulfill social obligations and perhaps to gain a bit of prestige in the process.

Cultural traditions dictate the manner and occasion of exchange. For example, when an animal is killed by a group of indigenous hunters in Australia, the meat is divided among the hunters' families and other relatives. Each person in the camp gets a share, the size depending on the nature of the person's kinship tie to the hunters. Typically, if the animal is a kangaroo, the left hind leg goes to the brother of the hunter, the tail to his father's brother's son, the loins and the fat to his father-in-law, the ribs to his mother-in-law, the forelegs to his father's younger sister, the head to his wife, and the entrails and the blood to the hunter. The hunter and his family seem to fare badly in this arrangement, but they have their turn when another man makes a kill. The giving and receiving are obligatory, as is the particularity of the distribution. Such sharing of food reinforces community bonds and ensures that everyone eats. By giving away part of a kill, the hunters get social credit for a similar amount of food in the future.

Reciprocity falls into several categories. The Australian food distribution example just noted constitutes an example of **generalized reciprocity**—exchange in which the value of what is given is not calculated, nor is the time of repayment specified. Gift giving, in the unselfish sense, also falls into this category. So, too, does the act of a kindhearted soul who stops to help a stranded motorist or someone else in distress and refuses payment with the admonition: "Pass it on to the next person in need."

Most generalized reciprocity, however, occurs among close kin or people who otherwise have very close ties with one another. Within such circles of intimacy, people give to others when they have the means and can count on receiving from others in time of need. Typically, participants will not consider such exchanges in economic terms but will couch them explicitly in terms of family and friendship social relations.

Balanced reciprocity differs in that it is not part of a long-term process. The giving and receiving, as well as the time involved, are more specific. One has a direct obligation to reciprocate promptly in equal value in order for the social relationship to continue. Examples of balanced reciprocity in contemporary North American society include such customary practices as hosting a

reciprocity The exchange of goods and services, of approximately equal value, between two parties.

generalized reciprocity A mode of exchange in which the value of what is given is not calculated, nor is the time of repayment specified.

balanced reciprocity A mode of exchange in which the giving and the receiving are specific as to the value of the goods and the time of their delivery.

Here we see a spectacular procession of the Three Wise Men or magician kings riding their camels into the Spanish city of Alcoi on the Eve of Epiphany. For this Roman Catholic holiday twelve days after Christmas, children write wish letters to these exotic kings from the east. Before going to bed on Epiphany night, youngsters place their shoes on the balcony or some other visible spot, along with food gifts for the kings' camels. Come morning, the children find presents left for them (supposedly) by the kings—a kind of ritualized gift "exchange" that represents balanced reciprocity.

Photo by Pamela Heywood

baby shower for young friends expecting their first baby, giving presents at birthdays and various other culturally prescribed special occasions, and buying drinks when one's turn comes at a gathering of friends and associates.

Giving, receiving, and sharing as so far described constitute a form of social security or insurance. A family contributes to others when they have the means and can count on receiving from others in time of need—promoting an egalitarian distribution of wealth over the long run. Exchanges that occur within a group of relatives or between friends generally take the form of generalized or balanced reciprocity.

Negative reciprocity is a third form of exchange, in which the aim is to get something for as little as possible. The parties involved have opposing interests and are not usually closely related; they may be strangers or even enemies. They are people with whom exchanges are often neither fair nor balanced and are usually not expected to be such. This type of reciprocity may involve hard bargaining, manipulation, or outright cheating. An extreme form of negative reciprocity is to take something by force, while realizing that one's victim may seek compensation or retribution for losses.

negative reciprocity A form of exchange in which the aim is to get something for as little as possible. Neither fair nor balanced, it may involve hard bargaining, manipulation, and outright cheating.

Sometimes elements of negative as well as balanced reciprocity are present in an exchange. Such is often the case with political fundraising in the United States, where big contributors expect their generosity will buy influence with a candidate, resulting in benefits of equal value. The politician may seek to do as little as possible in return, but not so little as to jeopardize future donations. Those who accept too much and/or give too much in return risk legal repercussions.

TRADE AND BARTER

Trade refers to a transaction in which two or more people are involved in an exchange of something—a quantity of food, fuel, clothing, jewelry, animals, or money, for example—for something else of equal value. In such a transaction, the value of the trade goods can be fixed by previous agreements or negotiated on the spot by the trading partners. When there is no money involved in the transaction, and the parties negotiate a direct exchange of one trade good for another, we may speak of *barter*. In barter, arguing about the price and terms of the deal may well be in the form of negative reciprocity, with each party aiming to get the better end of the deal. Relative value is calculated, and despite an outward show of indifference, sharp dealing is generally the rule, when compared to the more balanced nature of exchanges within a group.

An arrangement that combines elements of balanced reciprocity as well as barter existed in India between the Kota and three neighboring peoples. The Kota, the musicians and blacksmiths for the region, were able to provide their neighbors with tools and with music considered essential for ceremonial occasions. In exchange, the Toda, with whom they had an amicable relationship, offered *ghee* (a kind of butter used for certain ceremonies) and buffalo used for funerals. For grain, the Kota relied on the Badaga farmers, with whom they had a competitive relationship that sometimes led to one-sided trading practices (in which the Kota usually came out ahead). The forest-dwelling Kurumba, who were renowned as sorcerers, had honey, cane, and occasionally fruit to offer, but their main contribution was protection against the supernatural. The Kota feared the Kurumba, and the Kurumba took advantage of this in their dealings, so that they always got more than they gave. Thus great latent hostility existed between these two peoples.

One interesting mechanism for facilitating exchange between potentially antagonist groups is **silent trade** in which no verbal communication takes place. In fact, it may involve no actual face-to-face contact at all. Such cases have often characterized the dealings between food-foraging peoples and their food-producing neighbors—such as the Veddah of Sri Lanka's tropical forest, who traditionally offer wild honey to Sinhalese in exchange for metal tools. Another example of silent trade occurs with the Mbuti Pygmy of Congo's Ituri forest, who trade bushmeat for plantains and other crops grown by Bantu villagers on small farms. It works like this: People from the forest leave trade goods in a clearing, then retreat and wait. Agriculturalists come to the spot, survey the goods, leave what they think is a fair exchange of their own wares, and then leave. The forest people return, and if satisfied with the offer, take it with them. If not, they leave it untouched, signifying that they expect more. In this way, for 2,000 or so years, foragers have supplied various commodities in demand in a wider economy.[13]

To speculate about the reasons for silent trade, in some situations it may be silent for lack of a common language. More often silent trade may serve to control situations of distrust so as to keep relations peaceful. Good relations are maintained by preventing direct contact. Another possibility that does not exclude the others is that it makes exchange possible where problems of status might make verbal communication unthinkable. In any event, it provides for the exchange of goods between groups despite potential barriers.

KULA RING: GIFT GIVING AND TRADING IN THE SOUTH PACIFIC

Balanced reciprocity can take more complicated forms, whereby mutual gift giving serves to facilitate social interaction, smoothing relations between traders wanting to do business. One classic ethnographic example of balanced reciprocity between trading partners seeking to be friends and do business at the same time is the **Kula ring** in the southwestern Pacific Ocean. This practice was first described by Bronislaw Malinowski and involves thousands of seafarers going to great lengths to establish and maintain good trade relations; this centuries-old ceremonial exchange system continues to this day.[14]

Kula participants are men of influence who travel to islands within the Trobriand ring to exchange prestige items—red shell necklaces (*soulava*), which are circulated around the ring of islands in a clockwise direction, and white shell armbands (*mwali*), which are carried in the opposite direction (Figure 8.1). Each man in the Kula is

---

[14] Malinowski, B. (1922). *Argonauts of the western Pacific* (p. 94). London: Routledge & Kegan Paul; and see Weiner, A. B. (1988). *The Trobrianders of Papua New Guinea* (p. 156). New York: Holt, Reinhart & Winston.

silent trade A form of product exchange in which mutually distrusting ethnic groups avoid direct personal contact.

Kula ring A form of balanced reciprocity that reinforces trade relations among the seafaring Trobriand Islanders and other Melanesians.

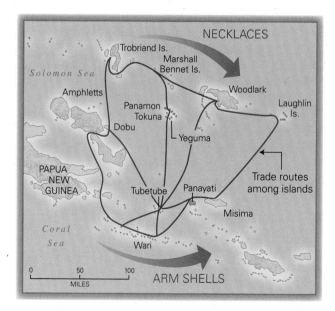

Figure 8.1 The ceremonial gift exchanges of shell necklaces and armbands in the Kula ring encourage trade and barter throughout the Melanesian islands.

---

[13] Turnbull. C. (1961), *The forest people.* New York: Simon & Schuster; Wilkie, D. S., & Curran, B. (1993). Historical trends in forager and farmer exchange in the Ituri rain forest of northeastern Zaïre. *Human Ecology* 21 (4), 389–417.

In Melanesia, men of influence paddle and sail within a large ring of islands in the southwestern Pacific off the eastern coast of Papua New Guinea to participate in the ceremonial trading of Kula shells, which smoothes trade relations and builds personal prestige.

linked to partners on the islands that neighbor his own. To a partner residing on an island in the clockwise direction, he offers a *soulava* and receives in return a *mwali*. He makes the reverse exchange of a *mwali* for a *soulava* to a partner living in the counterclockwise direction. Each of these trade partners eventually passes the object on to a Kula partner further along the chain of islands.

Soulava and *mwali* are ranked according to their size, their color, how finely they are polished, and their particular histories. Such is the fame of some that, when they appear in a village, they create a sensation.

Traditionally, men make their Kula journeys in elaborately carved dugout canoes, sailing and paddling these boats, which are 6 to 7.5 meters (20 to 25 feet) long, across open waters to shores some 100 kilometers (about 60 miles) or more away. The adventure is often dangerous and may take men away from their homes for several weeks, sometimes even months. Although men on Kula voyages may use the opportunity to trade for practical goods, acquiring such goods is not always the reason for these voyages—nor is Kula exchange a necessary part of regular trade expeditions.

Perhaps the best way to view the Kula is as an indigenous insurance policy in an economy fraught with danger and uncertainty. It establishes and reinforces social partnerships among traders doing business on distant shores, ensuring a welcome reception from people who have similar vested interests. This ceremonial exchange network does more than simply enhance the trade of foods and other goods essential for survival. Melanesians participating in the Kula ring have no doubt that

their social position has to do with the company they keep, the circles in which they move. They derive their social prestige from the reputations of their partners and the valuables that they circulate. By giving and receiving armbands and necklaces that accumulate the histories of their travels and the names of those who have possessed them, men proclaim their individual fame and talent, gaining considerable influence for themselves in the process.

Like other forms of currency, *soulava* and *mwali* must flow from hand to hand; once they stop flowing, they may lose their value. A man who takes these valuables out of their inter-island circuit invites criticism. Not only might he lose prestige or social capital as a man of influence, but he might become a target of sorcery for unraveling the cultural fabric that holds the islands together as a functioning social and economic order.

As this example from the South Pacific illustrates, the potential tension among trading partners may be resolved or lessened by participation in a ritual of balanced reciprocity. As an elaborate complex of ceremony, political relationships, economic exchange, travel, magic, and social integration, the Kula ring illustrates the inseparability of economic matters from the rest of culture. Although perhaps difficult to recognize, this is just as true in modern industrial societies as it is in traditional Trobriand society—as is evident when heads of state engage in ceremonial gift exchanges at official visits.

Redistribution

Redistribution is a form of exchange in which goods flow into a central place where they are sorted, counted, and reallocated. Commonly, it involves an element of power. In societies with a sufficient surplus to support

redistribution A form of exchange in which goods flow into a central place, where they are sorted, counted, and reallocated.

some sort of government, goods in the form of gifts, tribute, taxes, and the spoils of war are gathered into storehouses controlled by a chief or some other type of leader. From there they are handed out again. The leadership has three motives in redistributing this income: The first is to gain or maintain a position of power through a display of wealth and generosity; the second is to assure those who support the leadership an adequate standard of living by providing them with desired goods; and the third is to establish alliances with leaders of other groups by hosting them at lavish parties and giving them valuable goods.

The redistribution system of the ancient Inca empire in the Andean highlands of South America was one of the most efficient the world has ever known, both in the collection of tribute (obligatory contributions or gifts in the form of crops, goods, and services) and in its methods of administrative control.[15] Administrators kept inventories of resources and a census of the population, which at its peak reached 6 million. Each craft specialist had to produce a specific quota of goods from materials supplied by overseers. Required labor was used for some agricultural and mining work. Unpaid labor was also used in a program of public works that included a remarkable system of roads and bridges throughout the mountainous terrain, aqueducts that guaranteed a supply of water, temples for worship, and storehouses that held surplus food for times of famine.

Careful accounts were kept of income and expenditures. A central administration, regulated by the Inca emperor and his relatives, had the responsibility for ensuring that production was maintained and that commodities were distributed. Holding power over this command economy, the ruling elite lived in great luxury, but sufficient goods were redistributed to the common people to ensure that no one would be left in dire need or face the indignity of pauperism.

Taxes imposed by central governments of countries all around the world today are one form of redistribution—required payments typically based on a percentage of one's income and property value. Typically, a portion of the taxes goes toward supporting the government itself while the rest is redistributed either in cash (such as welfare payments and government loans or subsidies to businesses) or in the form of services (such as military defense, law enforcement, food and drug inspection, schools, highway construction, and the like). Tax codes vary greatly among countries. In many European countries, wealthy citizens are taxed at a considerably higher percentage of their income than are U.S. citizens.

SPENDING WEALTH TO GAIN PRESTIGE

In societies where people devote most of their time to subsistence activities, gradations of wealth are small, kept that way through various cultural mechanisms and systems of reciprocity that serve to spread quite fairly what little wealth exists. It is a different situation in ranked societies where substantial surpluses are produced, and the gap between the have-nots and the have-lots can be considerable. In these societies, showy display for social prestige—known as **conspicuous consumption**—is a strong motivator for the distribution of wealth.

Obviously, excessive efforts to impress others with one's wealth or status also play a prominent role in industrial and postindustrial societies, as individuals compete for prestige. Indeed, many North Americans and Europeans spend much of their lives trying to impress others. This requires the display of symbolic prestige items—designer clothes, substantial jewelry, mansions, expensive cars, private planes—and fits neatly into an economy based on consumer wants.

A form of conspicuous consumption also occurs in some crop-cultivating and foraging societies—as illustrated by potlatches hosted by the chiefs of various American Indian groups living along the Pacific Northwest coast, including the Tlingit, Haida, and Kwakwaka'wakw (Kwakiutl) peoples. A **potlatch** is a ceremonial event in which a village chief publicly gives away stockpiled food and other goods that signify wealth. (The term comes from the Chinook Indian word *patshatl*, which means "gift.")

Traditionally, a chief whose village had built up enough surplus to host such a feast for other villages in the region would give away large piles of sea otter furs, dried salmon, blankets, and other valuables while making boastful speeches about his generosity, greatness, and glorious ancestors. While other chiefs became indebted to him, he reaped the glory of successful and generous leadership and saw his prestige rise. In the future, his own village might face shortages, and he would find himself on the receiving end of a potlatch. Should that happen, he would have to listen to the self-serving and pompous speeches of rival chiefs. Obliged to receive, he would temporarily lose prestige and status.

In extreme displays of wealth, chiefs even destroyed some of their precious possessions. This occurred with some frequency in the second half of the 19th century, after European contact triggered a process of cultural change

conspicuous consumption A showy display of wealth for social prestige.

potlatch On the northwest coast of North America, a ceremonial event in which a village chief publicly gives away stockpiled food and other goods that signify wealth.

[15] Mason, J. A. (1957). *The ancient civilizations of Peru.* Baltimore: Penguin.

Among Native Americans living along the northwestern coast of North America, one gains prestige by giving away valuables at the potlatch feast. Here we see Tlingit clan members dressed in traditional Chilkat and Raven's Tail robes during a recent potlatch in Sitka, Alaska.

that included new trade wealth. Outsiders might view such grandiose displays as wasteful in the extreme. However, these extravagant giveaway ceremonies have played an ecologically adaptive role in a coastal region where villages alternately faced periods of scarcity and abundance and relied upon alliances and trade relations with one another for long-term survival. The potlatch provided a ceremonial opportunity to strategically redistribute surplus food and goods among allied villages in response to periodic fluctuations in fortune.

> **prestige economy** Creation of a surplus for the express purpose of gaining prestige through a public display of wealth that is given away as gifts.
>
> **leveling mechanism** A cultural obligation compelling prosperous members of a community to give away goods, host public feasts, provide free service, or otherwise demonstrate generosity so that no one permanently accumulates significantly more wealth than anyone else.

A strategy that features this sort of accumulation of surplus goods for the express purpose of displaying wealth and giving it away to raise one's status is known as a **prestige economy.** In contrast to conspicuous consumption in industrial and postindustrial societies, the emphasis is not on amassing goods that then become unavailable to others. Instead, it is on gaining wealth in order to give it away for the sake of prestige and status.

LEVELING MECHANISMS

The potlatch is an example of a **leveling mechanism**—a cultural obligation compelling prosperous members of a community to give away goods, host public feasts, provide free service, or otherwise demonstrate generosity so that no one permanently accumulates significantly more wealth than anyone else. With leveling mechanisms at work, greater wealth brings greater social pressure to spend and give generously. In exchange for such demonstrated altruism, a person not only increases his or her social standing in the community, but may also keep disruptive envy at bay.

Underscoring the value of collective well-being over individual self-interest, leveling mechanisms are important for the long-term survival of traditional communities. The potlatch is just one example of many cultural varieties of leveling mechanism.

By pressuring members into sharing their wealth in their own community rather than keeping it or privately investing it elsewhere, leveling mechanisms do more than keep resources in circulation. They also reduce social tensions among relatives, neighbors, and fellow town folk, promoting a collective sense of togetherness. An added practical benefit is that they ensure that necessary services within the community are performed.

Market Exchange

To an economist, **market exchange** has to do with the buying and selling of goods and services, with prices set by rules of supply and demand. Personal loyalties and moral values are not supposed to play a role, but they often do. Since the actual location of the transaction is not always relevant in today's world, we must distinguish between the *marketplace* and *market exchange*.

MARKETPLACE AND MARKET EXCHANGE

Typically, until well into the 20th century, market exchange was carried out in specific localities or marketplaces. This is still the case in much of the nonindustrial world and even in numerous centuries-old European and Asian towns and cities. In food-producing societies, marketplaces overseen by a centralized political authority provide the opportunity for farmers or peasants in the surrounding rural territories to exchange some of their livestock and produce for needed items manufactured in factories or in the workshops of craft specialists living (usually) in towns and cities. Thus markets require some sort of complex division of labor as well as centralized political organization.

The traditional market is local, specific, and contained. Prices are typically set on the basis of face-to-face bargaining rather than by unseen forces wholly removed from the transaction itself. Notably, sales do not necessarily involve money; instead, goods may be directly exchanged through some form of barter among the specific individuals involved.

In industrializing and industrial societies, many market transactions still take place in a specific identifiable location—including international trade fairs such as the semi-annual Canton Trade Fair in Guangzhou, China. In spring 2007, 13,000 Chinese enterprises participated in the event, offering 150,000 products and generating over $36 billion in export sales among 207,000 visitors. In 2009,

reflecting the international financial crisis, sales dropped to $26 billion, but the event remains China's largest trade fair by far. Notably, despite the overall slump, the number of e-commerce visitors to the fair rose 2.5 percent.[16]

It is increasingly common for people living in technologically wired parts of the world to buy and sell everything from cattle to cars without ever being in the same city, let alone the same space. For example, think of Internet companies such as eBay where all buying and selling occur electronically and irrespective of geographic distance. When people talk about a market in today's industrial or postindustrial world, the particular geographic location where something is bought or sold is often not important at all.

The faceless market exchanges that take place in industrial and postindustrial societies stand in stark contrast to experiences in the marketplaces of nonindustrial societies, which have much of the excitement of a fair. Traditional exchange centers are colorful places where a host of sights, sounds, and smells awaken the senses. Typically, vendors and/or their family members produced the goods they are selling, thereby personalizing the transactions. Dancers and musicians may perform, and feasting and fighting may mark the end of the day. In these markets social relationships and personal interactions are key elements, and noneconomic activities may overshadow economic ones. In short, such markets are gathering places where people renew friendships, see relatives, gossip, and keep up with the world, while procuring needed goods they cannot produce for themselves.[17]

MONEY AS MEANS OF EXCHANGE

Although there have been marketplaces without money of any sort, money does facilitate trade. **Money** may be defined as something used to make payments for other goods and services as well as to measure their value. Its critical attributes are durability, transportability, divisibility, recognizability, and interchangeability. Items that have been used as money in various societies include salt, shells, precious stones, special beads, livestock, and valuable metals,

[16] Xinhua News Agency. (2009, May 9). Canton Fair wraps up with export orders down 17 percent. *China Daily*.

[17] Plattner, S. (1989). Markets and marketplaces. In S. Plattner (Ed.), *Economic anthropology* (p. 171). Stanford, CA: Stanford University Press.

market exchange The buying and selling of goods and services, with prices set by rules of supply and demand.

money Something used to make payments for other goods and services as well as to measure their value.

Visual Counterpoint

In many societies, particularly in developing countries, the market is an important focus of social as well as economic activity, as shown in the photo of a crowded outdoor marketplace in Aswan, Egypt. In contrast, the packer pictured on the left works at an Amazon.com distribution center in Fernley, Nevada, preparing orders purchased on the Internet. With the advent of online shopping, people can buy and sell with no social interaction whatsoever.

such as iron, copper, silver, and gold. As revealed in this chapter's Biocultural Connection, cacao beans were also used as money—and more.

About 5,000 years ago, merchants and others in Mesopotamia (now part of Iraq) went beyond bartering in their trading activities and began using pieces of precious metal such as silver in their transactions. Once they agreed on the value of these pieces as a means of exchange (money), more complex commercial developments followed. As the means of exchange was standardized in terms of value, it became easier to accumulate, lend, or borrow money for specified amounts and periods against payment of interest. In due time, some merchants began to do business with money itself, and they became bankers.

As the use of money became widespread, the metal units were adapted to long-term use, easy storage, and long-distance transportation. In many cultures, such pieces of iron, copper, or silver were cast as miniature models of especially valuable implements like sword

blades, axes, or spades. But some 2,600 years ago in the ancient kingdom of Lydia (southwestern Turkey), they were molded into small flat discs conforming to different sizes and weights.[18] Over the next few centuries, metal coins were also standardized in terms of the metal's purity and value, such as 100 units of copper equal 10 units of silver or 1 of gold.

By about 2,000 years ago, the commercial use of such coins was spreading throughout much of Europe and becoming increasingly common in parts of Asia and Africa, especially along trade routes and in urban centers. Thus money set into motion radical economic changes in many traditional societies and introduced what has been called *merchant capitalism* in many parts of the world.[19]

---

[18] Davies, G. (2005). *A history of money from the earliest times to present day* (3rd ed.). Cardiff: University of Wales Press.

[19] See also Wolf, E. R. (1982). *Europe and the people without history* (pp. 135–141). Berkeley: University of California Press.

Cacao: The Love Bean in the Money Tree

Several thousand years ago Indians in the tropical lowlands of southern Mexico discovered how to produce a hot brew from ground roasted beans. They collected these beans from melon-shaped fruit pods growing in trees identified by today's scientists as *Theobroma cacao*. By adding honey, vanilla, and some flowers for flavoring, they produced a beverage that made them feel good and believed that these beans were gifts from their gods.

Soon, cacao beans became part of long-distance trade networks and appeared in the Mexican highlands, where the Aztec elite adopted this drink brewed from *cacahuatl,* calling it *chocolatl.* In fact, these beans were so highly valued that Aztecs also used them as money. When Spanish invaders conquered Guatemala and Mexico in the 1520s, they adopted the region's practice of using cacao beans as currency inside their new colony. They also embraced the custom of drinking chocolate, which they introduced to Europe, where it became a luxury drink as well as a medicine.[a]

In the next 500 years, chocolate developed into a $14-billion global business, with the United States as the top importer of cacao beans or cacao products. Women buy 75 percent of the chocolate products, and on Valentine's Day more than $1 billion worth of chocolate is sold.

What is it about chocolate that makes it a natural love drug? Other than carbohydrates, minerals, and vitamins, it contains about 300 chemicals, including some with mood-altering effects. For instance, cacao beans contain several chemical components that trigger feelings of pleasure in the human brain. In addition to tryptophan, which increases serotonin levels, chocolate also contains phenylethylamine, an amphetaminelike substance that stimulates the body's own dopamine and has slight antidepressant effects. Chocolate contains anandamide (*anan* means "bliss" in Sanskrit), a messenger molecule that triggers the brain's pleasure center. Also naturally produced in the brain, anandamide's mood-enhancing effect is the same as that obtained from marijuana leaves.[b] Finally, chocolate also contains a mild stimulant called theobromine ("food of god"), which stimulates the human brain's production of natural opiates, reducing pain and increasing feelings of satisfaction and even euphoria.

These chemicals help explain why the last Aztec ruler Montezuma drank so much chocolate. A Spanish eyewitness, who visited his royal palace in the Aztec capital in 1519, later reported that Montezuma's servants sometimes brought their powerful lord "in cups of pure gold a drink made from the cocoa-plant, which they said he took before visiting his wives. . . . I saw them bring in a good fifty large jugs of this chocolate, all frothed up, of which he would drink a little. They always served it with great reverence."[c]

BIOCULTURAL QUESTION

Viewed as a divine gift by Mexican Indians, chocolate stimulates our brain's pleasure center. Why would women buy this natural love drug in much greater quantities than men?

[a]For an excellent cultural history of chocolate, see Coe, S. D., & Coe, M. D. (1996). *The true history of chocolate.* New York: Thames and Hudson; Grivetti, L. E. (2005). From aphrodisiac to health food: A cultural history of chocolate. *Karger Gazette* (68).
[b]Personal communication, Lawrence C. Davis, Kansas State University.
[c]del Castillo, B. D. (1963). *The conquest of New Spain* (pp. 226–227) (translation and introduction by J. M. Cohen). New York: Penguin.

Local Economies and Global Capitalism

Failing to overcome cultural biases can have serious economic consequences, especially in this era of globalization. For example, it has led prosperous countries to impose inappropriate development schemes in parts of the world that they regard as economically underdeveloped. Typically, these schemes focus on increasing the target country's gross national product through large-scale production that all too often boosts the well-being of a few but results in poverty, poor health, discontent, and a host of other ills for many.

Among many examples of this scenario is the global production of soy, which has increased greatly in many parts of the world. Of particular note is Paraguay, where big landowners, in cooperation with large agribusinesses (most of which are owned by neighboring Brazilians), produce genetically modified seeds, developed and marketed by foreign companies, especially the U.S.-based multinational corporation Monsanto. Although these landowners and agribusinesses possess just 1 percent of the total number of Paraguayan farms, they own almost 80 percent of the country's agricultural land. Exporting the soy, they make hefty profits because production costs are low and international demand is high for cattle feed and biofuel. But there are victims of their "progress": hundreds of thousands of small farmers, landless peasants, rural laborers, and their families. Traditionally growing much of their own food (plus a bit extra for the local market) on small plots, many locals have been edged out and forced to work for hunger wages or to migrate to the city, or even abroad, in order to survive. Those who stay face malnutrition and other hardships, for they lack enough fertile land to feed their families and do not earn enough to buy basic foodstuffs.[20]

[20] Fogel, R., & Riquelme, M. A. (2005). *Enclave sorjero. Merma de soberania y pobreza.* Ascuncion: Centro de Estudios Rurales Interdisciplinarias; Bodley, J. H. (1990). *Victims of progress* (3rd ed., p. 141). Mountain View, CA: Mayfield.

A crowd of protestors demonstrated against World Trade Organization (WTO) policies favoring rich countries over poor ones during an informal meeting of trade officials from 35 countries hosted by India in its capital city, New Delhi, September 2009. Established in 1995 and headquartered in Geneva, the WTO is the only global international organization with rules of trade among its 153 member countries.

Such are the failures of many foreign-imposed economic development schemes in which powerful institutions and corporations primarily representing outside interests disregard or ignore a key anthropological fact: A culture is not a random happening. It is an integrated system (as illustrated by the barrel model), and therefore a shift in the infrastructure, or economic base, impacts interlinked elements of the society's social structure and superstructure. As the ethnographic examples of the potlatch and the Kula ring show, economic activities in traditional cultures are intricately intertwined with social and political relations and even involve spiritual elements. Agribusinesses and other large-scale economic operations or development schemes that do not take such structural complexities into consideration may have unintended negative consequences on a society.

Fortunately, there is now a growing awareness on the part of development officials that future projects are unlikely to succeed without the expertise that anthropologically trained people can bring to bear. And, in some parts of the world anthropologists with indigenous roots are taking leading roles in shaping development agendas that build on rather than destroy tradition—as relayed in this chapter's Anthropologist of Note about Rosita Worl, a Tlingit from Juneau, Alaska.

Achieving a cross-cultural understanding of the economic organizations of other peoples that is not distorted or limited by the logic, hopes, and expectations of one's own society has also become important for corporate executives in today's world. Recognizing how the economic structures are intertwined with other aspects of a culture could help business corporations avoid problems of the sort experienced by Gerber, when it began selling baby

food in Africa. As in the United States, Gerber's labels featured a picture of a smiling baby. Only later did company officials learn that, in Africa, businesses routinely put pictures of the products themselves on the outside label, since many people cannot read.[21]

As globalization increases so does corporate awareness of the cost of such cross-cultural miscues. So it is not surprising that business recruiters on college campuses in North America and elsewhere are now seeking job candidates with the kind of cross-cultural understanding of the world that anthropology provides.

When such work opportunities involve helping an enterprise more effectively exploit people for the sake of commercial gain, anthropologists have to deal with the profession's first ethical principle: Do no harm. It is important to note that powerful business corporations typically aim to make large profits. Their agenda is universally promoted through slogans such as "free trade," "free markets," and "free enterprise." The commercial success of such multinationals does not come without a price, and all too often that price is paid by still surviving indigenous foragers, small farmers, herders, fishermen, local artisans such as weavers and carpenters, and so on. From their viewpoint, such slogans of freedom have the ring of "savage capitalism," a term now often used in Latin America for a new world order in which the powerless feel condemned to misery.

Although political authorities in state-organized societies seek to govern and control economic activities for regulation and taxation purposes, they do not always

---

[21] "Madison Avenue relevance." (1999). *Anthropology Newsletter 40* (4), 32.

Rosita Worl

Photo: David Sheakley, Sealaska Heritage Institute.

Alaskan anthropologist **Rosita Worl,** whose Tlingit names are *Yeidiklats'akw* and *Kaa hani,* belongs to the Thunderbird Clan from the ancient village of Klukwan in southeastern Alaska. During her growing-up years by the Chilkat River, elders taught her to speak loudly so her words could be heard above the sound of crashing water. And her mother, a cannery union organizer, took her along to meetings.

As a university student, Worl led a public protest for the first time—successfully challenging a development scheme in Juneau detrimental to local

Tlingit. When she decided to pursue her anthropology doctorate at Harvard, she did so with a strong sense of purpose: "You have to be analytical about your culture," she says. "At one time, before coming into contact with other societies, we were just able to live our culture, but now we have to be able to keep it intact while integrating it into modern institutions. We have to be able to communicate our cultural values to others and understand how those modern institutions impact those values."

Worl's graduate studies included fieldwork among the Iñupiat of Alaska's North Slope region—research that resulted in her becoming a spokesperson at state, national, and international levels for the protection of whaling practices and the indigenous subsistence lifestyle. For over three decades now, she has fought to safeguard traditional rights to natural resources essential for survival, for current and future generations, including her own children and grandchildren.

A recognized leader in sustainable, culturally informed economic development, Worl has held several major positions at the Sealaska Corporation, a large Native-owned business enterprise with almost 18,000 shareholders primarily of Tlingit and neighboring Haida and Tsimshian descent. Created under the 1971 Alaska Native Claims Settlement Act, Sealaska is now the largest private landholder in southeastern Alaska. Its subsidiaries collectively employ over a thousand people and include

timber harvesting, marketing wood products, land and forest resource management, construction, and information technology. Putting the holistic perspective and analytical tools of anthropology to practice, Worl has spearheaded efforts to incorporate the cultural values of southeast Alaska Natives into Sealaska—including shareholding opportunities for employees.

Currently, Worl serves as president of Sealaska Heritage Institute, a Native nonprofit organization that seeks to perpetuate and enhance Tlingit, Haida, and Tsimshian cultures, including language preservation and revitalization. Also on the faculty of the University of Alaska Southeast, she has written extensively about indigenous Alaska for academic and general audiences. She founded the journal *Alaska Native News* to educate Native Alaskans on a range of issues and is deeply involved in the implementation of the 1990 Native American Graves Protection and Repatriation Act.

Sought for her knowledge and expertise, Worl has served on the board of directors of the Smithsonian Institution's National Museum of the American Indian, as well as Cultural Survival, Inc. She has earned many honors for her work, including the American Anthropological Association's Solon T. Kimball Award for Public and Applied Anthropology, received in 2008 in recognition of her exemplary career in applying anthropology to public life in Alaska and beyond.

succeed. Because of insufficient government resources, bureaucratic mismanagement, or official corruption, or because people are able to avoid government regulations and tax collectors, state-organized societies also possess a largely undocumented **informal economy**—a network of producing and circulating marketable commodities, labor, and services that for various reasons escapes government control (enumeration, regulation, or other types of public monitoring or auditing). Such enterprises may encompass a range of activities: house cleaning, child care, gardening, repair or construction work, making and selling alcoholic beverages, street peddling, money lending, begging, prostitution, gambling, drug dealing, pick-pocketing, and labor by illegal foreign workers, to mention just a few.

These off-the-books or black market activities have been known for a long time but generally have been

dismissed by economists as of marginal importance. Yet, in many countries of the world, the informal economy is, in fact, more important than the formal economy. In many places, large numbers of under- and unemployed people who have only limited access to the formal economic sector in effect improvise, "getting by" on scant resources. Meanwhile, more affluent members of society may dodge various regulations in order to maximize returns and/or to vent their frustrations at their perceived loss of self-determination in the face of increasing government regulation.

informal economy A network of producing and circulating marketable commodities, labor, and services that for various reasons escapes government control.

Globalscape

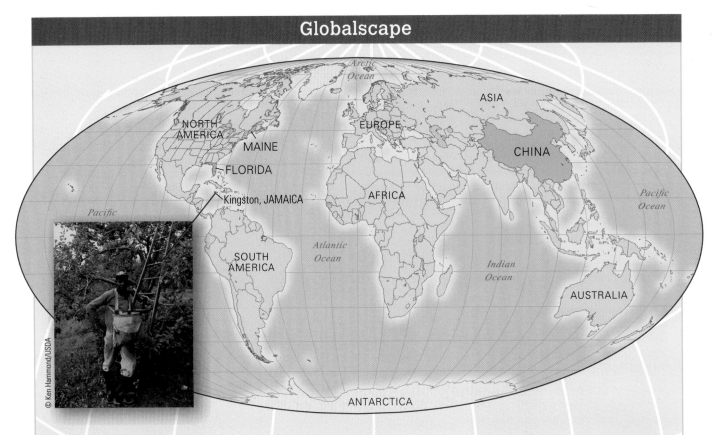

© Ken Hammond/USDA

How Much for a Red Delicious?

Each fall, about 600 Jamaicans migrate to Maine for the apple harvest.[a] While plucking the trees with speed and skill, they listen to reggae music that reminds them of home. Calling each other "brother," they go by nicknames like "Rasta." Most are poor peasants from mountain villages in the Caribbean where they grow yams. But their villages do not produce enough to feed their families, so they go elsewhere to earn cash.

Before leaving Jamaica, they must cut their dreadlocks and shave their beards. Screened and contracted by a labor recruiter in Kingston, they receive a temporary foreign farm workers visa from the U.S. embassy and then fly to Miami. Traveling northward by bus, many work on tobacco farms en route to Maine's orchards (and in Florida's

sugar cane fields on the way home). Earning the minimum hourly wage as regulated by the federal H-2A program for "temporary agricultural workers," they work seven days a week, up to 10 hours daily. Orchard owners value these foreigners, for they are twice as productive as local pickers. Moreover, hand-picked apples graded "extra fancy" earn farmers eight times the price of apples destined for processing.

While in the United States, the Jamaicans remain quite isolated, trying to save as much as they can to send more money home. Just before leaving the country, Rasta and his "brothers" buy things like a television, refrigerator, clothes, and shoes to take home as gifts or as goods to be resold for profit. Lately, their cash-earning opportunities in Maine are disappearing due to a tide of cheaper illegal

workers and a diminished demand for U.S.-grown apples due to increasing Chinese competition.

Although rural labor conditions for seasonal migrant workers in the United States have been likened to indentured service (causing some critics to call the federal H-2A program "rent-a-slave"), for Jamaicans like Rasta, it is an opportunity to escape from the dismal poverty on their Caribbean island.

Global Twister   When you take a big bite from your next apple, think of a brother like Rasta. What do you think is "fair value" anyway?

―――――――――

[a] See Rathke, L. (1989). To Maine for apples. *Salt Magazine 9* (4), 24–47.

Adult men and women from poor regions in the world may be forced to search for income far away from home. Those who cannot find a paying job within their own country seek cash-earning opportunities abroad. For multiple reasons such as visa requirements, most laborers who cross international borders legally get temporary work permits as "guest workers" but are not immigrants in that foreign country.

North Africa and Southwest Asia are cheap foreign labor reservoirs for the wealthy industrialized countries of western Europe, while Latin America and the Caribbean provide workers for the United States, which draws more migrant laborers than any other country in the world. These workers often send *remittances* (a portion of their earnings) to their families back in their home village or town abroad. A significant percentage of remittances flows through informal systems rather than through banks, so the sum total of these global transfers is unknown, but it is estimated to be well over $100 billion per year.

For a very poor country such as Jamaica, the total annual inflow of remittances is ten times greater than the foreign aid received and makes up almost 15 percent of that Caribbean island's income. Over a quarter of Jamaicans receive remittances from relatives working abroad, and the average value of such cash transfers for a typical Jamaican household is higher than the average per capita gross domestic product (GDP) in that island nation. For a specific example, see this chapter's Globalscape.

Concluding Remarks

Now that globalization is connecting national, regional, and local markets in which natural resources, commodities, and human labor are bought and sold, people everywhere in the world face new economic opportunities and confront new challenges. Not only are natural environments more quickly and radically transformed by means of new powerful technologies, but long-established subsistence practices, economic arrangements, social organizations, and associated ideas, beliefs, and values are also under enormous pressure.

Questions for Reflection

1. Imagine that you have gone to live with a group of nomadic foragers who meet the challenges of survival by hunting, fishing, and gathering, rather than by shopping. How would that way of life challenge your current attitude about social relations, possessions, and the natural environment?

2. Consider the differences between reciprocity and market exchange. What role does each play in your own society?

3. As the potlatch ceremony shows, prestige may be gained by giving away wealth. Does such a prestige-building mechanism exist in your own society? If so, how does it work?

4. When shopping for groceries in a supermarket, think of this chapter's Globalscape and try to imagine the great chain of human hands involved in getting something as simple as a nice red apple from a distant orchard to your own mouth. How many people do you think handled the fruit to get it to you?

5. Economic relations in traditional cultures are usually wrapped up in social, political, and even spiritual issues. Can you think of any examples in your own society in which the economic sphere is inextricably intertwined with other structures in the cultural system?

Suggested Readings

Blumberg, R. L. (1991). *Gender, family, and the economy: The triple overlap.* Newbury Park, CA: Sage.

The author presents a look at the interrelationship of gender, domestic life, and the economy.

Dalton, G. (1971). *Traditional tribal and peasant economies: An introductory survey of economic anthropology.* Reading, MA: Addison-Wesley.

This is just what the title says it is, by a major specialist in economic anthropology.

Mauss, M. (2000). *The gift: The form and reason for exchange in archaic societies* (translation by W. D. Halls and foreword by M. Douglas). New York: Norton.

Originally published as *Essai sur le don* in the French journal *Année Sociologique* (1923–1924), this short book remains the classic on reciprocity and traditional gift exchange.

Plattner, S. (Ed.). (1989). *Economic anthropology.* Stanford, CA: Stanford University Press.

This is a collection of essays from twelve scholars in the field concerning a variety of issues. These include economic behavior in various cultures, gender roles and common property resources, informal economics in industrial societies, and mass marketing in urban areas.

Wilk, R. R. (1996). *Economics and cultures: An introduction to economic anthropology.* Boulder, CO: Westview.

This lively primer traces the history of the dialogue between anthropology and economics and identifies the subdiscipline's basic practical and theoretical problems.

Challenge Issue All around the world humans face the challenge of managing sexual relations and establishing social alliances essential to the survival of individuals and their offspring. Adjusting to particular natural environments and facing distinct economic and political challenges, each group establishes its own specific social arrangements in terms of childrearing tasks, gender relations, household and family structures, and residence patterns. Because marriage and family, in various forms, play a fundamental role in determining these arrangements, wedding rituals are especially important cultural events. Whether private or public, sacred or secular, weddings reveal, confirm, and underscore important ideas and values of culture. Symbolically rich, they usually feature particular speech rituals, along with prescribed apparel, postures and gestures, food and drink, songs and dances—all passed down (with occasional alterations) through many generations. Here we see a traditional Japanese wedding at Tokyo's sacred Meiji shrine. Conforming to the ancient tradition of Shinto ("the way of the spirits"), the bride wears a white silk kimono as a profession of purity. Her white hood symbolically hides "horns of jealousy" from her new mother-in-law, who will have authority over her in the household she is joining.

CHAPTER 9

Sex, Marriage, and Family

Chapter Preview

What Is Marriage?

A nonethnocentric definition of marriage is a culturally sanctioned union between two or more people that establishes certain rights and obligations between the people, between them and their children, and between them and their in-laws. Although most marriages around the world involve unions between one woman and one man, numerous other arrangements exist. For example, many cultures not only permit but encourage marriage of one man to multiple wives. The specific form marriage takes is related to who has rights and obligations to offspring that may result from the marital union, as well as how property is distributed. In contrast to mating—the sexual bonding that all animal species do—marriage is a cultural institution, backed by economic, social, legal, and ideological forces.

What Is the Difference Between Family and Household?

Households are task-oriented residential units within which economic production, consumption, inheritance, childrearing, and shelter are organized and accomplished. In the vast majority of human societies, a household consists of a family or part of a family or their core members, even though some household members may not be relatives of the family around which it is built. In some societies, families may be less important to people than the households in which they live.

What Is the Family?

Although the idea of family means different things to different people, in anthropological terms it is a group of two or more people related by blood, marriage, or adoption. The family may take many forms, ranging from a single parent with one or more children, to a married couple or polygamous spouses with offspring, to several generations of parents and their children. The particular form family takes within a society is related to distinct social, historical, and ecological circumstances.

In contrast to individuals raised in traditional Shinto Japanese families featured in this chapter's opening photo, young people in the Trobriand Islands of the southern Pacific are traditionally unconstrained in premarital sexual explorations. By age 7 or 8, they begin playing erotic games and imitating adult seductive attitudes. Within another four or five years they start pursuing sexual partners in earnest—experimenting erotically with a variety of individuals.

Since attracting sexual partners is an important matter among young Trobrianders, they spend a great deal of time making themselves look attractive and seductive. Their daily conversations are loaded with sexual hints, and magical spells as well as small gifts are employed to entice a prospective sex partner to the beach at night or to the house in which boys sleep apart from their parents. Because girls, too, sleep apart from their parents, youths and adolescents have considerable freedom in arranging their erotic escapades. Boys and girls play this game as equals, with neither having an advantage over the other.

By the time Trobrianders are in their mid-teens, meetings between lovers may take up most of the night, and affairs are apt to last for several months. Ultimately, a young islander begins to meet the same partner again and again, rejecting the advances of others. When the couple is ready, they appear together one morning outside the young man's house as a way of announcing their intention to be married.

Until the latter part of the 20th century, the Trobriand attitude toward adolescent sexuality was in marked contrast to that of most Western cultures in Europe and North America where individuals were not supposed to have sexual relations before or outside of marriage. Since then, practices in much of Europe and North America have converged toward those of the Trobrianders, even though the traditional ideal of premarital abstinence has not been abandoned entirely.

Control of Sexual Relations

In the absence of effective birth control, the usual outcome of sexual activity between fertile individuals of the opposite sex is that, sooner or later, the woman becomes

To attract lovers, young Trobriand women and men must look as attractive and seductive as possible. This woman's beauty has been enhanced by face painting and adornments given by her father.

pregnant. Given the intricate array of social responsibilities involved in rearing the children that are born of sexual relations—and the potential for violent conflict resulting from unregulated sexual competition—it is not surprising that all societies have cultural rules that seek to regulate those relations.

However, the rules concerning when, how, and between whom sex takes place vary across cultures. For instance, in some societies, sexual intercourse during pregnancy is taboo, while in others it is looked upon positively as something that promotes the growth of the fetus. And while some cultures sharply condemn same-sex acts or relations, many others are indifferent and do not even have a special term to distinguish homosexuality as significant in its own right. In several cultures same-sex acts are not only accepted but even prescribed. Such is the case in some Papua societies in New Guinea, for example, where certain prescribed male-to-male sexual acts are part of initiation rituals required of all

Visual Counterpoint

Although homosexuality is a widespread phenomenon, in some societies homosexuals confront repression or ridicule. In parts of the United States, for example, public displays of same-sex affection between men in particular are often looked upon as distasteful or even disgusting. One nationwide exception is the football field, where an extreme measure of rough-and-tumble masculine behavior makes it possible for players to pat each other on the behind, exchange celebratory hugs, and even leap into each other's arms without bringing their sexual orientation into question.

boys to become respected adult men.[1] In those cultures, people traditionally see the transmission of semen from older to younger boys, through oral sex, as vital for building up the strength needed to protect against the supposedly debilitating effects of adult heterosexual intercourse.[2]

Despite longstanding culture-based opposition to homosexuality in many areas of the world, this sexual orientation exists within the wider range of human sexual relations, emotional attractions, and social identities, and it is far from uncommon. Homosexuality is found in diverse contexts—from lifelong loving relationships to casual sexual encounters, and from being fully open to being utterly private and secretive. During the past few decades, public denigration and condemnation of homosexuality have diminished in numerous countries, and same-sex relationships have become a publicly accepted part of the cosmopolitan lifestyle in metropolitan centers such as Amsterdam, Paris, Rio de Janeiro, and San Francisco. As recently as 2009, India decriminalized

homosexuality.[3] Clearly, the social rules and cultural meanings of all sexual behavior are subject to great variability not only across cultures but also across time.

Marriage and the Regulation of Sexual Relations

In much of Europe and North America, the traditional ideal was (and in some communities still is) that all sexual activity outside of marriage was taboo. Individuals were expected to establish a family through marriage, by which one gains an exclusive right of sexual access to another person. And while forbidding or disapproving of *premarital* sexual relations, these societies often criminalized *extramarital* affairs as adultery. According to strict Judeo-Christian law, as prescribed in the Book of Leviticus (20:10), adultery was punishable by death: "And the man that committeth adultery with another man's wife . . . , the adulterer and the adulteress shall surely be put to death." Deuteronomy (22:24) adds: "Then ye shall bring them

---

[1] Kirkpatrick, R. C. (2000). The evolution of human homosexual behavior. *Current Anthropology 41,* 385.

[2] Herdt, G. H. (1993). Semen transactions in Sambia culture. In D. N. Suggs & A. W. Mirade (Eds.), *Culture and human sexuality* (pp. 298–327). Pacific Grove, CA: Brooks/Cole.

[3] Timmons, H., & Kumar, H. (2009, July 3). Indian court overturns gay sex ban. *New York Times.*

both out unto the gate of that city, and ye shall stone them with stones that they die."

Many centuries later, among Christian fundamentalist colonists in 17th- and 18th-century New England, adultery by women remained a serious crime. While it did not lead to stoning, women so accused were shunned by the community and could even be imprisoned. As recounted in *The Scarlet Letter* by Nathaniel Hawthorne, the adulteress was forced to have the letter "A" stitched on her dress, publicly signifying her transgression.

Such restrictions exist today in many traditional Muslim societies in northern Africa and western Asia, where age-old Shariah law continues or has been reinstated to regulate social behavior in strict accordance with religious standards of morality. Under this law, women found guilty of having sexual relations outside marriage can be sentenced to death by stoning. In northern Nigeria, for example, a Muslim woman who committed adultery and had a child outside marriage was sentenced to death in 2002. Her sentence was ultimately overturned by an Islamic appeals court, but it nonetheless drove home the rule of Shariah law. Turning legal transgressions into a public spectacle, authorities reinforce public awareness of the rules of social conduct.

A positive side effect of such restrictive rules of sexual behavior is that they may limit the spread of sexually transmitted diseases. For instance, the global epidemic of HIV/AIDS has had dramatically less impact in North Africa's Muslim countries than in the non-Muslim states of sub-Saharan Africa, where the average infection rate among adults is almost 17 times higher. The statistics vividly illustrate the impact of religious and cultural prohibitions: The reported percentage of adults infected by the virus is 0.1 percent in Algeria, Morocco, and Tunisia, in contrast to 18.8 percent in South Africa, 24.1 percent in Botswana, and 33.8 percent in Swaziland.[4] Communities devastated by this sexually transmitted disease not only confront a serious public health problem but also face a cultural challenge in that they must create a new public awareness and adjust attitudes about sexual pleasure so that they do not endanger their collective well-being.

Yet most cultures in the world do not sharply regulate an individual's personal habits, including sexual practices.

Indeed, a majority of all cultures are considered sexually permissive or semi-permissive (the former having few or no restrictions on sexual experimentation before marriage, the latter allowing some experimentation but less openly). A minority of known societies—about 15 percent—have rules requiring that sexual involvement take place only within marriage.

This brings us to an anthropological definition of **marriage**—a culturally sanctioned union between two or more people that establishes certain rights and obligations between the people, between them and their children, and between them and their in-laws. Such marriage rights and obligations most often include, but are not limited to, sex, labor, property, childrearing, exchange, and status. Thus defined, marriage is universal. Notably, our definition of marriage refers to "people" rather than "a man and a woman" because in some countries same-sex marriages are socially acceptable and allowed by law, even though opposite-sex marriages are far more common. We will return to this point later in the chapter.

In many cultures, marriage is considered the central and most important social institution. In such cultures, people will spend considerable time and energy on maintaining this institution. They may do so in various ways, including highlighting the ritual moment when the wedding takes place, festively memorializing the event at designated times such as anniversaries, and making it difficult to divorce.

In some societies, however, marriage is a relatively marginal institution and is not considered central to the establishing and maintenance of family life and society. For instance, marriage has lost much of its traditional significance in the Scandinavian societies of Iceland, Norway, Sweden, and Denmark, in part due to changes in the political economy, more balanced gender relations, and shared public benefits of these capitalist welfare states.

Sexual and Marriage Practices among the Nayar

The relative unimportance of marriage as the major defining institution for establishing a family is not unique to wealthy European nations. For instance, historically, marriage has been of marginal significance in the family life of the Nayar people of Kerala in southwestern India. A landowning warrior caste, their estates are traditionally held by corporations made up of kinsmen related in the female line. These blood relatives live together in a large household, with the eldest male serving as manager.

Like Trobriand Islanders and contemporary Scandinavians noted above, the Nayar are a sexually permissive culture.[5] A classic anthropological study describes three

---

[4] AIDS Epidemic Update. (2007), p. 7. Geneva: Joint United Nations Program on HIV/AIDS (USAID) and World Health Organization. www.unaids.org; see also Gray, P. B. (2004, May). HIV and Islam: Is HIV prevalence lower among Muslims? *Social Science & Medicine* 58 (9), 1751–1756.

marriage A culturally sanctioned union between two or more people that establishes certain rights and obligations between the people, between them and their children, and between them and their in-laws. Such marriage rights and obligations most often include, but are not limited to, sex, labor, property, childrearing, exchange, and status.

[5] Our interpretation of the Nayar follows Goodenough, W. H. (1970). *Description and comparison in cultural anthropology* (pp. 6–11). Chicago: Aldine.

transactions related to customary Nayar sexual and marriage practices.[6] (Note that many of the practices described here have changed since the mid-20th century.) The first, taking place shortly before a girl experiences her first menstruation, involves a ceremony that joins her with a "ritual husband" in a temporary union. This union, which does not necessarily involve sexual relations, lasts for a few days and then breaks up. (Neither individual has any further obligation, although later, when the girl becomes a woman, she and her children typically participate in ritual mourning for the man when he dies.) This temporary union establishes the girl as an adult ready for motherhood and eligible for sexual activity with men approved by her household.

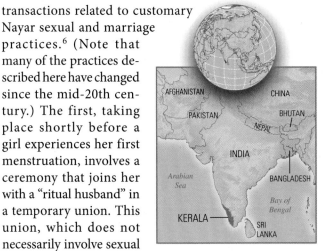

The second transaction takes place when a young Nayar woman enters into a continuing sexual liaison with a man approved by her family. This is a formal relationship that requires the man to present her with gifts three times each year until the relationship is terminated. In return, the man can spend nights with her. In spite of continuing sexual privileges, however, this "visiting husband" has no obligation to support his sex partner economically, nor is her home regarded as his home. In fact, she may have such an arrangement with more than one man at the same time. Regardless of the number of men with whom she is involved, this second transaction, the Nayar version of marriage, clearly specifies who has sexual rights to whom and includes rules that deter conflicts between the men.

If a Nayar woman becomes pregnant, one of the men with whom she has a relationship (who may or may not be the biological father) must formally acknowledge paternity. This third transaction, marked by the man giving gifts to the woman and the midwife, establishes the child's birth rights. In this sense, it is the counterpart of the registration of birth in Western societies, which clearly establishes motherhood and fatherhood. However, once a man has formally acknowledged fatherhood by gift giving, he may continue to take interest in the child, but he has no further obligations. Support and education for the child are the responsibility of the mother and her brothers with whom she and her offspring live.

Indeed, unlike most other cultural groups in the world, the traditional Nayar household includes only the mother,

her children, and her other blood relatives, technically known as **consanguineal kin.** It does not include any of the "husbands" or other people related through marriage—technically known as **affinal kin.** In other words, sisters and their offspring all live together with their brothers and their mother and her brothers. Historically, this arrangement addressed the need for security in a cultural group where warfare was common.

Among the Nayar, sexual relations are forbidden between consanguineal relatives and thus are permitted only with individuals who live in other households. This brings us to another human universal: the incest taboo.

The Incest Taboo

Just as marriage in its various forms is found in all cultures, so is the **incest taboo**—the prohibition of sexual contact between certain close relatives. But, what is defined as "close" is not the same in all cultures. Moreover, such definitions may be subject to change over time. While the scope and details of the taboo vary across cultures and time, almost all societies past and present strongly forbid sexual relations at least between parents and children and nearly always between siblings. In some societies the taboo extends to other close relatives, such as cousins, and even some relatives linked through marriage.

Anthropologists have long been fascinated by the incest taboo and have proposed many explanations for its cross-cultural existence and variation. The simplest explanation, based on the idea of "human nature," is that our species has an "instinctive" repulsion for incest. It has been documented that human beings raised together have less sexual attraction for one another. However, by itself this "familiarity breeds contempt" argument may simply substitute the result for the cause. The incest taboo ensures that children and their parents, who are constantly in close contact, avoid regarding one another as sexual objects. Besides this, if an instinctive horror of incest exists, how do we account for the far from rare violations of the incest taboo? (In the United States, for instance, an estimated 10 to 14 percent of children under 18 years of age have been involved in incestuous relations.[7])

---

[7] Whelehan, P. (1985). Review of incest, a biosocial view. *American Anthropologist 87,* 678; see also U.S. Department of Health and Human Services, Administration on Children, Youth, and Families. (2005). *Child maltreatment 2003.* Washington, DC: U.S. Government Printing Office.

consanguineal kin Biologically related relatives, commonly referred to as blood relatives.

affinal kin People related through marriage.

incest taboo The prohibition of sexual relations between specified individuals, usually parent and child and sibling relations at a minimum.

---

[6] Gough, K. (1959). The Nayars and the definition of marriage. *Journal of the Royal Anthropological Institute of Great Britain and Ireland 89,* 23–34.

Charles Darwin (founder of the theory of natural selection) and his first-cousin wife, Emma Wedgewood. Before proposing, Charles made a "pros and cons" list about marrying Emma. It said nothing about their close familial relationship. Rather, his concerns centered on the question of whether supporting a wife and children would compromise his scientific career. Ultimately, the idea of a "constant companion (& friend in old age) who will feel interested in one" won out. During their three-month engagement he wrote to her: "I think you will humanize me, & soon teach me there is greater happiness, than building theories, & accumulating facts in silence & solitude. . . ." Bonds of real affection linked the couple throughout their long lives.

Moreover, so-called instinctive repulsion does not explain institutionalized incest, such as a requirement that the divine ruler of the Inca empire in ancient Peru be married to his own (half) sister. Sharing the same father, both siblings belonged to the political dynasty that derived its sacred right to rule the empire from Inti, its ancestral Sun God. And by virtue of this royal lineage's godly origin, their children could claim the same sacred political status as their human-divine father and mother. Ancient emperors in Egypt also practiced such religiously prescribed incest based on a similar claim to godly status.

Early students of genetics argued that the incest taboo prevents the harmful effects of inbreeding. While this is so, it is also true that, as with domestic animals, inbreeding can increase desired characteristics as well as detrimental ones. Furthermore, undesirable effects will show up sooner than without inbreeding, so whatever genes are responsible for them are quickly eliminated from the population. That said, a preference for a genetically different mate does tend to maintain a higher level of genetic diversity within a population, and in evolution this variation works to a species' advantage. Without genetic diversity a species cannot adapt biologically to environmental change.

The inbreeding or biological-avoidance theory of incest can be challenged on several fronts. For instance, detailed census records made in Roman Egypt about 2,000 years ago show that brother–sister marriages were not uncommon in farming villages, and we have no evidence for linking this cultural practice to any biological imperatives.[8] To the contrary, some anthropologists have argued that the incest taboo exists as a cultural means to preserve the stability and integrity of the family, which is essential to maintaining social order. Sexual relations between members other than the husband and wife would introduce competition, destroying the harmony of a social unit fundamental to societal order. A truly convincing explanation of the incest taboo has yet to be advanced.[9]

Endogamy and Exogamy

Whatever its cause, the utility of the incest taboo can be seen by examining its effects on social structure. Closely related to prohibitions against incest are cultural rules against **endogamy** (from Greek *endon*, "within," and *gamos*, "marriage"), or marriage within a particular group of individuals (cousins and in-laws, for example). If the group is defined as one's immediate family alone, then societies generally prohibit or at least discourage endogamy, thereby promoting **exogamy** (*exo* is Greek for "outside"), or marriage outside the group. Yet, a society that practices exogamy at one level may practice endogamy at another. Among the Trobriand Islanders, for example, each

---

endogamy Marriage within a particular group or category of individuals.
exogamy Marriage outside the group.

[8] Leavitt, G. C. (1990). Sociobiological explanations of incest avoidance: A critical review of evidential claims. *American Anthropologist 92*, 982.
[9] In a sample of 129 societies, anthropologist Nancy Thornhill (1993) found that only fifty-seven had specific rules against parent–child or sibling incest. Twice that number (114) had explicit rules to control activity with cousins, in-laws, or both (quoted in Haviland, W. A., & Gordon, R. J. (Eds.), *Talking about people* (p. 127). Mountain View, CA: Mayfield). Absence of specific incest rules, however, does not mean sexual relations with close relatives were either common or condoned.

Marriage Prohibitions in the United States   *by Martin Ottenheimer*

In the United States, every state has laws prohibiting the marriage of some relatives. Every state forbids parent–child and sibling marriages, but there is considerable variation in prohibitions concerning more distant relatives. For example, although the majority of states ban marriage between first cousins, nineteen states allow it and others permit it under certain conditions. Notably, the United States is the only country in the Western world that has prohibitions against first-cousin marriage.

Many people in the United States believe that laws forbidding marriage between family members exist because parents who are too close biologically run the risk of producing children with mental and physical defects. Convinced that first cousins fall within this "too close" category, they believe laws against first-cousin marriage were established to protect families from the effects of harmful genes.

There are two major problems with this belief: First, cousin prohibitions were enacted in the United States long before the discovery of the genetic mechanisms of disease. Second, genetic research has shown that offspring of first-cousin couples do not have any significantly greater risk of negative results than offspring of very distantly related parents.

Why, then, do some North Americans maintain this belief? To answer this question, it helps to know that laws against first-cousin marriage first appeared in the United States right after the mid-1800s when evolutionary models of human behavior became fashionable. In particular, a pre-Darwinian model that explained social evolution as dependent upon biological factors gained popularity. It supposed that "progress from savagery to civilization" was possible when humans ceased inbreeding. Cousin marriage was thought to be characteristic of savagery, the lowest form of human social life, and it was believed to inhibit the intellectual and social development of humans. It became associated with "primitive" behavior and dreaded as a threat to a civilized America.

Thus, a powerful myth emerged in American popular culture, which has since become embedded in law. That myth is held and defended to this day, sometimes with great emotion despite being based on a discredited social evolutionary theory and contradicted by the results of modern genetic research.

Recently, a group of geneticists published the result of a study of consanguineous unions, estimating that there is "about a 1.7–2.8% increased risk for congenital defects above the population background risk."[a] Not only is this a high estimate, it is also well within the bounds of the margin of statistical error. But even so, it is a lower risk than that associated with offspring from women over the age of 40—who are not forbidden by the government to marry or bear children.

BIOCULTURAL QUESTION

What do you think is the underlying cultural logic that makes some societies traditionally forbid first cousins from marrying each other, whereas others, equally unfamiliar with genetics, accept or even prefer such marriages?

[a]Bennett, R. L., et al. (2002, April). Genetic counseling and screening of consanguineous couples and their offspring: Recommendations of the National Society of Genetic Counselors. *Journal of Genetic Counseling 11* (2), 97–119.

---

individual has to marry outside of his or her own clan and lineage (exogamy). However, since eligible sex partners are to be found within one's own community, village endogamy is commonly practiced.

Interestingly, societies vary widely concerning which relatives are or are not covered by rules of exogamy. For example, first cousins are prohibited from marrying each other in many countries where the Roman Catholic Church has long been a dominant institution. In the United States, laws against such marriages exist in thirty-one states, and there is a general assumption nationwide that these laws are rooted in genetics. Yet, in numerous other societies around the world, first cousins are preferred spouses,[10] and a recent report in the *Journal of Genetic Counseling* concludes that "cousins can have children together without running much greater risk than a 'normal' couple of their children having genetic abnormalities."[11] (See a discussion of U.S. marriage prohibitions in the Biocultural Connection.)

Early anthropologists suggested that our ancestors discovered the advantage of intermarriage as a means of creating bonds of friendship. French anthropologist Claude Lévi-Strauss elaborated on this idea. He saw exogamy as a form of intergroup social exchange in which "wife-giving" and "wife-taking" (or, as happens in communities with female-headed households, husband-giving and husband-taking) created social networks and alliances between distinct communities. By widening the human network, a larger number of people could pool natural resources and cultural information, including technology and other useful knowledge. (For more on this, see Anthropologist of Note.)

Building on the theory advanced by Lévi-Strauss, other anthropologists have proposed that exogamy is an

---

[10] Ottenheimer, M. (1996). *Forbidden relatives: The American myth of cousin marriage* (pp. 116–133). Champaign: University of Illinois Press.

[11] Grossman, J. (2002). Should the law be kinder to kissin' cousins? A genetic report should cause a rethinking of incest laws. *Find Law.* (accessed October 16, 2009)

Claude Lévi-Strauss (1908–2009)

Claude Lévi-Strauss lived to be 100. When he died, he was the most celebrated anthropologist in the world. Born in Belgium, where his father briefly worked as a portrait painter, he grew up in Paris. As a boy during World War I, Claude lived with his grandfather, a rabbi of Versailles.

He studied law and philosophy at the Sorbonne, married a young anthropologist named Dina Dreyfus, and became a philosophy teacher. In 1935 the couple ventured across the ocean to Brazil's University of São Paulo, where his wife taught anthropology and he sociology. Influenced by 18th-century romantic philosopher Rousseau and fascinated by historical accounts of Brazilian Indians, he preferred ethnographic research and lectured on tribal social organizations.

In 1937, he and his wife organized an expedition into the Amazon forest, visiting Bororo and other tribal villages and collecting artifacts for museums. In 1938, they made another journey and researched recently contacted Nambikwara Indians. Back in Paris together

in 1939, their marriage dissolved. That same year, the Second World War erupted, and the French army mobilized its soldiers, including Lévi-Strauss.

A year after Nazi Germany conquered France in 1940, Lévi-Strauss escaped to New York City, where he became an anthropology professor at the New School for Social Research. Teaching courses on South American Indians during the war years, he befriended other European exiles, including the linguist Roman Jakobson who pioneered the structural analysis of language.

After the war, Lévi-Strauss became French cultural consul in the United States, based in New York. Maintaining ties with the academic community, including anthropologist Margaret Mead, he completed his two-part doctoral thesis: *The Elementary Structures of Kinship* and *The Family and Social Life of the Nambikwara Indians*. Theoretically influenced by Jakobson's structural linguistics, his thesis analyzed the logical structures underlying the social relations of kin-ordered societies.

Building on Marcel Mauss's 1925 study of gift exchange as a means to build or maintain a social relationship, he applied the concept of reciprocity to kinship, arguing that marriage is based on the exchange relationship between kin-groups of "wife-givers" and "wife-takers."

Returning to France in late 1947, he became associate director of the ethnographic museum in Paris and successfully defended his thesis at the Sorbonne. His structural analysis was recognized as a pioneering study in kinship and marriage.

In 1949 Lévi-Strauss joined an international body of experts invited by UNESCO to discuss and define the "race" concept, a disputed term associated with discrimination and genocide. Three years later, he authored *Race and History,* a book that became instrumental in UNESCO's worldwide campaign against racism and ethnocentrism. By then, he had become an anthropology professor at the École Pratique des Hautes Études in Paris. Continuing his prolific writing, he published *Tristes Tropiques* (1955). This memoir about his ethnographic adventures among Amazonian Indians won him international fame. His next book, *Structural Anthropology* (1958), also became a classic. It presented his theoretical perspective that the human mind produces logical structures, classifying reality in terms of binary oppositions (such as light–dark, good–evil, nature–culture, and male–female) and that all humans share a mental demand for order expressed in a drive toward classification.

In 1959 Lévi-Strauss was appointed to a chair in social anthropology at the Collège de France and founded his own institute there. Specializing in the comparative study of religion, he undertook a massive comparative study and structural analysis of myths, resulting in a series of instantaneously classic books. In 1973, he was elected to the centuries-old Académie Française, a prestigious institution with just forty members known as "immortals." Countless other honors from around the world followed. Now, survived by his wife Monique and two sons, he lies in a small rural cemetery in Burgundy, near his old mansion where he liked to reflect on the human condition.

Bibliotèque nationale de France. © Marc Rochette

Renowned French anthropologist Claude Lévi-Strauss at age 100 in his home library.

important means of creating and maintaining political alliances and promoting trade between groups, thereby ensuring mutual protection and access to needed goods and resources not otherwise available. Forging wider kinship networks, exogamy also functions to integrate distinctive groups and thus potentially reduces violent conflict.

Distinction Between Marriage and Mating

Having defined marriage, in part, in terms of sexual access, we must make clear the distinction between marriage and mating. All animals, including humans, mate for

breeding—some for life and some not, some with a single individual and some with several or many. Among humans, mates are secured and held solely through personal effort and mutual consent.

In contrast to mating, which occurs when individuals join for purposes of sexual relations, marriage is a socially binding and culturally recognized relationship. Only marriage is backed by social, political, and ideological factors that regulate sexual relations as well as reproductive rights and obligations. Even among the Nayar, discussed above, where marriage seems to involve little other than a sexual relationship, a woman's husband is legally obligated to provide her with gifts at specified intervals. Nor may a

Nayar woman legally have sex with a man to whom she is not married.

Thus while mating is biological, marriage is cultural. This is evident when we consider the various forms of marriage around the world.

Forms of Marriage

Within societies, and all the more so across cultures, we see contrasts in the constructs and contracts of marriage. Indeed, as is evident in the definition of marriage given above, this institution comes in various forms—and these forms are distinct in terms of the number and gender of spouses involved.

Monogamy

Monogamy—marriage in which both partners have just one spouse—is the most common form of marriage worldwide. In North America and most of Europe, it is the only legally recognized form of marriage. In these places, not only are other forms prohibited, but systems of inheritance, whereby property and wealth are transferred from one generation to the next, are based on the institution of monogamous marriage. In some parts of the world (including Europe and North America), where divorce rates are high and people who have been divorced remarry, an increasingly common form of marriage is **serial monogamy,** whereby an individual marries a series of partners in succession.

Polygamy

Monogamy is the most common marriage form worldwide, but it is not the most culturally preferred. That distinction goes to **polygamy** (one individual having multiple spouses)—specifically to **polygyny,** in which a man is married to more than one woman (*gyne* is Greek for "woman" and "wife"). Favored in about 80 to 85 percent of the world's cultures, polygyny is commonly practiced in parts of Asia and much of sub-Saharan Africa.[12]

Although polygyny is the favored marriage form in these places, monogamy exceeds it, and the reason for this is economic rather than moral. In many polygynous societies, where a groom is usually expected to compensate a bride's family in cash or kind, a man must be

fairly wealthy to be able to afford more than one wife. Recent multiple surveys of twenty-five sub-Saharan African countries where polygyny is common show that it declined by about half between the 1970s and 2001. This dramatic decline has many reasons, one of which is related to families making an economic transition from traditional farming and herding to wage labor in cities. Nonetheless, polygyny remains highly significant with an overall average of 25 percent of married women in such unions.[13]

Polygyny is particularly common in traditional food-producing societies that support themselves by herding grazing animals or growing crops and where women do the bulk of cultivation. Under these conditions, women are valued both as workers and as child bearers. Because the labor of wives in polygynous households generates wealth and little support is required from husbands, the wives have a strong bargaining position within the household. Often, they have considerable freedom of movement and some economic independence from the sale of crafts or crops. Wealth-generating polygyny is found in its fullest elaboration in parts of sub-Saharan Africa and southwestern Asia, though it is known elsewhere as well.[14]

In societies practicing wealth-generating polygyny, most men and women do enter into polygynous marriages, although some are able to do so earlier in life than others. This is made possible by a female-biased sex ratio and/or a mean age at marriage for females that is significantly below that for males. In fact, this marriage pattern is frequently found in societies where violence, including war, is common and where many young males lose their lives in fighting. Their high combat mortality results in a population where women outnumber men.

By contrast, in societies where men are more heavily involved in productive work, generally only a small minority of marriages are polygynous. Under these circumstances,

---

[13] Ibid.

[14] White, D. R. (1988). Rethinking polygyny: Co-wives, codes, and cultural systems. *Current Anthropology 29,* 529–572.

---

monogamy Marriage in which both partners have just one spouse.

serial monogamy A marriage form in which a man or a woman marries or lives with a series of partners in succession.

polygamy One individual having multiple spouses at the same time; from the Greek words *poly* ("many") and *gamos* ("marriage").

polygyny Marriage of a man to two or more women at the same time; a form of polygamy.

---

[12] Lloyd, C. B. (Ed.). (2005). *Growing up global: The changing transitions to adulthood in developing countries* (pp. 450–453). Washington, DC: National Academies Press, Committee on Population, National Research Council, and Institute of Medicine of the National Academies.

A Christian polygamist with his three wives and children in front of their dormitory-style home in Utah, and a Baranarana man of Upper Guinea with his two wives and children.

women are more dependent on men for support, so they are valued as child bearers more than for the work they do. This is commonly the case in pastoral nomadic societies where men are the primary owners and tenders of livestock. This makes women especially vulnerable if they prove incapable of bearing children, which is one reason a man may seek another wife.

Another reason for a man to take on secondary wives is to demonstrate his high position in society. But where men do most of the productive work, they must work extremely hard to support more than one wife, and few actually do so. Usually, it is the exceptional hunter or male shaman ("medicine man") in a food-foraging society or a particularly wealthy man in a horticultural, agricultural, or pastoral society who is most apt to practice polygyny. When he does, it is usually of the *sororal* type, with the co-wives being sisters. Having lived their lives together before marriage, the sisters continue to do so with their husband, instead of occupying separate dwellings of their own.

Polygyny also occurs in a few places in Europe. In 1972, for example, English laws concerning marriage changed to accommodate immigrants who traditionally practiced polygyny. Since that time polygamous marriages have been legal in England for some specific religious minorities,

including Muslims and Sephardic Jews. According to one family law specialist, the real impetus behind this law change was a growing concern that "destitute immigrant wives, abandoned by their husbands, [were] overburdening the welfare state."[15]

Even in the United States where it is illegal, somewhere between 20,000 and 60,000 people in the Rocky Mountain states live in households made up of a man with two or more wives.[16] Most consider themselves Mormons, even though the official Mormon Church does not approve of the practice. A growing minority, however, call themselves "Christian polygamists," citing the Bible as justification.[17] Despite its illegality and concerns that the practice can jeopardize the rights and well-being of young women, regional law enforcement officials have adopted a "live and let live" attitude toward religious-based polygyny in their region. Women involved in the practice are sometimes outspoken in defending it. One woman—a lawyer and one

---

[15] Cretney, S. (2003). *Family law in the twentieth century: A history* (pp. 72–73). New York: Oxford University Press.

[16] Egan, T. (1999, February 28). The persistence of polygamy. *New York Times Magazine,* 52.

[17] Wolfson, H. (2000, January 22). Polygamists make the Christian connection. *Burlington Free Press,* 2c.

of nine co-wives—expresses her attitude toward polygyny as follows:

> I see it as the ideal way for a woman to have a career and children. In our family, the women can help each other care for the children. Women in monogamous relationships don't have that luxury. As I see it, if this lifestyle didn't already exist, it would have to be invented to accommodate career women.[18]

In some societies, if a man dies, leaving behind a wife and children, it is customary that one of his brothers marries the widowed sister-in-law—but this obligation does not preclude the brother having another wife then or in the future. This custom, called the *levirate* (from the Latin *levir,* which means "husband's brother"), not only provides security for the widow (and her children) but also is a way for the husband's family to maintain the established relationship with her family and their rights over her sexuality and her future children: It acts to preserve kin relationships between families previously established. The levirate also ensures that the deceased man's lineage will be perpetuated, as all children born to his remarried widow are formally acknowledged as *his* legitimate offspring, even though his brother is their biological father.

A related marriage tradition is the *sororate* (Latin *soror* means "sister"), in which a man has the right to marry a (usually younger) sister of his deceased wife. In some societies, the sororate also applies to a man who has married a woman who is unable to bear children. This custom entitles a man to a replacement wife from his in-laws. In societies that have the levirate and sororate—customary in many traditional foraging, farming, and herding cultures—the in-law relationship between the two families is maintained even after the spouse's death and secures an established alliance between two groups.

Although monogamy and polygyny are the most common forms of marriage in the world today, other forms do occur. **Polyandry,** the marriage of one woman to two or more men simultaneously, is known in only a few societies, perhaps in part because a woman's life expectancy is usually longer than a man's, and female infant mortality is somewhat lower, so a surplus of women in a society is likely.

Fewer than a dozen societies are known to have favored this form of marriage, but they involve people as widely separated as eastern Inuit (Eskimos) in Canada, Marquesan Islanders of Polynesia, and Tibetans in Central Asia. In Tibet, where inheritance is in the male line and arable land is limited, the marriage of brothers to a single woman (*fraternal polyandry*) keeps the land together by preventing it from being repeatedly subdivided among sons from one generation to the next. Unlike monogamy, it also holds down population growth, thereby avoiding increased pressures on resources. Finally, among Tibetans who practice a mixed economy of farming, herding, and trading in the Trans Himalayas, fraternal polyandry provides the household with an adequate pool of male labor for all three subsistence activities.[19]

Other Forms of Marriage

There are several other marriage forms, each with its own particular cultural expressions and reasons for being. For instance, the social practice of **group marriage** occurs in a few societies. Also known as *co-marriage,* this is a rare arrangement in which several men and women have sexual access to one another. Until a few decades ago, Iñupiat Eskimos in northern Alaska, for instance, engaged in "spouse exchange" (*nuliaqatigiit*) between non-kin, with two conjugal husband–wife couples being united by shared sexual access. Highly institutionalized arrangements, these intimate relationships implied ties of mutual aid and support across territorial boundaries and were expected to last throughout the lifetime of the participants.[20] The ties between the couples were so strong that their children retained a recognized relationship to one another.[21]

In contrast to group marriage, there are also arrangements anthropologists categorize as **fictive marriage**—marriage by proxy to the symbols of someone

---

[19] Levine, N. E., & Silk, J. B. (1997). Why polyandry fails. *Current Anthropology 38,* 375–398.

[20] Chance, N. A. (1990). *The Iñupiat and Arctic Alaska: An ethnography of development* (pp. 110–111). New York: Harcourt.

[21] Spencer, R. F. (1984). North Alaska Coast Eskimo. In D. Damas (Ed.), *Arctic: Handbook of North American Indians* (Vol. 5, pp. 320–337). Washington, DC: Smithsonian Institution.

polyandry Marriage of a woman to two or more men at one time; a form of polygamy.

group marriage Marriage in which several men and women have sexual access to one another; also called co-marriage.

fictive marriage Marriage by proxy to the symbols of someone not physically present to establish the social status of a spouse and heirs.

---

[18] Johnson, D. (1996). Polygamists emerge from secrecy, seeking not just peace but respect. In W. A. Haviland & R. J. Gordon (Eds.), *Talking about people* (2nd ed., pp. 129–131). Mountain View, CA: Mayfield.

not physically present in order to establish a social status for a spouse and heirs. One major reason for such a marriage is to control rights to property in the next generation. One type of fictive marriage occurs in several traditional African societies, most famously among Nuer cattle herders of southern Sudan, where a woman can marry a man who has died without heirs. In such situations the deceased man's brother may become his stand-in, or proxy, and marry a woman on his behalf. As in the case of the marriage custom of the sororate, discussed above, the biological offspring will be considered as having been fathered by the dead man's spirit. Recognized as his legitimate children, they are his rightful heirs. Because such spouses are absent in the flesh yet believed to exist in spirit form, anthropologists refer to these fictive unions as *ghost marriages*.[22]

Fictive marriage variations also exist outside Africa. For instance, a form of ghost marriage can be found in traditional Christianity, in particular Roman Catholic monasteries, where women who remain virgins devote their lives to religious service. When a young woman decides to become a nun, she may enter a religious order as a novice. Being promised in spiritual marriage to Jesus Christ, deemed to be the divine bridegroom, she makes vows of celibacy and chastity, abstaining from regular marriage and renouncing all sexual pleasures. In a special marriage by proxy ceremony, such women are "wedded" as spouses of Christ, who they believe died as a human but lives on as divine spirit in heaven. Veiled and clothed as divine spouses, these nuns also receive a new name, thus completely shedding their old social identities.[23]

Other cultural forms of wedding by proxy can be found throughout the world. In the Netherlands, for example, there is the legal custom known as "marriage with the glove" (*huwelijk met de handschoen*). In this official ceremony, just one of the marriage partners appears before the civil authorities—the other is represented symbolically by an imaginary glove and physically by someone formally authorized as a legal proxy. Traditionally, such proxy marriage ceremonies accommodated physically separated partners such as Dutch seafarers or nationals residing in remote territories.

In several places in the United States, including Colorado and Texas, we find yet another example of marriage by proxy. These marriages involve citizens who are incarcerated, deployed in the military, residing in a foreign country, or otherwise prevented from being physically present at the formal ceremony. In California, this wedding option became legal in 2004 but is restricted to members of the U.S. armed forces in wartime or to those who are deployed in combat operations abroad. Since the 1860s, a *double-proxy marriage* has been possible in Montana, where partners may become legally married in a civil wedding ceremony with neither party appearing before the official authorities.

The U.S. government recognizes legal proxy marriages, and as a result these ceremonies are becoming more common in the military, especially among troops deployed in dangerous overseas operations. In cases of injury or death, a military person married in a proxy wedding ceremony may leave a partner (with or without children) with full military benefits. Those who survive and return home may opt to celebrate their already legal marriage in a religious or otherwise meaningful ceremony with family and friends.[24]

Choice of Spouse

The Western egalitarian ideal that an individual should be free to marry whomever he or she chooses is a distinct arrangement, certainly not universally embraced. In many societies, marriage and the establishment of a family are considered far too important to be left to the whims of young people. The individual relationship of two people who are expected to spend their lives together and raise their children together is viewed as incidental to the more serious matter of making allies of two families through the marriage bond. Marriage involves a transfer of rights between families, including rights to property and rights over children, as well as sexual rights. Thus marriages tend to be arranged for the economic and political advantage of the family unit.

Although arranged marriages are rare in North American society, they do occur. Among ethnic minorities, they may serve to preserve traditional values that people fear might otherwise be lost. Among families of wealth and power, marriages may be arranged by segregating their children in private schools and carefully steering them toward appropriate spouses. The following Original Study illustrates how marriages may be arranged in cultures where such traditional practices remain commonplace.

[22] Evans-Pritchard, E. E. (1951). *Kinship and marriage among the Nuer.* New York: Oxford University Press.

[23] See also Pope Pius XII. (1954). *Sacra Virginitas. Encyclical on consecrated virginity.* The Catholic Encyclopedia Online: www.newadvent.org.

[24] Shane, L., III. (2005). Happy couple both no-show wedding: Deployed troops make use of double-proxy ceremony. *Stars & Stripes 3* (17), 6; see also www.MarriageByProxy.com.

Arranging Marriage in India   *by Serena Nanda*

Six years [after my first field trip to India] I returned to do fieldwork among the middle class in Bombay, a modern, sophisticated city. From the experience of my earlier visit, I decided to include a study of arranged marriages in my project. By this time I had met many Indian couples whose marriages had been arranged and who seemed very happy. Particularly in contrast to the fate of many of my married friends in the United States who were already in the process of divorce, the positive aspects of arranged marriages appeared to me to outweigh the negatives. In fact, I thought I might even participate in arranging a marriage myself. I had been fairly successful in the United States in "fixing up" many of my friends, and I was confident that my matchmaking skills could be easily applied to this new situation, once I learned the basic rules. "After all," I thought, "how complicated can it be?"

An opportunity presented itself almost immediately. A friend from my previous Indian trip was in the process of arranging for the marriage of her eldest son. Since my friend's family was eminently respectable and the boy himself personable, well educated, and nice looking, I was sure that by the end of my year's fieldwork, we would have found a match.

The basic rule seems to be that a family's reputation is most important. It is understood that matches would be arranged only within the

same caste and general social class, although some crossing of subcastes is permissible if the class positions of the bride's and groom's families are similar. Although dowry is now prohibited by law in India, extensive gift exchanges took place with every marriage. Even when the boy's family does not "make demands," every girl's family nevertheless feels the obligation to give the traditional gifts—to the girl, to the boy, and to the boy's family. Particularly when the couple would be living in the joint family—that is, with the boy's parents and his married brothers and their families, as well as with unmarried siblings, which is still very common even among the urban, upper-middle class in India—the girl's parents are anxious to establish smooth relations between their family and that of the boy. Offering the proper gifts, even when not called "dowry," is often an important factor in influencing the relationship between the bride's and groom's families and perhaps, also, the treatment of the bride in her new home.

In a society where divorce is still a scandal and where, in fact, the divorce rate is exceedingly low, an arranged marriage is the beginning of a lifetime relationship not just between the bride and groom but between their families as well. Thus, while a girl's looks are important, her character is even more so, for she is being judged as a prospective daughter-in-law as much as a prospective bride. . . .

My friend is a highly esteemed wife, mother, and daughter-in-law. She is religious, soft-spoken, modest, and deferential. She rarely gossips and never quarrels, two qualities highly desirable in a woman. A family that has the reputation for gossip and conflict among its womenfolk will not find it easy to get good wives for their sons. . . .

Originally from North India, my friend's family had lived for forty years in Bombay, where her husband owned a business. The family had delayed in seeking a match for their eldest son because he had been an air force pilot for several years, stationed in such remote places that it had seemed fruitless to try to find a girl who would be willing to

accompany him. In their social class, a military career, despite its economic security, has little prestige and is considered a drawback in finding a suitable bride. . . .

The son had recently left the military and joined his father's business. Since he was a college graduate, modern, and well traveled, from such a good family, and, I thought, quite handsome, it seemed to me that he, or rather his family, was in a position to pick and choose. I said as much to my friend. While she agreed that there were many advantages on their side, she also said, "We must keep in mind that my son is both short and dark; these are drawbacks in finding the right match." . . .

An important source of contacts in trying to arrange her son's marriage was my friend's social club in Bombay. Many of the women had daughters of the right age, and some had already expressed an interest in my friend's son. I was most enthusiastic about the possibilities of one particular family who had five daughters, all of whom were pretty, demure, and well educated. Their mother had told my friend, "You can have your pick for your son, whichever one of my daughters appeals to you most." I saw a match in sight. "Surely," I said to my friend, "we will find one there. Let's go visit and make our choice." But my friend held back; she did not seem to share my enthusiasm, for reasons I could not then fathom.

When I kept pressing for an explanation of her reluctance, she admitted, "See, Serena, here is the problem. The family has so many daughters, how will they be able to provide nicely for any of them? . . . Since this is our eldest son, it's best if we marry him to a girl who is the only daughter, then the wedding will truly be a gala affair." I argued that surely the quality of the girls themselves made up for any deficiency in the elaborateness of the wedding. My friend admitted this point but still seemed reluctant to proceed.

Is there something else," I asked her, "some factor I have missed?" "Well," she finally said, "there is one other thing. They have one daughter already married and living in Bombay. The mother is always complaining to me that

CONTINUED

CONTINUED

the girl's in-laws don't let her visit her own family often enough. So it makes me wonder, will she be that kind of mother who always wants her daughter at her own home? This will prevent the girl from adjusting to our house. It is not a good thing." And so, this family of five daughters was dropped as a possibility.

Somewhat disappointed, I nevertheless respected my friend's reasoning and geared up for the next prospect. This was also the daughter of a woman in my friend's social club. There was clear interest in this family and I could see why. The family's reputation was excellent; in fact, they came from a subcaste slightly higher than my friend's own. The girl, who was an only daughter, was pretty and well educated and had a brother studying in the United States. Yet, after expressing an interest to me in this family, all talk of them suddenly died down and the search began elsewhere.

"What happened to that girl as a prospect?" I asked one day. "You never mention her anymore. She is so pretty and so educated, what did you find wrong?"

"She is too educated. We've decided against it. My husband's father saw the girl on the bus the other day and thought her forward. A girl who 'roams about' the city by herself is not the girl for our family." My disappointment this time was even greater, as I thought the son would have liked the girl very much. . . . I learned that if the family of the girl has even a slightly higher social status than the family of the boy, the bride may think herself too good for them, and this too will cause problems. . . .

After one more candidate, who my friend decided was not attractive enough for her son, almost six months had passed and I had become anxious. My friend laughed at my impatience:

"Don't be so much in a hurry," she said. "You Americans want everything done so quickly. You get married quickly and then just as quickly get divorced. Here we take marriage more seriously. We must take all the factors into account. It is not enough for us to learn by our mistakes. This is too serious a business. If a mistake is made we have not only ruined the life of our son or daughter, but we have spoiled the reputation of our family as well. And that will make it much harder for their brothers and sisters to get married. So we must be very careful."

What she said was true and I promised myself to be more patient. I had really hoped and expected that the match would be made before my year in India was up. But it was not to be. When I left India my friend seemed no further along in finding a suitable match for her son than when I had arrived.

Two years later, I returned to India and still my friend had not found a girl for her son. By this time, he was close to 30, and I think she was a little worried. Since she knew I had friends all over India, and I was going to be there for a year, she asked me to "help her in this work" and keep an eye out for someone suitable. . . .

It was almost at the end of my year's stay in India that I met a family with a marriageable daughter whom I felt might be a good possibility for my friend's son. . . . This new family had a successful business in a medium-sized city in central India and were from the same subcaste as my friend. The daughter was pretty and chic; in fact, she had studied fashion design in college. Her parents would not allow her to go off by herself to any of the major cities in India where she could make a career, but they had compromised with her wish to work by allowing her to run a small dress-making

boutique from their home. In spite of her desire to have a career, the daughter was both modest and home-loving and had had a traditional, sheltered upbringing.

I mentioned the possibility of a match with my friend's son. The girl's parents were most interested. Although their daughter was not eager to marry just yet, the idea of living in Bombay—a sophisticated, extremely fashion-conscious city where she could continue her education in clothing design—was a great inducement. I gave the girl's father my friend's address and suggested that when they went to Bombay on some business or whatever, they look up the boy's family.

Returning to Bombay on my way to New York, I told my friend of this newly discovered possibility. She seemed to feel there was potential but, in spite of my urging, would not make any moves herself. She rather preferred to wait for the girl's family to call upon them.

A year later I received a letter from my friend. The family had indeed come to visit Bombay, and their daughter and my friend's daughter, who were near in age, had become very good friends. During that year, the two girls had frequently visited each other. I thought things looked promising.

Last week I received an invitation to a wedding: My friend's son and the girl were getting married. Since I had found the match, my presence was particularly requested at the wedding. I was thrilled. Success at last! As I prepared to leave for India, I began thinking, "Now, my friend's younger son, who do I know who has a nice girl for him . . . ?"

From Nanda, S. (1992). Arranging a marriage in India. In P. R. De Vita (Ed.). The naked anthropologist (pp. 139–143). Belmont, CA: Wadsworth.

Cousin Marriage

While cousin marriage is prohibited in some societies, certain cousins are the preferred marriage partners in others. A **parallel cousin** is the child of a father's brother or a mother's sister (Figure 9.1). In some societies, the preferred spouse for a man is his father's brother's daughter (or, from the woman's point of view, her father's brother's son). This is known as *patrilateral parallel-cousin marriage.*

Although not obligatory, such marriages have been favored historically among Arabs, the ancient Israelites, and the ancient Greeks. All of these societies are (or were) hierarchical in nature—that is, some people are ranked higher than others because they have more power and property—and although male dominance and descent are emphasized, property of value to men is inherited by daughters as well as sons. When a man marries his father's brother's daughter (or a woman marries her father's

parallel cousin Child of a father's brother or a mother's sister.

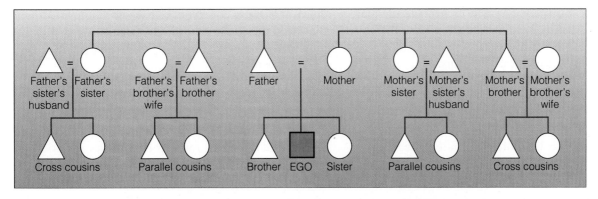

Figure 9.1 Anthropologists use diagrams of this sort to illustrate kinship relationships. This one shows the distinction between cross cousins and parallel cousins. In such diagrams, males are always shown as triangles, females as circles, marital ties by an equal sign (=), sibling relationships as a horizontal line, and parent–child relationships as a vertical line. Terms are given from the perspective of the individual labeled EGO, who can be male or female.

brother's son), property is retained within the single male line of descent. In these societies, generally speaking, the greater the property, the more this form of parallel-cousin marriage is apt to occur.

A **cross cousin** is the child of a mother's brother or a father's sister (see Figure 9.1). Some societies favor *matrilateral cross-cousin marriage*—marriage of a man to his mother's brother's daughter or a woman to her father's sister's son. This preference exists among food foragers (such as the Aborigines of Australia) and some farming cultures (including various peoples of South India). Among food foragers, who inherit relatively little in the way of property, such marriages help establish and maintain ties of solidarity between social groups. In agricultural societies, however, the transmission of property is an important determinant. In societies that trace descent exclusively in the female line, for instance, property and other important rights usually pass from a man to his sister's son; under cross-cousin marriage, the sister's son is also the man's daughter's husband.

Same-Sex Marriage

As noted earlier in this chapter, our definition of marriage refers to a union between "people" rather than "a man and a woman" because in some societies same-sex marriages are socially acceptable and officially allowed by law. Marriages between individuals of the same sex may provide a way of dealing with problems for which opposite-sex marriage offers no satisfactory solution. This is the case with woman–woman marriage, a practice permitted in many societies of sub-Saharan Africa, although in none does it involve more than a small minority of all women.

Details differ from one society to another, but woman–woman marriages among the Nandi people living in the highlands of the Rift Valley Province of western Kenya may

be taken as representative of such practices in Africa.[25] The Nandi are a pastoral people who also do considerable farming. Control of most significant property and the primary means of production—livestock and land—is exclusively in the hands of men and may only be transmitted to their male heirs, usually their sons. Since polygyny is the preferred form of marriage, a man's property is normally divided equally among his wives for their sons to inherit. Within the household, each wife has her own home in which she lives with her children, but all are under the authority of the husband, who is a remote and aloof figure within the household. In such situations, the position of a woman who bears no sons is difficult; not only does she not help perpetuate her husband's male line—a major concern among the Nandi— but also she has no one to inherit the proper share of her husband's property.

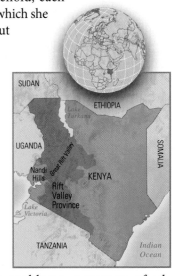

To get around these problems, a woman of advanced age who bore no sons may become a female husband by marrying a young woman. The purpose of this

---

[25] The following is based on Obler, R. S. (1982). Is the female husband a man? Woman/woman marriage among the Nandi of Kenya. *Ethnology 19,* 69–88.

cross cousin Child of a mother's brother or a father's sister.

arrangement is for the young wife to provide the male heirs her female husband could not. To accomplish this, the woman's wife enters into a sexual relationship with a man other than her female husband's male husband; usually it is one of his male relatives. No other obligations exist between this woman and her male sex partner, and her female husband is recognized as the social and legal father of any children born under these conditions.

In keeping with her role as female husband, this woman is expected to abandon her female gender identity and, ideally, dress and behave as a man. In practice, the ideal is not completely achieved, for the habits of a lifetime are difficult to reverse. Generally, it is in the context of domestic activities, which are most highly symbolic of female identity, that female husbands most completely assume a male identity.

The individuals who are parties to woman–woman marriages enjoy several advantages. By assuming male identity, a barren or sonless woman raises her status considerably and even achieves near equality with men, who otherwise occupy a far more favored position in Nandi society than women. A woman who marries a female husband is usually one who is unable to make a good marriage, often because she (the female husband's wife) has lost face as a consequence of premarital pregnancy. By marrying a female husband, she too raises her status and also secures legitimacy for her children. Moreover, a female husband is usually less harsh and demanding, spends more time with her, and allows her a greater say in decision making than a male husband does. The one thing she may not do is engage in sexual activity with her marriage partner. In fact, female husbands are expected to abandon sexual activity altogether, including with their male husbands to whom they remain married even though the women now have their own wives.

In contrast to woman–woman marriages among the Nandi are same-sex marriages that include sexual activity between partners. Over the past decade, the legal recognition of such unions has become a matter of vigorous debate in some parts of the world. Several countries—including Belgium, Canada, the Netherlands, Norway, South Africa, Spain, and Sweden—have passed laws legalizing gay marriages. Meanwhile, numerous U.S. states have adopted constitutional amendments barring same-sex marriage, while others—including Connecticut, Iowa, Massachusetts, New Hampshire, and Vermont—now legally recognize these unions. Additional states recognize same-sex marriage but do not allow official gay wedding ceremonies to take place within their boundaries. The issue of same-sex marriage remains unsettled in many parts of the world, with official policies sometimes swinging back and forth—evidence of the fact that cultures are dynamic and capable of change. In addition, close to a dozen U.S. states and about two dozen countries around the world recognize civil unions (also known as civil or domestic partnerships), which offer a varying range of marriage benefits.

The arguments most commonly marshaled by opponents of same-sex unions are, first, that marriage has always been between males and females—but as we have just seen, this is not true. Same-sex marriages have been documented not only for a number of societies in Africa but in other parts of the world as well. As among the Nandi, they provide acceptable positions in society for individuals who might otherwise be marginalized.

A second argument against same-sex unions is that they legitimize gays and lesbians, whose sexual orientations have been widely regarded as unnatural. But again, as discussed in earlier chapters, neither cross-cultural studies nor studies of other animal species suggest that homosexual behavior is unnatural.

A third argument, that the function of marriage is to produce children, is at best a partial truth, as marriage involves economic, political, and legal considerations as well. Moreover, it is increasingly common for same-sex partners (and growing numbers of heterosexual couples) to have children through adoption or by turning to modern reproductive technologies. There is also the fact that in many societies, such as the Nandi, there is a separation between the sexual and the reproductive attributes of women.

Marriage and Economic Exchange

In the Trobriand Islands, when a young couple decides to get married, they sit in public on the veranda of the young man's adolescent retreat, where all may see them. Here they remain until the bride's mother brings the couple cooked yams, which they then eat together, making their marriage official. A day later the bride is presented with three long skirts by the husband's sister, a symbol of the fact that the sexual freedom of adolescence is now over for the newlywed woman. This is followed by a large presentation of uncooked yams by the bride's father and her mother's brother, who represent both her father's lineage and her own.

Meanwhile, the groom's father and mother's brother collect such valuables as stone axe blades, clay pots, money, and the occasional Kula shell (see previous chapter) to present to the young wife's maternal kin and father. After the first year of the marriage, during which the bride's mother continues to provide the couple's meals of cooked yams, each of the young husband's relatives, who provided

In some societies, when a woman marries she receives her share of the family inheritance (her dowry), which she brings to her new family (unlike bride-price, which passes from the groom's family to the bride's family). Shown here are Slovakian women in a traditional farming village each carrying a trousseau (*výbava nevesty*)—consisting of the bride's clothes, linen, bedding, and other objects of her dowry—in a festive procession to her new home. Traditionally, the bride keeps her finer linen in a beautifully carved or painted dowry chest. In addition, her birth family contributes some livestock, land, or other form of wealth, which Slovaks call *veno*, to the new household. Held in her name, this property provides the woman with a measure of independence from her husband.

valuables for his father and mother's brother to present to the bride's relatives, will receive yams from her maternal relatives and father. All of this gift giving back and forth between the husband's and wife's lineages, as well as those of their fathers, serves to bind the four parties together in a way that makes people respect and honor the marriage and that creates obligations on the part of the woman's kin to take care of her husband in the future.

As among the Trobriand Islanders, marriages in many human societies are formalized by some sort of economic exchange. Among the Trobrianders, this takes the form of a gift exchange, as just described. Far more common is **bridewealth** (sometimes called *bride-price*), which involves payments of money or valuable goods to a bride's parents or other close kin. This usually happens in patrilineal societies where the bride will become a member of the household where her husband grew up; this household will benefit from her labor as well as from the offspring she produces. Thus her family must be compensated for their loss.

Not only is bride-price not a simple "buying and selling" of women, but the bride's parents may use the money to purchase jewelry or household furnishings for her or to finance an elaborate and costly wedding celebration. It also contributes to the stability of the marriage, because it usually must

be refunded if the couple separates. Other forms of compensation are an exchange of women between families—"My son will marry your daughter if your son will marry my daughter." Yet another is **bride service,** a period of time during which the groom works for the bride's family.

In a number of societies more or less restricted to the western, southern, and eastern margins of Eurasia, where the economy is based on agriculture, women often bring a **dowry** with them at marriage. A form of dowry in the United States is the custom of the bride's family paying the wedding expenses. Another example is that a Roman Catholic woman joining a religious order as a consecrated nun, and thus entering into a spiritual marriage as discussed earlier, also traditionally brings a dowry (*dos religiosa*) to that institution. In effect, a dowry

bridewealth Money or valuable goods paid by the groom or his family to the bride's family upon marriage; also called bride-price.

bride service A designated period of time when the groom works for the bride's family.

dowry Payment of a woman's inheritance at the time of her marriage, either to her or to her husband.

is a woman's share of parental property that, instead of passing to her upon her parents' death, is distributed to her at the time of her marriage. This does not mean that she retains control of this property after marriage. In some European countries, for example, a woman's property traditionally falls exclusively under her husband's control. Having benefited by what she has brought to the marriage, however, he is obligated to look out for her future well-being, including her security after his death.

One of the functions of dowry is to ensure a woman's support in widowhood (or after divorce), an important consideration in a society where men carry out the bulk of productive work, and women are valued for their reproductive potential rather than for the work they do. In such societies, women incapable of bearing children are especially vulnerable, but the dowry they bring with them at marriage helps protect them against desertion. Another function of dowry is to reflect the economic status of the woman in societies where differences in wealth are important. It also permits women, with the aid of their parents and kin, to compete through dowry for desirable (that is, wealthy) husbands.

Divorce

Like marriage, divorce in most societies is a matter of great concern to the couple's families as it impacts not only the individuals dissolving their marital relationship but also offspring, in-laws, other relatives, and sometimes entire communities. Indeed, divorce may have social, political, and economic consequences far beyond the breakup of a couple and their household.

Across cultures, divorce arrangements can be made for a variety of reasons and with varying degrees of difficulty. Among the Gusii farmers of western Kenya, for instance, sterility and impotence are grounds for a divorce. Among certain aboriginal peoples in northern Canada and Chenchu foragers in central India, divorce is traditionally discouraged after children are born; couples usually are urged by their families to adjust their differences. By contrast, in the southwestern United States, a traditional Hopi Indian woman in Arizona could divorce her husband at any time merely by placing his belongings outside the door to indicate he is no longer welcome. Among the most common reasons for divorce across cultures are infidelity, sterility, cruelty, and desertion.[26]

An adult unmarried woman is very rare in most non-Western societies where a divorced woman usually soon remarries. In many societies, economic considerations are often the strongest motivation to wed. On the island of New Guinea, a man does not marry because of sexual needs, which he can readily satisfy out of wedlock, but because there it is important to have a female partner to carry out tasks that traditionally fall to women—making pots and cooking his meals, fabricating nets, and weeding his plantings. Likewise, women in communities that depend for security upon males capable of fighting need husbands who are raised to be able warriors as well as good hunters.

Although divorce rates may be high in various parts of the world, they have become so high in Western industrial and postindustrial societies that many worry about the future of what they view as traditional and familiar forms of marriage and the family. It is interesting to note that although divorce was next to impossible in Western societies between 1000 and 1800, for the many generations in those centuries few marriages lasted more than about ten or twenty years, due to high mortality rates caused in part by inadequate health care and medical expertise.[27] For instance, women dying young in childbirth ended many marriages. With increased longevity, separation by death has diminished, and separation by legal action has grown. In the United States today, some 50 percent of first marriages end in divorce—twice the 1960 divorce rate but slightly less than the high point in the early 1980s.[28]

Family and Household

Dependence on group living for survival is a basic human characteristic. We have inherited this from primate ancestors, although we have developed it in our own distinctly human way—through culture. However each culture may define what constitutes a family, this social unit forms the basic cooperative structure that ensures an individual's primary needs and provides the necessary care for children to develop as healthy and productive members of the group and thereby help ensure its future.

Comparative historical and cross-cultural studies reveal a wide variety of family patterns, and these patterns may change over time. Thus the definition of **family** is

---

family Two or more people related by blood, marriage, or adoption. The family may take many forms, ranging from a single parent with one or more children, to a married couple or polygamous spouses with or without offspring, to several generations of parents and their children.

[26] Goodwin, R. (1999). *Personal relationships across cultures* (pp. 86–89). New York: Routledge; see also Betzig, L. (1989). Causes of conjugal dissolution: A cross-cultural study. *Current Anthropology 30*, 654–676.

[27] Stone, L. (1998). *Kinship and gender: An introduction* (p. 235). Boulder, CO: Westview.

[28] Whitehead, B. D., & Popenoe, D. (2004). *The state of our unions: The social health of marriage in America 2004.* Rutgers, NJ: Rutgers University National Marriage Project.

This is a celebration at the palace in the Yoruba City of Oyo, Nigeria. As is usual in societies with royalty, the Yoruba royal household includes many individuals not related to the ruler, as well as the royal family.

necessarily broad: two or more people related by blood, marriage, or adoption. The family may take many forms, ranging from a single parent with one or more children, to a married couple or polygamous spouses with offspring, to several generations of parents and their children.

In all known cultures, past and present, gender plays at least some role in determining the division of labor. An effective way to facilitate economic cooperation between men and women and simultaneously provide for a close bond between mother and child is by establishing residential groups that include adults of both sexes. The differing nature of male and female roles, as defined by different cultures, makes it advantageous in many cultures for a child to have an adult of the same sex available to serve as a proper model for the appropriate adult role. The presence of adult men and women in the same residential group provides for this. The men, however, need not be the women's husbands. In some societies they are the women's brothers—as in the case of the Nayar, discussed earlier in this chapter, where sisters and their children live together with their brothers and their mother and her brothers.

For purposes of cross-cultural comparison, anthropologists define the **household** as the basic residential unit where economic production, consumption, inheritance, childrearing, and shelter are organized and carried out. In the vast majority of human societies, most households are made up of families, but there are many other arrangements. For instance, among the Mundurucu Indians, a horticultural people living in the center of Brazil's Amazon rainforest, married men and women are members of separate households, meeting periodically for sexual activity. At age 13 boys join their fathers in the men's house. Meanwhile, their sisters continue to live with

their mothers and the younger boys in two or three houses grouped around the men's house. Thus the men's house constitutes one household inhabited by adult males and their sexually mature sons, and the women's houses, inhabited by adult women and prepubescent boys and girls, constitute others.

An array of other domestic arrangements can be found in other parts of the world, including situations in which co-residents of a household are not related biologically or by marriage—such as the service personnel in an elaborate royal household, apprentices in the household of craft specialists, low-status clients in the household of rich and powerful patrons, or groups of children being raised by paired teams of adult male and female community members in an Israeli kibbutz (a collectively owned and operated agricultural settlement). So it is that *family* and *household* are not always synonymous.

Forms of the Family

To discuss the various forms families take in response to particular social, historical, and ecological circumstances, we must, at the outset, make a distinction between a **conjugal family** (in Latin *conjugere* means "to join together"),

household The basic residential unit where economic production, consumption, inheritance, childrearing, and shelter are organized and carried out.

conjugal family A family established through marriage.

which is formed on the basis of marital ties, and a **consanguineal family** (based on the Latin word *consanguineus*, literally meaning "of the same blood"), which consists of related women, their brothers, and the women's offspring.

Consanguineal families are not common, but there are more examples than the classic case of the Nayar described earlier in the chapter. Among these are the Musuo of southwestern China and the Tory Islanders—a Roman Catholic, Gaelic-speaking fisherfolk living off the coast of Ireland. The Tory Islanders, who do not marry until they are in their late 20s or early 30s, look at it this way:

> Oh well, you get married at that age, it's too late to break up arrangements that you have already known for a long time. . . . You know, I have my sisters and brothers to look after, why should I leave home to go live with a husband? After all, he's got his sisters and his brothers looking after him.[29]

Because the Tory Island community numbers but a few hundred people, husbands and wives are within easy commuting distance of each other.

According to a cross-cultural survey of family types in 192 cultures around the world, the extended family is most common, present in about 48 percent of those cultures, compared to the nuclear family at 25 percent, and polygamy at 22 percent.[30] Each of these is discussed below.

The Nuclear Family

The smallest family unit is known as the **nuclear family,** a group consisting of one or two parents and dependent offspring, which may include a stepparent, stepsiblings, and adopted children (Figure 9.2). Until recently, the term *nuclear family* referred solely to the mother, father, and child(ren) unit—the family form that most North Americans, Europeans, and many others now regard as the normal or natural nucleus of larger family units. In the United States father–mother–child(ren) nuclear family households reached their highest frequency around 1950, when 60 percent of all households conformed to this model.[31] Today such families make up less than a quarter

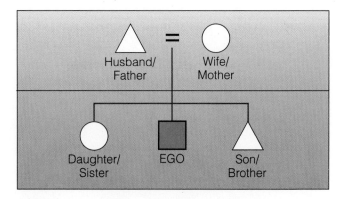

Figure 9.2 **This diagram shows the relationships in a traditional nuclear family, a form that is common but declining in North America and much of Europe.**

of U.S. households,[32] and the term *nuclear family* is used to cover the social reality of several types of small parent–child units, including single parents with children and same-sex couples with children.

Industrialization and market capitalism have played a historical role in shaping the nuclear family most of us are familiar with today. One reason for this is that factories, mining and transportation companies, warehouses, shops, and other businesses generally only pay individual wage earners for the jobs they are hired to do. Whether these workers are single, married, divorced, or have siblings or children is really not a concern to the profit-seeking companies. Because jobs may come and go, individual wage earners must remain mobile to adapt to the labor markets. And since few wage earners have the financial resources to support large numbers of relatives without incomes of their own, industrial or postindustrial societies do not favor the continuance of larger extended families (discussed below), which are standard in most societies traditionally dependent on pastoral nomadism, agriculture, or horticulture.

Interestingly, the nuclear family is also likely to be prominent in traditional foraging societies such as that of the Eskimo people who live in the barren Arctic environments of eastern Siberia (Russia), Alaska, Greenland, and Canada (where Eskimos are now known as Inuit). In the winter the traditional

---

[29] Fox, R. (1981, December 3). [Interview]. Coast Telecourses, Inc., Los Angeles.

[30] Winick, C. (Ed.). (1970). *Dictionary of anthropology* (p. 202). Totowa, NJ: Littlefield, Adams.

[31] Stacey, J. (1990). *Brave new families* (pp. 5, 10). New York: Basic.

---

consanguineal family A family of "blood relatives" consisting of related women, their brothers, and the women's offspring.

nuclear family A group consisting of one or two parents and dependent offspring, which may include a stepparent, stepsiblings, and adopted children. Until recently this term referred only to the father, mother, and child(ren) unit.

---

[32] Irvine, M. (1999, November 24). Mom-and-pop houses grow rare. *Burlington Free Press*; see also U.S. Census Bureau. (2008). *American Community Survey, 2006–2008.*

Among Inuit people in Canada who still hunt for much of their food, nuclear families, such as the one shown here, are typical. Their isolation from other relatives is usually temporary. Much of the time they are found in groups of at least a few related families.

Inuit husband and wife, with their children, roam the vast Arctic Canadian snowscape in their quest for food. The husband hunts and makes shelters. The wife cooks, is responsible for the children, and makes the clothing and keeps it in good repair. One of a wife's traditional chores is to chew her husband's boots to soften the leather for the next day so that he can resume his quest for game. The wife and her children could not survive without the husband, and life for a man is unimaginable without a wife.

Similar to nuclear families in industrial societies, those living under especially harsh environmental conditions must be prepared to fend for themselves. Such isolation comes with its own set of challenges, including the difficulties of rearing children without multigenerational support and a lack of familial care for the elderly. Nonetheless, this form of family is well adapted to a mode of subsistence that requires a high degree of geographic mobility. For the Inuit in Canada, this mobility permits the hunt for food; for other North Americans, the hunt for jobs and improved social status requires a mobile form of family unit.

Not even among the Inuit, however, is the nuclear family as independent from other kin as it has become among most non-Native North Americans. When Inuit families are off by themselves, it is regarded as a matter of temporary expediency; most of the time, they are found in groups of at least a few families together, with members of one family having relatives in all of the others.[33] Thus families cooperate with one another on a daily basis, sharing food and other resources, looking out for one another's children, and sometimes eating together.

The sense of shared responsibility for one another's children and for the general welfare in Inuit multifamily groups contrasts with families in the United States, which are basically "on their own." Here, individual families are responsible for their own child care and for the welfare of their own family members, with little assistance from outside.[34] To be sure, families can and often do help one another out, but they are under no obligation to do so; and even if they wish to, they may find it impossible due to geographic separation born of high mobility. In fact, once children reach the age of majority (18), parents have no further legal obligation to them, nor do the children to their parents.

The Extended Family

When two or more closely related nuclear families cluster together in a large domestic group, they form a unit known as the **extended family.** This larger family unit, common in traditional horticultural, agricultural, and pastoral societies around the world, typically consists of siblings with their spouses and offspring, and often their parents. All of these kin, some related by blood and some by marriage, live and work together for the common good and deal with outsiders as a single unit.

Because members of the younger generation bring their husbands or wives to live in the family, extended

[34] Collier, J., Rosaldo, M. Z., & Yanagisako, S. (1982). Is there a family? New anthropological views. In B. Thorne & M. Yalom (Eds.), *Rethinking the family: Some feminist questions* (pp. 34–35). New York: Longman.

[33] Graburn, N.H.H. (1969). *Eskimos without igloos: Social and economic development in Sugluk* (pp. 56–58). Boston: Little, Brown.

extended family Two or more closely related nuclear families clustered together in a large domestic group.

Extended family households exist in many parts of the world, including among the Maya people of Central America and Mexico.[35] In many of their communities, sons bring their wives to live in houses built on the edges of a small open plaza, on one edge of which their father's house already stands. Numerous household activities are carried out on this plaza—children play while adults weave, do some other productive work, or socialize with guests. The head of the family is the sons' father, who makes most of the important decisions. All members of the family work together for the common good and deal with outsiders as a single unit.

© Joe Cavanaugh/DDB Stock Photo

families have continuity through time. As older members die off, new members are born into the family. Extended families have built into them particular challenges. Among these are difficulties that the in-marrying spouse is likely to have in adjusting to his or her spouse's family.

In North America, extended families can still be found on many American Indian reservations. They also exist in some non-Indian communities, for example along the Maine coast,[36] where they developed in response to a unique economy featuring a mix of farming and seafaring, coupled with an ideal of self-sufficiency. Because family farms were incapable of providing self-sufficiency, seafaring was taken up as an economic alternative. Seagoing commerce, however, was periodically afflicted by depression, so family farming remained important as a cushion against hard economic times. The need for a sufficient labor pool to tend the farm—while at the same time furnish officers, crew, or both for locally owned vessels—was satisfied by the practice of a newly married couple settling on the farm of either the bride's or the groom's parents. Thus most people spent their lives cooperating on a day-to-day basis in economic activities with close relatives, all of whom lived together (even if in separate houses) on the same farm.

Nontraditional Families and Non-Family Households

In North America and parts of Europe, increasing numbers of people live in non-family households, either alone or with people who are not relatives. In fact, nearly 34 percent of households in the United States fall into this category[37] (Figure 9.3). Many others live as members of what are often called *nontraditional families*.

Increasingly common are *cohabitation* households, made up of unmarried couples. Since 1960, such households have increased in number dramatically especially among young couples in their 20s and early 30s in North America and parts of Europe. In Norway, over half of all live births now occur outside marriage. One reason for this is that Norwegian "cohabiting couples who have children together or have lived together for minimum two years will have many of the same rights and obligations to social security, pensions and taxation as their married counterparts."[38] For many others, however, cohabitation represents a relatively short-term domestic arrangement, since most cohabiting couples either marry or separate within two years.[39]

Cohabitation breakup has contributed to the growing number of single-parent households—as have increases in divorce, sexual activity outside marriage, declining marriage rates among women of childbearing age, and the number of women preferring single motherhood. In the United States, more than a third of all births occur outside of marriage.[40] There, the percentage of single-parent households has grown to nearly 10 percent, while the

[35] Vogt, E. Z. (1990). *The Zinacantecos of Mexico, A modern Maya way of life* (2nd ed., pp. 30–34). Fort Worth: Holt, Rinehart & Winston.

[36] Haviland, W. A. (1974). Farming, seafaring and bilocal residence on the coast of Maine. *Man in the Northeast 6*, 31–44.

[37] U.S. Census Bureau. (2008). *American Community Survey, 2006–2008.*

[38] Noack, T. (2001). Cohabitation in Norway: An accepted and gradually more regulated way of living. *International Journal of Law, Policy, and the Family 15* (1), 102–117.

[39] Forste, R. (2008). *Prelude to marriage, or alternative to marriage? A social demographic look at cohabitation in the U.S.* Working paper. Social Science Electronic Publishing, Inc. http://papers.ssrn.com/sol3/papers. cfm?abstract_id=269172.

[40] Stein, R., & St. George, D. (2009, May 13). Babies increasingly born to unwed mothers. *Washington Post.*

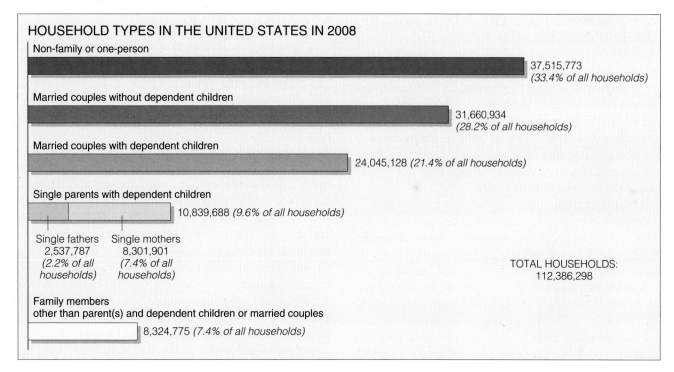

Figure 9.3 Household types in the United States, based on U.S. Census Bureau, *American Community Survey, 2006–2008.*

number comprised of married couples with children has dropped to just below 22 percent. Although single-parent households account for about 10 percent of all U.S. households, they are home to 30 percent of all children (under 18 years of age) in the country.[41]

In the vast majority of cases, a child in a single-parent household lives with the mother. Also significant today are the high numbers of *blended families,* comprised of a married couple together raising children from previous unions.

Single-parent households headed by women are neither new nor restricted to industrial or postindustrial societies. They have been known and studied for a long time in the countries of the Caribbean Sea, where men historically have been exploited as a cheap source of labor for sugar, coffee, or banana plantations. In more recent decades, many of these men are now also working as temporary migrant laborers in foreign countries, primarily in the United States—often living in temporary households comprised of fellow laborers.

Residence Patterns

Where some form of conjugal or extended family is the norm, family exogamy requires that either the husband or wife, if not both, must move to a new household upon marriage. There are several common patterns of residence that a newly married couple may adopt—the prime determinant

being ecological circumstances, although other factors enter in as well. Thus postmarital residence arrangements, far from being arbitrary, are adaptive in character. Here we will mention only the four most common patterns.

Patrilocal residence is when a married couple lives in the husband's father's place of residence. This arrangement is favorable in situations where men play a predominant role in subsistence, particularly if they own property that can be accumulated, if polygyny is customary, if warfare is prominent enough to make cooperation among men especially important, and if an elaborate political organization exists in which men wield authority. These conditions are most often found together in societies that rely on animal husbandry and/or intensive agriculture for their subsistence. Where patrilocal residence is customary, the bride often must move to a different band or community. In such cases, her parents' family is not only losing the services of a useful family member, but they are losing her potential offspring as well. Hence, some kind of compensation to her family, most commonly bride-price, is usual.

Matrilocal residence, in which a married couple lives in the wife's mother's place of residence, is likely if cultural ecological circumstances make the role of the woman

patrilocal residence A residence pattern in which a married couple lives in the husband's father's place of residence.

matrilocal residence A residence pattern in which a married couple lives in the wife's mother's place of residence.

---

[41] U.S. Census Bureau. (2008). *American Community Survey, 2006–2008.*

predominant for subsistence. It is found most often in horticultural societies, where political organization is relatively uncentralized and where cooperation among women is important. The Hopi Indians provide one example. Although it is the Hopi men who do the farming, the women control access to land and "own" the harvest. Indeed, men are not even allowed in the granaries. Under matrilocal residence, men usually do not move very far from the family in which they were raised so they are available to help out there from time to time. Therefore, marriage usually does not involve compensation to the groom's family.

Ambilocal residence (*ambi* in Latin means "both"), a pattern in which a married couple may choose either matrilocal or patrilocal residence, is adaptive in situations where the economic cooperation of more people than are available in the nuclear family is needed but where resources are limited in some way. Because the couple can join either the bride's or the groom's family, family membership is flexible, and the two can live where the resources look best or where their labor is most needed. This was once the situation on the peninsulas and islands along the coast of Maine, where, as already noted, extended family households were based upon ambilocal residence.

The same residential pattern is particularly common among food-foraging peoples, as among the Mbuti Pygmies of Africa's Ituri forest. Typically, a Mbuti marries someone from another band, so that one spouse always has in-laws who live elsewhere. If foraging is bad in their part of the tropical rainforest, the couple has somewhere else to go where food may be more readily available. Ambilocality greatly enhances the Mbutis' opportunity to find food. It also provides a place to go if a dispute breaks out with someone in the band where the couple is currently living. Consequently, Mbuti camps are constantly changing their composition as people split off to go live with their in-laws, while others are joining from other groups. For a people like food foragers, who find their food in nature and who maintain an egalitarian social order, ambilocal residence can be a crucial factor in both survival and conflict resolution.

Under **neolocal residence,** a married couple forms a household in a separate location. This occurs where the independence of the nuclear family is emphasized. In industrial societies such as the United States, where most economic activity occurs outside rather than inside the family and where it is important for individuals to be able to move where jobs can be found, neolocal residence is better suited than any of the other patterns.

---

ambilocal residence A residence pattern in which a married couple may choose either matrilocal or patrilocal residence.

neolocal residence A pattern in which a married couple establishes the household in a location apart from either the husband's or the wife's relatives.

Marriage, Family, and Households in a Globalized World

Large-scale emigration, modern technology, and multiple other factors in the emerging political economy of global capitalism also impact the cross-cultural mosaic of marriage, family, and household. For instance, electronic and digital communication by way of fiber optic cables and satellites has transformed how individuals express sexual attraction and engage in romantic courtship. Today, cross-cultural and transnational love relations bloom via the Internet. New technologies also permit the pursuit of traditionally prohibited relationships through clandestine text messaging of forbidden desires and tabooed intimacies—for example, across castes in India and between young unmarried men and women in traditional Muslim communities. Beyond sex and romance, many married couples and family members living far apart depend on satellite communications technology to stay in touch.

Adoption and New Reproductive Technologies

Although it has not been uncommon for childless couples in many cultures throughout human history to adopt children, including orphans and even captives, today it is a transnational practice for adults from industrial and postindustrial countries to travel across the world in search of infants to adopt, regardless of their ethnic heritage (see this chapter's Globalscape). Also increasingly common is open adoption, which makes it possible for a child to have a relationship with both the biological and the adoptive parents.

Among other contributing factors to today's diversity of families and households are *new reproductive technologies* (NRTs), including various forms of *in vitro fertilization* (IVF) in which an egg is fertilized in a laboratory. The embryo is then transferred into the uterus to begin a pregnancy or is frozen for future use. In cases of IVF with a surrogate mother using donor egg and sperm, a newborn essentially has five parents: the birth parents who provided the egg and sperm, the surrogate mother who carried the baby, and the parents who will raise the baby.

Migrant Workforces

Also of note in terms of new residential patterns is the ever-growing number of households comprised of temporary and migrant workers. Today, China alone has 114 million

Globalscape

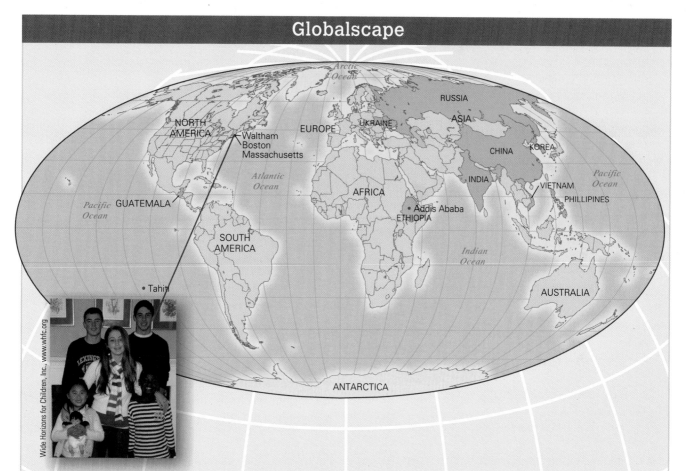

Wide Horizons for Children, Inc., www.whfc.org

Transnational Child Exchange?

Settling into her seat for the flight to Boston, Kathryn cradled the sleepy head of her newly adopted son, Mesay. As the plane lifted away from African soil and presented a sweeping view of Ethiopia's capital, tears slid down her cheeks. Were the tears for Ethiopia's loss of a boy, a boy's loss of Ethiopia, or her profound joy for the gift of adoption?

Child exchange is a universal phenomenon, taking place across the world and throughout human history. Just as marriage and kinship mean different things in different cultures, so does child exchange, referred to in the English language as "adoption." In some cultures, adoption is quite rare, while in others, such as in Polynesian communities in the Pacific Islands, it is very common. For instance, in a small village in Tahiti it was found that over 25 percent of children were raised by adoptive parents.

A cross-cultural understanding of adoption is vital now that child exchange has become part of the global flow, especially from poor countries in Africa, Latin America, Southeast Asia, and eastern Europe, to affluent countries in North America and western Europe. The global exchange of children initially involved war orphans after World War II. In recent decades, extreme poverty has become a major factor, as mothers confronting serious deprivation may feel forced to abandon, give away, or sometimes sell their children. Whether brokered by government or nongovernmental agencies, by for-profit or non-profit enterprises, global child exchange has become a big business—legal and illegal, moral and amoral, happifying and horrifying. This is especially true in poor countries where most workers earn less than a dollar a day, and a foreign adoption nets $12,000 to $35,000 in broker fees.

Since the early 1970s, about 500,000 foreign children have been adopted into families in the United States alone. A nearly equal number ended up in other wealthy countries. The global flow to the United States peaked in 2004 when nearly 23,000 arrived—most from China (30%), Russia (25%), Guatemala (14%), and Korea (7%), with 5,500 flown in from other poor countries such as India, Philippines, Ukraine, and Vietnam. Statistics vary (and shift) according to adoption rules. Some countries have shut the door on foreign adoptions due to accusations of "exporting" or even "selling" children. Others restrict or prohibit it for religious reasons. Sudan, for example, forbids foreign adoption of Muslim children and automatically classifies religiously unidentified orphans as Muslim.

A country that does not discriminate on the basis of religion is its neighbor, Ethiopia, which has gained popularity as an infant-provider country. One of six U.S. agencies officially approved to do foreign adoptions from Ethiopia is Wide Horizons for Children in Waltham, Massachusetts, which has placed many Ethiopian children with U.S. families. Among them is Mesay, now settled into his new life with Kathryn, her husband, and their four other children, including a sister about his age, adopted from China as an infant.

Global Twister How do you compare a European or North American woman who accepts a surrogate pregnancy fee of $115,000 to $150,000 to cover all costs of bearing a child for someone else to a Third World mother living in poverty, who decides to give up her child for adoption for a price?

Many of China's 114 million migrant laborers work in factories and live in factory dormitories such as the one shown here.

of them, mostly young people who have quit the peasant villages of their childhood and traveled to fast-growing cities to work in factories, shops, restaurants, and other such places. Some pile into apartments with friends or co-workers; others live in factory dormitories—new, single-generation households that stand in stark contrast to the multigeneration extended family households in which they were raised. Similar scenes are repeated all around the world as individuals in this transient workforce set up house together far away from home in order to make a living.

Although many countries have passed legislation intended to provide migrants with protections concerning housing—as well as work conditions and pay, such as the 1983 Migrant and Seasonal Agricultural Worker Protection Act in the United States—living conditions for these workers are often miserable.[42]

As the various ethnographic examples in this chapter illustrate, our species has invented a wide variety of marriage, family, and household forms, each in correspondence with related features in the social structure and conforming to the larger cultural system. In the face of new challenges, we explore and tinker in search of solutions, sometimes resulting in finding completely new forms, and other times returning to time-tested formulas of more traditional varieties.

---

[42] Chang, L. (2005, June 9). A migrant worker sees rural home in new light. *Wall Street Journal.*

Questions for Reflection

1. According to Shinto tradition in traditional Japanese society, a white wedding dress symbolizes the bride's purity. Many women living in less sexually restrictive societies also choose white bridal gowns. What do you think is the reason behind this—and the fact that the prescribed dress colors for Japanese grooms are black and gray? Does your culture have a similar color code?

2. Members of traditional communities in countries where the state is either weak or absent depend on consanguineal and affinal relatives to help meet the basic challenges of survival. In such traditional societies, why would it be risky to choose marriage partners exclusively on the basis of romantic love? Can you imagine other factors playing a role if the long-term survival of your community is at stake?

3. Although most women in Europe and North America probably view polygyny as a marriage practice exclusively benefiting men, women in cultures where such marriages are traditional may stress more positive sides of sharing a husband with several co-wives. Under which conditions do you think polygyny could be considered as relatively beneficial for women?

4. Many children in Europe and North America are raised in single-parent households. In contrast to the United States, where most children living with their unmarried mothers grow up in economically disadvantaged households, relatively few children raised by unmarried mothers in Norway face poverty. Why do you think that is?

5. Does your own society have cultural rules about alternative sexual orientations and sexual relations before or outside marriage? Have the rules become looser or tighter since your parents' generation? Do you expect economic and social changes will further alter ideas and attitudes toward sex and marriage? And if so, will they become more or less restrictive?

Suggested Readings

Coontz, S. (2005). *Marriage, a history: From obedience to intimacy, or how love conquered marriage.* New York: Viking Adult.

Challenging the idea that marriage is in crisis due to rising divorce rates, out-of-wedlock births, and same-sex unions, Coontz argues that marriage has always been in a state of flux and that "almost every marital and sexual arrangement we have seen in recent years . . . has been tried somewhere before." Placing current concepts of marriage in broad historical context, Coontz explains marriage as a political tool, a means of ensuring a domestic labor force, and a flexible reflection of changing social standards.

Hirsch, J. S., & Wardlow, H. (Eds.). (2006). *Modern loves: The anthropology of romantic courtship and companionate marriage.* Ann Arbor: University of Michigan Press.

This volume offers a political and economic understanding of changing ideals of romantic love, courtship, and marriage in the context of globalization. Through a cross-cultural sample of ethnographically rich descriptions, the book traces some of the sources of these shifts in mass media, missionization, and the spread of individualism.

Holy, L. (1996). *Anthropological perspectives on kinship.* London: Pluto.

Holy investigates changes in the conceptualization of kinship brought about by new reproductive technologies and the growing interest in culturally specific notions of personhood and gender. Considering the extent to which Western assumptions have guided anthropological studies of kinship, the author offers critical reflection on cultural bias in approaches to the subject.

Hutter, M. (Ed.). (2003). *The family experience: A reader in cultural diversity* (4th ed.). Boston: Allyn & Bacon.

This readable anthology examines the cultural diversity of the North American family by providing relevant articles integrating race, class, gender, and ethnicity. Taken as a whole, these readings reveal both historical trends and unique variations that widen our understanding of the diversity, patterns, and dynamics of the U.S. family.

Modell, J. (1994). *Kinship with strangers: Adoption and interpretations of kinship in American culture.* Berkeley: University of California Press.

The author, an adopter and an anthropologist, analyzes the "core symbols" of kinship in American culture—birth, biology, and blood—and examines their impact on people who experience the "fictive" kinship of adoption.

Stockard, J. E. (2002). *Marriage in culture: Practice and meaning across diverse societies.* Ft. Worth: Harcourt College.

This innovative, accessible text explores the meaning of marriage in different cultures, using compelling ethnographic accounts of the Ju/'hoansi (Bushmen), Chinese, Iroquois, and Tibetan societies to familiarize students with anthropologists' unique perspective on marriage in culture. Each chapter explores the ways in which different economic, political, family, and gender systems shape the practice and meaning of marriage.

Stone, L. (2005). *Kinship and gender: An introduction* (3rd ed.). Boulder, CO: Westview.

Focusing on gender, Stone considers the cross-cultural variations in marriage practices in the broader context of kinship studies. A particular strength is the inclusion of specific case studies to illustrate general principles. The book ends with a thought-provoking discussion of new reproductive technologies and their repercussions for both kinship and gender. This revised and updated edition features new case studies on primate kinship, U.S. kinship, and new reproductive technologies.

宗德流芳

Challenge Issue All humans face the challenge of creating and maintaining a social network that reaches beyond the capabilities of immediate family or household to provide security and support. On a basic level that network is arranged by kinship and may extend to distantly related individuals who claim descent from the same ancestor—living or long-deceased. Kin-groups are defined differently across cultures. For example, among the Han, the dominant ethnic majority in China, almost all ancestral temples, or clan houses, are dedicated to male forebears, reflecting the country's long-established patrilineal rules of descent and cultural values. Clan members affirm their place in the kin-group by making offerings to the ancestors in special ancestral halls or temples such as the one pictured here, located in a family home in Taishun, Zhejiang Province.

CHAPTER 10

Kinship and Descent

Chapter Preview

What Is Kinship?

Kinship is a social network of relatives within which individuals possess certain mutual rights and obligations. One's place in this network, or kinship status, determines what these rights and obligations are. Providing groups of relatives with a social structure, kinship helps shield them from the dangers of disorganization and fracture. Kinship is especially important in societies where a centralized government, a professional military, or financial institutions are absent or do not function effectively. In such societies, individuals must depend on a wide network of relatives for support and protection.

What Are Descent Groups?

A descent group is a kind of kinship group in which being in the direct line of descent from a particular real or mythical ancestor is a criterion of membership. Descent may be traced exclusively through men or women, or through either at the discretion of the individual. Two different means of tracing descent may be used at the same time to assign individuals to different groups for different purposes. In societies without descent groups, such as many food-foraging as well as industrial and postindustrial societies, people rely instead on the kindred: an individual's close blood relatives on the maternal and paternal sides of his or her family. Because each kindred is an ego-centered family group, it is a less stable social unit than the descent group.

What Are the Functions of Kin-Ordered Groups?

Kin-ordered groups are social networks of relatives organized to deal with specific challenges that commonly confront human societies: maintaining the integrity of resources that cannot be divided without being destroyed; providing workforces for tasks that require a labor pool larger than households can provide; and rallying support for purposes of self-defense or offensive attack. Kin-ordered organizations such as descent groups arise from extended family organization. Kinship terminology is affected by and adjusts to the kinds of descent or other kinship groups that are important in a society.

All societies rely on some form of family and/or household organization to meet basic human needs: securing food, shelter, and protection against danger, coordinating work, regulating sexual activities, and organizing childrearing. As efficient and flexible as family and household organization may be for meeting such challenges, many societies confront problems that are beyond the coping ability of family and household organization.

For example, members of one independent local group often need some means of interacting with people outside their immediate circle for defense against natural disasters or outside aggressors and for securing vitally important natural resources for food, fuel, and shelter. A wider circle may also be necessary in forming a cooperative workforce for tasks that require more participants than households alone can provide.

Humans have come up with many ways to widen their circles of support to meet such challenges. One is through a formal political system, with personnel to make and enforce laws, keep the peace, allocate resources, and perform other regulatory and societal functions. But the predominant way to build this support in societies that are not organized as political states—especially foraging, crop-cultivating, and pastoral

societies—is by means of **kinship,** a social network of relatives within which individuals possess certain mutual rights and obligations.

Descent Groups

A common way of organizing a society along kinship lines is by creating what anthropologists call descent groups. Found in many societies, a **descent group** is any kin-ordered social group with a membership in the direct line of descent from a real (historical) or fictional common ancestor. Members of such a group trace their shared connections back to such an ancestor through a chain of parent–child links. The addition of a few culturally meaningful obligations and taboos acts as a kind of glue to help hold the structured social group together.

Membership in a descent group provides individuals with a wider social network of relatives without whom it is difficult or even impossible to effectively deal with the multiple challenges of survival humans face, including securing vitally important natural resources for food, fuel, shelter, and other necessities. Although many important functions of the descent group are taken over by other institutions when a society becomes politically organized as a state, elements of such kin-ordered groups may continue. We see this with many traditional indigenous societies that have become part of larger state societies yet endure as distinctive kin-ordered communities.

So it is with the Maori of New Zealand, featured in this chapter's Biocultural Connection. Retaining key elements of their traditional social structure, they are still organized in about thirty large descent groups known

> **kinship** A network of relatives within which individuals possess certain mutual rights and obligations.
>
> **descent group** Any kin-ordered social group with a membership in the direct line of descent from a real (historical) or fictional common ancestor.

Biocultural Connection

Maori Origins: Ancestral Genes and Mythical Canoes

Anthropologists have been fascinated to find that the oral traditions of Maori people in New Zealand fit quite well with scientific findings. New Zealand, an island country whose dramatic geography served as the setting for the *Lord of the Rings* film trilogy, lies in a remote corner of the Pacific Ocean about 1,900 kilometers (1,200 miles) southeast of Australia. Named by Dutch seafarers who landed on its shores in 1642, it was claimed by the British as a colony about 150 years later. Maori, the country's indigenous people, fought back but were outgunned, outnumbered, and forced to lay down their arms in the

early 1870s. Today, nearly 600,000 of New Zealand's 4.1 million citizens claim some Maori ancestry.

Maori have an age-old legend about how they came to Aotearoa ("Land of the Long White Cloud"), their name for New Zealand: More than twenty-five generations ago, their Polynesian ancestors arrived in a great fleet of sailing canoes from Hawaiki, their mythical homeland sometimes identified with Tahiti where the native language closely resembles their own. According to chants and genealogies passed down through the ages, this fleet consisted of at least seven (perhaps up to thirteen) seafaring canoes. Estimated to weigh about 5 tons, each of these large dugouts had a single claw-shaped sail and may have carried 50 to 120 people, plus food supplies, plants, and animals.

As described by Maori anthropologist Te Rangi Hiroa (Peter Buck), the seafaring skills of these voyagers enabled them to navigate by currents, winds, and stars across vast ocean expanses.[a] Perhaps escaping warfare and tribute payments in Hawaiki, they probably made the 5-week-long voyage around 1350 AD, although there were earlier and later canoes as well.

Traditional Maori society is organized into about thirty different *iwis* ("tribes"), grouped into thirteen *wakas* ("canoes"), each with its own traditional territory. Today, prior to giving a formal talk, Maori still introduce themselves by identifying their *iwi,* their *waka,* and the major sacred places of their ancestral territory. Their genealogy connects them to their tribe's founding ancestor who was a crew member or perhaps even a chief in one of the giant canoes mentioned in the legend of the Great Fleet.[b]

Maori oral traditions about their origins fit quite well with scientific data based on anthropological and more recent genetic research. Study by outsiders can be controversial because Maori equate an individual's genes to his or her genealogy, which belongs to one's *iwi* or ancestral community. Considered sacred and entrusted to the tribal elders, genealogy is traditionally surrounded by *tapu* ("sacred prohibitions").[c] The Maori term for genealogy is *whakapapa* ("to set layer upon layer"), which is also a word for "gene." This Maori term captures something of the original *genous,* the Greek word for "begetting offspring." Another Maori word for gene is *ira tangata* ("life spirit of mortals"), and for them, a gene has *mauri* (a "life force"). Given these spiritual associations, genetic investigations of Maori human DNA could not proceed until the Maori themselves became actively involved in the research.

Together with other researchers, Maori geneticist Adele Whyte has examined sex-linked genetic markers, namely mitochondrial DNA in women and Y chromosomes in men.[d] She recently calculated that the number of Polynesian females required to found New Zealand's Maori population probably ranged between 170 and 230 women. If the original fleet sailing to Aotearoa consisted of seven large canoes, it may have carried a total of about 600 people (men, women, and children).

A comparison of the DNA of Maori with that of Polynesians across the Pacific Ocean and peoples from Southeast Asia reveals a genetic map of very ancient Maori migration routes. Mitochondrial DNA, which is passed along virtually unchanged from mothers to their children, provides a genetic clock linking today's Polynesians to southern Taiwan's indigenous coastal peoples, showing that female ancestors originally set out from that island off the southeast coast of China about 6,000 years ago.[e] In the next few thousand years, they migrated by way of the Philippines and then hopped south and east from island to island. Adding to their gene pool in the course of later generations, Melanesian males from New Guinea and elsewhere joined the migrating bands before arriving in Aotearoa. In short, Maori cultural traditions in New Zealand are generally substantiated by anthropological as well as molecular biological data.

BIOCULTURAL QUESTION

Why do you think the Maori view genealogy as sacred and attach certain prohibitions to it?

---

[a] Buck, P. H. (1938). *Vikings of the Pacific*. Chicago: University Press of Chicago.

[b] Hanson, A. (1989). The making of the Maori: Culture invention and its logic. *American Anthropologist 91* (4), 890–902.

[c] Mead, A. T. P. (1996). Genealogy, sacredness, and the commodities market. *Cultural Survival Quarterly 20* (2).

[d] Whyte, A. L. H. (2005). Human evolution in Polynesia. *Human Biology 77* (2), 157–177.

[e] "Gene study suggests Polynesians came from Taiwan." (2005, July 4). Reuters.

as *iwi* ("tribes"), which form part of larger social and territorial units known as *waka* ("canoes").

Descent group membership must be sharply defined in order to operate effectively in a kin-ordered society. If membership is allowed to overlap, it is unclear where someone's primary loyalty belongs, especially when different descent groups have conflicting interests. Membership can be restricted in a number of ways. The most common way is what anthropologists refer to as *unilineal descent*.

Unilineal Descent

Unilineal descent (sometimes called *unilateral descent*) establishes descent group membership by a direct line from a common ancestor exclusively through one's male or female ancestors, but not both. In this way, each individual is automatically assigned from the moment of birth to his or her mother's or father's group and to that group only.

In non-Western societies, unilineal descent groups are quite common. Depending on the culture, the individual is assigned at birth to membership in a specific descent group,

which may be traced either through the female line, that is by **matrilineal descent**, or through the male line, by **patrilineal descent.** In matrilineal societies females are culturally recognized as socially significant, for they are considered responsible for the group's continued existence. In patrilineal societies, this responsibility falls on the male members of the group, thereby enhancing their social importance.

The two major forms of a unilineal descent group (be it patrilineal or matrilineal) are the lineage and the clan. A **lineage** is a unilineal kinship group descended from a common ancestor or founder who lived four to six generations ago and in which relationships among members can be exactly stated in genealogical terms. A **clan** is an extended unilineal kinship group, often consisting of several lineages, whose members claim common descent from a remote ancestor, usually legendary or mythological.[1]

PATRILINEAL DESCENT AND ORGANIZATION: A CHINESE EXAMPLE

Patrilineal descent (sometimes called *agnatic* or *male descent*) is the more widespread of the two unilineal descent systems. Through forefathers, the male members of a patrilineal descent group trace their descent from a common ancestor (Figure 10.1). Brothers and sisters belong to the descent group of their father's father, their father, their father's siblings, and their father's brother's children. A man's son and daughter also trace their descent back through the male line to their common ancestor. In the typical patrilineal group, authority over the children rests with the father or his elder brother. A woman belongs to the same descent group as her father and his brothers, but her children cannot trace their descent through them.

Patrilineal kinship organization is traditionally embedded in many cultures throughout the world and often

---

unilineal descent Descent that establishes group membership exclusively through either the male or female line; also known as unilateral descent.

matrilineal descent Descent traced exclusively through the female line to establish group membership.

patrilineal descent Descent traced exclusively through the male line to establish group membership; also known as agnatic or male descent.

lineage A unilineal kinship group descended from a common ancestor or founder who lived four to six generations ago, and in which relationships among members can be exactly stated in genealogical terms.

clan An extended unilineal kinship group, often consisting of several lineages, whose members claim common descent from a remote ancestor, usually legendary or mythological.

---

[1] See Hoebel, E. A. (1949). *Man in the primitive world: An introduction to anthropology* (pp. 646, 652). New York: McGraw-Hill.

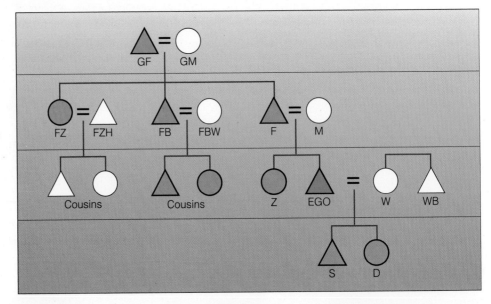

Figure 10.1 The path of patrilineal descent. Only the individuals symbolized by a filled-in circle or triangle are in the same descent group as EGO (the central person from whom the degree of each kinship relationship is traced). The abbreviation F stands for father, B for brother, H for husband, S for son, M for mother, Z for sister, W for wife, D for daughter, and G for grand.

endures despite radical political and economic changes. Such is also the case among the Han, the dominant ethnic majority in modern China. Until the communist takeover in 1949, most of rural Chinese society was strongly patrilineal, with a few exceptions such as the Mosuo of Yunnan Province in the southernmost part of the country (see photo on next page). Since then, considerable changes have occurred, although vestiges of the old system persist in different regions. Traditionally, the basic unit for economic cooperation among the Han Chinese was the large extended family, typically including aged parents and their sons, their sons' wives, and their sons' children.[2]

In places where tradition persists, residence is patrilocal, with Han Chinese children growing up in a household dominated by their father and his male relatives. The father is a source of discipline from whom a child would maintain a respectful social distance. Often, the father's brother and his sons are members of the same household. Thus

one's paternal uncle is like a second father and deserving of obedience and respect, while his sons are like one's brothers. Accordingly, the Han Chinese kinship term applied to one's own father is extended to the father's brother, and the term for a brother is extended to the father's brother's sons. When families become too large and unwieldy, as frequently happens, one or more sons would move elsewhere to establish separate households. When a son does so, however, the tie to the household in which he is born remains strong.

While family membership was important for each individual, the primary social unit is the lineage, or the *tsu,* as it is known among the Han in China. Each *tsu* consists of men who trace their ancestry back through the male line to a common ancestor, usually within about five generations. Although a woman belongs to her father's *tsu,* for all practical purposes she is absorbed by the *tsu* of her husband, with whom she lives after marriage. Nonetheless, members of her natal (birth) *tsu* retain some interest in her after her departure. Her mother, for example, would assist her in the birth of her children, and her brother or some other male relative would look after her interests, perhaps even intervening if her husband or other members of his family treat her badly.

The function of the *tsu* is to help its members economically and to gather on ceremonial occasions such as

weddings and funerals or to make offerings to the ancestors. Recently deceased ancestors, up to about three generations back, are given offerings of food and paper money on the anniversaries of their births and deaths, while more distant ancestors are collectively worshiped five times a year. Each *tsu* maintains its own shrine for storage of ancestral tablets on which the names of all members are recorded. In addition to its economic and ritual functions, the *tsu* also functions as a legal body, passing judgment on misbehaving members.

Just as families periodically split up into new ones, so would the larger descent groups periodically splinter along the lines of their main family branches. Causes for splits include disputes among brothers over management of landholdings and suspicion of unfair division of profits. When such fissions occur, a representative of the new *tsu* would return periodically to the ancestral temple in order to pay respect to the ancestors and record recent births and deaths in the official genealogy.

Ultimately, though the lineage tie to the old *tsu* still would be recognized, a copy of the old genealogy would be made and brought home to the younger *tsu,* and then only its births and deaths would be recorded. In this way, over many centuries, a whole hierarchy of descent groups develops, with all persons having the same surname considering themselves to be members of a great patrilineal clan. With this went surname exogamy, meaning that none of the many bearing the same clan name could marry anyone else within that large group. This marriage rule is still widely practiced today even though clan members no longer carry on ceremonial activities together.

Traditionally, the patrilineal system permeated all of rural Han Chinese social relations. Children owed obedience and respect to their fathers and older patrilineal relatives in life and had to marry whomever their parents chose for them. It was the duty of sons to care for their parents when they became old and helpless, and even after death sons had ceremonial obligations to them. Inheritance passed from fathers to sons, with an extra share going to the eldest, since he ordinarily made the greatest contribution to the household and had the greatest responsibility toward his parents after their death. Han Chinese women, by contrast, had no claims on their families' heritable property. Once married, a woman was in effect cast off by her own patrilineal kin (even though they might continue to take an interest in her) in order to produce children for her husband's family and *tsu.* Some of the obligations and attitudes of the traditional system persist today, minimally the obedience and respect owed by children to their fathers and older patrilineal relatives.

As the preceding suggests, a patrilineal society is very much a man's world. No matter how valued women may be, they inevitably find themselves in a difficult position. Far from resigning themselves to a subordinate position, however, they actively manipulate the system to their own advantage as best they can.

---

[2] Most of the following is from Hsiaotung, F. (1939). *Peasant life in China.* London: Kegan Paul.

Unlike the Han, the dominant ethnic majority in China who are patrilineal, several ethnic minorities in southern China are matrilineal, including the Mosuo. The women in the Mosuo family shown here are blood relatives of one another, and the men are their brothers. As among the Nayar, discussed in the previous chapter, Mosuo husbands live apart from their wives, in the households of their sisters.

MATRILINEAL DESCENT AND ORGANIZATION: AN AMERICAN INDIAN EXAMPLE

Matrilineal descent is traced exclusively through the female line (Figure 10.2), just as patrilineal descent is through the male line. However, the matrilineal pattern differs from the patrilineal in that it does not automatically confer gender authority. For example, among the just noted matrilineal Mosuo China, property passes through the female line, women are often heads of their households, and they are usually the ones making the business decisions—yet, political power tends to be in the hands of males.[3] Similar arrangements exist in a wide range of matrilineal societies worldwide, including some American Indian communities.

---

[3] Mathieu, C. (2003). *A history and anthropological study of the ancient kingdoms of the Sino-Tibetan borderland—Naxi and Mosuo*. New York: Mellen.

Figure 10.2 This diagram, which traces descent matrilineally, can be compared with that in Figure 10.1, showing patrilineal descent. The two patterns are virtually mirror images. Note that a man cannot transmit descent to his own children (just as a woman cannot transmit descent within the patrilineal system).

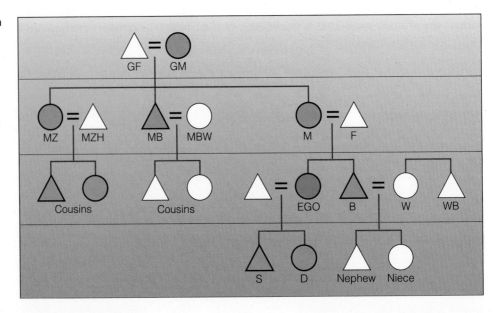

Indeed, while women in matrilineal societies may have considerable power, they do not hold exclusive authority in the descent group. They share it with men. Usually, these are the brothers, rather than the husbands, of the women through whom descent is traced. Apparently, a function of matrilineal systems is to provide continuous female solidarity within the female work group. Matrilineal systems are usually found in horticultural societies in which women perform much of the work in the house and nearby gardens. Matrilineal descent in part prevails because women's labor as crop cultivators is regarded as so important to the society.

In a matrilineal system, brothers and sisters belong to the descent group of the mother, the mother's mother, the mother's siblings, and the mother's sisters' children. Thus every male belongs to the same descent group as his mother, and a man's own children belong to his wife's descent group, not his.

Although not true of all matrilineal systems, a common feature is the relative weakness of the social tie between wife and husband. A woman's husband lacks authority in the household they share. Her brother, and not the husband-father, distributes goods, organizes work, settles disputes, supervises rituals, and administers inheritance and succession rules. Meanwhile, her husband fulfills the same role in his own sister's household. Furthermore, his property and status are inherited by his sister's son rather than his son. Thus brothers and sisters maintain lifelong ties with one another, whereas marital ties are easily severed. In matrilineal societies, unsatisfactory marriages are more easily ended than in patrilineal societies.

Among Hopi Indians, a farming people whose ancestors have lived in *pueblos* ("villages") in northeastern Arizona for many centuries, society is divided into a number of clans based strictly on matrilineal descent.[4] (This is also true of many other Native American groups, such as the White Mountain Apache living just south of the Hopi.) At birth, every Hopi is assigned to his or her mother's clan. This

affiliation is so important that, in a very real sense, a person has no social identity in the community apart from it. Two or more clans together constitute larger supra-clan units, which anthropologists refer to as *phratries* (discussed later in this chapter). There are nine phratries in Hopi society, and within each phratry member clans are expected to support one another and observe strict exogamy. Because people from all nine phratries can be found living in any given Hopi village, marriage partners usually can be found in one's home community. This same dispersal of membership provides individuals with rights of entry into villages other than their own.

Although phratries and clans are the major kinship units in Hopi culture, the actual functional social units consist of lineages, and there are several in each village. Each Hopi lineage is headed by a senior woman (usually the eldest), although it is her brother or mother's brother who keeps the sacred "medicine bundle" (objects of spiritual power considered essential for peoples' well-being) and plays an active role in running lineage affairs. However, the senior woman is no mere figurehead. She may act as mediator to help resolve disputes among group members. Also, although her brother and mother's brother have the right to offer her advice and criticism, they are equally obligated to listen to what she has to say, and she does not yield her authority to them.

Most female authority, however, is exerted within the household, which is the smallest distinct unit of Hopi society, and here men clearly take second place. These households consist of the women of the lineage with their husbands and unmarried sons, all of whom used to live in sets of adjacent rooms in single large buildings. Nowadays, nuclear families often live (frequently with a maternal relative or two) in separate houses, but motorized vehicles enable related households to maintain close contact and cooperation as before.

Hopi lineages function as landholding corporations, allocating land for the support of member households. These lands are farmed by "outsiders," the husbands of the women whose lineage owns the land, and the harvest belongs to these women. Thus Hopi men spend their lives laboring for their wives' lineages, and in return they are given food and shelter. Although sons learn from their fathers how to farm, a man has no real authority over his son. This is because a man's own children belong to his wife's lineage while his sister's children form part of his. When parents have difficulty with an unruly child, the mother's brother is called upon to mete out discipline. A man's loyalties are therefore divided between his wife's household on the one hand and his sisters' on the other. According to tradition, if a man is perceived as being an unsatisfactory husband, his wife merely has to place his

---

[4] Most of the following is from Connelly, J. C. (1979). Hopi social organization. In A. Ortiz (Ed.), *Handbook of North American Indians, Vol. 9, Southwest* (pp. 539–553). Washington, DC: Smithsonian Institution.

White Mountain Apaches in Arizona, like their Hopi neighbors, are organized in matrilineal clans. Closely related through the maternal line, small groups of these Apache Indian women traditionally live and work together, farming on stream banks in the mountains and gathering wild foods in ancestral territories. They trace their ancestry to *Is dzán naadleeshe'* (Changing Woman), a mythological founding mother. This photo shows three generations in prayer during a traditional puberty ceremony known as *na'ii'ees* ("getting her ready"), also called a Sunrise Dance. During this event, marking a girl's transition into womanhood, the sacred power of her clan's founding mother ritually passes to her.

personal belongings outside the door, and the marriage is over.

In addition to their economic and legal functions, lineages play a role in Hopi ceremonial activities. Although membership in the associations that actually perform ceremonies is open to all who have the proper qualifications, clans own and manage all the associations, and in each village a leading lineage acts as its clan's representative. This lineage owns a special house where the clan's religious paraphernalia are stored and cared for by the "clan mother." Together with her brother, the clan's "big uncle," she helps manage ceremonial activities.

Traditionally, each Hopi village is politically autonomous, with its own chief and all-male village council. Here again, however, descent group organization makes itself felt, for the council is made up of men who inherit their positions through their clans. Moreover, the powers of the chief and his council are limited; the chief's major job is to maintain harmony between his village and the spiritual world, and whatever authority he and his council wield is directed at coordination of community effort, not enforcement of official decrees. Decisions are made on a consensual basis, and women's views have to be considered, as well as those of men.

Once again, although men hold positions of authority, women have considerable control over their decisions in a behind-the-scenes way. These men, after all, live in households women control, and their positions within them depend largely on how well they get along with the senior women. Outside the household, women's refusal to play their part in the performance of ceremonies gives them

veto power. Small wonder, then, that Hopi men readily admit that "women usually get their way."[5]

Other Forms of Descent

Among Samoan Islanders (and numerous other cultures in the Pacific as well as in Southeast Asia) a person has the option of affiliating with either the mother's or the father's descent group. Known as *ambilineal descent,* such a kin-ordered system provides a measure of flexibility. However, this flexibility also introduces a possibility of dispute and conflict as unilineal groups compete for members.

This problem does not arise under *double descent,* or double unilineal descent, a very rare system in which descent is matrilineal for some purposes and patrilineal for others.

Generally, where double descent is traced, the matrilineal and patrilineal groups take action in different spheres of society. For example, among the Yakö of eastern Nigeria, property is divided into both patrilineal possessions and matrilineal possessions.[6] The patrilineage owns

5 Schlegel, A. (1977). Male and female in Hopi thought and action. In A. Schlegel (Ed.), *Sexual stratification* (p. 254). New York: Columbia University Press.

6 Forde, C. D. (1968). Double descent among the Yakö. In P. Bohannan & J. Middleton (Eds.), *Kinship and social organization* (pp. 179–191). Garden City, NY: Natural History.

perpetual productive resources, such as land, whereas the matrilineage owns consumable property, such as livestock. The legally weaker matriline is somewhat more important in religious matters than the patriline. Through double descent, a Yakö might inherit grazing lands from the father's patrilineal group and certain ritual privileges from the mother's matrilineal group.

Finally, when descent derives from both the mother's and father's families equally, anthropologists use the term *bilateral descent*. In such a system people trace their descent from all ancestors, regardless of their gender or side of the family. We may recognize bilateral descent when individuals apply the same genealogical terms to identify similarly related individuals on both sides of the family. For instance, when they speak of a "grandmother" or "grandfather," no indication is given whether these relatives are on the paternal or maternal side of the family.

Bilateral descent exists in various foraging cultures and is also quite common in many contemporary state societies with agricultural, industrial, or postindustrial economies. For example, although most people in Europe, Australia, and North America typically inherit their father's family name (indicative of a culture's history in which patrilineal descent is the norm), they usually consider themselves as much a member of their mother's as their father's family.

Descent Within the Larger Cultural System

There is a close relationship between the descent system and a cultural system's infrastructure. Generally, patrilineal descent predominates where male labor is considered of prime importance, as among pastoralists and agriculturalists. Matrilineal descent predominates mainly among horticulturalists in societies where female work in subsistence is especially important. Numerous matrilineal societies are found in southern Asia, one of the earliest cradles of food production in the world. They are also prominent in parts of indigenous North America, South America's tropical lowlands, and parts of Africa.

Regardless of how descent is traced, descent groups are usually more than mere sets of relatives providing emotional support and a sense of belonging. In nonindustrial societies they are tightly organized working units providing security and services in what can be a difficult, uncertain life. The tasks descent groups perform are manifold. Besides acting as economic units providing mutual aid to their members, they may act to support the aged and

infirm and help with marriages and deaths. Often, they play a role in determining whom an individual may or may not marry.

In many societies an individual has no legal or political status except as a lineage member. Since "citizenship" is derived from lineage membership and legal status depends on it, political powers are derived from it as well. Because a lineage endures after the deaths of members with new members continually born into it, it has a continuing existence that enables it to act like a corporation, as in owning property, organizing productive activities, distributing goods and labor power, assigning status, and regulating relations with other groups. The descent group also may act as a repository of religious traditions. Ancestor worship, for example, is often a powerful force acting to enhance group solidarity. Thus it is a strong, effective base of social organization.

Whatever form of descent predominates, the kin of both mother and father are important components of the social structure in all societies. Just because descent may be traced patrilineally this does not mean that matrilineal relatives are necessarily unimportant. It simply means that, for purposes of group membership, the mother's relatives are excluded. Similarly, under matrilineal descent, the father's relatives are excluded for purposes of group membership.

By way of example, among the matrilineal Trobriand Islanders in the southern Pacific, discussed in previous chapters, children belong to their mother's descent groups, yet fathers play an important role in their upbringing. Upon marriage, the bride and groom's paternal relatives contribute to the exchange of gifts, and, throughout life, a man may expect his paternal kin to help him improve his economic and political position in society. Eventually, sons may expect to inherit personal property from their fathers.

As a traditional institution in a kin-ordered society, the descent group often endures in state-organized societies where political institutions are ineffective or weakly developed. Such is the case in many countries of the world today, especially in remote mountain or desert villages difficult to reach by state authorities.

Also, because the cultural ideas, values, and practices associated with traditional descent groups may be deeply embedded, such patterns of culture often endure in *diasporic communities* (among immigrants who have relocated from their ancestral homelands and retain their distinct cultural identities as ethnic minority groups in their new host countries). In such situations, it is not uncommon for people to seek familiar, kin-ordered cultural solutions to challenges faced in unfamiliar state-organized settings. We see an example of this in the following Original Study on "honor killing" by a young female anthropologist in the Netherlands.

Honor Killings in the Netherlands *by Clementine van Eck*

When I first told my anthropology professors I wanted to write my dissertation on honor killing among Turkish immigrants in the Netherlands, they told me no way. It was the mid-1990s, and everyone seemed to feel that writing negative things about struggling immigrants was discriminatory. Better to choose a subject that would help them deal with the challenges of settling in Dutch society, such as the problems they experienced as foreigners in school or at work. But I was quite determined to investigate this issue and finally found a professor who shared my interest—Dr. Anton Blok. He himself was specialized in Italian mafia,[a] so quite used to violence of the cultural sort.

Before getting into some of the details of my research, I need to set the stage. Until the 1960s, the Netherlands was a relatively homogeneous society (despite its colonial past). The major differences among its people were not ethnic but religious, namely their distinct ties to Catholicism or Protestantism (of various kinds). The country's population makeup began to change dramatically after the economic boom of the 1960s created a need for cheap labor and led to an influx of migrants from poor areas in Mediterranean countries seeking wage-earning opportunities.

These newcomers came not as immigrants but as "guest laborers" (*gastarbeiders*) expected to return to their countries of origin, including Italy, Yugoslavia, Turkey, and Morocco. While

many did go back home, numerous others did not. In contrast to most of the guest workers from southern European nations, those from Turkey and Morocco are mainly Muslim. And unlike southern European workers who stayed on as immigrants and successfully assimilated into Dutch society, many of the Muslim newcomers formed isolated, diasporic communities.

During the past three decades, these communities have expanded in size and are concentrated in certain areas of various cities. Today, the Turkish population in the Netherlands is about 350,000. Most of them have become Dutch citizens, but they maintain some key cultural features of their historical "honor-and-shame" traditions. And this is what is at stake when we are dealing with the problem of honor killing.

Anthropologists have identified honor-and-shame traditions in many parts of the world, especially in remote traditional herding and farming societies where the power of the political state is either absent or ineffective. People in such areas, my professor, Dr. Blok, explained,

> cannot depend on stable centers of political control for the protection of life and patrimony. In the absence of effective state control, they have to rely on their own forces—on various forms of self-help. These conditions . . . put a premium on self-assertive qualities in men, involving the readiness and capacity to use physical force in order to guarantee the immunity of life and property, including women as the most precious and vulnerable part of the patrimony of men. The extremes of this sense of honour are reached when even merely glancing at a woman is felt as an affront, an incursion into a male domain, touching off a violent response.[b]

Beyond serving as a means of social control in isolated areas, honor-and-shame traditions may be used in situations where state mechanisms are alien to a certain group of people, as among some Turkish and Moroccan migrants in the Netherlands. Focusing on the latter, I tried to make sense of certain cultural practices that often baffle indigenous

Dutch citizens accustomed to a highly organized bureaucratic state where our personal security and justice are effectively managed by social workers, police, courts, and so on. Most of all, I wanted to understand honor killings.

Honor killings are murders in the form of a ritual and they are carried out to purify tarnished honor—specifically honor having to do with something Turks refer to as *namus*. Both men and women possess *namus*. For women and girls *namus* means chastity, while for men it means having chaste family members. A man is therefore dependent for his *namus* on the conduct of the womenfolk in his family. This means in effect that women and girls must not have illicit contact with a member of the opposite sex and must avoid becoming the subject of gossip, since gossip alone can impugn *namus*. The victim of an honor killing can be the girl or woman who tarnished her honor, or the man who did this to her (usually her boyfriend). The girl or woman is killed by her family members, the man is killed by the family of the girl/woman whose honor he has violated.

As I was wrapping up my PhD in 2000, Dutch society still didn't seem quite ready to acknowledge the phenomenon of honor killing. That year a Kurdish boy whose parents were born in Turkey tried to shoot the boyfriend of his sister. Because the attempt took place in a high school and resulted in injury to several students and a teacher, authorities focused on the issue of school safety rather than on the cultural reasons behind the murder attempt.

A shift in government and public awareness of honor killing took place in 2004. That year three Muslim Turkish women were killed by their former husbands on the street. Coming in quick succession, one after the other, these murders did not escape the attention of government officials or the media. Finally, honor killing was on the national agenda. In November of that year I was appointed as cultural anthropologist at the Dutch police force in The Hague district and began working with law enforcers on honor killing cases there (and soon in other areas of the country).

On 2 November 2004, the day I gave an opening speech about honor killings to colleagues at my new job, a radical Muslim migrant from Morocco shot the famous Dutch author and film director Theo van Gogh, well known for his critical, often mocking, views on Islam. Although his murder was not an honor killing, it had key elements of that cleansing ritual: It occurred in a public place (on the street) in front of many people, the victim had to die (injury would not suffice), the killer used many shots (or knife thrusts), the killing was planned (it was not the product of a sudden outburst), and the killer had no remorse.

Let me tell you about a recent and quite typical case. On a Friday evening the local police in an eastern Dutch community called in the help of our police team. A 17-year-old Turkish girl had run away to the family home of her Dutch boyfriend, also 17. Her father, who had discovered that this boy had a police record, telephoned his parents and asked them to send the daughter home. The parents tried to calm him down and told him his daughter was safe at their house. But as he saw it, she was in the most unsafe place in the world,

for she was with the boy she loved. This could only mean that her virginity was in jeopardy and therefore the *namus* of the whole family.

My colleagues and I concluded that the girl had to be taken out of her boyfriend's home that same night: the father knew the place, he didn't want the boy as a son-in-law, and he believed his daughter not mature enough to make a decision about something as important as marriage. ("Just having a boyfriend" was not allowed. You either marry or you don't have a boyfriend, at least not an obvious one.) Because of my honor killing research, I was well aware of similar situations that ended in honor killings. To leave the girl where she was would invite disaster.

After we persuaded the prosecutor that intervention was necessary, the girl was taken from her boyfriend's house and brought to a guarded shelter to prevent her from fleeing back to him the next day. This is anthropology-in-action. You cannot always just wait and see what will happen (although I admit that as a scholar this is very tempting); you have to take responsibility and take

action if you're convinced that a human life is at stake.

When I took up the study of cultural anthropology, I did so just because it intrigued me. I never imagined that what I learned might become really useful. So, what I would like to say to anthropology students is: Never give up on an interesting subject. One day it might just matter that you have become an expert in that area. At this moment I am analyzing all kinds of threatening cases and drawing up genealogies of the families involved—all in the effort to deepen our understanding of and help prevent honor killings.

[a] Blok, A. (1974). *The mafia of a Sicilian village 1860–1960.* New York: Harper & Row.
[b] Blok, A. (1981). Rams and billy-goats: A key to the Mediterranean code of honour. *Man, New Series 16* (3), 427–440. See also Van Eck, C. (2003). *Purified by blood: honour killings amongst Turks in the Netherlands.* Amsterdam: Amsterdam University Press.

Lineage Exogamy

A common characteristic of lineages is *exogamy*. As defined in the previous chapter, this means that lineage members must find their marriage partners in other lineages. One advantage of exogamy is that competition for desirable spouses within the group is curbed, promoting the group's internal cohesiveness. Lineage exogamy means that each marriage is more than a union between two individuals; it is also a new alliance between lineages. This helps to maintain them as components of larger social systems. Finally, lineage exogamy promotes open communication within a society, facilitating the diffusion of knowledge from one lineage to another.

In contemporary North American Indian communities, kinship and descent play an essential role in tribal membership—as illustrated in this chapter's Anthropology Applied.

From Lineage to Clan

In the course of time, as generation succeeds generation and new members are born into the lineage, the kinship group's membership may become too large to manage or may outgrow the lineage's resources. When this happens, as we have seen with the Chinese *tsu*, **fission** occurs; that

is, the original lineage splits into new, smaller lineages. Usually the members of the new lineages continue to recognize their original relationship to one another. The result of this process is the appearance of a larger kind of descent group: the clan.

As already noted, a clan—typically consisting of several lineages—is an extended unilineal descent group whose members claim common descent from a distant ancestor (usually legendary or mythological) but are unable to trace the precise genealogical links back to that ancestor. This stems from the great genealogical depth of the clan, whose founding ancestor lived so far in the past that the links must be assumed rather than known in detail. A clan differs from a lineage in another respect: It lacks the residential unity that is generally, although not always, characteristic of a lineage's core members. As with the lineage, descent may be patrilineal, matrilineal, or ambilineal.

Because clan membership is dispersed rather than localized, it usually does not involve a shared holding of tangible property. Instead, it involves shared participation in

fission The splitting of a descent group into two or more new descent groups.

Resolving a Native American Tribal Membership Dispute

by Harald E. L. Prins

In autumn 1998, I received a call from the tribal chief of the Aroostook band of Micmacs in northern Maine asking for help in resolving a bitter tribal membership dispute. The conflict centered on the fact that several hundred individuals had become tribal members without proper certification of their Micmac kinship status. Traditionalists in the community argued that their tribe's organization was being taken over by "non-Indians." With the formal status of so many members in question, the tribal administration could not properly determine who was entitled to benefit from the available health, housing, and education programs. After some hostile confrontations between the factions, tribal elders requested a formal inquiry into the membership controversy, and I was called in as a neutral party with a long history of working with the band.

My involvement as an advocacy anthropologist began in 1981, when these Micmacs (also spelled Mi'kmaq) first employed me, along with Bunny McBride, to help them achieve U.S. government recognition of their Indian status. At the time, the Micmacs formed a poor and landless community not yet officially recognized as a tribe. During that decade, we helped the band define its political strategies, which included petitioning for federal recognition of their Indian status; claiming their traditional rights to hunt, trap, and fish; and even demanding return of lost ancestral lands.

To generate popular support for the effort, I co-produced a film about the community (*Our Lives in Our Hands,* 1986). Most important, we gathered oral histories and detailed archival documentation to address kinship issues and other government criteria for tribal recognition. The latter included important genealogical records showing that most Micmac adults in the region were at least "half-blood" (having two of their grandparents officially recorded as Indians).

Based on this evidence, we effectively argued that Aroostook Micmacs could claim aboriginal title to lands in the region. Also, we were able to convince politicians in Washington, DC, to introduce a special bill to acknowledge their tribal status and settle their land claims. When

formal hearings were held in 1990, I testified in the U.S. Senate as an expert witness for the Micmacs. The following year, the Aroostook Band of Micmacs Settlement Act became federal law. This made the band eligible for the financial assistance (health, housing, education, and child welfare) and economic development loans that are available to all federally recognized tribes in the United States. Moreover, the law provided the band with funding to buy a 5,000-acre territorial base in Maine.

Flush with federal funding and rapidly expanding its activities, the 500-member band became overwhelmed by complex bureaucratic regulations now governing their existence. Without formally established ground rules determining who could apply for tribal membership, and overlooking federally imposed regulations, hundreds of new names were rather casually added to its tribal rolls.

By 1997, the Aroostook band population had ballooned to almost 1,200 members, and Micmac traditionalists were questioning the legitimacy of many whose names had been added to the band roster. With mounting tension threatening to destroy the band, the tribal chief invited me to evaluate critically the membership claims of more than half the tribe. In early 1999, I reviewed the kinship records submitted by hundreds of individuals whose membership on the tribal rolls was in question. Several months later, I offered my final report to the Micmac community.

After traditional prayers, sweetgrass burning, drumming, and a traditional meal of salmon and moose, I formally presented my findings. Based on the official criteria, about 100 lineal descendants of the original members and just over 150 newcomers met the minimum required qualifications for membership; several hundred others would have to be removed from the tribal roster. After singing, drumming, and closing prayers, the Micmac gathering dispersed.

Today, the band numbers about 850 members and is doing well. It has purchased several tracts of land (collectively over 600 acres), including a small residential reservation near Presque Isle, now home to about 200 Micmacs. Also located here are new tribal administration offices, a health clinic, and a cultural center.

© David Sanipass

The Sanipass-Lafford family cluster in Chapman, Maine, represents a traditional Micmac residential kin-group. Such extended families typically include grandchildren and bilaterally related family members such as in-laws, uncles, and aunts. Taken from the Sanipass family album, this picture shows a handful of members in the mid-1980s: Marline Sanipass Morey with two of her nephews and uncles.

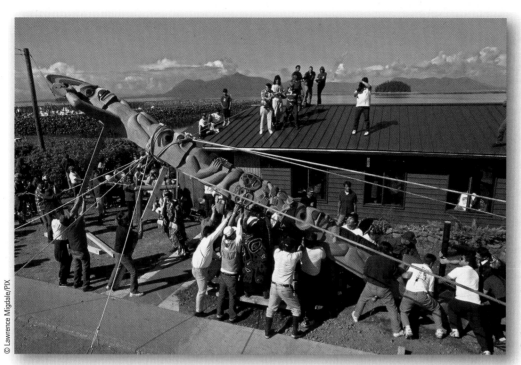

© Lawrence Migdale/PIX

Tsimishian people of Metlakatla, Alaska, raise a memorial totem pole gifted to the community by noted carver David Boxley, a member of the Eagle clan. The tradition of erecting totem poles to commemorate special events endures in several Native American communities in the Pacific Northwest. Carved from tall cedar trees, these spectacular monuments display a clan or lineage's ceremonial property and are prominently positioned as frontal house posts, as markers at grave sites, or at some other place of significance. Often depicting legendary ancestors and mythological animals, the painted carvings symbolically represent a descent group's cultural status and associated privileges in the community.

ceremonial and political matters. Only on special occasions will the membership gather together for specific purposes.

Clans, however, may handle important integrative functions. Like lineages, they may regulate marriage through exogamy. Because of their dispersed membership, clans give individuals the right of entry into associated local groups no matter where they are. Members usually are expected to give protection and hospitality to others in the clan. Hence, these can be expected in any local group that includes people who belong to a single clan.

Clans, lacking the residential unity of lineages, frequently depend on symbols—of animals, plants, natural forces, colors, and special objects—to provide members with solidarity and a ready means of identification. These symbols, called *totems,* often are associated with the clan's mythical origin and reinforce clan members' awareness of their common descent.

The word *totem* comes from the Ojibwa American Indian word *ototeman,* meaning "he is a relative of mine." **Totemism** was defined by the British anthropologist A. R. Radcliffe-Brown as a set of customary beliefs and practices that set up a special system of relations between the society and the plants, animals, and other natural objects that are important.[7]

Totemism varies among cultures. For example, Iroquois Indian matrilineal clans in New York carry such totemic names as Wolf, Bear, and Turtle. Families belonging to these clans can be found in different villages of the Mohawk or any other of the six Iroquois nations, and they act toward each other as if they are related as "brothers," "sisters," "sons," or "daughters." By this device, members of, say, a Bear clan in a Mohawk village can traditionally travel to a nearby Oneida village, or to more distant Onondaga, Cayuga, Tuscarora, or even Seneca villages some 200 miles west of their homeland, and be welcomed and hosted in any of these Iroquois settlements by members of local Bear clans.

In addition to the above-mentioned matrilineal clans (or matriclans), there are also patrilineal clans (or patriclans) tracing descent exclusively through men from a founding ancestor. Historically, a few dozen such clans existed in the Scottish highlands, often identified with the prefix "Mac" or "Mc" (from an old Celtic word meaning "son of"). During the past few hundred years, large Scottish clans such as McGregor and Mackenzie broke apart as many members moved away in search of economic opportunity. Today, their descendants are dispersed all across the globe, especially in Australia, Canada, England,

_____

[7] Radcliffe-Brown, A. R. (1931). Social organization of Australian tribes. *Oceana Monographs 1,* 29.

totemism The belief that people are related to particular animals, plants, or natural objects by virtue of descent from common ancestral spirits.

In the highlands of Scotland, as among many traditional peoples around the world, large kinship groups known as clans have been important units of social organization. Now dispersed all over the world, clan members gather and express their kinship with one another by wearing a tartan skirt, or kilt, with a distinct plaid identifying clan membership. Pictured here is a "parade of tartans"—a festive expression of group identity and ethnic pride during a gathering of the clans at Grandfather Mountain in North Carolina.

Clans among the Six Nations of the Iroquois confederacy in New York State are a kinship construct that, traditionally, facilitated free travel of clan members to multiple member villages. This portrait, made in 1710, shows Sa Ga Yeath Qua Pieth Tow, a chief of the Mohawk Nation. Behind him stands a bear, which represents his clan.

New Zealand, and the United States. During the past few decades, widely scattered descendants have sought to reestablish their kinship ties to ancestral clans, and many travel great distances to attend the annual gathering of their clan, preferably in their traditional ancient homeland in the highlands of Scotland. These clan members express their kinship with one another by wearing woolen shawls, kilts, or other pieces of clothing made of their clan tartan—a distinct plaid pattern and color identifying their particular clan membership.

A reductive variation of totemism may be found in contemporary industrial and postindustrial societies, where sports teams are often given the names of such powerful wild animals as bears, lions, and wildcats. In the United States, this extends to the Democratic Party's donkey and the Republican Party's elephant, and to the Elks, the Lions, and other fraternal and social organizations. These animal emblems, or mascots, however, do not involve the notion of biological descent and the strong sense of kinship that they symbolize for clans, nor are they linked with the traditional ritual observances associated with clan totems.

Phratries and Moieties

Larger kinds of descent groups are phratries and moieties (Figure 10.3). A **phratry** (after the Greek word for "brotherhood") is a unilineal descent group composed of

phratry A unilineal descent group composed of at least two clans that supposedly share a common ancestry, whether or not they really do.

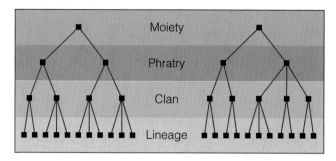

Figure 10.3 This diagram shows how lineages, clans, phratries, and moieties form an organizational hierarchy. Each moiety is subdivided into phratries, each phratry into clans, and each clan into lineages.

at least two clans that supposedly share a common ancestry, whether or not they really do. Like individuals in the clan, phratry members cannot trace precisely their descent links to a common ancestor, although they firmly believe such an ancestor existed.

If the entire society is divided into only two major descent groups, whether they are equivalent to clans or phratries, each group is called a **moiety** (after the French word *moitié*, for "half"). Members of the moiety believe themselves to share a common ancestor but cannot prove it through definite genealogical links. As a rule, the feelings of kinship among members of lineages and clans are stronger than those of members of phratries and moieties. This may be due to the much larger size and more diffuse nature of the latter groups.

Since feelings of kinship are often weaker between people from different clans, the moiety system is a cultural invention that keeps clan-based communities together by binding the clans into a social network of obligatory giving and receiving. That is to say, by institutionalizing reciprocity between groups of clans, the moiety system joins together families who otherwise would not be sufficiently invested in maintaining the commonwealth.

Like lineages and clans, phratries and moieties are often exogamous, and so these different kin-groups are bound together by marriages between their members. And like clans, they provide members rights of access to other communities, as among the Hopi. In a community that does not include one's clan members, one's phratry members are still there to turn to for hospitality. Finally, moieties may perform reciprocal services for one another. Among them, individuals turn to members of the opposite "half" in their community for the necessary mourning rituals when a member of their own moiety dies. Such interdependence between moieties, again, serves to maintain the cohesion of the entire society.

The principle of institutionalized reciprocity between groups of matrilineal clans organized into two equal halves, or moieties, is beautifully illustrated in the circular settlement pattern of many traditional Indian villages in the tropical forest of South America's Amazon region. Dwellings located in one-half of the village are those of clans belonging to one exogamous moiety, and those on the opposite side are the dwellings of clans belonging to the other. Since their clans are often matrilineal, the institutionalized rules of reciprocity in this kin-ordered

moiety Each group that results from a division of a society into two halves on the basis of descent.

Many Amazonian Indians in South America's tropical woodlands traditionally live in circular villages socially divided into moieties. Here we see the Canela Indians' Escalvado village as it was in 1970. (Behind it is a smaller abandoned village where part of the tribe lived before uniting under one chief.) The village is 300 meters (165 feet) wide. The community's "upper" moiety meets in the western part. Nearly all 1,800 members of the Canela tribe reside in the village during festival seasons, but otherwise they are largely dispersed into their smaller, farm-centered circular villages. (Missionaries built the landing strip.)

© Ray Roberts Brown/Smithsonian Institution

Figure 10.4 EGO and his or her kindred. The kindred designates a person's exact degree of being related by blood to other relatives in the family. This degree of blood relatedness determines not only one's social obligations toward relatives, but also one's rights. For instance, when a wealthy, widowed, and childless woman dies without a will, specific surviving members of her kindred will be legally entitled to inherit from her.

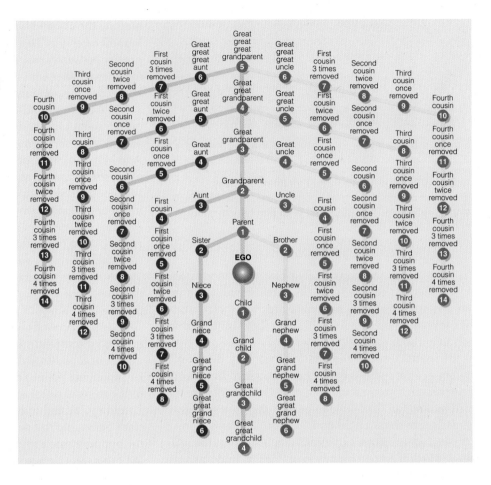

Bilateral Kinship and the Kindred

Important though descent groups are in many societies, they are not found in all societies, nor are they the only kinds of extended kinship groups to be found. *Bilateral*

community traditionally require that a woman marry a man from a clan house on the opposite side of the village, who then moves into her ancestral clan house. Their son, however, will one day have to find a wife from his father's original moiety and will have to move to his father's mother's side of the village. That is to say, the moiety system of institutionalized reciprocity functions like a social "zipper" between clans engaged in a repetitive cycle of exchange relations.

kindred An individual's close blood relatives on the maternal and paternal sides of his or her family.

EGO The central person from whom the degree of each relationship is traced.

kinship, a characteristic of most contemporary European and American societies as well as a number of food-foraging cultures, affiliates a person with genetically close relatives (but not in-laws) through both sexes. In other words, the individual traces descent through both parents, all four grandparents, and so forth, recognizing multiple ancestors. Theoretically, one is associated equally with all "blood" relatives on both the mother's and father's sides of the family. Thus this principle relates an individual lineally to all eight great-grandparents and laterally to all third and fourth cousins.

Since such a huge group is too big to be socially practical, it is usually reduced to a smaller circle of paternal and maternal relatives, called the kindred. The **kindred** may be defined as an individual's close blood relatives on the maternal and paternal side of his or her family. Since the kindred is laterally rather than lineally organized—that is, **EGO,** or the central person from whom the degree of each relationship is traced, is the center of the group — it is not a true descent group (Figure 10.4).

Most North Americans are familiar with the kindred; those who belong are simply referred to as relatives. It includes those blood relatives on both sides of the family who are seen on important occasions, such as family weddings, reunions, and funerals. In the United States, for example, nearly everyone can identify the members of their kindred up to grandparents and first cousins, and quite a few can also name their great grandparents.

Because of its bilateral structure, a kindred is never the same for any two people except siblings (brothers and sisters). And it is not self-perpetuating—it ceases with EGO's death. It has no constant leader, nor can it easily hold, administer, or pass on property. Because of its vagueness, temporary nature, and changing affiliation, the kindred cannot function as a group except in relation to EGO. In most cases, it cannot organize work, nor can it easily administer justice or assign status.

It can, however, be turned to for aid. In non-Western societies, for example, raiding or trading parties may be composed of kindreds. The group comes together to perform some particular function, shares the results, and then disbands. It also can act as a ceremonial group for rites of passage—initiation rituals and the like. Traditionally, the kindred is also of importance in many European cultures, where it may serve to help raise bail, compensate a victim's family, or carry out revenge for the murder or injury of a someone in one's kindred. Finally, kindreds also can regulate marriage through exogamy.

Kindreds are frequently found in industrial and postindustrial state societies where capitalist wage labor conditions promote mobility and individualism, thereby weakening the importance of a strong kinship organization. In societies where small domestic units—nuclear families or single-parent households—are of primary importance, bilateral kinship and kindred organization are likely to result. This can be seen in modern industrial and postindustrial societies, in newly emerging societies in the "underdeveloped" world, and in still-existing food-foraging societies throughout the world.

Kinship Terminology and Kinship Groups

Any system of organizing people who are relatives into different kinds of groups—whether kindreds, lineages, or clans—influences how relatives are labeled. Kinship terminology systems vary considerably across cultures, reflecting the positions individuals occupy within their respective societies and helping to differentiate one relative from another. Distinguishing factors include gender, generational differences, or genealogical differences. In the various systems of kinship terminology, any one of these factors may be emphasized at the expense of others.

By looking at the terms a particular society uses for their relatives, an anthropologist can tell how kinship

groups are structured, what relationships are considered especially important, and sometimes what the prevailing attitudes are concerning various relationships. For instance, a number of languages use the same term to identify a brother and a cousin, and others have a single word for cousin, niece, and nephew. Some cultures find it useful to distinguish an oldest brother from his younger brothers and have different words for these brothers. And unlike English, many languages distinguish between an aunt who is a mother's sister and one who is a father's sister.

Regardless of the factors emphasized, all kinship terminologies accomplish two important tasks. First, they classify similar kinds of individuals into single specific categories; second, they separate different kinds of individuals into distinct categories. Generally, two or more kin are merged under the same term when the individuals have more or less the same rights and obligations with respect to the person referring to them as such. This is the case among most English-speaking North Americans, for instance, when someone refers to a mother's sister and a father's sister both as an "aunt." As far as the speaker is concerned, both relatives possess a similar status.

Several different systems of kinship terminology result from the application of the above principles just mentioned, including the Eskimo, Hawaiian, Iroquois, Crow, Omaha, Sudanese, Kariera, and Aranda systems, each named after the ethnographic example first or best described by anthropologists. The latter five of these systems are fascinating in their complexity and are found among only a few of the world's societies. However, to illustrate some of the basic principles involved, we will focus our attention on the first three systems.

Eskimo System

The Eskimo system, comparatively rare among all the world's systems, is the one used by Euramericans, as well as by a number of food-foraging peoples (including the Inuit and other Eskimos; hence the name). Sometimes referred to as the *lineal system*, the **Eskimo system** emphasizes the nuclear family by specifically identifying mother, father, brother, and sister while lumping together all other relatives into a few large categories (Figure 10.5). For example, the father is distinguished from the father's brother (uncle), but the father's brother

Eskimo system Kinship reckoning in which the nuclear family is emphasized by specifically identifying the mother, father, brother, and sister, while lumping together all other relatives into broad categories such as uncle, aunt, and cousin; also known as a lineal system.

© B & C Alexander/ArcticPhoto

The Inuit in Canada are one of several large Eskimo groups inhabiting Arctic regions from Greenland to Alaska and eastern Siberia. Although they speak different languages and dialects, they share a traditional way of life primarily based on hunting and fishing in which the nuclear family is the primary social unit. As such, their kinship terminology system specifically identifies EGO's father, mother, brother, and sister and lumps all other relatives into a few broad categories that do not distinguish the side of the family from which they derive. Here we see the Taqqaugaq family in their outpost camp home at Iglurjuat on Baffin Island, Nunavut, Canada.

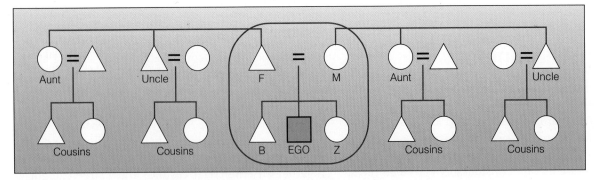

Figure 10.5 The Eskimo system of kinship terminology emphasizes the nuclear family (circled). EGO's father and mother are distinguished from EGO's aunts and uncles, as are siblings from cousins.

is not distinguished from the mother's brother (both are called "uncle"). The mother's sister and father's sister are treated similarly, both called "aunt." In addition, all the sons and daughters of aunts and uncles are called "cousin," thereby making a generational distinction but without indicating the side of the family to which they belong or even their gender.

Unlike other terminologies, the Eskimo system provides separate and distinct terms for the nuclear family members. This is probably because the Eskimo system is generally found in bilateral societies where the dominant kin-group is the kindred, in which only immediate family members are important in day-to-day affairs. This is especially true of modern North American societies, where many families are independent, living apart from, and not directly involved with, other relatives except on special occasions. Thus most North Americans (and others) generally distinguish between their closest kin (parents and siblings) but lump together (as aunts, uncles, cousins) other kin on both sides of the family.

Hawaiian System

The **Hawaiian system** of kinship terminology, common (as its name implies) in Hawaii and other islands in the southern central Pacific Ocean but found elsewhere as well, is the least complex system, in that it uses the fewest terms. The Hawaiian system is also called the *generational system,* since all relatives of the same generation and sex are referred to by the same term (Figure 10.6). For example, in one's parents' generation, the term used to refer to one's father is used as well for the father's brother and mother's brother. Similarly, one's mother, mother's sister, and father's sister are all lumped together under a single term. In EGO's generation, male and female cousins are distinguished by gender and are equated with brothers and sisters.

Hawaiian system Kinship reckoning in which all relatives of the same sex and generation are referred to by the same term.

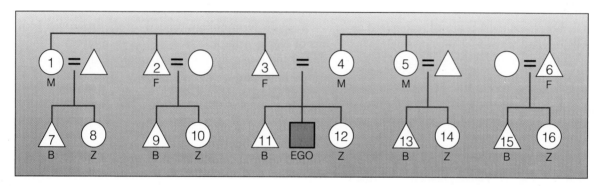

Figure 10.6 In the Hawaiian kinship system the men numbered 2 and 6 are called by the same term as father (3) by EGO; the women numbered 1 and 5 are called by the same term as mother (4). All cousins' of EGO's own generation (7–16) are considered brothers (B) and sisters (Z).

Polynesian societies throughout the Pacific Ocean are traditionally structured according to the Hawaiian system of kinship terminology. With so many relatives identified as their fathers and mothers, children growing up in hamlets on islands such as Hawaii, as well as Tahiti, Samoa, Tonga, or Figi, are welcome in many homes where they share meals and find a place to sleep like other brothers and sisters.

© Erica Heider

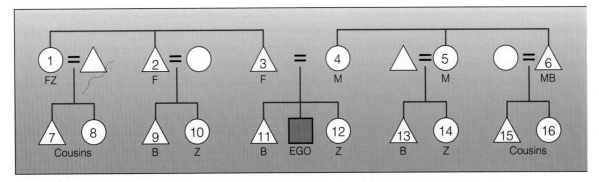

Figure 10.7 According to the Iroquois system of kinship terminology, EGO's father's brother (2) is called by the same term as the father (3); the mother's sister (5) is called by the same term as the mother (4); but the people numbered 1 and 6 are each referred to by a distinct term. Those people numbered 9 to 14 are all considered siblings, but 7, 8, 15, and 16 are considered cousins.

The Hawaiian system reflects the absence of strong unilineal descent, and members on both the father's and the mother's sides are viewed as more or less equal. The siblings of EGO's father and mother are all recognized as being similar relations and are merged under a single term appropriate for their gender. In like manner, the children belonging to the siblings of EGO's parents are related to EGO in the same way the brother and sister are. Falling under the incest taboo, they are ruled out as potential marriage partners.

Iroquois System

In the **Iroquois system** of kinship terminology, the father and father's brother are referred to by a single term, as are the mother and mother's sister; however, the father's sister and mother's brother are given separate terms (Figure 10.7). In one's own generation, brothers, sisters, and parallel cousins (offspring of parental siblings of the same sex—that is, the children of the mother's sister or father's brother) of the same sex are referred to by the same terms, which is logical enough considering that they are the offspring of people who are classified in the same category as EGO's actual mother and father. Cross cousins (offspring of parental siblings of opposite sex—that is, the children of the mother's brother or father's sister) are distinguished by terms that set them apart from all other

kin. In fact, cross cousins are often preferred as spouses, for marriage to them reaffirms alliances between related lineages or clans.

Iroquois terminology, named for the Iroquoian Indians of North America's woodlands, is in fact very widespread and is usually found with unilineal descent groups. It was, for example, the terminology in use until recently in rural Chinese Han society.

Making Relatives

In every culture—from kin-ordered foraging, herding, or farming communities to state-organized capitalist societies—people have developed ideas about the status of relatives. These ideas concern how someone becomes one of "us"—whether by birth, paternal recognition, or some other means. And although many languages may stress the biological, as the English term "blood relative" demonstrates, what ultimately matters is the *culturally defined social status* of a person who is recognized as kin, with all the specific rights and obligations that come with being a daughter, son, brother, or sister to someone else in that kin-group. That is what "being related" is all about and what gives it symbolic meaning with practical consequences. Each kin term marks out a specific set of rights and obligations for individuals socially identified by such a cultural label. In state societies governed by law, these rights may even be legally spelled out in detail.

Fictive Kin by Ritual Adoption

One example of "making relatives" of individuals who are not biologically related is adoption—as discussed in the previous chapter's Globalscape on the transnational

> **Iroquois system** Kinship reckoning in which a father and father's brother are referred to by a single term, as are a mother and mother's sister, but a father's sister and mother's brother are given separate terms. Parallel cousins are classified with brothers and sisters, while cross cousins are classified separately but not equated with relatives of some other generation.

adoption of children. Adoption is a longstanding and widespread cultural practice in many societies all across the world. For instance, it is not uncommon in kin-ordered tribal communities for the head of a clan or family to adopt an outsider, especially when such an individual is valued as a contributing member because of unique skills or contacts with the outside world.

Historically, families and clans facing exceptional challenges to their survival sometimes went to war to obtain human captives from other societies—sometimes young men, but especially women and children. These captives would then be adopted. This occurred among Iroquois Indians in northeastern America. In the 17th and 18th centuries, they often incorporated specially selected war captives and other valued strangers, including European colonists, into their kin-groups in order to make up for population losses due to warfare and disease. As soon as these newcomers were ceremonially naturalized, they acquired essentially the same birthright status as those actually born into one of the families and were henceforth identified by the same kin term as the member being replaced.

Today, it is still not uncommon in traditional societies, especially in kin-ordered communities, for the head of a clan or family to adopt an outsider, especially when such an individual is valued as a contributing member because of unique skills or contacts with the outside world. This may also befall an anthropologist, as noted in our fieldwork chapter, when she or he is doing long-term participant observation in a culture where such ritual incorporation into a kin-group is customary. As an outsider committed to learning the language and culture, the anthropologist may also offer valuable services in return, bringing useful gifts such as steel axes or machetes. As an adopted member of a family or clan, such an out/insider provides a useful linkage with powerful external forces, including international organizations with a mission to protect human rights.

A form of ritual adoption traditionally practiced in many parts of Europe—and spreading to other parts of the world through European colonization or settlement—is the institution of god-parenthood. Generally, this involves a mother and/or father of a newborn child inviting another adult, whether already a relative or not, to become the godfather or godmother to their newborn when it is baptized and formally named. One of the many variations of this institution is *compadrazgo,* or "co-parenthood." Especially common in Latin America, *compadrazgo* involves a child's father and/or mother and godfather and/or godmother becoming linked to each other through the

ritual of a Roman Catholic baptism; they thereby agree to certain mutual rights and obligations. In *compadrazgo,* the main emphasis is placed not on the child–godparent relationship but on the fictive kinship between the child's parents and the sponsor who becomes a ritual co-parent, or *compadre.* Historically common in South Europe and Latin America, such quasi-kinship is

> a pact for mutual support between the two *compadres,* co-parents, involved. Such a pact can be entered into between two *compadres* who are each other's equals in social and economic standing. Very often, however, it is formed between people, of whom one is wealthier, of higher social standing and more powerful politically than the other.[8]

Kinship and New Reproductive Technologies

Today's advances in reproductive technologies also pose new opportunities for kin-making. As defined in the previous chapter, *new reproductive technologies* (NRTs) are alternative means of reproduction such as surrogate motherhood and in vitro fertilization. Since 1978, when the world's first "test-tube baby" was created, thousands of babies have been created outside the womb, without sexual intercourse—and all kinds of new technologies have become part of the reproductive repertoire.

These technologies have opened up a mind-boggling array of reproductive possibilities and social relations. For example, if a child is conceived from a donor egg, implanted in another woman's womb, to be raised by yet another woman, who is its mother? To complicate matters even further, the egg may have been fertilized by sperm from a donor not married to, or in a sexual relationship with, any of these women. Indeed, it has been suggested that about a dozen different modern kin-type categories are embraced in the concepts of mother and father in today's changing societies.[9]

Clearly, NRTs challenge previously held notions of parenthood and kinship. They force us to rethink what being biologically "related" to others really means. Moreover, they drive home the point that the human capacity for securing relatives is not only impressive and ingenious but also fascinating.

[8] Wolf, E. R., & Hansen, E. C. (1972). *The human condition in Latin America* (pp. 131–132). New York: Oxford University Press.
[9] Stone, L. (1998). *Kinship and gender* (p. 272). Boulder, CO: Westview.

Questions for Reflection

1. Have you, for reasons of support and security, created and maintained a social network of relatives beyond your immediate family or household? How so?

2. People in modern industrial and postindustrial societies generally treasure ideas of personal freedom, individuality, and privacy as essential to their happiness. Considering the social functions of kinship relations in traditional nonstate societies, why do you think that such ideas may be considered unsociable and even dangerously selfish?

3. Why do you think that one of the simplest kinship terminology systems imaginable, namely the Eskimo system, is functionally adequate for most Europeans, North Americans, Australians, and others living in complex modern societies?

4. One major reason anthropologists are so interested in understanding a culture's kinship terminology system is that it offers a quick but crucially important insight into a group's social structure. Why do you think this is especially true for traditional communities of foragers, herders, and farmers but is less so for urban neighborhoods in industrial and postindustrial societies?

5. Why do you think that religious institutions such as the Roman Catholic Church and criminal associations such as the Mafia use kinship terms such as "father," "mother," "brother," "sister," "son," and "daughter" for members who are not relatives?

Suggested Readings

Carsten, J. (Ed.). (2008). *Cultures of relatedness: New approaches to the study of kinship*. Cambridge, England: Cambridge University Press.

A cross-cultural examination of what it means to be a relative at a time when established ideas about kinship are being transformed by radical changes in marriage arrangements and gender relations, as well as new reproductive technologies. This collection of contemporary studies—including cultures in Alaska, China, India, Madagascar, and Sudan—shows why we can no longer take it for granted that our most fundamental social relationships are grounded in biology or nature.

Finkler, K. (2000). *Experiencing the new genetics: Family and kinship on the medical frontier*. Philadelphia: University of Pennsylvania Press.

An exploration of medical and genetic aspects of kinship and debates concerning the social impact of modern medical and genetic knowledge and practices.

Fox, R. (1968). *Kinship and marriage in an anthropological perspective*. Baltimore: Penguin.

This classic book outlines some of the methods of analysis used in the anthropological treatment of kinship and marriage. It updates Radcliffe-Brown's *African Systems of Kinship and Marriage* and features a perspective focused on kinship groups and social organization.

Parkin, R. (1997). *Kinship: An introduction to basic concepts*. Cambridge, MA: Blackwell.

A solid, useful, readable text on the basics of kinship study.

Schusky, E. L. (1983). *Manual for kinship analysis* (2nd ed.). Lanham, MD: University Press of America.

This useful book discusses the elements of kinship, diagramming, systems classification, and descent with specific examples.

Challenge Issue   Beyond ties of kinship and household, people extend their social networks to cope with multiple challenges of human survival. These networks may take the form of groups based on gender, age, common interest, and social class. The latter—tied to ranking differences in wealth, status, and power—may range from relatively open to closed social classes such as estates, castes, or "races." Societies traditionally depending on armed self-defense for their security may meet this challenge by forming groups of young men who are mature enough to fight but still unmarried and childless. Such is the case among various East African herding societies, including the Samburu of Kenya, pictured here. Male teenagers of the same age set are collectively initiated as warriors, serving together for fifteen years in protecting their community and livestock from wild animals and enemies. Their long braids of hair, treated with red ochre clay, and ornaments distinguish them from other Samburu.

CHAPTER 11

Grouping by Gender, Age, Common Interest, and Social Class

Chapter Preview

What Principles Do People Use to Organize Societies?

Besides kinship and marriage, people in a society commonly group themselves by gender, age, common interest, and social rank to deal with problems not conveniently handled by marriage, the family and/or household, descent group, or kindred. Such social groups are not only formed within many societies all across the world, but some extend membership to eligible individuals in other societies for purposes of economic, social, and cultural exchange and international ties of friendship and alliance.

What Is Age Grading?

Age grading—the formation of groups on an age basis—is a widely used means of organizing people in societies, including those of Europe and North America. In addition to age grades, some societies feature age sets—formally established groups of people born during a certain time span who move through the series of age-grade categories together.

What Are Common-Interest Associations?

Common-interest associations are formed to deal with specific challenges or opportunities. Membership may be voluntary or compulsory. Common-interest associations have been a feature of human societies since the appearance of the first farming villages several thousand years ago. They have become especially prominent in contemporary postindustrial, industrial, or industrializing societies. Assisted by electronic media, associations are increasingly transnational in our globalizing world. Some are based on shared ethnic, religious, or regional background.

What Is Social Stratification?

Stratification is the division of society into two or more social classes of people who do not share equally in basic resources, status, or power. Such a hierarchical social structure is characteristic of all of the world's societies having large and heterogeneous populations with centralized political control. Among others, these include ancient kingdoms and empires, but also modern republics. Social classes can be relatively open, as in North America where membership is based primarily on personal achievement or wealth. They can also be closed, as in India where membership in hierarchically ranked groups known as castes is determined by birth and remains fixed for life.

Social organization based on kinship and marriage has received considerable attention from anthropologists. There are several reasons for this: In one way or another, kinship and marriage operate as organizing principles in all societies, and in the small stateless societies so often studied by anthropologists they are usually the most important organizational principles. There is, too, a certain fascination in the almost mathematical way kinship systems appear to work.

Yet, because ties of kinship and household are not always sufficient to handle all the challenges of human survival, people also form groups based on gender, age, common interest, and social status.

Grouping by Gender

As shown in preceding chapters, division of labor along gender lines occurs in all human societies. In some cultures—the previously discussed Ju/'hoansi in southern Africa for example—many tasks that men and women undertake may be shared. People may perform work normally assigned to the opposite sex without loss of face. In others, however, men and women are rigidly segregated in what they do. Such is the case in many maritime cultures, where seafarers aboard fishing, whaling, and trading ships are usually men. For instance, we find temporary all-male communities aboard ships of coastal Basque fishermen in northwest Spain, Yupik Eskimo whalers in Alaska, and Swahili merchants sailing along the East African coast.

These seafarers commonly leave their wives, mothers, and daughters behind in their home ports, sometimes for months at a time.

Clearly demarcated grouping by gender also occurs in many traditional horticultural societies. For instance, among the Mohawk, Oneida, Onondaga, Cayuga, Seneca, and Tuscarora Indians of New York—the famous Six Nations of the Iroquois—society was divided into two parts consisting of sedentary women on the one hand and highly mobile men on the other. Women who were blood relatives to one another lived in the same village and shared the job of growing the corn, beans, and squash that all Iroquois relied upon for subsistence. Although men built the houses and the wooden palisades that protected villages and also helped women clear fields for cultivation, they did their most important work some distance away from the villages. This consisted of hunting, fishing, trading, warring, and diplomacy. As a consequence, men were mostly transients in the villages, being present for only brief periods.

Although Iroquoian men were often absent from the village, when present they ate and slept with women. This contrasts with the habits of Mundurucu Indians of Brazil's Amazon rainforest. Mundurucu men and women work, eat, and sleep separately. From age 13 onward, males live together in one large house, while women, girls, and preteen boys occupy two or three houses grouped around the men's house. For all intents and purposes, men associate with men, and women with women.

Among the Mundurucu, relations between the sexes is not harmonious but rather one of opposition. According

Gender-based groups are common among the Mundurucu and numerous other Amazonian Indian nations such as the Yawalapiti pictured here, who live on the Tuatuari River in Brazil's upper Xingu region. Gender issues are symbolically worked out in their mythologies and ceremonial dances. One common theme concerns ownership of the sacred trumpets, which represent spiritual power and are played only by men. These trumpets are zealously guarded by the tribesmen, and only men are allowed to play them. Traditionally, women were even forbidden to see them.

to their belief, sex roles were once reversed: Women ruled over men and controlled the sacred trumpets that are the symbols of power and represent the reproductive capacities of women. But because women could not hunt, they could not supply the meat demanded by the ancient spirits that possessed the trumpets. This enabled the men to take the trumpets from the women, establishing their dominance in the process. Ever since, the trumpets have been carefully guarded and hidden in the men's house, and traditionally women were prohibited from even seeing them.

Thus Mundurucu men express fear and envy toward women and seek to control them by force. For their part, the women neither like nor accept a submissive status, and even though men occupy all formal positions of political and religious leadership, women are autonomous in the economic realm.

Alongside notable differences, there are also interesting similarities between the Mundurucu beliefs and those of traditional European and Euramerican cultures. For example, many 19th-century European and Euramerican intellectuals held to the idea that patriarchy (rule by men) had replaced an earlier state of matriarchy (rule by women). Moreover, the idea that men may use force to control women is deeply embedded in Judaic, Christian, and Muslim traditions.[1] This has changed significantly over the past few decades, but women in North America and other Western countries still have some distance to go before they achieve full parity with men in terms of income, status, and power.

Grouping by Age

Age grouping is so familiar and so important that it and sex have been called the only universal factors that determine a person's position in society. In North America today, for instance, a child's first friends are usually children of his or her own age. Starting preschool or kindergarten with age mates, children typically move through a dozen or more years in the educational system together. At specified ages they are allowed to see certain movies, drive a car, and do things reserved for adults, such as voting, drinking alcoholic beverages, and serving in the military. Ultimately, North Americans retire from their jobs at a specified age and, increasingly, spend the final years of their lives in retirement communities, segregated from the rest of society. As North Americans age, they are labeled "teenagers," "middle-aged," and "senior citizens"—whether they like it or not and for no other reason than the number of years they have lived.

Age classification also plays a significant role in non-Western societies. At a minimum, these cultures make distinctions among immature, mature, and older people whose physical powers are waning. In these societies old age often has profound significance, bringing with it the period of greatest respect (for women it may mean the first social equality with men). Rarely are the elderly shunted aside or abandoned. Even the Inuit of the Canadian Arctic, who are often cited as a people who literally abandon their aged relatives, do so only in truly desperate circumstances, when the group's physical survival is at stake. In all oral tradition societies, elders are the repositories of accumulated wisdom for their people. Recognized as such and no longer expected to carry out many subsistence activities, they play a major role in passing on cultural knowledge to their grandchildren.

In North America, however, elder status is becoming problematic because senior citizens 65 years and older now constitute 12 percent of the overall population, and experts predict their numbers will swell to about 70 million (20 percent of the overall population) by 2030.[2] With more and more people living longer, achieving old age seems less of an accomplishment than it once did and so commands less respect. Also, the youth-oriented society that prevails in the United States, and increasingly in many other industrialized countries, values independence, stigmatizes the less physically robust "autumn years" of life, and commonly laments the "economic burdens" of caring for the elderly.

All human societies recognize a number of life stages. The demarcation and duration of these stages vary across cultures. Each successive life stage provides distinctive social roles and comes with certain cultural features such as specific patterns of activity, attitudes, obligations, and prohibitions.

In many cultures, the social position of an individual in a specific life stage is also marked by a distinctive outward appearance in terms of dress, hairstyle, body paint, tattoos, insignia, or some other symbolic distinction. Typically, these stages are designed to help the transition from one age to another, to teach needed skills, or to lend economic assistance. Often they are taken as the basis for the formation of organized groups.

Institutions of Age Grouping

An organized category of people with membership on the basis of age is known as an **age grade**. Entry into and transfer out of age grades may be accomplished individually,

---

[1] For example, see the Torah and the Bible, Genesis 3:16, and the Koran 4:34.

[2] U.S. Census Bureau News. (2004, March 18).

age grade An organized category of people based on age; every individual passes through a series of such categories over his or her lifetime.

either by a biological distinction, such as puberty, or by a socially recognized status, such as marriage.

Whereas age-grade members may have much in common, may engage in similar activities, may cooperate with one another, and may share the same orientation and aspirations, their membership may not be entirely parallel with physiological aging. A specific time is often ritually established for moving from a younger to an older grade. An example of this is the traditional Jewish ceremony of the *bar mitzvah* (a Hebrew term meaning "son of the commandment"), marking that a 13-year-old boy has reached the age of religious duty and responsibility. *Bat mitzvah*, "daughter of the commandment," is the term for the equivalent ritual for a girl.

Although members of senior groups commonly expect deference from and acknowledge certain responsibilities to their juniors, this does not necessarily mean that one grade is seen as better, or worse, or even more important than another. There can be standardized competition (opposition) between age grades, such as that traditionally between first-year and second-year students on U.S. college campuses.

In addition to age grades, some societies feature age sets (sometimes referred to as *age classes*). An **age set** is a formally established group of people born during a certain time span who move through the series of age-grade categories together. Age sets, unlike age grades, end after a specified number of years; age-set members usually remain closely associated throughout their lives. This is akin to the broad and informal North American practice of identifying generation clusters comprised of all individuals born within a particular time frame—such as baby boomers (1946–1964), Gen-Xers (1961–1981), and the Millennial or Internet generation (1982–2000), also known as Generation Y (year spans approximate).

The age-set notion implies strong feelings of loyalty and mutual support. Because such groups may possess property, songs, shield designs, and rituals and are internally organized for collective decision making and leadership, age sets are distinct from simple age grades.

Theoretically, membership in an age grade ought to be automatic: One reaches the appropriate age and so is included, without question, in the particular age grade. Just such situations exist, for example, among the East African Tiriki, whose system we profile in the next section. Sometimes, though, individuals must buy their way into the age grade for which they are eligible. This was the case among some of the Indians of North America's Great Plains, who

required boys to purchase the appropriate costumes, dances, and songs for age-grade membership. In societies where entrance fees are expensive, not all people eligible for membership in a particular age grade may actually be able to join.

Age Grouping in East Africa

While age is a criterion for group membership in many parts of the world, its most varied and elaborate use is found in several pastoral groups in East Africa, such as the Maasai, Samburu, and Tiriki in Kenya.[3] In Tiriki society, each boy born within a fifteen-year period joins a particular age set. Seven named age sets exist, but only one is open for membership at a time. When it closes, the next one opens. And so it continues until the passage of 105 years (7 times 15), when the first set's membership is gone due to death, and it opens once again to take in new recruits.

Members of Tiriki age sets remain together for life as they move through four successive age grades: Advancement in age grades occurs at fifteen-year intervals, coinciding with the closing of the oldest age set and the opening of a new one. Each age group has its own particular duties and responsibilities. Traditionally, the first, or Warrior age grade, served as guardians of the country, and members gained renown through fighting. Under British colonial rule, however, this traditional function largely fell by the wayside with the decline of intergroup raiding and warfare; members of this age grade may now find excitement and adventure by leaving their community for extended employment or study elsewhere.

The next age grade, the Elder Warriors, had few specialized tasks in earlier days beyond learning skills they would need later on by assuming an increasing share of administrative activities. For example, they would chair the postfuneral gatherings held to settle property claims after someone's death. Traditionally, Elder Warriors also served as envoys between elders of different communities. Nowadays, they hold nearly all of the administrative and executive roles opened up by the creation and growth of a centralized Tiriki administrative bureaucracy.

Judicial Elders, the third age grade, traditionally handled most tasks connected with the administration and settlement of local disputes. Today, they still serve as the local judiciary body.

Members of the Ritual Elders, the senior age grade, used to preside over the priestly functions of ancestral shrine observances on the household level, at subclan meetings, at semiannual community appeals, and at rites of initiation into the various age grades. They also were

---

age set A formally established group of people born during a certain time span who move through the series of age-grade categories together.

[3] Sangree, W. H. (1965). The Bantu Tiriki of western Kenya. In J. L. Gibbs, Jr. (Ed.), *Peoples of Africa* (pp. 69–72). New York: Holt, Rinehart & Winston.

Maasai subclans of western Kenya at the opening parade of the elaborate *eunoto* ceremony, marking the coming of age of *morans* ("warriors"). At the end of the ceremony, these men will be in the next age grade—junior adults—ready to marry and start families. Members of the same age set, they were initiated together into the warrior age grade as teenagers. They spent their warrior years raiding cattle (an old tradition that is now illegal but nonetheless still practiced) and protecting their community homes and animal enclosures (from wild animals and other cattle raiders). The *eunoto* ceremony includes a ritual in which the warrior's mother shaves his head, marking the end of many freedoms and the passage to manhood.

credited with access to special magical powers. With the decline of ancestor worship over the past several decades, many of these traditional functions have been lost, and no new ones have arisen to take their places. Nonetheless, Ritual Elders continue to hold the most important positions in the initiation ceremonies, and their power as sorcerers and expungers of witchcraft is still recognized.

Grouping by Common Interest

The rise of urban, industrialized societies in which individuals are often separated from their kin has led to a proliferation of **common-interest associations**—associations that result from an act of joining and are based on sharing particular activities, objectives, values, or beliefs, sometimes rooted in common ethnic, religious, or regional background. Moreover, common-interest associations help people meet a range of needs from companionship to safe work conditions to learning a new language and customs upon moving from one country to another.

Because common-interest associations are flexible, they have often been turned to, both in cities and in traditional villages, as a way of meeting these needs. Common-interest associations are not, however, restricted to modernizing societies alone. They also are found in many

common-interest association An association that results from an act of joining based on sharing particular activities, objectives, values, or beliefs, sometimes rooted in common ethnic, religious, or regional background.

Visual Counterpoint

The range of common-interest associations is astounding, as suggested by these photos of Shriners and Crips. The Shriners are a secret fraternal order of middle-class males in the United States committed to "fun, fellowship, and service" and named after the Ancient Arabic Order of Nobles of the Mystic Shrine. The Crips are a violent urban gang, originating in poor Los Angeles neighborhoods. Their trademark is a blue bandana—in contrast to the red bandana of their rival gang, the Bloods. The notoriety of the Crips spread as a result of sensational stories in the media, spawning a network of independent satellite Crip gangs in other U.S. cities as well as in Europe, Asia, and Central America.

traditional societies, and there is reason to believe they arose with the emergence of the first horticultural villages. Furthermore, associations in traditional societies may be just as complex and highly organized as those of countries such as the United States and Canada.

Common-interest associations have often been referred to in the anthropological literature as voluntary associations, but this term is misleading. The act of joining may range from being fully voluntary to being required by law. For example, in the United States, under previous draft laws individuals often became members of the armed forces without choosing to join. And although it is not compulsory to join a labor union, unless one does, one cannot work in a union shop. What the term *voluntary association* really refers to are those associations not based on sex, age, kinship, marriage, or territory that result from an act of joining. The act of joining often may be voluntary, but it does not have to be.

Kinds of Common-Interest Associations

The variety of common-interest associations is astonishing. In the United States, they include sport, hobby, and civic service clubs; religious and spiritual organizations; political parties; labor unions; environmental organizations; urban gangs; private militias; women's and men's clubs of all sorts—the list could go on and on. Their goals may include the pursuit of friendship, recreation, and the

promotion of certain values, as well as governing, seeking peace on a local or global scale, and the pursuit or defense of economic interests.

Associations also have served to preserve traditional songs, history, language, moral beliefs, and other customs among members of various ethnic minorities. So it is among North American Indians, who since the late 1960s have been experiencing a resurgence of ethnic pride after generations of forced assimilation and schooling designed to stamp out their cultural identity. A satisfying way of publicly expressing pride in their ethnic identity and cultural heritage is by way of ceremonial gatherings known as *powwows,* which take place not only on reservations but also in cities where most American Indians now live. Usually pan-tribal, these festive gatherings feature American Indians from dozens of different nations or tribes dancing together in traditional regalia as songs and drumming fill the air. Gift offerings and the selling of Native crafts are part of the event, along with traditional Native foods such as frybread.[4]

The Original Study on the next page provides a detailed example of how another ethnic minority group establishes a sense of traditional community, even within modern cities, by means of symbolic geographic boundary markers.

---

[4] Ellis, C. (2006). *A dancing people: Powwow culture on the southern plains.* Lawrence: University Press of Kansas.

Common-interest associations sometimes grow out of shared ethnic background. Here we see "Black Indians" at the famous Mardi Gras carnival in New Orleans, Louisiana. Usually Americans of African descent and belonging to the poor working class, these "Indians" are members of neighborhood social clubs or "tribes" that are, in part, spiritual and secret. Mardi Gras (from the French word *mardi* for "Tuesday" and *gras* meaning "fat") is an ancient Roman Catholic feasting day just before Lent, traditionally a season of fasting and penitence before Easter. During carnival the normal social order of a stratified society is suspended and celebrated with masquerade balls and colorful street parades. In New Orleans, African American descendents of black slaves use Mardi Gras to publicly express ethnic pride in spectacular fashion.

Original Study

The Jewish *Eruv:* Symbolic Place in Public Space *by Susan Lees*

Cultural anthropologists are interested in how a geographic space becomes a culturally meaningful *place*—an area that we may think of as "our territory" or that we designate for one particular purpose or another, such as pasturing animals, playing sports, gardening, or worshiping. As in a baseball diamond, there are certain boundaries to such places. We may mark them off with lines or symbols not readily comprehensible to outsiders, who may not understand what makes a "foul ball" until we explain the rules and the symbols.

At times, different cultural groups may occupy the same geographic space, but each will see and divide it differently in terms that are meaningful only within their group. We see this on maps where international borders cut through traditional tribal or ethnic group territories, as with the Yupik Eskimos of Alaska and Siberia. And we see it in various urban communities that may divide up their

city spaces in ways perceptible only to themselves.

An example can be found among Orthodox Jews who ritually define the boundaries of their communities for the purpose of Sabbath observance: Once a week, on the seventh day religiously reserved for worship and obligatory rest, the area enclosed by the boundaries becomes, by definition, a single shared symbolic domain. This symbolically enclosed space is called an *eruv,* which means "combination" of public and private space—that is, the private spaces of the household and the public areas of the sidewalks, streets, and perhaps parks are combined on the Sabbath as one big communal household.

The purpose of the *eruv* for Orthodox communities is to accommodate one of the many Sabbath prohibitions on religiously defined "work": the work of "carrying" objects from a private domain

to a public one, or vice versa, or carrying objects for any distance in a public domain. On the Sabbath, if there is an *eruv,* observant Jews may carry within the entire *eruv* enclosure as if they were in their own homes. For instance, they are permitted to push a baby stroller or a wheelchair within the ritually enclosed neighborhood. This makes it possible for whole families—including small children and disabled individuals—to attend religious services in the synagogue or to socialize with one another and still be faithful to traditional law.

Historically, *eruv* boundaries were in fact the walls of houses and courtyards and city walls within which communities were enclosed. But today, where there are no walls, communities sometimes erect thin strings or wires, or sometimes just use wires already there on utility poles (such as phone or electricity wires) to demarcate the boundaries. These are

CONTINUED

CONTINUED

known to members of the community but usually are invisible to outsiders because they are part of the urban landscape anyway.

I was first drawn to the subject of the *eruv* nearly three decades ago, when I leafed through my mother's copy of the Code of Jewish Law still found in many Jewish households. Much of this text concerns rules about observing the Sabbath.

As an anthropologist, I was intrigued by explanations given for certain practices because they heightened awareness of the uniqueness of Jewish identity in a world where temptations to assimilate with the larger, dominant culture were strong. Most of all, the *eruv* captured my interest because it seemed to create, not just prohibit something. It transformed a group of diverse urban households into one common household, not just a community but a real "private" home. The symbolic "walls" around this collective domain were erected not to keep others out but to enclose its members and thus erase the actual walls of each individual household.

The ritual that creates an *eruv* requires that one member take a loaf of bread and make other members co-owners of that loaf; the symbolism of a household is shared ownership (not consumption) of this most symbolically meaningful food. The boundaries of the *eruv* "household" they co-inhabit must be contiguous, broken only by symbolic doorways through which they can pass as if through doorways of their individual homes. As long as the contiguity is maintained, they can extend the *eruv* to

incorporate hundreds or even thousands of other houses. It occurred to me then that in a highly urbanized mass society of mostly strangers, this symbolic unification of sometimes widely separated Jewish households was an extraordinary thing.

The majority of North American Jews who are members of religious congregations belong to Reform synagogues (the other major groups are Conservative and Orthodox), and American Reform Judaism officially abandoned the *eruv* as a Sabbath practice in 1846. When I first became interested in the subject, there were rather few *eruvin* anywhere.

But in the early 1970s, on the heels of the 1960s civil rights movement in the United States, a shift in Jewish identity issues occurred, and some younger generation Jews began to turn to traditional practices that distinguished them from mainstream society and more assimilated Jews. It was in this context that a proliferation of new *eruvin*

occurred in both urban and suburban contexts. Meanwhile, some Jews resisted this expression of difference, and within the wider Jewish community there was considerable strife over the question of the "authenticity" of the beliefs and practices of more assimilated Jews.

Most *eruvin* have been established without conflict, but a handful have been highly controversial. In my research, I was interested to find that Jews are among the principal parties on both sides of *eruv* conflicts. Opponents of the *eruv* appear to fear the creation, or re-creation, of ghettos of inassimilable Jews who neither conform to nor respect the ideals of the dominant or mainstream culture—who appear "foreign" in appearance and practices. Thus the *eruv* conflict appears on one level to be an argument among Jews adhering to different beliefs about how they should live in modern society with other groups and among themselves. Interestingly, when Jewish religious leaders were first developing the laws of the *eruv* more than 2,000 years ago, this problem of how Jews could maintain a communal identity while living as a diasporic group (dispersed from their ancestral homeland) was among their primary concerns.

The *eruv* is one symbolic device to reinforce community as neighborhood—to establish a meaningful place for a distinct group in a diverse society. Ethnic church parishes often have done the same for other urban groups. Neighborhood identities like these can be the basis for disputes about exclusivity, but they can also ease the maintenance of cultural traditions and humanize life in the city.

Boundaries of the Washington, DC, *eruv*—one of many symbolically enclosed spaces created by Orthodox Jews in cities around the world.

Men's and Women's Associations

In some societies women have not established formal common-interest associations to the extent men have because they live in male-dominated cultures that restrict them or because women are absorbed on the domestic front with a host of activities compatible with childrearing. Moreover, some functions of men's associations—such as military combat duties—often are culturally defined as fit only for adult males or repugnant to women. Still, as cross-cultural research makes clear, women often play important roles in associations of their own as well as in those in which men predominate. Moreover,

an ever-expanding feminist movement has directly or indirectly inspired and promoted the formation of professional organizations for women.

Throughout Africa, women's social clubs complement the men's and are linked to a variety of economic and social matters. These clubs provide information on wealth-generating opportunities, offer mutual support, and give spiritual counseling; they are also concerned with educating women, with promoting craftworks, and with charitable and wealth-generating activities. Increasingly, women's clubs are devoted to politics. In Sierra Leone, once-simple dancing societies have developed under urban conditions

These members of a women's craft association in Bakingili, Cameroon, in Africa are making tie-dyed fabric together.

Courtesy of Women's Promotion and Assistance Association of Cameroon. Photo by Mousa.

into complex organizations with a set of new objectives. The resulting dancing *compin* (Krio for "company") is comprised of young women (along with men) performing plays based on traditional music and dances and raising money for various mutual benefit causes.[5]

Women's rights organizations, consciousness-raising groups, and professional organizations are examples of some of the associations arising directly or indirectly out of feminist movements. These groups cover the entire range of association formation, from simple friendship and support groups to associations centered on politics, sports, the arts, spirituality, charity, and economic endeavors—on a national and even international scale. One example of a global female youth movement is the World Association of Girl Guides and Girl Scouts. Founded in England in 1928, this association supports young-female scouting organizations with a total membership of over 10 million girls and young women in 145 countries.

A far-reaching example on the economic front is India's Self-Employed Women's Association (SEWA), headquartered in the northwestern city of Ahmedabad. With more than half a million members, it is the single largest union of informal sector workers in the country. Working with 200 cooperatives and thousands of individual artisans, it has helped to establish supportive services vital to helping women achieve the goals of full employment and

self-reliance—services such as savings and credit, health care, child care, insurance, legal aid, capacity building, and communication services, which are important needs of poor women. Today, SEWA's Trade Facilitation Centre is being expanded into a global network aimed at making women's voices and contributions significant factors in world trade decisions.

Associations in the Postindustrial World

Despite the diversity and vitality of common-interest associations, some social analysts have noted a recent decline in participation in all sorts of these groups, at least in North America. Those who have observed this trend see it as part of a more general drop in civic participation. People are spending less time socializing with others in bars, at dinner parties, having friends over, and so on.

We can only speculate on the causes, but they likely include further isolation of individuals as people spend more and more of their free time with an ever-growing array of electronic and/or digital entertainment. For example, in the United States, people devote an average of nearly 5 hours each day watching television. And teens spend close to 3 hours a day viewing videos on the Internet, thanks to Hulu and YouTube.[6] Then, too, the frequency with which people move interferes with their ability to establish more

[5] Little, K. L. (1973). *African women in towns: an aspect of Africa's social revolution* (pp. 58–62). New York: Cambridge University Press. See Steady, F. C. (2001). *Women and the Amistad connection, Sierra Leone Krio Society* (pp. 71–80). Rochester, VT: Schenkman.

[6] "Average TV viewing for 2008–09 TV season at all-time high." (2009, November 10). blog.nielsen.com; "A pocket guide to social media and kids." (2009, November 2). blog.nielsen.com.

High-speed wireless networks in affluent Japan, as in many other parts
of the world, make it possible for
people to continually tap into information and exchange messages and
images by means of portable computers or, increasingly, web-enabled
mobile telephones. For Japanese
commuters, who spend hours staring
at tiny screens on their mobiles while
riding the world's most extensive
network of subways and commuter
trains, blogging is especially popular.

© David Sacks/Getty Images

than superficial friendships with others. Add to this the
fact that individuals in the United States generally work
longer hours, commute longer distances, and have fewer
days off on average than people in nearly all other industrialized countries, leaving less time for face-to-face socialization and participation in the neighborhood.

On the other hand, the digital communication revolution has radically restructured social relations, creating
rather than eliminating social connections, albeit many
of the virtual type. All those American teens who devote
hours to TV and Internet entertainment are also spending considerable time text messaging one another on their
cell phones. In fact, the average U.S. teenager texts about
2,000 times a month—a figure probably not much different from that of their age-mates in Japan, Australia, and
many other wealthy industrialized countries.[7]

People in societies all across the world now have direct
access to an ever-expanding range of relatively cheap digital communication tools—especially portable media players and mobile phones, which facilitate establishing new
social contacts and maintaining existing ones with relatives
and friends, regardless of where these people physically live.

In 2009, worldwide mobile telephone subscriptions reached
4.1 billion—about 60 percent of the global population.[8]

Whether accessed by computer or mobile phone, social
networking platforms—such as Facebook (with over 300
million users worldwide in 2009), MySpace (150 million),
Twitter (about 50 million), or Fanfou (a Chinese Twitter
replica)—enable individuals to text message and exchange
images with "friends," continually update their personal or
other information, and engage in micro-blogging.

These social platforms are now also used by office
managers, city mayors, and school principals for purposes
of quick communication and have become instrumental
in the functioning of many social groups. Importantly, in
highly mobile societies and globally interconnected cultures, these new social media make it possible to build and
expand social networks regardless of geographic distance
and across international boundaries.

Grouping by Social Status in Stratified Societies

Social stratification is a common and powerful structuring
force in many of the world's societies. Basically, **stratified
societies** are those in which people are hierarchically

[7] Ibid.

stratified society A society in which people are hierarchically
divided and ranked into social strata, or layers, and do not share
equally in the basic resources that support survival, influence,
and prestige.

[8] "4.1 billion mobile phone subscribers worldwide." (2009, March 27). www.
mocom2020.com/2009/03/41-billion-mobile-phone-subscribers-worldwide/

Anthropologists and Social Impact Assessment

Anthropologists frequently do a type of policy research called a *social impact assessment*, which entails collecting data about a community or neighborhood for planners of development projects. Such an assessment seeks to determine a project's effect by determining how and upon whom its impact will fall and whether the impact is likely to be positive or negative.

In the United States, any project requiring a federal permit or license, or using federal funds, by law must be preceded by a social impact assessment as part of the environmental review process. Examples of such projects include highway construction, urban renewal, water diversion schemes, and land reclamation. Often, such projects are sited so that their impact falls most heavily on neighborhoods or communities inhabited by people in low socioeconomic strata—sometimes because the projects are viewed as a way of improving the lives of poor people and sometimes because the poor people have less political power to block these proposals.

As an illustration of this kind of work, anthropologist Sue Ellen Jacobs was hired to do a social impact assessment of a water diversion project in New Mexico planned by the Bureau of Land Reclamation in cooperation with the Bureau

of Indian Affairs. This project proposed construction of a diversion dam and an extensive canal system for irrigation on the Rio Grande. The project would affect twenty-two communities inhabited by primarily Hispanic Americans, as well as two Indian pueblos. Unemployment was high in the region, and the project was seen as a way to promote urbanization, which theoretically would be associated with industrial development, while bringing new land into production for intensive agriculture.

What the planners failed to take into account was that both the Hispanic and Indian populations were heavily committed to farming for household consumption (with some surpluses raised for the market), using a system of irrigation canals that had been established for 300 years. These canals are maintained by elected supervisors familiar with the communities and knowledgeable about water laws, ditch management, and sustainable crop production. Such individuals can resolve conflicts concerning water allocation and land use—and often other issues as well. Under the proposed project, this system was to be given up in favor of one in which fewer people would control larger tracts of land, and water allocation would be in the hands of a government technocrat.

One of the strongest measures of local government would be lost.

Not surprisingly, Jacobs discovered widespread community opposition to this project, and her report helped convince Congress that any positive impact was far outweighed by negative effects. One of the major objections to the construction project was that it would obliterate the centuries-old irrigation system. Project planners did not seem to recognize the antiquity and cultural significance of these traditional irrigation structures, referring to them as "temporary diversion structures." The fact that the old dams associated with the ditches were attached to local descent groups was simply not acknowledged in the government documents.

Beyond infringing on local control, the project threatened the community with a range of negative side effects: problems linked to population growth and relocation, a loss of fishing and other river-related resources, and new health hazards, including increased threat of drowning, insect breeding, and airborne dust.

Adapted from van Willigen, J. (1986). Applied anthropology (p. 169). South Hadley, MA: Bergin & Garvey.

divided and ranked into social strata, or layers, and do not share equally in the basic resources that support income, status, and power. Members of the bottom strata typically have fewer resources, lower status, and less power than those in top-ranked strata. In addition, the restrictions and obligations imposed on those in the lowest-ranked strata are usually more strenuous or oppressive, and they must work harder for far less financial reward.

In short, social stratification amounts to culturally institutionalized inequality. In the United States, Hispanic, African American, and American Indian groups are among those who have struggled with their positions in the low-ranked strata. As profiled in this chapter's Anthropology Applied feature, their needs are often ignored in development efforts.

Stratified societies stand in sharp contrast to **egalitarian societies,** in which everyone has about equal rank, access to, and power over basic resources. In these societies, social values of communal sharing are culturally emphasized and approved; wealth hoarding and elitist pretensions are despised, belittled, or ridiculed. As we saw in earlier chapters,

foraging societies are characteristically egalitarian, although there are some exceptions.

Social Class and Caste

A **social class** may be defined as a category of individuals in a stratified society who enjoy equal or nearly equal prestige according to the system of evaluation. The qualification "nearly equal" is important, for a certain amount of inequality may occur even within a given class. Class distinctions are not always clear-cut and obvious in societies that have a wide and continuous range of differential privileges.

egalitarian society A society in which everyone has about equal rank, access to, and power over the basic resources that support survival, influence, and prestige.

social class A category of individuals in a stratified society who enjoy equal or nearly equal prestige according to the system of evaluation.

A **caste** is a closed social class in a stratified society in which membership is determined by birth and fixed for life. The opposite of the principle that all humans are born equal, the caste system is based on the principle that humans neither are nor can be equal. Castes are strongly endogamous, and offspring are automatically members of their parents' caste.

TRADITIONAL HINDU CASTE SYSTEM

The classic ethnographic example of a caste system is the traditional Hindu caste system of India (also found in other parts of Asia, including Nepal and Bali). Perhaps the world's longest surviving social hierarchy, it encompasses a complex ranking of social groups on the basis of "ritual purity." Each of some 2,000 different castes considers itself as a distinct community higher or lower than other castes, although their particular ranking varies among geographic regions and over time.

The different castes are associated with specific occupations and customs, such as food habits and styles of dress, along with rituals involving notions of purity and pollution. Traditional Hindus are taught to follow the ritual path of duty, or *dharma,* of the specific caste into which they are born, and learn to avoid everyone and everything considered taboo to their caste. For this reason, castes are always endogamous. Differences in caste rankings are traditionally justified by the Hindu religious doctrine of the transmigration of the soul, or *karma,* a belief that one's place in life is determined by one's deeds in previous lifetimes.

All of these castes, or *jatis,* are organized into four ranked orders, or *varnas* (literally meaning "colors"), distinguished partly by occupation and ranked in order of descending religious status of purity (Figure 11.1). The religious foundation for this social hierarchy is found in a sacred text known as the Laws of Manu, an ancient work about 2,000 years old and considered by traditional Hindus as the highest authority on their cultural institutions. It defines the Brahmans as the purest and therefore highest *varna.* As priests and lawgivers, Brahmans represent the world of religion and learning. Next come the fighters and rulers, known as the Kshatriyas. Below them are the Vaisyas (merchants and traders), who are engaged in commercial, agricultural, and pastoral pursuits. At the bottom are the Sudras (artisans and laborers), an order required to serve the other three *varnas* and who also make a living by handicrafts.

Falling outside the *varna* system is a fifth category of degraded individuals known as "Untouchables." These

"outcastes" are tasked with doing the "dirty work" in society—collecting garbage, removing animal carcasses, cleaning streets, and disposing of dung, sewage, and other refuse. Commonly associated with filth and discriminated against by fellow Hindus as ritually impure, Untouchables were historically prohibited from owning land or the tools of their trade. Brahmans (who view themselves as the most pure) and members of other *varnas* avoid direct contact with these Untouchables, due to the belief that touching or accepting food from such "dirty" persons—let alone having sexual relations with them—would result in ritual pollution.

Untouchables constitute a large pool of cheap labor at the beck and call of those controlling economic and political affairs. In an effort to bestow some dignity on these poverty-stricken victims of the caste system, Hindu nationalist leader Mahatma Gandhi renamed them *harijan* or "children of God."

Although India's national constitution of 1950 sought to abolish caste discrimination and the practice of Untouchability, the caste system remains deeply entrenched in Hindu culture and is still widespread throughout southern Asia, especially in rural India. In what has been called India's "hidden apartheid," entire villages in many Indian states remain completely segregated by caste. Traditionally powerless and desperately poor, members of this religious inferior underclass endure near complete social isolation, humiliation, and discrimination based exclusively on their birth status. Even the shadow of an Untouchable is believed to pollute the higher-ranking castes. They may not cross the line dividing their part of the village from that occupied by higher castes, drink water from public wells, or visit the same temples as the higher castes. Their children are still often made to sit at the back of classrooms, and in rural areas huge numbers still lack access to education altogether.[9] Over the past five decades, Untouchables,

---

[9] Committee on the Elimination of Racial Discrimination, India. (2007, March). Consideration of reports submitted by states parties under Article 9 of the International Convention on the Elimination of All Forms of Racial Discrimination, 70th Session (p. 3). www2.ohchr.org/english/bodies/cerd/cerds70.htm; see also "Hidden apartheid: Caste discrimination against India's Untouchables." (2007). Human Rights Watch and the Center for Human Rights and Global Justice.

---

caste A closed social class in a stratified society in which membership is determined by birth and fixed for life.

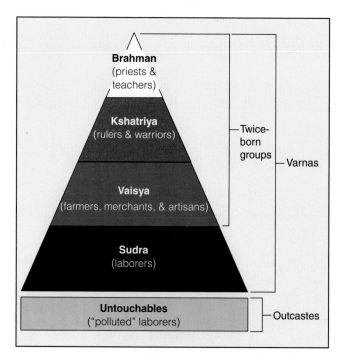

Figure 11.1 Hindu castes are organized into four "grades of being" called *varnas* ("colors"), which determine what members are permitted to do, touch, or eat; where they live; how they dress; and who they can marry. The highest-ranking order Brahman is associated with the color white, below which are the Kshatriya (red) and Vaisya (brown). Members born into these *varnas* are all believed to have been reincarnated from a morally correct earlier life in a lower-ranked order. Below these three are the Sudra (black), who make a living as laborers. Lower still are the "polluted" laborers—the Untouchables who are charged with cleaning the streets and with the collection and disposal of garbage, animal carcasses, and sewage. Brahmans and members of other *varnas* avoid direct contact with Untouchables, believing that touching or accepting food from them would result in ritual pollution.

in concert with the lowest-ranking Sudra castes, have built a civil rights movement—described later in this chapter.

Castelike situations are found in other places in the world. In Bolivia, Ecuador, and several other South and Central American countries, for example, the wealthy upper class is almost exclusively white and rarely intermarries with people of non-European descent. In contrast, the lower class of working poor in those countries is primarily made up of American Indian laborers and peasants. Likewise, most European stratified societies were historically organized in closed social classes known as *estates*—ranked as clergy, nobility, and citizens and each with distinctive political rights (privileges). These were hierarchically identified by titles and forms of address, and they

were publicly identified by distinctive dress and codes of behavior.

Historical Racial Segregation in South Africa and the United States

Other than social class, caste, and estate, the hierarchy in a stratified society may be based on ethnic origin or skin color. For instance, dark-skinned individuals culturally classified as "colored" or "black" may encounter social rules excluding them from certain jobs or neighborhoods and making it difficult if not impossible to befriend or marry someone with a lighter skin color.

One of the best-known historical examples of a pluralistic country with social stratification based on the notion of "race" is South Africa. From 1948 to 1994, a minority of 4.5 million people of European descent imposed a political regime of racial segregation and discrimination on 25 million indigenous Zulu, Sotho, Tswana, Xhosas, Khoi (Hottentot), Bushmen, and other ethnic groups. Known as *apartheid* (an Afrikaans-Dutch term meaning "segregation" or "separation"), this white superiority ideology officially relegated indigenous dark-skinned Africans to a low-ranking stratum. Similar to the Hindu caste system with its concepts of ritual purity and pollution, South African whites feared pollution of their purity through improper contact with blacks.

Until the mid-20th century, institutionalized racial segregation officially prevailed in the United States, where the country's ruling upper class was historically comprised exclusively of individuals of European ("Caucasian" or "white") descent. After the American Revolution, several states in New England joined Virginia and other southern states and made it illegal for whites to marry blacks or American Indians. After the federal government officially abolished slavery in 1863, these miscegenation laws remained in force in many states from Maine to Florida for decades.

In 1924, Virginia's General Assembly passed the Racial Integrity Act to prevent light-skinned individuals with some African ancestry from "passing" as whites. Known as the *one drop rule,* it codified the idea of white racial purity by classifying individuals as black if just one of their multiple ancestors was of African origin ("one drop of Negro blood").

However light-skinned, they were subject to a wide range of discriminatory practices not applicable to whites. Such institutionalized racial discrimination continued for a century after slavery was abolished, and today self-segregation exists in many parts of the United States.

Despite U.S. civil rights laws passed in the 1960s (prohibiting discrimination in accommodations, schools, employment, and voting for reasons of color, "race," religion, or national origin), economic inequality persists as the

During South Africa's apartheid regime (1948–1994), the white minority of European descent imposed strict racial segregation in that country, which not only dictated where "blacks" and "coloreds" were allowed to live or work, but also prohibited who they could marry, where they could worship and socialize, and even where they could swim.

typical African American household has 54 cents of income and 12 cents of wealth for every corresponding dollar in the typical white American household.[10] And, despite laws against it, discrimination continues, especially in former slave-holding states such as North Carolina. Recent research on that state's legal system showed that the life of a "white" person is more highly valued than a "non-white," as defendants whose victims are "white" are 3.5 times more likely to be sentenced to death than those with "non-white" victims.[11]

Indicators of Social Status

Social status in a stratified society, whether divided in open or closed classes, is manifested in several ways. One is through *verbal evaluation*—what people say about others in their own society. For this, anything can be singled out for attention and spoken of favorably or unfavorably: from a person's physical features, dress, social manners, and speech to his or her circle of friends, economic activities, political affiliations, church membership, and material possessions such as houses, cars, and so on. Cultures evaluate such identifying features differently, and what may be spoken of favorably in one may be spoken of unfavorably in another and ignored in a third.

Furthermore, cultural values may change, so that something regarded favorably at one time may not be so regarded at another. This is one reason why a researcher may be misled by verbal evaluation, for what people say may not correspond completely with social reality. As an example, the official language of Egypt is Classical Arabic, the language of the Koran (the holiest of Islamic texts). Though it is highly valued, no one in Egypt uses this language in daily interaction; rather, it is used for official documents or on formal occasions. Those most proficient in it are not of the upper class but, rather, of the lower middle classes. These are the people educated in the public schools (where Classical Arabic is the language of schooling) and who hold jobs in the government bureaucracy (which requires the most use of Classical Arabic). Upper-class Egyptians, by contrast, go to private schools, where they learn the foreign languages essential for success in diplomacy and in the global economy of business and industry.[12]

[10] Boshara, R. (2003, January/February). Wealth inequality: The $6,000 solution. *Atlantic Monthly*. See also Kennickell, A. B. (2003, November). *A rolling tide: Changes in the distribution of wealth in the U.S. 1989–2001*. Levy Economics Institute.

[11] Unah, I., & Boger, C. (2001, April). *Race and the death penalty in North Carolina*. www.common-sense.org/pdfs/NCDeathPenaltyReport2001.pdf.

[12] Haeri, N. (1997). The reproduction of symbolic capital: Language, state, and class in Egypt. *Current Anthropology 38*, 795–816.

Social status in a stratified society is also indicated through *patterns of association*—not just who interacts with whom but how and in what context. In Western society, informal, friendly relations take place mostly within one's own class. Relations with members of other classes tend to be more formal and occur in the context of specific situations. For example, a corporate executive and a janitor normally are members of different social classes. They may have frequent contact with each other, but it occurs in the setting of the corporate offices and usually requires certain stereotyped behavior patterns.

A third way social status is manifested is through *symbolic indicators*. For example, in the United States certain activities and possessions are indicative of class: occupation (a garbage collector has different class status than a medical specialist); wealth (rich people are generally in a higher social class than poor people); dress ("white collar" versus "blue collar"); form of recreation (people of the upper class are expected to play golf rather than shoot pool down at the pool hall—but they can shoot pool at home or in a club); residential location (people of the upper class do not ordinarily live in slums); kind of car; and so on. All sorts of status symbols are indicative of class position, including measures such as the number of bathrooms in a person's house. That said, class rankings do not fully correlate with economic status or pay scales. The local garbage collector or unionized factory laborer typically makes more money than an average college professor with a doctorate.

Symbolic indicators involve factors of lifestyle, but differences in life chances may also signal differences in class standing. Life is apt to be less hard for members of an upper class as opposed to a lower class. This shows up in a tendency for lower infant mortality and longer life expectancy for the upper class. There is also a tendency for greater physical stature and robustness among people of the upper class—the result of better diet and protection from serious illness in their growing-up years (see the Biocultural Connection).

Maintaining Stratification

In any system of stratification, those who dominate proclaim their supposedly superior status by means of a powerful ideology, commonly asserting it through intimidation or propaganda (in the form of gossip, media, religious doctrine, and so forth) that presents their position as normal, natural, divinely guided, or at least well-deserved. As anthropologist Laura Nader points out, "Systems of thought develop over time and reflect the interests of certain classes or groups in the society who manage to universalize their beliefs and values."[13]

So it is with certain religious ideologies that effectively assert that the social order is divinely fixed and therefore not to be questioned. With the aid of culturally institutionalized thought structures, religious and otherwise, those in power hope that members of the lower classes will thereby "know their place" and not contest their domination by the "chosen elite." If, however, this domination is contested, the elite usually control the power of the state and use its institutions to protect their privileged position.

In India, for example, Hindu belief in reincarnation and an incorruptible supernatural power that assigns people to a particular caste position, as a reward or punishment for the deeds and misdeeds of past lives, justifies one's position in this life. If, however, individuals faithfully perform the duties appropriate to their caste in this lifetime, then they can expect to be reborn into a higher caste in a future existence.

In the minds of orthodox Hindus, one's caste position is something earned rather than the accident of birth as it appears to outside observers. In contrast to India's traditional caste system, which explicitly recognizes (and accepts as legitimate) inequality among people, the principle of human equality is fundamental to the American worldview in the Unites States—despite the country's history of racial and gender discrimination and its stark disparities in wealth, status, and power.

Social Mobility

Most stratified societies offer at least some **social mobility**—upward or downward change in one's social class position. The prospects of improving status and wealth help to ease the strains inherent in any system of inequality.

Social mobility is most common in societies made up of independent nuclear families where the individual is closely tied to fewer people—especially when neolocal residence is the norm and it is assumed that individuals will leave their family of birth when they become adults. In such social settings—through hard work, occupational success, opportune marriage, and disassociation from the lower-class family in which they grew up—individuals can more easily move up in status and rank.

In societies where the extended family is the usual form, mobility tends to be more difficult, because each individual is strongly tied to many relatives. Typically,

---

[13] Nader, L. (1997). Controlling processes: Tracing the dynamic components of power. *Current Anthropology 38*, 271.

social mobility Upward or downward change in one's social class position in a stratified society.

Biocultural Connection

African Burial Ground Project   *by Michael Blakey*

In 1991, construction workers in lower Manhattan unearthed what turned out to be an African burial ground, the final resting place of some 10,000 enslaved African captives brought to New York in the 17th and 18th centuries to build the city and provide the labor for its thriving economy. The discovery sparked controversy as the African American public held protests and prayer vigils to stop the part of a federal building project that nearly destroyed the site.

As a biological anthropologist and African American, I had a unique opportunity to work together with the descendant African American community to develop a plan that included both extensive biocultural research and the humane retention of the sacred nature of the site, ultimately through reburial and the creation of a fitting memorial. The research also involved archaeological and historical studies that used a broad African diasporic context for understanding the lifetime experiences of these people who were enslaved and buried in New York.

Studying a sample population of 419 individuals from the burial ground, our team used an exhaustive range of skeletal biological methods, producing a database containing more than 200,000 observations of genetics, morphology, age, sex, growth and development, muscle development, trauma, nutrition, and disease. The bones revealed an unmistakable biocultural connection: physical wear and tear of an entire community brought on by the social institution of slavery.

We now know, based on this study, that life for Africans in colonial New York was characterized by poor nutrition, grueling physical labor that enlarged and often tore muscles, and death rates that were unusually high for 15- to 25-year-olds. Many of these young adults died soon after arriving on slaving ships. Few Africans lived past 40 years of age, and less than 2 percent lived beyond 55. Church records show strikingly different mortality trends for the Europeans of New York: About eight times as many English as Africans lived past 55 years of age, and mortality in adolescence and the early 20s was relatively low.

Skeletal research also showed that those Africans who died as children and were most likely to have been born in New York exhibited stunted and disrupted growth and exposure to high levels of lead pollution—unlike those who had been born in Africa (and were distinguishable because they had filed teeth). Fertility was very low among enslaved women in New York, and infant mortality was high. In these respects, this northern colonial city was very similar to South Carolina and the Caribbean to which its economy was tied—regions where conditions for African captives were among the harshest.

Individuals in this deeply troubling burial ground came from warring African states including Calibar, Asante, Benin, Dahomey, Congo, Madagascar, and many others—states that wrestled with the European demand for human chattel. They resisted their enslavement through rebellion, and they resisted their dehumanization by carefully burying their dead and preserving what they could of their cultures.

BIOCULTURAL QUESTION

Although few will question that slavery is an inhuman system of labor exploitation, was it economically rational for slave owners to mistreat their "human chattel," as indicated by the poor health, low fertility, and high mortality of African slaves in colonial New York?

© A. J. Giordano/Corbis SABA

Excavation of the African Burial Ground in lower Manhattan, New York City. The site is now a National Monument featuring a distinctive memorial that commemorates and communicates the story of this all-important historical archaeological project. The memorial is operated by the National Park Service.

Stratified societies are hierarchically structured into social classes that can be closed, like Hindu castes in traditional India, or open, as in the United States and most other industrialized societies based on capitalist economies. Either way, people ranking at the bottom of the social order tend to be powerless and poor. The open class system of the United States allows individuals to move upward in social rank and become one of the have-lots, but they may also slide down the social ladder and end up as have-nots. Today, almost 40 million women, men, and children (over 13 percent) in the United States are officially classified as "in poverty." About 3.5 million of these poor periodically experience being homeless in any given year, and about 150,000 are chronically homeless. A disproportionate number (40 percent) is African American, but most are Americans of European descent. Homelessness is growing due to a worsening global economy that has spiked unemployment and home foreclosures. Here we see a newly homeless couple cooking potatoes over a campfire at a homeless tent city in Sacramento, California.

if a person in such a society moves up to a higher social class, it is expected that he or she will help the rest of the family move up as well. In all likelihood, the extended families of the highly successful Ivory Coast soccer players described in this chapter's Globalscape have experienced upward social mobility through their ties to these athletes.

Societies that permit a great deal of upward and downward mobility are referred to as *open-class societies*—although the openness is apt to be less in practice than members hope or believe. In the United States, despite its rags-to-riches ideology, most mobility involves a move up or down only a notch; however, if this continues in a family over several generations, it may add up to a major change. Nonetheless, U.S. society makes much of the relatively rare examples of great upward mobility consistent with its cultural values and tends to overlook the numerous cases of little or no upward (not to mention downward) mobility.

Caste societies exemplify *closed-class societies* because of their severe institutionalized limits on social mobility. Yet, even the Hindu caste system, with its guiding ideology that all social hierarchies within it are eternally fixed, has a degree of flexibility and mobility. Although individuals cannot move up or down the caste hierarchy, whole groups can do so depending on claims they assert for higher ranking and on how well they can convince or manipulate others into acknowledging their claims.

Globalscape

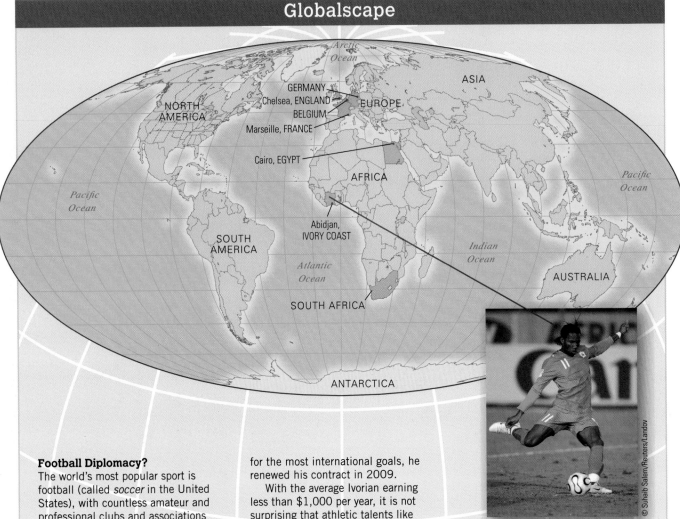

Football Diplomacy?

The world's most popular sport is football (called *soccer* in the United States), with countless amateur and professional clubs and associations on every continent. Globally, competitions are organized by the Federation Internationale de Football Association (FIFA), which organizes the World Cup every four years.

Football is a ticket to upward social mobility for many thousands of gifted, hardworking, and lucky players, including Didier Drogba, who plays for England's Chelsea Football Club and for his own country—the Ivory Coast national team, nicknamed "the Elephants." Born in Abidjan, the major city in this former French West African colony, Drogba is a southerner belonging to the Bete, one of the country's sixty-five ethnic groups. Recruited at an early age for a Belgian club and becoming a powerful striker, he was drafted by a French club in Marseille for $8 million. Chosen French Player of the Year in 2004, after just one season, he signed with England's champion team, Chelsea, for a record $42-million multi-year contract (not counting endorsements). Holding the team's record

for the most international goals, he renewed his contract in 2009.

With the average Ivorian earning less than $1,000 per year, it is not surprising that athletic talents like Drogba venture abroad for fortune and fame. In fact, all twenty-three members of the Ivory Coast national football team normally play abroad, most for wealthy European clubs. For the 2006 World Cup in Berlin, Germany, they trained together in Egypt, under a French coach. Meanwhile, their home country was wracked by a brutal civil war pitting southern ethnic groups against northern ones.

Ninety percent of the Ivory Coast's foreign exchange earnings come from cocoa beans. As a world-renowned sports star, Drogba appears in ads promoting the international sale of Ivorian chocolate. He also promotes peace: During the 2006 games, enthusiastically watched on television by millions of fellow Ivorians back home, team captain Drogba and his teammates (representing both southern and northern Ivory Coast) pleaded that the unity of the Elephants in the stadium would inspire fellow Ivorians to settle their conflict and reunite as a country. In 2007, a tentative

peace agreement was reached. That same year, Drogba became a Goodwill Ambassador for the United Nations Development Program, helping efforts to end extreme poverty in Africa.

Recently Drogba gained yet another opportunity to contribute to positive change: After years of facing anti-apartheid sporting boycotts, South Africa is proud to host the 2010 World Cup. Expected to draw a cumulative worldwide audience of 30 billion (more than the last Olympics), it promises to be the most spectacular sporting event of the year—and could be Drogba's biggest forum ever for inspiring international goodwill.

Global Twister How realistic is Drogba's idea that a national multi-ethnic soccer team competing for the World Cup can help unite its country's rival factions in a lasting way?

© Barcroft/Fame Pictures

Members of India's Gulabi Gang, sometimes referred to as "pink vigilantes." Poor rural woman, most of whom are Dalits (Untouchables and members of the lowest castes), they are collectively challenging the repressive status quo. Banding together, they demand justice—shaming and intimidating abusive men as well as corrupt officials who deny them equal access to water, farming supplies, and other resources.

During the past half century, political activism has stirred among members of India's vast underclass of Untouchables (outcasts) and lowest Sudra castes—collectively known as *Dalits*, a Sanskrit name meaning "crushed" or "suppressed." Historically discriminated against and economically exploited, they now number about 200 million scattered all across this vast South Asian country of 1.15 billion people. A growing political force, Dalits are now organizing themselves on local, regional, and even national levels. Their movement for civil rights is facilitated by increased access to digital communication technology.

Within the vast underclass of Dalits, women and children are especially vulnerable, barely surviving at the very bottom of Indian society. In recent years, however, Dalit women in many parts of India have joined hands with the intention of claiming social justice. Perhaps best known among them is a group in India's northern province of Uttar Pradesh who vigorously protest government discrimination and official corruption and strive to create opportunities for women. Dressed in vibrant pink saris and wielding traditional Indian fighting sticks known as

lathi, they are known as the Gulabi ("Pink") Gang. They demand justice—shaming and intimidating abusive men and corrupt officials who deny them equal access to water, farming supplies, and other resources. As one of these "pink vigilantes" puts it, "On my own I have no rights, but together, as the Gulabi Gang, we have power."[14]

The Dalit women's movement in India illustrates that even long-established and culturally entrenched hierarchical orders are not immune from being challenged, reformed, or even overthrown. Great disparities in wealth, power, and privilege may persist and even grow in many parts of the world, but there are notable social changes in the opposite direction. In the course of the 19th century, slavery was abolished and declared illegal nearly everywhere in the world. And in the last century, civil rights, women's rights, and other human rights movements resulted in social and legal reforms, as well as changes in ideas and values regarding hierarchical social orders in many countries.

---

[14] Dunbar, P. (2008, January 19). The pink vigilantes. www.dailymail.co.uk.

Questions for Reflection

1.   When young adults leave their parental home to go to college or find employment in a distant part of the country, they face the challenge of establishing new social relationships—ones that are not based on kinship but on common interest. To which common-interest associations do you belong and why?

2.   Do you use a networking platform such as Facebook or Twitter to stay in touch with relatives, friends, schoolmates, or colleagues? Where are these individuals in your digital social network geographically located? How often do you see them in real space, and is your interaction with them different in person than online?

3.   Do you think that members of an upper class or caste in a socially stratified system have a greater vested interest in the idea of law and order than those forced to exist on the bottom of such societies? Why or why not?

4.   Slavery in the United States was officially abolished in 1863, caste-based discrimination of Untouchables was constitutionally outlawed in India in 1950, and race-based segregation in South Africa officially ended with the abolition of apartheid in 1993. Considering these important political changes, do you think that social repression against these groups has now ended for good?

5.   In your own life, have you personally seen and experienced grouping by gender, age, and social status? What do you see as the positive and negative aspects of these groupings?

Suggested Readings

Bernardi, B. (1985). *Age class systems: Social institutions and policies based on age.* New York: Cambridge University Press.

This is a cross-cultural analysis of age as a device for organizing society and seeing to the distribution and rotation of power.

Bradfield, R. M. (1998). *A natural history of associations* (2nd ed.). New York: International Universities Press.

First published in 1973, this major anthropological study of common-interest associations attempts to provide a comprehensive theory of the origin of associations and their role in kin-based societies.

De Mott, B. (1990). *The imperial middle: Why Americans can't think straight about class.* New York: Morrow.

This critical commentary on the myth that the United States is a classless society demonstrates the great social and political costs of buying into that idea.

Price, T. D., & Feinman, G. M. (Eds.). (1995). *Foundations of social inequality.* New York: Plenum.

A collection of essays by various contributors examining the emergence of social inequality.

Sanday, P. R. (1981). *Female power and male dominance: On the origins of sexual inequality.* Cambridge, England: Cambridge University Press.

A cross-cultural study of various ways that male–female relations are organized in human societies. Demonstrating that male dominance is not inherent in those relations, the author suggests that dominance emerges in situations of stress as a result of chronic food shortages, migration, and colonial domination.

Smedley, A. (2007). *Race in North America: Origin and evolution of a worldview.* Boulder, CO: Westview.

A cultural historical analysis of the invention and development of the idea of race and the political ideological context from which it emerged. Smedley considers in this latest edition whether race is a universal concept, offers interpretations of the human genome, analyzes new racial categories on the U.S. census, including "mixed-race," and deftly counters claims of scientific racism.

Steady, F. C. (2005). *Women and collective action in Africa.* New York: Palgrave Macmillan.

This examination of women's movements and collective action in Africa begins in precolonial times and moves through to the present. It identifies and discusses the various arenas in which collective action has influenced and can influence, including women's traditional, mutual-aid, and religious associations.

Challenge Issue   In all societies, from the largest to the smallest, people face the challenge of who gets what, when, where, and how. This is the challenge of politics and involves mobilizing, contesting, and controlling power. In the political process, coalitions of individuals and groups defend or dispute an established social and economic order as they fight or negotiate with rival factions and foreign neighbors. Political organization takes many forms, of which the state is just one. State-organized societies are complex, large-scale, and stratified, with a centralized government supported by administrative bureaucracies largely paid for by society members or subjects. In traditional kin-ordered societies, such as tribes, political power is neither centralized nor monopolized, but shared by social networks of extended families, lineages, or clans. Representing their kinfolk, leaders gather periodically to discuss and resolve collective challenges. Among the Pashtun of Afghanistan and Pakistan, such a political assembly is known as a *jirga*—as shown in this photo of tribal elders attending a Loya Jirga (Grand Assembly) in Afghanistan's capital city of Kabul. Representing many different tribal communities, these elders are delegated to settle disputes, decide on treaties, discuss trade issues, and deal with other important political matters such as law and order in their war-torn homelands.

CHAPTER 12

Politics, Power, and Violence

Chapter Preview

How Are Power and Political Organization Different?

All human relations involve power, which refers to the ability of individuals or groups to impose their will upon others and make them do things even against their own wants or wishes. Power—from persuasion to violence—also operates on the societal level. The ability to impose or maintain order and to resolve conflicts requires political organization, which refers to the means by which a society maintains order internally and manages its affairs with other societies externally. It may be relatively uncentralized and informal, as in bands and tribes, or more centralized and formal, as in chiefdoms and states.

How Do Political Systems Obtain Support and Legitimacy?

In uncentralized systems, people depend primarily upon their kin-ordered local networks for support and protection. Politically represented by personally known leaders, they give loyalty and cooperation freely because there is power sharing in the political decision-making process. Centralized systems, by contrast, rely more heavily on institutionalized power, authority, and even coercion. Political organizations all over the world seek to justify their power as popularly mandated, divinely ordained, naturally given, or otherwise ideologically authorized.

How Are Social and Political Order Formed and Maintained?

Social controls may be internalized—in cultural values that are "built into" individuals—or externalized, in the form of sanctions. Positive sanctions encourage approved behavior, while negative sanctions discourage unacceptable behavior. Negative sanctions are called laws if they are formalized and enforced by an authorized political agency. Force or violence may be employed to impose or maintain order within a society or between groups. Although states and chiefdoms frequently practice warfare as a means of achieving political objectives, some groups condemn or avoid such organized violence.

Ironically, the social ties that facilitate human coexistence and cooperation also create the dynamics that may lead to social tension and possible violent conflict within and between groups. We see this in a wide range of situations: in riots among fans rooting for different soccer teams, in the gang violence in many North American cities, and in bloody conflicts between neighboring religious or ethnic groups such as Hindu Tamils and Buddhist Sinhalese, Muslim Palestinians and Jewish Israelis, and Roman Catholic Croats and Eastern Orthodox Serbs in southern Europe.

Therefore, every society must have ways and means for resolving internal conflicts and preventing a breakdown of its social order. Moreover, each society must possess the capacity to deal with neighboring societies in peaceful or troubled times. To meet these internal and external challenges, individuals and groups form coalitions capable of defending or contesting an established social and/or economic order and, if necessary, fighting or settling conflicts with rival factions and foreign neighbors. This is the business of *politics* (derived from the Greek word *polis,* referring to a self-governing "city").

Complex political structures known as *states* first began to emerge over 5,000 years ago. Commonly unstable, many have disappeared in the course of history, some temporarily and others forever. Some were annexed by other states, and others collapsed or fragmented into smaller political units. Although some present-day states are very old—such as Japan, which has endured as a state for almost 1,500 years—few are older than the United States, an independent country since 1783.

Despite the predominance of state societies today, there are still groups where political organization consists of flexible and informal kinship systems whose leaders lack real **power**—the ability of individuals or groups to impose their will upon others and make them do things even against their own wants or wishes. Between these two polarities of kin-ordered and state-organized political systems lies a world of variety.

---

power The ability of individuals or groups to impose their will upon others and make them do things even against their own wants or wishes.

political organization The way power is accumulated, arranged, executed, and structurally distributed and embedded in society; the means through which a society creates and maintains social order.

band A relatively small and loosely organized kin-ordered group that inhabits a common territory and that may split periodically into smaller extended family groups that are politically and economically independent.

Systems of Political Organization

The term **political organization** refers to the way power is accumulated, arranged, executed, and structurally embedded in society, whether in organizing a whale hunt, managing irrigated farmlands, staging a religious festival, or raising an army. In short, it is the means through which a society creates and maintains social order. It assumes a variety of forms among the peoples of the world, but anthropologists have simplified this complex subject by identifying four basic kinds of political systems: bands, tribes, chiefdoms, and states (Figure 12.1). The first two are uncentralized systems; the latter two are centralized.

Uncentralized Political Systems

Until recently, many non-Western peoples have had neither chiefs with established rights and duties nor any fixed form of government, as those who live in modern states understand the term. Instead, marriage and kinship have formed their principal means of social organization. The economies of these societies are primarily of a subsistence type, and populations are typically small.

Leaders do not have real power to force compliance with the society's customs or rules, but if individuals do not conform, they may become targets of scorn and gossip or even be banished. Important decisions are usually made in a collective manner by agreement among adults. Dissenting members may decide to act with the majority, or they may choose to adopt some other course of action, including leaving the group.

This egalitarian form of political organization provides great flexibility, which in many situations offers an adaptive advantage. Since power in these kin-ordered communities is shared, with nobody exercising exclusive control over collective resources or public affairs, individuals typically enjoy much more freedom than those who are part of larger and more complex political systems.

BANDS

The **band** is a relatively small and loosely organized kin-ordered group that inhabits a common territory and that may split periodically into smaller family groups that are politically and economically independent. Typically, bands are found among food foragers and other small-scale migratory communities where families organize into politically autonomous extended family groups that usually camp together as long as environmental and subsistence circumstances are favorable. Bands periodically break up into smaller groups to forage for food or visit other relatives. The band is probably the oldest form of political

TYPES OF POLITICAL ORGANIZATION
The symbol ➤ indicates that the attribute varies between less and more complex societies of that type.

	BAND	TRIBE	CHIEFDOM	STATE
MEMBERSHIP				
Number of people	Dozens and up	Hundreds and up	Thousands and up	Tens of thousands and up
Settlement pattern	Mobile	Mobile or fixed: 1 or more villages	Fixed: 2 or more villages	Fixed: Many villages and cities
Basis of relationships	Kin	Kin, descent groups	Kin, rank, and residence	Class and residence
Ethnicities and languages	1	1	1	1 or more
GOVERNMENT				
Decision making, leadership	"Egalitarian"	"Egalitarian" or Big Man	Centralized, hereditary	Centralized
Bureaucracy	None	None	None, or 1 or 2 levels	Many levels
Monopoly of force and information	No	No	No ➤ Yes	Yes
Conflict resolution	Informal	Informal	Centralized	Laws, judges
Hierarchy of settlement	No	No	No ➤ Paramount village or head town	Capital
ECONOMY				
Food production	No	No ➤ Yes	Yes ➤ Intensive	Intensive
Labor specialization	No	No	No ➤ Yes	Yes
Exchanges	Reciprocal	Reciprocal	Redistributive ("tribute")	Redistributive ("taxes")
Control of land	Band	Descent group	Chief	Various
SOCIETY				
Stratified	No	No	Yes, ranked by kin	Yes, by class or caste
Slavery	No	No	Some, small-scale	Some, large-scale
Luxury goods for elite	No	No	Yes	Yes
Public architecture	No	No	No ➤ Yes	Yes
Indigenous literacy	No	No	No ➤ Some	Often

Figure 12.1 This figure outlines the four basic types of political systems: bands, tribes, chiefdoms, and states. Bands and tribes are uncentralized political organizations; chiefdoms and states are centralized political organizations.

organization, since all humans were once food foragers and remained so until the development of farming and pastoralism over the past 10,000 years.

Since bands are egalitarian and small, numbering at most a few hundred people, no real need exists for formal, centralized political systems. Because everyone is related to—and knows on a personal basis—everyone else with whom dealings are required, there is high value placed on "getting along." Conflicts that do arise are usually settled informally through gossip, ridicule, direct negotiation, or mediation. When negotiation or mediation is used, the focus is on reaching a solution considered fair by all concerned parties, rather than on conforming to some abstract law or rule. Where all else fails, disgruntled individuals have the option of leaving to go live in another band where they have relatives or trying to establish a new community of their own.

Decisions affecting a band are made with the participation of all its adult members, with an emphasis on achieving consensus—a collective agreement—rather than a simple majority. Individuals become leaders by virtue of their abilities and serve in that capacity only as long as they retain the confidence of the community. They have no real power to force people to abide by their decisions. A leader who exceeds what people are willing to accept quickly loses followers.

An example of the informal nature of band leadership is found among the Ju/'hoansi Bushmen of the Kalahari Desert mentioned in earlier chapters. Each Ju/'hoansi band is composed of a group of families that live together, linked through kinship to one another and to the headman (or, less often, headwoman). Although each band has rights to the territory it occupies and the resources within it, two or more bands may range over the same land.

Toma, a Ju/'hoansi headman, is known to many people worldwide through the classic ethnographic film *The Hunters.*

The head, called the *kxau,* or "owner," is the focal point for the band's claims on the territory. He or she does not personally own the land or resources but symbolically represents the rights of band members to them. If the head leaves the area to live elsewhere, people turn to someone else to lead them.

The head coordinates band migration when resources are no longer adequate for subsistence in a particular habitat. This leader's major duty is to plan when and where the group will move, and when the move begins his or her position is at the head of the line. The leader selects the site for the new settlement and has the first choice of a spot for his or her own fire.

There are few other material rewards or duties. For example, a Ju/'hoansi head is not a judge and does not punish other band members. Wrongdoers are judged and held accountable by public opinion, usually expressed by gossip—which can play an important role in curbing socially unacceptable behavior. In small-scale communities where everyone is interdependent, public scolding or open expression of irritation may escalate into serious anger and lead to splits that jeopardize everyone's security.

Through gossip—talking behind someone's back and spreading rumors about behavior considered disruptive, shameful, or ridiculous—people accomplish several

objectives while avoiding the potential disruption of open confrontation. First, gossip underscores and reinforces the cultural standards of "normal" people who abide by the unwritten rules of proper conduct. At the same time, the gossip discredits those who violate standards of socially acceptable behavior. Furthermore, since gossip can damage a person's reputation and is often fueled by hidden jealousy or a secret desire to retaliate against someone considered too accomplished or successful, it may function like a leveling mechanism to reduce a real or perceived threat of someone becoming too dominant.

Another prime technique in small-scale societies for resolving disputes, or even avoiding them in the first place, is mobility. Those unable to get along with others of their group may feel pressured to move to another group where existing kinship ties give them rights of entry.

TRIBES

The second type of uncentralized authority system is the tribe. In anthropology, the term **tribe** refers to a wide range of kin-ordered groups that are politically integrated by some unifying factor and whose members share a common ancestry, identity, culture, language, and territory. Tribes may develop when a number of culturally related bands join together, peacefully settle disputes, participate in periodic visiting and communal feasting, and intermarry, for purposes of economic exchange and/or collective self-defense against common enemies.

Typically, though not invariably, a tribe has an economy based on some form of crop cultivation or herding. Since these subsistence methods usually yield more food than those of the food-foraging band, tribal membership is usually larger than band membership. While band population densities are usually less than one person per square mile, tribal population densities generally exceed that and may be as high as 250 per square mile. Greater population density brings a new set of problems to be solved as opportunities for bickering, begging, adultery, and theft increase markedly, especially among people living in permanent villages.

Each tribe consists of one or more self-supporting and self-governing local communities (including smaller kin-groups earlier discussed as bands) that may then form alliances with others for various purposes. As in the band, political organization in the tribe is informal and temporary. Whenever a situation requiring political integration of all or several groups within the tribe arises—perhaps for defense, to carry out a raid, to pool resources in times of scarcity, or to capitalize on a windfall that must be distributed quickly lest it spoil—groups come together to deal with the situation in a cooperative manner. When the problem is satisfactorily solved, each group then resumes autonomy.

In many tribal societies the organizing unit and seat of political authority is the clan, comprised of people

tribe In anthropology, refers to a range of kin-ordered groups that are politically integrated by some unifying factor and whose members share a common ancestry, identity, culture, language, and territory.

© Matt York/Associated Press

Shown here is a meeting of the Navajo Tribal Council, a nontraditional governing body created in response to requirements set by the U.S. government in order for the Navajo to exercise national sovereignty. Calling themselves *Dineh* ("the people"), the Navajo were traditionally organized in self-governing communities led by respected clan leaders known as *naat'aanii* ("the ones who orate"). These clan leaders led the collective decision-making process by their wise guidance and consensus building.

who consider themselves descended from a common ancestor. Within the clan, elders or headmen and/or headwomen regulate members' affairs and represent their clan in interactions with other clans. As a group, the elders of all the clans may form a council that acts within the community or for the community in dealings with outsiders. Because clan members usually do not all live together in a single community, clan organization facilitates joint action with members of related communities when necessary.

Leadership in tribal societies is also relatively informal, as is evident in a wide array of past and present examples. The Navajo Indians in the southwestern United States, for example, traditionally did not think of government as something fixed and all-powerful, and leadership was not vested in a central authority. A local leader was a man respected for his age, integrity, and wisdom. Therefore, people sought his advice frequently, but he had no formal means of control and could not force any decision on those who asked for his help. Group decisions were made by public consensus, although the most influential man usually played a key role in reaching a decision. Social mechanisms that induced members to abide by group decisions included gossip, criticism, withdrawal of cooperation, and the belief that antisocial actions caused sickness and other misfortune.

Another example of tribal leadership is the "Big Man." Common in the South Pacific, such men are leaders of localized descent groups or of a territorial group. The Big Man combines a measure of interest in his community's welfare with a great deal of cunning and calculation for his own personal gain. His political status is personal; he does not come to a position of power in any formal sense, nor is he elected. His prestige is the result of strategic acts that contribute to his political capital, raise him above most other tribe members, and attract to him a number of loyal followers who benefit from or depend on his success.

The Kapauku of Western New Guinea typify this form of political organization. Among them, the Big Man is called the *tonowi* or "rich one." To achieve this status, one must be male, wealthy, generous, and eloquent. Physical bravery and an ability to deal with the supernatural are also common *tonowi* characteristics, but they are not essential.

The *tonowi* functions as the headman of the village unit in a wide variety of situations within and beyond the community. He represents his group in dealing with outsiders and other villages and acts as negotiator and/or judge when disputes break out among his followers.

Because Kapauku culture places a high value on wealth, a well-to-do man is considered successful and admirable—provided he is also generous when it comes to making loans. Those who refuse to lend money to other

This Big Man from New Guinea is wearing his official regalia.

villagers may be ostracized, ridiculed, and, in extreme cases, actually executed by a group of warriors. Such responses to tightfistedness ensure that economic wealth is distributed throughout the group.

The *tonowi* acquires political power through his loans. Other villagers comply with his requests because they are in his debt (often interest-free) and they do not want to have to repay their loans. Those who have not yet borrowed from him may wish to do so in the future, so they, too, want to keep his goodwill.

The *tonowi* gains further support by taking into his household young male apprentices who receive business training along with food and shelter. He also gives them a loan that enables them to marry when the apprenticeship ends. In return, they act as messengers and bodyguards. After leaving, they remain tied to the *tonowi* by bonds of affection and gratitude. Political support also comes from the *tonowi*'s kinsmen, whose relationship brings with it varying obligations.

As discussed in an earlier chapter, the *tonowi*'s wealth comes from his success at breeding pigs, which is the focus of the entire Kapauku economy. It is not uncommon

for a *tonowi* to lose his fortune rapidly due to poor management or bad luck with his pigs. Thus the Kapauku political structure shifts frequently; as one man loses wealth and consequently power, another gains it and becomes a *tonowi*. By virtue of this flexibility in the political organization, no one *tonowi* accumulates much political capital or holds on to political power for too long.

Although it is far more common for tribal chiefs to be men, in some cultures women serve in such leadership positions, as discussed later in this chapter.

POLITICAL INTEGRATION BEYOND THE KIN-GROUP

Age sets, age grades, and common-interest groups discussed in the previous chapter are among the political integration mechanisms used by tribal societies. Cutting across territorial and kin-groupings, these organizations link members from different lineages and clans.

For example, among the Tiriki of East Africa (mentioned in the previous chapter) the Warrior age grade guards the village and grazing lands, while Judicial Elders resolve disputes. The oldest age grade, the Ritual Elders, advise on matters involving the well-being of all the Tiriki people. With the tribe's political affairs in the hands of the various age grades and their officers, this type of organization enables the largely independent kin-groups to solve conflicts and sometimes even avoid feuding between the lineages.

Another system of political integration found among tribes in many parts of the world is the common-interest association, also discussed in the previous chapter. For example, among many Indian peoples inhabiting North America's Great Plains in the 19th century, the band comprised the basic territorial and political unit within a tribe or ethnic group. In addition, however, there were a number of military societies or warrior clubs.

Among the Cheyenne, for instance, there were seven of these military societies. A boy might be invited to join one of these clubs when he achieved warrior status, whereupon he became familiar with the society's particular insignia, songs, and rituals. Beyond military functions, the warrior societies also had ceremonial and social functions.

The Cheyenne warriors' daily tasks consisted of overseeing activities in the village, protecting families on the move to the next camping site, and enforcing buffalo hunting rules. In addition, each warrior club had its own repertoire of dances, performed on special ceremonial occasions. Since each Cheyenne band had identical military societies bearing identical names, the societies served to integrate the entire tribe for military and political purposes.[1]

---

[1] Hoebel, E. A. (1960). *The Cheyennes: Indians of the Great Plains*. New York: Holt, Rinehart & Winston.

Centralized Political Systems

In bands and tribes, political authority is not centralized, and each group is economically and politically autonomous. Political organization is vested in kinship, age, and common-interest groups. Populations are small and relatively homogeneous, with people engaged for the most part in the same sorts of activities throughout their lives.

However, as a society's social life becomes more complex—as population rises, technology becomes more intricate, and specialization of labor and trade networks produce surplus goods—the opportunity increases for some individuals or groups to exercise control at the expense of others. In such societies, political authority and power are concentrated in a single individual (the chief) or in a body of individuals (the state).

CHIEFDOMS

A **chiefdom** is a regional polity (a politically organized society) in which two or more local groups are organized under a single ruling individual—the chief—who is at the head of a ranked hierarchy of people. An individual's status in such a polity is determined by the closeness of his or her relationship to the chief. Those closest are officially superior and receive deferential treatment from those of lower ranks.

The office of the chief is usually for life and often hereditary. Typically, it passes from a man to his son or his sister's son, depending on whether descent is traced patrilineally or matrilineally.

Unlike the headman or headwoman in bands and tribes, the leader of a chiefdom is generally a true authority figure, whose right to make final decisions, give commands, and enforce obedience serves to unite members in all affairs and at all times. For example, a chief can distribute land among community members and recruit people into military service.

Chiefdoms have a recognized hierarchy consisting of major and minor authorities who control major and minor subdivisions. Such an arrangement is, in effect, a chain of command, linking leaders at every level. It serves to bind groups in the heartland to the chief's headquarters, be it a mud and dung hut or a marble palace. Although leaders of chiefdoms are almost always men, in some cultures a politically astute wife, sister, or single daughter of a deceased male chief could inherit such a powerful position as well.

Chiefs usually control the economic activities of those who fall under their political rule. Typically, chiefdoms involve redistributive systems, and the chief has control over surplus goods and perhaps even over the community's labor force. Thus, he (and sometimes she) may demand a quota of rice from farmers, which will then be redistributed to the entire community. Similarly, laborers may be recruited to build irrigation works, a palace, or a temple.

The chief may also amass a great amount of personal wealth and pass it on to offspring. Land, cattle, and luxury goods produced by specialists can be collected by the chief and become part of the power base. Moreover, high-ranking families of the chiefdom may engage in the same practice and use their possessions as evidence of noble status.

An example of this form of political organization may be seen among the Kpelle of Liberia in West Africa.[2] Among them is a class of *paramount chiefs,* each of whom presides over one of the Kpelle chiefdoms (each chiefdom is now a district of the Liberian state). The paramount chiefs' traditional tasks are hearing disputes, preserving order, seeing to the upkeep of trails, and performing various other supervisory functions. In addition, they are now salaried officials of the Liberian government, mediating between it and their own people.

Also, a paramount chief receives government commissions on taxes and court fees collected within his chiefdom, plus a commission for providing laborers for the rubber plantations. Moreover, he gets a stipulated amount of rice from each household and gifts from people who come to request favors and intercessions. In keeping with his exalted station in life, a paramount chief has at his disposal uniformed messengers, a literate clerk, and the symbols of wealth: many wives, embroidered gowns, and freedom from manual labor.

In a ranked hierarchy beneath each Kpelle paramount chief are several lesser chiefs: one for each district within the chiefdom, one for each town within a district, and one for each quarter of all but the smallest towns. Each acts as a kind of lieutenant for his chief of the next higher rank and also serves as a liaison between him and those of lower rank. Unlike paramount or district chiefs, who are comparatively remote, town and quarter chiefs are readily accessible to people at the local level.

---

[2] Gibbs, J. L., Jr. (1965). The Kpelle of Liberia. In J. L. Gibbs, Jr. (Ed.), *Peoples of Africa* (pp. 216–218). New York: Holt, Rinehart & Winston.

chiefdom A regional polity in which two or more local groups are organized under a single chief, who is at the head of a ranked hierarchy of people.

A Kpelle chief in Liberia, West Africa, listens to a dispute in his district. Settling disputes is one of several ongoing traditional tasks that fall to paramount chiefs among Kpelle people.

Traditionally, chiefdoms in all parts of the world have been highly unstable, with lesser chiefs trying to take power from higher-ranking chiefs or paramount chiefs vying with one another for supreme power. In precolonial Hawaii, for example, war was the way to gain territory and maintain power; great chiefs set out to conquer one another in an effort to become paramount chief of all the islands. When one chief conquered another, the loser and all his nobles were dispossessed of all property and were lucky if they escaped alive. The new chief then appointed his own supporters to positions of political power. As a consequence, there was very little continuity of government or religious administration.

STATES

The **state** is a political institution established to manage and defend a complex, socially stratified society occupying a defined territory. The most formal of political systems, the state is organized and directed by a government that has the capacity and authority to make laws and to use military force to defend or expand its territories. Some of the smallest states today measure less than 2.59 square kilometers (1 square mile), while the largest cover over 15.5 million square kilometers (6 million square miles).

Often states are ruled by coalitions of well-connected and wealthy individuals or groups that have accumulated and fought over power. Possessing the resources (including

money, weapons, and manpower), these ruling elites exercise power by institutional means, such as a government and bureaucracy, which allow them to arrange and rearrange a society's social and economical order.

A large population in a state-organized society requires increased food production and wider distribution networks. Together, these lead to a transformation of the landscape by way of irrigation and terracing, carefully managed crop rotation cycles, and intensive competition for resources—such as clearly demarcated lands, roads, and enough farmers and other rural workers to support market systems and a specialized urban sector. Under such conditions, corporate groups that stress exclusive membership proliferate, ethnic differentiation and ethnocentrism become more pronounced, and the potential for social conflict increases dramatically. Given these circumstances, state institutions, which minimally involve a bureaucracy, a military, and (usually) an official religion, provide the means for numerous and diverse groups to function together as an integrated whole.

Every state, whatever its population, claims sovereign power over its subjects, controls social tension, represses or punishes violent protest by angry factions, and protects its territorial borders against hostile forces, including neighboring states. Throughout history, neighboring states have often had conflicts over territorial boundaries.

Since their first appearance some 5,000 years ago, political states have been anything but permanent. They are often unstable, and many have disappeared in the course of time, some temporarily and others forever. Some were annexed by other states, and others collapsed or fragmented into smaller political units. As already noted, while some present-day states are very old—such as Japan, which has

state In anthropology, a political institution established to manage and defend a complex, socially stratified society occupying a defined territory.

© Reuters/Corbis

After the British empire pulled out of South Asia over sixty years ago, that subcontinent erupted in warfare between Muslims and Hindus. The region was then carved up along religious lines into Pakistan and India. Since then, these countries have fought three wars against each other. The tense political relations between these nuclear-armed rivals are symbolically displayed in the military border-closing ritual at Wagah, pictured here. Every evening, Pakistani Pathan guards, dressed in black uniforms and fan-tailed headgear of the same color, face India's border guards, dressed in khaki uniforms and hats adorned with scarlet fan-tails. Brandishing rifles and parading in goose-step, they greet each other, lock gates, and lower their national flags.

been a state for almost 1,500 years—few are older than the United States. Nowhere have states even begun to show the staying power of less centralized political systems.[3]

From the perspective of the political elite in control, the state's formation and endurance are something positive—evidence of progress. This view is not necessarily shared by those who are not represented in the political decision-making process or who fail to benefit from the system. This is especially the case when subjects of the state are forced to pay for the maintenance of the bureaucracy and public works in the form of state-imposed taxes or tribute payments in goods or labor services.

An important distinction to make at this point is between state and nation. As noted in Chapter 1, a **nation** is a people who share a collective identity based on a common culture, language, territorial base, and history.[4] Today, there are roughly 200 internationally recognized states in the world, most of which did not exist before the end of World War II (1945). By contrast, there are about 5,000 nations (including tribes), many of which have existed since time immemorial. Rarely do state and nation coincide, as they do, for example, in Iceland, Japan, and Swaziland.

About 73 percent of the world's states are *pluralistic societies,* defined in an earlier chapter as societies in which two or more ethnic groups or nationalities are politically organized into one territorial state but maintain their cultural differences.[5] Often, smaller nations (including tribes) and other groups find themselves at the mercy of one or more dominant nations or ethnic groups controlling the state. Frequently facing discrimination or repression, some minority nations seek to improve their political position by founding an independent state. In the process, they usually encounter stiff opposition, with sometimes violent confrontations.

So it is with the Chechens, a small Sunni Muslim nation within the Russian Federation, for example, or the Palestinians (Sunni Muslims and Christians), who continue to struggle for political independence as a nation against the Jewish state of Israel, which dominates their homeland. And so it is with the Kurds, an Iranian-speaking Sunni Muslim nation whose homeland is subdivided between the modern states of Turkey, Iraq, and Iran. As members of a cross-border nation, many Kurds are willing to fight for political autonomy or even national independence,

[3] Diamond, J. (2005). *Collapse: How societies choose to fail or succeed.* New York: Viking Penguin.

[4] Clay, J. W. (1996). What's a nation? In W. A. Haviland & R. J. Gordon (Eds.), *Talking about people* (2nd ed., p. 188). Mountain View, CA: Mayfield.

[5] van den Berghe, P. L. (1992). The modern state: Nation builder or nation killer? *International Journal of Group Tensions 92* (3), 193.

nation A people who share a collective identity based on a common culture, language, territorial base, and history.

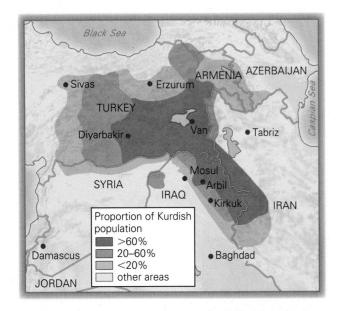

Figure 12.2 The Kurds—most of whom live in Turkey, Iran, and Iraq—are an example of a nation without a state. With a population of about 27 million, they are much more numerous than Australians, for example. In fact, the total population of the four Scandinavian countries—Denmark, Finland, Norway, and Sweden—is less than that of the Kurds who have no independent country of their own.

but they are forced to accept their minority status in these three neighboring states.

Covering almost 200,000 square kilometers (77 square miles), the cross-border region known as Kurdistan was historically organized in several semi-independent chiefdoms or principalities called *emirates*. After a series of long wars between the Safavid Iranian and Ottoman Turkish empires in the 16th century, these powerful rivals split the Kurdish homeland between them. After the First World War, several new states, including Iraq and Syria, were carved out of the collapsed Ottoman empire and split from what is now the Republic of Turkey. Kurds as well as Arabs, Armenians, Turks, and other minorities, and Muslims as well as Christians, coexist in Kurdistan (Figure 12.2).

Forming a new state is a political challenge. Violent confrontation is typically the way that some nations have forged their own state. Such armed struggle recently made it possible for Bosnia, a southern European country primarily inhabited by Sunni Muslims, to split from Serb-dominated Yugoslavia. But other nations have been able to peacefully establish statehood, as exemplified by Papua New Guinea in the southern Pacific, which became an independent state in 1975.

An important aspect of the state is its delegation of authority to maintain order within and outside its borders.

Police, foreign ministries, war ministries, and other bureaucracies function to control and punish disruptive acts of crime, dissension, and rebellion. By such agencies the state asserts authority impersonally and in a consistent, predictable manner. Western forms of government, like that of the United States, of course, are state governments, and their organization and workings are undoubtedly familiar to most everyone.

An example of a not-so-familiar state is Swaziland in southern Africa. One of the world's few true nation-states, it is home to the Swazi—a Bantu-speaking people.[6] Although the Swazi are primarily farmers, cattle raising is also practiced—and highly esteemed. In fact, the ritual, wealth, and power of their authority system are all intricately linked with cattle.

The traditional Swazi authority system was characterized by a highly developed dual monarchy (now a thing of the past), a hereditary aristocracy, and elaborate kinship rituals, as well as by statewide age sets. The king and his mother were the central figures of national activity, linking all the people of the Swazi state: They presided over higher courts, summoned national gatherings, controlled age classes, allocated land, disbursed national wealth, took precedence in ritual, and helped organize important social events.

Advising the king were the senior princes, who were usually his uncles and half-brothers. Between the king and the princes were two specially created *tinsila*, or blood brothers, who were chosen from certain common clans. These men were his shields, protecting him from evildoers and serving him in intimate personal situations. In addition, the king was guided by two *tindvuna*, or counselors, one civil and one military. The people of the state made their opinions known through two councils: the *liqoqo*, or privy council (dissolved in 1986), composed of senior princes, and the *libanda*, or council of state, composed of chiefs and headmen and open to all adult males of the state. The *liqoqo* could advise the king, make decisions, and carry them out. For example, they could rule on questions about land, education, traditional ritual, court procedure, and transport.

---

[6] Kuper, H. (1965). The Swazi of Swaziland. In J. L. Gibbs, Jr. (Ed.), *Peoples of Africa* (pp. 475–512). New York: Holt, Rinehart & Winston.

Swazi government extended from the smallest local unit—the homestead—upward to the central administration. The head of a homestead had legal and administrative powers; he was responsible for the crimes of those under him, controlled their property, and spoke for them before his superiors. On the district level, political organization was similar to that of the central government. The relationship between a district chief, however, and his subjects was personal and familiar; he knew all the families in his district. To prevent a district chief from becoming too autocratic, his subjects could easily transfer their allegiance to a more responsive chief. Swazi officials held their positions for life and were dismissed only for treason or witchcraft. Incompetence, drunkenness, and stupidity were frowned upon, but they were not considered to be sufficient grounds for dismissal.

Political Systems and the Question of Legitimacy

Whatever a society's political system, it must find some way to obtain and retain the people's allegiance. In uncentralized systems, where every adult participates in all decision making, loyalty and cooperation are freely given because each person is considered a part of the political system. As the group grows larger, however, and the organization becomes more formal, the problem of obtaining and keeping public support becomes more complicated.

Centralized political systems may rely upon coercion as a means of social control. This, however, carries a measure of risk since the personnel needed to apply force often must be numerous and may grow to be a political power. Also, the emphasis on force typically creates resentment and may lessen cooperation. Thus police states are generally short-lived; most societies choose less extreme forms of social coercion. In the United States, this tendency is reflected in the increasing emphasis placed on cultural controls, as we discuss later in this chapter. Laura Nader (see Anthropologist of Note) is well known for her anthropological research concerning issues of power, including social and cultural control.

Also basic to the political process is the concept of **legitimacy,** or the right of political leaders to govern—to hold, use, and allocate power. Legitimacy is a form of support for a political system; unlike force, legitimacy is based on the socially accepted customs, rules, or laws that bind and hold a people together as a collective whole. For example, among the Kapauku of Western New Guinea discussed a few pages back, the legitimacy of the *tonowi's*

power comes from his wealth; the head of the traditional Dahomey state in what is now Benin, West Africa, acquired legitimacy through his age, as he was always the oldest living male; and the kings of Hawaii and of France (before its bloody revolution in 1789) and the emperor of Japan (before being defeated by the Allies in 1945) were thought to have a divine right to rule.

Power based on legitimacy results in *authority*. It is distinct from power based solely on force: Obedience to authority results from the belief that obedience is "right"; compliance to power based on force results from fear of being deprived of liberty, physical well-being, life, or material property. Thus power based on legitimacy is symbolic and depends upon the positive expectations of those who recognize and accept it. If the expectations are not met regularly (if the head of state fails to deliver economic prosperity or the leader is continuously unsuccessful in preventing or dealing with calamities), the legitimacy of the recognized power figure erodes or may collapse altogether.

Politics and Religion

Religion is often intricately connected with politics. Frequently it is religion that legitimizes the political order and leadership. Religious beliefs may influence or provide authoritative approval to customary rules and laws. For example, acts that people believe to be sinful, such as murder, are often illegal as well.

In both industrial and nonindustrial societies, belief in the supernatural is important and is reflected in people's political institutions. One place where the effect of religion on politics was well exemplified was in medieval Europe: Holy wars were fought over the smallest matter; labor was mobilized to build immense cathedrals in honor of the Virgin Mary and other saints; kings and queens ruled by "divine right" and (in the West) pledged allegiance to the pope and asked his blessing in all important ventures, whether marital or martial.

In Peru, the divine ruler of the Inca empire proclaimed absolute authority based on the proposition that he was descended from the Sun God. Mexico's ancient Aztec state was also a politico-religious one, having a divine ruler and engaging in nearly constant warfare

legitimacy The right of political leaders to govern—to hold, use, and allocate power—on the socially accepted customs, rules, or laws that bind and hold a people together as a collective whole.

Laura Nader (b. 1930)

Laura Nader has stood out among her peers from the start of her career in 1960, when she became the first woman faculty member in the anthropology department at the University of California, Berkeley.

Nader and her three siblings grew up in Winsted, Connecticut, children of immigrants from Lebanon. As she recalls, "My dad left Lebanon for political reasons, and when he came to the land of the free, he took it seriously. So we were raised to believe that you should be involved in public issues." They were also taught to question assumptions. Both Nader and her younger brother Ralph have made careers of doing this. She is an anthropologist noted for her

Courtesy of Dr. Laura Nader

cross-cultural research on law, justice, and social control and their connection to power structures. He is a consumer advocate and frequent U.S. presidential candidate who is a watchdog on issues of public health and the safety and quality of life.

Laura Nader's undergraduate studies included a study-abroad year in Mexico. Later, while earning her doctorate in anthropology at Radcliffe College, she returned to Mexico to do fieldwork in a Zapotec Indian peasant village in the Sierra Madre Mountains of Oaxaca. Reflecting on this and subsequent research, she says, "In the 1950s, when I went to southern Mexico, I was studying how the Zapotec organize their lives, what they do with their problems, what they do when they go to court. And when I came back to this country, I started looking at American equivalents, at how Americans solve their consumer and service complaints."

Nader's first decade of teaching at Berkeley coincided with the Vietnam War, an era when the campus was in a perpetual state of turmoil with students demonstrating for peace and civil rights. Turning into a scholar-activist, she called upon colleagues to "study up" and do research on the world's power elite. "The study of man," she wrote in 1972, "is

confronted with an unprecedented situation: Never before have a few, by their actions and inactions, had the power of life and death over so many members of the species."

To date, the results of Nader's own research have appeared in over a hundred publications. Among these are her numerous books, including *Naked Science—Anthropological Inquiry into Boundaries, Power, and Knowledge* (1996) and *The Life of the Law: Anthropological Projects* (2002).

Playing a leading role in the development of the anthropology of law, Nader has taken on specialists in the fields of law, children's issues, nuclear energy, and science (including her own profession), critically questioning the basic assumptions ("central dogmas") under which these experts operate. She presses her students to do the same—to think critically, question authority, and break free from the "controlling processes" of the power elite. In 2000, Nader accepted one of the highest honors of the American Anthropological Association—an invitation to give the distinguished lecture at its annual gathering.

Adapted from "Interview with Laura Nader." (2000, November). California Monthly.

to procure captives for human sacrifices thought necessary to assuage or please the gods. Modern Iran was proclaimed an "Islamic republic" in the 1979 revolution that toppled the authoritarian regime of the shah, and its first head of state, Ayatollah Ruhollah Khomeini, was the most holy of all Shiite Muslim holy men. As the highest-ranking religious and political authority of the country, he was proclaimed its supreme leader, a position he held until his death ten years later. Since then, Iran remains a theocratic republic with a high-ranking Shia Muslim cleric, or ayatollah, as its most powerful authority. The country's democratically elected parliament and president are subordinate to the ayatollah.

The fact that the president of the United States takes the oath of office by swearing on the Bible is another instance of the use of religion to legitimize political power, as is the phrase "one nation, under God" in the Pledge of Allegiance. On U.S. coins is the phrase "In God We

Trust," many meetings of government bodies begin with a prayer or invocation, and the phrase "so help me God" is routinely used in legal proceedings. Despite an official separation of church and state, religious legitimization of government lingers.

Political Leadership and Gender

Irrespective of cultural configuration or type of political organization, women hold important positions of political leadership far less often than men. Furthermore, when they do occupy publicly recognized offices, their power and authority rarely exceed those of men. But significant exceptions occur. Historically, one might cite the female chiefs, or *sachems,* of Algonquian Indian

Visual Counterpoint

In contrast to countries such as the United States, where religion and state are constitutionally separated, countries such as Iran and Great Britain permit a much closer relationship between political and religious affairs. For instance, Iran's current religious leader, Ayatollah Ali Khamenei, is not only the supreme spiritual leader but also his country's highest political authority. In England, Queen Elizabeth is not only her country's nominal head of state but also "the Supreme Governor" of the Church of England, which entitles her to appoint the Anglican bishops in that state.

communities in southern New England, as well as powerful queens in several Asian, African, and European monarchies.

Perhaps most notable is Queen Victoria, the long-reigning queen of England, Scotland, Wales, and Ireland. Also recognized as monarch in a host of colonies all over the world, Victoria even acquired the title "Empress of India" and became the world's wealthiest and most powerful leader. During her reign from 1837 until 1901, the British empire encompassed 20 percent of the land area of the world and even more of its population. London, its capital, was the world's financial center.

In addition to inheriting high positions of political leadership, a growing number of women have also been elected as presidents, chancellors, or prime ministers. Countries with elected female heads of state now or in recent years include Argentina, Indonesia, Ireland, Sri Lanka, Norway, India, Liberia, Chile, Germany, and the Philippines, to mention just a few. While such high-profile female leadership is still relatively rare, women regularly

enjoy as much political power as men in a number of societies. In band societies, for example, it is common for females to have as much of a say in public affairs as males, even though more often than not men are the nominal leaders of their groups.

Among the Iroquois nations of New York State, all leadership positions above the household and clan levels were, without exception, filled by men. Thus men held all positions on the village and tribal councils, as well as on the great council of the Iroquois Confederacy. However, they were completely beholden to women, for only women could nominate men to high office. Moreover, women actively lobbied the men on the councils and could have someone removed from office whenever it suited them.

Lower visibility in politics does not necessarily indicate that women lack power in political affairs. And just as there are various ways in which women play a role behind the scenes, so it is when they have more visible roles, as in the traditional dual-sex system of the Igbo in Nigeria, West Africa. Among the Igbo, each political unit had separate

political institutions for men and women, so that both had an autonomous sphere of authority, as well as an area of shared responsibility.[7] At the head of each political unit was a male *obi,* considered the head of government although in fact he presided over the male community, and a female *omu,* the acknowledged mother of the whole community but in practice concerned with the female section. Unlike a queen (though both she and the *obi* were crowned), the *omu* was neither the *obi's* wife nor the previous *obi's* daughter.

Just as the *obi* had a council of dignitaries to advise him and act as a check against any arbitrary exercise of power, the *omu* was served by a council of women in equal number to the *obi's* male councilors. The duties of the *omu* and her councilors involved such tasks as establishing rules and regulations for the community market (marketing was a woman's activity) and hearing cases involving women brought to her from throughout the town or village. If such cases also involved men, then she and her council would cooperate with the *obi* and his council.

In the Igbo system, then, women managed their own affairs, and their interests were represented at all levels of government. Moreover, they had the right to enforce their decisions and rules with sanctions similar to those employed by men, including strikes, boycotts, and "sitting on" someone, including a man:

> To "sit on" or "make war on" a man involved gathering at his compound, sometimes late at night, dancing, singing scurrilous songs which detailed the women's grievances against him and often called his manhood into question, banging on his hut with the pestles women used for pounding yams, and perhaps demolishing his hut or plastering it with mud and roughing him up a bit. A man might be sanctioned in this way for mistreating his wife, for violating the women's market rules, or for letting his cows eat the women's crops. The women would stay at his hut throughout the day, and late into the night if necessary, until he repented and promised to mend his ways.[8]

When the British imposed colonial rule on the Igbo in the late 1800s, they failed to recognize the autonomy and power of the women. One reason for that oversight

---

[7] Okonjo, K. (1976). The dual-sex political system in operation: Igbo women and community politics in midwestern Nigeria. In N. Hafkin & E. Bay (Eds.), *Women in Africa.* Stanford, CA: Stanford University Press.

[8] Van Allen, J. (1997). Sitting on a man: Colonialism and the lost political institutions of Igbo women. In R. Grinker & C. Steiner (Eds.), *Perspectives on Africa* (p. 450). Boston: Blackwell.

Liberian President Ellen Johnson Sirleaf inspects members of the Liberian police after taking the presidential oath in January 2006. The first female president on the African continent, Sirleaf is a Harvard-educated economist who took the world by surprise when she won the top office in her war-torn and poverty-stricken country. Since becoming president, she has managed to eliminate most of Liberia's international debt, promote investment in the country, and significantly increase its economic output. Serious challenges continue, but she has done much to change Liberia's course.

was that the British were blinded by the cultural values of their own male-dominated society, in which the domestic sphere was seen as the ideal place for women. Ironically, as mentioned earlier, the powerful ruler of the British empire at the time was Queen Victoria. Nevertheless, the British introduced "reforms" that destroyed traditional forms of female autonomy and power without providing alternative forms in exchange. As a result, Igbo women lost much of their traditional equality and became subordinate to men.

Political Organization and the Maintenance of Order

Political organization always includes means of maintaining order that ensure people behave in acceptable ways and define what action will be taken when they do not. In chiefdoms and states, some sort of authority has the power to regulate the affairs of society. In bands and tribes, however, people behave generally as they are expected to, without the direct intervention of any centralized political authority. To a large degree, gossip, criticism, fear of supernatural forces, and the like serve as effective deterrents to antisocial behavior.

Internalized Controls

Individuals who are well-socialized and enculturated members of their own society typically acquire an internalized set of shared beliefs and values about what is proper and what is not. These values are so deeply ingrained that each person becomes personally responsible for his or her own conduct. **Cultural control** may be thought of as an internalized form of self-control, as opposed to **social control,** which involves external enforcement through open coercion.

Cultural controls are embedded in our consciousness and may rely on deterrents such as fear of supernatural punishment—ancestral spirits sabotaging the hunting, for example—and magical retaliation. Like the devout Christian who avoids sinning for fear of hell, the individual expects some sort of punishment, even though no one in the community may be aware of the wrongdoing.

Cultural controls can also be framed in positive terms, with customary ways and means that encourage individual sacrifice for the common good. For example, many cultures honor traditions of giving to, or volunteering for, charitable or humanitarian institutions. Performed out of a desire to help those in need, such personal sacrifices (from the Latin *sacer*, "holy," and *facere*, "making") may be motivated by a spiritual or religious worldview. Often deeply rooted in basic ideas of a wider community and reciprocity, they are also cultural controls against self-seeking, self-serving, greedy opportunism that threatens the well-being of a larger community.

INTERNALIZED CONTROLS AMONG THE WAPE OF PAPUA NEW GUINEA

As an example of how internalized controls serve to keep people in line, we may look at the Wape people of Papua New Guinea, who believe the spirits of deceased ancestors roam lineage lands, protecting them from trespassers and helping their hunting descendants by driving game their way.[9] These ancestral spirits also punish those who have wronged them or their descendants by preventing hunters from finding game or causing them to miss their shots, thereby depriving people of much needed meat.

Nowadays, the Wape hunt with shotguns, which the community purchases for the use of one man, whose job it is to hunt for all the others. The cartridges used in the hunt, however, are invariably supplied by individual community members. Thus if the gunman shoots and misses, it is not viewed as his failing. Rather, it is because the owner of the fired shell, or some close relative, has quarreled or wronged another person whose deceased relative is securing revenge by causing the hunter to miss. Or, if the gunman cannot even find game, it is because vengeful ancestors have chased the animals away. As a proxy hunter for the villagers, the gunman is potentially subject to sanctions by ancestral spirits in response to collective wrongs by those for whom he hunts.

For the Wape, then, successful hunting depends upon avoiding quarrels and maintaining tranquility within the community so as not to antagonize anybody's deceased ancestor. Unfortunately, complete harmony is impossible to achieve in any human community, and the Wape are no exception. When hunting is poor, the gunman must discover what quarrels and wrongs have occurred within his village to identify the proper ancestral spirits to appeal to for renewed success. Usually, this is done in a special meeting where confessions of wrongdoing may be forthcoming. If not, questioning accusations are bandied about until resolution occurs, but even with no resolution, the meeting must end amicably to prevent new antagonisms. In this way, everyone's behavior comes under public scrutiny, reminding all of what is expected of them and encouraging villagers to avoid acts that will cast them in an unfavorable light.

---

[9] Mitchell, W. E. (1973, December). A new weapon stirs up old ghosts. *Natural History Magazine,* 77–84.

---

cultural control Control through beliefs and values deeply internalized in the minds of individuals.
social control External control through open coercion.

Formal sanctions may involve some form of regulated combat, seen here as armed dancers near Mount Hagen in New Guinea demand redress for murder.

Externalized Controls

Because internalized controls are not wholly sufficient even in bands and tribes, every society develops externalized social controls known as **sanctions** designed to encourage conformity to social norms. Operating within social groups of all sizes and involving a mix of cultural and social controls, sanctions may vary significantly within a given society, but they fall into one of two categories: positive or negative. Positive sanctions consist of incentives to conformity such as awards, titles, and recognition by one's neighbors. Negative sanctions consist of threats such as imprisonment, fines, corporal punishment, or ostracism from the community for violation of social norms.

For sanctions to be effective, they must be applied consistently, and they must be generally known among members of the society. Even if some individuals are not convinced of the advantages of social conformity, they are still more likely to obey society's rules than to accept the consequences of not doing so.

Sanctions may also be either formal or informal, depending on whether or not a legal statute is involved. In the United States, the man who goes shirtless in shorts to a church service may be subject to a variety of informal sanctions, ranging from disapproving glances from the

clergy to the chuckling of other parishioners. If, however, he were to show up without any clothing at all, he would be subject to the formal negative sanction of arrest for indecent exposure. Only in the second instance would he have been guilty of breaking the law.

Formal sanctions, such as laws, are always organized, because they attempt to precisely and explicitly regulate people's behavior, whether they are peacefully trading with others or confronting others on a battlefield. Other examples of organized sanctions include, on the positive side, military decorations and monetary rewards. On the negative side are loss of face, exclusion from social life and its privileges, seizure of property, imprisonment, and even bodily mutilation or death.

Informal sanctions emphasize cultural control and are diffuse in nature, involving spontaneous expressions of approval or disapproval by members of the group or community. They are, nonetheless, very effective in enforcing a large number of seemingly unimportant customs. Because most people want to be accepted, they are willing to acquiesce to the rules that govern dress, eating, and conversation, even in the absence of actual laws.

Social Control Through Witchcraft

In societies with or without centralized political systems, witchcraft sometimes functions as an agent of social control and involves both internal and external controls. An individual will think twice before offending a neighbor if

sanction An externalized social control designed to encourage conformity to social norms.

convinced that the neighbor could retaliate by resorting to black magic. Similarly, individuals may not wish to be accused of practicing witchcraft, and so they behave with greater circumspection.

Among the Azande of the Sudan, people who think they have been bewitched may consult an oracle, who, after performing the appropriate mystical rites, then may establish or confirm the identity of the offending witch.[10] Confronted with this evidence, the witch will usually agree to cooperate in order to avoid any additional trouble. Should the victim die, the relatives of the deceased may choose to make magic against the witch, ultimately accepting the death of some villager as evidence of both guilt and the efficacy of their magic.

For the Azande, witchcraft provides not only a sanction against antisocial behavior but also a means of dealing with natural hostilities and death. No one wishes to be thought of as a witch, and surely no one wishes to be victimized by one. By institutionalizing their emotional responses, the Azande successfully maintain social order.

Social Control Through Law

In Western society, someone who commits an offense against another person may become subject to a series of complex legal proceedings. In criminal cases the primary concern is to assign and punish guilt rather than to help out the victim. The offender will be arrested by the police; tried before a judge and perhaps a jury; and,

---

[10] Evans-Pritchard, E. E. (1937). *Witchcraft, oracles and magic among the Azande.* London: Oxford University Press.

depending on the severity of the crime, may be fined, imprisoned, or even executed. Rarely does the victim receive restitution or compensation. Throughout this chain of events, the accused party is dealt with by police, judges, jurors, and jailers, who may have no personal acquaintance whatsoever with the plaintiff or the defendant.

By contrast, among traditional Inuit in northern Canada, all offenses are considered to involve disputes between individuals; thus, they must be settled between the disputants themselves. A traditional way of doing this is through a *song duel,* in which the individuals involved heap insults upon one another in songs specially composed for the occasion. Although society does not intervene, its interests are represented by spectators, whose applause determines the outcome. If, however, social harmony cannot be restored—and that is the goal, rather than assigning and punishing guilt—one or the other disputant may move to another band. Ultimately, there is no binding legal authority.

DEFINITION OF LAW

Once two Inuit settle a dispute by engaging in a singing contest, the affair is considered closed; no further action is expected. Would we choose to describe the outcome of such a contest as a *legal* decision? If every law is a sanction but not every sanction is a law, how are we to distinguish between social sanctions in general and those to which we apply the label "law"?

According to anthropologist E. Adamson Hoebel, an important pioneer in the cross-cultural study of law, "A social norm is legal if its neglect or infraction is regularly met, in threat or in fact, by the application of physical force by an individual or group possessing the socially recognized

Having a song duel is the traditional approach to dispute resolution among the Inuit of northern Canada.

© Bryan & Cherry Alexander/Arcticphoto

privilege of so acting."[11] In stressing the legitimate use of physical coercion, Hoebel deemphasized the traditional association of law with a centralized court system.

Although rules enacted by an authorized legislative body and enforced by the judicial mechanisms of the state are fundamental features of Western jurisprudence, they are not the universal backbone of human law. Can any concept of law be applied to societies for whom the notion of a centralized judiciary is virtually meaningless? How shall we categorize Inuit song duels and other socially condoned forms of dispute resolution that seem to meet some but not all of the criteria of law?

Ultimately, it is always of greatest value to consider each case within its cultural context. After all, law reflects a society's basic postulates, so to understand any society's laws, one must understand the underlying values and assumptions. Nonetheless, a working definition of law is useful for purposes of discussion and cross-cultural comparison, and for this, **law** is adequately characterized as formal rules of conduct that, when violated, lead to negative sanctions.

FUNCTIONS OF LAW

Anthropologists recognize several basic functions of law, in particular the following three: First, it defines relationships among society's members and marks out proper behavior under specified circumstances. Knowledge of the law permits each person to know his or her rights and duties with respect to every other member of society.

Second, law allocates the authority to employ coercion in the enforcement of sanctions. In societies with centralized political systems, such authority is generally vested in the government and its judiciary system. In societies that lack centralized political control, the authority to employ force may be allocated directly to the injured party.

Third, law functions to redefine social relations and to ensure social flexibility. As new situations arise, law must determine whether old rules and assumptions retain their validity and to what extent they must be altered. Law, if it is to operate efficiently, must allow room for change.

---

[11] Hoebel, E. A. (1954). *The law of primitive man: A study in comparative legal dynamics* (p. 28). Cambridge, MA: Harvard University Press.

---

law Formal rules of conduct that, when violated, effectuate negative sanctions.

negotiation The use of direct argument and compromise by the parties to a dispute to arrive voluntarily at a mutually satisfactory agreement.

mediation Settlement of a dispute through negotiation assisted by an unbiased third party.

In practice, law is never as neat as a written description about it. In any given society, people are usually members of various subgroups—and fall under the varied dictates of these diverse groups. For example, among the Kapauku of Papua New Guinea, discussed earlier in this chapter, each individual is simultaneously a member of a family, a household, a sublineage, and a confederacy—and is subject to all the (sometimes conflicting) rules and regulations of each. Furthermore, the power to employ sanctions may vary from level to level within a given society. Thus the head of a Kapauku household in Papua New Guinea may punish a household member by slapping or beating, but the authority to confiscate property is vested exclusively in the headman of the lineage. Analogous distinctions exist in the United States among municipal, state, and federal jurisdictions. The complexity of legal jurisdiction within each society makes it difficult to generalize about law.

Punishing Crimes and Settling Disputes

As we have observed, an important function of negative sanctions, legal or otherwise, is to discourage the breach of social norms. A person contemplating theft is aware of the possibility of being caught and punished. Yet, even in the face of severe sanctions, individuals in every society sometimes violate the norms and subject themselves to the consequences of their behavior.

In Western societies a clear distinction is made between offenses against the state and offenses against an individual. However, in non-state societies such as bands and tribes, all offenses are viewed as transgressions against individuals or kin-groups (families, lineages, clans, and so on).

Disputes between individuals or kin-groups may seriously disrupt the social order, especially in small groups where the number of disputants, though small in absolute numbers, may be a large percentage of the total population. For example, although the Inuit traditionally have no effective domestic or economic unit beyond the family, a dispute between two people will interfere with the ability of members of separate families to come to one another's aid when necessary and is consequently a matter of wider social concern. The goal of judicial proceedings in such instances is restoring social harmony rather than punishing an offender. When distinguishing between offenses of concern to the community as a whole and those of concern only to a few individuals, we may refer to them as *collective* or *personal*.

Basically, disputes are settled in one of two ways. First, disputing parties may, through argument and compromise, voluntarily arrive at a mutually satisfactory agreement. This form of settlement is referred to as **negotiation** or, if it involves the assistance of an unbiased third party, **mediation.** In bands and tribes a third-party mediator has no coercive power and thus cannot force disputants to abide by such a decision, but as a person who commands great personal respect, the mediator frequently may help bring about a settlement.

Second, in chiefdoms and states, an authorized third party may issue a binding decision that the disputing parties will be compelled to respect. This process is referred to as **adjudication.** The difference between mediation and adjudication is basically a difference in authorization. In a dispute settled by adjudication, the disputing parties present their positions as compellingly as they can to an authority with the requisite legal power right to hear the case, but they do not participate in the ultimate decision making. Although the adjudication process is not universally characteristic, every society employs some form of negotiation to settle disputes.

Often negotiation acts as a prerequisite or an alternative to adjudication. For example, in the resolution of U.S. labor disputes, striking workers may first negotiate with management, often with the mediation of a third party. If the state decides the strike constitutes a threat to the public welfare, the disputing parties may be forced to submit to adjudication. In this case, the responsibility for resolving the dispute is transferred to a presumably impartial judge.

The judge's work is difficult and complex. In addition to sifting through evidence presented, he or she must consider a wide range of norms, values, and earlier rulings to arrive at a decision intended to be considered just not only by the disputing parties but by the public and other judges as well.

In many politically centralized societies, incorruptible supernatural, or at least nonhuman, powers are thought to make judgments through a "trial by ordeal." For example, among the Kpelle of Liberia discussed earlier in this chapter, when guilt is in doubt an "ordeal operator" licensed by the government may apply a hot knife to a suspect's leg. If the leg is burned, the suspect is guilty; if not, innocence is assumed. But the operator does not merely heat the knife and apply it. After massaging the suspect's legs and determining the knife is hot enough, the operator then strokes his own leg with it without being burned, demonstrating that the innocent will escape injury. The knife is then applied to the suspect.

Up to this point—consciously or unconsciously—the operator has read the suspect's nonverbal cues: gestures, the degree of muscular tension, amount of perspiration, and so forth. From this the operator can judge whether or not the accused is showing so much anxiety as to indicate probable guilt; in effect, a psychological stress evaluation has been made. As the knife is applied, it is manipulated to either burn or not burn the suspect, once this judgment has been made. The operator does this manipulation easily by controlling how long the knife is

in the fire, as well as the pressure and angle at which it is pressed against the leg.[12]

Similar to this is the use of the lie detector (polygraph) in the United States, although the guiding ideology is scientific rather than supernaturalistic. Nevertheless, an incorruptible nonhuman agency is thought to establish who is lying and who is not, whereas in reality the polygraph operator cannot just "read" the needles of the machine. He or she must judge whether or not they are registering a high level of anxiety brought on by the testing situation, as opposed to the stress of guilt. Thus the polygraph operator has much in common with the Kpelle ordeal operator.

Restorative Justice and Conflict Resolution

Punitive justice, such as imprisonment, may be the most common approach to justice in North America, but it has not proven to be an effective way of changing criminal behavior. There are cultural alternatives.

Indigenous communities in Canada successfully urged their federal government to reform justice services to make them more consistent with indigenous values and traditions.[13] In particular, they have pressed for restorative justice techniques such as the Talking Circle, traditionally used in various forms by several Native American groups. For this, parties involved in a conflict come together in a circle with equal opportunity to express their views—one at a time, free of interruption. Usually, a "talking stick" (or an eagle feather or some other symbolic object) is held by whoever is speaking to signal that she or he has the right to talk at that moment and others have the responsibility to listen.

In North America over the past three decades there has been significant movement away from the courts in favor of outside negotiation and mediation to resolve a wide variety of disputes. Many jurists see this as a means to clear overloaded court dockets so as to concentrate on more important cases.

Today, leaders in the field of dispute resolution are finding effective ways to bring about balanced resolutions to conflict. An example of this appears in the Anthropology Applied feature.

---

[12] Gibbs, J. L., Jr. (1983). [Interview]. *Faces of culture: Program 18.* Fountain Valley, CA: Coast Telecourses.

[13] Criminal Code of Canada, §718.2(e).

---

adjudication Mediation with an unbiased third party making the ultimate decision.

Dispute Resolution and the Anthropologist

In an era when the consequences of violent approaches to dispute resolution are more far-reaching than ever, conflict management is of growing importance. A world leader in this profession is anthropologist William L. Ury, an independent negotiations specialist.

In his first year at graduate school, Ury began looking for ways to apply anthropology to practical problems, including conflicts of all dimensions. He wrote a paper about the role of anthropology in peacemaking and on a whim sent it to Roger Fisher, a law professor noted for his work in negotiation and world affairs. Fisher, in turn, invited the young graduate student to co-author a kind of how-to book for international mediators. The book they researched and wrote together turned out to have a far wider audience, for it presented basic principles of negotiation that could be applied to household spats, management–employee conflicts, or international crises. Titled *Getting to Yes: Negotiating Agreement Without Giving In* (1981), it sold millions of copies, was translated into twenty-one languages, and earned the nickname "the negotiator's bible."

While working on *Getting to Yes,* Ury and Fisher co-founded the Program on Negotiation (PON) at Harvard Law School, pulling together an interdisciplinary group of academics interested in new approaches to and applications of the negotiation process. Today this applied research center is a multiuniversity consortium that trains mediators, businesspeople, and government officials in negotiation skills. It has four key goals: (1) design, implement, and evaluate better dispute resolution practices; (2) promote collaboration among practitioners and scholars; (3) develop education programs and materials for instruction in negotiation and dispute resolution; (4) increase public awareness and understanding of successful conflict resolution efforts.

In 1982, Ury earned his doctorate in anthropology from Harvard with a dissertation titled "Talk Out or Walk Out: The Role and Control of Conflict in a Kentucky Coal Mine." Afterward, he taught for several years while maintaining a leadership role at PON. In particular, he devoted himself to PON's Global Negotiation Project (initially known as the Project on Avoiding War). Today, having left his teaching post at Harvard, Ury continues to serve as director of the Global Negotiation Project, writing, consulting, and running regular workshops on dealing with difficult people and situations.

Utilizing a cross-cultural perspective sharpened through years of anthropological research, he specializes in ethnic and secessionist disputes, including those between white and black South Africans, Serbs and Croats, Turks and Kurds, Catholics and Protestants in Northern Ireland, and Russians and Chechens in the former Soviet Union.

Among the most effective tools in Ury's applied anthropology work are the books he continues to write on dispute resolution—from his 1993 *Getting Past No* to his 2007 title, *The Power of a Positive No.* His 1999 book, *Getting to Peace: Transforming Conflict at Home, at Work, and in the World,* examines what he calls the "third side," which is the role that the surrounding community can play in preventing, resolving, and containing destructive conflict between two parties.[a]

His 2002 edited volume *Must We Fight?* challenges entrenched ideas that violence and war are inevitable and presents convincing evidence that human beings have as much inherent potential for cooperation and coexistence as they do for violent conflict. The key point in this book is that violence is a choice. In Ury's words, "Conflict is not going to end, but violence can."[b]

What Ury and others in this field are doing is helping create a culture of negotiation in a world where adversarial, win–lose attitudes are out of step with the increasingly interdependent relations between people.

---

[a]Pease, T. (2000, Spring). Taking the third side. *Andover Bulletin.*
[b]Ury, W. (2002, Winter). A global immune system. *Andover Bulletin*; see also www.pon.harvard.edu/

Violent Conflict and Warfare

Although the regulation of a society's internal affairs is an important function of any political system, it is by no means the sole function. Another is the management of its external affairs—relations not just among different states but among different bands, lineages, clans, or whatever the largest autonomous political unit may be. And just as force, threatened or actual, may be used to maintain or restore order within a society, such powerful pressures are also used in the conduct of external affairs.

Humans have a horrific track record when it comes to violence. Far more lethal than spontaneous and individual outbursts of aggression, organized violence in the form of war is responsible for enormous suffering and deliberate destruction of life and property. In the past 5,000 years or so, some 14,000 wars have been fought, resulting in many hundreds of millions of casualties. In the 20th century alone, an estimated 150 million people lost their lives due to human violence.

The scope of violent conflict is wide, ranging from individual fights, local feuds, raids, and piracy (see the Globalscape) to formally declared international wars fought by professional armed forces. In addition, we may distinguish among various civil wars (in which armies from different geographic areas, ethnic or religious groups, or political parties within the same state are pitted against each other), rebellions, and guerrilla warfare involving small-scale hit-and-run tactical operations instead of pitched battles.

Why War?

In addition to the varying scales and methods of warfare, there are different motives, strategic objectives, and political or moral justifications for it. Some societies engage in

Globalscape

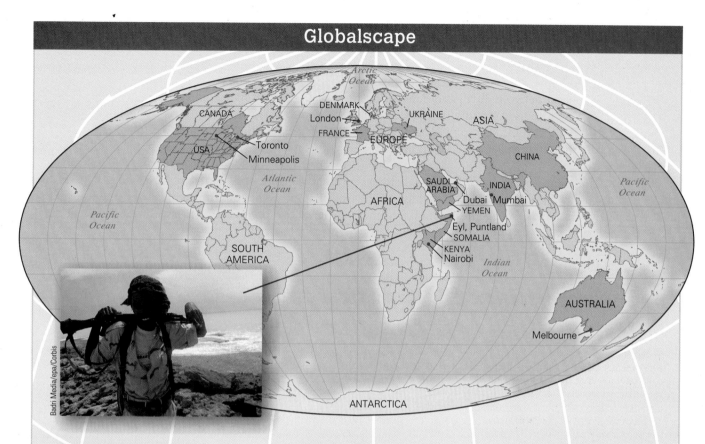

Badri Media/epa/Corbis

Pirate Pursuits in Puntland?

Abshir Boya, a towering Somali pirate, is active in coastal waters off the Horn of Africa, which juts deep into the Arabian Sea. He lives in the old fishing port of Eyl in Puntland, an autonomous territory in Somalia. By 2009, Eyl had become a pirate haven, holding a dozen hijacked foreign ships and their multinational crews.

Like Boya, most of the few hundred other pirates based in Puntland are Darod clansmen pressed out of their traditional fisheries by foreign commercial fleets polluting their coasts and depleting their fish stocks. Since 1991, Somalia has been splintered by rebellions, clan rivalries, and foreign armed interventions. It no longer has a centralized power system maintaining law and order for its citizens, who survive on an average annual income of $600. With a national

economy in tatters, Boyah and his clansmen spied the wealth passing through the Arabian Sea and decided to grab a share.

Bankrolled by emigrated Somali investors living in cities such as Melbourne, Dubai, Nairobi, London, Toronto, and Minneapolis, pirate gangs are equipped with radios, cell phones, and GPS, plus semi-automatic pistols, assault rifles, and rocket-propelled grenade launchers bought in Yemen. Speeding across open sea in skiffs, they chase cargo ships, oil tankers, and cruise ships from around the world, including the U.S., Canada, Denmark, France, Saudi Arabia, India, and China.

Some pirate captains have banked success, including Boyah who claims to have led over twenty-five hijackings. Ship owners pay huge ransoms, frequently topping $1 million per ship. Somali sea bandits—about a thousand

in total—collectively net between $80 and $150 million annually. They are obliged to pay their backers and share earnings with many poor relatives in their large clan. Far bigger profits go to Lloyd's of London, which earns an extra $400 million a year on piracy insurance for ships plying these dangerous waters.

The United Nations has called on nations with vessels in the area to repress piracy with military force. Today, a dozen navies patrol a million square miles of sea. Numerous Somali pirates have been killed or captured. Criminal prosecution of piracy in international waters is a big problem due to questions over jurisdiction, but many are now in jails in half a dozen foreign countries.

Global Twister   What is justice for Somali fishermen pressed into piracy?

---

defensive wars only and avoid armed confrontations with others unless seriously threatened or actually attacked. Others initiate aggressive wars to pursue particular strategic goals, including material benefits in the form of precious resources such as slaves, gold, or oil, as well as territorial expansion or control over trade routes. In some cultures, aggressive wars are waged for ideological reasons,

such as spreading one's own worldview or religion and defeating "evil" ideas or heresies elsewhere.

Beyond such explanations for warfare, is there something in our genetic makeup that makes it inevitable? Some argue that males of the human species are naturally aggressive. As evidence they point to aggressive group behavior exhibited by chimpanzees in Tanzania where researchers observed one group systematically destroy another and take over their territory. Also, they cite the "fierce" behavior of people such as the Yanomami Indians who inhabit the Amazon rainforest on either side of the border between Brazil and Venezuela. These tropical horticulturalists and foragers have been described as living in a chronic state of war, and some scientists suggest this exemplifies the way all humans once behaved.

Occasionally, archaeologists have discovered stone spear points embedded in ancient human skeletons. Also, here is ample evidence that armed conflicts in the form of deadly feuds and raids have long existed in stateless societies such as foraging bands, horticultural villagers, or nomadic herders. However, warfare among humans is likely to be situation specific rather than an unavoidable expression of genetic predisposition for violent behavior (see this chapter's Biocultural Connection).

Moreover, war is not a universal phenomenon, for in various parts of the world there are societies that do not practice warfare as we know it. Examples include people as diverse as the Ju/'hoansi Bushmen and Pygmy peoples of southern Africa, the Arapesh of New Guinea, and the Jain of India, as well as the Amish of North America. Among societies that do practice warfare, levels of violence may differ dramatically.

Biocultural Connection

Sex, Gender, and Human Violence

At the start of the 21st century, war and violence are no longer the strictly male domains that they were in many societies in the past. War has become embedded in civilian life in many parts of the world, and it impacts the daily lives of women and children. Moreover, women now serve in the military forces of several states, although their participation in combat is often limited. Some female soldiers in the United States argue that gender should not limit their participation in combat as they consider themselves as strong, capable, and well trained as their male counterparts. Others believe that biologically based sex differences make war a particularly male domain.

Scientists have long argued that males are more suited to combat because natural selection has made them on average larger and stronger than females. This idea, known as sexual selection, was first put forth by Darwin in the 19th century. At that time he proposed that the physical specializations of males in animal species—such as horns, vibrant plumage, and, in the case of humans, intelligence and tool use—demonstrate selection acting upon males to aid in the competition for mates. In these scenarios, male reproductive success is thought to be optimized through a strategy of "spreading seed"—in other words, by being sexually active with as many females as possible.

Females, on the other hand, are considered gatekeepers who optimize their reproductive success through caring for individual offspring. According to this theory of sexual selection, in species where male–male competition is high,

males will be considerably larger than females, and aggression will serve males well. In monogamous species, males and females will be of similar sizes.

Primatologist Richard Wrangham has taken the idea of sexual selection even further. In his book *Demonic Males,* he explores the idea that both male aggression and patriarchy have an evolutionary basis. He states that humans, like our close cousins the chimpanzees, are "party gang" species characterized by strong bonds among groups of males who have dominion over an expandable territory. These features "suffice to account for natural selection's ugly legacy, the tendency to look for killing opportunities when hostile neighbors meet."[a] Violence in turn generates a male-dominated social order: "Patriarchy comes from biology in the sense that it emerges from men's temperaments out of their evolutionarily derived efforts to control women and at the same time have solidarity with fellow males in competition against outsiders."[b] While Wrangham allows that evolutionary forces have shaped women as well, he suggests that females' evolutionary interests cannot be met without cooperation with males.

Feminist scholars have pointed out that these scientific models are "gendered" in that they incorporate the norms derived from the scientists' culture. Darwin's original model of sexual selection incorporated the Victorian gender norms of the passive female and active male. Primatologist Laura Fedigan suggests that in Darwinian models women evolved in positive directions only by a "coat tails" process whereby females were "pulled along"

toward improved biological states by virtue of the progress of the genes they shared with males.[c] Wrangham's more recent *Demonic Males* theory is similarly shaped by culture. It incorporates the dominant world order (military states) and the gender norms (aggressive males) it values. In both cases, the putatively scientific theory has created a natural basis for a series of social conventions.

This does not mean that biological differences between the sexes cannot be studied in the natural world. Instead, scientists studying sex differences must be especially sensitive to how they may project cultural beliefs onto nature. Meanwhile, the attitudes of some women soldiers continue to challenge generalizations regarding "military specialization" by gender.

BIOCULTURAL QUESTION

All across the world, males are far more likely to serve as warriors than females and, consequently, are far more likely to lose their lives on the battlefield. Do you think that there is any structural relationship between high male combat mortality rates and polygyny as the preferred marriage type in most traditional cultures?

---

[a]Wrangham, R., & Peterson, D. (1996). *Demonic males* (p. 168). Boston: Houghton Mifflin.

[b]Ibid., p. 125.

[c]Fedigan, L. M. (1986). The changing role of women in models of human evolution. *Annual Review of Anthropology 15,* 25–66.

We have ample reason to suppose that war—not to be confused with more limited forms of deadly violence such as raids—has become a problem only in the last 10,000 years, since the invention of food-production techniques and especially since the formation of centralized states 5,000 years ago. It has reached crisis proportions in the past 200 years, with the invention of modern weaponry and increased direction of violence against civilian populations.

Beginning in 1917 with military use of mustard gas—a chemical poison that causes blindness, large blisters on exposed skin, and (if inhaled) bleeding and blistering in mouth, throat, and lungs—the development of weapons of mass destruction has been horrendously effective. Today, the chemical, biological, and nuclear weapons arsenals stockpiled by many states are sufficient to wipe out all life on the planet, many times over.

Not surprisingly, given this development in the technology of death, casualties not just of civilians but also of *children* far outnumber those of soldiers. Indeed, because dangerous poisons, such as the anthrax bacterium or the nerve gas Sarin, are easy to produce and cheap, non-state groups, including terrorists, also seek to gain access to these modern weapons of mass destruction, if only to threaten to use them against more powerful opponents. Thus warfare on this level is not so much an age-old problem as it is a relatively recent one.

Among food foragers, with their uncentralized political systems, violence may erupt sporadically, but warfare was all but unknown until recent times. There are several reasons for this. First of all, since territorial boundaries and membership among food-foraging bands are usually fluid and loosely defined, a man who hunts with one band today may hunt with a neighboring band next month. This renders warfare impractical.

So, too, does the systematic exchange of marriage partners among food-foraging groups, which makes it likely that someone in each band will have a sibling, parent, or cousin in a neighboring band. Moreover, the absence of a food surplus among foragers makes prolonged combat difficult. In sum, where populations are small, food surpluses are absent, property ownership minimal, and no state organization exists, the likelihood of organized violence by one group against another is small.[14]

Despite the traditional view of the gardener or farmer as a gentle tiller of the soil, it is among such people, along with pastoralists, that warfare becomes prominent. One reason may be that food-producing peoples are much more likely to experience significant population growth, as opposed to food foragers whose numbers are generally maintained well below carrying capacity (the number of

people that the available resources can support at a given level of food-getting techniques). This population growth, if unchecked, can lead to resource depletion, one solution to which may be seizure of some other people's resources.

In addition, the commitment to a fixed piece of land inherent in farming makes such societies somewhat less fluid in their membership than those of food foragers. Instead of marrying distantly, farmers marry locally, depriving them of long-distance kin networks. In rigidly matrilocal or patrilocal societies, each new generation is bound to the same territory, no matter how small it may be or how large the group trying to live within it.

The availability of unoccupied lands may not serve as a sufficient detriment to the outbreak of war. Among swidden farmers, for example, competition for land cleared of old-growth forest frequently leads to hostility and armed conflict. The centralization of political control and the possession of valuable property among farming people provide many more stimuli for warfare.

It is among such peoples, especially those organized into states, where the violence of warfare is most apt to result in indiscriminate mass killing. This development has reached its peak in modern states. Indeed, much (but not all) of the warfare that has been observed in recent stateless societies (so-called tribal warfare) has been provoked by aggressively expanding states.[15]

Although competition for scarce resources may turn violent and lead to war, the motivations and justifications for war are often embedded in a society's worldview—the collective body of ideas that members of a culture generally share concerning the ultimate shape and substance of their reality. There are many historical examples of wars inspired or justified by religious ideas, ranging from the Crusades to Aztec Indian wars. More recently, the *jihad*—an Arabic word meaning "struggle" or Holy War—by Muslim fundamentalists called the Taliban in Afghanistan and Pakistan seeks to expel infidels (nonbelievers) from ancestral soil. An instructive comparison can be made between the two historical examples that follow.

Fighting for Worldview: The Crusades and Aztec Warfare

In 1095 the Roman Catholic Pope Urban II launched the first Crusade ("War of the Cross"), with a speech urging the Christian nobles of Europe to end their ceaseless wars against one another and instead direct their hostilities toward the infidels—in this case, Muslim Turks and Arabs in the Middle East. In the same speech the pope also alluded to the economic benefits to be realized by seizing

---

[14] Knauft, B. M. (1991). Violence and sociality in human evolution. *Current Anthropology 32,* 391–409.

[15] Whitehead, N. L., & Ferguson, R. B. (1993, November). Deceptive stereotypes about tribal warfare. *Chronicle of Higher Education,* A48.

the resources of the infidels. Although clearly the Crusades were motivated by more than religious ideology, they were justified as a holy war to liberate Jerusalem and the Holy Land from Muslims. However, the success of the Crusades was limited, and twenty years after the ninth and final Crusade (1271–1272), the last Christian stronghold in Palestine surrendered to a Muslim army.

Within the next few centuries, however, Europe's Christian powers turned their attention to state building and colonial expansion in other parts of the world. Along with this growth and outward expansion came advances in the technology and organization of warfare. With the emergence of states (not just in Europe but in other parts of the world as well) has come a dramatic increase in the scale of warfare. This is not surprising, given the state's acceptance of force as a legitimate tool for regulating human affairs and its ability to organize large numbers of people.

Consider, for example, the Aztec state in the central Mexican highlands, which engaged in continuous warfare from the mid-1400s until its demise in the early 1520s. By way of battle, the state collected tribute and achieved regional dominance. Moreover, by waging war against their neighbors, Aztecs obtained prisoners to use as offerings for their gods; the Aztecs believed their gods required human sacrifice to maintain the cosmic order: "The warrior slated for sacrifice was a *teomiqui*, 'he who dies in godlike fashion,' and would feed the sun so that it might shine upon the world and keep it in motion."[16]

Among Aztecs, this worldview justified, even sanctified, perpetual aggression. In fact, according to the noted anthropologist Eric Wolf, priests bearing the images of the Aztec war god Huitilopochtli and other deities walked ahead of the army and gave the signal to commence combat by lighting a fire and blowing on shell trumpets. The victory that followed, Wolf wrote, "always had the same results: Long lines of captives, wooden collars about their necks, made the long journey to Tenochtitlán to be offered upon the altars of the gods."[17]

Several thousand captives could be sacrificed after one of these Aztec military campaigns, and within a single year as many as 20,000 may have been offered to the gods in that capital city of the Aztec state. In fact, one major motive for the Aztecs to wage war against rival states was to obtain war captives for sacrificial rituals.

---

[16] Keen, B. (1971). *The Aztec image in Western thought* (p. 13). New Brunswick, NJ: Rutgers University Press.

[17] Wolf, E. R. (1999). *Envisioning power: Ideologies of dominance and crisis* (p. 263). Berkeley: University of California Press.

genocide The physical extermination of one people by another, either as a deliberate act or as the accidental outcome of activities carried out by one people with little regard for their impact on others.

War was glorified and associated with the beauty of flowers. Warriors were called "dancing flowers," and captives were known as "flowers of the heart," with the blood of warriors called "flower-water." Success in capturing warriors destined for sacrifice made an Aztec war hero "rich in flowers." For this reason, military expeditions to obtain war captives were known as "flowery wars."

The Aztec flowery wars and the Christian Crusades are just two of many examples of how religious motivations and ideological justifications for war are embedded in a society's worldview. We will discuss other aspects of worldview in the following chapter, which focuses on religion and the supernatural.

Genocide

As these cross-cultural examples of violent conflicts indicate, warfare often involves a complex dynamic of economic, political, and ideological interests. Such is especially the case when violence escalates into **genocide**—the physical extermination of one people by another, either as a deliberate act or as the accidental outcome of activities carried out by one people with little regard for their impact on others.

Genocide is not a new phenomenon. One of the most infamous 19th-century acts of genocide was the systematic killing of the indigenous inhabitants of Tasmania, a large island just south of Australia. British wool growers wanted the indigenous peoples removed so that they could take control of the sheep on the island. The government advanced their interests through military campaigns against the natives.

These campaigns failed to achieve the complete elimination of the Tasmanians, but what the military could not achieve was done by George Augustus Robinson, a British Protestant missionary. Rounding up the surviving natives, he brought them to his mission station, where they died from the combination of psychological depression and lack of resistance to European disease. Robinson retired to Britain to contemplate the horrible if unintended consequences of his actions, which secured Tasmania for the British commercial wool industry: the demise of the last full-blooded Tasmanians.

There are examples of genocide all across the world and throughout history. In North America, for example, European settlers massacred numerous indigenous communities from the 1500s up until the late 1800s in California. Among the many Californian Indian groups now extinct are the Yahi, a small tribe of foragers traditionally ranging the Sierra Nevada. Defending their territory from invading gold miners and settlers, most lost their lives. After a massacre in 1865, only thirty survived and went into hiding in the remote mountain wilderness. Some of them were killed by cattlemen, others died of other causes in the next forty years, until only one tribesman was left. Lonely, he straggled out and was discovered in a cattle

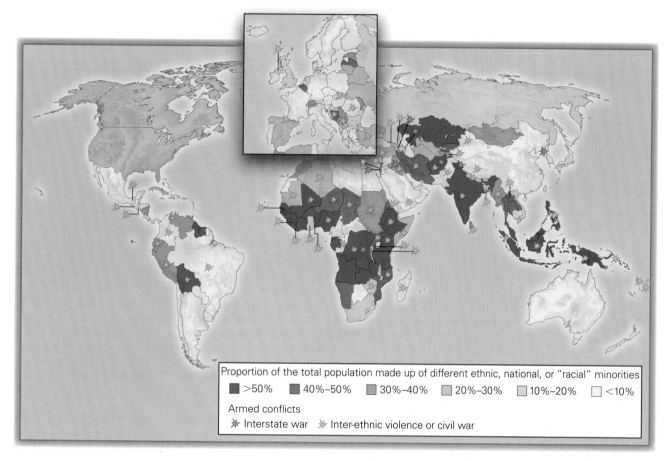

Proportion of the total population made up of different ethnic, national, or "racial" minorities

■ >50%   ■ 40%–50%   ■ 30%–40%   ■ 20%–30%   ■ 10%–20%   □ <10%

Armed conflicts
✳ Interstate war   ✳ Inter-ethnic violence or civil war

Figure 12.3 In pluralistic societies in which two or more ethnic groups or nationalities form part of the same political state, violent conflict between neighboring groups is not uncommon.

corral in the summer of 1911. Causing a sensation as the "last wild Indian," he was taken to the University of California in San Francisco. Never revealing his name because of a cultural taboo, he became known as Ishi, the word for "man" in his native language.[18]

The most widely known act of genocide in recent history was the attempt of the Nazis during World War II to wipe out European Jews and Roma (Gypsies) in the name of racial superiority and improvement of the human species. Unfortunately, referring to this atrocity as "*the* Holocaust"— as if it were something unique or at least exceptional—tends to blind us to the fact that this thoroughly monstrous act is but one example of an all-too-common phenomenon.

Among numerous more contemporary examples of mass murder, Khmer Rouge soldiers in Cambodia killed 1.7 million fellow citizens, or 20 percent of that country's population, between 1975 and 1979. During the next decade, government-sponsored terrorism against indigenous communities in Guatemala reached its height, and Saddam Hussein's government used poison gas against the Kurdish ethnic minority in northern Iraq. In 1994, more

than half a million Tutsi people were slaughtered by their Hutu neighbors in the African country of Rwanda.[19] Estimates vary, but during the 20th century as many as 83 million people have died of genocide.[20] The horrors continue in our current century with, among others, the genocidal campaign against the non-Arab black peoples in the Darfur desert region of western Sudan.

Wars Today

Currently, there are numerous wars going on in the world (Figure 12.3). They occur not only *between* countries but also *within* states where the political leadership and government bureaucracy are corrupt, repressive, ineffective, or without popular support. Notably, many armies around the world recruit not only adult men, but also women and children. Today, more than 250,000 child soldiers, many as young as 12 years old, are participating in armed conflicts around the world.[21]

[18] Starn, O. (2005). *Ishi's brain: In search of America's last "wild" Indian.* New York: Norton.

[19] www.hrw.org/reports/1999/rwanda.

[20] White, M. (2001). *Historical atlas of the twentieth century.* http://users. erols.com/mwhite28/20centry.htm; see also van den Berghe, p. 198.

[21] "Study estimates 250,000 active child soldiers." (2006, July 26). Associated Press.

Congo is one of Africa's failed states, the consequence of a century of ruthless colonial exploitation, many decades of government mismanagement, and an ill-equipped bureaucracy. With a wealth of precious natural resources—including gold, diamonds, and uranium, especially in the eastern frontier provinces far from the capital—the country risks splintering. Since 1998, a gruesome war has devastated the peoples living in eastern Congo. In addition to the deaths of almost 6 million people, millions more are homeless. Here we see a small part of the 200,000 refugees fleeing from the horrors of mass murder, pillage, famine, and rape.

The following examples offer some specific data on wars from the last decade of the 20th century to today. In the 1990s, between 2 and 3 million died due to separatist warfare in the southern Sudan. And since warfare erupted in eastern Congo in 1998, almost 6 million people have died and millions more have been forced to flee their home villages. Involving eight African states and about twenty-five armed forces, this gruesome war with mass murder and mass rape is also known as Africa's World War. Clashes between various government troops, ethnic rebel groups, and freelancing militias continue in Congo's lawless borderlands.

Moreover, the Middle East remains mired in political turmoil and violent strife, especially since the U.S.-led military invasion of Afghanistan in 2001, where a Muslim fundamentalist regime was removed from power as it provided a territorial base for an international terrorist organization. Two years later, the U.S. launched an invasion of Iraq, unseating Saddam Hussein whose dictatorship was deemed hostile to U.S. strategic interests in the oil-rich region. In addition to many tens of thousands of fatalities in both Iraq and Afghanistan, the vast majority of whom are noncombatants—children, women, and elders—there has also been massive destruction of roads, bridges, buildings, and livelihoods. Without a political leadership capable of effectively governing these pluralistic countries, providing security, and maintaining law and order, both war-torn countries seem doomed to be failed states.

Beyond these wars, there are numerous so-called low-intensity wars involving guerrilla organizations, rebel armies, resistance movements, terrorist cells, and a host of other armed groups engaged in violent conflict with official state-controlled armed forces. Every year, confrontations result in hundreds of hot spots and violent flashpoints, most of which are never reported in Western news media.[22]

As the above cross-cultural examples show, the causes of warfare are complex, involving economic, political, and ideological factors. The challenge of eliminating human warfare has never been greater than it is in today's world—nor has the cost of *not* finding a way to do so. In the First World War a new term, "crimes against humanity," was coined to identify inhumane acts such as the systematic persecution of one ethnic group by another, massive deportation or massacre of noncombatants, and other gruesome atrocities. Since 1945, the United Nations has been charged with the prosecution of this crime, albeit with mixed success.

In 2002, a permanent tribunal to prosecute crimes against humanity, genocide, and war crimes was established in The Hague, the Netherlands, called the International Criminal Court. So far, 110 states are members of this court, including all of South America, most of Europe, and about half the countries in Africa. Another forty-eight countries have signed but not ratified this international treaty. Some countries, however, refuse to join, including China, India, Israel, Russia, Sudan, and the United States. Nevertheless, the establishment of this court shows that almost a century after the start of the First World War, and more than half a century after the founding of the United Nations, issues of crime and punishment are now also recognized as global affairs.

---

[22] icasualties.org.

Questions for Reflection

1. In Afghanistan, a pluralistic society with many ethnic groups and tribes, the central government is so weak and has so little power that it cannot effectively manage, let alone protect, the country and its highly diverse population. Yet political ties among tribal communities are periodically reinforced by an ancient institution called the Loya Jirga, or Grand Council. Considering the geographic, political, economic, and cross-cultural challenges this poor Asian country faces, do you think Afghanistan has a better chance as a decentralized state, in which each region has considerable autonomy and is governed by tribal councils, than as a state with a centralized government?

2. Considering the comparative historical examples of the Crusades by European Christian armies and Aztec Indian warfare in Mexico, do you think there is a relationship between a profitable arms industry, promoting military dominance, and the pursuit of war as a means of solving conflicts? If so, what is the role of an ideology that asserts national and/or religious righteousness?

3. If political organization functions to impose or maintain order and to resolve conflicts, why do you think that a government in a country such as yours is so interested in legitimizing its power? What happens when a government loses such legitimacy?

4. Which nationalities or ethnic groups do you know that are dominant, and which can you identify that are in a minority position or are repressed? What is the basis for this inequality?

5. When your own government declares war against another country, on which basis does it seek to justify its decision to send soldiers into battle?

Suggested Readings

Cheater, A. (2005). *The anthropology of power.* London: Routledge.

The author presents case studies from a wide range of societies to examine the issues surrounding power and whether power can actually be transferred to the powerless. The book explores how traditionally disempowered groups gain influence in postcolonial and multicultural settings. Also, it surveys the relationships between empowerment and economic development, gender, and environmentalism.

Kertzer, D. I. (1989). *Ritual, politics, and power.* New Haven, CT: Yale University Press.

Using numerous examples from traditional and modern societies and writing in clear accessible prose, the author argues that political symbols manifested through rituals explain much of the political life of modern nations, contrary to the usual rational, utilitarian, and interest-group explanations. He discusses how elites use rituals to support the existing order, while revolutionaries use them to replace it.

Nader, L. (2002). *The life of the law: Anthropological projects.* Berkeley: University of California Press.

A renowned legal anthropologist, Nader presents a historical overview of the development of this specialization and explores the role of the law in the struggle for social and economic justice. Considering the profound impact of globalization on both the law and anthropology, she discusses the growing dominance of capitalist corporations and the prominence of neoliberal ideology and practice. Linking the growing popularity of the alternative dispute resolution movement, this critical theorist argues that mediation as an approach to conflict resolution is structured to favor powerful capitalist interests.

Ury, W. (Ed.). (2002). *Must we fight? From the battlefield to the schoolyard—A new perspective on violent conflict and its prevention.* Hoboken, NJ: Jossey-Bass.

This fresh exploration of the question of whether violence and war are inevitable presents evidence from leading anthropologists and other scholars that human beings have as much inherent potential for cooperation and coexistence as they do for violent conflict.

Vincent, J. (2002). *The anthropology of politics: A reader in ethnography, theory, and critique.* Boston: Blackwell.

This sweeping historical and theoretical introduction to the field features readings from noted anthropologists past and present, enriched by Vincent's insightful headnotes.

Whitehead, N., & Ferguson, R. B. (Eds.). (1992). *War in the tribal zone.* Santa Fe: School of American Research Press.

The central point of this book is that the transformation and intensification of war, as well as the formation of tribes, result from complex interaction in the "tribal zone" that begins where centralized authority makes contact with stateless people it does not rule. In such zones, newly introduced plants, animals, diseases, and technologies often spread widely, even before colonizers appear. These and other changes disrupt existing social and political relationships, fostering new alliances and creating conflicts.

Luca Invernizzi Tettoni/Photolibrary

Challenge Issue As self-aware and self-reflecting beings, humans face emotional and intellectual challenges born of the need to make sense of our place in the universe. We puzzle over human origin and destiny and truly big questions about time and space, as we wrestle with existential questions about our own fate, life, and death. Throughout time and across the globe, humans have creatively addressed these ponderings and worked out answers articulated in sacred narratives and associated ceremonies, rituals, and other cultural forms of religious or spiritual expression. One spectacular cultural example of people coming to terms with death is the Hindu cremation ceremony (*ngaben*) on the Indonesian island of Bali. After a death, relatives, friends, and neighbors transform emotional grief into a theatrical ceremony; everyone joyfully participates by making food and presenting offerings for the *ngaben*. For this dramatic ritual, the dead body is placed inside a wooden sarcophagus built in the shape of a bull (a sacred animal according to Hindu religion) and then set afire. Through cremation, the person's *roh* (spirit or soul) is believed to be ritually purified and freed from its material remains. As the *roh* takes wing and migrates to its next existence, the physical body continues to burn. Later, when the bones are no longer hot, they are collected and ground up while a priest chants prayers. The ashes are then taken to the island's coast and ceremonially released into the sea.

CHAPTER 13

Spirituality, Religion, and the Supernatural

Chapter Preview

What Are Religion and Spirituality?

Religion and spirituality form part of a cultural system's superstructure, which comprises a society's worldview. Religion is an organized system of ideas about spiritual reality, or the supernatural, along with associated beliefs and ceremonial practices. Spirituality, which also concerns the supernatural, involves less formalized beliefs and practices and is often individual rather than collective. Humans rely on both religion and spirituality to give meaning to the world and their place in it and to deal with problems that defy ordinary explanation or simple and direct solutions. To overcome these challenges, people appeal to, or seek to influence and even manipulate, spiritual or supernatural beings and powers.

What Are the Identifying Features of Religion and Spirituality?

Religion (and spiritual practices in general) consists of various beliefs and rituals—prayers, songs, dances, offerings, and sacrifices—that people use to interpret, appeal to, and manipulate supernatural beings and powers to their advantage. These beings and powers may be gods and goddesses, ancestral and other spirits, or impersonal powers, either by themselves or in various combinations. In all societies certain individuals are especially skilled at dealing with these beings and powers and assist other members of society in their ritual activities. A body of myths rationalizes or explains the system in a manner consistent with people's experience in the world in which they live. In many cultures, efforts to control supernatural powers include witchcraft and magic.

What Functions Do Religion and Spirituality Serve?

All religions serve a number of important social, psychological, and emotional functions, as well as ideological purposes: They help maintain social solidarity; they feature rituals that may be used to enhance the learning of oral traditions; they reduce anxieties by explaining the unknown; and they offer comfort with the belief that supernatural aid is available for healing and emotional relief in times of crisis. Religious systems also provide guidance about right and wrong, setting precedents for acceptable behavior and transferring the burden of decision making from individuals to supernatural powers. Spirituality also serves emotional, psychological, and social functions, but it tends to be fitted to more personal preferences, and its form and expression are often uniquely creative.

From an anthropological point of view, spirituality and religion are part of a cultural system's superstructure, earlier defined as the collective body of ideas, beliefs, and values by which a group of people makes sense of the world and their place in it. In contrast to other disciplines such as theology, for example, which may focus on questions concerning the nature of God or the idea of divine spirit and the interpretation of ancient sacred texts, anthropology examines spirituality and religion in terms of a society's **worldview**—the collective body of ideas that members of a culture generally share concerning the ultimate shape and substance of their reality. In their cross-cultural studies of different religious and spiritual beliefs and practices, anthropologists seek to remain unbiased regarding any particular historical tradition, belief, or ritual considered sacred by the people they study.

The Role of Religion and Spirituality

Among people in all cultures, particular spiritual or religious beliefs and practices fulfill numerous social and psychological needs, such as reducing anxiety by presenting an orderly view of the universe and answers to existential questions, including those concerning suffering and death. They can provide the path by which people transcend their burdensome and mortal existence and attain, if only momentarily, spiritual hope and relief.

In addition, a shared religion reinforces group norms, provides moral sanctions for individual conduct, and furnishes the ideology of common purpose and values that support the well-being of the community. Also of note, people often turn to religion or spirituality in the hope of reaching a specific goal, such as the healing of physical, emotional, or social ills.

Perhaps it is because they fulfill these and numerous other social and psychological needs shared by humans across cultures that supernatural beliefs are universal. While recognizing that not all individuals believe in a supernatural force or entity, anthropologists know of no group of people anywhere on the face of the earth who, at any time over the past 100,000 years, has been without some manifestation of spirituality or religion. Not even in countries such as China and North Korea, where atheism remains the communist state dogma and where powerful regimes have long suppressed religious institutions, did religion entirely disappear.

In the 19th century, the European intellectual tradition gave rise to the idea that modern science would ultimately replace religion by showing people the irrationality of their spiritual beliefs and practices. The expectation was that as valid scientific explanations became available, people would abandon their religious beliefs and rituals as superstitious myths and false worship. Although it is true that in wealthy northwestern European states such as Sweden the percentage of inhabitants who consider themselves atheist, agnostic, or simply non-believers in God is now the highest in the world, that secularist trend is by no means universal.[1] In fact, in many places, the opposite trend seems to prevail.

Far from causing religion's demise, and despite the enormous growth of scientific knowledge, modernization does not always lead to greater rationality or predictability in rapidly changing societies. In fact, globalization often leads to a destabilization of the established order. The upheaval in ordinary people's lives often produces new anxieties and raises new questions about human existence.

Although traditional, mainline Christian religions have shown some decline, nondenominational spirituality is on the rise. Also on the rise are fundamentalist religions, which often take a strong antiscience position. Examples include Islamic fundamentalism in countries such as Afghanistan, Algeria, and Iran; Jewish fundamentalism in Israel and the United States; and Hindu fundamentalism

---

[1] Zuckerman, P. (2005). Atheism: Contemporary rates and patterns. In M. Martin (Ed.), *The Cambridge companion to atheism*. Cambridge, England: Cambridge University Press.

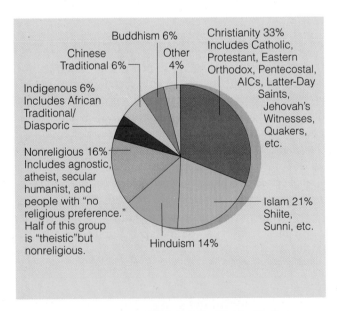

Figure 13.1 The major religions of the world with their percentages of believers. Note that the total adds up to more than 100 percent due to rounding and due to the upper-bound estimates used for each group. As we go to press, more recent comparative figures for all these groups are not available. However, a 2009 study by the Pew Research Center reports that the number of Muslims has grown to 1.57 billion, representing about 23 percent of the total global population. Sources: adherents.com; Pew Research Center, 2009.

---

worldview The collective body of ideas that members of a culture generally share concerning the ultimate shape and substance of their reality.

Members of the Church of Zion, an indigenous Christian church with a primarily Zulu congregation, perform a baptism in the Indian Ocean near Durban, South Africa. Over half of all Christian church members in South Africa belong to indigenous churches that combine some elements of their traditional African beliefs and rituals with those of Christianity.

in India. Christian fundamentalism is represented in the dramatic growth of evangelical denominations in the United States, Central America, and sub-Saharan Africa.

Among the fastest-growing religious communities in the world are the indigenous churches of Africa. Over the last half century, the number of registered indigenous denominations in southern Africa alone has doubled from about 5,000 to 10,000. There, it is estimated that more than half of Christian church members belong to indigenous churches, like the Amanazaretha Church founded by a Zulu prophet and popular among fellow Zulus in Natal.[2]

Within the United States, non-Christian religions are also growing: Islam (3 to 5 million followers—up from 527,000 in 1990), Buddhism (2 to 3 million—up from 401,000 in 1990), and Hinduism (1.28 million—up from 227,000 in 1990), not to mention various new age options such as Wicca (a modern, nature-oriented religion that draws upon ancient western European and pre-Christian beliefs and now counts about 310,000 adherents).[3]

Notably, just 16 percent of the adult population throughout the world claim to be nonreligious (Figure 13.1). This is not to say that those classified as nonreligious are all atheists, because this miscellaneous "negative" category actually includes many millions of individuals in dozens of countries who may reject or not fit under the label of any organized religion but who are metaphysically involved in creative arrangements of spiritual beliefs and practices of their own choosing.

Spiritual and religious beliefs do often change over time, but in whichever cultural form, faith in supernatural powers remains a dominant and dynamic force in most contemporary societies. It is not the responsibility of anthropologists to rank or pass judgment on the metaphysical truth of any particular faith system, but it is their task to show how each embodies a number of revealing facts about humans and the particular cultural superstructure within which these religious or spiritual beliefs are ideologically embedded.

The Anthropological Approach to Religion and Spirituality

Although people in different cultures—each with their own beliefs about the ultimate shape and substance of the supernatural—may have particular ideas about religion and spirituality, we offer a basic definition of both: **Religion is** an organized system of ideas about the spiritual sphere or the supernatural, along with associated

[2] Kunnie, J. (2007). *Umoya: The spirit in Africa.* Self-produced DVD, available at www.coh.arizona.edu/aas/aas.htm.

[3] U.S. Census 2000; www.adherents.com. See also *World almanac.* (2004). New York: Press Publishing.; and pluralism.org (the Pluralism Project, Harvard University).

religion An organized system of ideas about the spiritual sphere or the supernatural, along with associated ceremonial practices by which people try to interpret and/or influence aspects of the universe otherwise beyond their control.

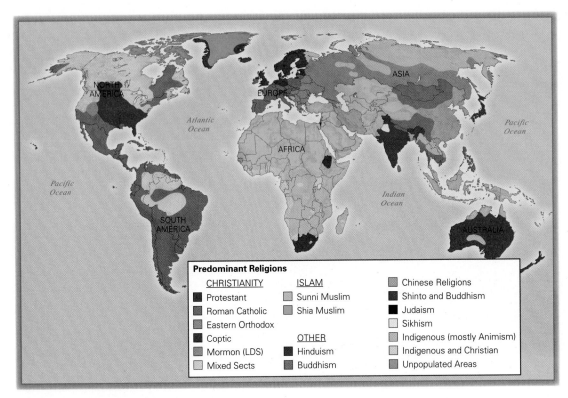

Figure 13.2 A half-page map cannot begin to convey the thousands of different religions and belief systems in the world or the complex dynamics of sectarian splinter groups. This one offers only a broad-stroke look at the global distribution of major religions, indicating where they are the majority. In some areas, the mixture of different religions is such that no single faith is shared by most of that region's inhabitants. Notably, this map is not detailed enough to depict geographic pockets with significant numbers of a particular faith. For instance, even though New York City is the second largest Jewish population center in the world and its 1.75 million Jewish adherents count for close to 10 percent of the total metropolitan area population, the city, like New York State, comprises mainly Roman Catholics (38 percent) and members of various Christian Protestant religions (30 percent). And many other significant religious groups are not individually represented here, such as Sikhism, with over 23 million members, Jehovah's Witnesses (7 million), Cao Dai in Vietnam (5 million), and Aladura in Nigeria (1 million).

ceremonial practices by which people try to interpret and/or influence aspects of the universe otherwise beyond their control. Similar to religion, **spirituality** is also concerned with the sacred, as distinguished from material matters, but it is often individual rather than collective and does not require a distinctive format or traditional organization. Both are indicators that many aspects of the human experience are thought to be beyond scientific or empirical explanation.

Since no known culture, including those of modern industrial and postindustrial societies, has achieved complete certainty in controlling existing or future conditions and circumstances, spirituality and/or religion play a role

> **spirituality** Concern with the sacred, as distinguished from material matters. In contrast to religion, spirituality is often individual rather than collective and does not require a distinctive format or traditional organization.

in all known cultures. However, considerable variability exists globally (Figure 13.2).

At one end of the spectrum are food-foraging peoples, whose technological ability to manipulate their environment is limited and who tend to see themselves as part of, rather than masters of, nature. This may be referred to as a *naturalistic worldview*. Among food foragers religion is likely to be inseparable from the rest of daily life. It also mirrors and confirms the egalitarian nature of social relations in their societies, in that individuals do not plead with high-ranking deities for aid the way members of stratified societies do.

At the other end of the spectrum is Western civilization, with its ideological commitment to overcoming problems through technological and organizational skills. Here religion is less a part of daily activities and is restricted to more specific occasions. Moreover, with its hierarchy of supernatural beings—for instance, God and (in some religions) the angels, saints, or holy people—it reflects and confirms the stratified nature of the society in which it is embedded.

Religious activity may be less prominent in the lives of social elites, who may see themselves as more in control of their own destinies, than it is in the lives of peasants or members of lower classes. Among the latter, religion may afford some compensation for a dependent position in society. Yet religion is still important to elite members of society, in that it rationalizes the system in such a way that less advantaged people are not as likely to question the existing social order as they might otherwise be. With hope for a better existence after death, one may be more willing to put up with a disadvantaged position in life. Thus religious beliefs serve to influence and perpetuate certain ideas about the relationships, if not the actual relations, between different classes of people.

Spiritual Forces and Supernatural Beings

A hallmark of religion is belief in spiritual forces and supernatural beings. In attempting to control by religious means what cannot be controlled in other ways, humans turn to prayer, sacrifice, and other religious or spiritual rituals. These presuppose the existence of spiritual forces that can be tapped into, or supernatural beings interested in human affairs and available for aid. In many cultures, these metaphysical forces or beings are associated with unique places such as extraordinary rocks, lakes, wells, waterfalls, or other special geographic locations valued as sacred sites.

Beginning with supernatural beings, we may divide them into three categories: major deities (gods and goddesses), ancestral spirits, and other sorts of spirit beings. Although the variety of deities and spirits recognized by the world's cultures is tremendous, it is possible to make certain generalizations about them.

Gods and Goddesses

Gods and goddesses are major deities, and as such they are more remote than other spirit beings. They are usually seen as controlling the universe. If more than one is recognized (known as **polytheism**), each has charge of a particular part of the universe. Such was the case with the gods and goddesses of ancient Greece: Zeus was lord of the sky, Poseidon was ruler of the sea, and Hades was lord of the underworld and ruler of the dead.

In addition to these three brothers, Greek mythology features a host of other deities, female as well as male, each similarly concerned with specific aspects of life and the universe. A **pantheon,** or the collection of gods and goddesses such as in Greek mythology, is common in non-Western

states as well. Since states typically have grown through conquest, often their pantheons have expanded as local deities of conquered peoples were incorporated into the official state pantheon.

Another frequent though not invariable feature of pantheons is the presence of a supreme deity, who may be all but totally ignored by humans. The Aztecs of the Mexican highlands, for instance, recognized a supreme pair to whom they paid little attention. After all, being so remote, this divine duo was unlikely to be interested in human affairs. The sensible practice, then, was to focus attention on less remote deities who were more directly concerned with human activities.

Whether or not a people recognize gods, goddesses, or both has to do with how men and women relate to each other in everyday life. Generally speaking, societies that subordinate women to men define the supreme deity in masculine terms. For instance, in traditional Christian religions believers speak of God as a "father" who had a divine "son" but do not entertain thoughts of God as a "mother" or of a divine "daughter." Such male-privileging religions developed in traditional societies with economies based on the herding of animals or intensive agriculture carried out or controlled by men, who are dominating figures to their children.

Goddesses, by contrast, are likely to be most prominent in societies where women play a significant role in the economy, where women enjoy relative equality with men, and where men are less controlling figures to their wives and children. Such societies are most often those that depend on crop cultivation carried out solely or mostly by women.

As an illustration, the early Israelites, like other pastoral nomadic groups of the Middle East, described their god in masculine, authoritarian terms. By contrast, goddesses played central roles in religious ritual and in the popular imagination of the region's farming peoples. Associated with these goddesses were concepts of light, fertility, and procreation. About 3,200 years ago, the Israelite tribes crossed the Jordan River and entered the land of Canaan (Palestine) where they began to till the soil and grow crops, requiring them to establish a new kind of relationship with the land. As they settled down and became sedentary, dependent upon rainfall and concerned about seasonal cycles and soil fertility (as the region's Canaanites already were), they adopted many of the region's already established Canaanite goddess cults. Although diametrically opposed to the original Israelite supreme male deity

polytheism Belief in several gods and/or goddesses (as contrasted with monotheism—belief in one god or goddess).
pantheon The several gods and goddesses of a people.

The patriarchal nature of traditional Euramerican society is culturally articulated and ideologically justified by its Judeo-Christian theology, in which a supreme male deity gives life to the first man, as depicted here on the ceiling of the Sistine Chapel in Rome. Only later is the first woman created—out of the rib of the first man.

© Visual Arts Library (London)/Albany

cult, worship of these Canaanite female deities appealed to the farming people's desire for security by seeking to control the forces of fertility.

Later, when the Israelite tribes sought national unity in the face of a military threat by neighboring nations and when they ethnocentrically strengthened their own identity as a supernaturally "chosen people," the goddess cults lost out to followers of the old masculine tribal god. This ancient masculine-authoritarian concept of god has been perpetuated down to the present, not just in the Judaic tradition but also by most Christians and Muslims, whose religions stem from the old Israelite religion. As a consequence, this masculine-authoritarian model has played an important role in perpetuating a relationship between men and women in which the latter traditionally have been expected to submit to the rule of men at every level of Jewish, Christian, and Islamic society.

Ancestral Spirits

A belief in ancestral spirits is consistent with the widespread notion that human beings are made up of two closely intertwined parts: a physical body and a mental component or spiritual self. For example, traditional belief of the Penobscot Indians in Maine holds that each person has a vital spirit capable of traveling apart from the body. Given such a concept, the idea of a spirit being freed from the body in trance and dreams or by death, and having an existence thereafter, seems quite reasonable. Frequently, where a belief in ancestral spirits exists, these beings are seen as retaining an active interest and even participation in society.

Belief in ancestral spirits of one sort or another is found in many parts of the world, especially among people having unilineal descent systems with their associated ancestor orientation. In several such African societies, the concept is highly elaborate. Here one

frequently finds ancestral spirits behaving just like humans. They are able to feel hot, cold, and pain, and they may be capable of dying a second death by drowning or burning. They even may participate in family and lineage affairs, and seats will be provided for them, even though the spirits are invisible. If they are annoyed, they may send sickness or death. Eventually, they are reborn as new members of their lineage, and, in societies that hold such beliefs, adults need to observe infants closely to determine just who has been reborn. Such beliefs provide a strong sense of continuity that links the past, present, and future.

Ancestor spirits played an important role in the patrilineal society of traditional China. For the gift of life, a boy was forever indebted to his parents, owing them obedience, deference, and a comfortable old age. Even after their death, he had to provide for them in the spirit world, offering them food, money, and incense on the anniversaries of their births and deaths. In addition, people collectively worshiped all lineage ancestors periodically throughout the year. Giving birth to sons was regarded as an obligation to the ancestors, because boys inherited their father's ancestral duties.

To fulfill his ancestors' needs for descendants (and his own need to be respectable in a culture that demanded satisfying the needs of one's ancestors), a man would go so far as to marry a girl who had been adopted into his family as an infant so she could be raised as a dutiful wife for him, even when this arrangement went against the wishes of both parties. Furthermore, a father readily would force his daughter to marry a man against her will. In fact, a female child raised to be cast out by her natal family might not find acceptance in her husband's family for years. Not until after death, when her vital spirit was carried in a tablet and placed in the shrine of her husband's family, was she an official member of it. As a consequence, once a son was born to her, a woman worked long and hard to establish the strongest possible tie between herself and her son to ensure she would be looked after in life.

Strong beliefs in ancestral spirits are particularly appropriate in a society of descent-based groups with their associated ancestor orientation. But, more than this, as noted above, these beliefs provide a strong sense of continuity that links the past, present, and future.

Other Types of Spiritual Forces and Supernatural Beings

ANIMISM

One of the most widespread concepts concerning supernatural beings is **animism,** a belief that nature is animated (enlivened or energized) by distinct personalized spirit beings separable from bodies. Spirits such as souls and ghosts are thought to dwell in humans and animals but also in human-made artifacts, plants, stones, mountains, wells, and other natural features. So too the woods may be full of a variety of unattached or free-ranging spirits.

The various spirit beings involved are a highly diverse lot. Generally speaking, though, they are less remote than gods and goddesses and are more involved in people's daily affairs. They may be benevolent, malevolent, or just plain neutral. They also may be awesome, terrifying, lovable, or mischievous. Since they may be pleased or irritated by human actions, people are obliged to be concerned about them.

Animism, a concept theoretically developed by the pioneering British anthropologist Sir Edward B. Tylor (1832–1917), is typical of those who see themselves as being a part of nature rather than superior to it. This includes most food foragers, as well as those food-producing peoples who acknowledge little qualitative difference between a human life and any living entity from turtles to trees, or even rivers and mountains. In such societies, gods and goddesses are relatively unimportant, but the woods are full of spirits. Gods and goddesses, if they exist at all, may be seen as having created the world and perhaps making it fit to live in; but in animism, spirits are the ones to beseech when ill, the ones to help or hinder the shaman, and the ones whom the ordinary hunter may meet when off in the woods.

ANIMATISM

Although supernatural power is often thought of as being vested in supernatural beings, it does not have to be. Such is the case with **animatism**—the belief that nature is enlivened or energized by an impersonal spiritual power or supernatural energy, which may make itself manifest in any special place, thing, or living creature. Although this concept is not universal, it is found in cultures on every continent.

The Melanesians, for example, think of *mana* as a spiritual force inherent in all objects—not unlike the idea of a cosmic energy passing into and through everything, affecting living and nonliving matter alike (similar to "the Force" in the *Star Wars* films). It is not in itself physical, but it can reveal itself physically. A warrior's success in fighting is not attributed to his own strength but to the *mana* contained in an amulet that hangs around his neck. Similarly, a farmer may know a great deal about horticulture, soil conditioning, and the correct time for sowing and harvesting but nevertheless depend upon *mana* for a successful crop, often building a simple altar to this power at one end of the field. If the crop is good, it is a sign that the farmer has in some way appropriated the necessary *mana*. Far from being a personalized spirit power, *mana* is abstract in the extreme, a spiritual force or metaphysical energy lying always just beyond reach of the senses.

This concept of impersonal potency or energy was widespread among North American Indians. The Algonquins called it *manitou;* to the Mohawk it was *orenda;* to the Lakota, *wakonda.* For instance, as discussed in the upcoming section on sacred sites, Bear Butte in the Black Hills is a mountain where Lakota believers feel a strong presence of spirit power, or *wakonda.*

In some cultures this impersonal spirit power, or metaphysical energy, is turned to for healing purposes. Notably, *animism* (as a belief in distinct spirit beings) and *animatism* (which lacks particular substance or individual form) are not mutually exclusive. They are often found in the same culture, as in Melanesian societies and also in North American Indian societies just mentioned.

People trying to comprehend beliefs in the supernatural beings and powers that others recognize frequently ask how such beliefs are maintained. In part, the answer is through manifestations of power. Given a belief in animatism and/or the powers of supernatural beings, one is predisposed to see what appear to be results of the application of such powers. For example, if a Melanesian warrior is convinced of his power because he possesses the necessary *mana* and he is successful, he is likely to interpret this success as proof of the power of *mana*. Beyond this, because of his confidence in his *mana*, he may be willing to take more chances in his fighting, and this indeed could mean the difference between success or failure.

Failures, of course, do occur, but they can be explained. Perhaps one's prayer was not answered because a deity or spirit was still angry about some past insult. Or perhaps

animism A belief that nature is animated (enlivened or energized) by distinct personalized spirit beings separable from bodies.

animatism A belief that nature is enlivened or energized by an impersonal spiritual power or supernatural potency.

An example of animism exists among Inuit of Arctic Canada, who believed that nature is animated by supernatural beings separable from the physical body or material substance they inhabit. Referring to such spirits as *anirniit* (singular *anirniq,* meaning "breath"), traditional Inuit still obey certain taboos and perform rituals when killing seal and other game animals and dividing the meat. This is to avoid offending the animal's spirit (which lives on and may take revenge on the hunter). Today, most Inuit are Christians and their concept of *anirniq* is akin to "soul." But traditional food rituals continue. In this photo, Inuit at Baffin Island, Nunavut, pray before a shared Easter feast of fish and seal meat.

B&C Alexander/ArcticPhoto

the Melanesian warrior lost his battle because he was not as successful in bringing *mana* to bear or his opponent had more of it. In any case, humans generally emphasize successes over failures, and long after many of the latter have been forgotten, tales will still be told of the workings of supernatural powers.

Beliefs are also maintained through myths—explanatory narratives that rationalize and reinforce religious beliefs and practices. We will discuss myths in more detail later in this chapter.

Sacred Places

In addition to revering special supernatural figures such as deities, ancestral spirits, and other special beings, some religious traditions consider certain geographic places to be spiritually significant or even sacred. Typically, such sites are rivers, lakes, waterfalls, islands, forests, caves, and—especially—mountains. Often, their status is due to some unique shape or outstanding feature, such as a conical volcano capped with snow. Numerous mountains around the world fall into this category. Often they are associated with origin myths as splendid abodes of the gods. Or they are revered as dwelling places for the spirits of the dead, heights where prophets received their divine directions, or retreats for prayer, meditation, and vision quests.

Three sacred mountains are shared by the Jewish, Christian, and Muslim traditions: Mount Ararat in the Caucasus Mountains, a multinational region between Russia and Turkey where the ark of the ancient patriarch Noah is said to have landed after the Great Flood; Mount Horeb, the

"mountain of God" in the Sinai Desert where the prophet Moses received the stone tablets from his god with the ten sacred rules of behavior; and Mount Moriah, also known as the Temple Mount, at the old city of Jerusalem. According to Jewish tradition, it was from this hilltop that God gathered "the dust of the ground" to create Adam, the ancestor of all human beings today. And it was there that Solomon, the Israelite king, is believed to have been divinely ordered to build the Great Temple almost 3,000 years ago.

Almost 1,500 years later, the prophet Muhammad came to this place on a mystic night journey in company with the angel Gabriel and riding a winged horse. After a prayer meeting with the prophets Abraham, Moses, and Jesus, Muhammad was led by Gabriel to the top of the rock and ascended on a ladder of golden light to heaven where Allah gave him his divine instructions. On this holy spot, the sacred shrine *Masjid Qubbat As-Sakhrah* ("Dome of the Rock") was built for Muslim pilgrims. Completed in 691 AD, it is the oldest Muslim building in existence and the third holiest site in Islam.

Similar traditions exist in many other cultures. For instance, the Japanese view the snow-capped perfect volcanic cone of Mount Fuji ("ever-lasting life") as a sacred place. Aztecs held several snow-capped volcanoes sacred, including Popocatepetl ("Smoking Mountain") just outside Mexico City. And the same can be said for Kirinyaga (Mount Kenya) in East Africa. Straddling the equator, it is seen as a holy place by the Kikuyu people who believe this "Mountain of Brightness" to be the earthly dwelling place of their creator god Ngai. Likewise, the ancient Greeks considered Mount Olympus to be the mythological abode of Zeus, the king of all their gods. In some religious traditions, such as among the Aymara of the Bolivian highlands, a volcanic mountain like Kaata is not only considered sacred, but is actually deified and worshiped as a living god.

Symbolic of the supreme being, or associated with various important deities or ancestral spirits, sacred mountains may feature in religious ceremonies or spiritual rituals. In some religious traditions, these towering geographic features are places of worship, like shrines, or are sacred destinations for spiritual journeys or pilgrimages. For example, as mentioned above, dozens of American Indian nations in the Great Plains consider Bear Butte in the Black Hills of South Dakota to be of great spiritual significance. They come to this domed mountain for meditation, prayers, and sacred vision quests. For outsiders

© Images & Stories, Turkey

Pilgrims at Mount Kailash in Tibet. Rising 6,700 meters (about 22,000 feet), this mountain has been held sacred for thousands of years by Hindus, Buddhists, Jains, and followers of Bön (Tibet's indigenous religion). They do not deify this peak, but they believe it to be the sacred abode of Lord Shiva, a member of the supreme divine trinity—so sacred that they would not even dream of trying to climb it. Year after year, thousands of pilgrims follow the ancient tradition of circling the mountain on foot. The rugged, 52-kilometer (32-mile) trek, known as *parikarma,* is seen as a holy ritual that removes sins and brings good fortune.

unfamiliar with (or unsympathetic to) the indigenous traditions, these sacred mountains may be valued for commercial or recreational purposes, thus leading to bitter controversies and unfortunate consequences.

Religious Specialists

Much of religion's value comes from the activities called for by its prescriptions and rules. Participation in religious ceremonies may bring a sense of personal lift—a wave of reassurance, a feeling of overwhelming joy, and even a sense of moving into a trancelike state—or a feeling of closeness to fellow participants. The beliefs and ceremonies of religions vary considerably, as do the individuals who guide others in these religious practices.

All human societies include individuals who guide and supplement the religious practices of others. Such individuals are seen to be highly skilled at contacting and influencing supernatural beings and manipulating or connecting to supernatural forces. Often their qualification is that they have undergone special training. In addition, they may display certain distinctive personality traits that make them particularly well suited to perform these tasks.

Priests and Priestesses

In societies with the resources to support a full-time occupational specialist, a **priest or priestess** will have the role of guiding religious practices and influencing the supernatural. He or she is the socially initiated, ceremonially inducted member of a recognized religious organization, with a rank and function that belong to him or her as the holder of a position others have held before. The sources of power are the society and the institution within which the priest or priestess functions.

The priest, if not the priestess, is a familiar figure in Western societies; he is the priest, minister, imam, lama, rabbi, or whatever the official title may be in an organized religion. With their god defined historically in masculine, authoritarian terms, it is not surprising that, in the Judaic, Christian, and Islamic religions, the most important positions traditionally have been filled by men. Female religious specialists are likely to be found only in societies where women are acknowledged to contribute in a major way to the economy and where gods

priest or priestess A full-time religious specialist formally recognized for his or her role in guiding the religious practices of others and for contacting and influencing supernatural powers.

Change Your Karma and Change Your Sex? *by Hillary Crane*

As Mahayana Buddhists, Taiwanese Chan (Zen) monastics believe that all humans are able to reach enlightenment and be released from reincarnation. But they believe it is easier for some because of the situation into which they are born—for example, if one is born in a country where Buddhism is practiced, in a family that teaches proper behavior, or with exceptional mental or physical gifts.

Chan monastics view contrasting human circumstances as the result of the karma accrued in previous lives. They believe certain behavior—such as diligently practicing Buddhism—improves karma and the chances of attaining spiritual goals in this lifetime or coming back in a better birth. Other behavior—such as killing a living being, eating meat, desiring or becoming attached to things or people—accrues bad karma.

One way karma manifests itself is in one's sex. Taiwanese Buddhists believe that being born female makes it harder to attain spiritual goals. This idea comes, in part, from the inferior status of women in Taiwan and the belief that their "complicated bodies" and monthly menstruation cycles can distract them. Moreover, they believe, women are more enmeshed in their families than men and their emotional ties keep them focused on worldly rather than spiritual tasks.

Taiwanese Buddhists who decide to become monks and nuns must break from their families to enter a monastery. Since women are thought to be more attached to their families than are men, leaving home is seen as a particularly big step for nuns and a sign that they are more like men than most women. In fact, a nun's character is considered masculine, unlike the frightened, indecisive, and emotional traits usually associated with women in Taiwan. When they leave home nuns even stop referring to themselves as women and call one another *shixiong* ("dharma brother"). They use this linguistic change to signal that they identify themselves as men and to remind one another to behave like men, particularly like the monks at the temple.

Monastics also reduce their attachments to worldly things like music and food. Nuns usually emphasize forsaking food and eat as little as possible. Their appearance, already quite masculine because they shave their heads and wear loose, gray clothing, becomes even more so when they lose weight—particularly in their hips, breasts, and thighs. Also, after becoming monastics, they often experience a slowing or stopping of their menses. Although these physical changes can be attributed to change in diet and lifestyle, the nuns point to them as signs they are becoming men, making progress toward their spiritual goals, and improving their karma.

BIOCULTURAL QUESTION

The Zen Buddhist ideal of enlightenment, realized when the soul is released from reincarnation, prescribes an extreme ascetic lifestyle for nuns that makes them physically incapable of biological reproduction. Do you think that their infertility allows these female monastics to emotionally adapt to a way of life that denies them motherhood?

For a more detailed treatment of this topic, see Crane, H (2001). Men in spirit: The masculinization of Taiwanese Buddhist nuns. *Doctoral dissertation, Brown University.*

---

and goddesses are both recognized. In western Europe and North America, for instance, where women are now wage earners in almost every profession and occupy leadership positions in the workforce, they have an increasing presence in the leadership of many Judeo-Christian religious groups.[4]

Although women still do not occupy the highest-ranking religious leadership positions in the Roman Catholic Church (headed by a male pope and his all-male council, the College of Cardinals), this Christian religion does recognize important female saints. Most significant among these is the Virgin Mary, held to be the human mother of God's son. In many places where Roman Catholicism has spread, worshipers have created cults around this female saint. Moreover, all around the world women devoted to a religious life have formed their own places for religious exclusion as nuns jointly belonging to a cloister or convent, headed by an abbess.

Such all-female religious institutions are not unique to Roman Catholicism. Convents of nuns are also part of Buddhist religious traditions. They can be found in several places around the world—in particular, Asian countries, including Thailand, as described by anthropologist Hillary Crane in this chapter's Biocultural Connection.

Shamans

Societies that lack full-time occupational specialization have existed far longer than those with such specialization, and they have always included individuals with special powers and skills that enable them to connect with and manipulate supernatural beings and forces. These powers

[4] Lehman, E. C., Jr. (2002, Fall). Women's path into the ministry. *Pulpit & Pew Research Reports 1*, 4.

have come to them through some personal experience, usually in solitude. In an altered state of consciousness, they receive a vision that empowers them to heal the sick, change the weather, control the movements of animals, and foretell the future. As they perfect these and related skills, they assume the role of shaman.

The word *shaman* originally referred to medical-religious specialists, or spiritual guides, among the Tungus and other Siberian pastoral nomads with animist beliefs. By means of various techniques such as fasting, drumming, chanting, or dancing, as well as hallucinogenic mushrooms, these Siberian shamans enter into a trance, or altered state of consciousness. While in this waking dream state, they experience visions of an alternate reality inhabited by spirit beings such as guardian animal spirits who may assist in the healing.

Cross-cultural research of shamanism shows that similar medical-religious healing practices also exist in traditional cultures outside Siberia. For that reason, the term *shaman* has also been applied to a variety of part-time spiritual leaders and traditional healers ("medicine men") active in North and South American indigenous communities and beyond.

As defined by anthropologist Michael Harner, famous for his participant observation among Shuar (or Jivaro) Indian shamans in the Amazon rainforest, a **shaman** is "a man or woman who enters an altered state of consciousness—at will—to contact and utilize an ordinarily hidden reality in order to acquire knowledge, power, and to help other persons. The shaman has at least one, and usually more, 'spirits' in his or her personal service."[5]

The term *shaman* has become so popular in recent decades that any non-Western local priest, healer, or diviner is often loosely referred to as one.[6] In the United States millions of people learned something about shamans through the popular autobiography of Black Elk, a traditional Lakota Indian holy man. Numerous other publications on shamanism have appeared over the past four decades, and some Euramericans have gone into practice as shamans, a development that has triggered considerable resentment among some Native Americans. ("They stole our land, now they are stealing our religion.") In addition to so-called new age enthusiasts, among whom shamanism is particularly popular, faith healers and other evangelists among fundamentalist Christians share many of the characteristics of shamanism.

Typically, one becomes a shaman by passing through stages of learning and practical experience, often involving psychological and emotional ordeals brought about by isolation, fasting, physical torture, sensory deprivation, and/or hallucinations. These hallucinations (derived from the Latin word for "mental wandering") occur when the shaman is in a trance, which may occur spontaneously but can also be induced by drumming or consuming mind-altering drugs such as psychoactive vines or mushrooms.

Among the Penobscot Indians in northern New England, for example, any person could become a shaman, since no formal institution provided rules and regulations to guide religious consciousness. The search for shamanic visions was pursued by most adult Penobscot males, who would go off alone and—through meditation, sensory deprivation, and hyperventilation—induce an altered state of consciousness in which they hoped to receive a vision. Not all were successful, but failure did not result in social disgrace. Those who did achieve success experienced a sense of being freed from their bodily existence in which they established a special relationship with a particular animal spirit that appeared in their trance state. This became the shaman's animal helper—a common element in shamanism—who thereafter would assist the individual in performing shamanic tasks.

Because shamanism is rooted in altered states of consciousness and the nervous system that produces these trance states is universal, individuals involved in shamanism experience similarly structured visual, auditory, somatic (touch), olfactory (smell), and gustatory (taste) hallucinations. The widespread occurrence of shamanism and the remarkable similarities among shamanic traditions everywhere are consequences of this universal neurological inheritance. At the same time, the meanings ascribed to sensations experienced in altered states and made of their content are culturally determined; hence, despite their overall similarities, local traditions always vary in their details.

The shaman is essentially a religious go-between who acts on behalf of some human client, often to bring about healing or to foretell some future event. To do so, the shaman intervenes to influence or impose his or her will on supernatural powers. The shaman can be contrasted with the priest or priestess, whose "clients" are the deities. Priests and priestesses frequently tell people what to do; the shaman tells supernatural beings what to do. In return for services rendered, the shaman may collect a fee—fresh meat, yams, or a favorite possession. In some cases, the added prestige, authority, and

---

[5] Harner, M. (1980). *The way of the shaman: A guide to power and healing* (p. 20). San Francisco: Harper & Row.

[6] Kehoe, A. (2000). *Shamans and religion: An anthropological exploration in critical thinking.* Prospect Heights, IL: Waveland.

shaman A person who enters an altered state of consciousness—at will—to contact and utilize an ordinarily hidden reality in order to acquire knowledge, power, and to help others.

Visual Counterpoint

Shamanism is by no means absent in modern industrial societies. Here we see a new age shaman in North America (left) and a traditional shaman in Mongolia. The Mongolian shaman's drum is crafted from the wood of a tree struck by lightning and covered with leather made from a female red deer. It is believed that when the shaman goes into a trance, her drum transforms into a magic steed that carries her into the dark sky of her ancestors.

social power attached to the shaman's status are reward enough.

When a shaman acts on behalf of a client, he or she may put on something of a show—one that heightens the basic drama with a sense of danger. Typically, the shaman enters a trance state, in which he or she experiences the sensation of traveling to the alternate world and seeing and interacting with spirit beings. The shaman tries to impose his or her will upon these spirits, an inherently dangerous contest, considering the superhuman powers that spirits are thought to possess.

An example of this can be seen in the trance dances of the Ju/'hoansi Bushmen of southern Africa's Kalahari Desert. Traditional Ju/'hoansi belief holds that illness and misfortune are caused by invisible arrows shot by spirits. The arrows can be removed by healers, men and women who possess the powerful healing force called *n/um* (the Ju/'hoansi equivalent of *mana*). Some healers can activate *n/um* by solo singing or instrument playing, but more often this is accomplished

through the medicinal curing ceremony or trance dance. To the sound of undulating melodies sung by women, healers dance around the fire, sometimes for hours. The music, the strenuous dancing, the smoke, the heat of the fire, and the healers' intense concentration cause their

n/um to heat up. When it comes to a boil, trance is achieved and *n/um* is available as a powerful healing force to serve the entire community. In trance, a healer lays hands on and ritually cures everyone sitting around the fire.[7]

In many human societies, sleight-of-hand tricks and ventriloquism occur at the same time as trancing. Among Arctic peoples, for example, a shaman may summon spirits in the dark and produce flapping noises and strange voices to impress the audience. Some Western observers regard this kind of trickery as evidence of the fraudulent nature of shamanism. However, those who have studied shamanic practices agree that even though shamans know perfectly well that they are manipulating people with their tricks, they really believe in their power to deal with supernatural forces and spirit beings. Their power, verified by the trance experience, gives them the right as well as the ability to manipulate people in minor technical matters. In short, the shaman regards his or her ability to perform extraordinary tricks as further proof of superior powers.

---

[7] Shostak, M. (1983). *Nisa: The life and words of a !Kung woman* (pp. 291–293). New York: Vintage.

Ju/'hoansi shaman healer and helper in trance dance.

Figure 13.3 The shamanic complex. Shamanic healing takes place within a "magic field" created when the shaman (A) and patient (B), as well as their community (C), are all convinced that the shaman is a genuine healing master using appropriate techniques that are effective and beneficial. Similar psychological processes are involved in Western medical treatments.

The importance of shamanism in a society should not be underestimated. It promotes, through the drama of performance, a trancelike feeling and a release of tension. And it provides psychological assurance that prevailing upon supernatural powers and spirits otherwise beyond human control can bring about invulnerability from attack, success at love, or the return of health. In fact, a frequent reason for a shamanic performance is poor health—a concept that is difficult to define effectively in cross-cultural terms. Not only do people in diverse cultures recognize and experience different types of illnesses, they may also view and explain them in different terms. The culturally defined diagnosis of an illness, in turn, determines how the patient will be treated according to the beliefs of the culture, in order to achieve healing.

Although the psychological effects of the shamanic treatment are not known, the connection between mind and body may contribute to the patient's recovery. From an anthropological perspective, shamanic healings can be understood by means of a three-cornered model: the *shamanic complex* (Figure 13.3). This triangle is created by the relationships among the shaman and the patient and the community to which both belong.

For healing to take place, the shaman needs to be convinced of the effectiveness of his or her spiritual powers and techniques. Likewise, the patient must see the shaman as a genuine healing master using appropriate techniques. Finally, to close the triangle's "magic field," the community within which the shaman operates on the patient must view the healing ceremony and its practitioner as potentially effective and beneficial.

Such dynamics are not unique to shamanic healing ceremonies, for similar social psychological processes are involved in Western medical treatments as well. Consider, for example, the *placebo effect*—the beneficial result a patient experiences after a particular treatment, due to his or her expectations concerning the treatment rather than from the treatment itself. Notably, some people involved in modern medicine work collaboratively with practitioners

Reconciling Modern Medicine with Traditional Beliefs in Swaziland

by Edward C. Green

Although the biomedical germ theory is generally known and accepted in Western societies today, this is not the case in many other societies around the world. In southern Africa's Swaziland, for example, many illnesses are generally thought to be caused by sorcery or by loss of ancestral protection. (Sexually transmitted diseases—STDs—and other contagious diseases are exceptions to these beliefs.)

Even where the effectiveness of Western medicine is recognized, the ultimate question remains: Why did a disease come to a particular person in the first place? Thus, for the treatment of disease, the Swazi have traditionally relied upon herbalists, diviner mediums through whom ancestor spirits are thought to work, and (more recently) Christian faith healers. Unfortunately, such individuals have usually been regarded as quacks and charlatans by the medical establishment. Yet, the herbal medicines used by traditional healers are effective in several ways, and the reassurance provided patient and family alike through rituals that reduce stress and anxiety plays an important role in the patient's recovery. In a country where there is one traditional healer for every 110 people, but only one physician for every 10,000, the potential benefit of cooperation between physicians and healers seems self-evident. Nevertheless, it was largely unrecognized until proposed by anthropologists D. M. Warren (in Ghana) and later, myself.

It was in 1981, when I was a Washington-based independent consultant, that I first went to Swaziland as a researcher for the Rural Water-Borne

Disease Control Project, funded by the United States Agency for International Development. Assigned the task of finding out about knowledge, attitudes, and practices related to water and sanitation, and aware of the serious deficiencies of conventional surveys that rely on precoded questionnaires, I used instead the traditional anthropological techniques of open-ended interviews with key informants, along with participant observation. The key informants were traditional healers, their patients, and rural health motivators (women chosen by communities to receive eight weeks of training in preventive health care in regional clinics). Without such anthropological research, it would have been impossible to design and interpret a reliable survey instrument, but the added payoff was that I learned a great deal about Swazi theories of illness and its treatment.

Disposed at the outset to recognize the positive value of many traditional practices, I could also see how cooperation with physicians might be achieved. For example, traditional healers already recognized the utility of Western medicines for treatment of diseases considered not indigenous to Africa, and traditional preventive medicines were routinely given to children through inhalation, something like childhood vaccinations. Thus, nontraditional medicines and vaccinations might be accepted, if presented in ways that resembled traditional medicine.

Realizing the suspicion existing on both sides, I and my Swazi associate Lydia Makhubu (a chemist who had studied the properties of indigenous

medicines) recommended to the minister of health a cooperative project focusing on a problem of concern to both health professionals and native healers: infant diarrheal diseases. These had recently become a health problem of high concern to the general public; healers wanted a means to prevent such diseases, and a means of treatment existed—oral rehydration therapy—that was compatible with traditional treatments for diarrhea (herbal preparations taken orally over a period of time). Packets of oral rehydration salts, along with instructions, were provided to healers in a pilot project, with positive results. This helped convince health professionals of the benefits of cooperation, while the healers saw the distribution of packets to them as a gesture of trust and cooperation on the part of their government.

Since then, further steps toward cooperation have been taken, such as work in prevention of AIDS, STDs, and TB. All of this demonstrates the importance of finding how to work in ways compatible with existing belief systems. Directly challenging traditional beliefs, as all too often happens, does little more than create stress, confusion, and resentment among people.

Adapted from Green, E. C. (1987). The planning of health education strategies in Swaziland, and the integration of modern and traditional health sectors in Swaziland. In R. M. Wulff & S. J. Fiske (Eds.), Anthropological praxis: Translating knowledge into action (pp. 15–25, 87–97). Boulder, CO: Westview.

of traditional belief systems toward the healing of various illnesses—as illustrated in this chapter's Anthropology Applied feature.

Sacred Performances: Rituals and Ceremonies

Rituals or ceremonial acts are not all religious in nature (consider, for example, college graduation ceremonies in North America), but those that are play a crucial role in religious activity. Religious ritual is the means through

which people relate to the supernatural; it is religion in action. Ritual serves to relieve social tensions and reinforce a group's collective bonds. More than this, it provides a means of marking many important events and lessening the social disruption and individual suffering of crises, such as death.

Anthropologists have classified several different types of ritual. These include rituals of purity, rites of passage, and rites of intensification. We begin with rituals of purity, which illustrate not only how members of a social group are bound together, but also how they reinforce the boundaries between the group and outsiders by means of cultural prohibitions known as taboos. Next come rituals

Exiled Tibetan monks at Drepunk Loseling monastery in India patiently create a mandala. Using narrow metal funnels, they spend many days placing millions of grains of fine colored sand into a geometric design that has deep spiritual significance in their Buddhist worldview. An ancient Sanskrit word, *mandala* means "circle-circumference" or "completion," referring to the enlightened mind of the Buddha. The ritual provides a visual framework for meditation toward establishing the radiant mental state. It is a tool for spiritual teaching, trance induction, and blessing the earth and all its creatures. Once complete, the sacred work is dismantled, and the sand is disseminated (usually in a body of running water) to spread the blessings.

for when individuals change their social status within their group. And finally, we briefly discuss rituals that allow members of a social group to strengthen their common identity in times of crisis.

Taboos: Cultural Prohibitions and Rituals of Purification

In many societies people follow certain culturally prescribed rules about what they can or cannot eat or drink, touch, or talk about. Many millions of Hindus, for example, eat pork but avoid beef because they regard the cow as a sacred animal. On the other hand, many millions of Muslims consume beef but avoid pork because in their religion swine is considered unclean. They share this pork taboo with Jews, both evoking the will of God (called Allah by Muslims and Yahweh by Jews) to justify their dietary laws. Christians accept the first books of the Bible as sacred and foundational, but ignore its laws prohibiting the eating of swine: "Their flesh you shall not eat, and

their carcasses you shall not touch."[8] And although Hindus, Muslims, Jews, and Christians all consider cannibalism offensive and even inhuman, there are societies that do not prohibit eating human flesh and provide certain cultural rules that categorize which types of human flesh can be consumed when, where, and how.

Taboo, the word used to describe these traditional prohibitions, is derived from the Polynesian term *tabu* (or *tapu*). Among Pacific Islanders such as Maoris or Samoans, this term refers to something that has supernatural power and is to be avoided. It can apply to an object (such as food), a person (such as a high-ranking noble), or a place (a shrine or temple). Especially applied to blood

---

[8] Deuteronomy 14: 3, 8. See also Leviticus 11: 7, 11.

taboo A prohibition, which, if not observed, leads to a penalty inflicted by magic, spiritual force, or religion.

and anything associated with sickness and death, taboos are taken very seriously. When a taboo is violated, believers expect supernatural punishment will follow. This penalty may come in magic form as misfortune—an unlucky accident, resulting in loss, sickness, or death. It is also possible that the taboo breaker will be punished by designated members in the community and may be ordered to undergo a purification ritual and make a sacrifice. Sometimes, the ultimate sacrifice is demanded and the offender is executed.

In the previous chapter, we discussed how the traditional hierarchy in the Hindu caste society is religiously reinforced by strict rules against ritual pollution that govern the lives of members of the different *varnas*. As members of the highest-ranking "grade of being," Brahmans are especially concerned about maintaining their "purity," which is symbolically associated with the color white and publicly visible in their dress. Like other traditional Hindus, they dutifully follow their ritually prescribed rules of conduct, known as *dharma* and thus avoid becoming "unclean." If they break a taboo, they are believed to have violated the fundamental Hindu principles of the cosmic order. And for someone who believes in reincarnation, such misconduct has consequences for one's *karma*, the soul's destiny or fate when it is reincarnated (literally, "returns into flesh") in the next life. Clearly, rules of ritual purity and pollution are embedded in this society's worldview and, as such, form part of a culture's superstructure.

Anthropologists specializing in comparative religion have been intrigued by the cross-cultural variation in cultural categories, classifying certain animals, plants, objects, or acts as unclean or "dirty," and others as dangerous or taboo.[9] Why do people make such prohibitions and deny themselves what others may enjoy as pleasures in life? In her classic study *Purity and Danger: An Analysis of Concepts of Pollution and Taboo*, British anthropologist Mary Douglas offers many insights originally based on her

research among the Lele in Congo: "Reflection on dirt involves reflection on the relation of order to disorder, being to non being, form to formlessness, life to death."[10]

Relating taboos involving rituals of purity to cultural classifications of the cosmic order, Douglas explains

> Dirt is essentially disorder. There is no such thing as absolute dirt: it exists in the eyes of the beholder. If we shun dirt, it is not because of craven fear, still less of dread of holy terror. . . . Dirt offends against order. Eliminating it is not a negative movement, but a positive effort to organise the environment. [Rituals] of purity and impurity create unity in experience. [By] their means, symbolic patterns are worked out and publicly displayed.[11]

Informed by their religious beliefs about the cosmic order and the laws that maintain its structure as a functioning system, members of a culture learn to find their proper place in society. Rules maintaining social order within the group, as well as defining these groups from others, are reinforced by rituals of purity and associated taboos. As such, these rituals not only serve to more effectively integrate individuals into that complex whole we call "culture," but also to help avoid mix-ups and mistakes that can cause chaos and thereby endanger the survival of the group.

Rites of Passage

Rites of passage are rituals that mark important stages in an individual's life cycle. In one of anthropology's classic works, German-French ethnographer Arnold van Gennep analyzed the rites of passage that mark an individual's crossing over from one social status to another. Such rituals help members of a society through the major social transitions or crucial crises in their lives, such as birth, puberty, graduation, marriage, parenthood, advancement to a higher official rank, and death.[12] Comparing these social transitions with "a territorial passage" in which travelers leave a country, cross its border (or limit), and enter another, he found it useful to divide ceremonies for all of these status transitions or life crises into three phases: pre-liminary (of separation), liminary (of marginality), and post-liminary (of admission). In anthropology today, this scheme is presented as three stages: **separation, transition,** and **incorporation;** the first being ritual removal of the individual from everyday society, followed by

---

[9] See, among others, Durkheim, E., & Mauss, M. (1963). *Primitive classification*. Chicago: University of Chicago Press. (orig. 1902); Lévi-Strauss, C. (1969). *The raw and the cooked*. New York: Harper & Row; Leach, E. (1964). Anthropological aspects of language: Animal categories and verbal abuse. In W. Lessa & E. Vogt (Eds.), *Reader in comparative religion* (4th ed.). New York: Harper & Row.

rite of passage   A ritual that marks an important stage in an individual's life cycle, such as birth, marriage, and death.

separation   In a rite of passage, the ritual removal of the individual from society.

transition   In a rite of passage, isolation of the individual following separation and prior to incorporation into society.

incorporation   In a rite of passage, reincorporation of the individual into society in his or her new status.

---

[10] Douglas, M. (1966). *Purity and danger: An analysis of concepts of pollution and taboo* (p. 6). London: Routledge & Kegan Paul.

[11] Ibid., pp. 2–3.

[12] Van Gennep, A. (1960). *The rites of passage*. Chicago: University of Chicago Press. (orig. [1909]. *Les rites de passage*. Paris: Émile Nourry)

a period of isolation, and, finally, formal return and read-mission back into society in his or her new status.

This sequence of stages is something that takes place in many forms in all cultures around the world, from military boot camps to college fraternity and sorority initiation ceremonies in the United States to a global array of puberty ceremonies that mark the transition from childhood to adulthood.

MALE INITIATION RITES

The Aborigines of Australia provide an example of a male initiation rite into manhood. When the elders decide the time for initiation, the boys are taken from the village (separation), while the women cry and make a ritual show of resistance. At a place distant from the camp, groups of men from many villages gather. The elders sing and dance, while the initiates act as though they are dead. The climax of this part of the ritual is a bodily operation, such as circumcision or the knocking out of a tooth. Australian anthropologist A. P. Elkin comments:

> This is partly a continuation of the drama of death. The tooth-knocking, circumcision or other symbolical act "killed" the novice; after this he does not return to the general camp and normally may not be seen by any woman. He is dead to the ordinary life of the tribe.[13]

In this transitional stage, the novice may be shown secret ceremonies and receive some instruction, but the most significant element is his complete removal from society. In the course of these Australian puberty rites, the initiate must learn the lore that all adult men are expected to know. The trauma of the occasion is a pedagogical technique that ensures he will learn and remember everything; in a nonliterate society the perpetuation of cultural traditions requires no less, and so effective teaching methods are necessary.

On his return to society (incorporation), the novice is welcomed with ceremonies, as though he had returned from the dead. This alerts the society at large to the individual's new status—people can expect him to act in certain ways, and in return they must act in the appropriate ways toward him. The individual's new rights and duties are thus clearly defined. He is spared, for example, the problems of a teenager in North America, whose status is ill defined as neither adult nor child.

In the Australian case just cited, boys are prepared not just for adulthood but also for manhood. In their society, for example, courage and endurance are considered important masculine virtues, and the pain of tooth-knocking and circumcision helps instill these in initiates.

FEMALE INITIATION RITES

In a similar way to the male initiation rite described above, female initiation rites help prepare Mende girls in West Africa for womanhood. After they have begun to menstruate, the girls are removed from society to spend weeks, or even months, in seclusion. There, they discard the clothes of childhood, smear their bodies with white clay, and dress in short skirts and many strands of beads.

Shortly after entering this transitional stage, the girls undergo clitoridectomy, a removal of the clitoris, viewed as the feminine version of the penis. The girls (and Mende in general) believe this form of female circumcision enhances their reproductive potential. While secluded, they are trained in the moral and practical responsibilities of potential child bearers by experienced women. With the training comes a good deal of singing, dancing, storytelling, and food—and a strong sense of sisterhood. The pain and danger of the surgery, endured in the context of intense social support from other women, serve as a metaphor for childbirth, which may well take place in the same place of seclusion, again with the support of experienced women. They emerge from their initiation as women in knowledgeable control of their sexuality, eligible for marriage and childbearing. Having gone through this ritual, a traditional Mende woman knows she is "all woman."

In recent decades, various activist groups in North America and western Europe, in particular, have identified clitoridectomy as one of several forms of female genital mutilation (FGM). Practiced in Africa and Asia especially, FGM has been condemned as a human rights violation, and committees to end the practice have been set up in twenty-two African countries.[14] Notably, women's breast implant surgery has been compared to FGM as Western industrialized society's version of what it takes to be "all woman."[15] The Original Study in the final chapter of this book addresses this issue in detail.

Rites of Intensification

Rites of intensification are rituals that take place during a crisis in the life of the group and serve to bind individuals together. Whatever the precise nature of the crisis—a

[14] "Female genital mutilation." (2000). Fact sheet no. 241. World Health Organization; Dirie, W., & Miller, C. (1998). *Desert flower: The extraordinary journey of a desert nomad* (pp. 218, 219). New York: Morrow.
[15] MacCormack, C. P. (1977). Biological events and cultural control. *Signs 3*, 98.

rite of intensification A ritual that takes place during a crisis in the life of the group and serves to bind individuals together.

[13] Elkin, A. P. (1964). *The Australian Aborigines.* Garden City, NY: Doubleday/Anchor.

drought that threatens crops, the sudden appearance of an enemy war party, the onset of an epidemic—mass ceremonies are performed to ease the sense of danger. This unites people in a common effort so that fear and confusion yield to collective action and a degree of optimism. The balance in the relations of all concerned is restored to normal, and the community's values are celebrated and affirmed.

While an individual's death might be regarded as the ultimate crisis in that person's life, it is, as well, a crisis for the entire group, particularly if the group is small. A member of the community has been removed, so its composition has been seriously altered. The survivors, therefore, must readjust and restore balance. They also need to reconcile themselves to the loss of someone to whom they were emotionally tied.

A remarkable cultural example of a rite of intensification is the Hindu cremation ceremony in Bali, depicted in this chapter's opening photograph. Sharing a worldview with a religious belief in the reincarnation of a deceased person's soul, the Balinese deal with death by turning what could be a painful emotional experience of grief and loss into a joyous celebration of life's progressive continuity by being reborn in a future existence. At the same time, as a social reminder of Hindu caste differences in Balinese stratified society, the family of a deceased relative uses this elaborate public ceremony to display its wealth and social rank. Everyone can see that some funeral pyres are bigger and more beautiful than others (such as those built for members of a noble or royal family on the island).

Funerary ceremonies, then, can be regarded as rites of intensification that permit the living to express in nondisruptive ways their upset over the death while providing for social readjustment. Frequently such ceremonies feature ambivalence toward the dead person. For example, one part of the funerary rites of certain Melanesians was the eating of the dead person's flesh. This ritual cannibalism, witnessed by anthropologist Bronislaw Malinowski, was performed with "extreme repugnance and dread and usually followed by a violent vomiting fit. At the same time it is felt to be a supreme act of reverence, love, and devotion."[16]

This custom and the emotions accompanying it clearly reveal ambivalence toward death: On the one hand, there is the survivors' desire to maintain the tie to the dead person, and, on the other hand, they feel disgust and fear at

Ritual cannibalism appears in various societies in diverse forms. In Christianity, it is symbolic rather than actual, although millions of orthodox believers subscribe to the doctrine of transubstantiation, which holds that in Holy Communion the consecrated red wine and wafer or bread actually change into the divine blood and flesh of Christ, the Son of God.

the transformation wrought by death. According to Malinowski, funeral ceremonies provide an approved collective means for individuals to express these feelings while maintaining social cohesiveness and preventing disruption of society.

Rites of intensification do not have to be limited to times of overt crisis. In regions with marked differences in seasons where human activities must change accordingly, these rites will take the form of annual ceremonies. These are particularly common among horticultural and agricultural peoples, with their planting and harvest ceremonies. Because these are critical times for such cultures, the ceremonies express reverence toward nature's generation and fertility upon which people's very existence depends.

Participation in rituals of reverence and celebration during planting and harvest seasons reinforces group involvement. It also serves as a kind of dress rehearsal for

---

[16] Malinowski, B. (1954). *Magic, science, and religion* (p. 50). Garden City, NY: Doubleday.

crisis situations by promoting the habit of relying on supernatural forces—a habit that may make a crucial difference under stressful circumstances when it is important not to give way to fear and despair.

Magic

Among the most fascinating of ritual practices is the belief that supernatural powers can be compelled to act in certain ways for good or evil purposes by recourse to specified formulas. This is a classical anthropological notion of magic. Many societies have magical rituals to ensure good crops, the replenishment of game, the fertility of domestic animals, and the avoidance or healing of illness.

Although many Western peoples today—seeking to objectify and demythologize their world—have tried to suppress magic mysteries in their own consciousness, they continue to be fascinated by them. Not only are books and films about demonic possession and witchcraft avidly devoured and discussed, but horoscope columns are a regular feature of daily newspapers in the United States. And magical rituals are still commonly practiced by many Westerners seeking some luck where the outcome is in doubt or beyond factual influence—from lighting a votive candle for someone going through a hard time, to wearing lucky boxers on a hot date, to the curious gesturing baseball pitchers perform before each throw.

In the 19th century British anthropologist Sir James George Frazer made a useful distinction between two fundamental principles of magic. The first principle, that "like produces like," he named **imitative magic** (sometimes called *sympathetic magic*). In Myanmar (Burma) in Southeast Asia, for example, a rejected lover might engage a sorcerer to make an image of his would-be love. If this image were tossed into water, to the accompaniment of certain charms, it was expected that the hapless girl would go mad. Thus the girl would suffer a fate similar to that of her image.

Frazer called the second principle of thought on which magic is based **contagious magic**—the idea that things or persons once in contact can influence each other after the contact is broken. The most common example of contagious magic is the permanent relationship between an individual and any part of his or her body, such as hair, fingernails, or teeth. Frazer cited the Basutos of Lesotho in southern Africa, who were careful to conceal their extracted teeth because these might fall into the hands of certain mythical beings who could harm the owners of the teeth by working magic on them. Related to this is the custom, in Western

A 100-year-old fetish from Congo in Central Africa, believed to possess harmful spirit power. Known as a *nkondi*, the power of the wooden carving comes in part from magic herbs hidden behind the mirror. During a special ritual (reflecting the principle of imitative magic), iron nails were driven into this figure to activate its power to destroy hostile evil spirits or hunt down wrongdoers and take vengeance.

societies, of treasuring things that have been touched by special people. Such things range from a saint's relics to possessions of other admired or idolized individuals, from rock stars to sport heroes to spiritual gurus.

imitative magic Magic based on the principle that like produces like; sometimes called sympathetic magic.

contagious magic Magic based on the principle that things or persons once in contact can influence each other after the contact is broken.

Witchcraft

In Salem, Massachusetts, 200 innocent citizens suspected of being witches were arrested in 1692; of these, thirteen women and six men were hanged, and one 80-year-old farmer was tortured to death. Despite awarding damages to descendants of some of the victims nineteen years later, it was not until 1957 that the last of the Salem witches were exonerated by the Massachusetts legislature. **Witchcraft** is an explanation of events based on the belief that certain individuals possess an innate psychic power capable of causing harm, including sickness and death.

> **witchcraft** An explanation of events based on the belief that certain individuals possess an innate psychic power capable of causing harm, including sickness and death.

In North America, interest in and practice of witchcraft have grown significantly over the past four decades, with the rise of Wicca among highly educated segments of society. Contrary to popular belief, witchcraft is *not* concerned exclusively, or even primarily, with working evil.

Although many North Americans suppose it to be something that belongs to a less enlightened past, witchcraft is alive and well in the United States today. Indeed, starting in the 1960s, a "witch cult" known as Wicca began to gain popularity, including among highly educated segments of U.S. society. Inspired by various pre-Christian western European beliefs, in particular the idea of a sacred Mother Earth, Wicca is a nature-centered religion. And, contrary to widespread but false rumor, its self-styled "witches" do not worship Satan and are not concerned with "working evil." In fact, Wicca's core ethical statement, known as the Wiccan Rede, states that it can "harm none, do what you will."

Ibibio Witchcraft

North Americans are not alone in having a contemporary interest in witchcraft. For example, as the Ibibio of Nigeria have become increasingly exposed to modern education and scientific training, their reliance on witchcraft as an explanation for misfortune has increased.[17] Furthermore, it is often the younger, more educated members of Ibibio society who accuse others of bewitching them. Frequently, the accused are older, more traditional members of society; thus we have an expression of the intergenerational hostility that often exists in fast-changing traditional societies.

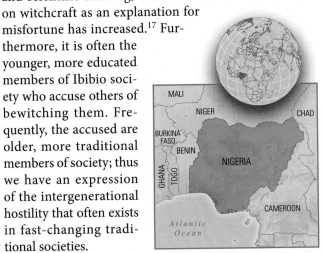

Ibibio witchcraft beliefs are highly developed and longstanding—as they are among most traditional peoples of sub-Saharan Africa. A rat that eats a person's crops is not really a rat but a witch that changed into one. If a young and enterprising man cannot get a job or fails an exam, he has been bewitched. If someone's money is wasted or if the person becomes sick, is bitten by a snake, or is struck by lightning, the reason is always the same—witchcraft.

Indeed, traditional Ibibio attribute virtually all misfortune, illness, or death to the malevolent activity of witches. The modern Ibibio's knowledge about the role of microorganisms in disease has little impact; after all, it says nothing about why these microorganisms were sent to the afflicted individual. Although Ibibio religious beliefs provide alternative explanations for misfortune, those carry

---

[17] Offiong, D. (1985). Witchcraft among the Ibibio of Nigeria. In A. C. Lehmann & J. E. Myers (Eds.), *Magic, witchcraft, and religion* (pp. 152–165). Palo Alto, CA: Mayfield.

negative connotations and do not elicit nearly as much sympathy from others. If evil befalls a person, witchcraft is a far more satisfying explanation than something such as offspring disobedience or violation of a taboo.

Ibibio witches are thought to be men or women who have within them a special substance acquired from another established witch. From swallowing this substance—made up of needles, colored threads, and other ingredients—one is believed to become endowed with a special psychic power that causes injury, even death, to others regardless of whether its possessor intends harm or not. It is believed to give them the ability to transform into animals and travel any distance at incredible speed to get at their unsuspecting victims, whom they may torture or kill by transferring the victim's soul or vital spirit into an animal, which is then eaten.

To identify a witch, an Ibibio looks for any person living in the region whose behavior is considered odd, out of the ordinary, immoral, or unsocial. Any combination of the following may cause someone to be labeled a witch: not being fond of greeting people; living alone in a place apart from others; charging too high a price for something; enjoying adultery or committing incest; walking about at night; not showing sufficient grief upon the death of a relative or other member of the community; taking improper care of one's parents, children, or wives; and being cold-hearted. Witches are apt to look and act mean and to be socially disruptive people in the sense that their behavior exceeds the range of variance considered acceptable.

The Ibibio make a distinction between *sorcerers,* whose acts are especially diabolical and destructive, and benign *witches,* whose witchcraft is relatively harmless, even though their powers are thought to be greater than those of their malevolent counterparts. Sorcerers are the very embodiment of a society's conception of evil—beings that flout the rules of sexual behavior and disregard every other standard of decency. Benign witches are often the community's non-conformists. Typically, they are morose, arrogant, and unfriendly people who keep to themselves but otherwise cause little disturbance. Such witches are thought to be dangerous when offended—likely to retaliate by causing sickness, death, crop failure, cattle disease, or any number of lesser ills. Not surprisingly, people viewed as witches are usually treated with considerable caution, respect, and even fear.[18]

Functions of Witchcraft

Why witchcraft? We might better ask, why not? In a world where there are few proven techniques for dealing with everyday crises, especially sickness, a belief in witches is not foolish; it is indispensable.[19] No one wants to resign oneself to illness, and if the malady is caused by a witch's curse, then magical countermeasures should cure it.

Not only does the idea of personalized evil answer the problem of unmerited suffering, but it also provides an explanation for many happenings for which no cause can be discovered. Witchcraft, then, cannot be refuted. Even if we could convince a person that his or her illness was due to natural causes, the victim would still ask, as the Ibibio do, Why me? Why now? Such a view leaves no room for pure chance; everything must be assigned a cause or meaning. Witchcraft offers an explanation and, in so doing, also provides both the basis and the means for taking counteraction.

Nor is witchcraft always entirely harmful. Its positive functions are noted in many African societies where people traditionally believe sickness, death, or other harm may be caused by witches. If people in the community agree that evildoing magic is in play, the ensuing search for the perpetrator of the misfortune becomes, in effect, a communal probe into dysfunctional social behavior. A witch-hunt is, in fact, a systematic investigation, through a public hearing, into all social relationships involving the victim of the sickness or death. Was a husband or wife unfaithful or a son lacking in the performance of his duties? Were an individual's friends uncooperative, or was the victim guilty of any of these wrongs? Accusations are reciprocal, and before long just about every unsocial or hostile act that has occurred in that society since the last outbreak of witchcraft (as manifested in sickness, death, or some other misfortune) is brought into the open.[20]

Through such periodic public scrutiny of behavior, people are reminded of what their society regards as both strengths and weaknesses of character. This encourages individuals to suppress as best they can those personality traits that are looked upon with disapproval, for if they do not, they at some time may be accused of being a witch. A belief in witchcraft thus serves as a broad control on antisocial behavior.

Witchcraft among the Navajo

Widely known among American Indians are the Navajo of the southwestern United States, who possess a highly developed concept of witchcraft. Several types of witchcraft are distinguished. Witchery encompasses the practices of witches, who are said to meet at night to practice cannibalism and kill people at a distance. Sorcery is distinguished from witchery only by the methods used by the sorcerer, who casts spells on individuals using the victim's

[18] See Mair, L. (1969). *Witchcraft* (p. 37). New York: McGraw-Hill.
[19] Ibid.

[20] Turnbull, C. M. (1983). *The human cycle* (p. 181). New York: Simon & Schuster.

fingernails, hair, or discarded clothing. Wizardry is not distinguished so much by its effects as by its manner of working: Wizards kill by injecting a cursed substance, such as a tooth from a corpse, into the victim's body.

Whether or not a particular illness results from Navajo witchcraft is determined by **divination**—a magical procedure or spiritual ritual designed to find out what is not knowable by ordinary means. Once a person is charged with witchcraft, he or she is publicly interrogated—in the past, possibly even tortured until there is a confession. It is believed the witch's own curse will turn against the witch once this happens, so it is expected that the witch will die within a year. Some confessed witches have been allowed to live in exile.

Navajo witchcraft serves to channel anxieties, tensions, and frustrations caused by the pressures from Euramericans.[21] The rigid rules of proper behavior among the Navajo allow little means for expression of hostility, except through accusations of witchcraft. Such accusations funnel pent-up negative emotions against individuals without upsetting the wider society. Another function of witchcraft accusations is that they permit direct expression of hostile feelings against people toward whom one ordinarily would be unable to express anger.

On a more positive note, individuals strive to behave in ways that will prevent them from being accused of witchcraft. Since excessive wealth is believed to result from witchcraft, individuals are encouraged to redistribute their assets among friends and relatives, thereby leveling economic differences. Similarly, because the Navajo believe elders, if neglected, will turn into witches, people are strongly motivated to take care of aged relatives. And because leaders are thought to be witches, people are understandably reluctant to go against their wishes, lest they suffer supernatural retribution.

The Consequences of Witchcraft

Anthropological research suggests that witchcraft, despite its often negative image, frequently functions in a very positive way to manage tensions within a society. Nonetheless, events may get out of hand, particularly in crisis situations, when widespread accusations may cause great

[21] Kluckhohn, C. (1944). Navajo witchcraft. *Papers of the Peabody Museum of American Archaeology and Ethnology 22* (2).

divination A magical procedure or spiritual ritual designed to find out what is not knowable by ordinary means, such as foretelling the future by interpreting omens.

suffering. This certainly was the case in the Salem witch trials, but even those pale in comparison to the half a million individuals executed as witches in Europe from the 15th through the 17th centuries. This was a time of profound change in European societies, marked by a good deal of political and religious conflict. At such times, it is all too easy to search out scapegoats to blame for what people believe are undesirable changes.

The Functions of Religion

Just as belief in witchcraft may serve a variety of psychological and social functions, so too do religious beliefs and practices in general. Here we may summarize these functions in a somewhat more systematic way.

One psychological function is to provide a model of the universe, which plays a key role in establishing orderly human behavior. Through special stories, or myths, people find answers to important questions such as: What does the universe look like, how does it work, and what is my place in it? To many Euramericans, the word *myth* conjures up the idea of an invented story about imaginary events, something that did not factually happen. This is not true for those people for whom a particular myth comprises part of their worldview. To them myths are sacred and true stories, not unlike historical documents in contemporary European or North American culture. And even in these literate societies, myths exist, such as the accounts of creation in the Book of Genesis. Invariably, myths are full of accounts about the doings of various supernatural beings and thus serve to reinforce beliefs in them.

Beyond this, by explaining the unknown and making it understandable, religion reduces the fears and anxieties of individuals. As we have seen, these explanations typically assume the existence of supernatural beings and powers, which people may potentially appeal to or manipulate as a means for dealing with crises. Thus at least theoretically, divine aid is available when all else fails.

A social function of religion is to prompt reflection concerning conduct. In this context, religion plays a role in social control, which, as we saw in the last chapter, does not rely on law alone. This is done through notions of right and wrong, good and evil. Right actions earn the approval of whatever supernatural powers are recognized by a particular culture. Wrong actions may cause revenge or punishment through supernatural agencies. In short, by deliberately raising people's feelings of guilt and anxiety about their actions, religion helps keep them in line.

Religion does more than this, though; it sets guidelines for acceptable behavior. We have noted already the

Many Bugis of Sulawesi—the third largest island in Indonesia, historically known as Celebes—are seafarers. Famous for their oceangoing schooners, these Muslims are excellent sailors who have long plied the trade routes between Australia and Malaysia and beyond, delivering spice and cargo to and from the thousands of islands to the major trading centers. Life at sea brings many risks—sudden storms, piracy, and other mishaps that may cause anxiety. Sustained by their faith, religion provides these mariners with a measure of psychological security. Here we see Bugis sailors praying in front of their schooners in the harbor of Jakarta on a holiday marking the end of Ramadan, the Islamic month of fasting, when Muslims refrain from eating, drinking, smoking, and sexual activities, from sunrise to sunset. This taboo serves to purify thought and build restraint for the sake of Allah.

connection between myths and religion. Usually, myths feature tales of extraordinary or supernatural beings that in various ways illustrate the society's ethical code in action. So it is that Gluskabe, the Penobscot Indian cultural hero, is portrayed in that society's traditions as tricking and punishing those who lie, mock others, behave greedily, overreact, or engage in other behaviors deemed inappropriate in Penobscot culture.

Moreover, the specific situations relayed in myths serve as guidelines for human behavior in similar circumstances. The Old and New Testaments of the Bible are rich in the same sort of material, as is the Koran. Related to this, by the models and morals it sets forth and advocates, religion serves to justify and perpetuate a particular social order. Thus in the Jewish, Christian, and Islamic traditions, a

masculine-authoritarian godhead along with a creation story that portrays a woman as responsible for a fall from grace serve to justify a social order in which men exercise control over women.

A psychological function also is tied up in this. A society's moral code, since it is considered to be divinely ordained, lifts the burden of responsibility from the shoulders of the society's individual members, at least in important situations. It can be a tremendous relief to individuals to know that the responsibility for the way things are rests with the gods or spirit forces rather than with themselves.

Another social function of religion is its role in the maintenance of social solidarity. In our discussion of shamans, we saw how such individuals provide a focus, thus

A Sufi *sema* (prayer dance) in Istanbul, Turkey. Sufism, a mystical Muslim movement that emerged in the late 10th century, borrowing ideas from Buddhism, Christianity, and Neoplatonism, emphasizes the surrender of individual ego and attachment to worldly things in order to be receptive to God's grace. Known as "Whirling Dervishes," these Sufi dancers are part of the Mevlevi brotherhood founded by Mevlana Rumi in the 13th century. According to Mevlevi tradition, during the *sema* the soul is freed from earthly ties and able to jubilantly commune with the divine. (*Dervish* literally means "doorway" and is thought to be an entrance from the material world to the spiritual.) The felt hat represents personal ego's tombstone, and the wide skirt symbolizes its shroud.

supplying one ingredient to help maintain group unity. In addition, common participation in rituals and a basic uniformity of beliefs bind people together and reinforce their identification with the group. Rituals are particularly effective for enhancing group solidarity, as the atmosphere is charged with emotion. The ecstatic feelings people experience in such circumstances positively reinforce their participation. Here, once again, we find religion providing psychological assurance while fulfilling the needs of society.

One other area in which religion serves a social function is education. In our discussion of rites of passage, we noted that puberty rituals of Aborigines in Australia served as a kind of crash course in traditional lore. By providing a memorable occasion, initiation rites can enhance learning and so help ensure the perpetuation of a nonliterate culture. And as we saw in the female initiation rites among the Mende, these girls will have the knowledge they will need to fulfill their adult roles in society.

> **revitalization movement** A movement for radical cultural reform in response to widespread social disruption and collective feelings of great stress and despair.
>
> **cargo cult** A spiritual movement (especially noted in Melanesia) in reaction to disruptive contact with Western capitalism, promising resurrection of deceased relatives, destruction or enslavement of white foreigners, and the magical arrival of utopian riches.

Rites of intensification can also be educational. Frequently, such rites involve dramas that portray matters of cultural importance. For example, among a food-foraging people, dances may imitate the movement of game and techniques of hunting. Among farmers a fixed round of ceremonies may emphasize the steps necessary for successful crops. All of this helps preserve knowledge important to a people's material well-being, gives expression to their worldview, and thereby reinforces their collective self-understanding. Finally, as noted earlier in this chapter, people often turn to established religion or follow prophets—spiritual leaders believed to be divinely inspired—in the hope of reaching a specific goal, such as the healing of physical, emotional, or social ills.

Religion in Cultural Change: Revitalization Movements

No anthropological consideration of religion is complete without some mention of **revitalization movements**—movements for radical cultural reform in response to widespread social disruption and collective feelings of great stress and despair. Many such movements developed in indigenous societies where European colonial exploitation caused enormous upheaval.

Among the various types of revitalization movements is the **cargo cult**—a spiritual movement (especially noted in Melanesia in the Southwest Pacific) in reaction to disruptive contact with Western capitalism, promising resurrection of deceased relatives, destruction or enslavement of white foreigners, and the magical arrival of utopian riches. Indigenous Melanesians referred to the white man's wealth as "cargo" (pidgin English for European trade goods). In times of great social stress, native prophets emerged, predicting that the time of suffering would come to an end and a new paradise on earth would soon arrive. Their deceased ancestors would return to life, and the rich white man would magically disappear—swallowed by an earthquake or swept away by a huge wave. However, their cargo would be left for the prophets and their cult followers who performed rituals to hasten this supernatural redistribution of wealth.[22]

One of many cargo cults took place in 1931 at Buka, in the Solomon Islands in the Pacific Ocean. A native religious movement suddenly emerged there when prophets predicted that a deluge would soon engulf all whites and a ship would then arrive filled with Western industrial commodities. The prophets told their followers to construct a storehouse for the goods and to prepare themselves to repulse the colonial police. They also spread word that the ship would come only after the natives had used up all their own supplies, and for this reason believers ceased working in the fields. Although the leaders of the movement were arrested, the cult continued for some years.

As deliberate efforts to construct a more satisfying culture, revitalization movements aim to reform not just the religious sphere of activity but an entire cultural system. Such drastic measures are taken when a group's anxiety and frustration have become so intense that the only way to reduce the stress is to overturn the entire social system and replace it with a new one. From the cargo cults of Melanesia to the 1890 Ghost Dance of many North American Indians to the Mau Mau of the Kikuyu in Kenya in the 1950s, extreme and sometimes violent religious reactions to European domination are so common that anthropologists have sought to formulate their underlying causes and general characteristics.

Revitalization movements are by no means restricted to the colonial world, and in the United States alone hundreds of them have sprung up. These range from Mormonism, which began in the 19th century, to the more recent Unification Church led by Reverend Sun Myung Moon, the Branch Davidians led by Seventh-Day Adventist prophet David Koresh, and the Black Muslims led by

Prophet Elijah Muhammad. Recent U.S. revitalization movements also include the American Indian revival of the spectacular Sun Dance ceremony, now held each summer at various reservations in the Great Plains.

Anthropologists now recognize a sequence common to all expressions of the revitalization process.[23] First is the normal state of society, in which stress is not too great and sufficient cultural means exist to satisfy needs. Under certain conditions, such as domination by a more powerful group or severe economic depression, stress and frustration are steadily amplified; this ushers in the second phase, or period of increased individual stress. If there are no significant adaptive changes, a period of cultural distortion follows in which stress becomes so chronic that socially approved methods of releasing tension begin to break down. This steady deterioration of the culture may be checked by a period of revitalization, during which a dynamic cult or religious movement grips a sizable portion of the population.

Sometimes the movement will be so out of touch with existing circumstances that it is doomed to failure from the beginning. This was the case with the Heaven's Gate cult, which mixed bits and pieces of apocalyptic Christian beliefs predicting destruction of the world at the end of the millennium with folk myths of contemporary North American culture, in particular those having to do with UFOs (alien spaceships). Its followers committed mass suicide out of a conviction that their spiritual essences would reunite with higher extraterrestrial beings in a spaceship that awaited them behind the tail of the Hale-Bopp comet, ready to take them "home."

More rarely, a movement may tap long-dormant adaptive forces underlying a culture, and an enduring religion may result. Such was the case with Mormonism. Though heavily persecuted at first and hounded from place to place, Mormons adapted to the point that their religion thrives in the United States today. Indeed, revitalization movements lie at the root of all known religions—Judaism, Christianity, and Islam included.

In Africa, during and following the period of foreign colonization and missionization, indigenous groups resisted or creatively revised Christian teachings and formed culturally appropriate religious movements. Since the 1970s, thousands of indigenous Christian churches have been founded. These churches are often born of alternative theological interpretations, new divinely inspired revelations, or cultural disagreements between African Christians and European or North American missionaries over inclusion of some traditional African practices, such as animism, ancestor worship, and polygyny. Today the African continent is as religiously and spiritually diverse

[22] For more on cargo cults, see Lindstrom, L. (1993). *Cargo cult: Strange stories of desire from Melanesia and beyond.* Honolulu: University of Hawaii Press; and Worsley, P. (1957). *The trumpet shall sound: A study of "cargo" cults in Melanesia.* London: Macgibbon & Kee.

[23] Wallace, A.F.C. (1970). *Culture and personality* (2nd ed., pp. 191–196). New York: Random House.

as ever. Although at least 40 percent of the population is Christian and more than another 40 percent is Muslim, African indigenous religions persist and are often merged with Christianity or Islam.

The Persistence of Religion

Interestingly, millions of people caught up by the radical upheaval of globalization are turning to religious precepts and practices to allay the anxiety of a world fraught with dangers and uncertainties. The need to find deeper meaning in life and to make sense of an increasingly complex, uncharted, and often confusing, even frightening world continues to drive human beings to explore not only scientifically, but also religiously and spiritually. As chronicled

in this chapter, this quest for metaphysical explanations and revelations occurs all around the globe. These signs are apparent from massive religious gatherings to the recurrent rise of new spiritual leaders and religious movements, growing interest and participation in pilgrimages and spiritual healing ceremonies, and persistent desires to safeguard certain buildings and natural places that people have designated as sacred sites.

However, the cultural boundary between the sacred and the ordinary is not always obvious. Indeed, one of the social functions of organized religion (and, in less formalized ways, spirituality) is that it provides ethical principles and guidelines for the faithful or inspired on how to morally conduct themselves in their daily social interactions, including business dealings. The following Original Study on Shariah-compliant banking demonstrates this point and closes our chapter.

Original Study

Sacred Law in Global Capitalism   *by Bill Maurer*

I will never forget my introduction to Islamic banking. It happened at a 1998 conference when I happened into a darkened room where the founder of an Islamic investment firm was showing a clip from the old Hollywood classic movie, *It's a Wonderful Life*. On the screen, George Bailey, played by Jimmy Stewart, faces an anxious crowd of Bedford Falls citizens, who have rushed into his Building and Loan, passbooks in hand, desperate to get their money. There is about to be a run on the bank.

One of the townspeople says he wants his money, *now*. George protests, "But you're thinking of this place all wrong—as if I had the money back in a safe. The money's not *here*. Why, your money's in Joe's house that's right next to yours, and in the Kennedy house, and Mrs. Macklin's house, and in a hundred others. You're lending them the money to build and then they're gonna pay it back to you as best they can. . . . Now, we can get through this thing all right. We've got to stick together, though. We've got to have faith in each other." The people cry, "I've got doctor's bills to pay!" "Can't feed my kids on faith!"

Then Mary, George's newlywed bride, shouts from behind the counter, "I've got two thousand dollars!" and holds up a wad of bills. It is the money for their honeymoon. George chimes in, "This'll tide us over until the bank reopens

tomorrow." He proceeds to disburse money based on people's stated needs ("Could I have $17.50?" one woman asks meekly) and guaranteed only by his trust in them.

Seconds before six o'clock, the last client leaves. George has just two dollars left. He, Mary, his Uncle Billy, and two cousins count down the seconds and then lock the doors. They have managed to stay in business for one more day. They place the two remaining dollars in a tray, and George offers a toast: "To Mama Dollar and to Papa Dollar, and if you want this old Building and Loan to stay in business you better have a family real quick." "I wish they were rabbits," says Cousin Tilly.

At this point in the film, the conference host paused the video and said, "This is the first *lariba* movie." A murmur went through the crowd. No one quite knew what he meant. Most of the audience was Muslim; this was a Christmas movie. What was our host trying to say?

I now know that *lariba* is Arabic for "no increase." The Koran invokes the term *riba* (increase) twenty times, and the term is often translated as interest or usury (excessive interest). Islamic banking and finance aim to avoid *riba* through profit-and-loss sharing, leasing, or other forms of equity- or asset-based financing.

We are all aware of the recent global financial crisis, which led to the collapse of major corporations, the nationalization of big banks and car companies,

massive unemployment, and unnerving insecurity for many people in the United States and around the world. One of the leading causes of the crisis was the marketing of debt to people who probably could not repay, and the packaging of those debts into complicated financial instruments that were supposed to curb risk but instead increased it.

What, you might ask, does anthropology have to contribute to the study of the financial markets, money, and the wider economy? Quite a lot, actually. Among other things, anthropologists have repeatedly demonstrated that economic decisions thought to be purely rational and self-interested are actually deeply embedded in social relationships, cultural values, and religious beliefs.

Take securitized debt instruments, for example—loans like mortgages, chopped up and rebundled together into salable commodities. When they started to go sour, many commentators blamed the instruments' complexity, and called for a return to an economy based on real things instead of abstract tradable debt. However, we know from our research across the globe that peoples in different cultures do not always differentiate the real from the abstract in the same way. A person's reputation might be deemed more solid and real than a piece of gold. And a piece of gold only has real value because people agree to it, as a convention.

After that 1998 conference, I began my study of global Islamic banking, including the efforts of American Muslims to create a new kind of "Islamic" mortgage that enables devout Muslims to buy a home in accordance with Islam's prohibition of interest. Instead of financing a home purchase with interest-bearing debt, Islamic alternatives rely on either leasing contracts (a sort of rent-to-own arrangement where the bank owns the house and the purchaser buys out the bank's share over time) or a partnership arrangement (like a joint business venture). Rather than having debt and interest at the center of the mortgage, as in a conventional loan, the house itself and its fair market rental value are at the center. The purchaser buys out the bank's share over time. At the center is the asset—the real thing—not the debt.

Of course, there is no reason why a joint partnership to own a piece of property is any more "real" or less "abstract" than bundling together debt. It depends on one's point of view, and one's precommitments to certain values—prohibiting interest and sharing risk, for example, or distributing risk onto others. In Islamic finance, the former is seen as "Shariah compliant," or in accord with Islamic law; and the latter, as unjust, for it offloads one's own share of risk onto others.

At the same time, Islamic mortgages often require relatively large down payments; this excludes poorer people from achieving the American dream of homeownership. So, we need to ask ourselves whether the virtues of adherence to the precepts of one's religion outweigh broader social goals of financial inclusion.

Global Islamic banking today owes much to the immigration of Middle Eastern and South Asian students and professionals to the United States and western Europe since the 1970s, and the consolidation of large U.S. Muslim organizations. The oil boom in the Middle East during the 1970s, which sparked renewed interest in Islamic banking in many Muslim-majority countries, also encouraged the development of a loosely knit interconnected network of Muslim international businessmen, who, working for oil and chemical companies as well as financial firms, gained experience in Western regulatory and business environments.

Islamic home financing expanded greatly after the 2001 terrorist attack on New York's World Trade Center and the Pentagon; these attacks sent shockwaves through the capitalist world system dominated by Wall Street. First of all, Americans in general, Muslims included, took their money out of the

stock market after the attack and started investing in real estate, buoyed by low interest rates and feeding the speculative real estate bubble. Second, Islamic mutual funds had been able to maintain their "Islamicity" in part by contributing a portion of their profits to charity in order to religiously "cleanse" the funds; however, as charities came under governmental suspicion for terrorist money laundering, many Muslims withdrew their investments from these funds. Third, home financing, American Muslims told me, is the cornerstone of the "American dream," and they were eager to demonstrate their commitment to that dream.

People involved in Islamic banking and finance are continually engaged in an effort to define precisely what their field is. Is *riba* simply Arabic for "interest," or does *riba* only refer to "excessive interest" or usury? Does the prohibition say something about justice, or does it moralize about proper market relationships? Like any aspect of culture—economy included—Islamic banking is always a field of debate. And more debate, not less, may help us all to find just, peaceful, and profitable ways out of the various catastrophes we continually make for ourselves, as we create the abstractions and realities that mutually determine our lives together.

Palani Mohan / The New York Times/Redux

Until the early 1990s, millions of Muslims throughout the world had few investment opportunities due to the ethics derived from Shariah law. Since then, hundreds of Islamic financial institutions have emerged in over fifty countries. Big American and European banks, including Citibank, have also entered the Islamic banking business in order to tap into the rising oil wealth. Today, Shariah-compliant banks manage well over $750 billion globally. Here we see three Muslim women in Kualu Lumpur, Malaysia.

Questions for Reflection

1. Beyond biological survival, humans need to find meaning in their existence. Do you ever ponder questions such as the meaning of your life and big issues such as the origin or destiny of the human species? How does your culture, including your religious or spiritual beliefs, offer you guidance in finding meaningful answers to such big questions?

2. Revitalization movements occur in reaction to the upheavals caused by rapid colonization and modernization. Do you think that the rise of Christian fundamentalism in the North American Bible Belt today is a response to such upheavals as well?

3. You have read about female genital mutilation as a rite of passage in some cultures. Do you know of any genital mutilation practices in your society? Why are so many boys in the United States circumcised immediately after their birth?

4. Do the basic dynamics of the shamanic complex also apply to preachers or priests in modern churches and medical doctors working in modern hospitals? Can you think of some similarities among the shaman, preacher, and medical doctor in terms of their respective fields of operation?

5. In postindustrial societies such as western Europe, the United States, and Canada, there is growing interest in shamanism and alternative healing techniques. Is there any relationship between globalization and this phenomenon?

Suggested Readings

Behrend, H., & Luig, U. (Eds.). (2000). *Spirit possession, modernity, and power in Africa.* Madison: University of Wisconsin Press.

This fascinating collection investigates how African spirit possession cults respond to local circumstances in a globalizing world. Contributors focus on power, histories, gender roles, and images of the other in shaping these beliefs and practices, introducing pantheons of new holy spirits—such as spirits of airplanes and guitars in Central Africa or Christian spirits with names like "Hitler" fighting against the government of Uganda.

Bowen, J. R. (2004). *Religions in practice: An approach to the anthropology of religion* (3rd ed.). Boston: Allyn & Bacon.

This author investigates how people from an array of spiritual traditions engage in special and everyday religious practices (prayer, sacrifice, pilgrimage, dress, rituals related to death) and discusses major issues of gender, states, and laws with respect to religion. The book also includes a review of religious studies theories from Hegel and Tylor to Geertz.

Bowie, F. (2006). *The anthropology of religion: An introduction* (2nd ed.). Malden, MA: Blackwell.

This readable introductory text presents the central theoretical ideas in the anthropology of religion, illustrating them with specific case studies. This edition features new chapters on mythology and pilgrimage, plus coverage of topics such as spirit possession and cargo cults.

Geertz, C. (2004). Religion as a cultural system. In M. Banton (Ed.), *Anthropological approaches to the study of religion* (pp. 1–46). London: Routledge. (orig. 1966)

In this gracefully written essay, Geertz describes religion as a cultural system of guidance, meaning, and authority in human affairs. Often cited in other disciplines as well, this is now regarded as a classic statement of the interpretive perspective on culture.

Lambek, M. (2002). *A reader in the anthropology of religion.* London: Blackwell.

This ambitious reader encompasses the breadth, depth, and complexity of anthropology's investigations into religion—and aims to create a conversation between Western and non-Western cultures, as well as between anthropology and other disciplines in the social sciences and humanities. It features a general introduction, a comprehensive range of classical and recent readings, and an extensive bibliography that is indexed according to both ethnographic region and religious topics and practices.

Tedlock, B. (2005). *The woman in the shaman's body: Reclaiming the feminine in religion and medicine.* New York: Random House.

Tracing the history of shamanism around the globe and illuminating the roles of women, the author integrates scholarship and her personal experience as a practicing shaman.

Challenge Issue   Humans in all cultures throughout time face the challenge of creatively articulating their feelings and ideas about themselves and the world around them. Although not all societies distinguish art as a special cultural domain, people everywhere have developed aesthetic forms—musical, visual, verbal, movement, and so on—to symbolically express, appreciate, and share sensations of beauty in all its variety. Art may be individual and personal. But it may also symbolically articulate, stimulate, and reinforce experiences and feelings of collective social identity, reminding and inspiring participants and observers alike of cultural values and ideals they share as members of a community. We see this when people join in a song of praise or devotion to an institution to which they belong, as in a national anthem. On such special occasions, processions may be staged in which people wear artfully designed clothing, carry banners, and march or dance to music, expressing important ideas and values. Such is the case here where we see the national army band of the small Buddhist kingdom of Bhutan. Band members wear traditional dress, but their instruments have been more recently adopted as a result of British colonial influence in South Asia. In addition to bagpipers shown here, the band features a brass section, which leads the way for singing the national anthem *Druk tsendhen* ("The Thunder Dragon Kingdom"), honoring the traditional *Druk Gylapo* (Dragon King) who serves as head of state.

The Arts

Chapter Preview

What Is Art?

Although difficult to define, art may be understood as the creative use of the human imagination to aesthetically interpret, express, and engage life, modifying experienced reality in the process. Many contemporary Western peoples consider art as exclusively aesthetic, serving no practical purpose, but most societies past and present have used art to give meaningful expression to almost every part of their culture, including ideas about religion, kinship, and ethnic identity. Almost anything can become an object of artistic creativity—skin, hair, dress, dwellings, vehicles, weapons, utensils, and so on.

Why Do Anthropologists Study Art?

Anthropologists have found that art often reflects a society's collective ideas, values, and concerns. From myths, songs, dances, paintings, carvings, and so on, anthropologists may learn how a people imagine their reality and understand themselves as well as other beings around them. Through the cross-cultural study of art and creativity, we discover much about different worldviews, religious beliefs, political ideas, social values, kinship structures, economic relations, and historical memory.

What Are the Functions of Art?

Aside from adding beauty and pleasure to everyday life, art serves a number of functions. Myths, for example, may offer basic explanations about the world and set cultural standards for right behavior. The verbal arts generally transmit and preserve a culture's customs and values. Songs, too, may do this within the structures imposed by musical form. And any art form, to the degree that it is characteristic of a particular society, may contribute to the cohesiveness or solidarity of that society. Yet, art may also express political themes and be used to influence events and create social change. Often it is created for religious purposes, to honor or beseech the aid of a divine power, a sacred being, an ancestral spirit, or an animal spirit.

Humans in all cultures throughout time have expressed feelings and ideas about themselves and the world around them through **art**—the creative use of the human imagination to aesthetically interpret, express, and engage life, modifying experienced reality in the process. Art comes in many forms: visual, verbal, musical, dance, and so on. Most societies, past and present, have used art to symbolically express almost every part of their culture, including ideas about religion, kinship, and ethnic identity.

In North America, the arts often are seen as a luxury, an aesthetic pleasure that people engage in for personal or collective enjoyment quite apart from more useful or productive pursuits. This attitude becomes apparent whenever public funds are in short supply. On the local level, for example, in battles over school budgets, art programs are often the first to be cut. On the national level, fiscal conservatives repeatedly seek to curb funds for theater performances, museum exhibits, concerts, and other fine arts to be enjoyed by the general public on the premise that these lack the practical importance of roads, sewers, police, warplanes, office bureaucracies, and other government priorities.

Indeed, a significant portion of the society views artists and their supporters as an elite group subsidized at the expense of "practical" tax-paying citizens. This is due in large part to the rather recent Western concept of fine art as a distinct cultural category of art for art's sake, unrelated to society at large but relished by specialists and wealthy collectors who chatter about, purchase, or even commission works of art for enjoyment in the privacy of their homes or showings in selective galleries and museums.

The idea of art serving purely aesthetic but impractical purposes seems firmly entrenched in the thinking of many contemporary Western peoples. Today, for example, the objects from the ancient tomb of the young Egyptian King Tutankhamen are on display in a museum, where they may be seen and admired as the exquisite works of art that they are. They were made, however, not for human eyes but to guarantee the eternal life of the king and protect him from evil forces that might enter his body and gain control over it.

Similarly, we may listen to the singing of a sea chantey purely for aesthetic pleasure, as a form of entertainment. But, in fact, in the days of sailing by wind power alone, sea chanteys served very useful and practical purposes. They set the appropriate rhythm for the performance of specific shipboard tasks such as hoisting or reefing sails, and the same qualities that make them pleasurable to listen to today served to coordinate these tasks and to relieve boredom.

art The creative use of the human imagination to aesthetically interpret, express, and engage life, modifying experienced reality in the process.

Such links between art and other aspects of everyday life are common in human societies around the world. This can also be seen in the way that art has been incorporated into everyday, functional objects—from pottery and baskets used to carry or store food to carpets and mats woven by nomadic herders to cover the ground inside their portable tent dwellings. Designs painted on or woven or carved into such objects typically express ideas, values, and things that have meaning to an entire community.

All of this goes to show that artistic expression is as basic to human beings as talking and is by no means limited to a special category of people called "artists." For example, all human beings adorn their bodies in certain ways and by doing so make a statement about who they are, both as individuals and as members of society. Similarly, people in all cultures tell stories in which they express their values, hopes, and concerns and in the process reveal much about themselves and the nature of the world as they see it. In short, all peoples engage in artistic expression. And, they have been doing this in countless ways for at least 40,000 years—from fashioning and playing bone flutes to painting animals on ancient rock walls to digital music jamming on iPhones.

Far from being a luxury to be afforded or appreciated by a minority of sophisticated experts or frivolous lovers of art, creativity is a necessary activity in which everyone participates in one way or another.

Whether a particular work of art is intended to be appreciated purely for beauty or to serve some practical purpose, it requires the same special combination of symbolic representation of form and expression of feeling that constitute the creative imagination. Because human creativity and the ability to symbolize are universal, art is an important subject for anthropological study.

The Anthropological Study of Art

Anthropologists have found that art often reflects a society's collective ideas, values, and concerns. Indeed, through the cross-cultural study of art—myths, songs, dances, paintings, carvings, designs, and so on—we may discover much about different worldviews and religious beliefs, as well as political ideas, social values, kinship structures, economic relations, and historical memory.

In approaching art as a cultural phenomenon, anthropologists have the pleasant task of cataloguing, photographing, recording, describing, and analyzing all possible forms of imaginative activity in any particular culture. An enormous variety of forms and modes of artistic expression exists in the world. Because people everywhere

Visual Counterpoint

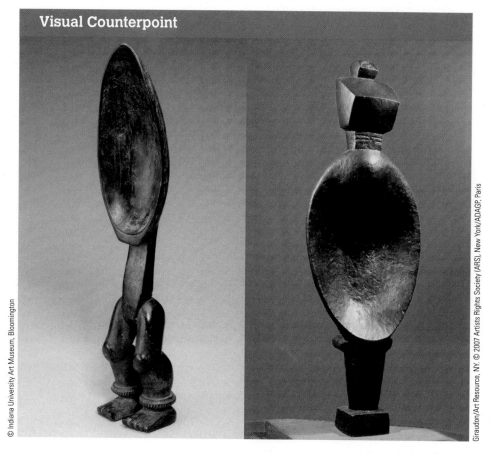

On the left is a wooden spoon used by the Dan people of Ivory Coast, West Africa, carver unknown. On the right is a bronze sculpture, *Spoon Woman,* created by the Italian artist Alberto Giacometti in 1926. Both may be beautiful, but one is functional and the other purely aesthetic. Usually, traditional utilitarian objects, no matter how exquisite, are identified only in terms of the "primitive" or "tribal" cultures in which they were made. In contrast, "works of art" created for the sake of art itself are typically tied to the name of the person who made them. How curious it is that this great modern piece credited to the famous Giacometti was inspired by a now-nameless West African.

continue to create and develop in ever-new ways, there is no end to the interesting process of collecting and describing the world's ornaments, ceremonial masks, body decorations, clothing variations, blanket and rug designs, pottery and basket styles, monuments, architectural embellishments, legends, work songs, dances, and other art forms—many of them rich with religious symbolism.

To study and analyze art, anthropologists employ a combination of aesthetic, narrative, and interpretive approaches. The distinctions among these methods can be illustrated through a brief look at a famous work of Western art, Leonardo da Vinci's painting *The Last Supper.*[1] A non-Christian viewing this late 15th-century mural in Italy will see thirteen people at a table, apparently enjoying a meal. Although one of the men clutches a bag of money and appears to have knocked over a dish of salt, nothing else in the scene seems out of the ordinary.

Aesthetically, our non-Christian observer may admire the way the composition fits the space available, how the attitudes of the men are depicted, and the means by which the artist conveys a sense of movement. As narrative, the painting may be seen as a record of customs, table manners, dress, and architecture. But to interpret this picture—to perceive its real meaning—the viewer must be aware that in Western culture money symbolizes the root of all evil, and spilling the salt symbolizes impending disaster. But even this is not enough; to fully understand this work of art, one must know something of the beliefs of Christianity. In other words, moving to the interpretive level of studying art requires knowledge of the symbols and beliefs of the people responsible for the art.

[1] This example is drawn from Lewis-Williams, J. D. (1990). *Discovering southern African rock art* (p. 9). Cape Town and Johannesburg: David Philip.

Detail of *The Last Supper* by the famous Italian artist Leonardo da Vinci (1452–1519). To really understand this painting, one must know something about Christianity and about the general cultural symbols and beliefs of the artist's place and time.

A good way to deepen our insight into the relationship between art and the rest of culture is to examine critically some of the generalizations that have already been made about specific art forms. Since it is impossible to cover all art forms in the space of a single chapter, we shall concentrate on just a few—visual, verbal, and musical—in that order.

Visual Art

For many people, the first thing that springs to mind in connection with the word *art* is some sort of visual image, be it a painting, drawing, sketch, or whatever. And indeed, in many parts of the world, people have been making pictures in one way or another for a very long time—etching in bone; engraving in rock; painting on cave walls and rock surfaces; carving and painting on wood, gourds, and clay pots; or painting on textiles, bark cloth, animal hide, or even their own bodies. Some form of visual art is a part of every historically known human culture, and extraordinary examples have been found at prehistoric sites dating back more than 35,000 years.

As a type of symbolic expression, visual art may be representational (imitating closely the forms of nature) or abstract (drawing from natural forms but representing only their basic patterns or arrangements). In some of the Indian art of North America's northwest coast, for example, animal figures may be so highly stylized as to be difficult for an outsider to identify. Although the art appears abstract, the artist has created it based on nature, even though he or she has exaggerated and deliberately transformed various shapes to express a particular feeling toward the animals. Because artists do these exaggerations and transformations according to the aesthetic principles of their Indian culture, their meanings are understood not just by the artist but by other members of the community as well.

This collective understanding of symbols is a hallmark in traditional art. Unlike modern Western art, which is judged in large part on its creative originality and the unique vision of an individual artist, traditional art is all about community and shared symbolism. Consider, for example symbols related to kinship. As discussed in earlier chapters, small-scale traditional societies—hunter-gatherers, nomadic herders, slash-and-burn horticulturists—are profoundly interested in kinship relations. In such societies, kinship may be symbolically expressed in stylized motifs and colorful designs etched or painted on human skin, animal hides or bones, pottery, wood, rocks, or almost any other surface

In the figure at left, the two rows of diagrams at the top show the stylized human figures that are the basic bricks used in the construction of genealogical patterns. Each figure is designed to be joined limb-and-limb with adjacent figures to illustrate descent or other kin relationships. The diagrams in the two bottom rows show how these basic figures are linked arm-and-leg with diagonally adjacent figures to depict descent. For thousands of years people all over the world have linked such figures together, creating the familiar geometric patterns that we see in countless art forms, from pottery to sculpture to weaving—patterns that informed eyes recognize as genealogical.

imaginable. To cultural outsiders these designs appear to be purely decorative, ornamental, or abstract, but they can actually be decoded in terms of genealogical iconography primarily illustrating social relations of marriage and descent.[2]

Shared symbolism has also been fundamental to the traditional art of tattooing—although that is changing

in some parts of the world, as discussed in the following Original Study.

[2] Schuster, C., & Carpenter, E. (1996). *Patterns that connect: Social symbolism in ancient and tribal art.* New York: Abrams; see also Prins, H.E.L. (1998). Book review of Schuster, C., & Carpenter, E. *American Anthropologist 100* (3), 841.

Original Study

The Modern Tattoo Community   *by Margo DeMello*

As an anthropology graduate student in the early 1990s, I had no idea what (or, more accurately, whom) to study for my field research. Working as an animal advocate, I had a house full of creatures to care for, which left me in no position for long-term travel to a far-off field site.

Then one of my professors suggested a topic that was literally under my nose—tattooing. I myself had several tattoos and

spent quite a bit of time with other tattooed people, including my husband who had just become a professional tattooist.

Early on in my research, I, along with my husband, strove to find a way to "join" what is known as the "tattoo community," finding that it was not as friendly and open as we had imagined it to be. As an anthropologist, I came to see that the sense of exclusion we felt

reflected the fact that we were on the lower rungs of a highly stratified social group in which an artist's status is based on such features as class, geography, and professional and artistic credentials, and a "fan" might be judged on the type and extent of his or her tattoos, the artist(s) who created them, the level of media coverage achieved, and more. This awareness led to one of the major

CONTINUED

CONTINUED

focuses of my work: how class and status increasingly came to define this once working-class art form.

Ultimately, I spent almost five years studying and writing about tattooing, finding my "community" wherever tattooed people talked about themselves and each other—within the pages of tattoo magazines and mainstream newspapers, on Internet newsgroups, and at tattoo-oriented events across the country. I spent countless hours in tattoo shops watching the artists work; I collected what I call "tattoo narratives," which are often elaborate, sometimes spiritual, stories that people tell about their tattoos; and I followed the careers of seminal artists. I even learned to tattoo a bit myself, placing a few particularly ugly images on my patient husband's body.

Tattoos are created by inserting ink or some other pigment through the epidermis (outer skin) into the dermis (the second layer of skin) through the use of needles. They may be beautiful as designs in and of themselves, but they can also express a multitude of meanings about the wearer and his or her place within the social group. Whether used in an overt punitive fashion (as in the tattooing of slaves or prisoners) or to mark clan or cult membership, religious or tribal affiliation, social status, or marital position, tattoos have historically been a social sign. They have long been one of the simplest ways of establishing humans as social beings. In fact, tattooing is one of the most persistent and universal forms of body art and may date back as far as the Upper Paleolithic era (10,000–40,000 years ago).

Tattoos as signs derive their communicative power from more than a simple sign-to-meaning correspondence: They also communicate through color, style, manner of execution, and location on the body. Traditionally inscribed on easily viewable parts of the body, tattoos were designed to be "read" by others and were part of a collectively understood system of inscription. However, for many middle-class North Americans today tattoos are more about private statement than public sign, and these individuals, especially women, tend to favor smaller tattoos in private spots.

The process by which tattooing has expanded in the United States from a working-class folk art into a more widespread and often refined aesthetic practice is related to a number of shifts in North American culture that occurred during the 1970s and 1980s. This time period saw the introduction of finely trained artists into tattooing, bringing with them radically different backgrounds and artistic sensibilities to draw from. More and more middle-class men and women began getting tattooed, attracted by the expanded artistic choices and the new, more spiritual context of body decoration.

Tattoos have been partially transformed into fine art by a process of redefinition and framing based on formal qualities (that is, the skill of the artist, the iconic content of the tattoo, the style in which the tattoo is executed, and so on) and ideological qualities (the discourses that surround "artistic" tattoos, discourses that point to some higher reality on which the tattoo is based). When it is judged that a tattoo has certain formal artistic qualities as well as expresses a higher, often spiritual, reality, then it is seen as art.

While it may seem as though tattoos are not good candidates to be defined as art, due to their lack of permanence (the body, after all, ages and dies) and their seeming inability to be displayed within a gallery setting, modern tattoo art shows get around these problems by photographing tattoos and displaying them in a way that showcases the "art" and often minimizes the body. By both literally and figuratively "framing" tattoos in a museum or gallery setting, or within an art book, the tattoo is removed from its social function and remade into art.

The basic working-class American tattoo designs (such as "Mother" or "Donna" inscribed alongside a heart) have been relegated to the bottom rung of today's tattoo hierarchy in the United States. Such tattoos are now seen by middle-class artists and fans as too literal, too transparently obvious, and too grounded in everyday experience and social life to qualify as art.

The modern, artistic tattoos that have increasingly gained favor are less "readable" and no longer have an easily recognizable function. Often derived from foreign (or "exotic") cultures (such as Polynesia) and custom-drawn for the wearer, they tend to eliminate the social aspect in favor of the highly individualistic. Some are purely decorative, and those that are intended to signify meaning often do so only for the individual or those in his or her intimate circle.

Tattoos in the United States have traveled a long way from the tattoo of old: brought to North America by way of British Captain James Cook's 18th-century explorations of the Pacific, moving, over time, from a mark of affiliation to a highly individual statement of personal identity, losing and regaining function, meaning, and content along the way. In our increasingly global world, tattoo designs and motifs move swiftly and easily across cultural boundaries. As this happens, their original, communal meanings are often lost—but they are not meaningless. An animal crest tattoo traditionally worn by Indians on the northwest coast of North America to signify clan membership may now be worn by a non-Native in Boston as an artful, often private, sign of rebellion against Western "coat and tie" consumer culture.

For more on this topic, see DeMello, M. (2000). Bodies of inscription: A cultural history of the modern tattoo community. (2000). Durham, NC: Duke University Press.

© Michael M. Phillips

For many U.S. Marines in Iraq, memorial tattoos have provided a way to give ink-and-skin permanence to fallen friends. In memory of fellow Marine Lance Cpl. Michael Torres, Curt Stiver of Oshkosh, Wisconsin, had a tattoo artist copy onto his left chest a photograph taken of Torres in infantry school.

Rock Art from Southern Africa

Rock art—paintings and engravings made on the faces of rock outcrops and on the interior walls of rock shelters—is one of the world's oldest art traditions. Bushmen in southern Africa practiced this art continually from at least 27,000 years ago until the beginning of the 20th century when European colonization led to the demise of their societies. Their art depicted humans and animals in highly sophisticated ways, sometimes in static poses but often in highly animated scenes. It also featured what appear to be abstract signs—dots, zigzags, nested curves, and the like. Until fairly recently, the significance of these abstract features puzzled non-Bushmen, as did the fact that new pictures were quite often created directly over existing images.

Because Bushman rock art, especially the paintings, are generally seen as beautiful and pleasurable to look at, it is not surprising that the specialists who first studied them took the aesthetic approach—analyzing how things were depicted. Investigating the various colored pigments, they found that the Bushmen had used charcoal and specularite (hematite mineral) for black; silica, china clay, and gypsum for white; and ferric oxide for red and reddish-brown hues—and that they had mixed the colors with fat, blood, and perhaps water. The paint had been applied to the rough rock with great skill. Indeed, the effectiveness of line and the way shading was used to suggest the contours of the animals' bodies elicit admiration, as does the realistic rendering of details such as the twist of an eland's horns or the black line running along its back.

Specialists also analyze Bushman rock art as "narrative," investigating *what* it depicts. Certainly, aspects of Bushman life are shown, as in several hunting scenes of men with bows, arrows, quivers, and hunting bags. Some depictions show hunting nets and also fish traps. Women are also portrayed—identifiable by their visible sexual characteristics and the stone-weighted digging sticks they carry.

In addition to aesthetic and narrative approaches, researchers study Bushman rock art from an interpretive angle—looking at it in light of contemporary ethnographic research among modern-day Bushman communities. Doing so, we see that certain designs relate to the shamanic trance dance. These include fly whisks, which are used to extract invisible arrows of sickness, and designs of hand-clapping women surrounding dancing men whose bodies are bent forward in the distinctive posture caused by the cramping of abdominal muscles as they go into trance. The designs also show dancers' arms outstretched behind their backs, which present-day Bushmen do to catch more *n/um*—supernatural power.

However, for a more complete interpretation of this scene, anthropologists have to go beyond ethnographic observation and description of the trance dance and learn about altered states of consciousness. Laboratory research shows that humans typically move through three stages when entering a trance. In the first stage, the nervous system generates images of luminous, pulsating, revolving, and constantly shifting geometric patterns known as *entoptic phenomena*—similar to images seen during a migraine headache. Usually these include dots, zigzags, grids, filigrees, nested curves, and parallel lines, often in a spiral pattern.

In the second stage, the brain tries to make sense of these abstract forms (a process known as *construal*). Here,

Bushmen in southern Africa created rock paintings and engravings depicting animals they believed possessed great supernatural powers, especially the eland. Many of these renderings also featured trance dancing, with shamans transforming into birds, appearing elongated and weightless as in flight or water—imagery based on altered states of consciousness experienced in trance.

Peyote Art: Divine Visions among the Huichol

For generations, Huichol Indians living in Mexico's mountainous western Sierra Madre region have created art remarkable for its vibrant colors. They are especially noted for their spectacular beadwork and embroidery. Although many people far and wide appreciate the intricate beauty of Huichol art, most are probably unaware that the colorful designs express a religious worldview tied to the chemical substance of a sacred plant: a small cactus "button" known as peyote (*Lophophora williamsii*).[a]

Among the many Huichol gods and goddesses, all addressed in kinship terms, is Our Grandfather Fire. His principal spirit helper is Our Elder Brother Deer, a messenger between the gods and humans. Serving the Huichol as their spiritual guide, this divine deer is also the peyote cactus itself. Huichol Indians refer to peyote as *yawéi hikuri,* the "divine flesh of Elder Brother Deer." Guided by their shamans on a pilgrimage to harvest peyote, they "hunt" this "deer" in Wirikúta, the sacred desert highlands where their ancestor deities dwell. Having found and "shot" the first cactus button with an arrow, they gather many more, later to be consumed in fresh, dried, or liquid form.

Participating in a holy communion with the creator god, Huichol shamans

Huichol artist Olivia Carrillo makes peyote-inspired art in Real de Catorce, a town in the mountains of central Mexico. About an hour's horseback ride away from the Huichol sacred mountain Wirikúta, the town is located in the peyote heartland.

© Russell Cobb/Dallas Observer

consume peyote (the divine flesh) as a sacrament. Doing so, they enter into an ecstatic trance. With the help of peyote, their spiritual guide, they become hawks or eagles soaring high in the sky. Having visions extending far across the world, they interact directly with their gods and seek advice on behalf of those who need help in dealing with illness and other misfortunes.

From a purely chemical point of view, peyote contains a psychotropic substance identified by scientists as an alkaloid. By consuming some of this toxic organic substance, the

Huichol move into an altered state of consciousness. In this dreamlike psychological state, which is also profoundly emotional, they experience religiously inspired, brilliantly colored visions from their spirit world.

These are reflected in Huichol art, such as the piece pictured here in which a stylized peyote button and deer have been rendered in rainbow-hued beadwork by Huichol artist Olivia Carrillo, who lives in the peyote heartland of central Mexico. The sacred cactus, with its flower- or starlike shape, is the most prominent symbolic design in Huichol art, beaded onto fabric and objects of all kinds or embroidered on clothing.

BIOCULTURAL QUESTION

In Huichol Indian art we often find vibrantly colored peyote buttons, articulating shamanic visions induced by this psychotropic cactus. What inspired traditional European artists painting Christian holy men and women with a halo—a silver- or gold-colored ring around or above their heads?

[a]Schaeffer, S. B., & Furst, P. T. (Eds.). (1996). *People of the peyote: Huichol Indian history, religion, and survival.* Albuquerque: University of New Mexico Press.

---

cultural influences come into play, so a trancing Bushman in southern Africa's Kalahari is likely to construe a grid pattern as markings on the skin of a giraffe, nested curves as a honeycomb (honey is a delicacy in the region), and so forth. A New York City police officer or a Chinese priest would construe the patterns in very different ways.

During the third and deepest trance stage, people tend to feel as if they are at one with their visions, passing into a rotating tunnel or vortex. Typically, the tunnel has lattice-like sides where **iconic images** of animals,

humans, and monsters appear, merging with the entoptic forms of the early trance stages. Because these iconic images are culture specific, individuals usually see things that have high significance within their culture. Thus Bushmen often see the eland, a massive antelope they believe carries supernatural powers for making rain. So, one of the things shamans try to do in trance is to "capture" these envisioned elands ("rain animals") for purposes of making rain.

All of this helps us understand why elands are so prominent in the Bushman rock art. Moreover, it reveals the significance of the zigzags, dots, grids, and so forth that are so often a part of the compositions. It also leads to an understanding of other puzzling features of the art. For example, the third trance stage includes such sensations

iconic images Culturally specific people, animals, and monsters seen in the deepest stage of trance.

as being stretched out or elongated, weightlessness as in flight or in the water, and difficulty breathing as when under water. Hence we find depictions in the art of humans who appear to be abnormally long, as well as individuals who appear to be swimming or flying.

Another well-documented trance phenomenon is the sensation of being transformed into some sort of animal. Such experiences are triggered in the deepest stage of trance if the individual sees or thinks of an animal. This sensation accounts for the part human–part animal (therianthrope) images in the art.

Finally, we are able to comprehend the layering of one work of art over another with the interpretative approach; not only are the visions seen in trance commonly superimposed on one another as they rotate and move, but if the trancer stares at a painting or engraving of an earlier vision, the new one will appear as if projected on the old.

The interpretive approach makes clear, then, that the rock art of southern Africa—even in the case of compositions that otherwise might appear to be scenes of everyday life—is intimately connected with the practices and beliefs of shamanism. After shamans came out of trance and reflected on their visions, they proceeded to paint or engrave their recollections on the rock faces. But these were more than records of important visions; they had their own innate power, owing to their supposed supernatural origin. This being so, when the need arose for a new trance experience, it might be held where the old vision was recorded to draw power from it.

A similar interpretive analysis is needed to fully understand the art of Huichol Indians living in Mexico, as profiled in this chapter's Biocultural Connection feature.

Verbal Art

The verbal arts include narratives, dramas, poetry, incantations, proverbs, riddles, word games—as well as naming procedures, compliments, and insults, when these take structured and special forms. Narratives, in particular, have received considerable attention from linguists and anthropologists.

In the 19th century, when the industrial revolution triggered a series of radical changes in the national cultural fabric of state societies, the pressures of modernization were also transforming the way of life in traditional communities of peasants and other rural folk. Although many folk communities still preserved their own unique historical heritage, their distinctive local customs—including legends, songs, dances, dress, and crafts—began to disappear without a trace. Alarmed about these vanishing traditions, some amateur scholars and professional academics began collecting the unwritten popular stories (and other artistic traditions) of rural peoples. They coined the word **folklore** to distinguish between "folk art" and the "fine art" of the

elite. Today, many linguists and anthropologists prefer to speak of a culture's oral traditions and verbal arts rather than its folklore and folktales, recognizing that the distinction between folk and fine art is a projection imposed by Western elites.

Generally, the narratives that make up the verbal arts have been divided into several basic and recurring categories, including myth, legend, and tale.

Myth

Derived from the Greek word *mythos,* meaning "speech" or "story," a **myth** is a sacred narrative that explains the fundamentals of human existence—where we and everything in our world came from, why we are here, and where we are going. Beyond this explanatory function, a myth provides a rationale for religious beliefs and practices and sets cultural standards for proper behavior. A typical creation or origin myth, traditional with the western Abenaki of northwestern New England and southern Quebec, goes as follows:

In the beginning, *Tabaldak,* "The Owner," created all living things but one—the spirit being who was to accomplish the final transformation of the earth. *Tabaldak* made man and woman out of a piece of stone, but he didn't like the result, their hearts being cold and hard. So, he broke them up, and their remains today can be seen in the many stones that litter the landscape of the Abenaki homeland. Then *Tabaldak* tried again, this time using living wood, and from this came all later Abenakis. Like the trees from which the wood came, these people were rooted in the earth and could dance as gracefully as trees swaying in the wind.

The one living thing not created by *Tabaldak* was *Odzihózo,* "He Makes Himself from Something." This transformer created himself out of dust, but he wasn't able to accomplish it all at once. At first, he managed only his head, body, and arms; the legs came later, growing slowly as legs do on a tadpole. Not waiting until his legs were grown, he set out to transform the shape of the earth. He dragged his body about with his hands, gouging channels that became the rivers. To make the mountains, he piled dirt up with his hands. Once his legs grew, *Odzihózo's* task was made easier; by merely extending his legs, he made the tributaries of the main stream. . . .

folklore A term coined by 19th-century scholars studying the unwritten stories and other artistic traditions of rural peoples to distinguish between "folk art" and the "fine art" of the literate elite.

myth A sacred narrative that explains the fundamentals of human existence—where we and everything in our world came from, why we are here, and where we are going.

The last work he made was Lake Champlain and liked it so well that he climbed onto a rock in Burlington Bay and changed himself into stone so he could sit there and enjoy his masterpiece through the ages. He is still there and he is still given offerings of tobacco as Abenakis pass this way. The Abenaki call the rock *Odzihózo*, since it is the Transformer himself.[3]

Such a myth, insofar as it is believed, accepted, and perpetuated in a culture, expresses part of a people's traditional worldview. This Abenaki myth accounts for the existence of rivers, mountains, lakes, and other features of the landscape, as well as of humans and all other living things. It also sanctions particular attitudes and behaviors. It is a product of creative imagination and is a work of art, as well as a potentially religious statement.

Extrapolating from the details of this particular Abenaki myth, we may conclude that these people recognize a kinship among all living things; after all, they were all part of the same creation, and humans even were made from living wood.

This idea of closeness among all living things led the Abenaki to show special respect to the animals they hunted in order to sustain their own lives. For example, before eating meat, they placed an offering of grease on the fire to thank Tabaldak.

A characteristic of myths such as this one is that the unknown is simplified and explained in terms of the known. The analysis of myths has been carried to great lengths, becoming a field of study almost unto itself. Myth making is an extremely significant kind of human creativity, and studying the myth-making process and its results can give valuable clues to the way people perceive and think about their world.

Legend

A **legend** is a story about a memorable event or figure handed down by tradition and told as true but without historical evidence. An example of a modern urban legend in the United States is one that was often told by Ronald Reagan when he was president, about an African American woman on welfare in Chicago. Supposedly, her ability to collect something like 103 welfare checks under different names enabled her to live lavishly. Although proved to

---

[3] Haviland, W. A., & Power, M. W. (1994). *The original Vermonters: Native inhabitants, past and present* (2nd ed., p. 193). Hanover, NH: University Press of New England.

legend A story about a memorable event or figure handed down by tradition and told as true but without historical evidence.

be false, the story was told as if true (by the president even after he was informed that it was not true) as legends are.

This particular legend illustrates a number of features all such narratives share: They cannot be attributed to any known author; they always exist in multiple versions, but, in spite of variation, they are told with sufficient detail to be plausible; and they tell us something about the cultures in which they are found. In this case, we learn something about popular anger against wasteful government spending of taxpayer dollars ("big government" policies to help the poor), mainstream society's views on self-reliant individualism and hard work (distrust, if not dislike, of the poor), and, last but not least, enduring racism in U.S. society (the story is told by whites, who identify the woman as African American).

Clearly, legends (no more than myths) are not confined to nonliterate, nonindustrialized societies. Legends commonly consist of pseudo-historical narratives that account for the deeds of heroes, the movements of peoples, and the establishment of local customs, typically with a mixture of realism and the supernatural or extraordinary. As stories, they are not necessarily believed or disbelieved, but they usually serve to entertain as well as to instruct and to inspire or bolster pride in family, community, or nation. Legends all around the world tell us something about the cultures in which they are found.

To a degree, in literate societies, the function of legends has been taken over by history. The trouble is that history does not always tell people what they want to hear about themselves, or, conversely, it tells them things that they would prefer not to hear. By projecting their culture's hopes and expectations onto the record of the past, they seize upon and even exaggerate some past events while ignoring or giving scant attention to others. Although this often takes place unconsciously, so strong is the motivation to transform history into legend that states have even gone so far as to deliberately rewrite it.

Not surprisingly, different groups often recall and recount the same historical event in highly contrasting ways. For instance, white colonists and their descendants who settled in New England portrayed the region's 17th-century Indian rebellion, led by Chief Metacomet (better known in American history books as King Philip), as a treacherous uprising and described the Indian defeat as a divinely guided military victory over heathen savages. In this violent conflict, thousands on both sides lost their lives. Although many Indian survivors found refuge among neighboring indigenous nations, hundreds of Indian captives were sold as slaves and died in foreign lands. Unable to resist English colonial land grabs and repression, Indians who were allowed to remain in their homeland were confined to small reservations where they came under the administrative control of white agents.

In public commemorations and written historical accounts, the Indian side of this conflict remains largely unvoiced and unknown to the general public.⁴ For this reason, American Indians sometimes joke bitterly about such one-sided versions of the past as "his story," and scholars attempting to separate historical fact from fiction frequently incur the wrath of people who refuse to abandon what they wish to believe is true, whether or not it really is.

A long, dramatic narrative recounting the celebrated deeds of a historic or legendary hero—often sung or recited in poetic language—is known as an **epic.** In parts of western and Central Africa, people hold remarkably elaborate and formalized recitations of extremely long legends, lasting several hours and even days. These long narratives have been described as veritable encyclopedias of a culture's most diverse aspects, with direct and indirect statements about history, institutions, relationships, values, and ideas. Epics are typically found in nonliterate societies with some form of state political organization; they serve to transmit and preserve a culture's legal and political precedents and practices.

Legends may incorporate mythological details, especially when they make an appeal to the supernatural, and are therefore not always clearly distinct from myth. Legends may also incorporate proverbs and incidental tales and thus be related to other forms of verbal art as well.

For the anthropologist, a major significance of the secular and apparently realistic portions of legends, whether long or short, is the clues they provide as to what constitutes a culture's approved or ideal ethical behavior. The subject matter of legends is essentially problem solving and mentoring, and the content is likely to include physical and psychological trials of many kinds. Certain questions may be answered explicitly or implicitly. In what circumstances, if any, does the culture permit homicide? What kinds of behavior are considered heroic or cowardly? Does the culture stress forgiveness over retaliation as an admirable trait?

Tale

A third type of creative narrative, the **tale,** is recognized as fiction that is for entertainment but may also draw a moral or teach a practical lesson. Consider this brief summary of a tale from Ghana in West Africa, known as "Father, Son, and Donkey":

> A father and his son farmed their corn, sold it, and spent part of the profit on a donkey. When the hot season came, they harvested their yams and prepared to take them to storage, using their donkey. The father mounted the donkey and they

A scene such as this may bring to mind the internationally popular "Father, Son, and Donkey" tale. Told in different versions featuring localized draft animals, this tale conveys a basic motif or story situation—father and son trying in vain to please everyone.

> all three proceeded on their way until they met some people. "What? You lazy man!" the people said to the father. "You let your young son walk barefoot on this hot ground while you ride on a donkey? For shame!" The father yielded his place to the son, and they proceeded until they came to an old woman. "What? You useless boy!" said the old woman. "You ride on the donkey and let your poor father walk barefoot on this hot ground? For shame!" The son dismounted, and both father and son walked on the road, leading the donkey behind them until they came to an old man. "What? You foolish people!" said the old man. "You have a donkey and you walk barefoot on the hot ground instead of riding?" And so it goes. Listen: when you are doing something and other people come along, just keep on doing what you like.

---

epic A long, dramatic narrative recounting the celebrated deeds of a historic or legendary hero—often sung or recited in poetic language.

tale A creative narrative that is recognized as fiction for entertainment but may also draw a moral or teach a practical lesson.

---

⁴ Calloway, C. (1997). Introduction: Surviving the dark ages. In C. G. Calloway (Ed.), *After King Philip's war: Presence and persistence in Indian New England* (pp. 1–28). Hanover, NH: University Press of New England.

This is precisely the kind of tale that is of special interest in traditional folklore studies. It is an internationally popular "numbskull" tale. Versions of it have been recorded in India, Southwest Asia, southern and western Europe, and North America, as well as in West Africa. It is classified or catalogued as exhibiting a basic **motif** or story situation—father and son trying to please everyone—one of the many thousands that have been found to recur in tales around the world. Despite variations in detail, every version follows the same basic structure in the sequence of events, sometimes called the syntax of the tale: A peasant father and son work together, a beast of burden is purchased, the three set out on a short excursion, the father rides and is criticized, the son rides and is criticized, both walk and are criticized, and a conclusion is drawn.

Tales of this sort (not to mention myths and legends) that are found to have wide geographic distribution raise the question: Where did they originate? Did the story arise only once and then pass from one culture to another (diffusion)? Or did the stories arise independently (independent invention) in response to like causes in similar settings, or perhaps as a consequence of inherited mental preferences and images deeply embedded in the evolutionary construction of the human brain? Or is it merely that there are logical limits to the structure of stories, so that, by coincidence, different cultures are bound to come up with similar motifs and syntax?[5]

A surprisingly large number of motifs in European and African tales are traceable to ancient sources in India, evidence of diffusion of tales. Of course, purely local tales also exist. Within any particular culture, anthropologists usually can categorize local types of tales: animal, human experience, trickster, dilemma, ghost, moral, scatological, nonsense tales, and so on. In West Africa, for example, there is a remarkable prevalence of stories with animal protagonists. Many were carried to the slaveholding areas of the Americas; the Uncle Remus stories about Brer Rabbit and Brer Fox may be part of this tradition.

The significance of tales for the anthropologist rests partly in this matter of their distribution. They provide evidence of either cultural contacts or cultural isolation and of limits of influence and cultural cohesion.

Anthropologists are interested, however, in more than these questions of distribution. Like legends, tales very often illustrate local solutions to universal human ethical problems, and in some sense they state a moral philosophy. Anthropologists recognize that regardless of where the tale of the father, the son, and the donkey originated, the very fact it is told in West Africa suggests that it states something valid for that culture. The tale's lesson of a necessary degree of self-confidence in the face of arbitrary social criticism is therefore something that can be found in the culture's values and beliefs.

Other Verbal Art

Myths, legends, and tales, prominent as they are in anthropological studies, in many cultures turn out to be no more important than many other verbal arts. In the culture of the Awlad 'Ali Bedouins of Egypt's western desert, for example, poetry is a lively and active verbal art, especially as a vehicle for personal expression and private communication. These Bedouins use two forms of poetry. One is the elaborately structured and heroic poems men chant or recite only on ceremonial occasions and in specific public contexts. The other is the *ghinnawas* or "little songs" that punctuate everyday conversations, especially of women. Simple in structure, these deal with personal matters and feelings more appropriate to informal social situations, and older men regard them as the unimportant productions of women and youths.

Despite this official devaluation in the male-dominated Bedouin society, however, "little songs" play a vital part in people's daily lives. In these poems individuals are shielded from the consequences of making statements and expressing sentiments that contravene the moral system. Paradoxically, by sharing these "immoral" sentiments only with intimates and veiling them in impersonal traditional formulas, those who recite them demonstrate that they have a certain control, which actually enhances their moral standing. As is often true of folklore in general, the "little songs" of the Awlad 'Ali provide a culturally appropriate outlet for otherwise taboo thoughts or opinions.[6] Disaster jokes are an example of this in contemporary North American society.

In all cultures the words of songs constitute a kind of poetry. Poetry and stories recited with gesture, movement, and props become drama. Drama combined with dance,

---

[5] Gould, S. J. (2000). The narthex of San Marco and the pangenetic paradigm. *Natural History 109* (6), 29.

---

motif A story situation in a tale.

---

[6] Abu-Lughod, L. (1986). *Veiled sentiments: Honor and poetry in a Bedouin society* (p. 252). Berkeley: University of California Press.

The *ghinnawas* or "little songs" of the Awlad 'Ali Bedouins in Egypt punctuate conversations carried out while the people perform everyday chores, such as making bread, as these young women are doing. Through these "little songs," they can express what otherwise are taboo subjects.

music, and spectacle becomes a public celebration. The more we look at the individual arts, the clearer it becomes that they often are interrelated and interdependent. The verbal arts are, in fact, simply differing manifestations of the same creative imagination that produces music and the other arts.

Musical Art

Evidence of humans making music reaches far back in time. Bone flutes and whistles that date back some 40,000 years and resemble today's recorders have been found by archaeologists. And historically known food-foraging peoples were not without music. In the Kalahari Desert, for example, a Ju/'hoansi hunter off by himself would play a tune on his bow simply to help wile away the time. (Long before anyone thought of beating swords into plowshares, some genius discovered that bows could be used not just to kill but to make music as well.) In northern New England, Abenaki shamans used cedar flutes to call game, lure enemies, and attract women. In addition, shamans would use

a drum—over which two rawhide strings were stretched to produce a buzzing sound, representing singing—to allow communication with the spirit world.

The study of music in specific cultural settings, or **ethnomusicology,** began in the 19th century with the collection of folksongs and has developed into a specialized subfield of anthropological study. Ethnomusicology studies the world's musics in their cultural contexts from a comparative and relativistic perspective.[7] Although early ethnomusicologists primarily focused on non-Western musical traditions in tribal cultures, some now also study folk music or music played and enjoyed in different ethnic communities within industrialized modern states.

---

[7] See Nettl, B. (2005). The study of ethnomusicology: Thirty-one issues and concepts (pp. 12–13). Chicago: University of Illinois Press.

ethnomusicology The study of a society's music in terms of its cultural setting.

What is of primary importance when distinguishing music from other modes of expression? Music to one person may be merely noise to another. Music is a form of communication that includes a nonverbal auditory component. The information it transmits is often abstract and emotional rather than concrete ideas and is experienced in a variety of ways by different listeners. Such factors make music tough to define. In fact, no single definition of music can be agreed upon, because different peoples may include or exclude different ideas within that category. Ethnomusicologists often distinguish between "music" and that which is "musical."

Much of the historical development of ethnomusicology has been based on musicology, which is primarily the study of European music. As a result of this history, music has been discussed in terms of elements considered important in European music (especially tonality, rhythm, melody), when these may be of little importance to the practitioner. European music is defined, primarily, in terms of the presence of melody and rhythm. Melody is a function of tonality, and rhythm is an organizing concept involving tempo, stress, and measured repetition. Although these can be addressed in non-European music, they may not be the defining characteristics of a performance.

In general, human music is said to differ from natural music—the songs of birds, wolves, and whales, for example—by being almost everywhere perceived in terms of a repertoire of tones at fixed or regular intervals: in other words, a scale. Scale systems and their modifications make up what is known as **tonality** in music. These vary cross-culturally, so it is not surprising that something that sounds musical to one group of people may come across as noise to another.

Humans make closed systems out of a formless range of possible sounds by dividing the distance between a tone and its first overtone or sympathetic vibration (which always has exactly twice as many vibrations as the basic tone) into a series of measured steps. In the Western or European system, the distance between the basic tone and the first overtone is called the *octave*; it consists of seven steps—five whole tones and two semitones. The whole tones are further divided into semitones for a total working scale of twelve tones. Interestingly, some birds pitch their songs to the same scale as Western music,[8] perhaps influencing the way these people developed their scale.

One of the most common alternatives to the semitonal system is the *pentatonic* (five-tone) system, which divides the scale into five nearly equidistant tones. Such scales may be found all over the world, including in much European folk music. Arabic and Persian music has smaller units of a third of a tone with scales of seventeen and twenty-four steps in the octave. Even quarter-tone scales are used in large parts of South Asia, North Africa, and the Middle East with subtleties of shading that are nearly indistinguishable to most Western ears. Small wonder, then, that even when Westerners can hear what sounds like melody and rhythm in these systems, the total result may sound peculiar to them, or "out of tune."

Like so many other cultural elements, musical instruments and even styles of playing and singing are now circulating around the globe, as are the artists themselves. One such example is West African musician Saliou "Zale" Seck, known for his "funky crisscrossing rhythms." A member of the Lébou tribe, Zale was born in the old fishing town of Yoff, just north of Senegal's capital city of Dakar. He performs Wolof percussive music on traditional skin-covered *djembe* (hand drum) and *sabar* (played with one hand and a stick). Coming from a long line of *griots* (oral historians-traditional storytellers), he transmits his people's memory through lyrics of love and humanity. Fluent in French (his country was a French colony for many years), he has toured Europe and played on radio and television in France. Recently, Zale relocated to the French-speaking Canadian city of Quebec to further pursue his musical career.

---

[8] Gray, P. M., et al. (2001). The music of nature and the nature of music. *Science 291*, 52.

tonality   In music, scale systems and their modifications.

Another organizing factor in music is rhythm. Involving tempo, stress, and measured repetition, it may be more important than tonality. One reason for this may be our constant exposure to natural pulses, such as our own heartbeat and rhythms of breathing and walking. Even before we are born, we are exposed to our mother's heartbeat and to the rhythms of her movements, and as infants we experience rhythmic touching, petting, stroking, and rocking.[9]

The rhythms of traditional European music are most often measured into recurrent patterns of two, three, and four beats, with combinations of weak and strong beats to mark the division and form patterns. Non-European music is likely to move in patterns of five, seven, or eleven beats, with complex arrangements of internal beats and sometimes *polyrhythms*: one instrument or singer using a pattern of three beats, for example, while another uses a pattern of five or seven. Polyrhythms are frequent in the drum music of West Africa, which shows remarkable precision in the overlapping of rhythmic lines. Non-European music also may contain *shifting rhythms*: a pattern of three beats, for example, followed by a pattern of two or five beats with little or no regular recurrence or repetition of any one pattern, although the patterns are fixed and identifiable as units.

Melody involves both tonality and rhythm, for it is a rhythmical succession of musical tones organized as a distinct phrase or sequence of phrases.

Functions of Art

Art in all its many forms has countless functions beyond providing aesthetic pleasure. For anthropologists and others seeking to understand cultures beyond their own, art offers insights into a culture's worldview, giving clues about everything from gender and kinship relations to religious beliefs, political ideas, historical memory, and so on.

For those within a society, art may serve to display social status, spiritual identity, and political power. An example of this can be seen in the totem poles of Indians living along North America's northwest coast. Erected in front of the homes of chiefs, these poles are inscribed with symbols that are visual reminders of the social hierarchy. Similarly, art is used to mark kinship ties, as seen in Scottish tartans designed to identify clan affiliation. It can also affirm group solidarity and identity beyond kinship lines, as evidenced in national emblems such as the dragon (Bhutan), bald eagle (United States), maple leaf (Canada), crescent moon (Turkey), and cedar tree (Lebanon) that typically appear on coins, government buildings, and so on. Sometimes art is employed to express political themes and influence events, as in the counter-culture rock and folk music of the 1960s in the United States. Other times it is used to transmit traditional culture and ancestral ties, as in epic poems passed down from generation to generation.

As an activity or behavior that contributes to human well-being and that helps give shape and significance to life, art is often intricately intertwined with religion and spirituality. Shamans drum to help create a trance state, Buddhist monks chant to focus their meditation, and Christians sing hymns to praise God. And in some parts of the world, artisans create funerary boxes that are so creative that they find their way into museums as art (see the Globalscape feature). In elaborate ceremonies involving ornamentation, masks, costumes, songs, dances, and effigies, it is not easy to say precisely where art stops and religion begins.

Furthermore, music, dance, and other arts may be used, like magic, to "enchant"—to take advantage of the emotional or psychological predispositions of another person or group so as to cause them to perceive reality in a way favorable to the interests of the "enchanter." Often it is created to honor or beseech the aid of a deity, an ancestral spirit, or an animal spirit. Indeed, the arts may be used to manipulate a seemingly inexhaustible list of human passions, including desire, terror, wonder, love, fantasy, and vanity.[10] (Marketing specialists, of course, are well aware of this, which is why they routinely employ certain music and images in their advertising.)

Clearly, art in all its varied forms is used in a vast number of ways for a great array of purposes. To simplify our discussion of its numerous functions, we will consider a particular art form as embedded in a cultural system: music.

Functions of Music

Music is a powerful identifier. Many marginalized groups have used it for purposes of self-identification—as a means of building group solidarity and distinguishing themselves from dominant culture and sometimes as a channel for direct social and political commentary. Examples of this range from ethnic groups sponsoring music festivals to rock bands such as Britain's Rolling Stones, Coldplay, and Radiohead to North American rap artists Kanye West, Eminem, and Jay-Z. Music plays an important role in

---

[9] Dissanayake, E. (2000). Birth of the arts. *Natural History 109* (10), 89.

[10] Gell, A. (1988). Technology and magic. *Anthropology Today 4* (2), 7; Lewis-Williams, J. D. (1997). Agency, art and altered consciousness: A motif in French (Quercy) upper Paleolithic parietal art. *Antiquity 71*, 810–830.

Globalscape

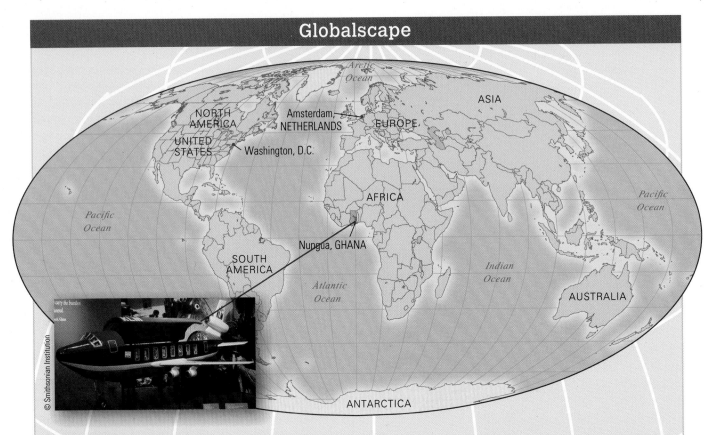

© Smithsonian Institution

Do Coffins Fly?

In his workshop in Nungua, Ghana, master carpenter Paa Joe makes unique painted wooden coffins for his clients in his Ga society and beyond. Some are spectacular, representing richly colored tropical fish or even luxury cars, such as Mercedes-Benz. Celebrating the life accomplishments of the deceased, these designer coffins show off the family's prominent status and wealth.

As a collective expression of culturally shared ideas about the afterlife, a Ga funeral ceremony reminds the mourners of important values embodied in the departed individual. Seeing the deceased off on a journey to the afterlife, Ga mourners call out praises to this person, and some may even

pour schnapps on the coffin. Henceforth, the deceased will continue to be ritually honored as an ancestor by descendants.

The 747 jumbo jet coffin pictured here confers upon the deceased the prestige and mystique of air travel. Its colors, blue and white, are those of the KLM Royal Dutch Airline, a long-time provider of air service between this West African country and the rest of the world. Its creator, Paa Joe, began working at age 15 for his cousin Kane Quaye, a carpenter known for designer coffins. Later, Joe started his own workshop, and before too long he began receiving orders from other parts of the world—not only from individuals but also from museums. Using wood, enamel paint,

satin, and Christmas wrapping paper, Joe created this KLM airplane coffin in 1997 for the Smithsonian National Museum of Natural History in Washington, DC, where millions of visitors from all over the globe now admire this Ghanian funereal ritual object.

Global Twister   When the Smithsonian Museum purchased one of Paa Joe's remarkable coffins for public display, did this West African funereal ritual object transform into a work of art?

Based on script for African Voices exhibition at NMNH, Smithsonian courtesy of Dr. Mari Jo Arnoldi.

Native American potlatches and powwows where Native American groups gather to reaffirm and celebrate their ethnic identities. And Scottish gatherings would not be Scottish without the sound of the highland bagpipes and the fiddle.

This power of music to shape identity has had varying consequences. The English understood that the

bagpipes created a strong sense of identity among the highland regiments of the British army and encouraged it within certain bounds, even as they suppressed piping in Scotland itself under the Disarming Act. Over time, the British military piping tradition was assimilated into the Scottish piping tradition and so was accepted and spread by Scottish pipers. As a result, much of the supposedly

Scottish piping one hears today consists of marches written within the conventions of the musical tradition of England, though shaped to fit the physical constraints of the instrument. Less often heard is the "classical" music known in Scottish Gaelic as Pibroch ("pipering") or, as some prefer to call traditional pipe music, Ceòl Mòr ("great music"). This more traditional Scottish pipe music has been revived over the past century and is now often romantically associated with rising cultural pride and even nationalist sentiment.

The English adoption of the highland bagpipe into Scottish regiments is an instance of those in authority employing music to further a political agenda. So, too, in Spain, former dictator Francisco Franco (who came to power in the 1930s) established community choruses in even the smallest towns to promote the singing of patriotic songs. Similarly, in Ireland Comhaltas Ceoltoiri Eireann has promoted the collection and performance of traditional Irish music, and in Brittany and Galicia, music is playing an important role in attempts to revive the spirits of the indigenous Celtic cultures in these regions of France and Spain.

The social function of music is perhaps most obvious in song, since these contain verbal text. Like other verbal forms, songs often express a group's values, beliefs, and concerns, but they do so with an increased formalism resulting from adherence to the systematic rules or conventions of pitch, rhythm, timbre, and musical genre. For this reason, music plays an important part in the cultural preservation and revitalization efforts of indigenous peoples around the world whose traditions were repressed or nearly exterminated through colonialism.

Work songs have played an important part in manual labor, serving to coordinate efforts in heavy or dangerous labor (such as weighing anchor and furling sail on board ships), to synchronize axe or hammer strokes, and to pass time and relieve tedium as with oyster-shucking songs. Songs also have been used to soothe babies to sleep, to charm animals into giving more milk, to keep witchcraft at bay, and to advertise goods. Songs may also serve social and political purposes, spreading particular ideas swiftly and effectively by giving them a special form involving poetic language and rhythm and by attaching a pleasing and appropriate tune, be it solemn or light.

In the United States numerous examples exist of marginalized social and ethnic groups attempting to gain a larger audience and more compassion for their plight through song. Perhaps no better example exists than African Americans, whose ancestors were captured and carried across the Atlantic Ocean to be sold as slaves. Out

Laborers in Mali, West Africa, working to the beat of a drum, which serves to set the pace of work, unify the workforce, and relieve boredom.

Visual Counterpoint

Aaron Smale/Ikon

Khampha Bouaphanh-2005 Fort Worth Star-Telegram

In cultures all across the world, people are not only concerned with making a living, but also with defending themselves against hostile outsiders. Those traditionally sent off to battle rely not only on their strength and weapons but may boost their own collective fighting spirits and intimidate and inspire fear in their rivals through musical rituals. Some of these traditional war rituals have been preserved and adapted for performance in theater or competitive male team sports. One spectacular example is the *haka,* a war dance (and song) originally performed by Maori warriors in New Zealand and now performed by rival rugby and football teams from many Pacific Ocean island nations. Opposite the photo showing Maori dancers performing the *haka* on stage, members of the Texas Trinity Trojans high school football team do it on the field. The Trojans have several outstanding players from Tonga, a large group of islands south of Samoa. Their families migrated to the United States for employment opportunities but maintain close contact and frequently visit home. For the Tongans and their teammates in Texas, jointly performing the *haka* minutes before the game makes them feel proud and inspires them to win. Among the first college football players from the Pacific to act out the war dance before a game were Samoan athletes at Kansas State University in the early 1980s.

of their experience emerged spirituals and, ultimately, gospel, jazz, blues, rock and roll, and rap. These forms all found their way into the North American mainstream, and white performers such as Elvis Presley and Benny Goodman (the latter with integrated bands—unusual in the 1930s) presented their own versions of this music to white audiences. Even composers of so-called serious music—ranging from Leonard Bernstein to George Gershwin to Antonin Dvorák to Francis Poulenc—were influenced by the music of African Americans. In short, music of a marginalized group of former slaves eventually captivated the entire world, even while the descendants of those slaves have had to struggle continually to escape their subordinate status.

In the 1950s and 1960s performers such as Pete Seeger and Joan Baez gained great visibility when supporting civil and human rights causes in the United States. Indeed, both performers' celebrity status led to the broader dissemination of their social and political beliefs. Such

celebrity status comes from skill in performing and communicating with the intended audience. So powerful a force was music in the civil rights and peace movements of the time that Seeger was targeted by right-wing Senator Joseph McCarthy's anticommunist crusade, which aimed to discredit the political left as anti-American and unpatriotic. Seeger became one of many performers blacklisted by the entertainment industry due to this political witch-hunt.

In Australia, certain ceremonial songs of the Aborigines have taken on a new legal function, as they are being introduced into court as evidence of early settlement patterns. These songs recount ancient adventures of mythic ancestors who lived in "Dreamtime" and created water holes, mountains, valleys, and other significant features in the landscape. The ancestors' tracks are known as *songlines,* and through ceremonial songs countless generations of Aborigines have passed on sacred ecological knowledge.

This oral tradition helps Aborigines to claim extensive indigenous land ownership, thus allowing them greater authority to use the land, as well as to negotiate and profit from the sale of natural resources. This had been impossible before. The British, upon their annexation of Australia, declared the land ownerless (*Terra Nullius*). Although the Aborigines had preserved their records of ownership in song and story, these were not admissible in the British courts.

In the early 1970s, however, the Aborigines exposed the injustice of the situation, and the Australian government began responding in a more favorable, if still limited, fashion, granting the claims of traditional ownership to groups in the Northern Territory. In 1992 the legitimacy of the concept of *Terra Nullius* was overturned, and native claims are now being presented in the other territories as well. These newer claimants are granted equal partnership with developers and others. Sacred sites are being recognized, and profits are being shared with the traditional owners. Proof of native ownership includes recordings of Aborigine songs indicative of traditional patterns of settlement, travel, and land use.[11]

Music gives basic human ideas a concrete form, made memorable and attractive with melody and rhythm. Whether a song's content is didactic, satiric, inspirational, religious, political, or purely emotional, the formless has been given form, and feelings hard to express in words alone are communicated in a symbolic and memorable way that can be repeated and shared. This, in turn, shapes and gives meaning to the community.

Art, Globalization, and Cultural Survival

Clearly, there is more to art than meets the eye or ear (not to mention the nose and tongue—consider how burning incense or tobacco is part of the artfulness of sacred ceremonies and imagine the cross-cultural array of smells and tastes in the cooking arts). In fact, art is such a significant part of any culture that many indigenous groups around the world whose lifeways have been threatened—first by colonialism and now by globalization—are using aesthetic expressions as part of a cultural survival strategy. They are finding that a traditional art form—a dance, a song, a dress, a basket, a carving, or anything that is distinctly beautiful and well made or performed—can serve as a powerful symbol that conveys the vital message, "We're still here, and we're still a culturally distinct people with our own particular beliefs and values."

There are many examples of art playing a role in indigenous rights efforts. Consider the Native rights case of the Aroostook band of Micmac Indians in northern Maine, described in the Anthropology Applied feature in the kinship and descent chapter. Building support for this particular case involved making a documentary film to inform politicians and the general public about the band's cultural identity and tribulations.[12] At the time, only a dozen or so families in this band still practiced traditional wood-splint basketry. However, it had been a common livelihood for many generations, and almost every band member had parents or grandparents who had made baskets.

Emblematic of Micmac identity, including their stubborn desire for self-determination, basketry became a focal point of the film, which ultimately played a key role in the success of the band's Native rights case. More than this, the film helped create a wider market for Micmac baskets, and by conveying the diligence and real skill involved in making them, it justified raising the prices of the baskets to levels that make the craft a viable livelihood. This, in turn, has prompted young people to take up basketry and strengthened their relationships with Micmac elders who are now passing on the age-old art to a new generation. A great array of similar examples of the link between art and cultural survival can be found all around the world. One of them is featured in the following Anthropology Applied feature, which closes out this chapter.

---

[11] Koch, G. (1997). Songs, land rights, and archives in Australia. *Cultural Survival Quarterly 20* (4). See also Berndt, R. M., & Berndt, C. H. (1989). *The speaking land: Myth and story in Aboriginal Australia.* New York: Penguin.

[12] Prins, H.E.L., & Carter, K. (1986). *Our lives in our hands.* Video and 16mm. Color. 50 min. Distributed by Watertown, MA: Documentary Educational Resources and Bucksport, ME: Northeast Historic Film; see also Prins, H.E.L. (2002). Visual media and the primitivist perplex: Colonial fantasies, indigenous imagination, and advocacy in North America. In F. D. Ginsburg et al. (Eds.), *Media worlds: Anthropology on new terrain* (pp. 58–74). Berkeley: University of California Press.

Bringing Back the Past *by Jennifer Sapiel Neptune*

Near the turn of the 20th century, a young Penobscot woman sat for a photograph, wearing a very old and elaborately beaded ceremonial chief's collar. She was the daughter of Joseph and Elizabeth Nicola and the descendant of a long line of tribal leaders. Her name was Florence Nicola, and she would go on to live a long life, marry Leo Shay, raise a family, and be remembered as a fine basketmaker and dedicated advocate for our tribe. Her efforts brought increased educational opportunities, the right for Native people in the state of Maine to vote in state and federal elections, and the first bridge that would connect our small village of Indian Island in the Penobscot River to the mainland.

Now, over one hundred years later, the photograph has resurfaced and found its way back to her son, Charles Shay. Charles brought the photograph of his mother to our tribal historian who recognized the collar as one he had seen in the book *Penobscot Man* by Frank G. Speck, and he was then able to trace it to the collections of the Smithsonian Institution's Museum of the American Indian.

In the late part of the nineteenth century the idea of the "vanishing Indian" took hold in anthropology—leading to a specialized field known as "salvage ethnography," which sought to save traditional knowledge, life ways, and material culture. Collecting examples of material culture to be sold into museum collections had become a business for some—which was how the collar Florence wore in the photograph came to be purchased by George Heye sometime before 1905 and then joined the collections of the museum. I have always found it ironic that we as a people and culture did not vanish; but during this time many of our tribes' most precious material objects did.

Bangor Daily News/Bridget Brown

Penobscot artist and cultural anthropologist Jennifer Neptune hugs tribal elder Charles Shay after giving him the traditional collar he commissioned. Modeled after a collar owned by his ancestors and now in the Smithsonian Institution's National Museum of the American Indian, the piece took Neptune more than 300 hours to make.

As a teenager I spent a lot of time in the library at the University of Maine looking through photographs in books of Penobscot beadwork, appliqué ribbon work, basketry, and carvings that were now in museums all over the world. I dreamed of being able to visit these objects, to study them up close, and to be able to find a way to bring them back into our world. It was for this reason that I went into anthropology, to learn how to research and write about my own culture. I started doing reproductions of the old beadwork designs, became a basketmaker, consulted on museum exhibitions, sold my own artwork, and worked with the Maine Indian Basketmakers Alliance promoting the work of basketmakers and artists from the four tribes in Maine.

In the spring of 2006 Charles showed me the photograph of his mother and asked me if I could make a reproduction of the collar for him.

As I worked on the collar, I was struck by how so much had changed since the late 18th century when the original collar was made. Back then the wool, silk ribbon, and beads its maker used had come by ship, horse, and foot from trade or treaty annuities; my materials were ordered over the Internet and came by UPS and FedEx. She worked by the light of the sun or fire; I worked mostly in the evenings with electric lights. Her world had northern forests still untouched by logging and filled with caribou and wolves; my world had airplanes, cars, and motor boats.

As I worked some more, I thought about what had stayed the same. We had lived and watched the sun rise and set on the same island our ancestors had for over 7,000 years. I wondered if we had stitched the same prayers into our work and if we used the same medicinal plants to soothe our aching hands and shoulders at the end of the day.

There are no words that can express how gratifying it was to hand over the finished collar to Charles—and to have played a part in returning to him, his family, and our tribe a part our history.

One hundred years ago when the collar left my community, anthropology seemed to be about taking objects, stories, and information away. As an anthropologist and artist I believe that I have a responsibility to use what I have learned to give back to my community. I have been so fortunate to be able to have spent time in museum collections visiting objects that most of my own people will never have the opportunity to see. What I learned from my time with the collar was that the objects that left still have a relationship with us today; they have a story that wants to be told, and they are waiting for someone to listen.

Questions for Reflection

1. All across the world and throughout human history, people have creatively expressed ideas and feelings through art, whether in music, dance, imagery, or sculpture. Do you know any specific forms of art originally created for, and performed by, or in, your own community? Do these art forms have any cultural meaning or social function?

2. Among the Maori in New Zealand, tattooing is a traditional form of skin art, and their tattoo designs are typically based on cultural symbols understood by all members in the community. Are the tattoo designs in your culture based on traditional motifs that have a shared symbolic meaning?

3. Because kinship relations are important in small-scale traditional societies, these relationships are often symbolically represented in artistic designs and motifs. What are some of the major concerns in your society, and are these concerns reflected in any of your culture's art forms?

4. In some cultures art is produced not to be preserved and enjoyed by the living but to be buried along with the dead. In fact, in some cultures highly valued art objects may also be burned or otherwise destroyed. Can you think of any reason for such seemingly irrational cultural practices?

5. Many museums and private collectors in Europe and North America are interested in so-called tribal art, such as African statues or American Indian masks originally used in sacred rituals. Are there sacred objects such as paintings or carvings in your religion that might also be collected, bought, or sold as art?

Suggested Readings

Buckland, T. J. (Ed.). (2007). *Dancing from past to present: Nation, culture, identities.* Madison: University of Wisconsin Press.

In this wide-ranging collection of ethnographic and historical essays, the reader will enjoy learning about the cultural significance and social role of dance in many different societies in all parts of the world—from England to India, Java, Korea, Macedonia, New Mexico, and Tonga in the southern Pacific.

Dundes, A. (1980). *Interpreting folklore.* Bloomington: Indiana University Press.

A collection of articles that assesses the materials folklorists have amassed and classified, this book seeks to broaden and refine traditional assumptions about the proper subject matter and methods of folklore.

Layton, R. (1991). *The anthropology of art* (2nd ed.). Cambridge, England: Cambridge University Press.

This readable introduction to the diversity of non-Western art deals with questions of aesthetic appreciation, the use of art, and the big question: What *is* art?

Morphy, H., & Perkins, M. (Eds.). (2006). *Anthropology of art: A reader.* Boston: Blackwell.

This illustrated anthology explores the art of different cultures at different times, covering the essential theoretical debates in the anthropology of art—including definitions of art and aesthetics, the nature of authenticity and representational processes, the primitivism controversy, and the history of trade and commodification.

Seeger, A. (2004). *Why Suyá sing: A musical anthropology.* Champaign: University of Illinois Press.

Examining the myth telling, speech making, and singing of Suyá Indians in Mato Grosso, Brazil, Seeger considers why music is important for them—and by extension for other groups. He reveals how Suyá singing creates euphoria out of silence, a village community out of a collection of houses, a socialized adult out of a boy, and contributes to the formation of ideas about time, space, and social identity.

Venbrux, E., Rosi, P. S., & Welsch, R. L. (Eds.). (2006). *Exploring world art.* Long Grove, IL: Waveland.

Ethnographic case studies examine the contemporary art world from local and comparative global perspectives, spanning topics such as artistic agency, new art forms and media, arenas of cultural production, and the role of gender in these innovative traditions.

Challenge Issue For long-term survival, human cultures must adapt to different environments and shifting circumstances. Today's technological and other major changes challenge us to adjust at an ever-faster pace. The challenge is all the more unsettling in traditional communities where changes are often imposed by powerful outside forces undermining customary ways of life. However, some cultures confront change on their own terms, even welcoming new ideas, products, and practices into their lives as improvements. This harbor scene in the small kingdom of Bahrain reflects the rapid changes occurring in many non-Western countries today. Strategically situated in the Persian Gulf, Bahrain has long been an international trading center. A former British protectorate, it is a multi-ethnic and multilingual country, historically dominated by Arab Muslims. Over half the workforce hails from Egypt, India, Iran, Pakistan, and beyond, consisting primarily of unskilled migrant laborers. Here we see the traditional Arab sailing *dhows* that share this busy sea lane with high-tech warships and the huge oil tankers that export this region's black liquid wealth. The splendid skyline behind them features ultra-modern buildings, including the Bahrain World Trade Center on the right, designed to resemble the silhouette of *dhows.* Its hi-tech, sail-shaped twin towers funnel sea breeze into turbines that produce 15 percent of the power needed to operate the offices of these 50-story buildings.

CHAPTER 15

Processes of Change

Chapter Preview

Why Do Cultures Change?

All cultures change at one time or another for a variety of reasons. Although people may deliberately alter their ways in response to problems or challenges, much change is unforeseen, unplanned, and undirected. Changes in existing values and behavior may also come about due to contact with other peoples who introduce new ideas or tools. This sometimes involves the massive imposition of foreign ideas and practices through conquest of one group by another. Through cultural change, societies can adapt to altered conditions; however, not all change is positive or adaptive.

What Is Modernization?

Modernization is a problematic term referring to a process of change by which traditional, nonindustrial societies acquire characteristics of technologically complex societies. Accelerated modernization interconnecting all parts of the world is known as globalization. Although commonly assumed to be a good thing, modernization has also led to the destruction of treasured customs and values, leaving many people unsettled, disoriented, and demoralized.

How Do Cultures Change?

The mechanisms of cultural change include innovation, diffusion, cultural loss, and acculturation. Innovation is the discovery or creation of something that is then accepted by fellow members in a society. Diffusion is the borrowing of something from another group, and cultural loss is the abandonment of an existing practice or trait, with or without replacement. Acculturation is a massive change that comes about in a group due to intensive firsthand contact with another, usually more powerful, group. Typically, it occurs when dominant societies forcefully expand their activities beyond their borders, pressuring other societies to abandon their traditional culture and replace it with the foreign one.

Culture has become the primary medium through which the human species adapts to changes and solves the problems of existence. Various cultural institutions—such as religion, kinship, marriage, and political and economic organization—mesh to form an integrated cultural system. Because systems generally work to maintain stability, cultures are often fairly steady and remain so unless there is a critical change in one or more significant factors such as natural environment, technology, population density—or in people's perceptions of the various conditions to which they are adapted.

Archaeological studies reveal how elements of a culture may persist for long periods. In northeastern North America, for example, the cultures of indigenous inhabitants remained relatively consistent over thousands of years because they successfully adapted to relatively minor fluctuations in their social conditions and natural environments, making changes from time to time in tools, utensils, and other material support.

Although stability may be a striking feature of many traditional cultures, all cultures are capable of adapting to changing conditions—climatic, economic, political, or ideological. Adaptation is a consequence of change that happens to work favorably for a population.

However, not all change is positive or adaptive, and not all cultures are equally well equipped for making the necessary adjustments in a timely fashion. In a stable society, change may occur gently and gradually, without altering in any fundamental way the culture's underlying structures, as was the case in much of North America before the European invasion several centuries ago. Sometimes, though, the pace of change may increase dramatically, to the point of destabilizing or even breaking up a cultural system. The modern world is full of examples of such radical changes, from the disintegration of the Soviet Union to the utter devastation of many indigenous communities in the Amazon caused by state efforts to develop Indian homelands and capitalize on the rainforest's natural resources.

The causes of change are many, including accidental discoveries, deliberate attempts to solve a perceived problem, and interaction with other peoples who introduce—or force—new ideas or tools or ways of life. Sometimes change is caused by the unexpected outcome of particular actions or events. Among countless examples is the establishment of European colonies in the homelands of Algonquian-speaking Natives in northeastern America nearly 500 years ago. Many people today assume this came about because the culture of the newcomers was better or more advanced than that of the region's original inhabitants. However, one could just as well argue that it was the reverse, for at the time these Indians had higher quality diets, enjoyed better health, and experienced less violence in their lives than did most Europeans.[1]

A deeper look at American history shows that the colonial settlements in New England were actually the outcome of a series of unrelated historical events that happened to coincide at a critical time. In the 1500s, economic and political developments in England drove large numbers of small farmers off the land during a period of population growth, thereby forcing an outward migration. By pure chance, this took place shortly after the European discovery of the Americas. Seeing the New World as an answer to its overpopulation, the English attempted to establish overseas colonies in lands they claimed and renamed New England. Early efforts failed, until an epidemic of unprecedented scope resulted in the sudden death of 75 to 90 percent of the indigenous inhabitants.

This devastating epidemic occurred because the region's Native communities were exposed to a host of foreign diseases through contact with European fishermen and traders. It left the weakened remnants of indigenous survivors with few defenses against aggressive colonizers, many of whom possessed natural immunity to the diseases. For centuries, Europeans had been living under conditions that were ideal for the incubation and spread of infectious diseases, which periodically killed off up to 80 percent of local populations. Since those who survived had a higher resistance to the diseases than those who succumbed, such resistance became more common in European populations over time. Indians at the time of the European invasion, by contrast, lacked all resistance to these diseases.

Although the crucial issue of immunity played a huge role in England's North American colonization efforts, it is unlikely the English could have dispossessed the surviving indigenous peoples from their land were it not for one other important factor: They crossed the Atlantic Ocean equipped with the political and military techniques for dominating other peoples—tactics previously used to impose rule over the Scots, Irish, and Welsh. In addition, they came with the ideology of a "just war," which they believed justified dispossessing America's indigenous peoples who fought back in defense.

Change imposed upon one group by another continues in much of the world today as culture contact intensifies between societies unequal in power. Among those who have the power to drive and direct change in their favor, it is typically referred to as "progress," which literally translates as "to move forward"—that is, in a positive direction. But progress is a relative term that implies improvement *as defined by the people who profit or otherwise benefit from the changes set into motion.* In other words, progress is in the eye of the beholder, for not everyone benefits from change. In fact, countless peoples (including traditional foraging, herding, and peasant communities in many parts of the world) have become the victims of progress, seeing their lives destroyed by powerful others focused on plucking almost all of the fruits for themselves.

---

[1] Stannard, D. E. (1992). *American holocaust* (pp. 57–67). Oxford, England: Oxford University Press.

Eric R. Wolf (1923–1999)

© Sydel Silverman

Like the millions of peasants about whom he wrote, **Eric Wolf** personally experienced radical upheaval in his life due to powerful outside political forces. A war refugee in his teens, he survived the battlefields and mass murders of Nazi-occupied Europe. Driven by the inequities and atrocities he witnessed during World War II, he turned to anthropology to sort through issues of power. Viewing anthropology as the most scientific of the humanities and the most humane of the sciences, he became famous for his comparative historical studies on peasants, power, and the transforming impact of capitalism on traditional nations.

Wolf's life began in Austria shortly after the First World War. During that terrible conflict, his Austrian father had been a prisoner of war in Siberia, where he met Wolf's mother, a Russian exile. When peace returned, the couple married and settled in Vienna, where Eric was born in 1923. Growing up in Austria's capital and then (because of his father's job) in Sudetenland in what is now the Czech Republic, young Eric enjoyed a life of relative ease. He relished summers spent in the Alps among local peasants in exotic costumes, and he drank in his mother's tales about her father's adventures with Siberian nomads.

Life changed for Eric in 1938 when Adolf Hitler grabbed power in Germany, annexed Austria and Sudetenland, and threatened Jews like the Wolfs. Seeking security for their 15-year-old son,

Eric's parents sent him to high school in England. In 1940, a year after World War II broke out, British authorities believed invasion was imminent and ordered aliens, including Eric, into an internment camp. There he met other refugees from Nazi-occupied Europe and had his first exposure to Marxist theories. Soon, he left England for New York City and enrolled at Queens College, where Professor Hortense Powdermaker, a former student of Malinowski, introduced him to anthropology.

In 1943, the 20-year-old refugee enlisted in the U.S. Army's 10th Mountain Division. Fighting in the mountains of Tuscany, Italy, he won a Silver Star for combat bravery. At the war's end, Wolf returned to the United States, completed his bachelor's degree, and

went on to graduate school at Columbia University, studying anthropology under Julian Steward and Ruth Benedict. After earning his doctorate in 1951, based on fieldwork in Puerto Rico, he did extensive research on Mexican peasants.

Following short stints at various U.S. universities, he became a professor at the University of Michigan in 1961. A prolific writer, Wolf gained tremendous recognition for his fourth book, *Peasant Wars of the Twentieth Century,* published in 1969 during the height of the Vietnam War. Against that war, he headed a newly founded ethics committee in the American Anthropological Association and helped expose counter-insurgency uses of anthropological research in Southeast Asia.

Wolf left Michigan in 1971, accepting a distinguished professorship at Lehman College in the Bronx, New York. There his classes were filled with working-class students of all ethnic backgrounds, including many who took the courses he taught in Spanish. In addition, he taught anthropology at the Graduate School of the City University of New York. After many more publications, Wolf wrote his award-winning book, *Europe and the People Without History* (1982). In 1990, he received a MacArthur "genius" prize. Shortly before his death of cancer in 1999, he published *Envisioning Power: Ideologies of Dominance and Crisis,* which explores how ideas and power are connected though the medium of culture.

In recent decades, some anthropologists have focused on the historical impact European capitalist expansionism has had on indigenous cultures around the world, radically changing or even destroying them. One of the first and most prominent among these anthropologists was Eric Wolf, who personally experienced the global havoc and upheaval of the 20th century (see Anthropologist of Note).

Mechanisms of Change

Anthropologists are not only interested in the structures of cultures as systems of adaptation, which help us understand how a population maintains itself in a certain habitat, but also in explaining processes of cultural change.

Some of the major mechanisms involved in cultural change are innovation, diffusion, and cultural loss. These types of change are typically voluntary and are not imposed on a population by outside forces.

Innovation

The ultimate source of all cultural change is innovation: any new idea, method, or device that gains widespread acceptance in society. **Primary innovation** is the creation, invention, or chance discovery of a completely new idea,

primary innovation The creation, invention, or chance discovery of a completely new idea, method, or device.

A Hopi Indian woman firing pottery vessels. The earliest discovery that firing clay vessels makes them more durable took place in Asia, probably when clay-lined basins next to cooking fires were accidentally fired. Later, a similar innovation took place in the Americas.

© Stephen Trimble

method, or device. A **secondary innovation** is a deliberate application or modification of an existing idea, method, or device.

An example of a primary innovation is the discovery that firing clay makes it permanently hard. Presumably, accidental firing of clay occurred frequently in ancient cooking fires—but a chance occurrence is of no consequence unless someone perceives an application for it. This discovery took place about 25,000 years ago, when people began making figurines of fired clay. However, it was not until about 10,000 years later that people recognized a highly practical application of fired clay and began using it to make pottery containers and cooking vessels—a secondary innovation.

The earliest known pottery was recently found in Yuchanyan Cave, an Upper Paleolithic site in southern China, where broken pieces of coarse, thick-walled, and low-fired ceramic vessels were dated to between 15,000 and 18,000 years ago.[2] Meanwhile, almost everywhere else in the world, people continued using baskets, animal-hide bags, and stone or wooden bowls for containers.

Scholarly reconstruction of the development of pottery suggests that it probably came about in the following way:[3] Thousands of years ago, people in parts of Asia were familiar with the working of clay, using it to build houses, line storage pits, and model figurines. In addition, their cooking areas included clay-lined basins built into the floor and clay ovens and hearths, making the accidental firing of clay inevitable. Once the significance of fired clay—the primary innovation—was understood, then the application of known techniques to it—secondary innovation—became possible. Clay could be modeled in the familiar way but now into the known shapes of existing containers. It could then be fired, either in an open fire or in the same facilities used for cooking food. Early pottery imitated leather and stone containers, but over time potters developed shapes and decorative techniques specifically suited to the new technology.

Archaeological research shows that the earliest known clay vessels produced were initially handmade, and the earliest furnaces or kilns were the same ovens used for cooking. As people became more adept at making pottery, they refined the technology. To aid in production, the clay could be modeled on a mat or other surface that could be turned as work progressed. Hence, the potter could sit in one place while working, without having to get up to move around the clay. A further refinement was to mount the

[2] Boaretto, E., et al. (2009, June 16). Radiocarbon dating of charcoal and bone collagen associated with early pottery at Yuchanyan Cave, Hunan Province, China. *Proceedings of the National Academy of Sciences, USA 106* (24), 9595–9600.

secondary innovation The deliberate application or modification of an existing idea, method, or device.

[3] Amiran, R. (1965). The beginnings of pottery-making in the Near East. In F. R. Matson (Ed.), *Ceramics and man* (pp. 240–247). Viking Fund Publications in Anthropology, 41.

Lefthand driving on London Bridge in England. Once one's reflexes become habituated to doing something one way, it becomes difficult to do it differently. An example is the custom of driving a vehicle on a particular side of the highway. Which is the correct side? About a third of the world's population is used to traveling on the left, while the rest is accustomed to the right. When a British, Australian, Indonesian, or Japanese tourist visits the United States, France, or Mexico, the experience of driving on the opposite ("wrong") side of the road is challenging and often disorienting.

movable surface on a vertical rotating shaft—an application of a known principle used for drills—creating the potter's wheel and permitting mass production. Kilns, too, were modified for better heat circulation by separating the firing chamber from the fire itself. By chance, these improved kilns produced enough heat to smelt metal ores such as copper, tin, gold, silver, and lead. Presumably, this discovery was made by accident—another primary innovation—and set the stage for the eventual development of the forced-draft furnace out of the earlier pottery kiln.

The accidental discoveries responsible for primary innovations are not generated by environmental change or some other need, nor are they necessarily adaptive. They are, however, given structure by the cultural context. Thus the outcome of the discovery of fired clay by migratory food foragers 25,000 years ago was very different from what it was when discovered later by more sedentary farmers in Southwest Asia, where it set off a cultural chain reaction as one invention led to another. Indeed, given particular sets of cultural goals, values, and knowledge, certain innovations are nearly inevitable.

Although a culture's internal dynamics may encourage particular innovative tendencies, they may discourage or remain neutral about others. Indeed, Polish astronomer Nicolaus Copernicus's discovery in the early 1500s of the rotation of the planets around the sun and the discovery of the basic laws of heredity in the early 1860s by Austrian botanist Gregor Mendel are instances of genuine creative insights out of step with the established needs, values, and goals of their times and places. In fact, Mendel's pioneering experiments in genetics remained obscure until sixteen years after his death, when three scientists working

independently rediscovered, all in the same year (1900), the same laws of heredity. In the context of turn-of-the-century Western culture, Mendel's laws were bound to be discovered, even if Mendel's botanical experiments had not revealed them earlier.

Although an innovation must be reasonably consistent with a society's needs, values, and goals in order to gain acceptance, it takes more than this. Force of custom or habit tends to obstruct ready acceptance of the new or unfamiliar, for people typically stick with what they are used to rather than adopt something strange that requires adjustment on their part.

Obviously, an innovation is not assured of acceptance simply because it is notably better than the thing, method, or idea it might replace. Much depends on the prestige of the innovator and potential adopters. If the innovator's prestige is high, this will help gain more general acceptance for the innovation. If it is low, acceptance is less likely, unless the innovator can attract a sponsor who has high prestige.

Diffusion

The spread of certain ideas, customs, or practices from one culture to another is known as **diffusion.** So common is cross-cultural borrowing that North American anthropologist Ralph Linton suggested that it accounts for as much as

---

diffusion The spread of certain ideas, customs, or practices from one culture to another.

Change, whether generated within a society or introduced from the outside, may encounter unexpected cultural obstacles. Such obstacles are often ideologically embedded in religious faith-based traditions, such as some conservative Mennonite sects in North America rejecting motorized vehicles in their rural communities. In several Asian and African countries primarily inhabited by Muslims, orthodox religious groups oppose modern development and the spread of what they consider immoral foreign influences. Instead, they seek to return to or maintain a society based on Muslim traditions. Here we see a class of traditional Muslim students in Lahore, Pakistan, studying the holy scriptures of the Koran at a *madrasah* (religious school).

90 percent of any culture's content. People are creative about their borrowing, however, picking and choosing from multiple possibilities and sources. Usually their selections are limited to those compatible with the existing culture.

In Guatemala in the 1960s, for example, Maya Indians, who then (as now) made up more than half of that country's population, would adopt Western ways if the practical advantage of what they adopted was self-evident and did not conflict with deeply rooted traditional values and customs. The use of metal hoes, shovels, and machetes became standard early on, for they are superior to stone tools and yet compatible with the cultivation of corn in the traditional way by men using hand tools.

Yet, other modern practices that might seem advantageous to the Maya were resisted if they were perceived to be in conflict with Indian tradition. Pursuing these practices could make one a social outcast. This happened to a young farmer who tried using chemical fertilizers and pesticides to grow cash crops of vegetables not eaten by the Maya to sell in the city. He found he could not secure a "good" woman for a wife—a "good" woman (in his cultural context) being one who has never had sex with another man and is hardworking, skilled at domestic chores, and willing to attend

to her husband's needs. However, after abandoning his unorthodox ways, he gained acceptance in his community as a "real" man—one who provides for his household by working steadily at farming and making charcoal in the traditional ways. No longer conspicuous as someone different from other local men, he married well within a short time.[4]

An awareness of the extent of cultural borrowing can be eye opening. Take, for example, the numerous things that people all around the globe have borrowed from American Indians. Domestic plants developed ("invented") by the Indians—potatoes, avocados, beans, squash, tomatoes, peanuts, manioc, chili peppers, chocolate, sweet potatoes, and corn (maize), to name a few—furnish a major portion of the world's food supply. In fact, American Indians are recognized as primary contributors to the world's varied cuisine and credited with developing the largest array of nutritious foods.[5]

---

[4] Reina, R. E. (1966). *The law of the saints* (pp. 65–68). Indianapolis: Bobbs-Merrill.

[5] Weatherford, J. (1988). *Indian givers: How the Indians of the Americas transformed the New World* (p. 115). New York: Ballantine.

Having spread from the tropics of the Mexican highlands to much of the rest of North and South America, corn diffused rapidly to the rest of the world after Italian explorer Christopher Columbus first crossed the Atlantic in 1492. A favorite dish in Italy is polenta (a thick mush made of cornmeal). Here we see it being made the traditional way: boiled in a big copper cauldron over a fire of hot coals and then spread out and cooled to firmness on a wooden or stone slab.

© Hubert Stadler/CORBIS

Take corn, for instance, also known as maize (derived from a Caribbean Indian word *maíz*). The English originally referred to this Native American cereal plant as "Indian corn." First cultivated by indigenous peoples in the Mexican highlands over 7,000 years ago, this food crop diffused to much of the rest of North, Central, and South America over the next few millennia. In 1493, the explorer Columbus returned from America to Spain with a sampling of maize. First planted in kitchen gardens in Andalusia, in the course of several decades maize spread to other parts of Spain and Portugal. From there it diffused southwest, reaching France and northern Italy by the late 1530s. Producing more calories per acre than traditional European crops, it was initially grown as green fodder to feed pigs and other livestock. However, forced by poverty and famine, peasants and other poor folk in southern Europe accepted this new food as cornmeal cakes or thick porridge. Portuguese traders introduced maize to western Africa and across the Indian Ocean to South Asia from where it spread to China before the mid-1500s.

Diffusing across the globe, maize has become one of the world's major staple foods and culturally incorporated under many different names. This dietary revolution not only completely altered people's lives but is also responsible for enormous population growth, especially since the 18th century.[6] Today, a greater weight of maize is produced each year than rice, wheat, or any other grain—about 800 million tons, with over half of the global production taking place in the United States and China.

In recent years, an enormous quantity of maize has been grown for biomass fuel, such as ethanol, as an alternative to nonrenewable fossil fuels such as oil. Moreover, the production of genetically engineered maize (manipulated with herbicide or drought-resistant genes) has been gaining ground, especially in the United States and many developing countries, but this practice is resisted by European farmers and consumers.

Another remarkable example of diffusion—across multiple language barriers and despite long-held local traditions—is the metric system for measuring length, weight, capacity, currency, and temperature. Based on a classification in which standard units of measurement are multiplied or divided by 10 in order to produce larger or smaller units, this rational system has simplified calculations and is practical on many levels of accounting and management. In 1795, three centuries after an engineer in the Netherlands first proposed the use of decimal fractions for measures, weights, and currency in everyday life, and just a few years after the French revolution toppled the monarchy, the French First Republic adopted the metric system as its official system of measurement. As a result of French military expansion under Napoleon, this system was forced upon conquered neighboring countries, standardizing a bewildering array of regional and local systems of measurement that had been traditionally used for generations.

[6] Braudel, F. (1979). *The structures of everyday life: Civilization and capitalism 15th–18th century* (vol. 1, pp. 163–167). New York: Harper & Row.

During the 1800s, the metric system gained acceptance in most of Europe and various other parts of the world, and by 1900 about forty countries had officially adopted it. The system continued to spread over the next century, despite initial reluctance or even resistance in some countries, such as Great Britain. Since the early 1970s, that country and most of its former colonies have made a full transition to the metric system. British law now defines each "Imperial unit" in terms of the metric equivalent, having adjusted the traditional currency system of pence (penny), sixpence, shilling (12-pence), and pound (20 shillings) by doing away with the sixpence and shilling and making the pound equivalent to 100 pence. Likewise, Imperial units of length—measured in terms of the inch, foot (12 inches), yard (36 inches), mile (63,360 inches), and league (190,080 inches)—were also officially declared obsolete (although many older Britons still hold on to traditional measurements in daily life). Today, at least officially, the metric system is almost universal, with the exception of Myanmar (Burma), Liberia, and, most notably, the United States.[7]

Despite the obvious importance of diffusion, an innovation from another culture probably faces more obstacles when it comes to being accepted than does one that is "homegrown." In the United States, for example, this is one reason why people have been so reluctant to abandon the cumbersome English system of weights and measures for the far more logical metric system. While all other countries in the world have essentially converted to metric, in the United States the switchover is still less than about 50 percent. Hence, ethnocentrism may act as a barrier to cultural diffusion.

Cultural Loss

Most often people look at cultural change as an accumulation of innovations. Frequently, however, the acceptance of a new innovation results in **cultural loss**—the abandonment of an existing practice or trait. For example, in ancient times chariots and carts were used widely in northern Africa and southwestern Asia, but wheeled vehicles virtually disappeared from Morocco to Afghanistan about 1,500 years ago. They were replaced by camels, not because of some reversion to the past but because camels used as pack animals worked better. The old Roman empire roads had deteriorated, and these sturdy animals traveled well with or without roads. Their endurance, longevity, and ability to ford rivers and traverse rough ground made pack camels admirably suited for the region. Plus, they were economical in terms of labor: A wagon required a man for every two draft animals, but a single person could manage up to six pack camels.

Reflecting on this, paleontologist Stephen Jay Gould commented that this surprises most Westerners because

> Wheels have come to symbolize in our culture . . . intelligent exploitation and technological progress. . . . The success of camels reemphasizes a fundamental theme. . . . Adaptation, be it biological or cultural, represents a better fit to specific, local environments, not an inevitable stage in a ladder of progress. Wheels were a formidable invention, and their uses are manifold. . . . But camels may work better in some circumstances. Wheels, like wings, fins, and brains, are exquisite devices for certain purposes, not signs of intrinsic superiority.[8]

Often overlooked is another facet of losing apparently useful traits: loss without replacement. An example of this is the historical absence of boats among the indigenous inhabitants of the Canary Islands, a group of small islands isolated off North Africa's Atlantic coastline. The ancestors of these people must have had boats, for without them they could never have transported themselves and their domestic livestock to the islands in the first place. Later, without boats, they had no way to communicate with other islands or with the mainland. This loss of something useful came about due to the islands' lack of stone suitable for making polished stone axes, which in turn limited the islanders' carpentry.[9]

Repressive Change

Innovation, diffusion, and cultural loss all may take place among peoples who are free to decide for themselves what changes they will or will not accept. Not always, however, do people have the liberty to make their own choices. Frequently, changes they would not willingly make have

---

[7] Cardarelli, F. (2003). *Encyclopaedia of scientific units, weights, and measures: Their SI equivalences and origins.* London: Springer.

cultural loss The abandonment of an existing practice or trait.

---

[8] Gould, S. J. (1983). *Hens' teeth and horses' toes* (p. 159). New York: Norton.
[9] Coon, C. S. (1954). *The story of man* (p. 174). New York: Knopf.

© Harald E. L. Prins

Until a few decades ago, these Ache Indians survived as traditional hunters and gatherers in the deep tropical forest of eastern Paraguay. Not unlike the Ju/'hoansi of southern Africa, they were organized in small migratory bands and rarely had contact with outsiders. Armed with spears and bows and arrows, they could not defend their homeland against large numbers of foreign invaders equipped with chainsaws, bulldozers, and firearms. Massacres and foreign diseases, coupled with massive deforestation of their hunting territories, almost annihilated these people in the 1950s and 1960s. Since then, they have been exposed to intensive acculturation. Here we see the break up of an Ache encampment in the middle of Asunción, Paraguay's capital city, where they lived during many weeks of protest against government policies.

been forced upon them by some other group, usually in the course of conquest and colonialism. A direct outcome in many cases is repressive change to a culture, which anthropologists call acculturation. The most radical form of repressive change is ethnocide.

Acculturation and Ethnocide

Acculturation is the massive culture change that occurs in a society when it experiences intensive firsthand contact with a more powerful society. It always involves an element of force, either directly, as in conquests, or indirectly, as in the implicit or explicit threat that force will be used if people refuse to make the demanded changes. Other variables include degree of cultural difference; circumstances, intensity, frequency, and hostility of contact; relative status of the agents of contact; who is dominant and who is submissive; and whether the nature of

the flow is reciprocal or nonreciprocal. *Acculturation* and *diffusion* are not equivalent terms; one culture can borrow from another without being in the least forced into change.

In the course of cultural contact, any number of things may happen. Merger or fusion occurs when two cultures lose their separate identities and form a single culture, as historically expressed by the melting pot ideology of English-speaking, Protestant Euramerican culture in the United States. Sometimes, though, one of the cultures loses its autonomy but retains its identity as a subculture in the form of a caste, class, or ethnic group.

acculturation Massive culture change that occurs in a society when it experiences intensive firsthand contact with a more powerful society.

This is typical of conquest or slavery situations, and the United States has examples of this despite its melting pot ideology—we need look no further than the nearest American Indian reservation.

Acculturation may occur as a result of military conquest, political and economic expansion, or massive invasion and breaking up of cultural structures by dominant newcomers who know or care nothing about the traditional beliefs and practices of the people they seek to control. Under the sway of powerful outsiders—and unable to effectively resist imposed changes and obstructed in carrying out many of their own social, religious, and economic activities—subordinated groups are forced into new social and cultural practices that tend to isolate individuals and destroy the integrity of their traditional communities.

In virtually all parts of the world today, people are faced with the tragedy of forced removal from their traditional homelands, as entire communities are uprooted to make way for hydroelectric projects, grazing lands for cattle, mining operations, or highway construction. In Brazil's rush to develop the vast Amazon rainforest, for instance, entire indigenous communities have been relocated to "national parks," where resources are inadequate for the number of people and where former enemies are often forced to live in close proximity.

Ethnocide, the violent eradication of an ethnic group's collective cultural identity as a distinctive people, occurs when a dominant society deliberately sets out to destroy another society's cultural heritage. This may take place when a powerful nation aggressively expands its territorial control by annexing neighboring peoples and their territories, incorporating the conquered groups as subjects. A policy of ethnocide typically includes forbidding a subjugated nation's ancestral language, criminalizing their traditional customs, destroying their religion and demolishing sacred places and practices, breaking up their social organizations, and dispossessing or removing the survivors from their homelands—in essence, stopping short of physical extermination while removing all traces of their unique culture.

One tragic current example is Tibet, which could not defend itself against an invasion by the Chinese communist army in 1950. The Chinese government then initiated its ethnocidal policies by means of systematic attacks against traditional Tibetan culture. Seeking to

stamp out deeply rooted religious beliefs and practices, it ordered the demolition of most Buddhist temples and monasteries. Following a mass uprising, hundreds of thousands of Tibetans were killed or forced into exile abroad. Seeking to annihilate Tibetan identity, China sought to turn the surviving Tibetans into political subjects who would culturally identify themselves as Chinese nationals.[10]

Ethnocide may also take place when so many carriers of a culture die that those who manage to survive become refugees, living among peoples of different cultures. Examples of this may be seen in many parts of the world today (Figure 15.1). A particularly well-documented case occurred in Brazil's Amazon basin in 1968, when developers hired killers to wipe out several Indian groups, using arsenic, dynamite, and machine guns from light planes.

Violence continues to be used in Brazil as a means of dealing with indigenous peoples. For example, according to conservative estimates, at least 1,500 Yanomami Indians died in the 1980s, many the victims of deliberate massacres, as cattle ranchers and gold miners poured into northern Brazil. By 1990, 70 percent of Yanomami land in Brazil had been illegally expropriated; fish supplies were poisoned by

mercury contamination of rivers; and malaria, venereal disease, and tuberculosis were running rampant. The Yanomami were dying at the rate of 10 percent a year, and their fertility had dropped to near zero. Many villages were left with no children or old people, and the survivors awaited their fate with a profound terror of extinction.[11]

The typical attitude of many Brazilians toward such situations is illustrated by their government's reaction to a diplomatic journey that two Kayapó Indian leaders and an anthropologist made to the United States. They ventured north to speak with World Bank authorities and

ethnocide The violent eradication of an ethnic group's collective cultural identity as a distinctive people; occurs when a dominant society deliberately sets out to destroy another society's cultural heritage.

[10] www.savetibet.org/tibet/us/proceedings/senatefrmauramoynihan.php. See also Avedon, J. F. (1997). *In exile from the land of snows: The definitive account of the Dalai Lama and Tibet since the Chinese conquest.* New York: Harper.

[11] Turner, T. (1991). Major shift in Brazilian Yanomami policy. *Anthropology Newsletter 32* (5), 1, 46.

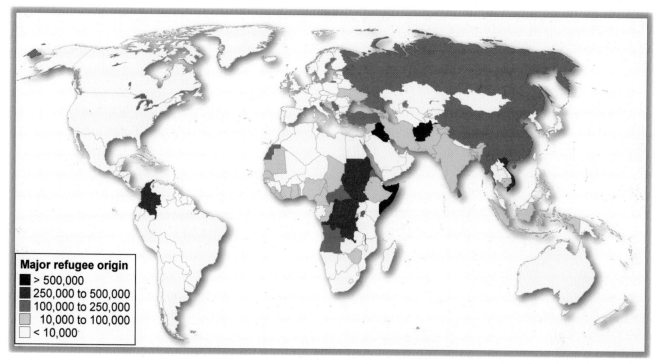

Figure 15.1 Maps and numbers cannot capture the plight of the 42 million forcibly displaced people in the world, most escaping violent conflict in pluralistic societies. Sixteen million have fled their homelands and many are now stuck in cramped and squalid refugee camps. One out of four refugees in the world escaped from Afghanistan (2.8 million). Today, Afghans are located in 69 different asylum countries. Iraqis are the second largest refugee group, with 1.9 million having sought refuge mainly in neighboring countries, in particular Syria.
Source: United Nations Refugee Agency.

various government officials in the U.S. Congress and State Department concerning the destruction of their land and way of life caused by internationally financed development projects. All three were charged with violating Brazil's Foreign Sedition Act, which prohibits foreigners from secretly stirring up discontent, resistance, or revolt against the government in power. This charge and other relevant atrocities provoked international outrage, which in turn prompted Brazilian authorities to recommend policy changes that could favorably impact the country's indigenous peoples. However, whether their recommendations will be sufficient to effect positive change, or will even be acted upon fully, remains to be seen.

Directed Change

Although the process of acculturation often unfolds without planning, powerful elites may devise and enforce programs of cultural change, directing immigrant or subordinated groups into learning and accepting dominant society's cultural beliefs and practices. So it was with the Ju/'hoansi of southern Africa. Rounded up by government

officials in the early 1960s, these Bushmen were confined to a reservation in Tsumkwe where they could not possibly provide for their own needs. The government supplied them with rations, but these were insufficient to meet basic nutritional needs.

In poor health and prevented from developing meaningful alternatives to traditional activities, the Ju/'hoansi became embittered and depressed, and their death rate came to exceed the birthrate. Within the next few years, however, surviving Ju/'hoansi began to take matters into their own hands. They returned to water holes in their traditional homeland, where, assisted by anthropologists and others concerned with their welfare, they are trying to sustain themselves by raising livestock. Whether this will succeed remains to be seen, as there are still many obstacles to overcome.

One byproduct of colonial dealings with indigenous peoples has been the growth of *applied anthropology,* originally concerned with the use of anthropological techniques and knowledge for the purpose of advising in government programs of directed cultural change and solving practical problems. For example, in the United States, the Bureau of American Ethnology was founded in 1876 to gather reliable data the government might use to formulate Indian policies. At the time, anthropologists were convinced of the practicality of their discipline, and many who did ethnographic work among Indians devoted a great deal of time, energy, and even money to assisting their informants, whose interests were frequently at risk.

In the 20th century, the scope and intent of applied anthropology expanded. In the first part of that century, the applied work of Franz Boas—who almost singlehandedly trained an entire generation of anthropologists in the United States—proved instrumental in reforming the country's immigration policies. With impressive statistical data based on comparative skull measurements and related physical anthropological studies, this German Jewish immigrant challenged popular race theories of the day. He demonstrated that theories privileging non-Jewish immigrants from western Europe and discrimination against Jews and others deemed undesirable were based not on fact but on deeply rooted racial prejudice.

In the 1930s, anthropologists with clearly pragmatic objectives did a number of studies in industrial and other institutional settings in the United States. With World War II came increased involvement in colonial administration beyond U.S. borders, especially in the Pacific, by American officers trained in anthropology. The rapid postwar recovery of Japan was due in no small measure to the influence of anthropologists in structuring the U.S. occupation. Anthropologists continue to play an active role today in administering U.S. trust territories in the Pacific.

All too often, however, states and other powerful institutions directly intervening in the affairs of different ethnic groups or foreign societies fail to seek professional advice from anthropologists who possess relevant cross-cultural expertise and deeper insights. Such failures have contributed to a host of avoidable errors in planning and executing nation-building programs in ethnically divided countries such as Iraq and Afghanistan, both of which are now devastated by war and violence.

Today, applied anthropologists are in growing demand in the field of international development because of their specialized knowledge of social structure, value systems, and the functional interrelatedness of cultures targeted for development. Those working in this arena face a particular challenge: As anthropologists, they are bound to respect other peoples' dignity and cultural

integrity, yet they are asked for advice on how to change certain aspects of those cultures. If the request comes from the people themselves, that is one thing, but more often than not, it comes from outsiders. Supposedly, the proposed change is for the good of the targeted population, yet members of that community do not always see it that way. Just how far applied anthropologists should go in advising outsiders how to manipulate people to embrace the changes proposed for them is a serious ethical question, especially when it concerns people without the power to resist.

In direct response to such critical questions concerning the application and benefits of anthropological research, an alternative type of practical anthropology has emerged during the last half century. Known by a variety of names—including action anthropology and committed, engaged, involved, and advocacy anthropology—this involves community-based research and action in collaboration and solidarity with indigenous societies, ethnic minorities, and other besieged or repressed groups. In sum, not only are the practical applications of anthropology necessary, but there is a growing demand for anthropologically informed pragmatic solutions.

Reactions to Repressive Change

The reactions of indigenous peoples to the changes outsiders have thrust upon them have varied considerably. Some have responded by moving to the nearest available forest, desert, or other remote place in hopes of being left alone. In Brazil, a number of communities once located near the coast took this option a few hundred years ago and were successful until the great push to develop the Amazon forest began in the 1960s. Others, like many Indians of North America, took up arms to fight back but were ultimately forced to sign treaties and surrender much of their ancestral lands, after which they were reduced to an impoverished underclass in their own land. Today, they continue to fight through nonviolent means to retain their identities as distinct peoples and to regain control over natural resources on their lands.

In addition, ethnic groups may try to retain their distinctive identities by maintaining cultural boundaries such as holding on to traditional language, festive ceremonies, customary dress, ritual songs and dances, unique food, and so on. Indeed, when facing modernization, people often seek emotional comfort from **tradition**—customary ideas and practices passed on from generation to generation, which in a modernizing society may form an obstacle to new ways of doing things.

tradition Customary ideas and practices passed on from generation to generation, which in a modernizing society may form an obstacle to new ways of doing things.

Indigenous peoples have reacted to colonialism in many different ways. When British missionaries pressed Trobriand Islanders of Melanesia to celebrate their regular yam harvests with a game of "civilized" cricket rather than traditional "wild" erotic dances, Trobrianders responded by transforming the staid British sport into an exuberant event that featured sexual chants and dances between innings. This is an example of syncretism—the creative blending of indigenous and foreign beliefs and practices into new cultural forms.

© Jerry Leach

Syncretism

When people are able to hold on to some of their traditions in the face of powerful outside domination, the result may be **syncretism**—the creative blending of indigenous and foreign beliefs and practices into new cultural forms. A fine illustration of this is the game of cricket as played by the Trobriand Islanders of Melanesia, some of whose practices we looked at in earlier chapters. When Trobrianders were under British rule, missionaries introduced them to this rather reserved British game to replace the erotic dancing and open sexuality that normally followed the yam harvests. Traditionally, this was the season when chiefs sought to spread their fame by hosting nights of dancing, providing food for the hundreds of young married people who participated. For several months, there would be night after night of provocative dancing, accompanied by chanting and shouting full of sexual innuendo, each night ending as couples disappeared into the bush together.

Since no chief wished to be outdone by any other (being outdone brought into question the strength of one's magic), the dancing had a strong competitive element, and fighting sometimes erupted. To the British Protestant missionaries, cricket seemed a good way to end all of this in a way that would encourage conformity to "civilized" comportment in dress, religion, and sportsmanship. The Trobrianders, however, were determined to "rubbish" (throw out) the British rules of the game. They did this by turning it into the same kind of distinctly Trobriand event that their thrilling dance competitions had once been.

Making cricket their own, Trobrianders added battle dress and battle magic and incorporated erotic dancing into the game. Instead of inviting dancers each night, chiefs now arrange cricket matches. Pitching has been modified from the British style to one closer to their old way of throwing a spear. Following the game, they hold massive feasts, where wealth is displayed to enhance their prestige.

Cricket, in its altered form, has been made to serve traditional systems of prestige and exchange. Neither primitive nor passively accepted in its original form, Trobriand cricket was thoughtfully and creatively adapted into a sophisticated activity reflecting the importance of basic indigenous cultural premises. Exuberance and pride are displayed by everyone associated with the sport, and the players are as much concerned with conveying the full meaning of who they are as with scoring well. From the sensual dressing in preparation for the game to the team chanting songs full of sexual metaphors to the erotic chorus-line dancing between the innings, it is clear that each participant is playing for his own importance, for the fame of his team, and for the hundreds of attractive young women who watch the game.

syncretism In acculturation, the creative blending of indigenous and foreign beliefs and practices into new cultural forms.

Revitalization Movements

Another common reaction to repressive change is revitalization. As noted in the chapter on religion and spirituality, *revitalization movements* are efforts for radical cultural reform in response to widespread social disruption and collective feelings of anxiety and despair. They are often, but not always, religiously or spiritually based. When primary ties of culture, social relationships, and activities are broken, and meaningless activity is imposed by outside forces, individuals and groups characteristically react by rejecting newly introduced cultural elements and reclaiming historical roots and traditional identity, along with a measure of spiritual imagination.

In the United States, revitalization movements have occurred often—whenever significant segments of the population have found their conditions in life to be at odds with the values of the American Dream. For example, the 1960s saw the emergence of revitalization movements among young people of middle-class and even upper-class families. In their case, the professed cultural values of peace, equality, and individual freedom were seen to be at odds with the realities of persistent war, poverty, and constraints on individual action imposed by a variety of impersonal institutions. Youths countered these realities by advocating free love, joining hippie communes, celebrating new forms of rock and folk music, using mind-altering drugs, challenging authority, growing their hair long, and wearing unconventional clothes.

By the 1980s revitalization movements were becoming prominent even among older, more affluent segments of U.S. society, as in the rise of the so-called religious right. In these cases, the reaction is not so much against a perceived failure of the American Dream as it is against perceived threats to that dream by dissenters and activists within their society, by foreign governments, by new ideas that challenge other ideas they prefer to believe, and by the sheer complexity of modern life.

Clearly, when value systems are out of step with existing realities, a condition of cultural crisis is likely to build up that may breed reactive movements. Not all suppressed, conquered, or colonized people eventually rebel against established authority, although why they do not is debatable. When they do, however, cultural resistance may take one of several forms, all of which are varieties of revitalization movements. Some of these revitalization movements take on a revolutionary character, as did the Taliban in Afghanistan.

rebellion Organized armed resistance to an established government or authority in power.

© AFP/Getty Images

The 2006 inauguration of Bolivia's first indigenous president, Evo Morales, shown here flanked by native spiritual leaders. The ceremony took place at the archaeological site of Tiwanaku, the ancient capital of a large indigenous empire in the Bolivian highlands surrounding Lake Titicaca. Wearing traditional royal clothing and speaking in his native Aymara tongue, Morales proclaimed, "Today begins a new era for the native peoples of the world." He chose this symbolic event to officially launch an indigenous cultural revitalization movement in a country where most citizens are Aymara, Quechua, or members of other indigenous nations. Long repressed, often dispossessed, and struggling against poverty, more than a dozen generations of Bolivian Indians have seen their ancestral traditions marginalized by Spanish-speaking European invaders and their descendants. True to his vow to establish a fairer distribution of wealth in South America's poorest country, Morales nationalized many companies and used the income to finance social programs. He won reelection in December 2009.

Rebellion and Revolution

When the scale of discontent within a society reaches a certain level, the possibilities are high for **rebellion**—organized armed resistance to an established government or authority in power. There have been many peasant rebellions around the world in the course of history. Often, such rebellions are triggered by repressive regimes imposing new taxes on the already struggling small farmers unable to feed their families under such unacceptable levels of exploitation.

One current example is the Zapatista Maya Indian uprising in southern Mexico, which began in the mid-1990s and has not yet been resolved. This rebellion involves thousands of poor Indian farmers whose livelihoods have been threatened by the disruptive changes imposed on them and whose human rights under the Mexican constitution have never been fully implemented.

In contrast to rebellions, which have rather limited objectives, a **revolution**—a radical change in a society or culture—involves a more dramatic transformation. Revolutions occur when the level of discontent in a society is very high. In the political arena, revolution involves the forced overthrow of an old government and the establishment of a completely new one.

Such was the case when Muslim fundamentalists in Iran toppled the imperial regime of the shah in 1979 and replaced him with Ayatollah Khomeini, a high-ranking Shiite Muslim religious leader. Returning to his homeland from exile and becoming Iran's new leader, he instituted a new social and political order based on Islamic fundamentalist principles.

The question of why revolutions erupt, as well as why they frequently fail to live up to the expectations of the people initiating them, is unsolved. It is clear, however, that the colonial policies of countries such as Britain, France, Spain, Portugal, and the United States during the 19th and early 20th centuries have created a worldwide situation in which revolution is nearly inevitable. Despite the political independence most colonies have gained since World War II, powerful countries continue to exploit many of these "underdeveloped" countries for their natural resources and cheap labor, causing a deep resentment of rulers beholden to foreign powers. Further discontent has been caused as governing elites in newly independent states try to assert their control over peoples living within their boundaries. By virtue of a common ancestry, possession of distinct cultures, persistent occupation of their own territories, and traditions

revolution Radical change in a society or culture. In the political arena, it involves the forced overthrow of an old government and establishment of a completely new one.

On New Year's Day 1994, when the North American Free Trade Agreement (NAFTA) went into effect, 3,000 armed peasants belonging to the Zapatista revolutionary movement invaded towns in southern Mexico. Mostly Maya Indians, they declared war on the Mexican government, claiming that globalization was destroying their rural communities. Strong Internet presence helped them build an international network of political support. Now committed to nonviolent resistance to Mexican state control, Zapatistas have created 32 self-governing municipalities and established their own local health, justice, and education services.

Matias Recart/AFP/GETTY

In China, women's labor has become critical to economic expansion. Much of this labor is controlled by male heads of families, who act as agents of the state in allocating labor.

© A. Ramey/PhotoEdit

of self-determination, the peoples they aim to control identify themselves as distinct nations and refuse to recognize the legitimacy of what they regard as a foreign government.

Thus in many a former colony, large numbers of people have taken up arms to resist annexation and absorption by imposed state governments run by people of other nationalities. As they attempt to make their multi-ethnic states into unified countries, ruling elites of one nationality set about stripping the peoples of other nations within their states of their lands, resources, and particular cultural identities. The phenomenon is so common that Belgian sociologist Pierre van den Berghe has renamed what modern states refer to as "nation building" as, in fact, "nation killing."[12]

One of the most important facts of our time is that the vast majority of the distinct peoples of the world have never consented to rule by the governments of states within which they find themselves living.[13] In many newly emerging countries, such peoples feel they have no other option than to take up weapons in armed protest and fight.

Apart from rebellions against authoritarian regimes, such as in the Chinese, French, and Russian revolutions, many revolutions in modern times have been insurgencies against political rule imposed by foreign powers. Such resistance usually takes the form of national independence movements that wage campaigns of armed defiance against colonial or imperial dominance. The Mexican war of liberation against Spain in the early 1800s and the Algerian struggle for independence from France in the 1950s are relevant examples.

Of the hundreds of armed conflicts in the world today, almost all are in the economically poor countries of Africa, Asia, and Latin America, many of which were at one time under European colonial domination. Of these wars, the majority are between the state and one or more nations or ethnic groups within the state's borders. These groups are seeking to maintain or regain control of their personal lives, communities, lands, and resources in the face of what they regard as repression or subjugation by a foreign power.[14]

Revolutions do not always accomplish what they set out to do. One of the stated goals of the 1949 Chinese communist revolution, for example, was to liberate women from the oppression of a strongly patriarchal society in which a woman owed lifelong obedience to some male relative—first her father, later her husband, and, after his death, her oldest son. Although changes were and continue to be made, the transformation overall has been frustrated by the cultural lens through which the revolutionaries viewed their work. A tradition of deeply rooted patriarchy extending back at least 2,200 years is not easily overcome and has influenced many of the decisions made by communist China's leaders since the revolution.

Despite the current rapid changes taking place in China today, in many rural parts of the country a woman's life is still largely determined by her relationship to a man—be it her father, husband, or son—rather than by

[12] van den Berghe, P. (1992). The modern state: Nation builder or nation killer? *International Journal of Group Tensions 22* (3), 191–207.

[13] Nietschmann, B. (1987). The third world war. *Cultural Survival Quarterly 11* (3), 3.

[14] Ibid.

her own efforts or failures. Moreover, many rural women face official local policies that identify their primary roles as wives and mothers. When they do work outside the house, it is generally at jobs with low pay, low status, and no benefits. Indeed, the 1990s saw a major outbreak of the abduction and sale of women from rural areas as brides and workers. Women's no-wage home labor (and low-wage outside labor) for their husbands' households have been essential to China's economic expansion, which relies on the allocation of labor by the heads of patrilineal households.[15]

This situation shows that the undermining of revolutionary goals, if it occurs, is not necessarily by political opponents. Rather, it may be a consequence of the revolutionaries' own traditional cultural background. In rural China, as long as women marry out and their labor is controlled by male heads of families, women will be seen as commodities.

It should be understood that revolution is a relatively recent phenomenon, occurring only during the past 5,000 years or so. The reason is that political rebellion requires a centralized political authority to rebel against, and states did not exist before 5,000 years ago. Obviously, then, in kin-ordered societies organized as tribes and bands, without a centralized government, there could be no rebellion or political revolution.

Modernization

One of the most frequently used terms to describe social and cultural changes as they are occurring today is **modernization.** This is most clearly defined as an all-encompassing and global process of political and socioeconomic change, whereby developing societies acquire some of the cultural characteristics common to Western industrial societies.

Derived from the Latin word *modo* ("just now"), modernization literally refers to something "in the present time." The dominant idea behind this concept is that "becoming modern" is becoming like European, North American, and other wealthy industrial or postindustrial societies, with the very clear implication that not to do so is to be stuck in the past—backward, inferior, and needing to be improved. It is unfortunate that the term modernization continues to be so widely used. Since we seem to be stuck with it, the best we can do at the moment is to recognize its problematic one-sidedness, even as we continue to use it.

The process of modernization may be best understood as consisting of five subprocesses, all interrelated with no fixed order of appearance:

- *Technological development:* In the course of modernization, traditional knowledge and techniques give way to the application of scientific knowledge and techniques borrowed mainly from the industrialized West.
- *Agricultural development:* This is represented by a shift in emphasis from subsistence farming to commercial farming. Instead of raising crops and livestock for their own use, people turn with growing frequency to the production of cash crops, with increased reliance on a cash economy and on global markets for selling farm products and purchasing goods.
- *Urbanization:* This subprocess is marked particularly by population movements from rural settlements into cities.
- *Industrialization:* Here human and animal power become less important, and greater emphasis is placed on material forms of energy—especially fossil fuels—to drive machines.
- *Telecommunication:* The fifth and most recent subprocess involves electronic and digital media processing and sharing of news, commodity prices, fashions, and entertainment, as well as political and religious opinions. Information is widely dispersed to a mass audience, far across national borders.

As modernization proceeds, other changes are likely to follow. In the political realm, political parties and some sort of electoral apparatus frequently appear, along with the development of an administrative bureaucracy. In formal education, institutional learning opportunities expand, literacy increases, and an indigenous educated elite develops. Formalized religion becomes less important in many areas of thought and behavior, as traditional beliefs and practices are undermined. Many long-held rights and duties connected with kinship are altered, if not eliminated, especially where distant relatives are concerned. Finally, where social stratification is a factor, social mobility increases as ascribed status becomes less important and personal achievement counts for more.

Self-Determination

A closer examination of traditional cultures that have felt the impact of modernization or other cultural changes will help to illustrate some of the problems such cultures have met. We will focus here on the Shuar Indians of Ecuador

[15] Gates, H. (1996). Buying brides in China—again. *Anthropology Today* 12 (4), 10.

modernization The process of political and socioeconomic change, whereby developing societies acquire some of the cultural characteristics of Western industrial societies.

and the Skolt Lapps, one of several groups of Saami people living in the Arctic and sub-Arctic tundra of northwest Russia and Scandinavia.

SAAMI HERDERS: THE SNOWMOBILE REVOLUTION AND ITS UNINTENDED CONSEQUENCES

In the 1960s Saami reindeer herders in Scandinavia eagerly adopted snowmobiles, expecting that the new technology would make herding physically easier and economically more advantageous. The choice to modernize was essentially theirs, but in Finland it backfired. As snowmobile technology replaced traditional skills, the ability of the Saami (historically also known as Lapps) to creatively survive on their own diminished, and their dependency on the outside world grew.

Given the high cost of buying, maintaining, and fueling the machines, they faced a sharp rise in their need for money. To obtain cash, men began going outside their communities for wage labor more than just occasionally, as had previously been the case.

One might argue that dependency on the larger economy and the need for cash are prices worth paying for an improved system of reindeer herding. However, snowmobiles contributed in a significant way to a disastrous decline in reindeer herding in some Saami communities, such as among the Skolt Lapps of northern Finland. Traditionally Skolt men tended the animals, moving about on wooden skis and associating closely with the herds—intensively from November to January and periodically from January to April. But once snowmobiles were introduced, the familiar, prolonged, and largely peaceful relationship between herder and beast changed into a noisy, traumatic one. The humans that reindeer encountered came speeding out of the woods on noisy, smelly machines that invariably chased the animals, often for long distances. Instead of helping the reindeer in their winter food quest, aiding does with their calves, and protecting the herd from predators, men appeared periodically, either to slaughter or to castrate the animals.

The reindeer became wary of people, resulting in de-domestication, with reindeer scattering and running off

In the 1960s, Saami reindeer herders in Scandinavia's Arctic tundra adopted newly invented snowmobiles, convinced that these modern machines would make traditional herding physically easier and economically more advantageous. Here a young Saami man stands beside his tent and snowmobile, searching for his reindeer with binoculars.

to less accessible areas. In addition, snowmobile harassment seemed to adversely affect birthing and the survival of calves. Within a decade the average size of the family herd among the Skolts had dropped from fifty to twelve—a number that is not economically viable.

This is a classic illustration that change, even when initiated by a community on its own volition, is not always advantageous. The financial cost of mechanized herding and the decline in domesticated herd size have led many to abandon herding altogether. Now, the majority of men are no longer herders at all. This constitutes a serious economic problem, since few local subsistence alternatives are available.[16]

SHUAR INDIANS AND CATTLE IN THE AMAZON: A SUCCESSFUL EXPERIMENT IN CONTROLLED ADAPTATION

In contrast to the Saami in northern Europe, the Shuar Indians of Ecuador's tropical forest deliberately avoided modernization until they felt that they had no other option, having seen whole societies destroyed elsewhere in the Amazon basin. Traditionally organized in small autonomous groups that engaged in constant feuding, the Shuar (historically better known as Jivaro) survived on a mixed subsistence strategy of foraging and gardening. In 1964, threatened with the loss of their land base as more and more Ecuadoran colonists intruded into their territory, leaders from the many, widely scattered Shuar communities came together and founded a fully independent ethnic organization—the Shuar Federation—to take control over their own future.

Recognized by Ecuador's government, albeit reluctantly, the federation is officially dedicated to promotion of the social, economic, and moral advancement of the growing Shuar population and to coordinating development with official government agencies. Since its founding, the federation has secured title to more than 96,000 hectares of communal land; established a cattle herd of more than 15,000 head as the people's primary source of income; taken control of their own education, using their own language and mostly Shuar teachers; and established their own bilingual radio station and a bilingual newspaper.

Obviously, all of this has transformed daily life among the Shuar, but they have been able to maintain a variety of distinctive cultural markers, including their language, communal land tenure, cooperative production and distribution, a basically egalitarian economy, and kin-based communities that retain maximum autonomy. For all the changes, they feel they are still Shuar and distinct from other Ecuadorans.[17]

The Shuar case shows that indigenous peoples are capable of taking control of their own destinies even in the face of intense outside pressures, *if* allowed to do so. Unfortunately, until recently, few have had that option. Prior to European invasions of the Amazon rainforest, more than 700 distinct ethnic groups inhabited this vast region. By 1900 in Brazil, the number was down to 270, and today something like 180 remain.[18] Many of these survivors find themselves in situations not unlike that of the Yanomami, described earlier in this chapter. Nevertheless, some are showing resourcefulness in resisting the outside forces of destruction arrayed against them. Some receive help from anthropologists, as discussed in the Anthropology Applied feature on the next page.

Globalization in the "Underdeveloped" World

Throughout the so-called underdeveloped world, in Africa, Asia, Latin America, and elsewhere, whole countries are in the throes of radical political and economic change and overall cultural transformation. In fact, inventions and major advances in industrial production, mass transportation, and communication and information technologies are transforming societies in Europe and North America as well. As discussed in Chapter 1, this worldwide process of accelerated modernization in which all parts of the earth are becoming interconnected in one vast interrelated and all-encompassing system is known as *globalization,* evidenced in global movements of natural resources, trade goods, human labor, finance capital, information, and infectious diseases.

All around the globe we are witnessing the removal of economic activities—or at least their control—from the family and community setting. And we are seeing the altered structure of the family in the face of the changing labor market: young children relying increasingly on parents alone for affection, instead of on the extended family; parental authority generally declining; schools replacing the family as the primary educational unit; old people spending their last days in nursing homes rather than with family members; and many other changes.

In many societies, this modernization process is now happening very fast, often without the necessary time to adjust. Changes that took generations to accomplish in Europe and North America are attempted within the span

[16] Pelto, P. J. (1973). *The snowmobile revolution: Technology and social change in the Arctic.* Menlo Park, CA: Cummings.

[17] Bodley, J. H. (1990). *Victims of progress* (3rd ed., pp. 160–162). Mountain View, CA: Mayfield.

[18] *Cultural Survival Quarterly.* (1991). *15* (4), 38.

Development Anthropology and Dams

Over a 35-year career in scholarly and applied work, Michael M. Horowitz, president and executive director of the Institute for Development Anthropology (IDA) and distinguished professor of anthropology at the State University of New York at Binghamton, has made pioneering contributions to applied anthropology. His work has focused on achieving equitable economic growth, environmental sustainability, conflict resolution, and participatory government in the former colonial world.

Since co-founding IDA in 1976, Horowitz has been its principal leader. He has played a key role in bringing anthropology forward as an applied science in international development organizations such as the World Bank, the United Nations Fund for Women, and the U.S. Agency for International Development (USAID), as well as nongovernmental organizations (NGOs) such as Oxfam and the International Union for the Conservation of Nature. He has mentored several generations of young scholars and professionals—paying particular attention to those from developing countries—encouraging the application of anthropology's comparative and holistic methodologies and theories to empower low-income majorities in the so-called underdeveloped world.

Horowitz's work with pastoralists and floodplain dwellers has had substantial positive impact on the well-being of small producers and landholders in developing countries. A clear example of this is the impact of his work on the lives and livelihoods of people living downstream of a hydropower dam in West Africa. Beginning in the 1980s, he and his IDA team carried out rigorous anthropological research along the Senegal River, which flows through Mali, Senegal, and Mauritania. Their study showed that traditional, pre-dam, flood-recession farming yielded better results than irrigated agriculture and was better for the environment.

This finding influenced decisions made by these countries and affiliated NGOs to manage the system with a controlled release from the Manatali Dam in Mali in order to reproduce as nearly as possible the pre-dam flow system. Horowitz's long-term field research demonstrated that seasonal flooding would provide economic, environmental, and sociocultural benefits for nearly a million small producers.

Recognized by national governments, NGOs, and development funding agencies, the work of Horowitz and his IDA colleagues on the Senegal River Basin Monitoring Activity (SRBMA) was a breakthrough in the concepts of resettlement and river management, and it continues to influence development policy. Prior to IDA's work in West Africa, no hydropower dam had ever been managed with a controlled flood. Since then, IDA has been asked to help apply the SRMBA model to other parts of the world, including the lower Zambezi River in Mozambique and the Mekong River in Laos, Cambodia, and Vietnam.

Visible from space, China's Three Gorges hydroelectric dam is the world's biggest and most powerful hydroelectric dam. About 2,300 meters (7,700 feet) long and 185 meters (330 feet) high, it controls the Yangtze, the world's third largest river. After fifteen years of construction with a price tag of $22 billion, it became operational in 2009. The dam was built to provide a clean energy alternative to coal and to control flooding along the Yangtze River. However, it has been controversial since its inception, flooding ancient archaeological and cultural sites, displacing more than 1.4 million people, and causing significant ecological changes, including risks of landslides that threaten some 4 million people. Unlike the dam described in this Anthropology Applied feature, not one social scientist was consulted in the planning and assessment phase of Three Gorges Dam.

Adapted from Young, W. (Ed.). (2000). Kimball Award winner. Anthropology News 41(8), 29, with update based on personal communication with IDA, November 2003.

of a single generation in developing countries. In the process cultures frequently face unforeseen disruptions and a rapid erosion of dearly held values they had no intention of giving up. Anthropologists doing fieldwork in distant communities throughout the world witness how these traditional cultures have been impacted, and often destroyed, by powerful global forces.

Commonly, the burden of modernization falls most heavily on women. For example, the commercialization of agriculture often involves land reforms that overlook or ignore women's traditional land rights. This reduces their control of and access to resources at the same time that mechanization of food production and processing drastically reduces their opportunities for employment. As a consequence, women are confined more and more to traditional domestic tasks, which are increasingly devalued as commercial production becomes the dominant concern.

Moreover, the domestic workload tends to increase, because men are less available to help out, while tasks such as fuel gathering and water collection are made more difficult as common land and resources come to be privately owned and as woodlands are reserved for commercial exploitation. As well, the growing of nonfood crops—such as cotton and sisal or luxury crops such as tea, coffee, and cacao (source of chocolate)—for the world market makes households vulnerable to wide price fluctuations. As a result, people cannot afford the high-quality diet that subsistence farming provided,

and they become malnourished. In short, with modernization, women frequently find themselves in an increasingly inferior position. As their workload increases, the value assigned to the work they do declines, as does their relative educational status, not to mention their health and nutrition.

Globalization: Must It Be Painful?

Most anthropologists see the radical changes that affect traditional non-Western peoples caught up in the modern technological world as an ordeal. Yet, the more common attitude in the industrial West has been that modernization is both inevitable and good—that however disagreeable the "medicine" may be, it is worth it for the "backward" people to become just like people in the West. (For a serious look at the consequences of these changes, see the Biocultural Connection.)

Biocultural Connection

Studying the Emergence of New Diseases

Since the Neolithic, humans have had to cope with a host of new diseases that began as a consequence of changes in human behavior. Recently, this has become a renewed source of concern following the resurgence of infectious diseases and the spread of a host of new and lethal diseases.[a]

All told, more than thirty diseases new to medicine have emerged in the past thirty years. Perhaps the best known of these is AIDS, which has become a top killer among infectious diseases. Since 1981, more than 25 million people have died of AIDS, and today some 33 million people around the world are living with AIDS/HIV.[b] But there are others—like Ebola hemorrhagic fever, which causes victims to bleed to death; other hemorrhagic fevers like dengue fever, Lassa fever, and hantavirus; invasive streptococcus A, which consumes the victims' flesh; Legionnaire's disease; and Lyme disease.

What has sparked the appearance and spread of these new diseases remains a mystery, but one theory is that some are the result of human activities. In particular, the intrusion of people into new ecological settings, such as rainforests, along with construction of roads and worldwide shipping and airplane traffic, allows viruses and other infectious microbes to spread rapidly to large numbers of people. It is now generally accepted that the HIV virus responsible for AIDS transferred to humans from chimpanzees in the tropical forests of the Democratic Republic of Congo as a

consequence of hunting and butchering these animals for food. For the first thirty years, few people were affected; it was not until people began congregating in quickly growing cities like Kinshasa that conditions were ripe for an epidemic.

In recognition of her research to gain a better understanding of the interplay between ecological disturbance and the emergence of new diseases, medical anthropologist Carol Jenkins received a MacArthur Foundation grant in 1993. From her base at the Papua New Guinea Institute of Medical Research, she has been tracking the health of local people in the wake of a massive logging operation, work that provides insights on questions such as how disease organisms spread from animal hosts to humans.

Since most of the "new" viruses that have suddenly afflicted humans are in fact old ones that have been present in animals like monkeys (monkey pox), rodents (hantavirus), deer (Lyme disease), and insects (West Nile virus), it appears that something new has enabled them to jump from their animal hosts to humans.

A recent example comes from Congo. Here civil war created a situation where villagers in the central part of the country were faced with starvation. Their response was to increase the hunting of animals, including monkeys, squirrels, and rats that carry a disease called monkey pox. Related to smallpox, the disease transfers easily to humans, resulting in the largest outbreak of this disease ever seen among humans. What

makes this outbreak even more serious is an apparently new strain of the infection, enabling it to spread from person to person, instead of only from an animal host.[c]

Large-scale habitat disturbance is an obvious candidate for such disease transfers. So far, however, it is hard to make more than a circumstantial case by looking back after a disease outbreak. The work of Jenkins and her team is unique in that she was able to get baseline health data on local people before their environment was disturbed. Thus she is in a position to follow events as they unfold.

It will be some time before conclusions can be drawn from Jenkins's study. Its importance is obvious; in an era of globalization, as air travel allows diseases to spread worldwide, we need a fuller understanding of how pathogens interact with their hosts if we are to devise effective preventive and therapeutic strategies to deal with them.

BIOCULTURAL QUESTION
Since some new viruses and bacteria are fast-spreading and lethal, what do you think of government-funded research and development of killer diseases for purposes of biological warfare?

[a]Gibbons, A. (1993). Where are new diseases born? *Science 261*, 680–681.
[b]See www.avert.org/worldstats.htm.
[c]Cohen, J. (1997). Is an old virus up to new tricks? *Science 277*, 312–313.

This Western view has little to do with the cold political and economic realities of the contemporary world. It overlooks the stark fact that the standard of middle- and upper-class living throughout the industrialized world (and increasingly in metropolitan areas worldwide) is based on a rate of consumption of nonrenewable resources whereby a small fraction of the world's population uses the vast majority of these precious resources. The imbalance continues, suggesting that it is impossible for most peoples of the world to achieve a material standard of living at all comparable to the majority of people in wealthy countries in the near future. At the very least, the peoples of the industrial and postindustrial parts of the world would have to cut drastically their unrelenting and often wasteful consumption of resources. So far, few have shown a willingness to seriously adjust their standard of living in order to do this.

In large part due to the influence of global media, along with mass tourism, countless people around the world today have been led to aspire to a material standard of living like that commonly enjoyed by people in industrialized and postindustrialized countries, even as the gap between rich and poor continues to widen among and within countries. Every year, many millions of people slide below the poverty level.[19] This has led to what has been called a "culture of discontent" in which aspirations far exceed the bounds of local opportunities.

No longer satisfied with traditional values and often unable to sustain themselves in the rural backlands, people all over the world are moving to the large cities to find a better life. All too often they live out their days in poor, congested, and diseased slums while attempting to achieve what is usually beyond their reach. Unfortunately, despite rosy predictions about a better future, hundreds of millions of people in our world remain trapped in a wretched reality, struggling against poverty, hunger, poor health, and other dangers. In the next and final chapter of this book, we further explore the underlying structures and deeper causes of these problems and look at the role anthropology can and does play in helping to meet these challenges.

---

[19] Paul Magnarella, cited in Kurth, P. (1998, October 14). Capitol crimes. *Seven Days*, 7.

Questions for Reflection

1. Globalization radically challenges most of us to adjust at an ever-faster pace within increasingly complex transnational settings. Do you feel that these changes are good for everyone? As exemplified by Bahrain, described in the chapter opener, which groups benefit the most, and which the least, from globalization?

2. Taking a close look at your clothing and your meals today, can you identify the places of geographic origin of any of the raw materials in what you wear and consume?

3. On a regular basis, the news media are reporting about violent uprisings or rebellion and armed conflicts that result in death and destruction. Why do you think many people feel the need to fight?

4. When societies become involved in the modernizing process, all levels of their cultural systems are affected by these changes. Do you think that people are fully aware of the long-term consequences of the changes they themselves may have welcomed? Can you come up with any examples of unforeseen changes in your own community or neighborhood?

5. In many Muslim countries, orthodox religious groups oppose modern developments that they associate with moral corruption and seek to maintain or return to a way of life more strictly based on Islamic traditions. Do you know Christian or Jewish fundamentalist groups having similar conservative values and ideals? What would be the future of your own family or community if a religious fundamentalist group became large enough to gain political power and rule the country?

Suggested Readings

Bodley, J. H. (2008). *Victims of progress* (5th ed.). Lanham, MD: Alta Mira.

In this compelling account of the effect of technology and development on "victims of progress," the author reviews major issues, including health and disease, oil development, global warming, and ecocide. He also discusses the political struggle for self-determination by indigenous peoples.

Inda, J. X., & Renato, R. (Eds.). (2001). *The anthropology of globalization: A reader.* Malden, MA, and Oxford: Blackwell.

This wide-ranging reader focuses simultaneously on the large-scale processes through which various cultures are increasingly interconnected and on the ways that people around the world—from Africa and Asia to the Caribbean and North America—mediate these processes in culturally specific ways.

Maybury-Lewis, D. (2001). *Indigenous peoples, ethnic groups, and the state* (2nd ed.). Boston: Allyn & Bacon.

The author, who founded the organization Cultural Survival, summarizes modernization's effect on "tribalism and ethnic parochialism." Revealing the peculiar situation of indigenous peoples as ethnic minorities alien to the states in which they live, he describes the worldwide proliferation of ethnic conflicts and the growing demand for indigenous rights. The book stands on its own, while serving as introduction to a series of individual ethnographies on indigenous peoples and their struggles.

Prins, H.E.L. (1996). *The Mi'kmaq: Resistance, accommodation, and cultural survival.* Belmont, CA: Wadsworth.

This content-rich case study spans 500 years of history, chronicling the endurance of a tribal nation—its ordeals in the face of colonialism, and its current struggle for self-determination and cultural revitalization. Rare for its multi-vocality.

Spindler, G., & Stockard, J. E. (Eds.). (2006). *Globalization and change in fifteen cultures.* Belmont, CA: Wadsworth.

This collection of original articles reflects a world changed by globalization and an anthropology committed to documenting the effects of the vast cultural flows of people, information, goods, and technology. Spindler and Stockard's introduction frames the topic of cultural change, and the fifteen anthropologists in the anthology take readers on a return visit to their original field sites, asking questions for a new era and writing of peoples familiar to them yet transformed by global forces.

Stannard, D. E. (1992). *American holocaust.* Oxford, England: Oxford University Press.

Stannard deals with 500 years of cultural change in the Americas arising from contact between European and Native cultures. In doing so, he focuses on genocide, relates it to the Holocaust of World War II, and demonstrates how deeply rooted the phenomenon is in Western culture and Christianity.

Challenge Issue For at least 10,000 years humans have met the challenges of survival not only by adapting to their natural environment but by transforming it to fit their needs. They have turned deserts, forests, swamps, and mountainsides into pastures, farmlands, and industrial centers, creating new survival opportunities (and often some unanticipated new challenges) for an ever-growing population. In the course of history thousands of cities have been built, and during the past half century the world's urban population has more than tripled, rising from 750 million to 2.9 billion. In 2000 there were nearly 400 cities in the world with 1 million or more residents. Urban areas are gaining about 67 million people per year—about 1.3 million every week. As the global population grows, the number of big cities will grow substantially, with the majority located in coastal areas of developing countries. One of the world's largest and most violent cities is Rio de Janeiro, a metropolitan area in coastal Brazil. Almost half of its multi-ethnic population of 14 million is poor, living in crowded slums and shantytowns with unsanitary conditions and inadequate health care. Remarkably, even in the face of hardship, humans find ways to celebrate. In Rio, citizens from all walks of life participate in the annual carnival, forgetting the challenges of survival during a few days of abundant feasting and revelry before Lent. With the motto "Everyone is free," hundreds of thousands of people, citizens and tourists alike, sing and dance around multicolored parade floats, carried away by Afro-Brazilian drumming and music and briefly enjoying a happy feeling of community.

CHAPTER 16

Global Challenges, Local Responses, and the Role of Anthropology

Chapter Preview

What Can Anthropologists Tell Us of the Future?

Although anthropologists cannot entirely predict future cultural forms, they can identify patterns and trends and foresee some of their consequences if they continue. Moreover, they can shed light on already identified problems by showing how they relate to each other and to cultural features and structures that may not be obvious to experts in other disciplines. This ability to systematically consider cultural facts and their underlying structures in a wider context and from a comparative perspective is a recognized anthropological specialty.

What Are the Cultural Trends in Today's World?

One major cultural trend is globalization, including worldwide adoption of the products, technologies, ideas, and cultural practices of powerful Western countries. This move toward a homogenized, global culture is countered by an opposite trend of ethnic and religious groups all over the world reasserting their distinctive cultural identities and emphasizing their unique historical traditions. A third trend is the growing concern that rising populations, spiraling energy use, and expanding consumption are devastating our natural resources, overwhelming us with waste, and poisoning our environment.

What Problems Must Be Solved for Humans to Have a Viable Future?

Creative, effective, and responsible solutions need to be found to deal with a host of serious problems posed by vanishing natural resources, environmental destruction, ever-more powerful technologies, and unequal distribution of wealth. Today's huge demographic shifts are also problematic—explosive population growth in many poorer parts of the world, lowering birth rates leading to population decline in some of the wealthiest countries, and movements of individuals or entire families escaping poverty or violence in their homelands. Many people fail to recognize that most of the problems facing us are interconnected. Anthropology provides us with a critical and realistic understanding of the emergence of a global cultural system and its radical impact on local communities. Its cross-cultural and historically informed perspective is essential for solving problems and ensuring a future in which all peoples enjoy basic human rights.

Anthropology is superficially described by those who know little about it as an exotic discipline interested mainly in what happened long ago and far away. The most common popular stereotype is that anthropologists devote all of their attention to digging up the past and describing the last surviving tribal peoples with traditional ways of life. Yet, as noted throughout this book, anthropologists also investigate the ways and workings of industrial and postindustrial societies. Indeed, anthropologists are interested in the entire range of human cultures past and present—in their similarities and differences and in the multiple ways they influence one another.

In this era, marked by rapid and radical change all around the world, many anthropologists wonder what today's globalizing processes will create and what will be transformed, disrupted, or damaged beyond repair. When traditional communities are exposed to intense contact with more powerful groups, their cultures may change with unprecedented speed, often for the worse, becoming disintegrated and less supportive. Since globalization seems unstoppable, we are compelled to ask: How can the thousands of different societies, having existed for centuries if not millennia, maintain their distinctive cultural identities and deal successfully with the multiple challenges hurled at them?

The Future of Humanity

To comprehend anthropology's role in understanding and solving problems in times to come, we must look at flaws frequently seen in publications and planning efforts focused on the future, especially in the 21st century. First of all, given the current speed and complexity of worldwide changes, it is nearly impossible to predict and plan for more than about fifty years ahead. Even that time span is tricky since projections of future trends are usually based on recent historical trajectories and cannot factor in all the possible inventions or events (including catastrophes) that determine the course of human history. While we must try to anticipate and plan for future needs and challenges, long-term predictions are bound to be problematic. As one anthropologist quipped: "It is worth recalling the story of the person who leaped from a very tall building and on being asked how things were going as he passed the 20th floor replied 'Fine, so far.'"[1]

A second flaw typical in futurist projections is a tendency to treat subjects in isolation, without reference to pertinent trends outside an expert's field of competence. For example,

agricultural planning is often based on the assumption that a certain amount of water is available for irrigation, whether or not urban planners or others have designs upon that same water. Thus people may be counting on natural resources in the future that will not, in fact, be available.

This brings us to a third flaw common among futurists: The tendency to project the hopes and expectations of one's own group or culture into the future interferes with the scientific objectivity necessary to see and address emerging problems. A recent example is the war in Iraq, where the goals of the official U.S. and British planners blinded them to the complex problems that would emerge.

Against this background, anthropology's contribution to our understanding of the future is clear. Anthropologists bring a perspective that is not only long term, but also holistic, integrative, and comparative. With more than a hundred years of cross-cultural research behind them—based on ancient archaeological finds, linguistic information, biological data, as well as participant observation within living cultures—anthropologists have a comprehensive view on short-term trends and recognize culture-bound assertions when they encounter them. Moreover, they are familiar with alternative ways of dealing with a wide variety of problems.

A Global, Transnational Culture?

Despite vast geographic distance, human populations have always interacted. The interaction intensified about 500 years ago, when the first sailing ship successfully circumnavigated the entire globe—an almost three-year journey that was completed in 1522, but at great cost. Four of the five Spanish ships perished, as did most of the crew, as well as the seafarer Ferdinand Magellan who led this epic voyage of discovery.

Since then, peoples inhabiting every far-flung corner of the world have come in contact with one another, directly or indirectly. Many benefited from the new opportunities and prospered, enjoying the new commodities, such as sugar, spices, tobacco, silk, and other exotic luxuries. Millions, however, died in terrible epidemics or brutal warfare. Millions more were forced into slave labor or lost their independence and self-determination under colonial rule.

About two centuries ago, the invention of steam engines and other machinery brought about the industrial revolution, with large-scale factory production and an expanding transportation network of steam-powered trains and ships. Modern mass transportation, along with recent revolutions in telecommunication technology—from print media to telegraph and telephone to radio, television, satellites, and the Internet—makes it possible to exchange more information with more people faster and over greater distances. Obviously, this global flow of

---

[1] Cowgill, G. L. (1980). Letter. *Science 210*, 1305.

When McDonald's was first introduced to Hong Kong in 1975, the Chinese name for this fast-food restaurant was *Mai-Dang-Nu*, chosen to phonetically approximate the English brand name. However, since this translates "wheat-becomes-slaves," the U.S.-based global corporation altered it slightly to *Mai-Dang-Lao* when opening franchises in Taiwan and mainland China. This also caused confusion as it means "wheat-becomes-work." By 2009, McDonald's had more than 2,000 restaurants in China and plans to launch hundreds more in the next few years. Many people see the worldwide spread of giants like McDonald's, Kentucky Fried Chicken, Pepsi, and Coca-Cola as a sign of a homogeneous global culture.

humans, their products, and their ideas plays a major role in culture change.

A popular belief since the mid-1900s has been that humanity's future will feature a single homogenous global culture. This idea is based largely on the observation that technological developments in communication, transportation, and trade are causing peoples of the world to increasingly watch the same television programs, read the same newspapers, eat the same foods, wear the same types of clothes, and communicate via satellites and the Internet.

The continuation of such trends, so this thinking goes, would mean that North Americans who travel a hundred years from now to Botswana, Colombia, or Denmark would find the local inhabitants living in a manner identical or similar to theirs. Yet, as we look at ethnic conflicts around the world, this forecast seems unlikely.

Certainly it is striking—the extent to which such items as Western-style fast food, soft drinks, clothing, music, and movies have spread to virtually all parts of the world. Daily serving nearly 50 million customers in 31,000 restaurants in almost 120 countries, the U.S.-based global corporation McDonald's operates the world's largest fast-food chain. Famous for its "Big Mac" hamburger, it has become emblematic of the homogenizing of the world's different cultures in the age of globalization, sometimes referred to as the "McDonaldization" of societies.[2] And

_____

[2] Referring to the "process by which institutions in society become standardized and focused on efficiency and predictability," this term was first coined by George Ritzer in his 1983 article "The McDonaldization of Society," *Journal of American Culture* 6 (1), 100–107. Since the 1990s, this term has also been used by antiglobalization activists seeking to safeguard their traditional cultures against the onslaught of modernization.

many countries—Costa Rica or Japan, for example—appear to have gone a long way toward becoming Westernized. Moreover, looking at the past 5,000 years of human history, we see that political units have tended to become larger, more all-encompassing, and fewer in number. The logical outcome of this trend would be a further reduction of autonomous political units into a single one taking in the entire globe.

However, anthropologists call attention to something that all large states throughout time have had in common: a tendency to come apart. Not only have the great empires of the past, without exception, broken up into numbers of smaller independent states, but states in virtually all parts of the world today show this same tendency to fragment, usually along major geographic and ethnic divisions.

The threat of political collapse is ever-present in multi-ethnic states, especially when these countries are large, difficult to travel in, and lack unifying cultural features such as a common national language. Such has been the case, for instance, with Afghanistan. This vast, mountainous country is inhabited by several major ethnic groups, including Pashtun who live mainly in the south, and Tajik, Uzbek, Hazara, and Turkmen who live mainly in the north. Although the Pashtun are greatest in number and most dominant in the past 200 years, they have never been able to successfully impose their political will on the other ethnic groups who maintain a great deal of independence. Nor have they succeeded in making their own native tongue, Pashto, the country's national language.

The tendency of multi-ethnic states to break apart has been especially noteworthy since the end of the Cold War between the United States and the former Soviet Union after the fall of the Berlin Wall in 1989. For example, 1991 saw the dramatic breakup of the Soviet Union into about a dozen independent republics—Russia, Armenia, Belarus, Estonia, Ukraine, and Georgia, among others. In 2008, about seventeen years after Georgia gained its own independence as an internationally recognized state, this multi-ethnic republic diminished in size when two of its ethnically distinct regions, South Ossetia and Abkhazia, officially split after years of separatist pressure. Declaring independence, Abkhazia and South Ossetia both seek international recognition as small sovereign republics. While Russia and a few allies now recognize both mini republics as independent states, most other UN member countries do not.

The splintering tendency of multi-ethnic states can also be seen in separatist movements such as that of French-speaking peoples in Canada, Basques in Spain, Tibetans in China, Karen in Myanmar (Burma), Kurds in Turkey and Iraq, and so on—this list is far from exhaustive. Nor is the United States immune, as can be seen in Native American nations seeking to secure greater political self-determination on their reservations. We may have reached the point where the tendency for political units to grow in size while decreasing in number is being canceled out by their tendency to fragment into a greater number of smaller ones.

Despite these examples, there are also a few instances of reunification. Best known among these is the 1990 reunification of Germany, divided since the end of World War II as East and West Germany, into one large federal republic. Another notable exception is the recent integration of twenty-seven European countries into the European Union—however hindered by linguistic differences, distinctive cultural traditions, and bureaucratic red tape.

Also, many global integrative mechanisms have been developed to counteract the centrifugal forces at work. These include international sporting events from Wimbledon to the Olympics, plus organizations ranging from UNESCO to Rotary Clubs, Boy Scouts, and Girl Guides, as well as humanitarian aid organizations such as Doctors Without Borders and Save the Children. Notably, while such mechanisms connect people all around the world, they do not represent a global transnational culture.

The Problem of a Global Culture

The idea of a shared global culture may have a degree of popular appeal in certain circles. A common language, for instance, would greatly facilitate international exchange, and a shared ideology (with everyone having similar political ideals and religious beliefs) might lessen cross-cultural misunderstandings and conflicting viewpoints that have led so often to violence over the past several hundred years.

However, anthropologists greet this prognosis with skepticism, suspecting that distinctive worldviews will persist, even in the face of massive changes. Moreover, new worldviews are emerging, and those that are changing are not necessarily changing in the same fashion. In fact, given the intensified interactions among people in the world today, especially where competing interests are involved, it is more likely that the potential for serious conflict is actually growing.

Although the forces of globalization impact almost every society, not all peoples react the same way to the changes on their doorstep. Those who are willing and

Olympic Games are unique among the many strands in today's global web. Inspired by the ancient Greek sporting event held at Olympia 2,000 years ago, the games have become a global spectacle, with thousands of athletes from all around the world competing in a different country every four years. In today's world—where powerful states have conquered and destroyed many smaller nations and tens of millions have been killed in warfare worldwide—this global sports gathering is a crucial ritual, celebrating international peace in a friendly rivalry for medals and prestige. Pictured here is the opening ceremony of the 2008 Olympics in China.

Paul Gilham/Getty Images

able to make the required adjustments may actually benefit from the transformation in their cultures, whereas others less well positioned for the changes may resist and/or have a deeply troubling experience. In short, globalization is a complex and dynamic process with a vast range of national, regional, and even local cultural reactions and adjustments.

Some have argued that perhaps a generalized world culture would be desirable in the future, because some traditional cultures may be too specialized to adjust to a changed environment. For instance, when Amazonian Indians pursuing traditional ways of life that are well adapted to South America's tropical rainforest are confronted with sudden, radical changes brought on by foreign invaders, their long-established cultures often collapse. The reason for this, it is argued, is that the forest-dwellers' traditions and political and social organizations are not adapted to modern ways and that they are naturally destined to give way to the new. The problem with this argument is that, far from being unable to adapt, such traditional peoples have been robbed repeatedly of the opportunity to work out their own adaptations according to their own priorities. Their demise is caused not by laws of nature but rather by the political and economic choices of powerful outside forces.

Pluralistic Societies and Multiculturalism

If a single homogenous global culture is not necessarily the wave of the future, what is? Some predict a world in which ethnic groups will become more nationalistic in response to globalization, each group stressing its unique cultural heritage and emphasizing differences with neighboring groups. But not all ethnic groups organize themselves politically as distinctive sovereign nations with their own independent state. In fact, it has been common for two or more neighboring ethnic groups or nations to draw together in a loose political union while maintaining their particular cultural identities. One complex example is Russia. Geographically the largest country in the world, it is a federation consisting of twenty-one autonomous republics. Representing territories of non-Russian ethnicity, such as Tatarstan and Yakutia, these republics may have their own national language.

However, because such *pluralistic societies* lack a common cultural identity and heritage, and often do not share the same language or religion, political relationships between them can be fraught with tension. When feelings of ethnonationalism are not far from the surface, political pressure may build up and result in separation and independence. For instance, over the past two decades Chechen nationalists have waged wars and insurgencies to split the republic of Chechnya (an area in the northern

Caucasus Mountains primarily inhabited by Sunni Muslim Chechens) from the Russian Federation.

One way of curbing divisive pressures in pluralistic or multi-ethnic societies is the adoption of a public policy based on mutual respect and tolerance for cultural differences. Known as **multiculturalism,** such an official policy asserts the value of different cultures coexisting within a country and stresses the reciprocal responsibility of all citizens to accept the rights of others to freely express their views and values. In contrast to state policies in which a dominant ethnic group uses its power to impose its own culture as the national standard, forcing other groups within the same state to assimilate, multiculturalism involves a public policy for managing a society's cultural diversity. Examples of long-established multiculturalism may be seen in states such as Switzerland (where German-, French-, Italian-, and Romansh-speaking peoples coexist under the same government) and Canada (where French- and English-speaking Canadians as well as dozens of indigenous nations live side by side).

Although cultural pluralism is still more common than multiculturalism, several multi-ethnic countries have recently changed their official melting pot ideology and associated policies of assimilation. One example of a country that is moving toward multiculturalism is the United States, which now has over 120 different ethnic groups within its borders, in addition to hundreds of federally recognized American Indian groups. Another is Australia, now counting over a hundred ethnic groups and with eighty languages spoken within its territorial boundaries. Similar changes are also under way in many European countries where millions of foreign immigrants have settled during the past few decades. Such changes are not easy, however, and often engender protests along the way.

We cannot ignore the fact that what historically has been called "nation building" in all parts of the world almost always involves attempts to subordinate or even destroy the cultures of peoples whose nationalities differ from those in control of the government.[3] During the last two decades of the 20th century, states were borrowing more money to fight peoples within their own boundaries than for all other programs combined. Nearly all state debt in Africa and

---

[3] van den Berghe, P. (1992). The modern state: Nation builder or nation killer? *International Journal of Group Tensions 22* (3), 194–198.

multiculturalism Public policy for managing cultural diversity in a multi-ethnic society, officially stressing mutual respect and tolerance for cultural differences within a country's borders.

Although South Africa's apartheid regime was abolished in 1993 and that pluralistic country is no longer politically dominated by a white minority, social tensions between different ethnic groups remain. With few opportunities to earn money, many of the 8 million people living in Johannesburg's squalid townships and squatter camps are unemployed and impoverished, and they blame foreign immigrants for their misery. This *xenophobia* ("fear of strangers") has frequently turned violent, resulting in bloody assaults against foreigners, many of whom are from poor neighboring countries such as Zimbabwe and Mozambique. Dozens have been killed, hundreds cruelly beaten and butchered, and thousands forced to flee. But there is a counter voice: Here we see a demonstration of South Africans and immigrants protesting the brutal murder of forty foreign laborers in Johannesburg in 2008.

nearly half of all other debt in "underdeveloped" countries comes from the cost of weapons purchased by states to fight their own citizens.[4] The more divergent cultural traditions are, the more difficult it is to make pluralism work.

Pluralistic Societies and Ethnocentrism

A major obstacle to the successful functioning of a pluralistic society is the loyalty each ethnic group has toward its distinctive language and unique cultural traditions, from which its members derive psychological support and a firm social bond to their community. Such ethnic pride is often tied to ethnocentrism, the belief that the ways of one's own culture are the only proper ones. To overcome this cultural superiority complex, a pluralistic society may have to develop a common superstructure with an ideology that binds different peoples together in a collective identity and destiny.

As illustrated again and again in this book, ethnic pride and loyalty are often turned into an ethnocentric charter

for denigrating people with different cultural practices and exploiting them for the benefit of one's own group. Although this is not an inevitable result, when it does occur, unrest, hostility, and violence commonly ensue.[5] This is evident in a growing nationalist intolerance toward foreign laborers and recent immigrants in many parts of the world today, especially where economies are in decline and local populations become agitated about survival and security.

Transnational Cultural Flows in a Global Environment

Anthropologist Arjun Appadurai, born in India, has developed theoretical concepts to help us understand the complex and largely unpredictable processes currently rearranging human relations and restructuring cultural

[4] *Cultural Survival Quarterly* (1991). *15* (4), 38.

[5] Nieftagodien, N. (2008, June 18). Incoherent response to crisis. *The Star*, Johannesburg. http://web.wits.ac.za/NewsRoom/NewsItems/Noor+Nieftag odien+xenophobia+opinion.htm

systems worldwide. Although most people in today's world still function within geographically defined communities, Appadurai points out that territorial borders have become increasingly irrelevant given the "cultural flows" in our emerging global environment. He marks out five global spaces or dimensions in which transnational cultural flows occur, identifying them as "scapes" (meaning something crafted, configured, or transformed by humans):

- *Ethnoscapes:* the fluid and shifting landscape of migrants, refugees, exiles, tourists, and other moving groups and people.
- *Technoscapes:* the global configuration of technologies moving at high speeds across previously restrictive borders.
- *Financescapes:* the global crossroads of currency speculation and financial transfers.
- *Mediascapes:* the distribution of electronic media capabilities to produce and spread information, plus the large complex repertoire of narratives and visual images generated by these media.
- *Ideoscapes:* ideologies produced by the state and alternative ideologies developed by non-state and counter-hegemonic forces, around which societies organize their political cultures and collective cultural identities.

Each of these "scapes" plays a significant role in structural power, the topic of our next section.[6] Notably, Appadurai's "scape" concept inspired the Globalscape feature in this textbook.

Structural Power in the Age of Globalization

A new form of expansive international capitalism has emerged since the mid-1900s. Operating under the banner of globalization, it builds on earlier cultural structures of worldwide trade networks, and it is the successor to a system of colonialism in which a handful of powerful, mainly European, capitalist states ruled and exploited foreign nations inhabiting distant territories.

Enormously complex and turbulent, globalization is a dynamically structured process in which individuals, business corporations, and political institutions actively rearrange and restructure the political field to their own competitive advantage, vying for increasingly scarce natural resources, cheap labor, new commercial markets, and ever-larger profits. This restructuring occurs in a vast arena spanning the entire globe. Doing this, of course, requires a great deal of power.

As discussed previously, power refers to the ability of individuals or groups to impose their will upon others and make them do things even against their own wants or wishes. Power plays a major role in coordinating and regulating collective behavior toward imposing or maintaining law and order within—and beyond—a particular community or society.

There are different levels of power within societies, as well as among societies. Anthropologist Eric Wolf pointed out the importance of understanding a macro level of power that he referred to as **structural power**—power that organizes and orchestrates the systemic interaction within and among societies, directing economic and political forces on the one hand and ideological forces that shape public ideas, values, and beliefs on the other.[7] The concept of structural power applies not only to regional political organizations such as chiefdoms or states but also captures the complex new cultural formations currently restructuring and transfiguring societies and environments everywhere on earth.

Joseph Nye—a political scientist, international security specialist, and former assistant secretary of defense in the U.S. government—refers to these two major interacting forces in the worldwide arena as "hard power" and "soft power."[8] **Hard power** is the kind of coercive power that is backed up by economic and military force. **Soft power** is cooptive rather than coercive, pressing others through attraction and persuasion to change their ideas, beliefs, values, and behaviors. Although propaganda is a form of soft power, the exercise of ideological influence (the global struggle for hearts and minds) also operates through more subtle means, such as foreign aid, international diplomacy,

[6] Appadurai, A. (1990). Disjuncture and difference in the global cultural economy. *Public Culture 2*, 1–24.

[7] Wolf, E. (1999). *Envisioning power: Ideologies of dominance and crisis* (p. 5). Berkeley: University of California Press.

[8] Nye, J. (2002). *The paradox of American power: Why the world's only superpower can't go it alone.* New York: Oxford University Press.

structural power Power that organizes and orchestrates the systemic interaction within and among societies, directing economic and political forces on the one hand and ideological forces that shape public ideas, values, and beliefs on the other.

hard power Coercive power that is backed up by economic and military force.

soft power Cooptive power that presses others through attraction and persuasion to change their ideas, beliefs, values, and behaviors.

news media, sports, entertainment, museum exhibits, and academic exchanges.

Military Hard Power

Today the United States has more hard power at its disposal than any of its allies or rivals worldwide. It is the global leader in military expenditure, spending $711 billion in 2008, followed by Europe ($289 billion), and China ($122 billion). In fact, as the world's still-dominant superpower, the United States is responsible for almost half of the $1.473 trillion spent on arms worldwide[9] (Figure 16.1).

Moreover, although there are seven other nuclear weapons states (Britain, France, and China, as well as Israel, India, Pakistan, and North Korea, collectively possessing nearly 900 active nuclear warheads), Russia and the United States have by far the largest nuclear arsenals at their disposal—minimally 5,830 and 5,735 operational warheads, respectively. (There are also nearly 16,000 intact but nonoperational warheads, almost all in the hands of the United States and Russia.)[10]

In addition to military might, hard power involves using economic strength as a political instrument of coercion or intimidation in the global structuring process. Among other things, this means that economic size and productivity, technological capability, and finance capital

---

[9] www.globalissue.org.

[10] Norris, R. S., & Kristensen, H. M. (2006, July/August). Global nuclear stockpiles, 1945–2006. *Bulletin of the Atomic Scientists 62* (4), 64–66.

may be brought to bear on the global market, forcing less powerful states to weaken the systems protecting their workers, natural resources, and local markets.

As the world's largest economy and leading exporter, the United States has long pushed for free trade for its corporations doing business on a global scale. Sometimes it uses military power to impose changes on a foreign political landscape by means of armed interventions or full-scale invasions. For instance, when the United Fruit Company (later bought by Del Monte), owner of enormous banana plantations in Guatemala, saw its economic interests threatened by that country's democratically elected government, the U.S. government engineered a military coup in 1954 that resulted in a dictatorship favorable to U.S.-based corporations.

Through history, the United States (like several other powerful countries, including Russia, Britain, and France) has engaged in such military interventions around the world. Because of this, many see the United States as an ever-present threat, apt to use overwhelming military force in order to benefit its corporate interests from fruit to fuel, from microchips to automobiles. The corporations, in turn, wield enormous political and financial power over governments and international organizations, including the World Trade Organization, headquartered in Geneva, and global banking institutions such as the International Monetary Fund (IMF) and World Bank, both based in Washington, DC.

The IMF is a specialized agency of the United Nations, but it functions virtually independently of UN control. Specializing in short-term loans to assist poor or developing countries, its financial resources weigh in at more than $500 billion. The five wealthiest countries in the world (United States, Japan, Germany, France, and Britain) control 40 percent of this global fund and dominate its executive board. As the global lender of last resort, the IMF's structural power is evident not only in which development projects and policies it chooses to support financially, but also in its surveillance practices, which involve monitoring a borrower's economic and financial developments.

The World Bank is an independent specialized agency of the UN as well as a member and observer in many UN bodies. It makes long-term loans ($20 billion annually) for economic development projects such as roads, schools, and health systems to reduce poverty in about a hundred developing countries. Like the IMF, it is largely controlled by a handful of powerful capitalist states. Operating under geopolitical constraints, these global banking institutions strategically direct capital flows to projects in certain parts of the world, financially supporting some governments and withholding capital from others.

Both the IMF and the World Bank have been accused of being insensitive to the political and cultural

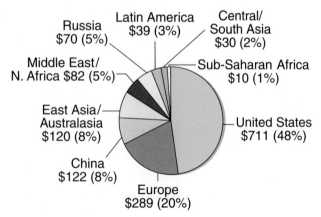

U.S. Military Spending vs. the World, 2008 (in billions of U.S. dollars)

Russia $70 (5%)
Latin America $39 (3%)
Central/South Asia $30 (2%)
Middle East/N. Africa $82 (5%)
Sub-Saharan Africa $10 (1%)
East Asia/Australasia $120 (8%)
United States $711 (48%)
China $122 (8%)
Europe $289 (20%)

Figure 16.1 The United States is responsible for nearly half of the $1.473 trillion spent on arms worldwide.
Source: Center for Arms Control and Non-Proliferation, 2008.

consequences of the projects they support. For example, in the 1990s the World Bank provided loans to a hydropower project in southern Chile to build dams in the upper Bio-Bio River without considering the human rights of local Pehuenche Indians. The dam flooded a large part of the Pehuenche's ancestral lands, forcing hundreds to be resettled against their own will.

Likewise, the World Bank approved a $40-million loan to the Chinese government to relocate almost 60,000 poor Han Chinese farmers to more fertile land in Qinghai, territory that Tibetans consider part of their homeland. Pro-Tibetan groups around the world protested that the bank was supporting China's effort to weaken the Tibetan ethnic minority population in that region. Due to these protests, the bank delayed funding, pending investigation. When the investigative panel concluded that regulations had been violated, the Chinese government took offense and withdrew its loan application from the Bank, declaring that it would use its own financial resources to implement the Qinghai component of the China Western Poverty Reduction Project.

Globalization does more than create a worldwide arena in which megacorporations reap megaprofits. It also wreaks havoc in many traditional cultures and disrupts long-established social organizations everywhere. By the early 21st century, the global trend of economic inequality has become quite clear: The poor are becoming poorer, and the rich are becoming richer.

Home to more global corporations than any other country, the United States is endeavoring to protect its interests by investing in what it refers to as a "global security environment." Numerous other countries, unable to afford expensive weapons systems or blocked from developing or acquiring them, have invested in biological or chemical weaponry. Still others, including relatively powerless political groups, have resorted to insurgencies, guerrilla tactics, or even terrorism.

Economic Hard Power

Global corporations, rare before the latter half of the 20th century, now are a far-reaching economic and political force in the world. Modern-day business giants such as General Electric, Shell, and Toyota are actually clusters of several corporations joined by ties of common ownership and responsive to a common management strategy. Usually tightly controlled by a head office in one country, megacorporations organize and integrate production across the international boundaries of different countries for interests formulated in corporate boardrooms, irrespective of whether these are consistent with the interests of people in the countries where they operate. These megacorporations are the products of the technological revolution, for without mass transportation, sophisticated data processing equipment, and telecommunication, they could not conduct or manage their transnational capitalist operations.

Though typically thought of as responding impersonally to outside market forces, megacorporations are in fact controlled by an increasingly smaller number of wealthy capitalists who benefit directly from their operations. Yet, unlike political leaders, the world's largest individual stockholders and most powerful directors are virtually unknown to the general public. For that matter, most people cannot even name the world's ten leading global corporations, which include Wal-Mart, Shell, and Toyota (Figure 16.2). Each of the top ten business giants currently generates annual revenues well over $200 billion, and three of them top the $400 billion mark.[11]

So great is the power of large businesses operating all across the globe that they increasingly thwart the wishes of national governments or international organizations such as the United Nations, Red Cross, and the International Court of Justice. Because megacorporations restrict information about their operations, it can be difficult for governments to make informed policy decisions. It took years for the U.S. Congress to extract information from tobacco companies to decide what to do about tobacco legislation, and it is nearly as slow-going today getting energy and media companies to provide data needed for regulatory purposes.

Beyond this, global corporations have repeatedly shown they can overrule foreign policy decisions. While some might see this as a hopeful signal for getting beyond ethnocentric motivations, it raises the unsettling issue of whether the global arena should be controlled by immense powerful private corporations interested only in financial profits. According to one market research organization:

> Today, the top 100 companies control 33 percent of the world's assets, but employ only one percent of the world's workforce. General Motors is larger than Denmark, Wal-Mart bigger than South Africa. The mega-corporations roam freely around the globe, lobbying legislators, bankrolling elections and playing governments off against each other to get the best deals. Their private hands control the bulk of the world's news and information flows.[12]

---

[11] Forbes International 500 List for 2008.

[12] www.adbusters.org. See also Hertz, N. (2001). *The silent takeover: Global capitalism and the death of democracy* (p. 43). New York: Arrow.

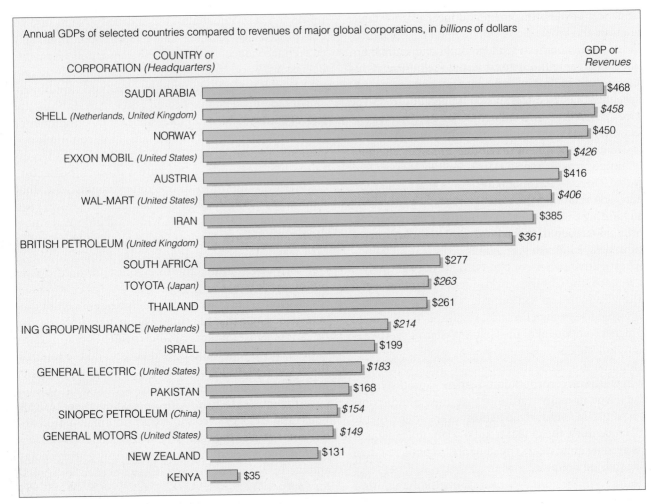

Annual GDPs of selected countries compared to revenues of major global corporations, in *billions* of dollars

COUNTRY or
CORPORATION *(Headquarters)*

GDP or
Revenues

SAUDI ARABIA	$468
SHELL *(Netherlands, United Kingdom)*	*$458*
NORWAY	$450
EXXON MOBIL *(United States)*	*$426*
AUSTRIA	$416
WAL-MART *(United States)*	*$406*
IRAN	$385
BRITISH PETROLEUM *(United Kingdom)*	*$361*
SOUTH AFRICA	$277
TOYOTA *(Japan)*	*$263*
THAILAND	$261
ING GROUP/INSURANCE *(Netherlands)*	*$214*
ISRAEL	$199
GENERAL ELECTRIC *(United States)*	*$183*
PAKISTAN	$168
SINOPEC PETROLEUM *(China)*	*$154*
GENERAL MOTORS *(United States)*	*$149*
NEW ZEALAND	$131
KENYA	$35

Figure 16.2 In today's consumer-driven world, it is not uncommon for the yearly revenues of large multinational corporations to equal and even exceed the total value of all goods and services produced within many countries per year, known as a country's gross domestic product (GDP). This graph shows the annual GDPs of selected countries alongside the annual revenues of leading global corporations. Notably, Shell revenues exceed the GDPs of 172 of the world's 195 countries. Not shown here are the countries with the highest and lowest GDPs. About half have GDPs under $18 billion, and thirty fall below $1 billion. Only fourteen countries surpass $1 trillion, including the United States at $14 trillion, with Japan in second place at nearly $5 trillion. (Note: GDP says nothing about the unequal distribution of wealth within a country.)
Source: Based on the global 500 sales figures for 2008 listed on www.forbes.com and the 2008 GDP figures provided on www.worldbank.org.

Global corporations are changing the shape of the world and the lives of individuals from every walk of life, including those they employ. In the never-ending search for cheap labor, these megacorporations have returned to a practice once common in the textile mills of 19th-century Britain and New England, but now on a much larger scale. More than ever before, they have come to favor women for low-skilled assembly jobs. In so-called underdeveloped countries, as subsistence farming gives way to mechanized agriculture for production of crops for export, women are less able to contribute to their families'

survival. Together with the devaluation of domestic work, women are pressured to seek jobs outside the household to contribute to its support. Since most women in these countries do not have the time or resources to get an education or to develop special job skills, only low-paying jobs are open to them.

Big business has created problems for consumers as well as workers. In a ten-year intensive study of relations between producers and consumers of products and services, anthropologist Laura Nader found repeated, documented offenses by North American businesses that could not be handled by existing complaint mechanisms, either in or out of court.[13]

Faceless relations between producers and consumers, among whom there is a grossly unequal distribution of power, have exacted a high cost: a terrible sense of indifference, apathy, even a loss of faith in the dehumanized system itself. When workers do not trust their bosses and bosses do not trust one another, production and trade relations on every level are damaged or ruined. This alienation may ultimately lead to a systemic breakdown. With production, trading, and banking operations on a global scale, the breakdown in one part of the system may trigger a worldwide chain reaction of failures. Such was the global crisis triggered by the bankruptcy of a handful of mismanaged Wall Street firms in 2008.[14]

Soft Power: A Global Media Environment

In addition to reliance on military and economic hard power in the global quest for dominance and profit, competing states and corporations utilize the ideological persuasion of soft power as transmitted through electronic and digital media, communication satellites, and other information technology. One of the major tasks of soft power is to sell the general idea of globalization as something positive and progressive (as "freedom," "free" trade, "free" market) and to frame or brand anything that opposes capitalism in negative terms.

The far-reaching capabilities of modern electronic and digital technologies have led to the creation of a global media environment that plays a major role in how individuals and even societies view themselves and their place in the world. Together with radio and television, the Internet is now the dominant means of mass communication around the world. The global flow of information made possible by fiber optic cables and communication satellites orbiting the earth is almost entirely digital-electronic, taking place in a new boundless cultural space identified earlier in this chapter as a "global mediascape."

In recent years, the power of corporations has become all the greater through media expansion. Over the past two decades, a global commercial media system has developed, dominated by a few megacorporations (such as

The poorest people in the world, such as this Maka Indian woman in Paraguay, often wear clothing discarded by those who are better off—and people from all walks of life can be found wearing clothes with corporate logos. The power that big business (such as the Disney media corporation) has over individuals is illustrated by the ability of corporations to get consumers to pay for goods that advertise corporate products.

General Electric and Disney), most based in the United States. Control of television and other media, as well as the advertising industry, gives global corporations enormous influence on the ideas and behavior of hundreds of millions of ordinary people across the world.

Consider, for example, the powerful marketing messages that shape cultural standards concerning the ideal human body. The widespread nature of this concern is evident in the abundance of TV infomercials selling workout equipment and "age-defying" cosmetic products, as well as in the highly popular TV drama *Nip/Tuck* and the much-watched reality program *Dr. 90210* (which follows the stories of plastic surgery patients and doctors in Beverly Hills, California). The following Original Study offers details on what has become a lucrative cosmetic surgery industry.

---

[13] Nader, L. (Ed). (1981). *No access to law: Alternatives to the American judicial system.* New York: Academic.

[14] Notably, as Brazilian anthropologist Gustavo Lins Ribeiro points out, today even informal economies, burgeoning in Latin America and elsewhere, are globalized. See Ribeiro, G. L. (2009). Non-hegemonic globalizations: Alternative transnational processes and agents. *Anthropological Theory 9* (3), 297–329.

Original Study

Standardizing the Body: The Question of Choice *by Laura Nader*

The question of choice is central to the story of how medicine and business generate controlling processes in the shaping of women's bodies. Images of the body appear natural within their specific cultural milieus. For example, breast implants are not seen as odd within the cultural milieu of the United States, and female circumcision and infibulation (also known as female genital mutilation or FGM) are not considered odd among people from the Sudan and several other African countries. However, many feminist writers differentiate FGM from breast implantation by arguing that North American women *choose* to have breast implants whereas in Africa women are presumably subject to indoctrination since they experience circumcision as young girls.

One of the most heated debates arising from the public health concern over breast implants is whether the recipients are freely situated—that is, whether their decision is voluntary or whether control is disguised as free will.

An informed response to the free choice argument requires knowing how the beauty-industrial complex works. Toward this end, corporate accountability researcher Linda Coco carried out fieldwork in multiple sites, gaining insights into the inner workings of a multibillion-dollar industry that segments the female body and manufactures commodities of and for the body.

Coco's research shows how some women get caught in the official beauty ideology, and in the case of silicone-gel breast implants some hundreds of thousands of women have been ensnared. But who gets caught and when are important to an understanding of the ecology of power. The average age of a woman having breast implantation is 36 years, and she has an average of two children. She is the beauty industry's insecure consumer recast as a patient

with an illness the industry defines as hypertrophy (small breasts).

Coco quotes a past president of the American Society of Plastic and Reconstructive Surgery (ASPRS):

> There is substantial and enlarging medical knowledge to the effect that these deformities [small breasts] are really a disease which result in the patient's feelings of inadequacies, lack of self-confidence, distortion of body image, and a total lack of well-being due to a lack of self-perceived femininity. . . .

Enlargement . . . is therefore . . . necessary to ensure the quality of life for the patient.

In other words, cosmetic surgery is necessary to the patient's psychological health.

The plastic surgeon regards the construction of the official breast as art, the aim being to reform the female body according to the ideals of classic Western art. One surgeon pioneering procedures for correcting deformity took as his ideal female figure that of ancient Greek statues, which he carefully measured, noticing the exact size and shape of the breasts, their vertical location between the third and seventh ribs, the horizontal between the line of the sternal (breast bone) border and the anterior axillary line, and so forth. In Coco's analysis the exercise of the plastic surgeon's technoart recreates a particular static, official breast shape and applies this creation ostensibly to relieve women's mental suffering. The surgeon becomes a psychological healer as well as an artist.

Along with art and psychology, there is, of course, the business of organized plastic surgery, which responds to the demands and opportunities of market economics [see figure]. By the late 1970s and early 1980s there was a glut of plastic surgeons. The ASPRS began to operate like a commercial enterprise instead of a medical society, saturating the media with ads and even providing low-cost financing. The discourse became a sales pitch. Women "seek" breast implants to keep their husbands or their jobs, to attract men, or to become socially acceptable. Coco calls this "patriarchal capitalism" and questions whether this is free choice or "mind colonization."

Understanding "choice" led Coco to an examination of the power both in the doctor–patient relationship and in the control of information.

PROCEDURE	NUMBER DONE 2008	PERCENT DONE FOR WOMEN
Facial resurfacing and fillers (chemical peel, laser, collagen, etc.)	4,260,000	91%
Brow lift	42,000	89%
Eyelid surgery	221,000	86%
Nose reshaping	279,000	73%
Botox injection	5,000,000	94%
Face lift	113,000	91%
Upper arm lift	14,000	98%
Breast enlargement	307,000	100%
Tummy tuck	122,000	96%
Liposuction	245,000	89%
Leg veins/laser	222,000	88%

Selected cosmetic surgical and nonsurgical procedures in the United States (2008) and the percentage carried out for women. In total 1.7 million cosmetic surgeries were done and 10.4 million nonsurgical procedures (chemical peels, laser treatments, Botox injections, and so on) at a total cost of about $10.3 billion. Overall, the number of procedures is up 882 percent since 1992, and 63 percent since 2000.

She found that women "were told by the media, plastic surgeons, women's magazines, other women, and the business world that they could enhance their lives by enhancing their bust lines . . . the social imperative for appearance was personalized, psychologized, and normalized." Social surveys indicate that, to the extent that women internalize the social imperative, they feel they are making the decision on their own.

Not surprisingly, women whose surgery resulted in medical complications often came to recognize the external processes of coercive persuasion that had led them to seek implants. In some ways, they resembled former cult members who had been deprogrammed: Their disillusionment caused them to question the system that had encouraged them to make the decision in the first place. The result was a gradual building of protest against the industry, expressed in networks, newsletters, support groups, workshops, and seminars. As have some former cult members, women have brought suit, testified before lawmakers, and challenged in other ways some of the largest corporations and insurance companies in the land.

The choice of implants, they learn, is part of a matrix of controlling processes in which women are subjects. Given the right circumstances it could happen to anyone. In the Sudan, the young girl is told that FGM procedures are done for her and not to her. In the United States the mutilation of natural breasts is also done for the recreation of femininity. Although power is exercised differently in these two cases, Coco notes the similarity: "The operation on the female breast in [North] America holds much of the same social symbolism and expression of cultural mandate as does FGM in Sudan. Thus, the question of why women choose breast augmentation becomes moot."

Breast implantation is now spreading elsewhere, most notably to China. Will it become a functional equivalent to foot-binding in China as part of the competition between patriarchies East and West? Whatever the answer, many social thinkers agree that people are always more vulnerable to intense persuasion during periods of historical dislocation—a break with structures and symbols familiar to the life cycle—in which the media can bring us images and ideas originating in past, contemporary, or even imaginary worlds.

Feminist researchers have sought to crack controlling paradigms such as those that define women's capacities and those that construct a standardized body shape and determine what is beautiful in women. Some of their writings are attempts to free the mind from the beauty constructions of cosmetic industries and fashion magazines. Others relay how the one model of Western beauty is affecting members of ethnic groups who aspire to look the way advertisements say they should. Choice is an illusion, since the restructuring of taste is inextricably linked to shifts in the organization of consumption.

Adapted from Nader, L. (1997). Controlling processes: Tracing the dynamics of power. Current Anthropology 38, *715–717.*

Problems of Structural Violence

Structural power and its associated concepts of hard and soft power enable us to better understand the global arena in which local communities throughout the world are now compelled to operate and the unequal the distribution of wealth, health, and power in today's world. When structural power undermines the well-being of others, we may speak of **structural violence**—physical and/or psychological harm (including repression, environmental destruction, poverty, hunger, illness, and premature death) caused by impersonal, exploitative, and unjust social, political, and economic systems.[15]

A useful baseline for identifying structural violence is provided by the Universal Declaration of Human Rights, officially adopted by all members of the United Nations in 1948. Anthropologists played a key role in drafting this important document. The declaration's preamble begins with the statement that "recognition of the inherent dignity and of the equal and inalienable rights of all members of the human family is the foundation of freedom, justice, and peace in the world."[16] Generally speaking, structural violence concerns the impersonal systemic violation of the human rights of individuals and communities to a healthy, peaceful, and dignified life.

Although human rights abuses are nothing new, globalization has enormously expanded and intensified structural violence. For instance, it is leading to an ever-widening gap between the wealthiest and poorest peoples, the powerful and powerless. In 1960 the average income for the twenty wealthiest countries in the world was fifteen times that of the twenty poorest. Today it is thirty times higher.[17]

Notably, these figures fail to indicate that some of the poorest countries in the world have a small number of very rich citizens, and that very wealthy countries include many poor inhabitants. In fact, the income disparity between rich and poor within many countries has been widening in recent years—as evident in the "income inequality index" annually posted by the United Nations. The index ranges from 0 to 100, with 0 corresponding to perfect equality (where everyone has the same income) and 100 corresponding to perfect inequality (where one person has all the income and everyone else has zero

---

[15] See Farmer, P. (1996). On suffering and structural violence: A view from below. *Daedelus 125 (1)*, 261–283.

[16] Universal Declaration of Human Rights. www.ccnmtl.columbia.edu/projects/mmt/udhr.

---

[17] www.worldbank.org/poverty. (2005 statistics).

---

structural violence Physical and/or psychological harm (including repression, environmental destruction, poverty, hunger, illness, and premature death) caused by impersonal, exploitative, and unjust social, political, and economic systems.

income). Measuring the gap between the richest and poorest 10 percent of the population in China, for example, the income inequality index shows that the world's largest communist country is even more unequal (21.5) than the United States, the world's largest capitalist country (15.9). By comparison, other wealthy industrialized countries have a much more equal income distribution, including Germany (6.9) and Japan (4.5).

On the other hand, the greatest income disparities between the richest and poorest 10 percent can be found in some of the poorest countries, including Paraguay (65.4), the Central African Republic (69.2), and Haiti (71.7).[18] However, the United States now has the highest income inequality in the wealthy industrialized world, and the big gap between rich and poor is widening.

Measured on a global scale, the wealth of the ultra-rich has reached stratospheric proportions. Today, the world's 225 richest individuals have a combined wealth equal to the annual income of the poorest 47 percent of the entire world population. In dramatic contrast, nearly half of all people in the world get by on less than $2.50 per day. Measuring the gap in another way reveals that the richest 20 percent of the human population enjoys 77 percent of all goods and services in the world. The other 80 percent of humanity has the benefit of only 23 percent—and the poorest 20 percent gets a mere 1.5 percent of those goods and services.[19]

Structural violence has countless manifestations in addition to widespread poverty. These range from the cultural destruction already indicated to hunger and obesity, and environmental degradation, all discussed in the remaining pages of this chapter.

Overpopulation and Poverty

In 1750, 1 billion people lived on earth. Over the next two centuries our numbers climbed to nearly 2.5 billion. And between 1950 and 2000 the world population soared above 6 billion. Today, India and China each have more than 1 billion inhabitants. Such increases are highly significant because population growth increases the scale of hunger and pollution—and the many problems tied to these two big issues. Although controlling population growth does not eliminate the other problems, we are unlikely to be able to solve them unless population growth is stopped or even reversed.

For a population to hold steady, there must be a balance between birthrates and death rates. In other words, people must produce only enough offspring to replace themselves when they die. This is known as **replacement reproduction.** Prior to 1976, birthrates around the world generally exceeded death rates, with the exception of European and North American populations. Poor people, in particular, have tended to have large families because children have been their main resource. Children can provide a needed labor pool to work farms, and they are the only source of security for the elderly. Historically, people were apt to limit the size of their families only when they became wealthy enough that their money replaced children as their main resource; at that point, children actually *cost* them money. Given this, we can see why birthrates remained high for so long in the world's poorer countries. To those who live in poverty, children are seen as potentially valuable contributors to the household income.

Since the mid-1970s, birthrates have dropped below replacement level (which is about 2.1 children per woman) in virtually every industrialized country and also in nineteen developing countries—including China, the world's most populous country. Even in much of Africa, as well as South Asia and Central and South America (home to most of the world's poorer nations), birthrates have also declined but far less dramatically.[20]

Despite progress, the worldwide population continues to grow. Projections are extremely tricky, given variables such as AIDS, but current estimates suggest that global population will peak around 2050 at about 9.37 billion people. The severity of the situation becomes clear with the realization that the present world population of more than 6 billion people can be sustained only by using up nonrenewable resources such as oil, which is like living off income-producing capital. It works for a time, but once the capital is gone, so is the possibility of even having an income to live on.

Hunger and Obesity

As frequently dramatized in media reports, hundreds of millions of people face hunger on a regular basis, leading to a variety of health problems, premature death, and other forms of suffering. Today, over a quarter of the world's countries do not produce enough food to feed their populations and cannot afford to import what is

---

[18] http://en.wikipedia.org/wiki/List_of_countries_by_income_equality.This site features a list of countries by income inequality, drawing wealth figures from various sources, including the United Nations and the U.S. Central Intelligence Agency. See also: Davies, J. B., et al. (2007). *The world distribution of household wealth.* University of California, Santa Cruz, Mapping Global Inequalities, Center for Global, International, and Regional Studies.

[19] Kurth, P. (1998, October 14). Capital crimes. *Seven Days,* 7; Swaminathan, M. S. (2000). Science in response to basic human needs. *Science 287,* 425. See also World Bank Development Indicators, 2008, and Human Development Report 2002, *Deepening democracy in a fragmented world,* United Nations Development Program.

replacement reproduction   The point at which birthrates and death rates are in equilibrium; people producing only enough offspring to replace themselves when they die.

---

[20] Bongaarts, J. (1998). Demographic consequences of declining fertility. *Science 282,* 419; Wattenberg, B. J. (1997, November 23). The population explosion is over. *New York Times Magazine,* 60.

© Monica Almeida/The New York Times/Redux

The Gila River Indian community canal. In the 19th century Pima Indians in southwest Arizona, who call them-selves *Akimel O'otham,* or "river people," lost the river that had for generations sustained their farming culture when white farmers upstream siphoned it off. The theft of the river—combined with U.S. federal government rations of lard (pig fat), canned meats, and sugary processed foods—unhinged traditional Pima life and conspired with genetic anomalies to sow an obesity epidemic that has left this reservation community with among the high-est diabetes rates in the world. In 2004, after decades of litigation, the Pima and neighboring Maricopa Indians achieved the largest Indian water rights settlement ever. Water is once again beginning to flow by way of irrigation canals, making it possible to reestablish vegetable farms with the hope of boosting Pima economy and restoring a healthier lifestyle. The question is whether this can repair the damage of generations of structural violence.

needed. In fact, our species has now reached a disturbing historic milestone with well over 1 billion humans going hungry every day. Most (almost 650 million) of these un-fortunates live in Asia and the Pacific islands. Next comes sub-Saharan Africa with about 265 million, followed by the Middle East and North Africa with 53 million, and an-other 15 million in the world's wealthy countries.[21]

Hunger is caused not only by drought and pests, but also by violent ethnic, religious, or political conflicts that uproot families and by a food production and distribution system geared to satisfy the demands of the world's most powerful countries. During the 20th century, 44 million people died due to human-made famine.[22] For example, in several sub-Saharan African countries plagued by chronic civil strife, it has been almost impossible to raise and har-vest crops, for hordes of hungry refugees, roaming militias, and underpaid soldiers constantly raid fields.

Without adequate nutrition, humans lose their ability to resist disease. And without access to adequate health care, many of the poverty-stricken sick have little chance to survive. For the poor—especially in refugee camps, slums, and other places with miserable living conditions—suffering is a normal condition of life, and death looms everywhere. Such is the case, for example, in Sudan's eth-nic war-torn Darfur region. Since 2003, the conflict in Sudan has claimed a half-million lives and chased more than 2.5 million people from their homes to camps where hunger, thirst, and disease are daily threats.

Today, nearly one out of every six human beings ex-periences chronic hunger. Every year, famine claims the lives of some 6 million children aged 5 and under, and those who survive it often suffer from physical and men-tal impairment.[23] These are victims of structural violence, because the increasing rate of starvation is not only due to environmental calamities or warfare, but also to the col-lapse of local markets caused by foreign imports, massive job cuts, and growing poverty rates.

[21] Food and Agriculture Organization (FAO), United Nations. (2009). *1.02 billion people hungry: One sixth of humanity undernourished—more than ever before.* http://www.fao.org/news/story/en/item/20568/icode/

[22] Hunger Project. (2003). www.thp.org; White, M. (2001). *Historical atlas of the twentieth century.* http://users.erols.com/mwhite28/20centry.htm.

[23] Hunger Project; Swaminathan.

The high cost of western farming practices, such as spraying chemicals to increase yields and decrease various pests and blights, is prohibitive for the world's small-scale farmers. Moreover, the practice trades short-term benefits for long-term pollution and health problems.

Another problem is that millions of acres in Africa, Asia, and Latin America once devoted to subsistence farming have been given over to the raising of cash crops for export. This has enriched members of elite social classes in these parts of the world, while satisfying the appetites of people in developed countries for coffee, tea, chocolate, bananas, and beef. Those who used to farm the land for their own food needs have been relocated—either to urban areas, where all too often there is no employment for them, or to areas ecologically unsuited for farming.

In Africa, such lands are often occupied seasonally by pastoral nomads, and turning them over to cultivation has reduced pasture available for livestock and led to overgrazing. The increase in cleared land, coupled with overgrazing, has depleted both soil and water, with disastrous consequences to nomad and farmer alike. So it is that more than 250 million people can no longer grow crops on their farms, and 1 billion people in about a hundred countries are in danger of losing their ability to grow crops.[24]

One strategy urged upon so-called underdeveloped countries, especially by government officials and development advisors from Europe and the United States, has been to adopt practices that have made agriculture in industrialized societies incredibly productive. However, this strategy ignores the crucial fact that these large-scale, commercial farming practices require a financial investment that small farmers and poor countries cannot afford—a substantial outlay of cash for chemical fertilizers, pesticides, and

herbicides, not to mention fossil fuels needed to run all the mechanized equipment. Despite its spectacular short-term success, serious questions arise about whether such a profligate food production system can be sustained over the centuries, even in North America.

Yet another problem with the idea of copying U.S. farming styles has to do with subsidies. Despite official rhetoric about free markets, governments of the wealthiest capitalist states in North America and western Europe spend between $100 billion and $300 billion annually on agriculture subsidies. In the United States, the world's largest agricultural exporter, 75 percent of these go to the wealthiest 10 percent of the farmers and large agricultural corporations.

Small farmers in poor countries cannot compete with subsidized agribusinesses that are selling mass-produced and often genetically engineered crops. Many small farmers have been forced to quit farming, leave their villages, and seek work in cities or as migrant workers abroad.

Such is the fate of many Maya Indians today. Since the early 1980s, when so many fled Guatemala's violence and poverty, thousands have made their way to places like southeastern Florida and taken low-paying jobs as illegal immigrants. Because of endemic poverty in their homeland where they would face starvation, these victims of structural violence have no choice but to remain where they are, condemned to an uncertain life in exile as cheap laborers without civil rights, Social Security, or health insurance.

Ironically, while many millions are starving in some parts of the world, many millions of others are overeating—quite literally eating themselves to death. In

[24] Godfrey, T. (2000, December 27). Biotech threatening biodiversity. *Burlington Free Press,* 10A.

© MARKA/Alamy

On the South Pacific island of Nauru, the world's smallest independent republic, about 80 percent of the 14,000 inhabitants are now classified as obese. This island nation in Micronesia also has the world's highest rate of diabetes.

fact, the number of overfed people now exceeds those who are underfed. According to the World Watch Institute in Washington, DC, more than 1.1 billion people worldwide are now overweight. And over 350 million of these are obese, but still often malnourished in that their diets lack certain nutrients.

Seriously concerned about the sharp rise in associated health problems (including stroke, diabetes, cancer, and heart disease), the World Health Organization classifies obesity as a global epidemic. Overeating is particularly dangerous for individuals living in societies where machines have eased the physical burdens of work and other human activities, which helps explain why more than half of the people in some industrial and postindustrial countries are overweight.

However, the obesity epidemic is not due solely to excessive eating and lack of physical activity. A key factor is the high sugar and fat content of mass-marketed foods. Thus in Japan, where food habits differ significantly from those in the United States, obesity plagues just over 3 percent of the population, compared to the U.S. rate of 32 percent. In fact, U.S. obesity figures have doubled over the past three decades, placing it at the top of the obesity chart among wealthy industrialized countries. Obesity rates differ between men and women, higher and lower income groups, and among various ethnic groups. The highest U.S. rate is among African American women, half of whom suffer obesity.[25]

The problem of obesity has become a serious concern even in some developing countries, especially where people have switched to a diet based on processed or canned fast food. The highest obesity rates worldwide can now be found among Pacific Island nations such as Fiji, Samoa, and Tonga, where being fat is traditionally associated with cultural ideals of beauty, good health, and high status.

Topping the world's obesity prevalence list is the island of Nauru, formerly known as Pleasant Island. Traditionally, Nauruans valued food as a symbol of well-being and social pride, considered fat as a sign of beauty, and associated large body size with strength and prosperity.[26] In the days when Nauruans still depended largely on fishing and gathering for most of their food, obesity was not a medical

---

[25] Centers for Disease Control and Prevention. (2009). Differences in prevalence of obesity among black, white, and Hispanic adults—United States, 2006–2008. *Morbidity and Mortality Weekly Report 58* (27), 740–744. Drewnowski, A., & Specter, S. E. (2004). Poverty and obesity: the role of energy density and energy costs. *American Journal of Clinical Nutrition 79* (1), 6–16.

[26] Pollock, N. J. (1995). Social fattening patterns in the Pacific—the positive side of obesity. A Nauru case study. In I. DeGarine & N. J. Pollock (Eds.), *Social aspects of obesity* (pp. 87–109). London: Routledge.

problem. However, when royalties from phosphate mining provided each family with large amounts of cash, their diets and lifestyles changed radically for the worse. Today, phosphate wealth has disappeared, but the junk food diet remains, and 80 percent of the indigenous population of this small island republic in Micronesia has become obese; about 30 percent of them now have diabetes.[27]

Pollution and Global Warming

The effects of corporate agribusiness practices are part of larger problems of environmental degradation in which pollution is tolerated for the sake of higher profits that benefit specific individuals and societies. Industrial activities are producing highly toxic waste at unprecedented rates, and factory emissions are poisoning the air. For example, smokestack gases are clearly implicated in acid rain, which is damaging lakes and forests all over northeastern North America. Air containing water vapor with a high acid content is, of course, harmful to the lungs, but the health hazard is greater than this. As ground and surface water becomes more acidic, the solubility of lead, cadmium, mercury, and aluminum, all of them toxic, rises sharply. For instance, aluminum contamination is high enough on 17 percent of the world's farmland to be toxic to plants—and has been linked to senile dementia, Alzheimer's, and Parkinson's diseases, three major health problems in industrial countries.

Finding their way into the world's oceans, toxic substances also create hazards for seafood consumers. For instance, Canadian Inuit face health problems related to eating fish and sea mammals that feed in waters contaminated by industrial chemical waste such as polychlorinated biphenyls (PCBs) (see the Biocultural Connection).[28] Obviously, environmental poisoning affects peoples all across the globe (Figure 16.3).

---

[27] That said, not all people who are overweight or obese are so because they eat too much junk food and do too little exercise. In addition to cultural factors, being overweight or obese can also have genetic or other biological causes.

[28] Inuit Tapiirit Kanatami. http://www.tapirisat.ca/english_text/ itk/ departments/enviro/ncp.

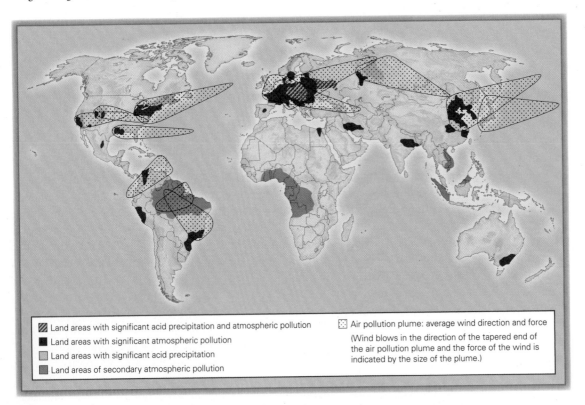

Land areas with significant acid precipitation and atmospheric pollution
Land areas with significant atmospheric pollution
Land areas with significant acid precipitation
Land areas of secondary atmospheric pollution

Air pollution plume: average wind direction and force
(Wind blows in the direction of the tapered end of the air pollution plume and the force of the wind is indicated by the size of the plume.)

Figure 16.3 Almost all processes of physical geography begin and end with flows of energy and matter among land, sea, and air. Because of the primacy of the atmosphere in this exchange system, air pollution is potentially one of the most dangerous human modifications in environmental systems. Pollutants such as various oxides of nitrogen or sulfur cause the development of acid precipitation, which damages soil, vegetation, and wildlife. Air pollution in the form of smog is often dangerous for human health. And most atmospheric scientists believe that the efficiency of the atmosphere in retaining heat—the greenhouse effect—is being enhanced by increased carbon dioxide, methane, and other gases produced by industrial and agricultural activities. The result, a period of global warming, threatens to dramatically alter climates in all parts of the world.

Source: *Student Atlas of Anthropology* by J. L. Allen & A. C. Shalinsky, p. 132. ©2003 McGraw-Hill/Dushkin Publishing.

Toxic Breast Milk Threatens Arctic Culture

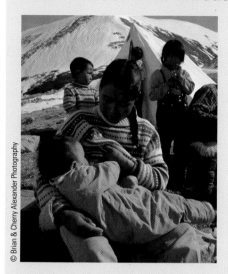

© Brian & Cherry Alexander Photography

Asked to picture the Inuit people inhabiting the Arctic coasts of Canada, Greenland, and Labrador, you are likely to envision them dressed in fur parkas and moving across a pristine, snow-covered landscape on dogsleds—perhaps coming home from hunting seal, walrus, or whale.

Such imaginings are still true—except for the pristine part. Although Inuit live nearer to the North Pole than to any city, factory, or farm, they are not isolated from the pollutants of modern society. Chemicals originating in the cities and farms of North America, Europe, and Asia travel thousands of miles to Inuit territories via winds, rivers, and ocean currents. These toxins have a long life in the Arctic, breaking down very slowly due to icy temperatures and low sunlight. Ingested by zooplankton, the chemicals spread through the seafood chain as one species consumes another. The result is alarming levels of pesticides, mercury, and industrial chemicals in Arctic animals—and in the Inuit people who rely on fishing and hunting for food.

Of particular note are toxic chemicals known as PCBs (polychlorinated

biphenyls), used widely over several decades for numerous purposes, such as industrial lubricants, insulating materials, and paint stabilizers. Research shows a widespread presence of PCBs in the breast milk of women around the globe. But nowhere on earth is the concentration higher than among the Inuit—on average seven times that of nursing mothers in Canada's biggest cities.[a]

PCBs have been linked to a wide range of health problems, from liver damage to weakened immune systems to cancer. Studies of children exposed to PCBs in the womb and through breast milk show impaired learning and memory functions. Beyond having a destructive impact on the health of humans (and other animal species), PCBs are impacting the economy, social organization, and psychological well-being of Arctic peoples. Nowhere is this more true than among the 450 Inuit living on Broughton Island, near Canada's Baffin Island. Here, word of skyrocketing PCB levels cost the community its valuable market for Arctic char fish. Other Inuits refer to them as "PCB people," and it is said that Inuit men now avoid marrying women from the island.[b]

The suggestion that the answer to these problems is a change of diet is soundly rejected by Inuit people, who have no real alternatives for affordable food. Abandoning the consumption of traditional seafood would destroy a 4,000-year-old culture based on hunting and fishing. Countless aspects of traditional Inuit culture—from worldview and social arrangements to vocabularies and myths—are linked to Arctic animals and the skills it takes to rely on them for food and so many other things. As one Inuit put it: "Our foods do more than nourish our bodies. They feed our souls. When I eat Inuit foods, I know who I am."[c]

The manufacture of PCBs is now banned in many Western countries (including the United States), and PCB

levels are gradually declining worldwide. However, because of their persistence (and widespread presence in remnant industrial goods such as fluorescent lighting fixtures and electrical appliances), they are still the highest-concentration toxins in breast milk, even among mothers born after the ban.

And even as PCBs decline, other commercial chemicals are finding their way northward. To date, about 200 hazardous compounds originating in industrialized regions have been detected in the bodies of Arctic peoples.[d] Global warming is fueling the problem, because as glaciers and snow melt, long-stored toxins are released.

BIOCULTURAL QUESTION

Since corporations are able to profit from large-scale and long-distance commercial activities, we should not be surprised that their operations may also cause serious damage to fellow humans in remote natural environments. What do you think of the profiteering of structural violence?

[a] Colborn, T., et al. (1997). *Our stolen future* (pp. 107–108). New York: Plume/Penguin.

[b] Arctic Monitoring Assessment Project (AMAP). (2003). *AMAP assessment 2002: Human health in the Arctic* (pp. xii–xiii, 22–23). Oslo: Author.

[c] Ingmar Egede, quoted in Cone, M. (2005). *Silent snow: The slow poisoning of the Arctic* (p. 1). New York: Grove.

[d] Additional sources: Johansen, B. E. (2002). The Inuit's struggle with dioxins and other organic pollutants. *American Indian Quarterly 26* (3), 479–490; Natural Resources Defense Council. (2005, March 25). Healthy milk, healthy baby: Chemical pollution and mother's milk. www.NRDC.org; Williams, F. (2005, January 9). Toxic breast milk? *New York Times Magazine.*

Added to this is the problem of climatic change, in particular global warming—the greenhouse effect—caused primarily by the burning of fossil fuels (oil, gas, and coal). During the past 200 years, global cultural development has relied on burning increasing quantities of these fuels, with dire results: massive deforestation and desertification, along with severe air, water, and soil pollution threatening the health of all life. Fossil fuel use has dramatically increased carbon dioxide levels, trapping more heat in the earth's atmosphere. Rising temperatures are causing more

Malé is one of many low-lying islands threatened by rising sea levels brought on by global warming. It is the capital island of the Maldives, an Indian Ocean archipelago comprised of 1,200 low-lying islands (199 inhabited), home to about 375,000 people. Climate change and rising sea levels are of great concern to the Maldivians, since their country is only 2.4 meters (8 feet) above sea level at its highest point. As global warming causes the polar ice caps to melt and sea levels to rise, the entire country could disappear. In recent years, the government had a $60-million seawall built around Malé and undertook the construction of a nearby artificial island where the land and buildings are several feet higher than the rest of the Maldives.

© Yann Arthus-Bertrand/Corbis

and greater storms, droughts, and heat waves, devastating populations in vulnerable areas. And if the massive meltdown of Arctic ice now under way continues, rising sea levels will inundate low coastal areas worldwide. Entire islands may soon disappear, including thousands of villages and even large cities.

Although much is unknown about the extent of global warming, scientists now overwhelmingly agree it is real and poses a serious challenge. Experts predict that it will lead to an expansion of the geographic ranges of tropical diseases and increase the incidence of respiratory diseases due to additional smog caused by warmer temperatures. Also, they expect an increase in deaths due to heat waves, as witnessed in the 52,000 deaths attributed to the 2003 heat wave in Europe.[29]

Structural violence also manifests itself in the shifting of manufacturing and hazardous waste disposal from developed to developing countries. In the late 1980s, a tightening of environmental regulations in industrialized countries led to a dramatic rise in the cost of hazardous waste disposal. Seeking cheaper ways to get rid of the wastes, "toxic traders" began shipping hazardous waste to eastern Europe and especially to poor and underdeveloped countries in western Africa (see the Globalscape). When news of this became public, international outrage about the poisoning of soil, air, and water in these poor countries led to the drafting and adoption of the Basel Convention to prohibit the export of hazardous wastes and to minimize their generation.

Today, the scope of the convention is severely limited by the fact that the United States, the largest toxic residue producer in the world, has not ratified the agreement.[30] Moreover, unscrupulous entrepreneurs and corrupt government officials have found ways to circumvent international treaty obligations.

Whereas a small number of wealthy countries—primarily in western Europe and North America—have reaped many economic benefits of early industrialization and global trade, they are also responsible for an estimated two-thirds of the atmospheric buildup of heat-trapping carbon dioxide (CO_2). By contrast, all of Africa, a huge continent three times larger than all of Europe, is responsible for less than 3 percent of the global CO_2 emissions in the past hundred years. Measuring the inequality in human terms, each person in North America adds, on average, 20 tons of carbon dioxide (a greenhouse gas) a year to the atmosphere. In "underdeveloped" countries, less than 3 tons per person are emitted.[31] And one North American consumes hundreds of times the resources of a single African, with all that implies with respect to waste disposal and environmental degradation (Figure 16.4). According to botanist Peter Raven, "if everyone lived like Americans, you'd need three planet earths . . . to sustain that level of consumption."[32]

[29] Larsen, J. (2006, July 28). *Setting the record straight*. Earth Policy Institute, Eco-economy updates.

[30] "Hazardous waste trafficking." www.Choike.org.

[31] Broecker, W. S. (1992, April). Global warming on trial. *Natural History*, 14.

[32] Quoted in Becker, J. (2004, March). *National Geographic*, 90.

Globalscape

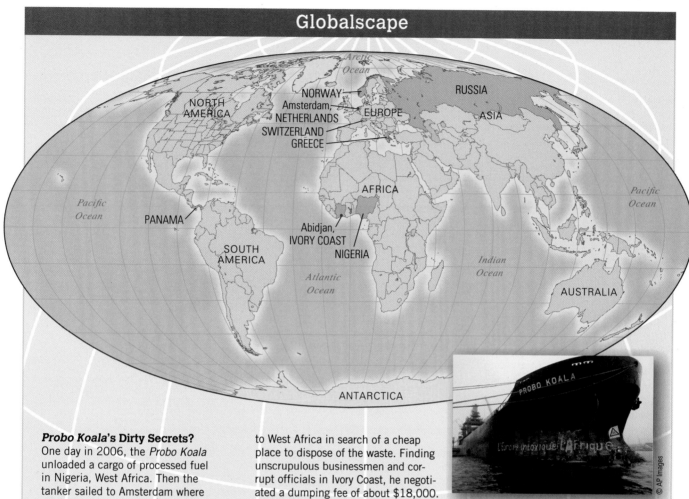

© AP Images

Probo Koala's Dirty Secrets?

One day in 2006, the *Probo Koala* unloaded a cargo of processed fuel in Nigeria, West Africa. Then the tanker sailed to Amsterdam where a Dutch treatment plant was to process its 400 tons of leftover toxic sludge. Navigating the oceans under the Panamanian flag, this ship's all-Russian crew serves under a Greek captain. Managed and operated by a Greek maritime company, the ship's registered owner is based in Norway. For this journey, it was chartered by a Dutch subsidiary of Trafigura, a multinational company headquartered in Switzerland that specializes in transporting oil and mineral products.

When port authorities in Amsterdam discovered that the *Probo Koala*'s captain had underreported the poison levels in his cargo, the cost of treating the waste jumped to $600,000. Unwilling to pay the higher fee, the captain ordered his ship back to West Africa in search of a cheap place to dispose of the waste. Finding unscrupulous businessmen and corrupt officials in Ivory Coast, he negotiated a dumping fee of about $18,000. Deposited in open-air waste pits on the edge of Abidjan (population 5 million), the substance gave off toxic gas that burned lungs and skin and caused severe headaches and vomiting—injuring at least 30,000 people and killing seventeen.

The *Probo Koala* forms part of a profitable global business network capitalizing on the more than 350 million tons of hazardous waste generated annually, primarily by industrial societies. Although most of this waste is now properly disposed, some companies avoid environmental regulations and high treatment costs within Europe and North America, seeking cheap (possibly illegal) options—including dumping at sea. Many millions of tons of hazardous waste are transported across the oceans to underdeveloped countries.

In a 2009 out-of-court settlement, Trafigura agreed to pay a total of $43,000 to cover all claims, but many see this as a slap on the hand that does not begin to match the gravity of the crime. Greenpeace has determined to take the company to court, claiming that Trafigura knew the toxicity and illegality of the dump.

Global Twister   Although hazardous waste dumping by the *Probo Koala* resulted in the arrest of several African businessmen in Ivory Coast, should the other participants in this global crime be judged and punished? If so, under which laws?

Yet, millions of peasants, herders, fishermen, and other folk inhabiting the world's developing countries in Africa, Asia, and Latin America find themselves paying for the progress enjoyed by fellow human beings who have reaped the benefits of industrialization for several generations. They now suffer from global-induced droughts and floods, but lack the capital to effectively deal with them. As President Yoweri Mueseveni of Uganda told an African Union

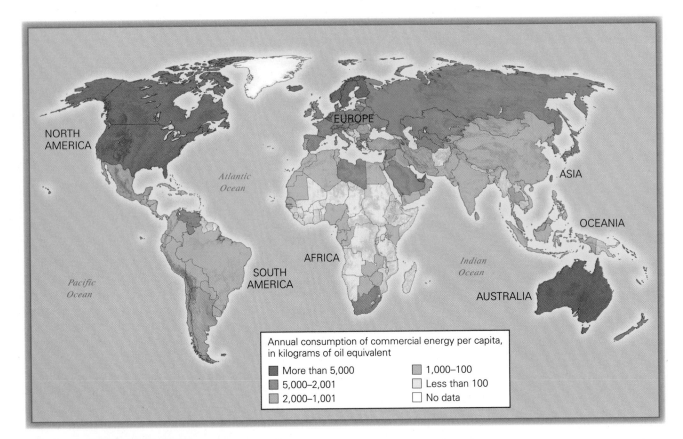

Annual consumption of commercial energy per capita, in kilograms of oil equivalent

- More than 5,000
- 5,000–2,001
- 2,000–1,001
- 1,000–100
- Less than 100
- No data

Figure 16.4 Most of the world's highest energy consumers are in North America and western Europe where at least 100 gigajoules of commercial energy per year are consumed by each person. (A gigajoule is the equivalent of about 3.5 metric tons of coal.) In some of these countries, such as the United States and Canada, the consumption rates are in the 300-gigajoule range. At the other end of the scale are low-income countries, whose consumption rates are often less than 1 percent of those in the United States. These figures do not include the consumption of noncommercial energy—the traditional fuels of firewood, animal dung, and other organic matter widely used in the less developed parts of the world.

Source: *Student Atlas of Anthropology* by J. L. Allen & A. C. Shalinsky, p. 126. ©2004, McGraw-Hill/Dushkin Publishing.

summit in Ethiopia in 2007, "We have a message here to tell these [wealthy industrialized] countries, that you are causing aggression to us by causing global warming."[33]

Reactions to Globalization

No matter how effectively a dominant state or corporation combines its hard and soft power, globalization does run into opposition. Pockets of resistance exist within the wealthy industrial and postindustrial states as well as elsewhere in the world. This resistance may be manifested in the rise of traditionalism and revitalization movements—efforts to return to life as it was (or how people think it was) before the familiar order became unhinged and people became unsettled. Some of these reactionary movements may take the form of resurgent ethnonationalism or religious fundamentalist movements. Others may find expression in alternative grassroots movements from radical environmental groups to peace groups.

While it is true that states and big corporations have expanded their power and influence through electronic communication technologies, it is also true that these same technologies present opportunities to those who have traditionally been powerless. They provide a means of distributing information and promoting activities that are distinct from or in opposition to those of dominant society.

One striking case of a cultural reaction to globalization is the Taliban, a group of Muslim religious fundamentalists

[33]UN's Intergovernmental Panel on Climate Change in 2007. Cited by Friedman, T. (2007, April). *New York Times.*

in Afghanistan. The Taliban (the Pashto word for "students," specifically of Islam) helped to force the Russian army out of their country and end the subsequent civil war; then they rose to power in the 1990s and imposed a radical version of traditional Islamic law (Shariah) in an effort to create an Islamic republic based on strict religious values.

In the United States, there has been a similar, though less radical, reaction against modernity. "Born again" and other fundamentalist citizens seek to shape or transform not only their towns but also states and even the entire country by electing politicians committed to forging a national culture based on what they see as American patriotism, English-only legislation, and traditional Christian values.[34]

Ethnic Minorities and Indigenous Peoples: Struggles for Human Rights

Throughout this book, we have discussed a wide range of cultures all across the globe. Many of our examples involve peoples who see themselves as members of distinct nations by virtue of their birth and their cultural and territorial heritage—nations over whom peoples of some other ethnic background have tried to assert political control. An estimated 5,000 such national groups exist in the world today, as opposed to a mere 192 states formally admitted as members of the United Nations (nearly four times the original fifty-one members at its founding in 1945).[35] Although some of these national or ethnic groups are small in population and area—100 or so people living on a few acres—many others are quite large. The Karen people inhabiting southern Myanmar (Burma), for example, number some 4.5 to 5 million, exceeding the population of nearly half of the countries in the world. And Kurds, living in Turkey, Iran, and Iraq, number about 30 million.

The reactions of such groups to forced annexation and domination by state regimes controlled by people of other nations range all the way from the nonviolence of the Saami in Scandinavia, Inuit of Nunavut in northern Canada, or Maori of New Zealand to bloody fights for national independence by Basque separatists in Spain, Karen in eastern Myanmar (Burma), Chechens in southern Russia, or Palestinians in the Middle East. In pursuit of self-determination, national autonomy, independence, or whatever their political objectives, some struggles have been going on for decades.

Since the mid-1900s, global institutions such as the United Nations have tried to address the problem of discrimination, repression, and crimes against humanity, in particular genocide. For example, even though it often fails to act on it, the UN General Assembly's 1966 Covenant of Human Rights states unequivocally:

> In those states in which ethnic, religious or linguistic minorities exist, persons belonging to such minorities shall not be denied the rights, in community with the other members of their group, to enjoy their own culture, to profess and practice their own religion or to use their own language.[36]

This covenant applies not only to minority groups, but also to the world's indigenous peoples, who make up about 5 percent of humanity's population. Nearly all indigenous groups are relatively small nations. Typically, they have suffered repression or discrimination by ethnically different, more powerful, and almost always more heavily populated groups that have gained control over their ancestral homelands.

In the early 1970s indigenous peoples began to organize self-determination movements, resisting acculturation and challenging violations of their human rights. Joining forces across international borders, they established the World Council of Indigenous Peoples in 1975.

In 2007, after many years of popular media campaigns, political lobbying, and diplomatic pressure by hundreds of indigenous leaders and other activists all around the globe, the UN General Assembly finally adopted the Declaration of the Rights of Indigenous Peoples. A foundational document in the global human rights struggle, it contains some 150 articles urging respect for indigenous cultural heritages, calling for official recognition of indigenous land titles and rights of self-determination, and demanding an end to all forms of oppression and discrimination as a principle of international law.

Global Migrations: Refugees, Migrants, and Diasporic Communities

Structural power and structural violence may both be involved in human migration. Throughout human history, individuals, families, and sometimes entire communities have migrated in pursuit of food, safety, and opportunity. Migration has always had a significant effect on world social geography, contributing to cultural change and development, to the diffusion of ideas and innovations, and to

---

[34] Marsella, A. J. (1982). Pulling it together: Discussion and comments. In S. Pastner & W. A. Haviland (Eds.), *Confronting the creationists* (pp. 79–80). *Northeaster Anthropological Association, Occasional Proceedings* 1.

[35] *Cultural Survival Quarterly*. (1992). 15(4), 38.

[36] Quoted in Bodley, J. H. (1990). *Victims of progress* (3rd ed., p. 99). Mountain View, CA: Mayfield.

In 1982 the UN Sub-
Commission on the Promo-
tion and Protection of Human
Rights established a Working
Group on Indigenous Populations (WGIP). Eleven years
later WGIP completed a draft
of the Declaration of the
Rights of Indigenous Peoples,
ratified in 2007. Here we see
delegates from Japan's ethnic
Ainu community in the UN
assembly hall at a recent
WGIP gathering.

the complex mixture of peoples and cultures found in the world today.

Internal migration occurs within the boundaries of a country. Unable to sustain themselves in the rural back-lands, people all over the world continue to move to large urban areas, hoping to find a better life. All too often they live out their days in poor, congested, and diseased slums while attempting to achieve what is usually beyond their reach.

External migration is movement from one country to another. Such migration may be voluntary (people seeking better conditions and opportunities), but all too often it may be involuntary, forced, or imposed—people who have been taken as slaves or prisoners, or driven from their homelands by war, political unrest, religious persecution, or environment disasters. Figure 16.5 shows the patterns of worldwide migration.

Today, about 42 million people in almost half of the world's countries are either internally displaced or have crossed international borders as refugees. Some 9 million of these people have been forced outside their countries, most of them suffering in makeshift camps where they cannot make a living. In some cases, large numbers of an

ethnic group are forced to abandon their homes and flee for their lives. For instance, some 18 million Africans are currently uprooted. In war-torn Sudan alone, more than 2.5 million people have been driven from their homes.

In addition to such forced displacements, tens of thousands of people migrate to wealthy countries every year in search of wage labor and a better future for themselves and their offspring. While most cross international borders as legal immigrants, seeking work permits and ultimately citizenship in their new homeland, untold numbers of others are illegal and do not enjoy many important rights and benefits.

Legal or not, many of these immigrants face great challenges as poor newcomers in these societies—all the more so because they may encounter racism and discrimination. As a consequence, many newcomers form or join communities of people who have come from the same part of the world. Modern transportation and telecommunication technology make it possible for these *diasporic communities,* which exist all across the globe, to remain in contact with relatives and friends who have settled elsewhere, as well as with their country of origin. Indicative of this aspect of globalization is that today about 200 million people (almost 3 percent of the world's population) live outside their countries of birth—not as refugees or immigrants, but as transnationals who earn their living in one country while remaining citizens of another.[37]

internal migration   Movement within the boundaries of a country.
external migration   Movement from one country to another. It may be voluntary or involuntary.

---

[37] UN. Global Commission on International Migration, 2005.

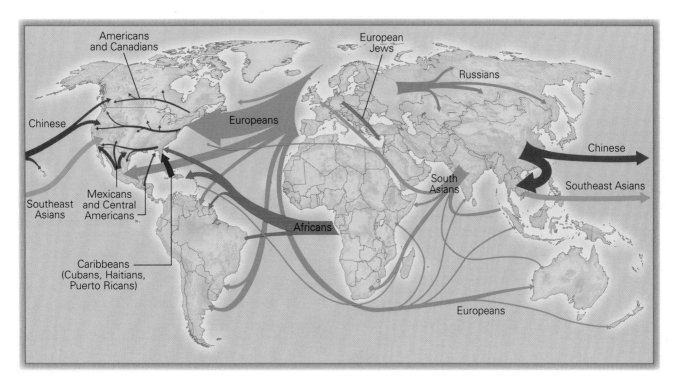

Figure 16.5 Migration has had and continues to have a significant effect on world social geography, contributing to cultural change and development, to the diffusion of ideas and innovations, and to the complex mixture of people and cultures found in the world today. Internal migration occurs within the boundaries of a country; external migration is movement from one country or region to another. Not shown here are recent migration waves from Africa and Turkey to Europe.

Source: From *Student Atlas of Anthropology* by J. L. Allen & A. C. Shalinsky, p. 73. Copyright © 2003 McGraw-Hill/ Dushkin Publishing.

Over the past few decades, mass migration across international borders has dramatically changed the ethnic composition of affluent societies in western Europe and North America. Since indigenous peoples such as the Cree or Navajo (just to mention two of more than 500 remaining tribal nations) are the original inhabitants of North America, nearly everyone else (almost 99 percent) is either immigrant offspring or a more recent newcomer. The 13 million Mexicans residing in the United States represent about one fourth of all foreign-born newcomers. As the largest and fastest-growing group of immigrants in the United States, they are settled primarily in California and Texas where many form Spanish-speaking ethnic enclaves. In addition there are over 25 million other immigrants from Asian countries, such as China and India, and African countries, such as Nigeria and Ethiopia. Today, almost 2 million African immigrants live in the United States, a 55-fold increase since the 1960s, with large clusters of different nationalities from that continent concentrated in Washington, DC, New York City, Atlanta, and other major metropolitan areas.

In contrast to former European colonies such as the settler societies of Australia, Canada, and the United States, in which indigenous peoples make up a very small proportion of the population, countries such as Germany, England, and France are traditionally inhabited by closely related ethnic groups historically unified and culturally integrated as nations. Accordingly, massive immigration into Europe by foreigners primarily from Asia and Africa has resulted in considerable upheaval, with the host countries facing unfamiliar problems with cultural integration. Such is the case with Germany, where almost 4 million people of Turkish origin now live and work.

Initially needed as cheap, unskilled laborers, Turks were hired as "guest workers" in highly industrialized urban areas. Since most of them remained, the authorities instituted a family reunification policy, which resulted in hundreds of thousands of Turkish relatives entering the country. Even after several decades in Germany, the vast majority of German Turks do not possess citizenship and have not become culturally integrated into

© Véronique de Viguerie

Two decades of clan feuds, violence, and warfare have wreaked havoc on the Republic of Somalia in East Africa. Its weakened central government is powerless to safeguard coastal waters from foreign trawlers depriving Somali fishermen of their livelihood. Nor can it stop local fishermen from turning to piracy for subsistence. Many Somali citizens rely on foreign aid, along with a flow of cash from fellow clan members living abroad, some of whom invest in piracy for profit. Piracy is a booming, multimillion-dollar enterprise in the country's informal economy. Pirates based in the coastal village of Hobyo get supplies 200 kilometers (125 miles) inland at this shop in Gaalkacyo. Its façade features symbols that reflect the globalized business of piracy in this region. Pirates call in their orders by cell phone, and the owner sends them out by truck, charging twice the normal price.

German society. Turkish, spoken by Germany's largest ethnic minority, has become that country's second language.

The ethnic composition in France has also dramatically changed in the past few decades. About 1.5 million Africans and another 2 million people from other parts of the world, mainly from former colonial territories, now live in that country. As with the Turks in Germany, many of these foreigners come in search of economic opportunity but do not become culturally integrated into French society. The same is true for England, now home to over 1.5 million South Asians, plus another 1.3 million people of African descent who hail primarily from the former British colonies.

Although migrants may experience *xenophobia* ("fear of strangers"), hostility, hardship, disappointment, and sometimes failure in their new countries, those who remain trapped in their troubled homelands often face worse challenges: malnutrition, hunger, chronic disease, and violence, resulting in a low life expectancy for many.

As mentioned in an earlier chapter, one fascinating aspect of this global movement of wage-earning workers is the electronic transfer of money in the form of remittances to relatives and friends still living in ancestral cities or villages abroad. For example, Mexicans working in the United States send an estimated $26 billion of their yearly

U.S. earnings by means of money transfers to relatives left behind in their home regions. Without these payments, many local communities throughout Mexico would face major economic problems. Worldwide, remittances total some $330 billion per year.[38] While still high, remittances have declined due to the global recession, causing real hardship in the impoverished communities that have come to depend on them.

Concluding Remarks

As defined in Chapter 1, anthropology is the comparative study of humankind everywhere and throughout time. It seeks to produce reliable knowledge about different peoples and cultures, their ideas and behaviors. Since the beginning of the discipline in the mid-1800s, generations of anthropologists have studied our species in all its cultural and biological variation. In the process, they described in great detail an enormous number and range of different cultures, and they collected a staggering volume of biological data

---

[38] www.worldbank.org/prospects/migrationandremittances.

Questions for Reflection

1. Given that the number of big cities is growing worldwide, especially in developing countries, do you know of any public festival other than carnival that brings people together from all walks of life for a few hours or a day? Can you think of any social integrative functions of such as public feast?

2. Reflecting on the human condition past and present, and the challenges facing your own family in the age of globalization, do you imagine the future in terms of continued progress? How do you measure that and by which cultural standard?

3. Considering the relationship between structural power and structural violence, does your own lifestyle in terms of buying clothes and food, driving cars, and so on reflect or have an effect on the globalization process?

4. In the global mediascape, television viewers and Internet users are not only consumers of news and entertainment but are also exposed to soft power. Can you think of an example of soft power in your daily life? And at which point does such influence turn into propaganda or manipulation?

5. The World Health Organization, UNESCO, Oxfam, and Amnesty International are global institutions concerned with structural violence and human rights violations. Confronted with genocidal conflicts, famines, epidemics, and torture of political prisoners, people active in these organizations try to improve the human condition. Why do you think that an anthropological perspective on such worldwide problems might be of practical use? Can you think of an example?

Suggested Readings

Appadurai, A. (1996). *Modernity at large: Cultural dimensions of globalization.* Minneapolis: University of Minnesota Press.

In this fundamental contribution to how globalization works, a leading anthropologist discusses how forces such as migration and electronic mediation acquire shaping roles in the production of contemporary culture.

Bodley, J. H. (2007). *Anthropology and contemporary human problems* (5th ed.). Lanham, MD: Alta Mira.

Anthropologist Bodley examines some of the most serious problems in the world today: overconsumption, resource depletion, hunger and starvation, overpopulation, violence, and war.

Farmer, P. (2003). *Pathologies of power: Health, human rights, and the new war on the poor.* Berkeley: University of California Press.

Farmer argues that promoting the social and economic rights of the world's poor is the most important human rights struggle of our time. Based on eyewitness accounts from Russian prisons and poor peasant communities in Haiti, Mexico, and Peru, his book exposes relationships between political and economic injustice and the suffering of the powerless. Linking the painful experiences of individual victims to a broader analysis of structural violence, Farmer hopes that new medical and social technologies will develop in conjunction with a more informed sense of social justice.

Ginsburg, F. D., Abu-Lughod, L., & Larkin, B. (Eds.). (2009). *Media worlds: Anthropology on new terrain.* Berkeley: University of California Press.

Groundbreaking essays by pioneers of media studies in anthropology, discussing the place and function of film, video, radio, television, and cinema in different cultures and showing that contemporary peoples and cultures cannot be understood without the mediascapes they inhabit.

Lewellen, T. C. (2002). *The anthropology of globalization: Cultural anthropology enters the 21st century.* Westport, CT: Greenwood.

Readable introduction, summary, and critique of globalization with telling and timely ethnographic examples.

Ong, A. (1999). *Flexible citizenship: The cultural logics of transnationality.* Durham, NC: Duke University Press.

Ong demonstrates how the Chinese transnational community confounds notions of peripheral non-Westerners and argues that the contemporary world is creating the context for the rise of China.

Trouillot, M. R. (2003). *Global transformations: Anthropology and the modern world.* New York: Palgrave Macmillan.

Examining anthropology's history and discussing future possibilities for the discipline, the author challenges colleagues to question dominant narratives of globalization and to radically rethink key concepts of anthropology.

Glossary

acculturation Massive culture change that occurs in a society when it experiences intensive firsthand contact with a more powerful society.

adaptation A series of beneficial adjustments of organisms to their environment.

adjudication Mediation with an unbiased third party making the ultimate decision.

advocacy anthropology Research that is community based and politically involved.

affinal kin People related through marriage.

age grade An organized category of people based on age; every individual passes through a series of such categories over his or her lifetime.

age set A formally established group of people born during a certain time span who move through the series of age-grade categories together.

agribusiness Large-scale businesses involved in food production, including farming, contract farming, seed supply, agrichemicals, farm machinery, distribution, processing, and marketing. Also known as corporate farming, it stands in contrast to smaller family-owned farms.

agriculture The cultivation of food plants in soil prepared and maintained for crop production. Involves using technologies other than hand tools, such as irrigation, fertilizers, and the wooden or metal plow pulled by harnessed draft animals.

alphabet A series of symbols representing the sounds of a language arranged in a traditional order.

ambilocal residence A residence pattern in which a married couple may choose either matrilocal or patrilocal residence.

animatism A belief that nature is enlivened or energized by an impersonal spiritual power or supernatural potency.

animism A belief that nature is animated (enlivened or energized) by distinct personalized spirit beings separable from bodies.

anthropology The study of humankind in all times and places.

applied anthropology The use of anthropological knowledge and methods to solve practical problems, often for a specific client.

archaeology The study of human cultures through the recovery and analysis of material remains and environmental data.

art The creative use of the human imagination to aesthetically interpret, express, and engage life, modifying experienced reality in the process.

Australopithecus The genus including several species of early bipeds from southern, eastern, and Central Africa (Chad) living between about 1.1 and 4.4 million years ago, one of whom was directly ancestral to humans.

balanced reciprocity A mode of exchange in which the giving and the receiving are specific as to the value of the goods and the time of their delivery.

band A relatively small and loosely organized kin-ordered group that inhabits a common territory and that may split periodically into smaller extended family groups that are politically and economically independent.

bioarchaeology The archaeological study of human remains emphasizing the preservation of cultural and social processes in the skeleton.

biocultural Focusing on the interaction of biology and culture.

bipedalism "Two-footed"—walking upright on both hind legs—a characteristic of humans and their ancestors.

bridewealth Money or valuable goods paid by the groom or his family to the bride's family upon marriage; also called bride-price.

cargo cult A spiritual movement (especially noted in Melanesia) in reaction to disruptive contact with Western capitalism, promising resurrection of deceased relatives, destruction or enslavement of white foreigners, and the magical arrival of utopian riches.

carrying capacity The number of people that the available resources can support at a given level of food-getting techniques.

caste A closed social class in a stratified society in which membership is determined by birth and fixed for life.

chiefdom A regional polity in which two or more local groups are organized under a single chief, who is at the head of a ranked hierarchy of people.

clan An extended unilineal kinship group, often consisting of several lineages, whose members claim common descent from a remote ancestor, usually legendary or mythological.

code switching Changing from one mode of speech to another as the situation demands, whether from one language to another or from one dialect of a language to another.

common-interest association An association that results from an act of joining based on sharing particular activities, objectives, values, or beliefs, sometimes rooted in common ethnic, religious, or regional background.

conjugal family A family established through marriage.

consanguineal family A family of "blood relatives" consisting of related women, their brothers, and the women's offspring.

consanguineal kin Biologically related relatives, commonly referred to as blood relatives.

conspicuous consumption A showy display of wealth for social prestige.

contagious magic Magic based on the principle that things or persons once in contact can influence each other after the contact is broken.

convergent evolution In cultural evolution, the development of similar cultural adaptations to similar environmental conditions by different peoples with different ancestral cultures.

core values Those values especially promoted by a particular culture.

core vocabulary The most basic and long-lasting words in any language—pronouns, lower numerals, and names for body parts and natural objects.

cross cousin Child of a mother's brother or a father's sister.

cultural adaptation A complex of ideas, activities, and technologies that enable people to survive and even thrive in their environment.

cultural anthropology The study of customary patterns in human behavior, thought, and feelings. It focuses on humans as culture-producing and culture-reproducing creatures. Also known as social or sociocultural anthropology.

cultural control Control through beliefs and values deeply internalized in the minds of individuals.

cultural evolution Cultural change over time; not to be confused with progress.

cultural loss The abandonment of an existing practice or trait.

cultural relativism The idea that one must suspend judgment of other people's practices in order to understand them in their own cultural terms.

cultural resource management A branch of archaeology tied to government policies for the protection of cultural resources and involving surveying and/or excavating archaeological and historical remains threatened by construction or development.

culture A society's shared and socially transmitted ideas, values, and perceptions, which are used to make sense of experience and generate behavior and are reflected in that behavior.

culture area A geographic region in which a number of societies follow similar patterns of life.

culture core Cultural features that are fundamental in the society's way of making its living—including food-producing techniques, knowledge of available resources, and the work arrangements involved in applying those techniques to the local environment.

culture-bound Describing theories about the world and reality based on the assumptions and values of one's own culture.

culture-bound syndrome A mental disorder specific to a particular cultural group.

dependence training Childrearing practices that foster compliance in the performance of assigned tasks and dependence on the domestic group, rather than reliance on oneself.

descent group Any kin-ordered social group with a membership in the direct line of descent from a real (historical) or fictional common ancestor.

dialects Varying forms of a language that reflect particular regions, occupations, or social classes and that are similar enough to be mutually intelligible.

diffusion The spread of certain ideas, customs, or practices from one culture to another.

digital ethnography The use of digital technologies (audio and visual) for the collection, analysis, and representation of ethnographic data.

discourse An extended communication on a particular subject.

displacement Referring to things and events removed in time and space.

divination A magical procedure or spiritual ritual designed to find out what is not knowable by ordinary means, such as foretelling the future by interpreting omens.

doctrine An assertion of opinion or belief formally handed down by an authority as true and indisputable.

dowry Payment of a woman's inheritance at the time of her marriage, either to her or to her husband.

economic system An organized arrangement for producing, distributing, and consuming goods.

ecosystem A system, or a functioning whole, composed of both the natural environment and all the organisms living within it.

egalitarian society A society in which everyone has about equal rank, access to, and power over the basic resources that support survival, influence, and prestige.

EGO The central person from whom the degree of each relationship is traced.

eliciting device An activity or object used to draw out individuals and encourage them to recall and share information.

empirical Based on observations of the world rather than on intuition or faith.

enculturation The process by which a society's culture is passed on from one generation to the next and individuals become members of their society.

endogamy Marriage within a particular group or category of individuals.

epic A long, dramatic narrative recounting the celebrated deeds of a historic or legendary hero—often sung or recited in poetic language.

Eskimo system Kinship reckoning in which the nuclear family is emphasized by specifically identifying the mother, father, brother, and sister, while lumping together all other relatives into broad categories such as uncle, aunt, and cousin; also known as a lineal system.

ethnic group People who collectively and publicly identify themselves as a distinct group based on cultural features such as common origin, language, customs, and traditional beliefs.

ethnicity This term, rooted in the Greek word *ethnikos* ("nation") and related to *ethnos* ("custom"), is the expression of the set of cultural ideas held by an ethnic group.

ethnocentrism The belief that the ways of one's own culture are the only proper ones.

ethnocide The violent eradication of an ethnic group's collective cultural identity as a distinctive people; occurs when a dominant society deliberately sets out to destroy another society's cultural heritage.

ethnographic fieldwork Extended on-location research to gather detailed and in-depth information on a society's customary ideas, values, and practices through participation in its collective social life.

ethnography A detailed description of a particular culture primarily based on fieldwork.

ethnohistory A study of cultures of the recent past through oral histories; accounts of explorers, missionaries, and traders; and through analysis of records such as land titles, birth and death records, and other archival materials.

ethnolinguistics A branch of linguistics that studies the relationships between language and culture and how they mutually influence and inform each other.

ethnology The study and analysis of different cultures from a comparative or historical point of view, utilizing ethnographic accounts and developing anthropological theories that help explain why certain important differences or similarities occur among groups.

ethnomusicology The study of a society's music in terms of its cultural setting.

evolution Changes in the genetic makeup of a population over generations.

exogamy Marriage outside the group.

extended family Two or more closely related nuclear families clustered together into a large domestic group.

external migration Movement from one country to another. It may be voluntary or involuntary.

family Two or more people related by blood, marriage, or adoption. The family may take many forms, ranging from a single parent with one or more children, to a married couple or polygamous spouses with or without offspring, to several generations of parents and their children.

fictive marriage Marriage by proxy to the symbols of someone not physically present to establish the social status of a spouse and heirs.

fieldwork The term anthropologists use for on-location research.

fission The splitting of a descent group into two or more new descent groups.

folklore A term coined by 19th-century scholars studying the unwritten stories and other artistic traditions of rural peoples to distinguish between "folk art" and the "fine art" of the literate elite.

food foraging Hunting, fishing, and gathering wild plant foods.

forensic anthropology Applied subfield of physical anthropology that specializes in the identification of human skeletal remains for legal purposes.

formal interview A structured question/answer session carefully notated as it occurs and based on prepared questions.

gender The cultural elaborations and meanings assigned to the biological differentiation between the sexes.

gendered speech Distinct male and female speech patterns, which vary across social and cultural settings.

generalized reciprocity A mode of exchange in which the value of what is given is not calculated, nor is the time of repayment specified.

genes The basic physical units of heredity that specify the biological traits and characteristics of each organism.

genocide The physical extermination of one people by another, either as a deliberate act or as the accidental outcome of activities carried out by one people with little regard for their impact on others.

gesture Facial expressions and body postures and motions that convey intended as well as subconscious messages.

globalization Worldwide interconnectedness, evidenced in global movements of natural resources, trade goods, human labor, finance capital, information, and infectious diseases.

glottochronology In linguistics, a method for identifying the approximate time that languages branched off from a common ancestor; based on analyzing core vocabularies.

grammar The entire formal structure of a language, including morphology and syntax.

group marriage Marriage in which several men and women have sexual access to one another; also called co-marriage.

hard power Coercive power that is backed up by economic and military force.

Hawaiian system Kinship reckoning in which all relatives of the same sex and generation are referred to by the same term.

holistic perspective A fundamental principle of anthropology: that the various parts of human culture and biology must be viewed in the broadest possible context in order to understand their interconnections and interdependence.

hominoid The broad-shouldered tailless group of primates that includes all living and extinct apes and humans.

Homo erectus "Upright man." A species within the genus *Homo* first appearing just after 2 million years ago in Africa and ultimately spreading throughout the Old World.

Homo habilis "Handy man." The first fossil members of the genus *Homo* appearing 2.5 to 2.6 million years ago, with larger brains and smaller faces than australopithecines.

horticulture Cultivation of crops carried out with simple hand tools such as digging sticks or hoes.

household The basic residential unit where economic production, consumption, inheritance, childrearing, and shelter are organized and carried out.

Human Relations Area Files (HRAF) A vast collection of cross-indexed ethnographic and archaeological data catalogued by cultural characteristics and geographic locations; archived in about 300 libraries (on microfiche or online).

hypothesis A tentative explanation of the relation between certain phenomena.

iconic images Culturally specific people, animals, and monsters seen in the deepest stage of trance.

idealist perspective A theoretical approach stressing the primacy of superstructure in cultural research and analysis.

imitative magic Magic based on the principle that like produces like; sometimes called sympathetic magic.

incest taboo The prohibition of sexual relations between specified individuals, usually parent and child and sibling relations at a minimum.

incorporation In a rite of passage, reincorporation of the individual into society in his or her new status.

independence training Childrearing practices that foster independence, self-reliance, and personal achievement.

informal economy A network of producing and circulating marketable commodities, labor, and services that for various reasons escape government control.

informal interview An unstructured, open-ended conversation in everyday life.

informed consent Formal recorded agreement to participate in research; federally mandated for all research in the United States and Europe.

infrastructure The economic foundation of a society, including its subsistence practices and the tools and other material equipment used to make a living.

internal migration Movement within the boundaries of a country.

intersexual A person born with reproductive organs, genitalia, and/or sex chromosomes that are not exclusively male or female.

Iroquois system Kinship reckoning in which a father and father's brother are referred to by a single term, as are a mother and mother's sister, but a father's sister and mother's brother are given separate terms. Parallel cousins are classified with brothers and sisters, while cross cousins are classified separately but not equated with relatives of some other generation.

key consultant A member of the society being studied who provides information that helps researchers understand the meaning of what they observe; early anthropologists referred to such individuals as informants.

kindred An individual's close blood relatives on the maternal and paternal sides of his or her family.

kinesics A system of notating and analyzing postures, facial expressions, and body motions that convey messages.

kinship A network of relatives within which individuals possess certain mutual rights and obligations.

Kula ring A form of balanced reciprocity that reinforces trade relations among the seafaring Trobriand Islanders and other Melanesians.

language A system of communication using sounds or gestures that are put together in meaningful ways according to a set of rules.

language family A group of languages descended from a single ancestral language.

law Formal rules of conduct that, when violated, effectuate negative sanctions.

legend A story about a memorable event or figure handed down by tradition and told as true but without historical evidence.

legitimacy The right of political leaders to govern—to hold, use, and allocate power—on the socially accepted customs, rules, or laws that bind and hold a people together as a collective whole.

leveling mechanism A cultural obligation compelling prosperous members of a community to give away goods, host public feasts, provide free service, or otherwise demonstrate generosity so that no one permanently accumulates significantly more wealth than anyone else.

lineage A unilineal kinship group descended from a common ancestor or founder who lived four to six generations ago, and in which relationships among members can be exactly stated in genealogical terms.

linguistic anthropology The study of human languages—looking at their structure, history, and relation to social and cultural contexts.

linguistic determinism The idea that language to some extent shapes the way in which we view and think about the world around us.

linguistic divergence The development of different languages from a single ancestral language.

linguistic nationalism The attempt by ethnic minorities and even countries to proclaim independence by purging their language of foreign terms.

linguistic relativity The idea that distinctions encoded in one language are unique to that language.

linguistics The modern scientific study of all aspects of language.

Lower Paleolithic The first part of the Old Stone Age spanning from about 200,000 or 250,000 to 2.6 million years ago.

market exchange The buying and selling of goods and services, with prices set by rules of supply and demand.

marriage A culturally sanctioned union between two or more people that establishes certain rights and obligations between the people, between them and their children, and between them and their in-laws. Such marriage rights and obligations most often include, but are not limited to, sex, labor, property, childrearing, exchange, and status.

materialist perspective A theoretical approach stressing the primacy of infrastructure (material conditions) in cultural research and analysis.

matrilineal descent Descent traced exclusively through the female line to establish group membership.

matrilocal residence A residence pattern in which a married couple lives in the wife's mother's place of residence.

mediation Settlement of a dispute through ..egotiation assisted by an unbiased third party.

medical anthropology A specialization in anthropology that combines theoretical and applied approaches from cultural and biological anthropology with the study of human health and disease.

modal personality Those character traits that occur with the highest frequency in a social group and are therefore the most representative of its culture.

modernization The process of political and socioeconomic change, whereby developing societies acquire some of the cultural characteristics of Western industrial societies.

moiety Each group that results from a division of a society into two halves on the basis of descent.

molecular anthropology A branch of biological anthropology that uses genetic and biochemical techniques to test hypotheses about human evolution, adaptation, and variation.

money Something used to make payments for other goods and services as well as to measure their value.

monogamy Marriage in which both partners have just one spouse.

morphemes The smallest units of sound that carry a meaning in language. They are distinct from phonemes, which can alter meaning but have no meaning by themselves.

morphology The study of the patterns or rules of word formation in a language (including such things as rules concerning verb tense, pluralization, and compound words).

motif A story situation in a tale.

Mousterian tool tradition The tool industry found among Neandertals in Europe and Southwest Asia, and their human contemporaries in northern Africa, during the Middle Paleolithic, generally dating from about 40,000 to 125,000 years ago.

multiculturalism Public policy for managing cultural diversity in a multi-ethnic society, officially stressing mutual respect and tolerance for cultural differences within a country's borders.

multiregional hypothesis The hypothesis that modern humans originated through a process of simultaneous local transition from *Homo erectus* to *Homo sapiens* throughout the inhabited world.

multi-sited ethnography The investigation and documentation of peoples and cultures embedded in the larger structures of a globalizing world, utilizing a range of methods in various locations of time and space.

myth A sacred narrative that explains the fundamentals of human existence—where we and everything in our world came from, why we are here, and where we are going.

naming ceremony A special event or ritual to mark the naming of a child.

nation A people who share a collective identity based on a common culture, language, territorial base, and history.

natural selection The principle or mechanism by which individuals having biological characteristics best suited to a particular environment survive and reproduce with greater frequency than individuals without those characteristics.

Neandertals A distinct group within the genus *Homo* inhabiting Europe and Southwest Asia from approximately 30,000 to 125,000 years ago.

negative reciprocity A form of exchange in which the aim is to get something for as little as possible. Neither fair nor balanced, it may involve hard bargaining, manipulation, and outright cheating.

negotiation The use of direct argument and compromise by the parties to a dispute to arrive voluntarily at a mutually satisfactory agreement.

Neolithic The New Stone Age; prehistoric period beginning about 10,000 years ago in which peoples possessed stone-based technologies and depended on domesticated plants and/or animals.

Neolithic revolution The profound cultural change beginning about 10,000 years ago and associated with the early domestication of plants and animals and settlement in permanent villages. Sometimes referred to as the Neolithic transition.

neolocal residence A pattern in which a married couple establishes the household in a location apart from either the husband's or the wife's relatives.

nuclear family A group consisting of one or two parents and dependent offspring, which may include a stepparent, stepsiblings, and adopted children. Until recently this term referred only to the father, mother, and child(ren) unit.

Oldowan tool tradition The first stone tool industry, beginning between 2.5 and 2.6 million years ago at the start of the Lower Paleolithic.

paleoanthropology The study of the origins and predecessors of the present human species; the study of human evolution.

pantheon The several gods and goddesses of a people.

paralanguage Voice effects that accompany language and convey meaning. These include vocalizations such as giggling, groaning, or sighing, as well as voice qualities such as pitch and tempo.

parallel cousin Child of a father's brother or a mother's sister.

parallel evolution In cultural evolution, the development of similar cultural adaptations to similar environmental conditions by peoples whose ancestral cultures were already somewhat alike.

participant observation In ethnography, the technique of learning a people's culture through social participation and personal observation within the community being studied, as well as interviews and discussion with individual members of the group over an extended period of time.

pastoralism Breeding and managing large herds of domesticated grazing and browsing animals, such as goats, sheep, cattle, horses, llamas, or camels.

patrilineal descent Descent traced exclusively through the male line to establish group membership; also known as agnatic or male descent.

patrilocal residence A residence pattern in which a married couple lives in the husband's father's place of residence.

peasant A rural cultivator whose surpluses are transferred to a dominant group of rulers that uses the surpluses both to underwrite its own standard of living and to distribute the remainder to groups in society that do not farm but must be fed for their specific goods and services in turn.

personality The distinctive way a person thinks, feels, and behaves.

phonemes The smallest units of sound that make a difference in meaning in a language.

phonetics The systematic identification and description of distinctive speech sounds in a language.

phonology The study of language sounds.

phratry A unilineal descent group composed of at least two clans that supposedly share a common ancestry, whether or not they really do.

physical anthropology The systematic study of humans as biological organisms; also known as biological anthropology.

pluralistic society A society in which two or more ethnic groups or nationalities are politically organized into one territorial state but maintain their cultural differences.

political organization The way power is accumulated, arranged, executed, and structurally distributed and embedded in society; the means through which a society creates and maintains social order.

polyandry Marriage of a woman to two or more men at one time; a form of polygamy.

polygamy One individual having multiple spouses at the same time; from the Greek words *poly* ("many") and *gamos* ("marriage").

polygyny Marriage of a man to two or more women at the same time; a form of polygamy.

polytheism Belief in several gods and/or goddesses (as contrasted with monotheism—belief in one god or goddess).

potlatch On the northwest coast of North America, a ceremonial event in which a village chief publicly gives away stockpiled food and other goods that signify wealth.

power The ability of individuals or groups to impose their will upon others and make them do things even against their own wants or wishes.

prestige economy Creation of a surplus for the express purpose of gaining prestige through a public display of wealth that is given away as gifts.

priest or priestess A full-time religious specialist formally recognized for his or her role in guiding the religious practices of others and for contacting and influencing supernatural powers.

primary innovation The creation, invention, or chance discovery of a completely new idea, method, or device.

primate The subgroup of mammals that includes lemurs, lorises, tarsiers, monkeys, apes, and humans.

primatology The study of living and fossil primates.

progress The notion that humans are moving forward to a better, more advanced stage in their cultural development toward perfection.

proxemics The cross-cultural study of people's perception and use of space.

qualitative data Nonstatistical information such as personal life stories and customary beliefs and practices.

quantitative data Statistical or measurable information, such as demographic composition, the types and quantities of crops grown, or the ratio of spouses born and raised within or outside the community.

race In biology, a subgroup within a species, not scientifically applicable to humans because there exist no subspecies within modern *Homo sapiens*.

rebellion Organized armed resistance to an established government or authority in power.

recent African origins hypothesis The hypothesis that all modern people are derived from one single population of archaic *Homo sapiens* from Africa who migrated out of Africa after 100,000 years ago, replacing all other archaic forms due to their superior cultural capabilities; also called the Eve or out of Africa hypothesis.

reciprocity The exchange of goods and services, of approximately equal value, between two parties.

redistribution A form of exchange in which goods flow into a central place, where they are sorted, counted, and reallocated.

religion An organized system of ideas about the spiritual sphere or the supernatural, along with associated ceremonial practices by which people try to interpret and/or influence aspects of the universe otherwise beyond their control.

replacement reproduction The point at which birthrates and death rates are in equilibrium; people producing only enough offspring to replace themselves when they die.

revitalization movement A movement for radical cultural reform in response to widespread social disruption and collective feelings of great stress and despair.

revolution Radical change in a society or culture. In the political arena, it involves the forced overthrow of an old government and establishment of a completely new one.

rite of intensification A ritual that takes place during a crisis in the life of the group and serves to bind individuals together.

rite of passage A ritual that marks an important stage in an individual's life cycle, such as birth, marriage, and death.

sanction An externalized social control designed to encourage conformity to social norms.

secondary innovation The deliberate application or modification of an existing idea, method, or device.

self-awareness The ability to identify oneself as an individual, to reflect on oneself, and to evaluate oneself.

separation In a rite of passage, the ritual removal of the individual from society.

serial monogamy A marriage form in which a man or a woman marries or lives with a series of partners in succession.

shaman A person who enters an altered state of consciousness—at will—to contact and utilize an ordinarily hidden reality in order to acquire knowledge, power, and to help others.

signal An instinctive sound or gesture that has a natural or self-evident meaning.

silent trade A form of product exchange in which mutually distrusting ethnic groups avoid direct personal contact.

slash-and-burn cultivation An extensive form of horticulture in which the natural vegetation is cut, the slash is subsequently burned, and crops are then planted among the ashes; also known as swidden farming.

social class A category of individuals in a stratified society who enjoy equal or nearly equal prestige according to the system of evaluation.

social control External control through open coercion.

social mobility Upward or downward change in one's social class position in a stratified society.

social structure The rule-governed relationships—with all their rights and obligations—that hold members of a society together. This includes households, families, associations, and power relations, including politics.

society An organized group or groups of interdependent people who generally share a common territory, language, and culture and who act together for collective survival and well-being.

sociolinguistics The study of the relationship between language and society through examining how social categories (such as age, gender, ethnicity, religion, occupation, and class) influence the use and significance of distinctive styles of speech.

soft power Cooptive power that presses others through attraction and persuasion to change their ideas, beliefs, values, and behaviors.

species A population or group of populations having common attributes and the ability to interbreed and produce live, fertile offspring. Different species are reproductively isolated from one another.

spirituality Concern with the sacred, as distinguished from material matters. In contrast to religion, spirituality is often individual rather than collective and does not require a distinctive format or traditional organization.

state In anthropology, a political institution established to manage and defend a complex, socially stratified society occupying a defined territory.

stratified society A society in which people are hierarchically divided and ranked into social strata, or layers, and do not share equally in the basic resources that support survival, influence, and prestige.

structural power Power that organizes and orchestrates the systemic interaction within and among societies, directing economic and political forces on the one hand and ideological forces that shape public ideas, values, and beliefs on the other.

structural violence Physical and/or psychological harm (including repression, environmental destruction, poverty, hunger, illness, and premature death) caused by impersonal, exploitative, and unjust social, political, and economic systems.

subculture A distinctive set of ideas, values, and behavior patterns by which a group within a larger society operates, while still sharing common standards with that larger society.

superstructure A society's shared sense of identity and worldview. The collective body of ideas, beliefs, and values by which members of a society make sense of the world—its shape, challenges, and opportunities—and understand their place in it. This includes religion and national ideology.

symbol A mark, sound, gesture, motion, or other sign that is arbitrarily linked to something else and represents it in a meaningful way.

syncretism In acculturation, the creative blending of indigenous and foreign beliefs and practices into new cultural forms.

syntax The patterns or rules by which words are arranged into phrases and sentences.

taboo A prohibition, which, if not observed, leads to a penalty inflicted by magic, spiritual force, or religion.

tale A creative narrative that is recognized as fiction for entertainment but may also draw a moral or teach a practical lesson.

technology Tools and other material equipment, together with the knowledge of how to make and use them.

theory In science, an explanation of natural phenomena, supported by a reliable body of data.

tonal language A language in which the sound pitch of a spoken word is an essential part of its pronunciation and meaning.

tonality In music, scale systems and their modifications.

totemism The belief that people are related to particular animals, plants, or natural objects by virtue of descent from common ancestral spirits.

tradition Customary ideas and practices passed on from generation to generation, which in a modernizing society may form an obstacle to new ways of doing things.

transgender A person who crosses over or occupies an alternative position in the binary male–female gender construction.

transition In a rite of passage, isolation of the individual following separation and prior to incorporation into society.

tribe In anthropology, refers to a range of kin-ordered groups that are politically integrated by some unifying factor and whose members share a common ancestry, identity, culture, language, and territory.

unilineal descent Descent that establishes group membership exclusively through either the male or female line; also known as unilateral descent.

Upper Paleolithic The last part (10,000–40,000 years ago) of the Old Stone Age, featuring tool industries characterized by long slim blades and an explosion of creative symbolic forms.

urgent anthropology Ethnographic research that documents endangered cultures; also known as salvage ethnography.

whistled speech An exchange of whistled words using a phonetic emulation of the sounds produced in spoken voice; also known as whistled language.

witchcraft An explanation of events based on the belief that certain individuals possess an innate psychic power capable of causing harm, including sickness and death.

worldview The collective body of ideas that members of a culture generally share concerning the ultimate shape and substance of their reality.

writing system A set of visible or tactile signs used to represent units of language in a systematic way.

Bibliography

Abbot, E. (2001). *A history of celibacy*. Cambridge, MA: Da Capo.

Aberle, D. F., Bronfenbrenner, U., Hess, E. H., Miller, D. R., Schneider, D. H., & Spuhler, J. N. (1963). The incest taboo and the mating patterns of animals. *American Anthropologist 65*, 253–265.

Abu-Lughod, L. (1986). *Veiled sentiments: Honor and poetry in a Bedouin society*. Berkeley: University of California Press.

Adams, R.E.W. (1977). *Prehistoric Mesoamerica*. Boston: Little, Brown.

Adams, R. M. (1966). *The evolution of urban society*. Chicago: Aldine.

Adbusters. www.adbusters.org

Adherents. www.adherents.com

Adler, S. (1959). Darwin's illness. *Nature*, 1102–1103.

AIDS Epidemic Update. (2007), p. 7. Geneva: Joint United Nations Program on HIV/AIDS (USAID) and World Health Organization. www.unaids.org

Alemseged, Z., et al. (2006, September 21). *Nature 443*, 296–301.

Alland, A., Jr. (1970). *Adaptation in cultural evolution: An approach to medical anthropology*. New York: Columbia University Press.

Alland, A., Jr. (1971). *Human diversity*. New York: Columbia University Press.

Allen, J. L., & Shalinsky, A. C. (2004). *Student atlas of anthropology*. New York: McGraw-Hill.

Allen, J. S., & Cheer, S. M. (1996). The non-thrifty genotype. *Current Anthropology 37*, 831–842.

Alper, J. S., Ard, C., Asch, A., Beckwith, J., Conrad, P., & Geller, L. N. (Eds.). (2002). *The double-edged helix: Social implications of genetics in a diverse society*. Baltimore: Johns Hopkins University Press.

Alvard, M. S., & Kuznar, L. (2001). Deferred harvest: The transition from hunting to animal husbandry. *American Anthropologist 103* (2), 295–311.

Ambrose, S. H. (2001). Paleolithic technology and human evolution. *Science 291*, 1748–1753.

American Anthropological Association. (1998). Statement on "race." www.ameranthassn.org

American Anthropological Association. (2007). Executive board statement on the Human Terrain System Project. http://www.aaanet.org/pdf/EB_Resolution_110807.pdf

Amiran, R. (1965). The beginnings of pottery-making in the Near East. In F. R. Matson (Ed.), *Ceramics and man* (pp. 240–247). Viking Fund Publications in Anthropology, 41.

Anderson, A. (2002). Faunal collapse, landscape change, and settlement history in Remote Oceania. *World Archaeology 33* (3), 375–390.

Andrews, L. B., & Nelkin, D. (1996). The Bell Curve: A statement. *Science 271*, 13.

Angrosino, M. V. (2004). *Projects in ethnographic research*. Long Grove, IL: Waveland.

"A pocket guide to social media and kids." (2009, November 2). blog.nielsen.com.

Appadurai, A. (1990). Disjuncture and difference in the global cultural economy. *Public Culture 2*, 1–24.

Appadurai, A. (1996). *Modernity at large: Cultural dimensions of globalization*. Minneapolis: University of Minnesota Press.

Appenzeller, T. (1998). Art: Evolution or revolution? *Science 282*, 1451–1454.

Arctic Monitoring Assessment Project (AMAP). (2003). *AMAP assessment 2002: Human health in the Arctic*. Oslo: Author.

Armstrong, D. F., Stokoe, W. C., & Wilcox, S. E. (1993). Signs of the origin of syntax. *Current Anthropology 34*, 349–368.

Ashmore, W. (Ed.). (1981). *Lowland Maya settlement patterns*. Albuquerque: University of New Mexico Press.

Aureli, F., & de Waal, F.B.M. (2000). *Natural conflict resolution*. Berkeley: University of California Press.

Avedon, J. F. (1997). *In exile from the land of snows: The definitive account of the Dalai Lama and Tibet since the Chinese conquest*. New York: Harper.

"Average TV viewing for 2008–09 TV season at all-time high." (2009, November 10). blog.nielsen.com.

Bailey, R. C., & Aunger, R. (1989). Net hunters vs. archers: Variation in women's subsistence strategies in the Ituri forest. *Human Ecology 17*, 273–297.

Baker, P. (Ed.). (1978). *The biology of high altitude peoples*. London: Cambridge University Press.

Balikci, A. (1970). *The Netsilik Eskimo*. Garden City, NY: Natural History.

Balter, M. (1998). On world AIDS day, a shadow looms over southern Africa. *Science 282*, 1790.

Balter, M. (1998). Why settle down? The mystery of communities. *Science 282*, 1442–1444.

Balter, M. (2001). Did plaster hold Neolithic society together? *Science 294*, 2278–2281.

Balter, M. (2001). In search of the first Europeans. *Science 291*, 1724.

Banton, M. (1968). Voluntary association: Anthropological aspects. In *International encyclopedia of the social sciences* (Vol. 16, pp. 357–362). New York: Macmillan.

Barham, L. S. (1998). Possible early pigment use in South-Central Africa. *Current Anthropology 39*, 703–710.

Barnard, A. (1995). Monboddo's *Orang Outang* and the definition of man. In R. Corbey & B. Theunissen (Eds.), *Ape, man, apeman: Changing views since 1600* (pp. 71–85). Leiden: Department of Prehistory, Leiden University.

Barnouw, V. (1985). *Culture and personality* (4th ed.). Homewood, IL: Dorsey.

Barr, R. G. (1997, October). The crying game. *Natural History*, 47.

Barth, F. (1961). *Nomads of South Persia: The Basseri tribe of the Khamseh confederacy*. Boston: Little, Brown.

Barth, F. (1962). Nomadism in the mountain and plateau areas of Southwest Asia. *The problems of the arid zone* (pp. 341–355). Paris: UNESCO.

Bar-Yosef, O. (1986). The walls of Jericho: An alternative interpretation. *Current Anthropology 27*, 160.

Bar-Yosef, O., Vandermeesch, B., Arensburg, B., Belfer-Cohen, A., Goldberg, P., Laville, H., Meignen, L., Rak, Y., Speth, J. D., Tchernov, E., Tillier, A-M., & Weiner, S. (1992). The excavations in Kebara Cave, Mt. Carmel. *Current Anthropology 33*, 497–550.

Bascom, W. (1969). *The Yoruba of southwestern Nigeria*. New York: Holt, Rinehart & Winston.

Bates, D. G. (2001). *Human adaptive strategies: Ecology, culture, and politics* (2nd ed.). Boston: Allyn & Bacon.

Bates, D. G., & Plog, F. (1991). *Human adaptive strategies*. New York: McGraw-Hill.

Bayer, R. (1987). *Homosexuality and American psychiatry: The politics of diagnosis*. Princeton, NJ: Princeton University Press.

Becker, J. (2004, March). *National Geographic*, 90.

Bednarik, R. G. (1995). Concept-mediated marking in the Lower Paleolithic. *Current Anthropology 36*, 606.

Beeman, W. O. (2000). Introduction: Margaret Mead, cultural studies, and international understanding. In M. Mead & R. Métraux (Eds.), *The study of culture at a distance* (pp. xiv–xxxi). New York and Oxford: Berghahn.

Behrend, H., & Luig, U. (Eds.). (2000). *Spirit possession, modernity, and power in Africa*. Madison: University of Wisconsin Press.

Behrensmeyer, A. K., Todd, N. E., Potts, R., & McBrinn, G. E. (1997). Late Pliocene faunal turnover in the Turkana basin, Kenya, and Ethiopia. *Science 278*, 1589–1594.

Bekoff, M., et al. (Eds.). (2002). *The cognitive animal: Empirical and theoretical perspectives on animal cognition*. Cambridge, MA: MIT Press.

Belshaw, C. S. (1958). The significance of modern cults in Melanesian development. In W. Lessa & E. Z. Vogt (Eds.), *Reader in comparative religion: An anthropological approach*. New York: Harper & Row.

Benedict, R. (1934). *Patterns of culture*. Boston: Houghton Mifflin.

Bennett, M. R., Harris, J.W.K., Richmond, B. G., Braun, D. R., Mbua, E., Kiura, P., Olago, D., Kibunjia, M., Omuombo, C., Behrensmeyer, A. K., Huddart, D., & Gonzalez, S. (2009). Early hominim foot morphology based on 1.5-million-year-old footprints from Ileret, Kenya. *Science 323* (5918), 1197–1201.

Bennett, R. L., et al. (2002, April). Genetic counseling and screening of consanguineous couples and their offspring: Recommendations of the National Society of Genetic Counselors. *Journal of Genetic Counseling 11* (2), 97–119.

Bergendorff, S. (2009). *Simple lives, cultural complexity: Rethinking culture in terms of complexity theory*. Lanham, MD: Rowman & Littlefield.

Bermúdez de Castro, J. M., Arsuaga, J. L., Cabonell, E., Rosas, A., Martinez, I., & Mosquera, M. (1997). A hominid from the lower Pleistocene of Atapuerca, Spain: Possible ancestor to Neandertals and modern humans. *Science 276*, 1392–1395.

Bernard, H. R. (2002). *Research methods in anthropology: Qualitative and quantitative approaches* (3rd ed.). Walnut Creek, CA: Altamira.

Bernardi, B. (1985). *Age class systems: Social institutions and policies based on age*. New York: Cambridge University Press.

Berndt, R. M., & Berndt, C. H. (1989). *The speaking land: Myth and story in Aboriginal Australia*. New York: Penguin.

Bernstein, R. E., Child, P., Famous, P., & South, A. (1984). Darwin's illness: Chagas' disease resurgens. *Journal of the Royal Society of Medicine 77*, 608–609.

Berra, T. M. (1990). *Evolution and the myth of creationism.* Stanford, CA: Stanford University Press.

Betzig, L. (1989). Causes of conjugal dissolution: A cross-cultural study. *Current Anthropology 30*, 654–676.

Bicchieri, M. G. (Ed.). (1972). *Hunters and gatherers today: A socioeconomic study of eleven such cultures in the twentieth century.* New York: Holt, Rinehart & Winston.

Binford, L. R. (1972). *An archaeological perspective.* New York: Seminar.

Binford, L. R., & Chuan, K. H. (1985). Taphonomy at a distance: Zhoukoudian, the cave home of Beijing man? *Current Anthropology 26*, 413–442.

Birdsell, J. H. (1977). The recalibration of a paradigm for the first peopling of Greater Australia. In J. Allen, J. Golson, & R. Jones (Eds.), *Sunda and Sahul: Prehistoric studies in Southeast Asia, Melanesia, and Australia* (pp. 113–167). New York: Academic.

Blackless, M., et al. (2000). How sexually dimorphic are we? Review and synthesis. *American Journal of Human Biology 12*, 151–166.

Blakey, M. (2003). *African Burial Ground Project.* Department of Anthropology, College of William & Mary.

Blok, A. (1974). *The mafia of a Sicilian village 1860–1960.* New York: Harper & Row.

Blok, A. (1981). Rams and billy-goats: A key to the Mediterranean code of honour. *Man, New Series 16* (3), 427–440.

Blok, A. (1992). Beyond the bounds of anthropology. In J. Abbink & H. Vermeulen (Eds.), *History and culture: Essays on the work of Eric R. Wolf* (pp. 5–20). Amsterdam: Het Spinhuis.

Blumberg, R. L. (1991). *Gender, family, and the economy: The triple overlap.* Newbury Park, CA: Sage.

Blumer, M. A., & Byrne, R. (1991). The ecological genetics and domestication and the origins of agriculture. *Current Anthropology 32*, 30.

Boaretto, E., Wu, X., Yuan, J., Bar-Yosef, O., Chu, V., Pan, Y., Liu, K., Cohen, D., Jiao, T., Li, S., Gu, H., Goldberg, P., & Weiner, S. (2009). Radiocarbon dating of charcoal and bone collagen associated with early pottery at Yuchanyan Cave, Hunan Province, China. *Proceedings of the National Academy of Sciences, USA 106* (24), 9595–9600.

Boas, F. (1962). *Primitive art.* Gloucester, MA: Peter Smith.

Boas, F. (1966). *Race, language and culture.* New York: Free Press.

Bodley, J. H. (2007). *Anthropology and contemporary human problems* (5th ed.). Lanham, MD: Alta Mira.

Bodley, J. H. (2008). *Victims of progress* (5th ed.). Lanham, MD: Alta Mira.

Boehm, C. (1984). *Blood revenge.* Lawrence: University of Kansas Press.

Boehm, C. (2000). The evolution of moral communities. *School of American Research, 2000 Annual Report, 7.*

Bogucki, P. (1999). *The origins of human society.* Oxford, England: Blackwell.

Bohannan, P. (Ed.). (1967). *Law and warfare: Studies in the anthropology of conflict.* Garden City, NY: Natural History.

Bohannan, P., & Middleton, J. (Eds.). (1968). *Kinship and social organization.* Garden City, NY: Natural History.

Bohannan, P., & Middleton, J. (Eds.). (1968). *Marriage, family, and residence.* Garden City, NY: Natural History.

Bolinger, D. (1968). *Aspects of language.* New York: Harcourt.

Bongaarts, J. (1998). Demographic consequences of declining fertility. *Science 182*, 419.

Bonn-Muller, E. (2009). Oldest oil paintings: Bamiyan, Afghanistan. *Archaeology 62* (1).

Bonvillain, N. (2007). *Language, culture, and communication: The meaning of messages* (5th ed.). Upper Saddle River, NJ: Prentice-Hall.

Bordes, F. (1972). *A tale of two caves.* New York: Harper & Row.

Bornstein, M. H. (1975). The influence of visual perception on culture. *American Anthropologist 77* (4), 774–798.

Boshara, R. (2003, January/February). Wealth inequality: The $6,000 solution. *Atlantic Monthly.*

Bošković, A. (Ed.). (2009). *Other people's anthropologies: Ethnographic practice on the margins.* Oxford, England: Berghahn.

Bowen, J. R. (2004). *Religions in practice: An approach to the anthropology of religion* (3rd ed.). Boston: Allyn & Bacon.

Bowie, F. (2006). *The anthropology of religion: An introduction* (2nd ed.). Malden, MA: Blackwell.

Brace, C. L. (1981). Tales of the phylogenetic woods: The evolution and significance of phylogenetic trees. *American Journal of Physical Anthropology 56*, 411–429.

Brace, C. L. (1997). Cro-Magnons "R" us? *Anthropology Newsletter 38* (8), 1, 4.

Brace, C. L. (2000). *Evolution in an anthropological view.* Walnut Creek, CA: Altamira.

Brace, C. L., Nelson, H., & Korn, N. (1979). *Atlas of human evolution* (2nd ed.). New York: Holt, Rinehart & Winston.

Bradfield, R. M. (1998). *A natural history of associations* (2nd ed.). New York: International Universities Press.

Bradford, P. V., & Blume, H. (1992). *Ota Benga: The Pygmy in the zoo.* New York: St. Martin's.

Braidwood, R. J. (1960). The agricultural revolution. *Scientific American 203*, 130–141.

Braidwood, R. J. (1975). *Prehistoric men* (8th ed.). Glenview, IL: Scott, Foresman.

Brain, C. K. (1968). Who killed the Swartkrans apemen? *South African Museums Association Bulletin 9*, 127–139.

Brain, C. K. (1969). The contribution of Namib Desert Hottentots to an understanding of australopithecine bone accumulations. *Scientific Papers of the Namib Desert Research Station, 13.*

Branda, R. F., & Eatoil, J. W. (1978). Skin color and photolysis: An evolutionary hypothesis. *Science 201*, 625–626.

Braudel, F. (1979). *The structures of everyday life: Civilization and capitalism 15th–18th century* (vol. 1, pp. 163–167). New York: Harper & Row.

Brettell, C. B., & Sargent, C. F. (Eds.). (2000). *Gender in cross-cultural perspective* (3rd ed.). Upper Saddle River, NJ: Prentice-Hall.

Brew, J. O. (1968). *One hundred years of anthropology.* Cambridge, MA: Harvard University Press.

Brody, H. (1981). *Maps and dreams.* New York: Pantheon.

Broecker, W. S. (1992, April). Global warming on trial. *Natural History, 14.*

Brown, B., Walker, A., Ward, C. V., & Leakey, R. E. (1993). New *Australopithecus boisei* calvaria from East Lake Turkana, Kenya. *American Journal of Physical Anthropology 91*, 137–159.

Brown, D. E. (1991). *Human universals.* New York: McGraw-Hill.

Brown, P., et al. (2004). A new small-bodied hominin from the Late Pleistocene of Flores, Indonesia. *Nature 431*, 1055–1061.

Brues, A. M. (1977). *People and races.* New York: Macmillan.

Brunet, M., Beauvilain, A., Coppens, Y., Heintz, E., Moutaye, A. H., & Pilbeam, D. (1995). The first australopithecine 2,500 kilometers west of the Rift Valley (Chad). *Nature 16*, 378 (6554), 273–275.

Brunet, M., et al. (2002). A new hominid from the Upper Miocene of Chad, Central Africa. *Nature 418*, 145–151.

Buck, P. H. (1938). *Vikings of the Pacific.* Chicago: University Press of Chicago.

Buckland, T. J. (Ed.). (2007). *Dancing from past to present: Nation, culture, identities.* Madison: University of Wisconsin Press.

Burling, R. (1969). Linguistics and ethnographic description. *American Anthropologist 71*, 817–827.

Burling, R. (1970). *Man's many voices: Language in its cultural context.* New York: Holt, Rinehart & Winston.

Burling, R. (1993). Primate calls, human language, and nonverbal communication. *Current Anthropology 34*, 25–53.

Burling, R. (2005). *The talking ape: How language evolved.* Oxford: Oxford University Press.

Butanayev, V. (n.d.). *Xooray attari* [Xakas names]. Cited by Harrison, K. D. (2002). Naming practices and ethnic identity in Tuva. *Proceedings of the Chicago Linguistics Society 35* (2).

Butynski, T. M. (2001). Africa's great apes. In B. Beck et al. (Eds.), *Great apes and humans: The ethics of co-existence* (pp. 3–56). Washington, DC: Smithsonian Institution.

Butzer, K. (1971). *Environment and anthropology: An ecological approach to prehistory* (2nd ed.). Chicago: Aldine.

Byers, D. S. (Ed.). (1967). *The prehistory of the Tehuacan Valley: Vol. 1. Environment and subsistence.* Austin: University of Texas Press.

Cachel, S. (1997). Dietary shifts and the European Upper Paleolithic transition. *Current Anthropology 38*, 590.

Calloway, C. (1997). Introduction: Surviving the dark ages. In C. G. Calloway (Ed.), *After King Philip's war: Presence and persistence in Indian New England* (pp. 1–28). Hanover, NH: University Press of New England.

Cardarelli, F. (2003). *Encyclopaedia of scientific units, weights, and measures: Their SI equivalences and origins.* London: Springer.

Carneiro, R. L. (1970). A theory of the origin of the state. *Science 169*, 733–738.

Carneiro, R. L. (2003). *Evolutionism in cultural anthropology: A critical history.* Boulder, CO: Westview.

Caroulis, J. (1996). Food for thought. *Pennsylvania Gazette 95* (3),16.

Carroll, J. B. (Ed.). (1956). *Language, thought and reality: Selected writings of Benjamin Lee Whorf* (p. 148). Cambridge, MA: MIT Press.

Carroll, S. B. (2005). *Endless forms most beautiful: The new science of evo devo.* New York: Norton.

Carson, R. C., Butcher, J. N., & Coleman, J. C. (1990). *Abnormal psychology and modern life* (8th ed.). Glenview, IL: Scott Foresman.

Carsten, J. (Ed.). (2008). *Cultures of relatedness: New approaches to the study of kinship.* Cambridge, England: Cambridge University Press.

Cartmill, M. (1998). The gift of gab. *Discover 19* (11), 64.

Cashdan, E. (1989). Hunters and gatherers: Economic behavior in bands. In S. Plattner (Ed.), *Economic anthropology* (pp. 21–48). Stanford, CA: Stanford University Press.

Catford, J. C. (1988). *A practical introduction to phonetics.* Oxford, England: Clarendon.

Caton, S. C. (1999). *Lawrence of Arabia: A film's anthropology.* Berkeley: University of California Press.

Cavalieri, P., & Singer, P. (1994). *The Great Ape Project: Equality beyond humanity.* New York: St. Martin's.

Cavalli-Sforza, L. L. (1977). *Elements of human genetics.* Menlo Park, CA: Benjamin.

Centers for Disease Control and Prevention. (2009). Differences in prevalence of obesity among black, white, and Hispanic adults—United States, 2006–2008. *Morbidity and Mortality Weekly Report 58* (27), 740–744.

Chagnon, N. A. (1988). Life histories, blood revenge, and warfare in a tribal population. *Science 239*, 935–992.

Chagnon, N. A. (1988). *Yanomamo: The fierce people* (3rd ed.). New York: Holt, Rinehart & Winston.

Chambers, R. (1983). *Rural development: Putting the last first.* New York: Longman.

Chan, J.W.C., & Vernon, P. E. (1988). Individual differences among the peoples of China. In J. W. Berry (Ed.), *Human abilities in cultural context* (pp. 340–357). Cambridge, England: Cambridge University Press.

Chance, N. A. (1990). *The Iñupiat and Arctic Alaska: An ethnography of development.* New York: Harcourt.

Chang, K. C. (Ed.). (1968). *Settlement archaeology.* Palo Alto, CA: National.

Chang, L. (2005, June 9). A migrant worker sees rural home in new light. *Wall Street Journal.*

Charpentier, M.J.E., Van Horn, R. C., Altmann, J., & Alberts, S. C. (2008). *Proceeding of the National Academy of Sciences, USA.* doi: 10.1073/pnas.0711219105.

Chase, C. (1998). Hermaphrodites with attitude. *Gay and Lesbian Quarterly 4* (2), 189–211.

Chasin, B. H., & Franke, R. W. (1983). US farming: A world model? *Global Reporter 1* (2), 10.

Chatty, D. (1996). *Mobile pastoralists: Development planning and social change in Oman.* New York: Columbia University Press.

Cheater, A. (2005). *The anthropology of power.* London: Routledge.

Childe, V. G. (1951). *Man makes himself.* New York: New American Library. (orig. 1936)

Ciochon, R. L., & Fleagle, J. G. (Eds.). (1987). *Primate evolution and human origins.* Hawthorne, NY: Aldine.

Ciochon, R. L., & Fleagle, J. G. (1993). *The human evolution source book.* Englewood Cliffs, NJ: Prentice-Hall.

Clark, E. E. (1966). *Indian legends of the Pacific Northwest.* Berkeley: University of California Press.

Clark, G. (1967). *The stone age hunters.* New York: McGraw-Hill.

Clark, G. A. (1997). Neandertal genetics. *Science 277,* 1024.

Clark, G. A. (2002). Neandertal archaeology: Implications for our origins. *American Anthropologist 104* (1), 50–67.

Clark, W.E.L. (1960). *The antecedents of man.* Chicago: Quadrangle.

Clark, W.E.L. (1966). *History of the primates* (5th ed.). Chicago: University of Chicago Press.

Clark, W.E.L. (1967). *Man-apes or ape-men? The story of discoveries in Africa.* New York: Holt, Rinehart & Winston.

Clarke, R. J. (1998). First ever discovery of a well preserved skull and associated skeleton of *Australopithecus. South African Journal of Science 94,* 460–464.

Clarke, R. J., & Tobias, P. V. (1995). Sterkfontein member 2 foot bones of the oldest South African hominid. *Science 269,* 521–524.

Clay, J. W. (1996). What's a nation? In W. A. Haviland & R. J. Gordon (Eds.), *Talking about people* (2nd ed., p. 188). Mountain View, CA: Mayfield

Clottes, J., & Bennett, G. (2002). *World rock art* (conservation and cultural heritage series). San Francisco: Getty Trust Publication.

Coe, S. D. (1994). *America's first cuisines.* Austin: University of Texas Press.

Coe, S. D., & Coe, M. D. (1996). *The true history of chocolate.* New York: Thames and Hudson.

Coe, W. R. (1967). *Tikal: A handbook of the ancient Maya ruins.* Philadelphia: University of Pennsylvania Museum.

Coe, W. R., & Haviland, W. A. (1982). *Introduction to the archaeology of Tikal.* Philadelphia: University Museum.

Cohen, M. N. (1977). *The food crisis in prehistory.* New Haven, CT: Yale University Press.

Cohen, M. N. (1995). Anthropology and race: The Bell Curve phenomenon. *General Anthropology 2* (1), 1–4.

Cohen, M. N. (1998). *Culture of intolerance: Chauvinism, class, and racism in the United States.* New Haven, CT: Yale University Press.

Cohen, M. N., & Armelagos, G. J. (1984). *Paleopathology at the origins of agriculture.* Orlando: Academic.

Colborn, T., et al. (1997). *Our stolen future.* New York: Plume/Penguin.

Colburn, T., Dumanoski, D., & Myers, J. P. (1996). Hormonal sabotage. *Natural History 3,* 45–46.

Cole, J. W., & Wolf, E. R. (1999). *The hidden frontier: Ecology and ethnicity in an alpine valley* (with a new introduction). Berkeley: University of California Press.

Cole, S. (1975). *Leakey's luck: The life of Louis Seymour Bazett Leakey. 1903–1972.* New York: Harcourt Brace Jovanovich.

Collier, J., & Collier, M. (1986). *Visual anthropology: Photography as a research method.* Albuquerque: University of New Mexico Press.

Collier, J., Rosaldo, M. Z., & Yanagisako, S. (1982). Is there a family? New anthropological views. In B. Thorne & M. Yalom (Eds.), *Rethinking the family: Some feminist questions* (pp. 25–39). New York: Longman.

Collier, J. F., & Yanagisako, S. J. (Eds.). (1987). *Gender and kinship: Essays toward a unified analysis.* Stanford, CA: Stanford University Press.

Committee on the Elimination of Racial Discrimination, India. (2007, March). Consideration of reports submitted by states parties under Article 9 of the International Convention on the Elimination of All Forms of Racial Discrimination, 70th Session. www2.ohchr.org/english/bodies/cerd/cerds70.htm

Conard., N. J. (2009). A female figurine from the basal Aurignacian deposits of Hohle Fels Cave in southwestern Germany. *Nature 459* (7244), 248.

Conard, N. J., Malina, M., & Münzel, S. C. (2009). New flutes document the earliest musical tradition in southwestern Germany. *Nature.* doi:10.1038/nature08169.

Cone, M. (2005) *Silent snow: The slow poisoning of the Arctic.* New York: Grove.

Connelly, J. C. (1979). Hopi social organization. In A. Ortiz (Ed.), *Handbook of North American Indians, Vol. 9, Southwest* (pp. 539–553). Washington, DC: Smithsonian Institution.

Conroy, G. C. (1997). *Reconstructing human origins: A modern synthesis.* New York: Norton.

Coon, C. S. (1954). *The story of man.* New York: Knopf.

Coon, C. S. (1958). *Caravan: The story of the Middle East* (2nd ed.). New York: Holt, Rinehart & Winston.

Coon, C. S. (1962). *The origins of races.* New York: Knopf.

Coontz, S. (2005). *Marriage, a history: From obedience to intimacy, or how love conquered marriage.* New York: Viking Adult.

Cooper, A., Poinar, H. N., Pääbo, S., Radovci, C. J., Debénath, A., Caparros, M., Barroso-Ruiz, C., Bertranpetit, J., Nielsen-March, C., Hedges, R.E.M., & Sykes, B. (1997). Neanderthal genetics. *Science 277,* 1021–1024.

Coppa, A., et al. (2006). Early Neolithic tradition of dentistry. *Nature 440,* 755–756.

Coppens, Y., Howell, F. C., Isaac, G. L., & Leakey, R.E.F. (Eds.). (1976). *Earliest man and environments in the Lake Rudolf Basin: Stratigraphy, paleoecology, and evolution.* Chicago: University of Chicago Press.

Corballis, M. C. (2003). *From hand to mouth: The origins of human language.* Princeton, NJ: Princeton University Press.

Corbey, R. (1995). Introduction: Missing links, or the ape's place in nature. In R. Corbey & B. Theunissen (Eds.), *Ape, man, apeman: Changing views since 1600* (p.1). Leiden: Department of Prehistory, Leiden University.

Cornwell, T. (1995, November 10). Skeleton staff. *Times Higher Education,* 20. http://www.timeshighereducation.co.uk/story.asp?storyCode=96035&sectioncode=26

Corruccini, R. S. (1992). Metrical reconsideration of the Skhul IV and IX and Border Cave I crania in the context of modern human origins. *American Journal of Physical Anthropology 87,* 433–445.

Cotte, M. (2008). *Journal of Analytical Atomic Spectrometry.* doi: 10.1039/b801358f.

Cowgill, G. L. (1980). Letter. *Science 210,* 1305.

Crane, H. (2001). *Men in spirit: The masculinization of Taiwanese Buddhist nuns.* Doctoral dissertation, Brown University.

Crane, L. B., Yeager, E., & Whitman, R. L. (1981). *An introduction to linguistics.* Boston: Little, Brown.

Cretney, S. (2003). *Family law in the twentieth century: A history.* New York: Oxford University Press.

Crocker, W. H., & Crocker, J. G. (1994). *The Canela, bonding through kinship, ritual, and sex.* Fort Worth: Harcourt Brace.

Crocker, W. H., & Crocker, J. G. (2004). *The Canela: Kinship, ritual, and sex in an Amazonian tribe.* Belmont, CA: Wadsworth.

Cultural Survival Quarterly. (1991). *15* (4).

Dalton, G. (Ed.). (1967). *Tribal and peasant economics: Readings in economic anthropology.* Garden City, NY: Natural History.

Dalton, G. (1971). *Traditional tribal and peasant economies: An introductory survey of economic anthropology.* Reading, MA: Addison-Wesley.

Daniel, G. (1970). *The first civilizations: The archaeology of their origins.* New York: Apollo Editions.

Dalton, G. (1971). *Traditional tribal and peasant economics: An introductory survey of economic anthropology.* Reading, MA: Addison-Wesley.

Darwin, C. (1887). *Autobiography.* Reprinted in F. Darwin (Ed.), (1902), *The life and letters of Charles Darwin.* London: John Murray.

Darwin, C. (1936). *The descent of man and selection in relation to sex.* New York: Random House (Modern Library). (orig. 1871)

Darwin, C. (2007). *On the origin of species by means of natural selection, or the preservation of favoured races in the struggle for life.* New York: Cosimo. (orig. 1859)

Davenport, W. (1959). Linear descent and descent groups. *American Anthropologist 61,* 557–573.

Davies, G. (2005). *A history of money from the earliest times to present day* (3rd ed.). Cardiff: University of Wales Press.

Davies, J. B., et al. (2007). *The world distribution of household wealth.* University of California, Santa Cruz, Mapping Global Inequalities, Center for Global, International, and Regional Studies.

Davis, S. H. (1982). *Victims of the miracle.* Cambridge, England: Cambridge University Press.

Deetz, J. (1977). *In small things forgotten: The archaeology of early American life.* Garden City, NY: Anchor/Doubleday.

del Carmen Rodríguez Martínez, M., et al. (2006). Oldest writing in the New World. *Science 313* (5793), 1610–1614.

del Castillo, B. D. (1963). *The conquest of New Spain* (translation and introduction by J. M. Cohen). New York: Penguin.

Delson, E., Tattersal, I., Brooks, A., & Van Couvering, J. (1999). *Encyclopedia of human evolution and prehistory.* New York: Garland.

DeMello, M. (2000). *Bodies of inscription: A cultural history of the modern tattoo community.* Durham: Duke University Press.

De Mott, B. (1990). *The imperial middle: Why Americans can't think straight about class.* New York: Morrow.

d'Errico, F., Zilhão, J., Julien, M., Baffier, D., & Pelegrin, J. (1998). Neandertal acculturation in western Europe? *Current Anthropology 39,* 521.

Dettwyler, K. A. (1994). *Dancing skeletons: Life and death in West Africa.* Prospect Heights, IL: Waveland.

Dettwyler, K. A. (1997, October). When to wean. *Natural History,* 49.

DeVore, I. (Ed.). (1965). *Primate behavior: Field studies of monkeys and apes.* New York: Holt, Rinehart & Winston.

de Waal, F.B.M. (1998). Comment. *Current Anthropology 39,* 407.

de Waal, F.B.M. (2000). Primates—A natural heritage of conflict resolution. *Science 28,* 586–590.

de Waal, F.B.M. (2001). *The ape and the sushi master.* New York: Basic.

de Waal, F.B.M. (2001). Sing the song of evolution. *Natural History 110* (8), 77.

de Waal, F.B.M., & Johanowicz, D. L. (1993). Modification of reconciliation behavior through social experience: An experiment with two macaque species. *Child Development 64,* 897–908.

Diamond, J. (1996). Empire of uniformity. *Discover 17* (3), 83–84.

Diamond, J. (1997). *Guns, germs, and steel.* New York: Norton.

Diamond, J. (1998). Ants, crops, and history. *Science 281,* 1974–1975.

Diamond, J. (2005). *Collapse: How societies choose to fail or succeed.* New York: Penguin.

Dicks, B., et al. (2005). *Qualitative research and hypermedia: Ethnography for the digital age (New technologies for social research).* Thousand Oaks, CA: Sage.

Dillehay, T. D. (2001). *The settlement of the Americas.* New York: Basic.

Dirie, W., & Miller, C. (1998). *Desert flower: The extraordinary journey of a desert nomad.* New York: Morrow.

Dissanayake, E. (2000). Birth of the arts. *Natural History 109* (10), 89.

Dixon, J. E., Cann, J. R., & Renfrew, C. (1968). Obsidian and the origins of trade. *Scientific American 218,* 38–46.

Dobyns, H. F., Doughty, P. L., & Lasswell, H. D. (Eds.). (1971). *Peasants, power, and applied social change.* London: Sage.

Dobzhansky, T. (1962). *Mankind evolving.* New Haven, CT: Yale University Press.

Douglas, M. (1966). *Purity and danger: An analysis of concepts of pollution and taboo.* London: Routledge & Kegan Paul.

Dozier, E. (1970). *The Pueblo Indians of North America.* New York: Holt, Rinehart & Winston.

Draper, P. (1975). !Kung women: Contrasts in sexual egalitarianism in foraging and sedentary contexts. In R. Reiter (Ed.), *Toward an anthropology of women* (pp. 77–109). New York: Monthly Review.

Drewnowski, A., & Specter, S. E. (2004). Poverty and obesity: the role of energy density and energy costs. *American Journal of Clinical Nutrition 79* (1), 6–16.

Driver, H. (1964). *Indians of North America.* Chicago: University of Chicago Press.

Dubos, R. (1968). *So human an animal.* New York: Scribner.

Dumurat-Dreger, A. (1998, May/June). "Ambiguous sex" or ambivalent medicine? *Hastings Center Report 28* (3), 2435 (posted on the website for Intersex Society of North America: www.isna.org)

Dunbar, P. (2008, January 19). The pink vigilantes. www.dailymail.co.uk

Dundes, A. (1980). *Interpreting folklore.* Bloomington: Indiana University Press.

Durant, J. C. (2000, April 23). Everybody into the gene pool. *New York Times Book Review,* 11.

Duranti, A. (2001). Linguistic anthropology: History, ideas, and issues. In A. Duranti (Ed.), *Linguistic anthropology: A reader* (pp. 1–38). Oxford: Blackwell.

Durkheim, E. (1964). *The division of labor in society.* New York: Free Press. (orig. 1893)

Durkheim, E. (1965). *The elementary forms of the religious life.* New York: Free Press. (orig. 1912)

Durkheim, E., & Mauss, M. (1963). *Primitive classification.* Chicago: University of Chicago Press. (orig. 1902)

duToit, B. M. (1991). *Human sexuality: Cross cultural readings.* New York: McGraw-Hill.

Eastman, C. M. (1990). *Aspects of language and culture* (2nd ed.). Novato, CA: Chandler & Sharp.

Eaton, S. B., Konner, M., & Shostak, M. (1988). Stone-agers in the fast lane: Chronic degenerative diseases in evolutionary perspective. *American Journal of Medicine 84* (4), 739–749.

Edwards, J. (Ed.). (1999). *Technologies of procreation: Kinship in the age of assisted conception.* New York: Routledge.

Edwards, S. W. (1978). Nonutilitarian activities on the Lower Paleolithic: A look at the two kinds of evidence. *Current Anthropology 19* (l), 135–137.

Egan, T. (1999, February 28). The persistence of polygamy. *New York Times Magazine,* 52.

Ehrlich, P. R., & Ehrlich, A. H. (2008). *The dominant animal: Human evolution and the environment.* Washington, DC: Island.

Eiseley, L. (1958). *Darwin's century: Evolution and the men who discovered it.* New York: Doubleday.

Eisenstadt, S. N. (1956). *From generation to generation: Age groups and social structure.* New York: Free Press.

El Guindi, F. (2004). *Visual anthropology: Essential method and theory.* Walnut Creek, CA: Altamira.

Elkin, A. P. (1964). *The Australian Aborigines.* Garden City, NY: Doubleday/Anchor.

Ellis, C. (2006). *A dancing people: Powwow culture on the southern plains.* Lawrence: University Press of Kansas.

Ellison, P. T. (2003). *On fertile ground: A natural history of human reproduction.* Cambridge, MA: Harvard University Press.

Ember, C. R., & Ember, M. (1996). What have we learned from cross-cultural research? *General Anthropology 2* (2), 5.

Enard, W., et al. (2002). Molecular evolution of FOXP2, a gene involved in speech and language. *Nature 418,* 869–872.

Erickson, P. A., & Murphy, L. D. (2003). *A history of anthropological theory* (2nd ed.). Peterborough, Ontario: Broadview.

Errington, F. K., & Gewertz, D. B. (2001). *Cultural alternatives and a feminist anthropology: An analysis of culturally constructed gender interests in Papua New Guinea.* Cambridge, England, and New York: Cambridge University Press.

Ervin-Tripp, S. (1973). *Language acquisition and communicative choice.* Stanford, CA: Stanford University Press.

Esber, G. S. (1987). Designing Apache houses with Apaches. In R. M. Wulff & S. J. Fiske (Eds.), *Anthropological praxis: Translating knowledge into action* (pp. 187–196). Boulder, CO: Westview.

Evans-Pritchard, E. E. (1937). *Witchcraft, oracles and magic among the Azande.* London: Oxford University Press.

Evans-Pritchard, E. E. (1951). *Kinship and marriage among the Nuer.* New York: Oxford University Press.

Evans-Pritchard, E. E. (1968). *The Nuer: A description of the modes of livelihood and political institutions of a Nilotic people.* London: Oxford University Press.

Evershed, R. P., et al. (2008). Earliest date for milk use in the Near East and southeastern Europe linked to cattle herding. *Nature.* doi:10.1038/nature07180.

Fagan, B. M. (1995). *People of the earth* (8th ed.). New York: HarperCollins.

Fagan, B. M. (2000). *Ancient lives: An introduction to archaeology.* Englewood Cliffs, NJ: Prentice-Hall.

Fagan, B. M. (2005). *Archaeology: A brief introduction* (9th ed.). New York: Longman.

Fagan, B. M., Beck, C., & Silberman, N. A. (1998). *The Oxford companion to archaeology.* New York: Oxford University Press.

Falk, D. (1975). Comparative anatomy of the larynx in man and the chimpanzee: Implications for language in Neanderthal. *American Journal of Physical Anthropology 43* (1), 123–132.

Falk, D. (1989). Apelike endocast of "ape-man" Taung. *American Journal of Physical Anthropology 80,* 335–339.

Falk, D. (1993). A good brain is hard to cool. *Natural History 102* (8), 65.

Falk, D. (1993). Hominid paleoneurology. In R. L. Ciochon & J. G. Fleagle (Eds.), *The human evolution source book.* Englewood Cliffs, NJ: Prentice-Hall.

Falk, D. (2004). *Braindance: New discoveries about human origins and brain evolution—revised and updated.* Gainesville: University Press of Florida.

Farmer, P. (1992). *AIDS and accusation: Haiti and the geography of blame.* Berkeley: University of California Press.

Farmer, P. (1996). On suffering and structural violence: A view from below. *Daedelus 125* (1), 261–283.

Farmer, P. (2001). *Infections and inequalities: The modern plagues.* Berkeley: University of California Press.

Farmer, P. (2003). *Pathologies of power: Health, human rights, and the new war on the poor.* Berkeley: University of California Press.

Farmer, P. (2004, June). An anthropology of structural violence. *Current Anthropology 45,* 3.

Farnell, B. (1995). *Do you see what I mean? Plains Indian sign talk and the embodiment of action.* Austin: University of Texas Press.

Fausto-Sterling, A. (1993, March/April). The five sexes: Why male and female are not enough. *The Sciences 33* (2), 20–24.

Fausto-Sterling, A. (2000, July/August). The five sexes revisited. *The Sciences 40* (4), 19–24.

Fausto-Sterling, A. (2003, August 2). Personal e-mail communication.

Feder, K. L. (2008). *Frauds, myths, and mysteries: Science and pseudoscience in archaeology* (6th ed.). New York: McGraw-Hill.

Fedigan, L. M. (1992). *Primate paradigms: Sex roles and social bonds.* Chicago: University of Chicago Press.

"Female genital mutilation." (2000). Fact sheet no. 241. World Health Organization.

Fernandez-Carriba, S., & Loeches, A. (2001). Fruit smearing by captive chimpanzees: A newly observed food-processing behavior. *Current Anthropology 42,* 143–147.

Ferrie, H. (1997). An interview with C. Loring Brace. *Current Anthropology 38,* 851–869.

Field, L. W. (2004). Beyond "applied" anthropology. In T. Biolsi (Ed.), *A companion to the anthropology of American Indians* (pp. 472–489). Oxford: Blackwell.

Finkler, K. (2000). *Experiencing the new genetics: Family and kinship on the medical frontier.* Philadelphia: University of Pennsylvania Press.

"The first Americans, ca. 20,000 B.C." (1998). *Discover 19* (6), 24.

Firth, R. (1946). *Malay fishermen: Their peasant economy.* London: Kegan Paul.

Firth, R. (1952). *Elements of social organization.* London: Watts.

Firth, R. (1957). *Man and culture: An evaluation of Bronislaw Malinowski.* London: Routledge.

Firth, R. (Ed.). (1967). *Themes in economic anthropology.* London: Tavistock.

Fisher, R., & Ury, W. L. (1991). *Getting to yes: Negotiating agreement without giving in* (2nd ed.). Boston: Houghton Mifflin.

Flannery, K. V. (1973). The origins of agriculture. In B. J. Siegel, A. R. Beals, & S. A. Tyler (Eds.), *Annual Review of Anthropology* (Vol. 2, pp. 271–310). Palo Alto, CA: Annual Reviews.

Flannery, K. V. (Ed.). (1976). *The Mesoamerican village.* New York: Seminar.

Fleagle, J. (1998). *Primate adaptation and evolution.* New York: Academic.

Fogel, R, & Riquelme, M. A. (2005). *Enclave sorjero. Merma de soberania y pobreza.* Asuncion: Centro de Estudios Rurales Interdisciplinarias.

Folger, T. (1993). The naked and the bipedal. *Discover 14* (11), 34–35.

Food and Agriculture Organization (FAO), United Nations. (2009). *1.02 billion people hungry: One sixth of humanity undernourished—more than ever before.* http://www.fao.org/news/story/en/item/20568/icode/

Forbes, J. D. (1964). *The Indian in America's past.* Englewood Cliffs, NJ: Prentice-Hall.

Forbes International 500 List. (2008).

Forde, C. D. (1955). The Nupe. In D. Forde (Ed.), *Peoples of the Niger-Benue confluence.* London: International African Institute (Ethnographic Survey of Africa. Western Africa, part 10).

Forde, C. D. (1968). Double descent among the Yakö. In P. Bohannan & J. Middleton (Eds.), *Kinship and social organization* (pp. 179–191). Garden City, NY: Natural History.

Forste, R. (2008). *Prelude to marriage, or alternative to marriage? A social demographic look at cohabitation in the U.S.* Working paper. Social Science Electronic Publishing, Inc. http://papers.ssrn.com/sol3/papers.cfm?abstract_id=269172.

Fortes, M. (1950). Kinship and marriage among the Ashanti. In A. R. Radcliffe-Brown & C. D. Forde (Eds.), *African systems of kinship and marriage.* London: Oxford University Press.

Fortes, M. (1969). *Kinship and the social order: The legacy of Lewis Henry Morgan.* Chicago: Aldine.

Fortes, M., & Evans-Prichard, E. E. (Eds.). (1962). *African political systems.* London: Oxford University Press. (orig. 1940)

Fossey, D. (1983). *Gorillas in the mist.* Burlington, MA: Houghton Mifflin.

Foster, G. M. (1955). Peasant society and the image of the limited good. *American Anthropologist 67,* 293–315.

Fountain, H. (2000, January 30). Now the ancient ways are less mysterious. *New York Times,* 5.

"4.1 billion mobile phone subscribers world-wide." (2009, March 27). www.mocom2020.com/2009/03/41-billion-mobile-phone-subscribers-worldwide/

Fouts, R. S., & Waters, G. (2001). Chimpanzee sign language and Darwinian continuity: Evidence for a neurology continuity of language. *Neurological Research 23,* 787–794.

Fox, R. (1968). *Encounter with anthropology.* New York: Dell.

Fox, R. (1968). *Kinship and marriage in an anthropological perspective.* Baltimore: Penguin.

Fox, R. (1981, December 3). [Interview]. Coast Telecourses, Inc., Los Angeles.

Frake, C. O. (1992). Lessons of the Mayan sky. In A. F. Aveni (Ed.), *The sky in Mayan literature* (pp. 274–291). New York: Oxford University Press.

Fraser, D. (Ed.). (1966). *The many faces of primitive art: A critical anthology.* Englewood Cliffs, NJ: Prentice-Hall.

Frayer, D. W. (1981). Body size, weapon use, and natural selection in the European Upper Paleolithic and Mesolithic. *American Anthropologist 83,* 57–73.

Frazer, Sir J. G. (1961 reissue). *The new golden bough.* New York: Doubleday, Anchor.

Freeman, J. D. (1960). The Iban of western Borneo. In G. P. Murdock (Ed.), *Social structure in Southeast Asia.* Chicago: Quadrangle.

Freeman, L. G. (1992). *Ambrona and Torralba: New evidence and interpretation.* Paper presented at the 91st Annual Meeting, American Anthropological Association.

Fried, M. (1967). *The evolution of political society: An essay in political anthropology.* New York: Random House.

Fried, M., Harris, M., & Murphy, R. (1968). *War: The anthropology of armed conflict and aggression.* Garden City, NY: Natural History.

Friedl, E. (1975). *Women and men: An anthropologist's view.* New York: Holt, Rinehart & Winston.

Friedman, J. (Ed.). (2003). *Globalization, the state, and violence.* Walnut Creek, CA: Altamira.

Friedman, T. (2007, April). *New York Times.*

Frisch, R. (2002). *Female fertility and the body fat connection.* Chicago: University of Chicago Press.

Frye, D. P. (2000). Conflict management in cross-cultural perspective. In F. Aureli & F.B.M. de Waal (Eds.), *Natural conflict resolution* (pp. 334–351). Berkeley: University of California Press.

Furst, P. T. (1976). *Hallucinogens and culture* (p. 7). Novato, CA: Chandler & Sharp.

Gamble, C. (1986). *The Paleolithic settlement of Europe.* Cambridge, England: Cambridge University Press.

Gardner, R. A., Gardner, B. T., & Van Cantfort, T. E. (Eds.). (1989). *Teaching sign language to chimpanzees.* Albany: State University of New York Press.

Garn, S. M. (1970). *Human races* (3rd ed.). Springfield, IL: Thomas.

Gates, H. (1996). Buying brides in China—again. *Anthropology Today 12* (4), 10.

Geertz, C. (1965). The impact of the concept of culture on the concept of man. In J. R. Platt (Ed.), *New views of man.* Chicago: University of Chicago Press.

Geertz, C. (1973). *The interpretation of culture.* London: Hutchinson.

Geertz, C. (1984). Distinguished lecture: Anti anti-relativism. *American Anthropologist 86,* 263–278.

Geertz, C. (2004). Religion as a cultural system. In M. Banton (Ed.), *Anthropological approaches to the study of religion* (pp. 1–46). London: Routledge. (orig. 1966)

Gell, A. (1988). Technology and magic. *Anthropology Today 4* (2), 6–9.

"Gene study suggests Polynesians came from Taiwan." (2005, July 4). Reuters.

Gero, J. M., & Conkey, M. W. (Eds.). (1991). *Engendering archaeology: Women and prehistory.* New York: Wiley-Blackwell.

Gibbons, A. (1993). Where are new diseases born? *Science 261,* 680–681.

Gibbons, A. (1997). Ideas on human origins evolve at anthropology gathering. *Science 276,* 535–536.

Gibbons, A. (1998). Ancient island tools suggest *Homo erectus* was a seafarer. *Science 279,* 1635.

Gibbons, A. (2001). The riddle of coexistence. *Science 291,* 1726.

Gibbons, A. (2001). Studying humans—and their cousins and parasites. *Science 292,* 627.

Gibbs, J. L., Jr. (1965). The Kpelle of Liberia. In J. L. Gibbs, Jr. (Ed.), *Peoples of Africa* (pp. 216–218). New York: Holt, Rinehart & Winston.

Gibbs, J. L., Jr. (1983). [Interview]. *Faces of culture: Program 18.* Fountain Valley, CA: Coast Telecourses.

Giddens, A. (1990). *The consequences of modernity.* Stanford, CA: Stanford University Press.

Ginsburg, F. D., Abu-Lughod, L., & Larkin, B. (Eds.). (2009). *Media worlds: Anthropology on new terrain.* Berkeley: University of California Press.

Gladdol, D. (2006). *English next.* London: British Council.

Gledhill, J. (2000). *Power and its disguises: Anthropological perspectives on politics* (2nd ed.). Boulder, CO: Pluto.

Godfrey, T. (2000, December 27). Biotech threatening biodiversity. *Burlington Free Press,* 10A.

Godlier, M. (1971). Salt currency and the circulation of commodities among the Baruya of New Guinea. In G. Dalton (Ed.), *Studies in economic anthropology.* Washington, DC: American Anthropological Association (Anthropological Studies No. 7).

González, R. J. (2009). *American counterinsurgency: Human science and the human terrain.* Chicago: University of Chicago Press.

Goodall, J. (1986). *The chimpanzees of Gombe: Patterns of behavior.* Cambridge, MA: Belknap.

Goodall, J. (1990). *Through a window: My thirty years with the chimpanzees of Gombe.* Boston: Houghton Mifflin.

Goodall, J. (2000). *Reason for hope: A spiritual journey.* New York: Warner.

Goodenough, W. (Ed.). (1964). *Explorations in cultural anthropology: Essays in honor of George Murdock.* New York: McGraw–Hill.

Goodenough, W. (1965). Rethinking status and role: Toward a general model of the cultural organization of social relationships. In M. Benton (Ed.), *The relevance of models for social anthropology.* New York: Praeger.

Goodenough, W. H. (1970). *Description and comparison in cultural anthropology.* Chicago: Aldine.

Goodenough, W. H. (1990). Evolution of the human capacity for beliefs. *American Anthropologist 92,* 601.

Goodman, A., & Armelagos, G. J. (1985). Death and disease at Dr. Dickson's mounds. *Natural History 94* (9), 12–18.

Goodman, M., Bailey, W. J., Hayasaka, K., Stanhope, M. J., Slightom J., & Czelusniak, J. (1994). Molecular evidence on primate phylogeny from DNA sequences. *American Journal of Physical Anthropology 94,* 7.

Goodwin, R. (1999). *Personal relationships across cultures.* New York: Routledge.

Goody, J. (1969). *Comparative studies in kinship.* Stanford, CA: Stanford University Press.

Goody, J. (1976). *Production and reproduction: A comparative study of the domestic domain.* Cambridge, MA: Cambridge University Press.

Goody, J. (1983). *The development of the family and marriage in Europe.* Cambridge, MA: Cambridge University Press.

Gordon, R. (2000). *Eating disorders: Anatomy of a social epidemic* (2nd ed.). New York: Wiley-Blackwell.

Gordon, R., Lyons, H., & Lyons, A. (Eds.). (2010). *Fifty key anthropologists.* New York: Routledge.

Gordon, R. J. (1992). *The Bushman myth: The making of a Namibian underclass.* Boulder, CO: Westview.

Gordon, R. J., & Megitt, M. J. (1985). *Law and order in the New Guinea highlands.* Hanover, NH: University Press of New England.

Gough, K. (1959). The Nayars and the definition of marriage. *Journal of the Royal Anthropological Institute of Great Britain and Ireland 89,* 23–34.

Gould, S. J. (1983). *Hen's teeth and horses' toes.* New York: Norton.

Gould, S. J. (1985). *The flamingo's smile: Reflections in natural history.* New York: Norton.

Gould, S. J. (1989). *Wonderful life.* New York: Norton.

Gould, S. J. (1991). *Bully for brontosaurus.* New York: Norton.

Gould, S. J. (1994). The geometer of race. *Discover 15* (11), 65–69.

Gould, S. J. (1996). *Full house: The spread of excellence from Plato to Darwin.* New York: Harmony.

Gould, S. J. (1996). *The mismeasure of man* (2nd ed.). New York: Norton.

Gould, S. J. (2000). The narthex of San Marco and the pangenetic paradigm. *Natural History 109* (6), 29.

Gould, S. J. (2000). What does the dreaded "E" word mean anyway? *Natural History 109* (1), 34–36.

Graburn, N.H.H. (1969). *Eskimos without igloos: Social and economic development in Sugluk.* Boston: Little, Brown.

Graburn, N. H. (1971). *Readings in kinship and social structure.* New York: Harper & Row.

Graves, J. L. (2001). *The emperor's new clothes: Biological theories of race at the millennium.* New Brunswick, NJ: Rutgers University Press.

Graves, P. (1991). New models and metaphors for the Neanderthal debate. *Current Anthropology 32*(5), 513–543.

Gray, P. B. (2004, May). HIV and Islam: Is HIV prevalence lower among Muslims? *Social Science & Medicine 58* (9), 1751–1756.

Gray, P. M., Krause, B., Atema, J., Payne, R., Krumhansl, C., & Baptista, L. (2001). The music of nature and the nature of music. *Science 291,* 52.

Green, E. C. (1987). The planning of health education strategies in Swaziland, and the integration of modern and traditional health sectors in Swaziland. In R. M. Wulff & S. J. Fiske (Eds.), *Anthropological praxis: Translating knowledge into action* (pp. 15–25, 87–97). Boulder, CO: Westview.

Greenberg, J. H. (1968). *Anthropological linguistics: An introduction.* New York: Random House.

Greymorning, S. N. (2001). Reflections on the Arapaho Language Project or, when Bambi spoke Arapaho and other tales of Arapaho language revitalization efforts. In K. Hale & L. Hinton (Eds.), *The green book of language revitalization in practice* (pp. 287–297). New York: Academic.

Grine, F. E. (1993). Australopithecine taxonomy and phylogeny: Historical background and recent interpretation. In R. L. Ciochon & J. G. Fleagle (Eds.), *The human evolution source book.* Englewood Cliffs, NJ: Prentice-Hall.

Grivetti, L. E. (2005). From aphrodisiac to health food: A cultural history of chocolate. *Karger Gazette,* 68.

Grossman, J. (2002). Should the law be kinder to kissin' cousins? A genetic report should cause a rethinking of incest laws. *Find Law.* (accessed October 16, 2009)

Grün, R., & Thorne, A. (1997). Dating the Ngandong humans. *Science 276,* 1575.

Guthrie, S. (1993). *Faces in the clouds: A new theory of religions.* New York: Oxford University Press.

Gutin, J. A. (1995). Do Kenya tools root birth of modern thought in Africa? *Science 270,* 1118–1119.

Haeri, N. (1997). The reproduction of symbolic capital: Language, state and class in Egypt. *Current Anthropology 38,* 795–816.

Hafkin, N., & Bay, E. (Eds.). (1976). *Women in Africa.* Stanford, CA: Stanford University Press.

Hager, L. (1989). *The evolution of sex differences in the hominid bony pelvis.* Ph.D. dissertation, University of California, Berkeley.

Haglund, W. D., Conner, M., & Scott, D. D. (2001). The archaeology of contemporary mass graves. *Historical Archaeology 35* (1), 57–69.

Hahn, R. A. (1992). The state of federal health statistics on racial and ethnic groups. *Journal of the American Medica Association 267* (2), 268–271.

Hall, E. T. (1959). *The silent language.* Garden City, NY: Anchor/Doubleday.

Hall, E. T., & Hall, M. R. (1986). The sounds of silence. In E. Angeloni (Ed.), *Anthropology 86/87* (pp. 65–70). Guilford, CT: Dushkin.

Hallowell, A. I. (1955). *Culture and experience.* Philadelphia: University of Pennsylvania Press.

Halperin, R. H. (1994). *Cultural economies: Past and present.* Austin: University of Texas Press.

Halverson, J. (1989). Review of the book *Altamira Revisited and other essays on early art. American Antiquity 54,* 883.

Handwerk, B. (2005, March 8). King Tut not murdered violently, CT scans show. *National Geographic News,* 2.

Hannah, J. L. (1988). *Dance, sex and gender.* Chicago: University of Chicago Press.

Hanson, A. (1989). The making of the Maori: Culture invention and its logic. *American Anthropologist 91* (4), 890–902.

Harlow, H. F. (1962). Social deprivation in monkeys. *Scientific America 206,* 1–10.

Harner, M. (1980). *The way of the shaman: A guide to power and healing.* San Francisco: Harper & Row.

Harpending, H., & Cochran, G. (2002). In our genes. *Proceedings of the National Academy of Sciences, USA 99* (1), 10–12.

Harpending, J. H., & Harpending, H. C. (1995). Ancient differences in population can mimic a recent African origin of modern humans. *Current Anthropology 36,* 667–674.

Harris, M. (1965). The cultural ecology of India's sacred cattle. *Current Anthropology 7,* 51–66.

Harris, M. (1968). *The rise of anthropological theory: A history of theories of culture.* New York: Crowell.

Harris, M. (1979). *Cultural materialism: The struggle for a science of culture.* New York: Random House.

Harris, M. (1989). *Cows, pigs, wars, and witches: The riddles of culture.* New York: Vintage/Random House.

Harrison, G. G. (1975). Primary adult lactase deficiency: A problem in anthropological genetics. *American Anthropologist 77,* 815–819.

Harrison, K. D. (2008). *When languages die: The extinction of the world's languages and the erosion of human knowledge.* New York: Oxford University Press.

Harrison, K. D. *Pop!Tech 2008: Scarcity and abundance: Global and local trends in language extinction.* www.poptech.org/popcasts/k_david_harrison__poptech_2008

Hart, C. W., Pilling, A. R., & Goodale, J. (1988). *Tiwi of North Australia* (3rd ed.). New York: Holt, Rinehart & Winston.

Hart, D., & Sussman, R. W. (2005). *Man the hunted: Primates, predators, and human evolution.* Boulder, CO: Westview.

Hartwig, W. C. (2002). *The primate fossil record.* New York: Cambridge University Press.

Hartwig, W. C., & Doneski, K. (1998). Evolution of the hominid hand and toolmaking behavior. *American Journal of Physical Anthropology 106,* 401–402.

Hatch, E. (1983). *Culture and morality: The relativity of values in anthropology.* New York: Columbia University Press.

Hatcher, E. P. (1985). *Art as culture, an introduction to the anthropology of art.* New York: University Press of America.

Haviland, W. A. (1967). Stature at Tikal, Guatemala: Implications for ancient Maya, demography, and social organization. *American Antiquity 32,* 316–325.

Haviland, W. A. (1970). Tikal, Guatemala and Mesoamerican urbanism. *World Archaeology 2,* 186–198.

Haviland, W. A. (1972). A new look at Classic Maya social organization at Tikal. *Ceramica de Cultura Maya 8,* 1–16.

Haviland, W. A. (1974). Farming, seafaring and bilocal residence on the coast of Maine. *Man in the Northeast 6,* 31–44.

Haviland, W. A. (1997). Cleansing young minds, or what should we be doing in introductory anthropology? In C. P. Kottak, J. J. White, R. H. Furlow, & P. C. Rice (Eds.), *The teaching of anthropology: Problems, issues, and decisions* (p. 35). Mountain View, CA: Mayfield.

Haviland, W. A. (1997). The rise and fall of sexual inequality: Death and gender at Tikal, Guatemala. *Ancient Mesoamerica 8,* 1–12.

Haviland, W. A. (2002). Settlement, society and demography at Tikal. In J. Sabloff (Ed.), *Tikal.* Santa Fe: School of American Research.

Haviland, W. A. (2003). *Tikal, Guatemala: A Maya way to urbanism.* Paper prepared for 3rd INAH/Penn State Conference on Mesoamerican Urbanism.

Haviland, W. A., & Gordon, R. J. (Eds.). (1993). *Talking about people.* Mountain View, CA: Mayfield.

Haviland, W. A., et al. (1985). *Excavations in small residential groups of Tikal: Groups 4F-1 and 4F-2.* Philadelphia: University Museum.

Haviland, W. A., & Moholy-Nagy, H. (1992). Distinguishing the high and mighty from the hoi polloi at Tikal, Guatemala. In A. F. Chase & D. Z. Chase (Eds.), *Mesoamerican elites: An archaeological assessment.* Norman: Oklahoma University Press.

Haviland, W. A., & Power, M. W. (1994). *The original Vermonters: Native inhabitants, past and present* (2nd ed.). Hanover, NH: University Press of New England.

Hawkes, K., O'Connell, J. F., & Blurton Jones, N. G. (1997). Hadza women's time allocation, offspring, provisioning, and the evolution of long postmenopausal life spans. *Current Anthropology 38,* 551–577.

Hawks, J. (2006, July 21). Neandertal Genome Project. http://johnhawks.net/weblog.

"Hazardous waste trafficking." www.Choike.org

Heilbroner, R. L., & Thurow, L. C. (1981). *The economic problem* (6th ed.). Englewood Cliffs, NJ: Prentice-Hall.

Heitzman, J., & Wordem, R. L. (Eds.). (2006). *India: A country study* (sect. 2, 5th ed.). Washington, DC: Federal Research Division, Library of Congress.

Helm, J. (1962). The ecological approach in anthropology. *American Journal of Sociology 67,* 630–649.

Henry, D. O., et al. (2004). Human behavioral organization in the Middle Paleolithic: Were Neandertals different? *American Anthropologist 107* (1), 17–31.

Henry, J. (1974). A theory for an anthropological analysis of American culture. In J. G. Jorgensen & M. Truzzi (Eds.), *Anthropology and American life.* Englewood Cliffs, NJ: Prentice-Hall.

Herdt, G. (Ed.). (1996). *Third sex, third gender: Beyond sexual dimorphism in culture and history.* New York: Zone.

Herdt, G. H. (1993). Semen transactions in Sambia culture. In D. N. Suggs & A. W. Mirade (Eds.), *Culture and human sexuality* (pp. 298–327). Pacific Grove, CA: Brooks/Cole.

Herskovits, M. J. (1952). *Economic anthropology: A study in comparative economics* (2nd ed.). New York: Knopf.

Hertz, N. (2001). *The silent takeover: Global capitalism and the death of democracy.* New York: Arrow.

Hewes, G. W. (1973). Primate communication and the gestural origin of language. *Current Anthropology 14,* 5–24.

"Hidden apartheid: Caste discrimination against India's Untouchables." (2007). Human Rights Watch and the Center for Human Rights and Global Justice.

Himmelfarb, E. J. (2000, January/February). First alphabet found in Egypt. Newsbrief. *Archaeology 53* (1).

Hirsch, J. S., & Wardlow, H. (Eds.). (2006). *Modern loves: The anthropology of romantic courtship and companionate marriage.* Ann Arbor: University of Michigan Press.

Historical atlas of the twentieth century. http://users.erols.com/mwhite28/20centry.htm

Hitchcock, R. K., & Enghoff, M. (2004). *Capacity-building of first people of the Kalahari, Botswana: An evaluation.* Copenhagen: International Work Group for Indigenous Affairs.

Hodgen, M. (1964). *Early anthropology in the sixteenth and seventeenth centuries.* Philadelphia: University of Pennsylvania Press.

Hoebel, E. A. (1954). *The law of primitive man: A study in comparative legal dynamics.* Cambridge, MA: Harvard University Press.

Hoebel, E. A. (1958). *Man in the primitive world: An introduction to anthropology.* New York: McGraw-Hill.

Hoebel, E. A. (1960). *The Cheyennes: Indians of the Great Plains.* New York: Holt, Rinehart & Winston.

Holden, C. (1999). Ancient child burial uncovered in Portugal. *Science 283,* 169.

Hole, F. (1966). Investigating the origins of Mesopotamian civilization. *Science 153,* 605–611.

Hole, F., & Heizer, R. F. (1969). *An introduction to prehistoric archeology.* New York: Holt, Rinehart & Winston.

Holloway, R. L. (1980). The O. H. 7 (Olduvai Gorge, Tanzania) hominid partial brain endocast revisited. *American Journal of Physical Anthropology 53,* 267–274.

Holloway, R. L. (1981). The Indonesian *Homo erectus* brain endocast revisited. *American Journal of Physical Anthropology 55,* 503–521.

Holloway, R. L. (1981). Volumetric and asymmetry determinations on recent hominid endocasts: Spy I and II, Djebel Jhroud 1, and the Salb *Homo erectus* specimens, with some notes on Neanderthal brain size. *American Journal of Physical Anthropology 55,* 385–393.

Holloway, R. L., & de LaCoste-Lareymondie, M. C. (1982). Brain endocast asymmetry in pongids and hominids: Some preliminary findings on the paleontology of cerebral dominance. *American Journal of Physical Anthropology 58,* 101–110.

Holmes, L. D. (2000). *Paradise bent* (film review). *American Anthropologist 102* (3), 604–605.

Holy, L. (1996). *Anthropological perspectives on kinship.* London: Pluto.

Horst, H. A., & Miller, D. (Eds.). (2006). *The cell phone: An anthropology of communication.* New York: Berg.

Hostetler, J., & Huntington, G. (1971). *Children in Amish society.* New York: Holt, Rinehart & Winston.

Howell, F. C. (1970). *Early man.* New York: Time-Life.

Hrdy, S. B. (1999). Body fat and birth control. *Natural History 108* (8), 88.

Hsiaotung, F. (1939). *Peasant life in China.* London: Kegan, Paul.

Hsu, F. L. (1961). *Psychological anthropology: Approaches to culture and personality.* Homewood, IL: Dorsey.

Hsu, F.L.K. (1979). The cultural problems of the cultural anthropologist. *American Anthropologist 81,* 517–532.

Hubert, H., & Mauss, M. (1964). *Sacrifice.* Chicago: University of Chicago Press.

Human development report. (2002). *Deepening democracy in a fragmented world.* United Nations Development Program.

Hunger Project. (2003). www.thp.org

Hunt, R. C. (Ed.). (1967). *Personalities and cultures: Readings in psychological anthropology.* Garden City, NY: Natural History.

Hutter, M. (Ed.). (2003). *The family experience: A reader in cultural diversity* (4th ed.). Boston: Allyn & Bacon.

Hymes, D. (1964). *Language in culture and society: A reader in linguistics and anthropology.* New York: Harper & Row.

Hymes, D. (Ed.). (1972). *Reinventing anthropology.* New York: Pantheon. icasualties.org.

Hymes, D. (1974). *Foundations in sociolinguistics: An ethnographic approach.* Philadelphia: University of Pennsylvania Press.

Imanishi, K., & Asquith, P. (2002). *Japanese view of nature: The world of living things.* New York: Routledge/Curzon.

Inda, J. X., & Rosaldo, R. (Eds.). (2001). *The anthropology of globalization: A reader.* Malden, MA, and Oxford: Blackwell.

Ingmanson, E. J. (1998). Comment. *Current Anthropology 39,* 409.

Inkeles, A., & Levinson, D. J. (1954). National character: The study of modal personality and sociocultural systems. In G. Lindzey (Ed.), *Handbook of social psychology.* Reading, MA: Addison-Wesley.

International Lesbian, Gay, Bisexual, Trans and Intersex Association (ILGA). (2009). The *2009 report on state-sponsored homophobia.*

Internet World Stats. (2009). www.internetworldstats.com

"Interview with Laura Nader." (2000, November). *California Monthly.*

Inuit Tapiirit Katami. http://www.taprisat.ca/english-text/itk/departments/enviro/ncp

Irvine, M. (1999, November 24). Mom-and-pop houses grow rare. *Burlington Free Press.*

"Italy-Germany verbal war hots up." (2003, July 9). *Deccan Herald* (Bangalore, India).

"It's the law: Child labor protection." (1997, November/December). *Peace and Justice News,* 11.

Jacobs, S. E. (1994). Native American two-spirits. *Anthropology Newsletter 35* (8), 7.

Jacoby, R., & Glauberman, N. (Eds.). (1995). *The Bell Curve debate.* New York: Random House.

Jane Goodall Institute. http://www.janegoodall.org/jane/study-corner/Jane/bio.asp (accessed June 16, 2009)

Jennings, F. (1976). *The invasion of America.* New York: Norton.

Jennings, J. D. (1974). *Prehistory of North America* (2nd ed.). New York: McGraw-Hill.

Johansen, B. E. (2002). The Inuit's struggle with dioxins and other organic pollutants. *American Indian Quarterly 26* (3), 479–490.

Johanson, D., & Shreeve, J. (1989). *Lucy's child: The discovery of a human ancestor.* New York: Avon.

Johanson, D. C., & Edey, M. (1981). *Lucy, the beginnings of humankind.* New York: Simon & Schuster.

Johanson, D. C, Edgar, B., & Brill, D. (1996). *From Lucy to language.* New York: Simon & Schuster.

Johanson, D. C., & White, T. D. (1979). A systematic assessment of early African hominids. *Science 203,* 321–330.

Johanson, D. C., & Wong, K. (2009). *Lucy's legacy: The quest for human origins.* New York: Harmony.

John, V. (1971). Whose is the failure? In C. L. Brace, G. R. Gamble, & J. T. Bond (Eds.), *Race and intelligence.* Washington, DC: American Anthropological Association.

Johnson, A. (1989). Horticulturalists: Economic behavior in tribes. In S. Plattner (Ed.), *Economic anthropology* (pp. 49–77). Stanford, CA: Stanford University Press.

Johnson, A. W., & Earle, T. (1987). *The evolution of human societies, from foraging group to agrarian state.* Stanford, CA: Stanford University Press.

Johnson, D. (1996). Polygamists emerge from secrecy, seeking not just peace but respect. In W. A. Haviland & R. J. Gordon (Eds.), *Talking about people* (2nd ed., pp. 129–131). Mountain View, CA: Mayfield.

Johnson, N. B. (1984). Sex, color, and rites of passage in ethnographic research. *Human Organization 43* (2), 108–120.

Jolly, A. (1985). *The evolution of primate behavior* (2nd ed.). New York: Macmillan.

Jolly, A. (1991). Thinking like a vervet. *Science 251,* 574.

Jolly, C. J. (1970). The seed eaters: A new model of hominid differentiation based on a baboon analogy. *Man 5,* 5–26.

Jones, S. (2005). Transhumance re-examined. *Journal of the Royal Anthropological Institute 11* (4), 841–842.

Jones, S., Martin, R., & Pilbeam, D. (Eds.). (1994). *The Cambridge encyclopedia of human evolution.* New York: Cambridge University Press.

Jorgensen, J. (1972). *The sun dance religion.* Chicago: University of Chicago Press.

Joukowsky, M. A. (1980). *A complete field manual of archaeology: Tools and techniques of field work for archaeologists.* Englewood Cliffs, NJ: Prentice-Hall.

Kalwet, H. (1988). *Dreamtime and inner space: The world of the shaman.* New York: Random House.

Kaplan, D. (1972). *Culture theory.* Englewood Cliffs, NJ: Prentice-Hall (Foundations of Modern Anthropology).

Kaplan, D. (2000). The darker side of the original affluent society. *Journal of Anthropological Research 53*(3), 301–324.

Kaplan, M. (2008, August 5). Almost half of primate species face extinction. doi: 10.1038/news.2008.1013.

Karavani, I., & Smith, F. H. (2000). More on the Neanderthal problem: The Vindija case. *Current Anthropology 41,* 839.

Kedia, S., & Van Willigen, J. (2005). *Applied anthropology: Domains of application.* New York: Praeger.

Keen, B. (1971). *The Aztec image in western thought.* New Brunswick, NJ: Rutgers University Press.

Kehoe, A. (1989). *The ghost dance: Ethno-history and revitalization.* Fort Worth: Holt, Rinehart & Winston.

Kehoe, A. (2000). *Shamans and religion: An anthropological exploration in critical thinking.* Prospect Heights, IL: Waveland.

Keiser, L. (1991). *Friend by day, enemy by night: Organized vengeance in a Kohistani community.* Fort Worth: Holt, Rinehart & Winston.

Kelly, T. L. (2006). *Sadhus, the great renouncers.* Photography exhibit, Indigo Gallery, Naxal, Kathmandu, Nepal. www.asianart.com/exhibitions/sadhus/index.html

Kendall, L. (1990, October). In the company of witches. *Natural History,* 92.

Kennickell, A. B. (2003, November). *A rolling tide: Changes in the distribution of wealth in the U.S. 1989–2001.* Levy Economics Institute.

Kertzer, D. I. (1988). *Ritual, politics, and power.* New Haven, CT: Yale University Press.

Key, M. R. (1975). *Paralanguage and kinesics: Nonverbal communication.* Metuchen, NJ: Scarecrow.

Kidder, T. (2003). *Mountains beyond mountains: The quest of Dr. Paul Farmer, a man who would cure the world.* New York: Random House.

Kirkpatrick, R. C. (2000). The evolution of human homosexual behavior. *Current Anthropology 41,* 384.

Klass, M. (1995). *Ordered universes: Approaches to the anthropology of religion.* Boulder, CO: Westview.

Klass, M., & Weisgrau, M. (Eds.). (1999). *Across the boundaries of belief: Contemporary issues in the anthropology of religion.* Boulder, CO: Westview.

Klein, R. (2002). *The dawn of human culture.* New York: Wiley.

Klein, R. G., & Edgar, B. (2002). *The dawn of human culture.* New York: Wiley.

Kluckhohn, C. (1970). *Mirror for man.* Greenwich, CT: Fawcett.

Kluckhohn, C. (1994). Navajo witchcraft. *Papers of the Peabody Museum of American Archaeology and Ethnology 22* (2).

Knauft, B. M. (1991). Violence and sociality in human evolution. *Current Anthropology 32,* 391–409.

Koch, G. (1997). Songs, land rights, and archives in Australia. *Cultural Survival Quarterly 20* (4).

Komai, T., & Fukuoka, G. (1934, October). Postnatal growth disparity in monozygotic twins. *Journal of Heredity 25,* 423–430.

Konner, M., & Worthman, C. (1980). Nursing frequency, gonadal function, and birth spacing among !Kung hunter-gatherers. *Science 207,* 788–791.

Krader, L. (1968). *Formation of the state.* Englewood Cliffs, NJ: Prentice-Hall.

Krajick, K. (1998). Greenfarming by the Incas? *Science 281,* 323.

Kramer, P. A. (1998). The costs of human locomotion: Maternal investment in child transport. *American Journal of Physical Anthropology 107,* 71–85.

Kraybill, D. B. (2001). *The riddle of Amish culture.* Baltimore: Johns Hopkins University Press.

Kroeber, A. (1958). Totem and taboo: An ethnologic psycho-analysis. In W. Lessa & E. Z. Vogt (Eds.), *Reader in comparative religion: An anthropological approach.* New York: Harper & Row.

Kroeber, A. L. (1939). Cultural and natural areas of native North America. *American Archaeology and Ethnology* (Vol. 38). Berkeley: University of California Press.

Kroeber, A. L. (1963). *Anthropology: Cultural processes and patterns.* New York: Harcourt.

Kroeber, A. L., & Kluckhohn, C. (1952). *Culture: A critical review of concepts and definitions.* Cambridge, MA: Harvard University Press (*Papers of the Peabody Museum of American Archaeology and Ethnology, 47*).

Kruger, J., et al. (2005, December). Egocentrism over e-mail: Can people communicate as well as they think? *Journal of Personality and Social Psychology 89* (6), 925–936.

Kummer, H. (1971). *Primate societies: Group techniques of ecological adaptation.* Chicago: Aldine.

Kunnie, J. (2003). Africa's fast growing indigenous churches. http://coh.arizona.edu/newandnotable/kunnie/kunnie.html

Kunnie, J. (2007). *Umoya: The spirit in Africa.* Self-produced DVD, available at www.coh.arizona.edu/aas/aas.htm

Kuper, H. (1965). The Swazi of Swaziland. In J. L. Gibbs (Ed.), *Peoples of Africa* (pp. 479–511). New York: Holt, Rinehart & Winston.

Kurth, P. (1998, October 14). Capital crimes. *Seven Days,* 7.

Kurtz, D. V. (2001). *Political anthropology: Paradigms and power.* Boulder, CO: Westview.

Kushner, G. (1969). *Anthropology of complex societies.* Stanford, CA: Stanford University Press.

LaFont, S. (Ed.). (2003). *Constructing sexualities: Readings in sexuality, gender, and culture.* Upper Saddle River, NJ: Prentice-Hall.

Lakoff, R. T. (2004). *Language and woman's place.* M. Bucholtz (Ed.). New York: Oxford University Press.

Lambek, M. (2002). *A reader in the anthropology of religion.* London: Blackwell.

Lancaster, J. B. (1975). *Primate behavior and the emergence of human culture.* New York: Holt, Rinehart & Winston.

Landau, M. (1991). *Narratives of human evolution.* New Haven, CT: Yale University Press.

Lang, I. A., et al. (2008). Association of urinary bisphenol A concentration with medical disorders and laboratory abnormalities in adults. *Journal of the American Medical Association 300* (11), 1303–1310.

Langan, P., & Harlow, C. (1994). *Child rape victims, 1992.* Washington, DC: Bureau of Justice Statistics, U.S. Department of Justice.

Lanning, E. P. (1967). *Peru before the Incas.* Englewood Cliffs, NJ: Prentice-Hall.

Larsen, C. S., Matter, R. M., & Gebo, D. L. (1998). *Human origins: The fossil record.* Long Grove, IL: Waveland.

Larsen, J. (2006, July 28). *Setting the record straight.* Earth Policy Institute, Eco-economy updates.

Lawler, A. (2001). Writing gets a rewrite. *Science 292,* 2419.

Layton, R. (1991). *The anthropology of art* (2nd ed.). Cambridge, MA: Cambridge University Press.

Leach, E. (1961). *Rethinking anthropology.* London: Athione.

Leach, E. (1962). The determinants of differential cross-cousin marriage. *Man 62,* 238.

Leach, E. (1962). On certain unconsidered aspects of double descent systems. *Man 214,* 13–34.

Leach, E. (1964). Anthropological aspects of language: Animal categories and verbal abuse. In W. Lessa & E. Vogt (Eds.), *Reader in comparative religion* (4th ed.). New York: Harper & Row.

Leach, E. (1982). *Social anthropology.* Glasgow: Fontana.

Leacock, E. (1981). *Myths of male dominance: Collected articles on women cross culturally.* New York: Monthly Review.

Leacock, E. (1981). Women's status in egalitarian society: Implications for social evolution. In *Myths of male dominance: Collected articles on women cross culturally*. New York: Monthly Review.

Leakey, L.S.B. (1965). *Olduvai Gorge, 1951–1961* (Vol. 1). London: Cambridge University Press.

Leakey, L.S.B., Tobias, P. B., & Napier, J. R. (1964). A new species of the genus *Homo* from Olduvai Gorge. *Nature 202*, 7–9.

Leakey, M. D. (1971). *Olduvai Gorge: Excavations in Beds I and II. 1960–1963*. London and New York: Cambridge University Press.

Leakey, M. G., Spoor, F., Brown, F. H., Gathogo, P. N., Kiare, C., Leakey, L. N., & McDougal, I. (2001). New hominin genus from eastern Africa shows diverse middle Pliocene lineages. *Nature 410*, 433–440.

Leap, W. L. (1987). Tribally controlled culture change: The Northern Ute language revival project. In R. M. Wulff & S. J. Fiske (Eds.), *Anthropological praxis: Translating knowledge into action* (pp. 197–211). Boulder, CO: Westview.

Leavitt, G. C. (1990). Sociobiological explanations of incest avoidance: A critical review of evidential claims. *American Anthropologist 92*, 982.

Leclerc-Madlala, S. (2002). Bodies and politics: Healing rituals in the democratic South Africa. In V. Faure (Ed.), *Les cahiers de l'IFAS*, No. 2. Johannesburg: French Institute.

Lee, R. B. (1993). *The Dobe Ju/'hoansi*. Ft. Worth: Harcourt Brace.

Lee, R. B., & Daly, R. H. (1999). *The Cambridge encyclopedia of hunters and gatherers*. New York: Cambridge University Press.

Lee, R. B., & DeVore, I. (Eds.). (1968). *Man the hunter*. Chicago: Aldine.

Lees, R. (1953). The basis of glottochronology. *Language 29*, 113–127.

Lehman, E. C., Jr. (2002, Fall). Women's path into the ministry. *Pulpit & Pew Research Reports 1*, 4.

Lehmann, A. C., & Myers, J. E. (Eds.). (2000). *Magic, witchcraft, and religion: An anthropological study of the supernatural* (5th ed.). Mountain View, CA: Mayfield.

Lehmann, J., & Joseph, S. (2009). *Biochar for environmental management: Science and technology*. London: Earthscan.

Leigh, S. R., & Park, P. B. (1998). Evolution of human growth prolongation. *American Journal of Physical Anthropology 107*, 331–350.

Leinhardt, G. (1964). *Social anthropology*. London: Oxford University Press.

LeMay, M. (1975). The language capability of Neanderthal man. *American Journal of Physical Anthropology 43* (1), 9–14.

Lenski, G. (1966). *Power and privilege: A theory of social stratification*. New York: McGraw-Hill.

Leroi-Gourhan, A. (1968). The evolution of Paleolithic art. *Scientific American 218*, 58ff.

Lestel, D. (1998). How chimpanzees have domesticated humans. *Anthropology Today 12* (3).

Leth, P. M. (2007). The use of CT scanning in forensic autopsy. *Forensic Science, Medicine, and Pathology 3* (1), 65–69.

Levine, N. E., & Silk, J. B. (1997). Why polyandry fails. *Current Anthropology 38*, 375–398.

Levine, R. A. (2007). Ethnographic studies of childhood: A historical overview. *American Anthropologist 109* (2), 247–260.

Lévi-Strauss, C. (1963). The sorcerer and his magic. In *Structural anthropology*. New York: Basic.

Lévi-Strauss, C. (1969). *The raw and the cooked*. New York: Harper & Row.

Lewellen, T. C. (2002). *The anthropology of globalization: Cultural anthropology enters the 21st century*. Westport, CT: Greenwood.

Lewin, R. (1987). Four legs bad, two legs good. *Science 235*, 969.

Lewin, R. (1993). Paleolithic paint job. *Discover 14* (7), 64–70.

Lewis, I. M. (1976). *Social anthropology in perspective*. Harmondsworth, England: Penguin.

Lewis-Williams, J. D. (1990). *Discovering southern African rock art*. Cape Town and Johannesburg: David Philip.

Lewis-Williams, J. D. (1997). Agency, art, and altered consciousness: A motif in French (Quercy) Upper Paleolithic parietal art. *Antiquity 71*, 810–830.

Lewis-Williams, J. D., & Dowson, T. A. (1988). Signs of all times: Entoptic phenomena in Upper Paleolithic art. *Current Anthropology 29*, 201–245.

Lewis-Williams, J. D., & Dowson, T. A. (1993). On vision and power in the Neolithic: Evidence from the decorated monuments. *Current Anthropology 34*, 55–65.

Lewis-Williams, J. D., Dowson, T. A., & Deacon, J. (1993). Rock art and changing perceptions of Southern Africa's past: Ezeljagdspoort reviewed. *Antiquity 67*, 273–291.

Lewontin, R. C. (1972). The apportionment of human diversity. In T. Dobzhansky et al. (Eds.), *Evolutionary biology* (pp. 381–398). New York: Plenum.

Lewontin, R. C., Rose, S., & Kamin, L. J. (1984). *Not in our genes*. New York: Pantheon.

Li, X., Harbottle, G., Zhang, J., & Wang, C. (2003). The earliest writing? Sign use in the seventh millennium bc at Jiahu, Henan Province, China. *Antiquity 77*, 31–44.

Lieberman, P. (2006). *Toward an evolutionary biology of language*. Cambridge, MA: Belknap.

Lindenbaum, S. (1978). *Kuru sorcery: Disease and danger in the New Guinea highlands*. New York: McGraw-Hill.

Lindstrom, L. (1993). *Cargo cult: Strange stories of desire from Melanesia and beyond*. Honolulu: University of Hawaii Press.

Little, K. L. (1973). *African women in towns: An aspect of Africa's social revolution*. New York: Cambridge University Press.

Littlewood, R. (2004). Commentary: Globalization, culture, body image, and eating disorders. *Culture, Medicine, and Psychiatry 28* (4), 597–602.

Livingstone, F. B. (1973). The distribution of abnormal hemoglobin genes and their significance for human evolution. In C. Loring Brace & J. Metress (Eds.), *Man in evolutionary perspective*. New York: Wiley.

Living Tongues. www.livingtongues.org/background.html

Lloyd, C. B. (Ed.). (2005). *Growing up global: The changing transitions to adulthood in developing countries* (pp. 450–453). Washington, DC: National Academies Press, Committee on Population, National Research Council, and Institute of Medicine of the National Academies.

Lock, M. (2001). *Twice dead: Organ transplants and the reinvention of death*. Berkeley: University of California Press.

Lorenzo, C., Carretero, J. M., Arsuaga, J. L., Gracia, A., & Martinez, I. (1998). Intrapopulational body size variation and cranial capacity variation in middle Pleistocene humans: The Sima de los Huesos sample (Sierra de Atapuerca, Spain). *American Journal of Physical Anthropology 106*, 19–33.

Loubser, J.H.N. (2003). *Archaeology: The comic*. Lanham, MD: Altamira.

Louckey, J., & Carlsen, R. (1991). Massacre in Santiago Atitlán. *Cultural Survival Quarterly 15* (3), 70.

Louie, A. (2004). *Chineseness across borders: Renegotiating Chinese identities in China and the United States*. Durham and London: Duke University Press.

Lounsbury, F. (1964). The structural analysis of kinship semantics. In H. G. Lunt (Ed.), *Proceedings of the Ninth International Congress of Linguists*. The Hague: Mouton.

Lovejoy, C. O. (1981). Origin of man. *Science 211*, 341–350.

Lowie, R. H. (1948). *Social organization*. New York: Holt, Rinehart & Winston.

Lowie, R. H. (1956). *Crow Indians*. New York: Holt, Rinehart & Winston. (orig. 1935)

Lucy, J. A. (1997). Linguistic relativity. *Annual Review of Anthropology 26*, 291–312.

Luhrmann, T. M. (2001). *Of two minds: An anthropologist looks at American psychiatry*. New York: Vintage.

Lurie, N. O. (1973). Action anthropology and the American Indian. In *Anthropology and the American Indian: A symposium*. San Francisco: Indian Historical.

MacCormack, C. P. (1977). Biological events and cultural control. *Signs 3*, 93–100.

MacLarnon, A. M., & Hewitt, G. P. (1999). The evolution of human speech: The role of enhanced breathing control. *American Journal of Physical Anthropology 109*, 341–363.

MacNeish, R. S. (1992). *The origins of agriculture and settled life*. Norman: University of Oklahoma Press.

"Madison Avenue relevance." (1999). *Anthropology Newsletter 40* (4), 32.

Mair, L. (1957). *An introduction to social anthropology*. London: Oxford University Press.

Mair, L. (1969). *Witchcraft*. New York: McGraw-Hill.

Mair, L. (1971). *Marriage*. Baltimore: Penguin.

Malefijt, A. de W. (1969). *Religion and culture: An introduction to anthropology of religion*. London: Macmillan.

Malinowski, B. (1945). *The dynamics of culture change: An inquiry into race relations in Africa*. New Haven, CT: Yale University Press.

Malinowski, B. (1951). *Crime and custom in savage society*. London: Routledge.

Malinowski, B. (1954). *Magic, science, and religion*. Garden City, NY: Doubleday.

Malinowski, B. (1961). *Argonauts of the western Pacific*. New York: Dutton. (orig. 1922)

Mann, A., Lampl, M., & Monge, J. (1990). Patterns of ontogeny in human evolution: Evidence from dental development. *Yearbook of Physical Anthropology 33*, 111–150.

Mann, C. C. (2000). Misconduct alleged in Yanomamo studies. *Science 289* (2), 253.

Mann, C. C. (2002). The real dirt on rainforest fertility. *Science 297*, 920–923.

Mann, C. C. (2005). *1491: New revelations of the Americas before Columbus*. New York: Knopf.

Marcus, G. (1995). Ethnography in/of the world system: The emergence of multi-sited ethnography. *Annual Review of Anthropology 24*, 95–117.

Marcus, J., & Flannery, K. V. (1996). *Zapotec civilization: How urban society evolved in Mexico's Oaxaca Valley*. New York: Thames & Hudson.

Marks, J. (1995). *Human biodiversity: Genes, race and history*. Hawthorne, NY: Aldine.

Marks, J. (2000, April 8). A feckless quest for the basketball gene. *New York Times*.

Marks, J. (2002). *What it means to be 98 percent chimpanzee: Apes, people, and their genes*. Berkeley: University of California Press.

Marks, J. (2009). *Why I am not a scientist: Anthropology and modern knowledge*. Berkeley: University of California Press.

Marsella, A. J. (1982). Pulling it together: Discussion and comments. In S. Pastner & W. A. Haviland (Eds.), *Confronting the creationists* (pp. 79–80). *Northeastern Anthropological Association, Occasional Proceedings 1*.

Marsella, A. J., & White, G. (1982). *Cultural conceptions of mental health and therapy*. New York: Springer.

Marshack, A. (1976). Some implications of the Paleolithic symbolic evidence for the origin of language. *Current Anthropology 17* (2), 274–282.

Marshack, A. (1989). Evolution of the human capacity: The symbolic evidence. *Yearbook of Physical Anthropology 32*, 1–34.

Marshall, E. (2001). Preclovis sites fight for acceptance. *Science 291*, 1732.

Marshall, L. (1961). Sharing, talking and giving: Relief of social tensions among !Kung bushmen. *Africa 31*, 231–249.

Marshall, M. (1990). Two tales from the Trukese taproom. In P. R. DeVita (Ed.), *The humbled anthropologist* (pp. 12–17). Belmont, CA: Wadsworth.

Martin, E. (1994). *Flexible bodies: Tracking immunity in American culture—from the days of polio to the age of AIDS*. Boston: Beacon.

Martin, E. (1999). Flexible survivors. *Anthropology News 40* (6), 5–7.

Martorell, R. (1988). Body size, adaptation, and function. *GDP*, 335–347.

Mascia-Lees, F. E., & Black, N. J. (2000). *Gender and anthropology*. Prospect Heights, IL: Waveland.

Mason, J. A. (1957). *The ancient civilizations of Peru*. Baltimore: Penguin.

Mathieu, C. (2003). *A history and anthropological study of the ancient kingdoms of the Sino-Tibetan borderland—Naxi and Mosuo*. New York: Mellen.

Matthews, G. (2006). Happiness and the pursuit of a life worth living: An anthropological approach. In Y.-K. Ng & L. S. Ho (Eds.), *Happiness and public policy* (pp. 147–168). Hampshire, England: Palgrave Macmillan.

Mauss, M. (2000). *The gift: The form and reason for exchange in archaic societies* (translation by W. D. Halls and foreword by M. Douglas). New York: Norton.

Maybury-Lewis, D. (1960). Parallel descent and the Apinaye anomaly. *Southwestern Journal of Anthropology 16*, 191–216.

Maybury-Lewis, D. (1984). The prospects for plural societies. *1982 Proceedings of the American Ethnological Society*.

Maybury-Lewis, D. (1993, fall). A new world dilemma: The Indian question in the Americas. *Symbols*, 17–23.

Maybury-Lewis, D. (2001). *Indigenous peoples, ethnic groups, and the state* (2nd ed.). Boston: Allyn & Bacon.

Maybury-Lewis, D.H.P. (1993). A special sort of pleading. In W. A. Haviland & R. J. Gordon (Eds.), *Talking about people* (2nd ed., p. 17). Mountain View, CA: Mayfield.

Mayo Clinic. http://www.mayoclinic.com/

Mayr, E., & Diamond, J. (2002). *What evolution is*. New York: Basic.

McBride, B. (1980). *Eric. R. Wolf interview. Between subjectivity and objectivity*. Unpublished masters thesis, anthropology department, Columbia University.

McCorriston, J., & Hole, F. (1991). The ecology of seasonal stress and the origins of agriculture in the Near East. *American Anthropologist 93*, 46–69.

McDermott, L. (1996). Self-representation in Upper Paleolithic female figurines. *Current Anthropology 37*, 227–276.

McElroy, A., & Townsend, P. K. (2003). *Medical anthropology in ecological perspective*. Boulder, CO: Westview.

McFate, M. (2007). *Role and effectiveness of sociocultural knowledge for counterinsurgency*. Alexandria, VA: Institute for Defense Analysis.

McFee, M. (1972). *Modern Blackfeet: Montanans on a reservation*. New York: Holt, Rinehart & Winston.

McHenry, H. (1975). Fossils and the mosaic nature of human evolution. *Science 190*, 524–431.

McHenry, H. M. (1992). Body size and proportions in early hominids. *American Journal of Physical Anthropology 87*, 407–431.

McKenna, J. J. (1999). Co-sleeping and SIDS. In W. Trevathan, E. O. Smith, & J. J. McKenna (Eds.), *Evolutionary medicine*. London: Oxford University Press.

McKenna, J. J. (2002, September–October). Breast-feeding and bedsharing. *Mothering*, 28–37.

McKenna, J. J., & McDade, T. (2005, June). Why babies should never sleep alone: A review of the co-sleeping controversy in relation to SIDS, bed-sharing, and breast feeding. *Pediatric Respiratory Reviews 6* (2), 134–152.

McNeill, W. (1992). *Plagues and people*. New York: Anchor.

Mead, A.T.P. (1996). Genealogy, sacredness, and the commodities market. *Cultural Survival Quarterly 20* (2).

Mead, M. (1928). *Coming of age in Samoa: A psychological study of primitive youth for western civilization*. New York: Morrow.

Mead, M. (1960). Anthropology among the sciences. *American Anthropologist 63*, 475–482.

Mead, M. (1963). *Sex and temperament in three primitive societies* (3rd ed.). New York: Morrow. (orig. 1935)

Mead, M., & Metraux, R. (Eds.). (1953). *The study of culture at a distance*. Chicago: University of Chicago Press.

Medicine, B. (1994). Gender. In M. B. Davis (Ed.), *Native America in the twentieth century*. New York: Garland.

Mellars, P. (1989). Major issues in the emergence of modern humans. *Current Anthropology 30*, 356–357.

Meltzer, D., Fowler, D., & Sabloff, J. (Eds.). (1986). *American archaeology: Past & future*. Washington, DC: Smithsonian Institution.

Merin, Y. (2002). *Equality for same-sex couples: The legal recognition of gay partnerships in Europe and the United States*. Chicago: University of Chicago Press.

Merriam, A. P. (1964). *The anthropology of music*. Chicago: Northwestern University Press.

Mesghinua, H. M. (1966). Salt mining in Enderta. *Journal of Ethiopian Studies 4* (2).

Métraux, A. (1953). Applied anthropology in government: United Nations. In A. A. Kroeber (Ed.), *Anthropology today: An encyclopedic inventory* (pp. 880–894).Chicago: University of Chicago Press.

Meyer, J. (2008). Typology and acoustic strategies of whistled languages: Phonetic comparison and perceptual cues of whistled vowels. *Journal of the International Phonetic Association 38*, 69–94.

Meyer J., & Gautheron, B. (2006). Whistled speech and whistled languages. In K. Brown (Ed.), *Encyclopedia of language & linguistics* (2nd ed., vol. 13, pp. 573–576). Oxford, England: Elsevier.

Meyer, J., Meunier, F., & Dentel, L. (2007). Identification of natural whistled vowels by non-whistlers. *Proceedings of Interspeech 2007* (pp. 1593–1596). Antwerpen, Belgium.

Miles, H.L.W. (1993). Language and the orangutan: The "old person" of the forest. In P. Cavalieri & P. Singer (Eds.), *The Great Ape Project* (pp. 45–50). New York: St. Martin's.

Miller, J.M.A. (2000). Craniofacial variation in *Homo habilis*: An analysis of the evidence for multiple species. *American Journal of Physical Anthropology 112*, 122.

Mintz, S. (1996). A taste of history. In W. A. Haviland & R. J. Gordon (Eds.), *Talking about people* (2nd ed., pp. 81–82). Mountain View, CA: Mayfield.

Minugh-Purvis, N. (1992). The inhabitants of Ice Age Europe. *Expedition 34* (3), 23–36.

Mitchell, W. E. (1973, December). A new weapon stirs up old ghosts. *Natural History*, 77–84.

Modell, J. (1994). *Kinship with strangers: Adoption and interpretations of kinship in American culture*. Berkeley: University of California Press.

Molnar, S. (1992). *Human variation: Races, types and ethnic groups* (3rd ed.). Englewood Cliffs, NJ: Prentice-Hall.

Monaghan, L., Hinton, L., & Kephart, R. (1997). Can't teach a dog to be a cat? The dialogue on ebonics. *Anthropology Newsletter 38* (3), 1, 8, 9.

Montagu, A. (1964). *The concept of race*. London: Macmillan.

Montagu, A. (1964). *Man's most dangerous myth: The fallacy of race* (4th ed.) New York: World Publishing.

Montagu, A. (1975). *Race and IQ*. New York: Oxford University Press.

Moore, J. (1998). Comment. *Current Anthropology 39*, 412.

Morgan, L. H. (1877). *Ancient society*. New York: World Publishing.

Morphy, H., & Perkins, M. (Eds.). (2006). *Anthropology of art: A reader*. Boston: Blackwell.

Morse, D., et al. (1979). *Gestures: Their origins and distribution*. New York: Stein & Day.

Moscati, S. (1962). *The face of the ancient orient*. New York: Doubleday.

Murdock, G. P. (1960). Cognatic forms of social organization. In G. P. Murdock (Ed.), *Social structure in Southeast Asia* (pp. 1–14). Chicago: Quadrangle Books.

Murdock, G. P. (1965). *Social structure*. New York: Free Press.

Murphy, R. (1971). *The dialectics of social life: Alarms and excursions in anthropological theory*. New York: Basic.

Murphy, R., & Kasdan, L. (1959). The structure of parallel cousin marriage. *American Anthropologist 61*, 17–29.

Mydens, S. (2001, August 12). He's not hairy, he's my brother. *New York Times*, sec. 4, 5.

Myrdal, G. (1974). Challenge to affluence: The emergence of an "under-class." In J. G. Jorgensen & M. Truzzi (Eds.), *Anthropology and American life*. Englewood Cliffs, NJ: Prentice-Hall.

Nader, L. (Ed.). (1965). The ethnography of law, part II. *American Anthropologist 67* (6).

Nader, L. (Ed.). (1969). *Law in culture and society*. Chicago: Aldine.

Nader, L. (Ed.). (1981). *No access to law: Alternatives to the American judicial system*. New York: Academic.

Nader, L. (Ed.). (1996). *Naked science: Anthropological inquiry into boundaries, power, and knowledge*. New York: Routledge.

Nader, L. (1997). Controlling processes: Tracing the dynamics of power. *Current Anthropology 38*, 715–717.

Nader, L. (Ed.). (1997). *Law in culture and society*. Berkeley: University of California Press.

Nader, L. (2002). *The life of the law: Anthropological projects*. Berkeley: University of California Press.

Nader, L., & Todd, Jr., H. F. (1978). *The disputing process: Law in ten societies*. New York: Columbia University Press.

Nanda, S. (1990). *Neither man nor woman: The hijras of India*. Belmont, CA: Wadsworth.

Nanda, S. (1992). Arranging a marriage in India. In P. R. De Vita (Ed.), *The naked anthropologist* (pp. 139–143). Belmont, CA: Wadsworth.

Nash, J. (1976). Ethnology in a revolutionary setting. In M. A. Rynkiewich & J. P. Spradley (Eds.), *Ethics and anthropology: Dilemmas in fieldwork* (pp. 148–166). New York: Wiley.

Natadecha-Sponsal, P. (1993). The young, the rich and the famous: Individualism as an American cultural value. In P. R. DeVita & J. D. Armstrong (Eds.), *Distant mirrors: America as a foreign culture* (pp. 46–53). Belmont, CA: Wadsworth.

NationMaster.com. http://www.nationmaster.com/graph/mor_eat_dis-mortality-eating-disorders

Natural Resources Defense Council. (2005, March 25). Healthy milk, healthy baby: Chemical pollution and mother's milk. www.NRDC.org

Needham, R. (Ed.). (1971). *Rethinking kinship and marriage*. London: Tavistock.

Needham, R. (1972). *Belief, language and experience*. Chicago: University of Chicago Press.

Neer, R. M. (1975). The evolutionary significance of vitamin D, skin pigment, and ultraviolet light. *American Journal of Physical Anthropology 43*, 409–416.

Nesbitt, L. M. (1935). *Hell-hole of creation*. New York: Knopf.

Nesse, R. M., & Williams, G. C. (1996). *Why we get sick*. New York: Vintage.

Netting, R. M., Wilk, R. R., & Arnould, E. J. (Eds.). (1984). *Households: Comparative and historical studies of the domestic group*. Berkeley: University of California Press.

Nettl, B. (2005). *The study of ethnomusicology: Thirty-one issues and concepts*. Chicago: University of Illinois Press.

Nieftagodien, N. (2008, June 18). Incoherent response to crisis. *The Star*, Johannesburg. http://web.wits.ac.za/NewsRoom/NewsItems/Noor+Nieftagodien+xenophobia+opinion.htm

Nietschmann, B. (1987). The third world war. *Cultural Survival Quarterly 11* (3), 1–16.

Noack, T. (2001). Cohabitation in Norway: An accepted and gradually more regulated way of living. *International Journal of Law, Policy, and the Family 15* (1), 102–117.

Norris, R. S., & Kristensen, H. M. (2006, July/August). Global nuclear stockpiles, 1945–2006. *Bulletin of the Atomic Scientists 62* (4), 64–66.

Nye, J. (2002). *The paradox of American power: Why the world's only superpower can't go it alone*. New York: Oxford University Press.

Oakley, K. P. (1964). *Man the tool-maker.* Chicago: University of Chicago Press.

O'Barr, W. M., & Conley, J. M. (1993). When a juror watches a lawyer. In W. A. Haviland & R. J. Gordon (Eds.), *Talking about people* (2nd ed., pp. 42–45). Mountain View, CA: Mayfield.

Obler, R. S. (1982). Is the female husband a man? Woman/woman marriage among the Nandi of Kenya. *Ethnology 19,* 69–88.

O'Carroll, E. (2008, June 27). Spain to grant some human rights to apes. *Christian Science Monitor.*

Offiong, D. (1985). Witchcraft among the Ibibio of Nigeria. In A. C. Lehmann & J. E. Myers (Eds.), *Magic, witchcraft, and religion* (pp. 152–165). Palo Alto, CA: Mayfield.

Okonjo, K. (1976). The dual-sex political system in operation: Igbo women and community politics in midwestern Nigeria. In N. Hafkin & E. Bay (Eds.), *Women in Africa.* Stanford, CA: Stanford University Press.

Olszewki, D. I. (1991). Comment. *Current Anthropology 32,* 43.

O'Mahoney, K. (1970). The salt trade. *Journal of Ethiopian Studies 8* (2).

Ong, A. (1999). *Flexible citizenship: The cultural logics of transnationality.* Durham, NC: Duke University Press.

Orlando, L., et al. (6 June 2006). Correspondence: Revisiting Neandertal diversity with a 100,000 year old mtDNA sequence. *Current Biology 16,* 400–402.

Oswalt, W. H. (1972). *Habitat and technology.* New York: Holt, Rinehart & Winston.

Otte, M. (2000). On the suggested bone flute from Slovenia. *Current Anthropology 41,* 271.

Otten, C. M. (1971). *Anthropology and art: Readings in cross-cultural aesthetics.* Garden City, NY: Natural History.

Ottenberg, P. (1965). The Afikpo Ibo of eastern Nigeria. In J. L. Gibbs (Ed.), *Peoples of Africa.* New York: Holt, Rinehart & Winston.

Ottenheimer, M. (1996). *Forbidden relatives: The American myth of cousin marriage.* Chicago: University of Illinois Press.

Otterbein, K. F. (1971). *The evolution of war.* New Haven, CT: HRAF Press.

Pandian, J. (1998). *Culture, religion, and the sacred self: A critical introduction to the anthropological study of religion.* Englewood Cliffs, NJ: Prentice-Hall.

Paredes, J. A., & Purdum, E. D. (1990). "Bye, bye Ted . . . " *Anthropology Today 6* (2), 9.

Parés, J. M., Perez-Gonzalez, A., Weil, A. B., & Arsuaga, J. L. (2000). On the age of hominid fossils at the Sima de los Huesos, Sierra de Atapuerca, Spain: Paleomagnetic evidence. *American Journal of Physical Anthropology 111,* 451–461.

Parish, A. R. (1998). Comment. *Current Anthropology 39,* 414.

Parker, R. G. (1991). *Bodies, pleasures, and passions: Sexual culture in contemporary Brazil.* Boston: Beacon.

Parkin, R. (1997). *Kinship: An introduction to basic concepts.* Cambridge, MA: Blackwell.

Parnell, R. (1999). Gorilla exposé. *Natural History 108* (8), 43.

Partridge, W. (Ed.). (1984). *Training manual in development anthropology.* Washington, DC: American Anthropological Association.

Patterson, F.G.P., & Gordon, W. (2002). Twenty-seven years of Project Koko and Michael. In B. Galdikas et al. (Eds.), *All apes great and small* (vol. 1): *Chimpanzees, bonobos, and gorillas* (pp. 165–176). New York: Kluwer Academic.

Patterson, F., & Linden, E. (1981). *The education of Koko.* New York: Holt, Rinehart & Winston.

Peacock, J. L. (2002). *The anthropological lens: Harsh light, soft focus* (2nd ed.). New York: Cambridge University Press.

Pease, T. (2000, Spring). Taking the third side. *Andover Bulletin.*

Pelto, G. H., Goodman, A. H., & Dufour, D. L. (Eds.). (2000). *Nutritional anthropology: Biocultural perspectives on food and nutrition.* Mountain View, CA: Mayfield.

Pelto, P. J. (1973). *The snowmobile revolution: Technology and social change in the Arctic.* Menlo Park, CA: Cummings.

Pennisi, E. (1999). Genetic study shakes up out of Africa theory. *Science 283,* 1828.

Peters, C. R. (1979). Toward an ecological model of African Plio-Pleistocene hominid adaptations. *American Anthropologist 81*(2), 261–278.

Pew Research Center. (2007). *Global attitudes survey.*

Pew Research Center. (2009). Mapping the global Muslim population: A report on the size and distribution of the world's Muslim population. http://pewforum.org/newassets/images/reports/Muslimpopulation/Muslimpopulation.pdf

Pfeiffer, J. E. (1978). *The emergence of man.* New York: Harper & Row.

Pfeiffer, J. E. (1985). *The creative explosion.* Ithaca, NY: Cornell University Press.

Piddocke, S. (1965). The potlatch system of the southern Kwakiutl: A new perspective. *Southwestern Journal of Anthropology 21,* 244–264.

Piggott, S. (1965). *Ancient Europe.* Chicago: Aldine.

Pilbeam, D. R. (1987). Rethinking human origins. In R. L. Ciochon & J. G. Fleagle (Eds.), *Primate evolution and human origins* (p. 217). Hawthorne, NY: Aldine.

Pimentel, D. (1991). Response. *Science 252,* 358.

Pimentel, D., Hurd, L. E., Bellotti, A. C., Forster, M. J., Oka, I. N., Sholes, O. D., & Whitman, R. J. (1973). Food production and the energy crisis. *Science,* 182.

Pink, S. (2001). *Doing visual ethnography: Images, media and representation in research.* Thousand Oaks, CA: Sage.

Pinker, S. (1994). *The language instinct: How the mind creates language.* New York: Morrow.

Piperno, D. R., & Fritz, G. J. (1994). On the emergence of agriculture in the new world. *Current Anthropology 35,* 637–643.

Pitts, V. (2003). *In the flesh: The cultural politics of body modification.* New York: Palgrave Macmillan.

Plane, A. M. (1996). Putting a face on colonization: Factionalism and gender politics in the life history of Awashunkes, the "Squaw Sachem" of Saconnet. In R. S. Grumet (Ed.), *Northeastern Indian lives, 1632–1816* (pp.140–175). Amherst: University of Massachusetts Press.

Plattner, S. (Ed.). (1989). *Economic anthropology.* Stanford, CA: Stanford University Press.

Plattner, S. (1989). Markets and marketplaces. In S. Plattner (Ed.), *Economic anthropology.* Stanford, CA: Stanford University Press.

Pluralism Project, Harvard University. pluralism.org

Pohl, M.E.D., Pope, K. O., & von Nagy, C. (2002). Olmec origins of Mesoamerican writing. *Science 298,* 1984–1987.

Polanyi, K. (1968). The economy as instituted process. In E. E. LeClair, Jr., & H. K. Schneider (Eds.), *Economic anthropology: Readings in theory and analysis* (pp. 127–138). New York: Holt, Rinehart & Winston.

Pollan, M. (2001). *The botany of desire: A plant's-eye view of the world.* New York: Random House.

Pollan, M. (2008). *In defense of food: An eater's manifesto.* New York: Penguin.

Pollock, N. J. (1995). Social fattening patterns in the Pacific—the positive side of obesity. A Nauru case study. In I. DeGarine & N. J. Pollock (Eds.), *Social aspects of obesity* (pp. 87–109). London: Routledge.

Pope, G. G. (1992). Craniofacial evidence for the origin of modern humans in China. *Yearbook of Physical Anthropology 35,* 243–298.

Pope Pius XII. (1954). *Sacra Virginitas. Encyclical on consecrated virginity.* The Catholic Encyclopedia Online: www.newadvent.org

Pospisil, L. (1963). *The Kapauku Papuans of west New Guinea.* New York: Holt, Rinehart & Winston.

Pospisil, L. (1971). *Anthropology of law: A comparative theory.* New York: Harper & Row.

Potts, R. (1997). *Humanity's descent: The consequences of ecological instability.* New York: Avon.

Powdermaker, H. (1939). *After freedom: A cultural study in the Deep South.* New York: Viking.

Powdermaker, H. (1976). *Stranger and friend: The way of an anthropologist.* London: Secker and Warburg.

Power, M. G. (1995). Gombe revisited: Are chimpanzees violent and hierarchical in the free state? *General Anthropology 2* (1), 5–9.

Premack, A. J., & Premack, D. (1972). Teaching language to an ape. *Scientific American 277*(4), 92–99.

Price, T. D., & Feinman, G. M. (Eds.). (1995). *Foundations of social inequality.* New York: Plenum.

Pringle, H. (1997). Ice Age communities may be earliest known net hunters. *Science 277,* 1203–1204.

Pringle, H. (1998). The slow birth of agriculture. *Science 282,* 1449.

Prins, A.H.J. (1953). *East African class systems.* Groningen, the Netherlands: J. B. Wolters.

Prins, H.E.L. (1996). *The Mi'kmaq: Resistance, accommodation, and cultural survival* (p. 106). Orlando: Harcourt Brace.

Prins, H.E.L. (1998). Book review of Schuster, C., & Carpenter, E. *American Anthropologist 100* (3), 841.

Prins, H.E.L. (2002). Visual media and the primitivist perplex: Colonial fantasies, indigenous imagination, and advocacy in North America. In F. D. Ginsburg et al. (Eds.), *Media worlds: Anthropology on new terrain* (pp. 58–74). Berkeley: University of California Press.

Prins, H.E.L., & Carter, K. (1986). *Our lives in our hands.* Video and 16mm. Color. 50 min. Distributed by Watertown, MA: Documentary Educational Resources and Bucksport, ME: Northeast Historic Film

Prins, H.E.L., & Krebs, E. (2006). Toward a land without evil: Alfred Métraux a UNESCO anthropologist 1948–1962. In *60 years of UNESCO history. Proceedings of the international symposium in Paris, 16–18 November 2005.* Paris: UNESCO.

Pruetz, J. D., & Bertolani, P. (2007, March 6). Savanna chimpanzees, *Pan troglodytes verus,* hunt with tools. *Current Biology 17,* 412–417.

Puleston, D. E. (1983). *The settlement survey of Tikal.* Philadelphia: University Museum.

Quinn, N. (2005). Universals of child rearing. *Anthropological Theory 5,* 475–514.

Radcliffe-Brown, A. R. (1931). Social organization of Australian tribes. *Oceana Monographs 1,* 29.

Radcliffe-Brown, A. R., & Forde, C. D. (Eds.). (1950). *African systems of kinship and marriage.* London: Oxford University Press.

Radin, P. (1923). The Winnebago tribe. In *37th annual report of the Bureau of American Ethnology, 1915–1916* (pp. 33–550). Washington, DC: Government Printing Office.

Rapp, R. (1999). *Testing women, testing the fetus: The social impact of amniocentesis in America.* New York: Routledge.

Rappaport, R. A. (1969). Ritual regulation of environmental relations among a New Guinea people. In A. P. Vayda (Ed.), *Environment and cultural behavior* (pp. 181–201). Garden City, NY: Natural History.

Rappaport, R. A. (1984). *Pigs for the ancestors* (Enl. ed.). New Haven, CT: Yale University Press.

Rappaport, R. A. (1999). *Holiness and humanity: Ritual in the making of religious life.* New York: Cambridge University Press.

Rathje, W. L. (1974). The garbage project: A new way of looking at the problems of archaeology. *Archaeology 27,* 236–241.

Rathje, W. L. (1993). Rubbish! In W. A. Haviland & R. J. Gordon (Eds.), *Talking about people: Readings in contemporary cultural anthropology.* Mountain View, CA: Mayfield.

Rathke, L. (1989). To Maine for apples. *Salt Magazine 9* (4), 24–47.

Read-Martin, C. E., & Read, D. W. (1975). Australopithecine scavenging and human evolution: An approach from faunal analysis. *Current Anthropology 16* (3), 359–368.

Recent demographic developments in Europe—2000. Council of Europe.

Recer, P. (1998, February 16). Apes shown to communicate in the wild. *Burlington Free Press*, 12A.

Redfield, R. (1953). *The primitive world and its transformations*. Ithaca, NY: Cornell University Press.

Redman, C. L. (1978). *The rise of civilization: From early farmers to urban society in the ancient Near East*. San Francisco: Freeman.

Reid, J. J., Schiffer, M. B., & Rathje, W. L. (1975). Behavioral archaeology: Four strategies. *American Anthropologist 77*, 864–869.

Reina, R. E. (1966). *The law of the saints*. Indianapolis: Bobbs-Merrill.

Relethford, J. H. (2001). Absence of regional affinities of Neandertal DNA with living humans does not reject multiregional evolution. *American Journal of Physical Anthropology 115*, 95–98.

Relethford, J. H., & Harpending, H. C. (1994). Craniometric variation, genetic theory, and modern human origins. *American Journal of Physical Anthropology 95*, 249–270.

Renfrew, C. (1973). *Before civilization: The radiocarbon revolution and prehistoric Europe*. London: Jonathan Cape.

"Return to the African Burial Ground: An interview with physical anthropologist Michael L. Blakey." (2003, November 20). *Archaeology*. http://www.archaeology.org/online/interviews/blakey/

Ribeiro, G. L. (2009). Non-hegemonic globalizations: Alternative transnational processes and agents. *Anthropological Theory 9* (3), 297–329.

Richter, C. A., et al. (2007). In vivo effects of bisphenol A in laboratory rodent studies. *Reproductive Toxicology 24* (2), 199–224.

Ridley, M. (1999). *Genome: The autobiography of a species in 23 chapters*. New York: HarperCollins.

Rightmire, G. P. (1990). *The evolution of Homo erectus: Comparative anatomical studies of an extinct human species*. Cambridge, MA: Cambridge University Press.

Rightmire, G. P. (1998). Evidence from facial morphology for similarity of Asian and African representatives of *Homo erectus. American Journal of Physical Anthropology 106*, 61–85.

Rindos, D. (1984). *The origins of agriculture: An evolutionary perspective*. Orlando: Academic.

Ritzer, G. (1983). The McDonaldization of society, *Journal of American Culture 6* (1), 100–107.

Ritzer, G. (2007). *The coming of post-industrial society* (2nd ed.). New York: McGraw-Hill.

Robben, A.C.G.M. (2007). Fieldwork identity: Introduction. In A.C.G.M. Robben & J. A. Sluka (Eds.), *Ethnographic fieldwork: An anthropological reader* (pp. 59–63). Malden, MA: Blackwell.

Robben, A.C.G.M. (2007). Reflexive ethnography: Introduction. In A.C.G.M. Robben & J. A. Sluka (Eds.), *Ethnographic fieldwork: An anthropological reader* (pp. 443–446). Malden, MA: Blackwell.

Robben, A.C.G.M., & Sluka, J. A. (Eds.). (2007). *Ethnographic fieldwork: An anthropological reader*. Malden, MA: Blackwell.

Rogers, J. (1994). Levels of the genealogical hierarchy and the problem of hominid phylogeny. *American Journal of Physical Anthropology 94*, 81–88.

Rosas, A., & Bermdez de Castro, J. M. (1998). On the taxonomic affinities of the Dmanisi mandible (Georgia). *American Journal of Physical Anthropology 107*, 145–162.

Roscoe, P. B. (1995). The perils of "positivism" in cultural anthropology. *American Anthropologist 97*, 497.

Roscoe, W. (1991). *Zuni man-woman*. Albuquerque: University of New Mexico Press.

Ruhlen, M. (1994). *The origin of language: Tracing the evolution of the mother tongue*. New York: Wiley.

Rupert, J. L., & Hochachka, P. W. (2001). The evidence for hereditary factors contributing to high altitude adaptation in Andean natives: A review. *High Altitude Medicine & Biology 2* (2), 235–256.

Ruvdo, M. (1994). Molecular evolutionary processes and conflicting gene trees: The hominoid case. *American Journal of Physical Anthropology 94*, 89–113.

Sabloff, J. A. (1997). *The cities of ancient Mexico* (rev. ed.). New York: Thames & Hudson.

Sabloff, J. A., & Lambert-Karlovsky, C. C. (Eds.). (1974). *The rise and fall of civilizations, modern archaeological approaches to ancient cultures*. Menlo Park, CA: Cummings.

Sahlins, M. (1961). The segmentary lineage: An organization of predatory expansion. *American Anthropologist 63*, 322–343.

Sahlins, M. (1968). *Tribesmen*. Englewood Cliffs, NJ: Prentice-Hall (Foundations of Modern Anthropology).

Sahlins, M. (1972). *Stone age economics*. Chicago: Aldine.

Salzman, P. C. (1967). Political organization among nomadic peoples. *Proceedings of the American Philosophical Society 111*, 115–131.

Sanday, P. R. (1975). On the causes of IQ differences between groups and implications for social policy. In M.F.A. Montagu (Ed.), *Race and IQ* (pp. 232–238). New York: Oxford.

Sanday, P. R. (1981). *Female power and male dominance: On the origins of sexual inequality*. Cambridge, England: Cambridge University Press.

Sanday, P. R. (2002). *Women at the center: Life in a modern matriarchy*. Ithaca: Cornell University Press.

Sangree, W. H. (1965). The Bantu Tiriki of western Kenya. In J. L. Gibbs, Jr. (Ed.), *Peoples of Africa* (pp. 69–72). New York: Holt, Rinehart & Winston.

Sanjek, R. (1990). On ethnographic validity. In R. Sanjek (Ed.), *Field notes*. Ithaca, NY: Cornell University Press.

Sapir, E. (1921). *Language*. New York: Harcourt.

Sapolsky, R. (2002). *A primate's memoir: Love, death, and baboons in East Africa*. New York: Vintage.

Savage-Rumbaugh, S., & Lewin, R. (1994). *Kanzi: The ape at the brink of the human mind*. New York: Wiley.

Scaglion, R. (1987). Contemporary law development in Papua New Guinea. In R. M. Wulff & S. J. Fiske (Eds.), *Anthropological praxis: Translating knowledge into action*. Boulder, CO: Westview.

Schaeffer, S. B., & Furst, P. T. (Eds.). (1996). *People of the peyote: Huichol Indian history, religion, and survival*. Albuquerque: University of New Mexico Press.

Scheflen, A. E. (1972). *Body language and the social order*. Englewood Cliffs, NJ: Prentice-Hall.

Schepartz, L.A. (1993). Language and human origins. *Yearbook of Physical Anthropology 36*, 91–126.

Scheper-Hughes, N., & Waquant, L. (2002). *Commodifying bodies*. London: Sage (Theory, Culture, and Society series).

Schlegel, A. (1977). Male and female in Hopi thought and action. In A. Schlegel (Ed.), *Sexual stratification* (pp. 245–269). New York: Columbia University Press.

Schoepfle, M. (2001). Ethnographic resource inventory and the National Park Service. *Cultural Resource Management 5*, 1–7.

Schrire, C. (Ed.). (1984). *Past and present in hunter-gatherer studies*. Orlando: Academic.

Schusky, E. L. (1983). *Manual for kinship analysis* (2nd ed.). Lanham, MD: University Press of America.

Schuster, C., & Carpenter, E. (1996). *Patterns that connect: Social symbolism in ancient and tribal art*. New York: Abrams.

Schuster, G., Smits, W., & Ullal, J. (2008). *Thinkers of the jungle: The orangutan report*. H. F. Uhlmann.

Schwartz, J. H. (1984). Hominoid evolution: A review and a reassessment. *Current Anthropology 25* (5), 655–672.

Schwartz, M. (1997). *A history of dogs in the early Americas*. New Haven: Yale University Press.

Scully, T. (2008). Online anthropology draws protest from aboriginal group. *Nature 453*, 1155.

Scupin, R. (Ed.). (2000). *Religion and culture: An anthropological focus*. Upper Saddle River, NJ: Prentice-Hall.

Seeger, A. (2004). *Why Suyá sing: A musical anthropology*. Champaign: University of Illinois Press.

Sellen, D. W., & Mace, R. (1997). Fertility and mode of subsistence: A phylogenetic analysis. *Current Anthropology 38*, 886.

Senut, B., Pickford, M., Gommery, D., Mein, P., Cheboi, K., & Coppens, Y. (2001). First hominid from the Miocene (Lukeino Formation, Kenya). *Comptes Rendus de l'Académie de Sciences 332*, 137–144.

Seyfarth, R. M., Cheney, D. L., & Marler, P. (1980). Vervet monkey alarm calls: Semantic communication in a free-ranging primate. *Animal Behavior 28* (4),1070–1094.

Seyfarth, R. M., et al. (1980). Monkey responses to three different alarm calls: Evidence for predator classification and semantic communication. *Science 210*, 801–803.

Seymour, D. Z. (1986). Black children, black speech. In P. Escholz, A. Rosa, & V. Clark (Eds.), *Language awareness* (4th ed.). New York: St. Martin's.

Shane, L., III. (2005). Happy couple both no-show wedding: Deployed troops make use of double-proxy ceremony. *Stars & Stripes 3* (17), 6.

Shapiro, H. (Ed.). (1971). *Man, culture and society* (2nd ed.). New York: Oxford University Press.

Sharer, R. J., & Ashmore, W. (2007). *Archaeology: Discovering our past* (4th ed.). New York: McGraw-Hill.

Shaw, D. G. (1984). A light at the end of the tunnel: Anthropological contributions toward global competence. *Anthropology Newsletter 25*, 16.

Shearer, R. R., & Gould, S. J. (1999). Of two minds and one nature. *Science 286*, 1093.

Sheets, P. D. (1993). Dawn of a new Stone Age in eye surgery. In R. J. Sharer & W. Ashmore (Eds.), *Archaeology: Discovering our past* (2nd ed.). Palo Alto, CA: Mayfield.

Shipman, P. (1993). *Life history of a fossil: An introduction to taphonomy and paleoecology*. Cambridge, MA: Harvard University Press.

Shook, J. R., et al. (Eds.). (2004). *Dictionary of modern American philosophers, 1860–1960*. Bristol, England: Thoemmes.

Shore, B. (1996). *Culture in mind: Meaning, construction, and cultural cognition*. New York: Oxford University Press.

Shostak, M. (1983). *Nisa: The life and words of a !Kung woman*. New York: Vintage.

Shreeve, J. (1994). Terms of estrangement. *Discover 15* (11), 60.

Shreeve, J. (1995). *The Neandertal enigma: Solving the mystery of modern human origins*. New York: William Morrow.

Shuey, A. M. (1966). *The testing of Negro intelligence*. New York: Social Science.

Sillen, A., & Brain, C. K. (1990). Old flame. *Natural History 4*, 6–10.

Simons, E. L. (1972). *Primate evolution*. New York: Macmillan.

Simons, E. L. (1989) Human origins. *Science 245*, 1349.

Simons, R. C., & Hughes, C. C. (Eds.). (1985). *The culture-bound syndromes: Folk illnesses of psychiatric and anthropological interest*. Dordrecht, Netherlands: Reidel.

Simpson, G. G. (1949). *The meaning of evolution*. New Haven, CT: Yale University Press.

Simpson, S. W., Quade, J., Levin, N. E., Butler, R., Dupont-Nivet, G., Everett, M., & Semaw, S. (2008). A female *Homo erectus* pelvis from Gona, Ethiopia. *Science 322* (5904), 1089–1092.

Sjoberg, G. (1960). *The preindustrial city*. New York: Free Press.

Sluka, J. A. (2007). Fieldwork relations and rapport: Introduction. In A.C.G.M. Robben & J. A. Sluka (Eds.), *Ethnographic fieldwork: An anthropological reader*. Malden, MA: Blackwell.

Small, M. F. (1997). Making connections. *American Scientist 85*, 503.

Small, M. F. (2000). Kinship envy. *Natural History 109* (2), 88.

Smedley, A. (2007). *Race in North America: Origin and evolution of a worldview*. Boulder, CO: Westview.

Smith, P.E.L. (1976). *Food production and its consequences* (2nd ed.). Menlo Park, CA: Cummings.

Snowden, C. T. (1990). Language capabilities of nonhuman animals. *Yearbook of Physical Anthropology 33*, 215–243.

Speck, F. G. (1920). Penobscot shamanism. *Memoirs of the American Anthropological Association 6*, 239–288.

Speck, F. G. (1970). *Penobscot man: The life history of a forest tribe in Maine.* New York: Octagon.

Spencer, F., & Smith, F. H. (1981). The significance of Ales Hrdlicka's "Neanderthal phase of man": A historical and current assessment. *American Journal of Physical Anthropology 56*, 435–459.

Spencer, H. (1896). *Principles of sociology.* New York: Appleton.

Spencer, R. F. (1984). North Alaska Coast Eskimo. In D. Damas (Ed.), *Arctic: Handbook of North American Indians* (Vol. 5, pp. 320–337). Washington, DC: Smithsonian Institution.

Spindler, G., & Stockard, J. E. (Eds.). (2006). *Globalization and change in fifteen cultures.* Belmont, CA: Wadsworth.

Spradley, J. P. (1979). *The ethnographic interview.* New York: Holt, Rinehart & Winston.

Spradley, J. P. (1980). *Participant observation.* New York: Holt, Rinehart & Winston.

Stacey, J. (1990). *Brave new families.* New York: Basic.

Stahl, A. B. (1984). Hominid dietary selection before fire. *Current Anthropology 25*, 151–168.

Standing Bear, L. (1975). *My people the Sioux.* Lincoln: University of Nebraska Press.

Stanford, C. B. (2001). *Chimpanzee and red colobus: The ecology of predator and prey.* Cambridge, MA: Harvard University Press.

Stanford, C. B. (2001). *The hunting apes: Meat eating and the origins of human behavior.* Princeton, NJ: Princeton University Press.

Stannard, D. E. (1992). *American holocaust.* Oxford, England: Oxford University Press.

Starn, O. (2005). *Ishi's brain: In search of America's last "wild" Indian.* New York: Norton.

Steady, F. C. (2001). *Women and the Amistad connection, Sierra Leone Krio Society.* Rochester, VT: Schenkman.

Steady, F. C. (2005). *Women and collective action in Africa.* New York: Palgrave Macmillan.

Stedman, H. H., et al. (2004). Myosin gene mutation correlates with anatomical changes in the human lineage. *Nature 428*, 415–418.

Stein, R., & St. George, D. (2009, May 13). Babies increasingly born to unwed mothers. *Washington Post.*

Stein, R. L., & Stein, P. L. (2004). *Anthropology of religion, magic, and witchcraft.* Boston: Allyn & Bacon.

Steward, J. H. (1972). *Theory of culture change: The methodology of multilinear evolution.* Urbana: University of Illinois Press.

Stiglitz, J. E. (2003). *Globalization and its discontents.* New York: Norton.

Stiles, D. (1979). Early Acheulean and developed Oldowan. *Current Anthropology 20* (l), 126–129.

Stockard, J. E. (2002). *Marriage in culture: Practice and meaning across diverse societies.* Ft. Worth: Harcourt College.

Stocking, G. W., Jr. (1968). *Race, culture and evolution: Essays in the history of anthropology.* New York: Free Press.

Stone, L. (2005). *Kinship and gender: An introduction* (3rd ed.). Boulder, CO: Westview.

Stone, R. (1995). If the mercury soars, so may health hazards. *Science 267*, 958.

Straus, W. L., & Cave, A.J.E. (1957). Pathology and the posture of Neanderthal man. *Quarterly Review of Biology, 32.*

Stringer, C. B., & McKie, R. (1996). *African exodus: The origins of modern humanity.* London: Jonathan Cape.

Stuart-MacAdam, P., & Dettwyler, K. A. (Eds.). (1995). *Breastfeeding: Biocultural perspectives.* New York: Aldine.

"Study estimates 250,000 active child soldiers."(2006, July 26). Associated Press.

Suarez-Orozoco, M. M., Spindler, G., & Spindler, L. (1994). *The making of psychological anthropology, II.* Fort Worth: Harcourt Brace.

Suwa, G., et al. (2007, August 23). A new species of great ape from the late Miocene epoch in Ethiopia. *Nature 448*, 921–924.

Swadesh, M. (1959). Linguistics as an instrument of prehistory. *Southwestern Journal of Anthropology 15*, 20–35.

Swaminathan, M. S. (2000). Science in response to basic human needs. *Science 287*, 425.

Swisher III, C. C., Curtis, G. H., Jacob, T., Getty, A. G., Suprijo, A., & Widiasmoro. (1994). Age of the earliest known hominids in Java, Indonesia. *Science 263*, 1118–1121.

Tapper, M. (1999). *In the blood: Sickle-cell anemia and the politics of race.* Philadelphia: University of Pennsylvania Press.

Tattersal, I. (1998). *Becoming human: Evolution and human uniqueness.* New York: Harcourt Brace.

Tattersall, I., & Schwartz, J. H. (1999). Hominids and hybrids: The place of Neanderthals in human evolution. *Proceedings of the National Academy of Science 96* (13), 7117–7119.

Tax, S. (1953). *Penny capitalism: A Guatemalan Indian economy.* Washington, DC: Smithsonian Institution, Institute of Social Anthropology, Pub. No. 16.

Taylor, G. (2000). *Castration: Abbreviated history of western manhood.* New York: Routledge.

Tedlock, B. (2005). *The woman in the shaman's body: Reclaiming the feminine in religion and medicine.* New York: Random House.

Templeton, A. R. (1994). Eve: Hypothesis compatibility versus hypothesis testing. *American Anthropologist 96* (1), 141–147.

Templeton, A. R. (1995). The "Eve" hypothesis: A genetic critique and re-analysis. *American Anthropologist 95* (1), 51–72.

Terashima, H. (1983). Mota and other hunting activities of the Mbuti archers: A socio-ecological study of subsistence technology. *African Studies Monograph* (Kyoto), 71–85.

Thin, N. (2007). "Realising the substance of their happiness": How anthropology forgot about *Homo gauisus.* In A. C. Jimenez (Ed.), *Culture and the politics of freedom: The anthropology of wellbeing.* London: Pluto

Thomas, E. M. (1994). *The tribe of the tiger: Cats and their culture* (pp. 109–186). New York: Simon & Schuster.

Thompson, P. (2009, March 6). Sign of the times: Jobless pitch "tent city" in Sacramento. *Mail Online* (London). http://obrag.org/?p=5008

Thomson, K. S. (1997). Natural selection and evolution's smoking gun. *American Scientist 85*, 516–518.

Thorne, A. G., & Wolpoff, M.D.H. (1981). Regional continuity in Australasian Pleistocene hominid evolution. *American Journal of Physical Anthropology 55*, 337–349.

Thornhill, N. (1993). Quoted in W. A. Haviland & R. J. Gordon (Eds.), *Talking about people* (p. 127). Mountain View, CA: Mayfield.

Timmons, H., & Kumar, H. (2009, July 3). Indian court overturns gay sex ban. *New York Times.*

Tobias, P. V., & von Konigswald, G.H.R. (1964). A comparison between the Olduvai hominines and those of Java and some implications for hominid phylogeny. *Nature 204*, 515–518.

Toth, N., Schick, K. D., Savage-Rumbaugh, E. S., Sevcik, R. A., & Rumbaugh, D. M. (1993–2001). Pan the tool-maker: Investigations into the stone tool-making and tool-using capabilities of a bonobo (*Pan panisicus*). *Journal of Archaeological Science 20* (1), 81–91.

Trevathan, W., Smith, E. O., & McKenna, J. J. (Eds.). (1999). *Evolutionary medicine.* London: Oxford University Press.

Trinkaus, E. (1986). The Neanderthals and modern human origins. *Annual Review of Anthropology 15*, 197.

Trinkaus, E., & Shipman, P. (1992). *The Neandertals: Changing the image of mankind.* New York: Knopf.

Trouillot, M. R. (1996). Culture, color, and politics in Haiti. In S. Gregory & R. Sanjek (Eds.), *Race.* New Brunswick, NJ: Rutgers University Press.

Trouillot, M. R. (2003). *Global transformations: Anthropology and the modern world.* New York: Palgrave Macmillan.

Tumin, M. M. (1967). *Social stratification: The forms and functions of inequality.* Englewood Cliffs, NJ: Prentice-Hall (Foundations of Modern Sociology).

Turnbull, C. M. (1961). *The forest people.* New York: Simon & Schuster.

Turnbull, C. M. (1983). *The human cycle.* New York: Simon & Schuster.

Turnbull, C. M. (1983). *Mbuti Pygmies: Change and adaptation.* New York: Holt, Rinehart & Winston.

Turner, T. (1991). Major shift in Brazilian Yanomami policy. *Anthropology Newsletter 32* (5), 1, 46.

Turner, V. W. (1957). *Schism and continuity in an African society.* Manchester, England: University Press.

Turner, V. W. (1969). *The ritual process.* Chicago: Aldine.

Tylor, E. B. (1871). *Primitive culture: Researches into the development of mythology, philosophy, religion, language, art and customs.* London: Murray.

Tylor, Sir E. B. (1931). Animism. In V. F. Calverton (Ed.), *The making of man: An outline of anthropology.* New York: Modern Library.

Unah, I., & Boger, C. (2001, April). *Race and the death penalty in North Carolina.* www.commonsense.org/pdfs/NCDeathPenaltyReport2001.pdf

UNESCO. www.unesco.org/webworld/babel

UNESCO. www.unesco.org/education/litdecade

UNESCO Institute for Statistics. (2007). http://stats.uis.unesco.org

"UN food agency warns G8 ministers of unparalleled hunger crisis as funding falls." (2009, June 12). http://www.un.org/apps/news/story.asp?NewsID=31116&Cr=WFP&Cr1=hunger

United Nations, World Tourism Organization. www.unwto.org

Universal Declaration of Human Rights. www.ccnmtl.columbia.edu/projects/mmt/udhr

Urban, G. (2001). *Metaculture: How cultures move through the modern world.* Westport, CT: Greenwood.

Ury, W. L. (1993). *Getting past no: Negotiating your way from confrontation.* New York: Bantam.

Ury, W. L. (1999). *Getting to peace: Transforming conflict at home, at work, and in the world.* New York: Viking.

Ury, W. (2002, Winter). A global immune system. *Andover Bulletin.*

Ury, W. (Ed.). (2002). *Must we fight? From the battlefield to the schoolyard—A new perspective on violent conflict and its prevention.* Hoboken, NJ: Jossey-Bass.

U.S. Census Bureau. (2002). *Current population survey.*

U.S. Census Bureau. (2008). *American Community Survey, 2006–2008.*

U.S. Census Bureau News. (2004, March 18).

U.S. Department of Health and Human Services, Administration on Children, Youth, and Families. (2005). *Child maltreatment 2003.* Washington, DC: U.S. Government Printing Office.

Van Allen, J. (1997). Sitting on a man: Colonialism and the lost political institutions of Igbo women. In R. Grinker & C. Steiner (Eds.), *Perspectives on Africa* (p. 450). Boston: Blackwell.

van den Berghe, P. (1992). The modern state: Nation builder or nation killer? *International Journal of Group Tensions 22* (3), 191–207.

Van Eck, C. (2003). *Purified by blood: Honour killings amongst Turks in the Netherlands.* Amsterdam: Amsterdam University Press.

Van Gennep, A. (1960). *The rites of passage.* Chicago: University of Chicago Press. (orig. [1909]. *Les rites de passage.* Paris: Émile Nourry)

Van Tilburg, J. A. (1994). *Easter Island: Archaeology, ecology, and culture.* London: British Museum.

Van Willigen, J. (1986). *Applied anthropology.* South Hadley, MA: Bergin & Garvey.

Veenhoven, R. (1993). *Happiness in nations: Subjective appreciation of life in 56 nations 1946–1992.* Rotterdam: RISBO.

Venbrux, E., Rosi, P. S., & Welsch, R. L. (Eds.). (2006). *Exploring world art.* Longrove, IL: Waveland.

Vincent, J. (2002). *The anthropology of politics: A reader in ethnography, theory, and critique.* Boston: Blackwell.

Vogt, E. Z. (1990). *The Zinacantecos of Mexico: A modern Maya way of life* (2nd ed.). Fort Worth: Holt, Rinehart & Winston.

vom Saal, F. S., & Myers, J. P. (2008). Bisphenol A and risk of metabolic disorders. *Journal of the American Medical Association, 300* (11), 1353–1355.

Walker, A., & Shipman, P. (1997). *The wisdom of the bones: In search of human origins.* New York: Vintage.

Wallace, A.F.C. (1956). Revitalization movements. *American Anthropologist 58,* 264–281.

Wallace, A.F.C. (1966). *Religion: An anthropological view.* New York: Random House.

Wallace, A.F.C. (1970). *Culture and personality* (2nd ed.). New York: Random House.

Wallace, E., & Hoebel, E. A. (1952). *The Comanches.* Norman: University of Oklahoma Press.

Walrath, D. (2002). Decoding the discourses: Feminism and science, review essay. *American Anthropologist 104* (1), 327–330.

Walrath, D. (2003). Rethinking pelvic typologies and the human birth mechanism. *Current Anthropology 44* (1), 5–31.

Walrath, D. (2006). Gender, genes, and the evolution of human birth. In P. L. Geller & M. K. Stockett (Eds.), *Feminist anthropology: Past, present, and future.* Philadelphia: University of Pennsylvania Press.

Washburn, S. L., & Moore, R. (1980). *Ape into human: A study of human evolution* (2nd ed.). Boston: Little, Brown.

Wattenberg, B. J. (1997, November 23). The population explosion is over. *New York Times Magazine,* 60.

Weatherford, J. (1988). *Indian givers: How the Indians of the Americas transformed the world.* New York: Ballantine.

Weiner, A. B. (1977). Review of Trobriand cricket: An ingenious response to colonialism. *American Anthropologist 79,* 506.

Weiner, A. B. (1988). *The Trobrianders of Papua New Guinea.* New York: Holt, Rinehart & Winston.

Weiner, J. S. (1955). *The Piltdown forgery.* Oxford, England: Oxford University Press.

Weiss, M. L., & Mann, A. E. (1990). *Human biology and behavior* (5th ed.). Boston: Little, Brown.

Wells, S. (2002). *The journey of man: A genetic odyssey.* Princeton, NJ: Princeton University Press.

Werner, D. (1990). *Amazon journey.* Englewood Cliffs, NJ: Prentice-Hall.

Wheeler, P. (1993). Human ancestors walked tall, stayed cool. *Natural History 102* (8), 65–66.

Whelehan, P. (1985). Review of incest, a biosocial view. *American Anthropologist 87,* 678.

White, D. R. (1988). Rethinking polygyny: Co-wives, codes, and cultural systems. *Current Anthropology 29,* 529–572.

White, L. (1949). *The science of culture: A study of man and civilization.* New York: Farrar, Straus.

White, L. (1959). *The evolution of culture: The development of civilization to the fall of Rome.* New York: McGraw-Hill.

White, M. (2001). *Historical atlas of the twentieth century.* http://users.erols.com/mwhite28/20centry.htm

White, R. (2003). *Prehistoric art: The symbolic journey of humankind.* New York: Abrams.

White, T., Asfaw, B., Degusta, D., Gilbert, H., Richards, G., Suwa, G., & Howell, F. C. (2003). Pleistocene *Homo sapiens* from the Middle Awash, Ethiopia. *Nature 423,* 742–747.

White, T. D. (1979). Evolutionary implications of Pliocene hominid footprints. *Science 208,* 175–176.

White, T. D. (2003). Early hominids—diversity or distortion? *Science 299,* 1994–1997.

White, T. D., Asfaw, B., Beyne, Y., Haile-Selassie, Y., Lovejoy, C. O., Suwa, G., & Wolde Gabriel, G. (2009, October). *Ardipithecus ramidus* and the paleobiology of early hominids. *Science 326* (5949), 64, 75–86.

White, T. D., & Toth, N. (2000). Cutmarks on a Plio-Pleistocene hominid from Sterkfontein, South Africa. *American Journal of Physical Anthropology 111,* 579–584.

Whitehead, B. D., & Popenoe, D. (2004). *The state of our unions: The social health of marriage in America 2004.* Rutgers, NJ: Rutgers University National Marriage Project.

Whitehead, N., & Ferguson, R. B. (Eds.). (1992). *War in the tribal zone.* Santa Fe: School of American Research.

Whitehead, N. L., & Ferguson, R. B. (1993, November). Deceptive stereotypes about tribal warfare. *Chronicle of Higher Education,* A48.

Whiting, B. B. (Ed.). (1963). *Six cultures: Studies of child rearing.* New York: Wiley.

Whiting, J.W.M., & Child, I. L. (1953). *Child training and personality: A cross-cultural study.* New Haven, CT: Yale University Press.

Whiting, J.W.M., Sodergem, J. A., & Stigler, S. M. (1982). Winter temperature as a constraint to the migration of preindustrial peoples. *American Anthropologist 84,* 289.

Whorf, B. (1941). The relation of habitual thought and behavior to language. In L. Spier, A. I. Hallowell, & S. S. Newman (Eds.), *Language, culture, and personality: Essays in memory of Edward Sapir* (pp. 75–93). Menasha, WI: Sapir Memorial Publication Fund.

Whyte, A.L.H. (2005). Human evolution in Polynesia. *Human Biology 77* (2), 157–177.

Wiley, A. S. (2004). *An ecology of high-altitude infancy: A biocultural perspective.* Cambridge, England: Cambridge University Press.

Wilk, R. R. (1996). *Economics and cultures: An introduction to economic anthropology.* Boulder, CO: Westview.

Wilkie, D. S., & Curran, B. (1993). Historical trends in forager and farmer exchange in the Ituri rain forest of northeastern Zaïre. *Human Ecology 21* (4), 389–417.

Willey, G. R. (1966). *An introduction to American archaeology: Vol. 1. North America.* Englewood Cliffs, NJ: Prentice-Hall.

Willey, G. R. (1971). *An introduction to American archaeology, Vol. 2: South America.* Englewood Cliffs, NJ: Prentice-Hall.

Williams, F. (2005, January 9). Toxic breast milk? *New York Times Magazine.*

Williamson, R. K. (1995). The blessed curse: Spirituality and sexual difference as viewed by Euramerican and Native American cultures. *The College News 18* (4).

Wills, C. (1994). The skin we're in. *Discover 15* (11), 79.

Wilson, A. K., & Sarich, V. M. (1969). A molecular time scale for human evolution. *Proceedings of the National Academy of Science 63,* 1,089–1,093.

Wingert, P. (1965). *Primitive art: Its tradition and styles.* New York: World.

Winick, C. (Ed.). (1970). *Dictionary of anthropology.* Totowa, NJ: Littlefield, Adams.

Wirsing, R. L. (1985). The health of traditional societies and the effects of acculturation. *Current Anthropology 26* (3), 303–322.

Wittfogel, K. A. (1957). *Oriental despotism, a comparative study of total power.* New Haven, CT: Yale University Press.

Wolf, E. R. (1966). *Peasants.* Englewood Cliffs, NJ: Prentice-Hall.

Wolf, E. R. (1969). *Peasant wars of the twentieth century.* New York: Harper & Row.

Wolf, E. R. (1982). *Europe and the people without history.* Berkeley: University of California Press.

Wolf, E. R. (1999). *Envisioning power: Ideologies of dominance and crisis.* Berkeley: University of California Press.

Wolf, E. R., & Hansen, E. C. (1972). *The human condition in Latin America.* New York: Oxford University Press.

Wolf, E. R., & Trager, G. L. (1971). Hortense Powdermaker 1900–1970. *American Anthropologist 73* (3), 784.

Wolf, M. (1985). *Revolution postponed: Women in contemporary China.* Stanford, CA: Stanford University Press.

Wolffe, R., Ramirez, J., & Bartholet, J. (2008, March 31). *Newsweek.*

Wolfson, H. (2000, January 22). Polygamists make the Christian connection. *Burlington Free Press,* 2c.

Wolpoff, M. H. (1993). Evolution in *Homo erectus:* The question of stasis. In R. L. Ciochon & J. G. Fleagle (Eds.), *The human evolution source book.* Englewood Cliffs, NJ: Prentice-Hall.

Wolpoff, M. H. (1993). Multiregional evolution: The fossil alternative to Eden. In R. L. Ciochon & J. G. Fleagle (Eds.), *The human evolution source book.* Englewood Cliffs, NJ: Prentice-Hall.

Wolpoff, M. (1996). *Australopithecus:* A new look at an old ancestor. *General Anthropology 3* (1), 2.

Wolpoff, M., & Caspari, R. (1997). *Race and human evolution: A fatal attraction.* New York: Simon & Schuster.

Wolpoff, M. H., Wu, X. Z., & Thorne, A. G. (1984). Modern *Homo sapiens* origins: A general theory of hominid evolution involving fossil evidence from east Asia. In F. H. Smith and F. Spencer (Eds.), *The origins of modern humans* (pp. 411–483). New York: Alan R. Liss.

Wood, B., Wood, C., & Konigsberg, L. (1994). *Paranthropus boisei:* An example of evolutionary stasis? *American Journal of Physical Anthropology 95,* 117–136.

Woolfson, P. (1972). Language, thought, and culture. In V. P. Clark, P. A. Escholz, & A. F. Rosa (Eds.), *Language.* New York: St. Martin's.

World almanac. (2004). New York: Press Publishing.

World Bank. www.worldbank.org/poverty

World Bank Development Indicators. (2008).

World Health Organization. http://www.who.int/about/definition/en

World Health Organization. (2003). *Global strategy on infant and young child feeding.* Geneva: Author.

World Health Organization. (2004). Statistical information system.

World Meteorological Organization. (2003). Increasing heat waves and other health hazards. greenpeaceusa.org/climate/index.fpl/7096/article/907.html

World Travel & Tourism Council. www.wttc.org

Worsley, P. (1957). *The trumpet shall sound: A study of "cargo" cults in Melanesia.* London: Macgibbon & Kee.

Worsley, P. (1959). Cargo cults. *Scientific American 200* (May), 117–128.

Wrangham, R., & Peterson, D. (1996). *Demonic males.* Boston: Houghton Mifflin.

Wulff, R. M., & Fiske, S. J. (1987). *Anthropological praxis: Translating knowledge into action.* Boulder, CO: Westview.

Xinhua News Agency. (2009, May 9). Canton Fair wraps up with export orders down 17 percent. *China Daily.*

Yip, M. (2002). *Tone.* New York: Cambridge University Press.

Young, W. (Ed.). (2000). Kimball award winner. *Anthropology News 41* (8), 29.

Zeresenay, A., Spoor, F., Kimbel, W. H., Bobe, R., Geraads, D., Reed, D., & Wynn, J. G. (2006). A juvenile early hominin skeleton from Dikika, Ethiopia. *Nature 443,* 296–301.

Zilhão, J. (2000). Fate of the Neandertals. *Archaeology 53* (4), 30.

Zimmer, C. (1999). New date for the dawn of dream time. *Science 284,* 1243.

Zimmer, C. (2001). *Evolution: The triumph of an idea.* New York: HarperCollins.

Zimmer, C. (2005) *Smithsonian intimate guide to human origins.* New York: HarperCollins.

Zohary, D., & Hopf, M. (1993). *Domestication of plants in the Old World* (2nd ed.). Oxford: Clarenden.

Zuckerman, P. (2005). Atheism: Contemporary rates and patterns. In M. Martin (Ed.), *The Cambridge companion to atheism.* Cambridge, England: Cambridge University Press.

Photo Credits

Associated Press; **p. 288:** © George Holton/Photo Researchers, Inc.; **p. 290:** © Jacques Jangoux/Peter Arnold, Inc.; **p. 291:** © Reuters/Corbis; **p. 294:** Courtesy of Dr. Laura Nader; **p. 295 (left):** © Reuters/Corbis; **p. 295 (right):** © K. Prouse/Pressnet/Topham/The Image Works; **p. 296:** © AFP/Getty Images; **p. 298:** © Fred McConnaughey/Photo Researchers, Inc.; **p. 299:** © Bryan & Cherry Alexander/Arctic-Photo **p. 303:** © Badri Media/epa/Corbis; **p. 308:** © Karel Prinsloo/AP Photo

CHAPTER 13

p. 310: Luca Invernizzi Tettoni/Photolibrary; **p. 313:** © Ed Kashi/Corbis; **p. 316:** © Visual Arts Library (London)/Alamy; **p. 318:** © B&C Alexander/ArcticPhoto; **p. 319:** © Images & Stories, Turkey; **p. 322 (left):** © Dan Budnick/Woodfin Camp & Associates; **p. 322 (right):** © Hamid Sardar/Corbis; **p. 323:** © Irven DeVore/Anthro-Photo; **p. 325:** © Waltraoud Grubitzsch/DPA/Landov; **p. 328:** © Mike Goldwater/Alamy; **p. 329:** © SSPL/The Image Works; **p. 330:** © Floris Leeuwenberg/The Cover Story/Corbis; **p. 333:** © AP/Ed Wray; **p. 334:** © Francois Daburon/Corbis; **p. 337:** © Palani Mohan/The New York Times/Redux

CHAPTER 14

p. 340: Pedro Ugarta/AFP/Getty Images; **p. 343 (left):** © Indiana University Art Museum, Bloomington; **p. 343 (right):** Giraudon/Art Resource, NY. © 2007 Artists Rights Society (ARS) New York/ADAGP/Paris; **p. 344:** © SCALA/Art Resource, NY; **p. 345 (left):** © The Rock Foundation. Courtesy of Edmund Carpenter; **p. 345 (right):** Gemeente Musea Delft, Collectie Museum Nusantara; **p. 346 (both):** © Michael Phillips; **p. 347:** Anthony Bannister/Gallo Images/Corbis; **p. 348:** © Russell Cobb/Dallas Observer; **p. 351:** © Kevin Kelly; **p. 353:** © Anthro-Photo; **p. 354:** © Zale Seck; **p. 356:** African Voices National Museum of Natural History, Smithsonian. Photograph by Donald Hurlbert; **p. 357:** © R. Todd Hoffman; **p. 358 (left):** © Aaron Smale/IKON; **p. 358 (right):** © Khampha Bouaphanh, 2005 Fort Worth Star-Telegram; **p. 360:** © Bangor Daily News/Bridget Brown

CHAPTER 15

p. 362: Jochan Tack/Photolibrary; **p. 365:** © Sydel Silverman; **p. 366:** © Stephen Trimble; **p. 367:** © Nicholas Asfouri/AFP/Getty Images; **p. 368:** © Reuters/Moshin Raza/Landov; **p. 369:** © Hubert Sadler/Corbis; **p. 371:** © Harald E. L. Prins; **p. 375:**

© Jerry Leach; **p. 376:** © AFP/Getty Images; **p. 377:** Matias Recart/AFP/Getty Images; **p. 378:** © A. Ramey/PhotoEdit; **p. 380:** © Staffen Widstrand/Corbis; **p. 382:** © Earth Observatory–NASA

CHAPTER 16

p. 386: © Andreas Valentin/Latin Content/Getty Images; **p. 389:** © Reuters/China Photo; **p. 390:** © Paul Gilham/Getty Images; **p. 392:** © John Moore/Getty Images; **p. 397:** © Harald E. L. Prins; **p. 401:** © Monica Almeida/The New York Times/Redux; **p. 402:** © Tony Freeman/PhotoEdit; **p. 403:** © MARKA/Alamy; **p. 405:** © Bryan & Cherry Alexander Photography; **p. 406:** © Yann Arthus-Bertrand/Corbis; **p. 407:** © AP Images; **p. 410:** © EPA/Laurent Gillieron/Corbis; **p. 412:** © Veronique de Viguerie; **p. 414:** Mark Rosenberg 8-2001 Andrew Marx

Index

Italic page numbers indicate charts, figures, and maps.